River City and Valley Life

AN ENVIRONMENTAL HISTORY
OF THE SACRAMENTO REGION

EDITED BY

Christopher J. Castaneda AND Lee M. A. Simpson

UNIVERSITY OF PITTSBURGH PRESS

Published by the University of Pittsburgh Press, Pittsburgh, Pa., 15260
Copyright © 2013, University of Pittsburgh Press
Manufactured in the United States of America
Printed on acid-free paper
10 9 8 7 6 5 4 3 2 1

Library of Congress Cataloging-in-Publication Data

River City and Valley Life: An Environmental History of the Sacramento Region / edited by
Christopher J. Castaneda and Lee M. A. Simpson.
     pages cm. — (History of the Urban Environment)
ISBN 978-0-8229-6250-2 (paper)
1. Sacramento (Calif.)—Environmental conditions. 2. Sacramento Valley (Calif.)—Environmental
conditions. 3. Sacramento (Calif.)—History. 4. Sacramento Valley (Calif.)—History. 5. City
planning—Environmental aspects—California—Sacramento—History. 6. Urbanization—
Environmental aspects—California—Sacramento—History. 7. Suburbs—Environmental
aspects—California—Sacramento—History. 8. Nature—Effect of human beings on—California—
Sacramento—History. 9. Landscape changes—California—Sacramento—History. 10. Landscape
changes—California—Sacramento Valley—History. I. Castaneda, Christopher James, 1959– II.
Simpson, Lee M. A.
GE155.C2R58 2013
304.209794'5—dc23   2013033572

CONTENTS

Preface   *vii*

Introduction: The Indomitable City and Its Environmental Context   1
STEVEN M. AVELLA

Part I. Boomtown Sacramento

1. John A. Sutter and the Indian Business   13
ALBERT L. HURTADO

2. River City: Sacramento's Gold Rush Birth and Transfiguration   31
KENNETH N. OWENS

3. "We Must Give the World Confidence in the Stability and Permanence of the Place": Planning Sacramento's Townsite, 1853–1870   61
NATHAN HALLAM

4. Railroads and the Urban Environment: Sacramento's Story   77
RICHARD J. ORSI

Part II. Valley Reclamation

5. The Perils of Agriculture in Sacramento's Untamed Hinterland   103
DAVID VAUGHT

6. Rivers of Gold, Valley of Conquest: The Business of Levees and Dams in the Capital City   117
TODD HOLMES

7. Forging Transcontinental Alliances: The Sacramento River Valley in National Drainage and Flood Control Politics, 1900–1917   135
ANTHONY E. CARLSON

8. Both "Country Town" and "Bustling Metropolis": How Boosterism, Suburbs, and Narrative Helped Shape Sacramento's Identity and Environmental Sensibilities   158
PAUL J. P. SANDUL

Part III. Government Town

9. Unseen Investment: New Deal Sacramento   185
GRAY BRECHIN AND LEE M. A. SIMPSON

10. The Legacy of War: Sacramento's Military Bases   200
    RAND HERBERT

11. Recalling Rancho Seco: Voicing a Nuclear Past   216
    CHRISTOPHER J. CASTANEDA

Part IV. Reclaiming the Past

12. Dreams, Realizations, and Nightmares: The American River Parkway's
    Tumultuous Life, 1915–2011   241
    ALFRED E. HOLLAND, JR.

13. Thunder over the Valley: Environmental Politics and Indian Gaming in
    California   267
    TANIS C. THORNE

14. The Invention of Old Sacramento: A Past for the Future   290
    LEE M. A. SIMPSON AND LISA C. PRINCE

Epilogue: Sacramento, Before and After the Gold Rush   313
    TY O. SMITH

Notes   *321*

Contributors   *385*

Index   *389*

PREFACE

This book grew out of a brief discussion between series editor Martin Melosi and Chris Castaneda at the Organization of American Historians conference in San Jose, California, during 2005. Being familiar with the region, Marty was enthusiastic about the idea of a volume on Sacramento's urban and environmental history. Lee M. A. Simpson soon thereafter agreed to coedit with Castaneda, and we began the process of conceptualizing the manuscript.

As we put together the initial outline of potential chapter topics, we became increasingly excited about the project, as no such comprehensive historical study of the Sacramento region exists. We identified within a chronological structure what we believed to be the major thematic episodes in the Sacramento region's urban environmental history, and then we began contacting potential authors based on their expertise in those areas. Although it was not our original intention, the process of inviting contributors inevitably focused on historians who have a professional, and in many cases personal, connection with the Sacramento area. We also wanted to include established and prominent scholars as well as promising ones beginning their careers. While most of the contributors are employed within academia, not all are, and that helps provide a wider and fresher perspective. We believe that the collection of essays in this volume provides some of the best and most insightful writing about the Sacramento region to date.

As faculty at California State University, Sacramento (CSUS), we are acutely aware of the superb work done over the years by faculty and former students of this university. A dedication to local and regional history advanced by Prof. Joseph McGowan and his students and continued by Kenneth Owens, Joseph Pitti, and Charles Roberts in a large sense set the stage for this book. Many of the contributors have studied and worked with these influential faculty, and all of the contributors have a professional, if not personal, tie to the area. We are gratified that this volume contains the work of historians who care deeply about history and place and that they have focused their attention on Sacramento for this book.

We are also grateful to the University of Pittsburgh Press for supporting and encouraging us in this project. In particular, former director Cynthia Miller guided us through the long process that begins with developing an idea and results in a book manuscript; thanks also to Kelly Hope Johovic, Alex Wolfe, Lowell Britson, David Bowmann, and our freelance copy editor, Maureen Bemko. Series editors Marty Melosi and Joel Tarr supported our efforts throughout and provided this forum for the ideas and research herein to become this volume. Two anonymous readers of an early manuscript proposal gave us valuable suggestions and guidance, and two readers of the draft manuscript provided invaluable guidance as well. We thank them for their insight.

Many others have assisted in a variety of ways, and we thank all of you (including those we unintentionally neglect to mention here by name), including the Center for Sacramento History (Marcia Eymann, Patricia Johnson, Dylan MacDonald, and Rebecca Crowther), where many of us did research and acquired photographs. Other persons and institutions who assisted include Heather Downey and Janessa West; the collections of California State Parks; Sacramento City Library; California State Library, Special Collections and University Archives at CSU, Sacramento (Sheila O'Neill, Julie Thomas, and Chris Rockwell); and the California State Archives. We also are grateful for the ongoing support and collegiality offered by the Department of History at CSU, Sacramento, as well as by the department's Oral History Program and Public History Program (directed by Patrick Ettinger), department chair Aaron Cohen, and administrative support coordinators (Julie Cahill and Loriann Rodriguez).

RIVER CITY AND VALLEY LIFE

The Indomitable City and
Its Environmental Context

Steven M. Avella

Sacramentans, like all city dwellers, live each day with the realities of their
natural setting. Embraced by two rivers, area residents swim, fish, inner-tube,
and sail up and down the sometimes treacherous waters of the American and the
Sacramento. They note the rivers' low flow in the hot summer months and (especially since Hurricane Katrina breached critical levees and inundated New Orleans)
worry about their rapid rise during the rainy season and when the Sierra Nevada
snow-melt cascades down the mountains and into the flat valley. Sacramentans
know that their city, sometimes referred to as the Big Tomato or, in the past, Sacra-
tomato, is part of an agricultural processing center. Along the highways, motorists
travel behind huge trucks filled with ripe, red tomatoes grown on valley farms
and destined for processing into sauce, ketchup, and salsa. Visitors to the city tour
the famous Blue Diamond almond plant, which processes tons of nuts harvested
from the myriad groves up and down the valley. Travelers landing at Sacramento's
airport see the expansive green rice paddies that are along the flight paths of most
incoming aircraft into the city. Joggers, walkers, and bicyclists maintain an uneasy
truce along the American River Parkway, which carves paths for exercise enthusiasts and occasionally provides a safe shelter for the city's homeless.

But Sacramentans are also aware of how they have pushed back nature. They
walk along the high levees and see the dams and weirs and floodgates that stand
like guardians against periodic threats of inundation. Areas of the city are the
sites of erstwhile industrial and military facilities that once brought hundreds of
thousands to work and live in the community and also polluted the soil and the
water. The city and the remaining legacy of the ranchos that became unincorporated towns are crisscrossed by freeways and smaller roads that cut through old
neighborhoods and open up a pathway to the recreational areas of the mountains.

Causeways cross floodplains and propel commuters and tourists west through Yolo and Solano Counties toward Berkeley, Oakland, and San Francisco.

Sacramento's history is a virtual case study of urban environmental development in California and other communities of the American West. It was first inhabited by native peoples, who created their own distinct tribal cultures in the area, then explored by Spain, traversed by early Anglo visitors, and carved up into Mexican land grants—one of which was secured by the Swiss adventurer Johann Augustus Sutter. Sacramento "took off" as a gateway to the gold fields of the Sierra, which made the settlement an "instant city" on the banks of the Sacramento River. Over the years it recreated itself again and again, refusing to be dominated or pushed out by the forces of nature or the whims of human decision making. Although raised in chaos, the solid, middle-class core of its residents displayed enough moxie to land the state capital. It became the western terminus for the Central Pacific Railroad, whose repair shops became the economic mainstay of the city for many years. As a railroad hub, Sacramento provided industrial jobs and created a food-processing and packaging center that drew from the abundant produce of the fields, orchards, and farms of the Sacramento Valley. Parallel to its manufacturing and agricultural growth was its rising significance as the capital city of the growing state of California. Although its most dynamic population surge took place after World War II, Sacramento enhanced its respectability by erecting a magnificent capitol building and eventually installing activist governors and legislators who transformed the valley community into a city of rank. While it never replicated the charm of San Francisco or the fast-paced sprawl of Los Angeles, it held sway in California's growing interior as a good place to live and prosper. Yet, the Sacramento region's unique sense of place and interaction with its surrounding environment was not often appreciated or understood by many of the state's residents.

In short, human interaction with nature has been an ever-present theme in Sacramento's history. Sacramento provides an instructive example of how "Nature and culture are always entangled."[1] And what Louis Warren has written of environmental history in general is specifically true of Sacramento. Sacramento's history is the story of how its inhabitants "have lived in the natural systems of the planet and how they have perceived nature and reshaped it to suit their own ideas of good living."[2] Indeed, the development of Sacramento fits well into the construct identified by William Cronon in *Nature's Metropolis: Chicago and the Great West,* which examines the intense interplay between countryside and city.[3] Even though these authors disentangle respective dimensions of the larger story, the collective impact of this volume should provide a fresh look at Sacramento's history and a new appreciation of the complex environmental history of the region.

The Sacramento region's history is far from unknown, but at the same time it has not received a comprehensive treatment; this collection of chapters is a start. The authors seek to understand the city's identity and examine the historical context of some of the significant issues of the environment and urban growth. Sacramento and its region have not lacked historians concerned with the interplay of city and environment; one of the earliest was Joseph McGowan, a faculty member at Sacramento State, who produced two substantive and still helpful volumes on the Sacramento Valley.[4] McGowan had engaged his own students in this research and examined the dynamic exchange that took place between the city of Sacramento and the northern part of the Great Central Valley. He repeatedly demonstrated the linkages between valley agriculture, climate, and land use, and the rise of Sacramento. His work was the first phase of a wider environmental history of Sacramento.

The rivers that embrace the California capital have both punished and rewarded. They created terrible floods and carried waterborne diseases like cholera but also helped to fashion the "earthly Eden," as one booster described Sacramento. All Sacramento historians have to pay tribute to the rivers and their dynamic impact on the environment and the culture of the River City. Robert Kelley's *Battling the Inland Sea* (1989) provides some of the richest descriptions of the Janus-faced impact of the rivers and the creation of the complex system of water controls that enables Sacramento and its watershed to survive and thrive. Other historians and students have also explored various aspects of this region's "commingling" with nature. Yet, this collection attempts to weave together an even more comprehensive narrative of Sacramento's dynamic interaction with its environment.

A metropolis that emerges from the hinterland can be explained in terms of urban development. Although not addressing Sacramento in particular, urban historian Carl Abbott argues that three themes characterize the history of western cities. First, western cities viewed themselves as "central and centralizing points" in a global economy. Self-consciously planned or "imagined" western cities matured into modern metroplexes that still sell themselves as centers of commerce and innovation in direct competition with both their neighbors and the cities of the world. Second, western city growth, especially in the second half of the twentieth century, forced a "cumulative rebalancing" of influence in North America as western cities accounted for eight of the twenty largest cities in the nation. Third, as western cities have grown, they have ceased to be imitators of eastern culture and capital and have come forward as innovators.[5] Abbott notes, "These decades have vaulted western North America into a new global position, central rather than peripheral to global circuits of trade and migration. In the process, its cities have filled the valleys with houses, contoured the hillsides with freeways and lined the highways with the lights of commerce."[6] As part II of this volume argues, this process of western urban growth and innovation, as seen in Sacramento, must be understood in the context of an emerging federal/city partnership.

While environmental and urban historians often aim their scholarship directly at public policy makers concerned with land usage, urban sprawl, and the use of scarce resources, these chapters follow a more straightforward approach. Given the relative dearth of scholarly historical work on Sacramento and the vacuum that exists in knowledge of Sacramento even by local inhabitants, these thematic chapters follow a rough chronological sequence and deploy a narrative style that will both inform and hopefully stimulate critical thinking about the future of nature and culture in the Sacramento region.

This book is divided into four thematic sections, each of which identifies major, overarching themes in the history of the Sacramento region. In part I, titled "Boomtown Sacramento," the authors examine the origins and early entrepreneurial development of Sacramento. In describing the prehistory of Sacramento, Albert Hurtado, the authoritative voice on both California Indians and Johann (John) Sutter and his Mexican land-grant settlement at what became Sacramento, singles out the extensive work done by local Indians (Miwok and Yokuts) in creating Sutter's economic advance; they constituted a "native labor pool" familiar with the rhythms of climate, soil, and food gathering and processing in the Sacramento Valley.

During the gold rush "Days of '49," many profit-motivated entrepreneurs bypassed the safer ground of Sutter's Fort and set up warehouses and shops on the low ground just south of the confluence of the rivers to outfit those heading to the rich gold fields of the eastern Sierra. Riverboats and barges hauled tons of goods and materials to and from Sacramento, transforming the river itself into a profitable superhighway. This combination of location, entrepreneurial risk-taking, and perhaps the urge to be literally at the center of things led people to this early boomtown to build the nucleus of a city that would become the commercial and political center of northern California. "Sacramento," as Mark A. Eifler writes in *Gold Rush Capitalists: Greed and Growth in Sacramento,* "in its own fast-paced and dramatic way, thus reflected the struggles throughout the United States in the nineteenth century of a rural people transforming themselves. . . . We see the collision of two different cultural systems: one based on rural resource extraction and the other on the urban buying and selling of commodities."[7]

The inchoate settlement soon evolved into a city, and the rivers formed the plumb line for the original grid superimposed on the flat ground fronting the north and west banks of the Sacramento and American Rivers. In 1854, the state of California planted its wandering capital in the River City. Creating a city and a governmental center on this location proved to be a perilous decision. Nature punished the heedless decisions of the get-rich-quick merchants and violently asserted itself with horrendous flooding that overwhelmed the city in its early years (and threatens occasionally down to the present day). Fires, sparked in the wooden buildings and fueled by the oppressive heat of summer, devastated the community while waterborne diseases caused inhabitants to flee to the salubrious air of the mountains along the sea coast. The Sacramento region was not conducive to the development of urban life. That circumstance did not daunt Sacramentans, who would "reengineer and refashion" Sacramento to deal with the rivers, the climate, and the topography. Sometimes we know the names of the human agents who made this reengineering possible, but often, as Kenneth Owens notes in his chapter here, the work was done through the efforts of Sacramento's middle-class merchants, professionals, and laborers, whose work Owens hails as the "unheralded, quiet accomplishments of ordinary people."

Establishing the city of Sacramento was an act of defiance against nature. Nathan Hallam lays out with clarity the now familiar story of how economic rather than geographically strategic forces placed it on a floodplain. An improvident Johann Sutter had surrendered his claims to the demands of his many debtors, and the new city's land was platted and gridded for easy sale. When the liabilities of its low ground became evident during winter's rains and the rising of the river's waters, Sacramentans raised the city grade rather than abandon what had been chosen in haste. Citizens taxed themselves nearly to urban death to pay for the ambitious street raising that figuratively hitched the skirts of infant "Sacramento City" above the floodwaters. Sacramento survived—a repeated refrain of its long, indomitable history.

The new city's locale would be a choice from which there was no turning back; its doughty inhabitants "altered" nature by building levees. When these barricades proved inadequate, the city's visionaries entered into a compact with the imaginative engineers of the Central Pacific Railroad, the western leg of the famous transcontinental railroad, who, in exchange for land and rail access, transformed "unruly" nature by redirecting the American River and erecting and improving stronger new levees. The railroad also created a symbiotic relationship between Sacramento and the fertile hinterland, both near and far. Agriculture became and is still an important mainstay of Sacramento's livelihood. The fields provided millions of tons of rice, hops, and other grains for the city's processing plants. Orchards, groves, and farms transferred vast quantities of fruits, nuts, and vegetables to Sacramento's food-processing, boxing, and shipping enterprises.

Richard Orsi's chapter in this volume details how the railroad filled in (and polluted) land that became the city's major industrial complex and its chief source of wage-earning jobs for many years. It cut through city neighborhoods, spewing noise and pollution, but while it destroyed and altered the lands around it, the railroad also helped to preserve the city and the rivers from ruination. Railroad interests aided the city in a long but eventually successful battle against hydraulic miners in the far-off hills of the eastern Sierra whose high-pressure hoses dumped tons of destructive slickens into the riverbeds, overspreading the fields and orchards on which Sacramento relied for a part of its economic life. Orsi's chapter represents the paradoxical nature of Sacramento's "commingling" of nature and culture. The railroad contributed to the "disordered environmental patterns" (including congestion, pollution, landscape degradation, and space allocation) that afflicted Sacramento. But it also "created or encouraged more balanced, sustainable human-nature" relationships. Although pilloried as a greedy and parasitic "Octopus" by Sacramento journalists such as C. K. McClatchy, the railroad ultimately gave as much as it took from Sacramento: jobs, economic stability, and critical assistance in taming the waters and assuring the city that it could survive and prosper.

Part II, "Valley Reclamation," highlights the overarching role of the agricultural impetus and, in particular, the realities and politics of river control—a by-product of the wider need to provide stability and predictability for the region's agricultural economy. Sacramento became "nature's metropolis," as David Vaught argues, because of the purposeful intervention of individual farmers, engineers, land speculators, and legislators who produced an array of land policies and created agencies to tame the landscape and alter the natural environment to make it economically productive. Todd Holmes and Anthony E. Carlson detail with great specificity the twists and turns of policy makers who pressed for a more coordinated, equitable, and efficacious use of Sacramento's water, for navigability of the rivers, and for the rights of all who lived "whithersoever the river cometh." Sacramentans threw bridges over the rivers to connect the city with nearby Yolo County's factories in the field and with the truck farms and orchards of the eastern part of the county. The rivers provided a test ground for the efforts of the emerging Progressive state, which undertook to rationalize water-use policies not only for flood control but to ensure the equitable usage of water resources. The reclaimed lands provided by dams, levees, and the huge Thor and Hercules dredgers of the Natomas Company also provided agricultural produce and work for the Sacramento food-processing plants. The rivers were the point of reference for city buildings and public space, and they gave, in the biblical phrase, "joy to the city" by providing bucolic pathways for walking, jogging, or biking, lovely vistas for elegant homes, recreational boating for summer months, and water for drinking, maintaining lawns, and filling swimming pools. No longer an "island community," Sacramento developed a version of the organizational revolution that drew on the advice of professionals who rationalized the use of the river systems. Reclaiming the valley also required the creation of a new identity for the Sacramento region. This effort was the work of local booster organizations such as the chamber of commerce and other development associations. Paul J. P. Sandul argues in his chapter that Sacramento's boosters and real estate speculators touted the area's rural-urban combination as a heaven on earth. The siren song of temperate days, of abundant citrus fruit, and health and prosperity had for many years enticed weather-battered easterners and midwesterners to the California capital. Sacramento boosters like the McClatchy brothers (Charles and Valentine, owners of the *Sacramento Bee* who themselves had landholdings in the area) pressed the natural advantages of the region—its water, sunlight, and benign weather. They even argued that northern California citrus ripened before the more widely advertised fruits of the south—and tasted better.

Inevitably, Sacramento, like all of California, was drawn more and more into the orbit of the ever-widening influence of the federal government. The third part of this book, "Government Town," lays heavier emphasis on the instrumentality of human agency than on the earlier themes of "commingling." In the contributions of part III, the effective action of the federal government is highlighted as a critical element in shaping Sacramento's environment and providing the engine for its most dramatic period of population growth. In the Progressive era, the state government was already transforming Sacramento as more and more of the city's workforce labored in state and local bureaucracies (with some of these workers summoned to the city from San Francisco). California, like most of the American West, was dramatically transformed by the huge transfers of federal dollars into infrastructure, defense, and other kinds of discretionary spending. Sacramento became more than ever a government town, with a local economy heavily dependent on paychecks from federal, state, or local government sources. Gray Brechin and Lee Simpson lay bare federal efforts to rescue the city from the worst ravages of the Great Depression. Public works sponsored by the alphabet soup agencies of the New Deal—the Public Works Administration (PWA), the Civil Works Administration (CWA), the Civilian Conservation Corps (CCC), and the Works Progress Administration (WPA)—poured millions of dollars into Sacramento and employed hundreds of Sacramentans. These efforts left behind visible monuments, including two high schools, an array of public buildings, a popular band shell, water towers, a rock garden in the city's most prominent public park, military structures, and the Tower Bridge. Less visible, these and other federal agencies also repaired roads, cleaned out weed-choked culverts, and literally sheltered hundreds of homeless and starving people who camped out in the city's various Hoovervilles and took advantage of its benign climate. Brechin is one of the foremost scholars working to re-awaken millions of historically illiterate Americans to the ubiquity and effectiveness of federal intervention. Sacramentans who labor under neoconservative myths that private enterprise created local infrastructure will find Brechin and Simpson's conclusions quite challenging.

Rand Herbert's chapter discusses the creation of the Sacramento region's defense economy, which supplanted the railroads as the economic mainstay of the region. The military already had selected California's sunny skies as the best place to train neophyte airmen during World War I. Later, as relations with Japan deteriorated during the 1930s, American defense planners girded for war by locating critical supply depots well inland from vulnerable coastal installations. Sacramento, sufficiently distant from the ocean and protected in part by mountain redoubts, was a natural location—shrewdly advanced by local booster Arthur S. Dudley. The new military installations—McClellan Field, Mather Field, the Army Signal Depot, and Camp Kohler—helped Sacramento play its role in "Fortress California." They also transformed once placid pasturelands into thriving workplaces, thus depositing millions of dollars into the local economy. These same military installations continued to perform such duties during the cold war and sprouted infrastructure and suburbs like mushrooms. Aerospace testing also shook the environs of the eastern part of the county as mighty rocket engines were tested with distressing regularity.

These facilities flourished and sustained Sacramento's economy, causing it to grow dramatically in the middle years of the twentieth century. However, when political machinations and a changing international climate undercut their usefulness, their time ended, and, like the railroads, when they closed they also left behind pollution and surplus buildings.

New people meant additional demands on outdated energy systems. Power generation, an increasing need since the late nineteenth century, began simply, with a small dam near Folsom. Sixty years later, two new dams—higher and more awe inspiring than ever—held back the fast-flowing American River at two points, thus providing protection from floods and generating hydroelectric power and recreation for Sacramento's fast-growing postwar population. But some argued that the region needed even more power. Chris Castaneda's astute distillation of oral histories provides us with an important examination of Sacramento County's municipal utility and an ultimately ill-fated attempt to harness atomic power for the region. But the problem-plagued history of nuclear energy in Sacramento and the interplay between local government and environmental politics, combined with the accidents at Three Mile Island and Chernobyl, helped a cadre of activists to persuade Sacramentans to shut down the facility.

The last section of the book, "Reclaiming the Past," reflects the impact of the environmental movement and the aligned interests in historical preservation and heritage tourism.[8] The twin impact of these developments caused a rethinking of how the Sacramento region allocated its public space and resources. Part IV offers a thoughtful examination of the concerted efforts of Sacramentans to reclaim a world they had lost or freely bartered away in exchange for continued urban viability. Sacramento had early on lamented its loss of trees, which gave way to efforts to control the rivers and to build the city. In particular, the long, hot summers were even more difficult to bear without the natural cooling of shade trees. Likewise, the dusty streets were unattractive, particularly to state legislators, who sometimes felt condemned to hell during the sessions of the legislature. My own work on Charles K. McClatchy, editor of the city's most widely circulated daily, the *Sacramento Bee*, recounts his front-page scolding of those who cut down trees and his relentless insistence that Sacramento needed tree-lined commercial streets and neighborhoods to provide shade and beauty to the California capital. A restful and memorial-filled park took shape around the state capitol, and Sacramentans could then find shade and peace as they walked through the giant granite pillars that stood as guardians around the statehouse. Later generations would call for small, postage-stamp-size parks—green spaces in the relentless grid and also places for youth to engage the physical culture that eugenicist Charles Goethe insisted was essential for the health and vitality of the American race.

Urban planners dreamed of diagonal boulevards emanating from the state capitol. City parks were an issue of great contention when William Land, the hotelier and former mayor (not to mention gambler), bequeathed a small fortune to purchase land for a large park where Sacramentans could picnic, recreate, and meet each other. Suburban development also had a green-belt flavor to it as small communities of agricultural gentleman farmers set up colonies to plant citrus orchards, delicately swaying olive trees, and fields of hops and barley. Even the giant Natomas Company planted vineyards and fields on reclaimed land. As Al Holland's chapter indicates, other dreamers sought to preserve the natural habitat of the riverbanks to the advantage of the growing city. The American River Parkway attempted to preserve the ecosystem's diverse wildlife and flora as a perpetual treasure for all Sacramentans. Denizens hike or bicycle along the parkway's winding paths or float gently down the river's chilly waters on hot Sacramento afternoons.

Returning to the legacy of the area's first inhabitants, Tanis Thorne explains how the native peoples first engaged the forces of nature—taking and receiving— and found themselves reborn and reinvested in their ancestral lands. In a twist of fate, they imitated the early gold rush era entrepreneurs by setting up a thriving gaming industry that provided a rich—if at times contentious—source of revenue for these tribes who had earlier been deprived of their land and very existence. Lee Simpson and Lisa Prince then turn to the city's other riverbank, along the Sacramento, to describe the complex and historically challenging reconstruction of Old Sacramento. The riverbank, once a railroad property and a deteriorating skid row, was one of the first transformed by the urban renewal and historic preservation policies of the federal government. Simpson and Prince not only provide the outline of the interesting policy history that created Old Sacramento but also raise deeper questions about the reconstruction of Sacramento's historical past. How does one accurately and honestly capture the historical memory of a community that has so often—by necessity—had to rediscover and reinvent itself? Where does one "freeze-frame" the history of Sacramento: in the gold rush period, in the railroad era, in its shuttered military bases or the capitol, or in the modernizing midtown?

These chapters each accentuate in their own way the tensions between humans and the natural environment that created Sacramento and that still inform contemporary urban realities. Sacramentans, like most Americans, are more conscious of the fragility of the environment than ever before. Reducing or undoing some of the ecological damage of the past, living more harmoniously with the natural environment, and conserving resources has been written into Sacramento's daily existence by law and public consensus. Economic changes in the city also have created new realities. The railroad yards are long gone—now mostly detoxified and awaiting the political will and money to transform them into commercial and/or urban use. Gone, too, are the military installations with their large workforces and distinct demands on the region. Sacramentans relish their proximity to the relatively tamed rivers that frame the city, but since Hurricane Katrina, they worry even more that an excessively wet winter will make the Sacramento Valley a replica of post-2005 New Orleans. These chapters will contribute to a sense of continuity in understanding human interaction with the regional environment. Nature and culture will continue to "commingle" in this area but perhaps with more thought and foresight, assisted by the perspective that these chapters bring. This book is the contribution of the work of an assortment of historians who have dedicated significant time and energy—and in some cases a full career's worth—to the study of the Sacramento region. If that indefatigable "lover of the place" Charles K. McClatchy were still alive, he would no doubt confer a rare accolade on this circle of scholars: "More power to your elbow!"

As this volume goes to press, renewed efforts to reuse land once developed by the all-powerful railroad move forward in the fits and starts that have always accompanied progress in the California capital. Renewed appreciation for the virtues of living in Sacramento's sometimes pulsating downtown has refurbished old neighborhoods and created new venues for entertainment and dining. This current season of re-creation focuses on streets and entertainment corridors once used by businesses and the railroad. However, it also extends to open concern for those left behind by the instability of the local economy—the homeless, who daily congregate in large numbers for free meals, showers, and respite from the perils of indigence. They, too, are part of the "environment," camping on the riverfronts, occupying the vacant spaces in the downtown, milling around the businesses and enterprises of the middle class, who are still the bedrock of Sacramento's vitality. Perhaps the same indomitability that led the denizens of Sacramento to fight flood, fire, disease, and the dislocations created by business enterprises will one day be applied to helping those who often cannot help themselves so that the city born at the meeting of two rivers may be a place fit for habitation by all.

PART I

Boomtown Sacramento

CHAPTER 1

John A. Sutter and the Indian Business

Albert L. Hurtado

John Sutter, as he frequently explained to anyone who might listen, was a man of no small ambitions. Though he arrived in the Sacramento Valley all but destitute, with a tangled record of past financial failure, he expected to accumulate a fortune by building a profitable, flourishing business enterprise in this most remote borderland of Mexican California.[1] Some people would have seen the valley as a wilderness, a place unsettled and untamed, but it was far from that. While Hispanic peoples had only explored this isolated region, native peoples had lived there and exploited its resources for untold generations. Now Sutter wished to take those resources for his own use. Thus, central to Sutter's grand, vastly optimistic plan was his reliance on the native people of the Sacramento region. Indian labor was the key to transforming native resources into commodities for a growing, worldwide, capitalist marketplace. Sutter's contemporaries appreciated this reality, although later writers and historical commentators often ignored it. If we return to a pre–gold rush appreciation of the importance of the Indian business as a basis for making money out of natural resources in the early West, we will have a truer view of Sutter and the enterprise he called New Helvetia.

In taking up this topic, my intent is to demonstrate the different ways in which Sutter used the Sacramento Valley's Indian resources for his own advantage. Along the way, I hope to clarify Sutter's purpose in coming to this region in the first place, describe some of the models of Indian labor relations that he had observed, and examine the methods that he used to control his Indian labor force. From this inquiry we should gain a fuller appreciation of John Sutter and his times. By focusing on the Indian business, we will be able to define more clearly the historical portrait of Sacramento's pioneer founder and also gain a fresh perspective concerning the larger human community upon which the current one was founded.

Building Blocks of Nascent Capitalism

Sutter did not invent the Indian business. He was a copyist who sought to imitate the success of others who had made fortunes with Indian labor. When Sutter arrived in the United States in 1834, the fur trade was the most obvious of several ways to profit from Indian work. From Hudson's Bay to the Pacific Ocean, large fur companies employed and traded with Indians. Traders happily extended credit to Indian clients who promised to pay up in furs. This arrangement tied Indians and their labor to a commercial economy. Beaver furs were the staple commodity produced by the fur trade. In the early nineteenth century, these pelts were made into high-quality felt for hats in the United States and Europe. American otter furs ornamented expensive clothing in China, as well as in the Occident. Buffalo hides were fashioned into robes for New England sleigh rides. Deer and other hides were sold far outside the western regions that produced them. Indian labor produced these commodities. While the mountain man, dressed in skins and perhaps wearing a coonskin hat, became the stock image of the American fur trade, Indian labor produced most of the animal skins that entered the world market. These items were often exchanged in a system of barter that was controlled by powerful businesses such as the Hudson's Bay Company, John Jacob Astor's American Fur Company, and lesser companies.[2] Within the United States, it should be added, the federal government cheerfully acted as a bill collector for traders—who were paid when federal agents distributed annual Indian annuities—and the federal government also used Indian indebtedness as a lever to force tribes to cede more land to the young republic.[3] Indian agricultural labor also supported the fur trade; Mandan and Hidatsa farmers peddled food to the traders at the posts on the upper Missouri River.[4]

Indian labor was thus fundamental to the fur trade—a considerable American industry during the early nineteenth century. The wealthy New Yorker John Jacob Astor founded his mighty fortune on the fur trade. Sutter scarcely could have failed to notice that Astor, a fellow immigrant of Germanic origin, was the wealthiest man of his age.[5]

In New Mexico, which, like California, was part of the Republic of Mexico until 1848, Indian labor was vital to the pastoral economy. Pueblo Indian shepherds tended flocks for missionaries, rancheros, and themselves and wove woolen and cotton fabric for trade with Mexican and Anglo American merchants who came down the Santa Fe Trail from Missouri. In two centuries of intermittent war, Spaniards, Mexicans, and their Pueblo Indian allies had taken slaves from among the Apaches, Navajos, and Utes. Some Indian prisoners were sold south to work in the silver mines of Zacatecas, and a few luckless Apaches even reached the auction block in Cuba. Captive children were frequently taken into prosperous New Mexican households, where they worked as servants while learning Spanish and Catholic customs. Numerous enough to form their own community, the progeny of these slaves were known as *genizaros*, which now literally means half-breed but then probably characterized the mixed cultural ancestry of these people. This combination of free and coerced labor reflected labor practices that had provided an economic underpinning for the Spanish Empire from the time of Columbus.[6]

California under Spain (1697–1821) and Mexico (1821–1848) also relied on Indian labor. The Franciscan missions, which served material as well as religious purposes, were the most important economic institutions in old California. The twenty thousand neophytes who lived and labored in these religious establishments provided the brawn that tended herds, tilled gardens, and made the mission shops hum. When mission properties came into private ownership following Mexican independence, much of the Indian workforce as well as mission lands wound up in the hands of rancheros—who were not above attacking native communities in the Central Valley to draft more Indian workers. Here, too, Sutter found a combination of free labor, slaves, and peons, all laboring among the golden hills of Mexican California in the halcyon days of the hide and tallow trade.[7]

Truly, when Sutter came to America, Indian workers from the Great Lakes to the Pacific and from Mexico to Hudson's Bay were among the building blocks of nascent capitalism. They were not the freeholding farmers that Thomas Jefferson revered nor the merchant capitalists and factory operatives that Alexander Hamilton believed would create in the United States a commercial empire to rival that of Europe. Yet Indian workers were there in fields, in pastures, in forests, and, yes, even in workshops of the American frontier. Away from America's burgeoning cities and towns, out on the edges of Indian country, in the shaggy fringes of frontier society, native labor was an undeniable part of the scene. Indians took a modest role in some places; in others they were indispensable to the primary purpose of frontier entrepreneurs: to bring western land and resources into the marketplace while reaping profits for themselves. Because this process was distant from eastern cities, new arrivals from Europe might overlook the possibilities of native labor in the continent-wide Indian business, but John A. Sutter had his eyes wide open when he reached the United States, and soon he was in a position to see for himself.

A Tour of Western Enterprise

Although the basic facts of Sutter's American experience before he reached California are well known, a brief summary will emphasize an important point: Sutter was thoroughly schooled in the Indian business before he arrived in the Sacramento Valley. If he had purposely set out to obtain such an education, he could scarcely have done a better job. After coming to the United States, Sutter did not stay long in New York but headed for Missouri, whose western border faced Indian country and opened to the Santa Fe and Oregon Trails. Sutter would see it all.

To mask his business and legal problems in Switzerland, Sutter fabricated an impressive résumé that included a bogus captaincy. With this fictional identity, he soon carved out a niche in the German colony near Saint Louis. Looking for quicker profits than a settled life could provide, Sutter joined the 1835 Santa Fe caravan. He was not disappointed. Trade was brisk in the Mexican town, and Sutter gained the impression that commercial success was an easy matter. A second Santa Fe trip in 1836 disabused him of naïve notions about the profitability of the Southwest. He lost not only his own money but that of other investors as well. Sutter recouped some of his losses by purchasing stolen mustangs from Apaches and selling them to the German burghers who farmed the Missouri bottoms. It was a transaction that ultimately must have proved less than satisfactory for buyers who were unfamiliar with the dangers of working with truly wild horses.

Having worn out a welcome among his compatriots, Sutter moved to Westport, now the site of Kansas City, and traded with the Shawnee and Delaware Indians—a trade that, contrary to US law, included whiskey. By 1838, Sutter was again broke and anxious to leave his debts behind. Determined to put as much distance as possible between himself and his creditors, he decided to go to California, making the first leg of the journey with the American Fur Company's caravan to the Rocky Mountain rendezvous, an annual fur trade fair where mountain men and Indians from all over the region congregated, drank, sported, and did business. On the way to California, he purchased an Indian boy for one hundred dollars, a "large price," according to Sutter.[8] Kit Carson had once owned the boy, who spoke tolerable English and was familiar with some parts of the transcontinental route. It is even possible that the boy was a California native, since Carson had earlier fought Indians and trapped furs within California. Whatever the young man's origins, Sutter took him to the rendezvous; from there he trekked west to Oregon's Willamette valley, then north to the Hudson's Bay Company Pacific headquarters at Fort Vancouver.

From the Oregon country, Sutter had intended to head directly south to California, but Hudson's Bay Company men convinced him that he would be foolhardy to attempt such a route through Indian country with the small party that accompanied him. It would be much safer, he was informed, to sail to Hawaii and then to California. Sutter agreed and, with eight followers who also wanted to go to California, took passage on the "honorable company's" bark *Columbia*. The ship dropped anchor in Honolulu, where he and his party waited for a vessel bound for the mainland.

They waited for several months, but no California-bound ship appeared. In the meantime, as Sutter later claimed, he so impressed the Hawaiian monarch, Kamehameha III, that he received an offer to take command of the island's native army. When Sutter refused, the disappointed king nonetheless provided him with indentured servants—two women and "eight men, all experienced seamen—for three years."[9] Sutter rewrote his own history, as he often did. He actually acquired the servants from another high-born Hawaiian, who expected to receive a share of the ten-dollar-per-month wage that Sutter paid them.[10]

Anxious to get to California, Sutter decided to sign on as supercargo of a trading ship bound for the Russian-American Company's headquarters at New Archangel (Sitka), Alaska. The Russian-American Company was a fur outfit specializing in sea otter and seal pelts. Besides the Alaskan operations, as Sutter learned, the Russians also had established Ross Colony in California, an agricultural settlement with its headquarters at Fort Ross, north of Bodega Bay. In Alaska, the Russians wined and dined their visitor and revealed more about Sutter's elusive destination.

Finally, Sutter and his small band of followers sailed to California, arriving in San Francisco Bay, then going on to Monterey. Before he embarked for the interior, Sutter visited Fort Ross and stopped at Mariano Vallejo's Sonoma rancho. He also briefly inspected some of the Franciscan mission properties in northern California, where the process of secularization was bringing to an end the missionaries' control over their native converts.

By the time the Swiss entrepreneur and his party paddled up the Sacramento River, Sutter had seen virtually every aspect of the Indian business. He had traded with the Apaches, Shawnees, and Delawares. At Fort Hall, Bent's Fort, Fort Vancouver, and in Alaska, he had seen the fur trade as practiced by Anglo Americans, Britons, and Russians. He had seen California's missions and ranchos with their Indian labor forces in plain view, and he had witnessed Indian-Hispanic labor relations in Santa Fe. He had seen Indian slaves—and purchased one—as well as indentured servants and free workers. A small force of indentured Hawaiians was at his disposal. Surely, in the summer of 1839 there was not a better prepared person to engage in the Indian business in the Sacramento Valley.

Besides accumulating information at the various stops on his grand tour of frontier enterprises, Sutter gathered letters of recommendation from respected westerners.[11] Some of Sutter's biographers have portrayed this exercise as a kind of con game.[12] Certainly, Sutter embellished his reputation, his financial condition, and his business prospects, but the men who endorsed him did not do so because they had been fooled. They recommended him to the attention of their frontier peers precisely because they were *not* fooled. They did not see him as green and untried, a visionary with utopian ideas. They recognized in him a man who appeared as calculating and ruthless as they were. They saw him as a practical man—someone who was quite capable of imitating their own accomplishments. And that is precisely what Sutter did.

Central Valley Indian Resources

Chief among valley resources was the Indian population that Sutter needed in order to exploit the region's other resources. In 1839, perhaps forty thousand to fifty thousand Indians lived in the Sacramento Valley, with a like number in the San Joaquin.[13] Before the arrival of Europeans, the people of central California hunted, fished, and gathered wild foods. They did not practice agriculture because they had no need for it. The temperate climate and a variety of food resources made for

FIGURE I.I. A typical Indian community in the Sacramento Valley before Sutter's arrival. This could have been a Miwok or Nisenan village. Note the conical gathering baskets that women would have used to gather acorns, seeds, and other wild plant foods. Several barrel-shaped granaries are scattered among the dwellings. Clothing was optional during warm weather. Courtesy Center for Sacramento History, Eleanor McClatchy Collection.

FIGURE I.2. An Indian fisherman. Salmon were among the staple foods of the valley Indians before Sutter came. This image depicts one of several traditional means of catching salmon and other fish. Courtesy Center for Sacramento History.

FIGURE 1.3. A young Indian woman grinding acorns. Acorns were an important part of the Indian diet. Women gathered and milled them into meal that was used in soup and made into bread. Sutter insisted that Indians who worked for him wear clothing such as this simple shift. Self-interest as well as prudery motivated him; he sold clothing at his trade store. Courtesy Center for Sacramento History.

an abundant and relatively easy life without tilling the fertile valley land. This is not to say that California Indians were lazy or somehow backward. They took each plant and game animal in its season, following a fairly constant round of activity from spring through fall, and during the winter they devoted much time to the cycle of religious ceremonies and dancing now known as the Kuksu cult. To live through the lean winter, of course, Indians had to amass surplus food during the warm seasons—a fact that argues well for their industriousness. The absence of agriculture did not reflect a lack of Indian ambition or aptitude but demonstrated how well they practiced the life of hunting and gathering.[14]

Indians divided labor according to gender. Women's work revolved around the gathering and preparation of grass seeds, berries, tubers, and the ubiquitous acorn. This latter food the women ground into flour with a stone muller or with a pestle in a bowl or a bedrock mortar. Then they placed the flour in a sandy depression near a stream and poured water through it to leach out the bitter tannin. The women cooked the flour as a kind of nutritious mush and prepared other foods from it as well. They also cooked the fish and meat that the men brought back from the hunt. Besides undertaking culinary duties, women also made baskets and other utensils from grasses and willow bark. California Indians still are noted basket weavers; the traditional basketry skull cap symbolized women's work and the weaver's skill throughout the region.

Men's work included hunting deer, elk, and antelope that grazed on the valley's vast grasslands. Before the advent of metal goods, men chipped stone projectile points for their hunting arrows and lances. Likewise, they made stone knives and scrapers with which to butcher animals for meat and dress the skins. Indians fished with spears, traps, and nets. To improve their efficiency, Indian fishermen built substantial weirs (or fish dams) to concentrate their prey. Central California natives also relied on small game, rodents, and insects as sources of protein, often using fire as an aid to their hunting and gathering.[15]

Indians did not farm the land, but they did cultivate it. Fire was their principal tool. Indians periodically set fires to clear underbrush, encourage the growth of grass, and open the oak lands to make them more productive sources for game animals. The Sacramento Valley was not an untamed wilderness but an environment that Indians shaped to make it richer and more productive.[16]

The traditional skills of California Indians did not immediately become obsolete when Europeans appeared. Native technology and knowledge of local ecology were important resources on a raw, isolated frontier, and Europeans were prepared to take full advantage of them until other resources were available. Long before Sutter came, however, Indians had added new skills to their credentials as workers. At the end of the eighteenth century, Franciscan missionaries began to recruit neophytes in the California interior. Until the Mexican civil government issued secularization orders in 1834, thousands of Plains Miwok and Valley Yokuts went to the missions in the coastal region. Missions were supposed to teach Indians European trades as well as the Catholic faith. Accordingly, former interior Indians learned to plant and harvest crops, ride horses, tend cattle, weave textiles, make adobe blocks, and build the structures that were the architectural hallmark of the California missions.[17]

Many Miwok and Yokuts neophytes became disenchanted with the missions and returned to the Central Valley. Often they took livestock from mission herds; horses were their favorite target. In training a labor force, Hispanic Californians had thus taught Indians a body of skills that made them formidable enemies and very efficient horse thieves. Established on the tributaries of the San Joaquin River, the so-called horse-thief Indians were the bane of Spanish, Mexican, and early Anglo American California. The Miwok who lived between the Cosumnes and Stanislaus Rivers were the most vigorous of these raiders, and the Muquelemne Miwok were the most feared.

In 1827, Jedediah Smith opened California to the Anglo American fur trade and introduced interior Indians to mountain men and their ways. Beaver pelts were the primary object of Smith and those who followed in his wake, but they also noticed another valuable California resource: horses and mules. Some traders, like Smith, purchased horses from Mexican owners and sold them at the annual trappers' rendezvous and at points as far east as Missouri. Other, less scrupulous traders—Jedediah Smith reputedly carried a Bible, did not swear, and lived an otherwise upstanding Christian life—did not bother to secure legal title to California horses. Instead, they traded with the Miwok and Yokuts raiders who rustled from Mexican herds. In the 1830s and 1840s, Anglo American traders and their Indian accomplices made off with thousands of California horses, destined for markets east of the Rocky Mountains. Thus, California blood stock contributed to the ancestry of the famed Missouri mule.

Though it was illicit from the Mexican perspective, rustling was a part of the California Indian business. The Indians who worked at this dangerous trade had skills that should not be underestimated. To steal a herd of horses and ride fast and hard over long distances through broken terrain at night, while eluding pursuing California vaqueros (according to some admirers, the finest light horsemen in the world), was not an easy trick. Hispanic Californians were unable to put a stop to this long-distance rustling, and Anglo American authorities did no better until the gold rush shifted the demographic balance of the Indian and white populations.[18]

Sutter intended to make use of many of the same resources that Indians had used for generations, but he did not necessarily see them in the same way. For Indians, oak trees were an invaluable source of food that should be preserved. In the oak parklands that spread over the valley, Sutter saw cordwood for fuel and winter warmth, barrel staves, building material, and charcoal. He intended to mine those resources, not farm them. Grasslands provided Indians with food and material for making baskets. They also fed antelope and elk that added protein to the native diet. Sutter wanted to convert these natural pastures to forage for his horses, cattle, and sheep. Some land would be cleared to plant farm crops like wheat, beans, and other crops. The Sacramento River fed Indians with countless spawning salmon. Sutter intended to salt them, pack them in barrels, and ship them to markets around the Pacific basin.

From Sutter's perspective, the interior Indians were a labor resource with a variety of traditional and new skills that enhanced their value as workers. Some among these people offered the prospect of a basic native labor pool already familiar with agriculture and livestock herding. But as Sutter would soon learn, these native Californians could be a useful labor force but challenging to manage. They had already gained plenty of experience with white men, and they had their own ideas about the utility of Sutter's New Helvetia project.

Musket, Lash, and Gibbet

Sutter had no illusions about finding docile Indians in the Sacramento Valley. He intended to establish friendly relations with them, but he realized that force might be needed to maintain his small group of intruders. Though the Nisenan Indians were initially friendly, the lord of New Helvetia came equipped with brass cannons that his men mounted and prepared for firing when they made camp on the American River. Upon the departure of the vessels that had carried him up the Sacramento, Sutter had his cannoneers fire a nine-gun salute that made a lasting impression on William Heath Davis: "A large number of deer, elk and other animals on the plains were startled, running to and fro, stopping to listen, their heads raised, full of curiosity and wonder, seemingly attracted and fascinated to the spot, while from the interior of the adjacent wood the howls of wolves and coyotes filled the air, and immense flocks of waterfowl flew wildly over the camp."[19]

Sutter remembered firing his cannons, too, but not merely to salute the departing boats. "To show the Indians the effect of powder & ball," Sutter recalled, "I planted my guns and fired at a target. They did not care to have them tried on them."[20] Sutter, it should go without saying, had not brought cannons to the Sacramento Valley to hunt deer but to overpower Indians who resisted his authority.

Sutter was either lucky or wise in his selection of the site for New Helvetia. He settled in Nisenan country near the villages of Pusune and Momol, just north of Miwok territory. Occupying a borderland between the Miwok and the Nisenan, Sutter was able to play off these groups against each other.[21] Indian responses to Sutter were divided more or less along tribal lines, but it must be admitted that some Nisenan never accepted Sutter and some Miwok readily joined the coterie of Indians, Mexicans, British and Anglo American fur traders, and Hawaiians who founded Sacramento's modern multiethnic society. He first made contact with Gualacomne and Ochejamne Miwoks about ten miles south of the American River. Some of these Indians had fled from the Franciscan missions. The Miwoks had been in contact with the mountain men and horse rustlers who plagued the Mexican ranchos on the coast. They accompanied Sutter as he went farther north into Nisenan country. The Nisenans retreated north of the American River while Sutter established his first settlement near the south bank of the same river. Thus, Miwoks helped to clear Nisenans from their customary territory and became Sutter's indispensable allies and laborers.[22] Farther to the south, other Miwoks (notably the Muquelemne) stayed aloof from Sutter, occasionally raiding his herds, although some of them eventually established amicable relations with Sutter.

The Nisenan had been in contact with Anglo American and British fur traders and had suffered greatly from a malaria epidemic that swept the valley in 1833.[23] Unlike the Miwok, Nisenan people had not entered the Spanish missions, though some former mission Indians had evidently settled among them. Despite a few early attempts to oust Sutter, the Nisenan for the most part quickly accommodated, joined his workforce, and helped him to assert his influence among interior Indians. Indians who accepted Sutter responded not only to force but also to the advantages that Sutter's presence offered: a steady supply of trade goods and protection from Indian and Mexican enemies. Moreover, new diseases like malaria, smallpox, and measles had ravaged the Indian population, leaving them in a debilitated condition and less able to resist. Sutter, of course, was not a social experimenter bent on creating a new community based on racial equality but a hardhearted realist determined to put the valley's human capital to work. Wage labor was an important part of Sutter's master plan; whenever he could, he paid Indians for their labor. He did not do so, however, merely because he believed in an honest day's pay for an honest day's labor but because the payment of wages and the extension of credit provided Sutter with more control over Indian workers. His system was simple and

FIGURE I.4. An Indian dwelling in the mid-nineteenth century. This illustration shows continuity and change after Sutter's time. Indians wore European clothes, a practice that Sutter initiated. Baskets and granaries remained a part of the Indians' technological kit. Courtesy Center for Sacramento History, Eleanor McClatchy Collection.

effective. He issued metal disks to Indian workers, who wore them as pendants on necklaces. After they had worked for a standard period of time, Sutter punched a distinctive hole in the disk. Each hole represented a monetary value that Indians could redeem only at Sutter's store. Heinrich Lienhard, one of Sutter's white overseers, recalled that Indians had to work about two weeks to receive enough credit to purchase a pair of cotton trousers or a plain muslin shirt. Other trade goods— metalware, blankets, weapons—were no doubt priced accordingly.[24] Like other Indian traders, Sutter extended credit to his customers and secured a lien on Indian labor in the future. Thus, Sutter created a primitive form of currency and a system of debt and credit with which he controlled wages and prices in New Helvetia.

Because we are all now caught in the web of money, debt, and credit, some may ask whether that was such a bad thing for Indians. For some individual Indians, such a system might have worked well because it provided a fairly reliable livelihood. However, labor in New Helvetia drew adult male Indians away from *rancherías,* leaving the women, children, and elderly unprotected. The Indian working days symbolized in Sutter's tin currency were not available for traditional Indian pursuits. Blankets, clothing, and beads could not replace traditional foods, which went unharvested at the proper times. However attractive the short-term rewards, wage labor in the long run thus tended to break down Indian community life while undercutting the customary native economy.

And what did Indian workers do for Sutter at New Helvetia? The short answer is that they did virtually everything. They caught fish and salted and packed them in barrels for shipment to South America. They trapped beaver and otters and cured the pelts for the fur trade. They killed deer and elk, rendered tallow, and stored salted meat in barrels. They tanned hides, made leather goods, produced felt, blocked hats, wove blankets, and distilled brandy from native grapes. Indians mixed mud and straw, which they shaped into bricks then laid in courses to form the walls of Sutter's Fort. They dug ditches, plowed furrows, and sowed, weeded, reaped, threshed, winnowed, and gleaned Sutter's wheat. Indian hands bagged, stored, and ground grain to flour, which they baked into bread. Indian vaqueros herded, branded, killed, and butchered New Helvetia cattle.[25]

Sutter provided a frank description of the magnitude and variety of his Indian workforce: "Business increased until I had in the harvest 600 men, & to feed them I had to kill four oxen, sometimes five daily. . . . I had at the same time twelve thousand head of cattle and two thousand horses, and ten or fifteen thousand sheep. I had all the Indians I could employ. There were thirty plows with fresh oxen running every morning. I had looms and taught the natives to weave blankets and [to make] hats. My best days were just before the gold discovery."[26] When Sutter reminisced about the flush days of early California, he thought of a time when he had all the Indians he could employ. Even in old age, Sutter still appreciated the simple calculus of the Indian business. Cheap Indian labor plus abundant natural resources made profits. Sutter hired white skilled labor and overseers whenever he could, and historians have emphasized the presence of the few white craftsmen who worked at the fort.[27] But it was the labor of the Indian majority that created a demand for the services of the white minority. What, we might ask, would a cooper do at Sutter's Fort without the agricultural production of those hundreds of Indian hands? And we can also imagine that Indians helped white craftsmen, cleaned the shops, stoked the blacksmith's fires, drew the water, cut the wood, and attended to the dozens of errands that arose in the course of any craftsman's work day.

Sutter's great success at New Helvetia was in managing the local Indian population for his own purposes. In this, he replicated the achievements of Anglo American, British, and Russian traders and trappers, Franciscan missionaries, California rancheros, and sundry others who relied on Indian labor in the far West. Indian labor was at the very center of Captain Sutter's vision for a vast and thriving New Helvetia, and his fortunes rose and fell with his ability to command native workers.

Nobody, of course, understood this better than Sutter. His correspondence is full of references to his Indian labor needs. Determined to secure that labor, he was willing to use any means at his disposal to get it.[28] The fort was emblematic of Sutter's ambition and authority, and it remains so today. But the fort was not merely a symbol, for it housed an Indian army of perhaps two hundred men supervised by white officers. After Sutter purchased Fort Ross, he dressed his army in Russian uniforms of blue and green.[29] It was an outlandish image yet was part of the daily routine at Sutter's Fort.

This Indian army was a vital part of Sutter's Indian business and a force to be reckoned with in Mexican California. It enabled him to protect his fort, fields, and herds against Miwok raiders. He marched his army against the troublesome Muquelemne Miwok to the south and recounted these exploits with pride.[30] When disaffected *californios* rebelled against the Mexican government, Gov. Manuel Micheltorena called Sutter and his army to service in southern California. Though the army was not defeated, Sutter managed to blunder into enemy hands, and his force surrendered.[31] Nevertheless, the victorious *californios* permitted Sutter and his Indian troops to return to the Sacramento Valley, where they protected Mexican herds in the coastal valleys against the forays of Miwok horse raiders. During the US-Mexico War, these Indians enlisted in the American army and helped to secure California for the United States. Thus, Nisenan and Miwok soldiers became unheralded veterans of a war between foreigners in their native land.[32]

The primary purpose of this Indian force, however, was to control Indians in the Sacramento and San Joaquin Valleys. As Sutter explained to his overseer, Pierson B. Reading, if the Indians were "not kept strickly under fear, it will be no good."[33] Indian communities that violated New Helvetia's unwritten laws risked armed attack, and individual Indians faced corporal punishment from Sutter. Nevertheless, Indians defied Sutter's authority, fled from his service, and instigated rebellions.

Rufino and Raphero, two Miwok men, became central figures in the most dramatic example of Sutter's use of violence to control the Indians at Sutter's Fort. Rufino worked for Sutter while his kinsman Raphero followed the life of a horse raider with the Muquelemne Miwok. Sutter captured Raphero, executed him, and affixed his head over the gate of Sutter's Fort, where one of Sutter's employees saw "the long black hair and skull."[34] Sutter no doubt intended this grisly trophy to deter Indian rebellion; it remained on display for some time. Sutter misjudged the impact of his actions, however, for the execution of Raphero outraged Rufino. In apparent retaliation, Rufino killed his own brother-in-law, a loyal member of Sutter's army, and fled from New Helvetia. For months Sutter hunted for Rufino, who was finally captured and killed in September 1845. But the lord of New Helvetia did not put Rufino's head on display next to Raphero's.[35] Evidently, Sutter decided not to push his luck again.

Sutter recorded Rufino's execution in his *New Helvetia Diary* with a single terse sentence that mixed punishment and business with hardly a pause: "Rufino chief of the Moquelumnes, was tried for murder, found guilty, and executed."[36] Then, without a pause, Sutter recorded that he sent one of his employees for lumber. In Sutter's world, the execution of an Indian and the execution of his orders to employees were prosaic acts. Life went on at New Helvetia. The killing of an Indian was just a part of daily affairs at the fort, a matter of fact and barely remarkable. We do not even know if Sutter built a gallows and hanged Rufino or put him up against one of the fort's walls before an Indian firing squad. Perhaps the killing was perfunctory, unaccompanied by the grim pomp and ceremony of public execution and now just a footnote to Sutter's Indian business.

The Trade in Indian Persons

One more aspect of Sutter's Indian business must be given attention, and that is Indian slavery. While it is true that Sutter paid his Indian workers most of the time, he also used his Indian army to capture native people who were reluctant to work voluntarily. Sometimes he held these dragooned workers in stock pens; when there was space, he locked them in rooms at the fort to keep them from escaping at night.[37] Indian labor was in greatest demand at harvest time. Without machinery, Sutter was utterly dependent on stoop labor to get in his wheat and other crops, and he was always at pains to find enough workers during the long harvest season.

John Bidwell, another of Sutter's employees, has left us a compelling description of Indians at this backbreaking work: "Imagine three or four hundred wild Indians in a grain field armed, some with sickles, some with butcher-knives, some with pieces of hoop iron roughly fashioned into shapes like sickles, but others having only their hands with which to gather up by small handfuls the dry and brittle grain; and as their hands would become sore, they resorted to dry willow sticks, which were split to sever the straw."[38] No wonder that some Indians were unwilling to volunteer for this work. No wonder that Sutter used his army to drive shanghaied workers into the fields.

But Sutter's use of Indian slaves did not stop there. He also found profit in selling and leasing Indians to other landholders. Little documentary evidence remains of these transactions, although what does exist suggests that at one point Sutter derived about one-third of his income from leasing Indians to others.[39] Ordinarily, Sutter fed his Indian workers, and he insisted that those who leased his labor force do likewise. But when times were hard, Sutter could neither feed nor clothe Indian laborers. John Marsh complained in 1845 that one gang of these leased workers arrived at his place "as usual, dying of hunger."[40]

Records of the outright sale of Indians are sketchy. John Chamberlain, Sutter's blacksmith, reported that it was "customary for Capt Sutter to buy and sell Indian boys and girls at New Helvetia."[41] Sutter's correspondence suggests some unsavory aspects of this trade. He promised to send one Mexican ranchero thirty young Indians after a "campaign against the horse-thieves."[42] We may assume that these captives were not free agents competing in an open marketplace. Some of Sutter's clients requested young girls, and Sutter complied, although he evidently had some misgivings. In sending two girls to William Leidesdorff, he wrote that Leidesdorff should take the one "which you like the best, the *other* is for Mr. Ridley, whom I promised one longer as two year's ago." And then he continued, "As this shall never be considered an article of trade [I] make you a present with this girl."[43] Sutter's logic is difficult to comprehend in this matter. When he turned the young girls into gifts for his male friends, they did indeed become "articles of trade." One does not make a gift of a free human being.

It is tempting to compare New Helvetia Indian labor to the slave-based plantation economy in the antebellum South, but the comparison does not quite work. Certainly there were similarities: slavery, the lash, a trade in Indian persons. But New Helvetia did not depend primarily on a slave labor system. Probably the majority, perhaps a large majority, of Indian workers were free. No doubt some of these workers opted for wage labor because of the ever-present threat of force, but some (we will never know how many) freely chose to work for Sutter because it seemed to be advantageous. Wage labor gave Indians access to new material goods at Sutter's store. And, after all, Indians who entered the labor force were by no means unique. People the world over have been abandoning barter and subsistence economies for hundreds of years. I will stop short of saying that it is human nature to do so, but this movement into commercial, money-based economies is one of the major themes of human history. Indians who worked for Sutter showed that they were flexible and that they shared some of the traits of other people, in other times, who have made similar choices.[44]

Free Indian workers, however, did not live in a world of unlimited choices. Under Sutter's aegis, the valley environment was transformed. Indians' customary ways of making a living could no longer be followed because the resource base had been altered by the Indian labor that Sutter had employed. Many "free" workers took up wage labor because they had no other viable choice. Environmental transformation was a form of "soft coercion" that drove Indians into the marketplace as free laborers.

Although individual Indians may have benefited from wage labor, overall the New Helvetia economy had a negative influence on the Indian population. Census records show that Sutter employed far more men than women; women, children, and old people were thus left unprotected when men were at work. Slave raiders from the coast found these defenseless villages tempting targets, though Sutter tried to restrain such invasions.[45]

In addition, Indians who worked for Sutter risked infection with many newly introduced diseases. Because of their centuries of biological isolation from Europe, Asia, and Africa, America's native peoples lacked any genetic resistance or acquired immunities to a wide range of illnesses unknown in the Western Hemisphere before the Euro-American invasion. As a result, smallpox, measles, influenza, and other communicable epidemic disease killed Indians in immense numbers throughout the hemisphere. Locally, in addition to the earlier introduction of malaria, the consequences of this disease frontier were dramatically revealed when a measles epidemic swept the valley in the summer of 1847. Sutter recorded the disease's progress, along with his repeated attempts to recruit replacements for his sick and dying labor force. To his credit, Sutter employed a physician to cure sick Indians, but of course mid-nineteenth-century medicine was totally ineffective against this and similar outbreaks.[46] Thus, employment with Sutter also imposed a mortal tax on the Indian population, a tax that fell due with dreadful regularity.

The gold rush rapidly changed the California economy. Sutter's primitive monetary monopoly quickly ended as gold dust, coin, and regular currency came into circulation. At first, he tried to benefit by contracting Indian labor to early mine operators.[47] But, as more and more white newcomers entered the Mother Lode region and insisted—often by force of arms—that they would not tolerate the competition of any nonwhite, servile workforce in the placer diggings, Indian labor quickly fell out of favor. Finally, Sutter retired to Hock Farm on the Feather River, where he continued to rely on Indian labor. Much to his surprise, however, the conditions of employment for Indian farm workers were also changing. Native workers demanded cash, while Sutter preferred to give them old clothes, just as he had done at Sutter's Fort. Consequently, Sutter was unable to secure their services—at least not on the terms that he remembered so fondly from his best years in New Helvetia.

In 1856, Sutter was nearly broke and about to lose his farm. With creditors pressing from every side, he made a last-ditch attempt to resurrect the labor patterns of the past. He wrote to the superintendent of Indian affairs for California, Thomas Henley, the official responsible for carrying out federal Indian policy in the Golden State. The Indians near his farm, Sutter claimed, were out of control. They refused to work for less than a dollar a day and, in Sutter's opinion, spent their money unwisely on liquor in Marysville. Many of them preferred to work for wages in the town rather than in Sutter's fields. As Sutter put it in his characteristic, broken English, "nothing as the Dollars could bring them to work." The Nisenan, who had formerly worked willingly for the lord of New Helvetia, "don't like more to work unless they are paid more as they earn."[48]

A little translation is in order here. Sutter was upset because Indians demanded an honest day's wages for a long day's work. They wanted to be free to work for whomever they pleased and to spend their cash on whatever they wanted. This simply would not do for Sutter's purposes, and he had a remedy in mind. He advised the superintendent to take the most troublesome Nisenan to a reservation and "give me the Control *only of the* Hock and Yukulme Indians, I would make them work and pay them a reasonable compensation in food and Clothing. And when they know that it is your Order, they will do so, in preference of leaving the Grounds where they are born and where their Ancestors have dwelled."[49]

Though this request contravened federal Indian policy, the superintendent acceded to Sutter's wishes because, as Henley recorded, Sutter was "the Pioneer of California; and his character for hospitality, generosity, and true friendship for the Indians is proverbial."[50] In 1856, Sutter's credentials in the Indian business were impeccable with federal officials, if not with Indians. However, this arrangement did not save Sutter, since his debtors foreclosed on the Hock Farm property in 1857. Somehow, he managed to redeem his property, and he remained in California until 1865, when an arsonist burned him out. Poverty-stricken and dispirited, and relying on a pension from the state government, he then left California for good.[51] By then, Sutter had been in the Indian business for about thirty years.

During those decades Sutter was renowned for his hospitality to immigrants, and he was also respected for his ability to work with Indians. Whites regarded him as a model: just as he at first copied the techniques of the leading frontier entrepreneurs of his age, newcomers had imitated Sutter. John Bidwell, Pierson Reading, and other white employees of Sutter acquired ranchos and Indian workers much as he had done. Charles Weber and Thomas Savage opened the southern mines and employed Indians in mines and on ranchos.[52] Even the federal government noticed Sutter's success and appointed him Indian agent during the US-Mexico War, a position that he resigned due to the press of business affairs after gold was discovered.[53]

The first federal reservations in California were meant to be self-sufficient using Indian labor, an idea inspired in part by the missions and partly by Sutter's operations at New Helvetia.[54] So Sutter's fame and influence as the leading California pioneer were based largely on his success in the Indian business—which was the main business of New Helvetia.

A few figures help to underscore that basic point. In 1847, about 280 white men, women, and children were associated in one way or another with New Helvetia. At the same time, the New Helvetia area was home to about 2,800 Indian men, women, and children.[55] Some were workers, some were soldiers, and there were many women and children carrying on traditional pursuits in their rancherias. In effect, even nonworkers subsidized New Helvetia by providing a population from which workers could be drawn and by providing sustenance for workers when they were not employed. The native villages, in other words, offered to Sutter a rudimentary system of unemployment compensation, medical care, and disability and retirement support—all at no cost. One way or another, Indians were New Helvetia. None of its work, none of Sutter's accomplishments would have been possible without the Indian majority who furnished labor, food, and even a market for Sutter's trade goods.

Land and Life

Sutter controlled the southern reaches of the Sacramento Valley for scarcely a decade, but he profoundly influenced the land and the people who lived there. When he arrived, the valley was connected to the outside world primarily through the fur trade and horse rustling. At the time of the gold discovery, the region was dotted with farms and ranchos in addition to Sutter's own establishment. Ocean-going vessels anchored at his landing on the Sacramento River. Overland immigrants made their way to his fort and then took up farmsteads in the surrounding country.

Domestic livestock grazed on land that had once supported wild game. Instead of Indian country that supported a hunting and gathering economy, the Sacramento Valley was increasingly connected to a global capitalist marketplace. Sutter ultimately failed because of his own poor business acumen, but that should not obscure the transformation that he envisioned and set in motion.

As the land was transformed, so were the Indians who lived there. One way or another, Sutter's presence compelled them to become useful to his purposes or to go elsewhere if they could. Even the possibility of retreat became less viable as Sutter's enterprise extended its reach. As time went by, most Indians chose to accommodate to new circumstances. Thus, Indian labor exacerbated the conditions that led to Indian dispossession and dependence. The case of Sutter and the Indian business therefore reminds us that changes to the land ultimately mean changes for human life that are not easy to calculate beforehand.

CHAPTER 2   River City

SACRAMENTO'S GOLD RUSH BIRTH

AND TRANSFIGURATION

Kenneth N. Owens

Two hundred miles inland from the Pacific Ocean and San Francisco Bay, the Sierra Nevada range extends over four hundred miles north and south, defining an eastern boundary for most of northern and central California. The Sierra is an immense granite mass fractured and uplifted along its eastern edge, raised by ancient tectonic pressures, topped by ridges and peaks that form a virtually unbroken barrier to the passage of plants, animals, and peoples across its heights. The passage from the high arid deserts on the east side to the Sierra summit is abrupt; early travelers who headed across the Great Basin for California found themselves faced with imposing walls of snow-covered rock reaching ten thousand to twelve thousand feet above sea level—a baffling, often terrifying sight. Coming from the west, the transition from the floor of California's Central Valley into the Sierra is gradual. From grassy foothills dotted with valley oak trees, the country rises by moderate grades through a landscape of digger pine and black oak into a yellow pine belt above three thousand feet. The venturesome can reach the Ponderosa pine belt above five thousand feet, with redwood and Douglas fir still higher. Except in a few favored locations, the soils of this mountainous region are thin, composed in large part of gravels and easily eroded red clay. But the heart of the Sierra Nevada's western slope is gold country, the Mother Lode region—a four-hundred-mile-long belt of gold-bearing granite more extensive and richer in mineral than any comparable area on the earth's surface.

The prevailing weather systems for northern California blow in from the Pacific Ocean, carried from west to east by high wind currents that tend to flow from the central and southern Pacific in spring and summer, and from the Gulf of Alaska in the late fall and winter. The result is a strongly seasonal climate pattern, hot and dry during the summer months, relatively cool, wet, and stormy during the winter and spring: a Mediterranean climate in the terminology of weather observers. From early May until late October or November in most years, the region lacks any precipitation. The specific weather sequence is unpredictable; cycles of drought and flooding alternate in irregular fashion. Yet, residents expect heavy rain and, at higher elevations, snow throughout the winter, accumulating a Sierra snowpack that will provide abundant runoff throughout the dry season. Snow on the Sierra remains the most vital natural resource for life in the valley below. But every so often powerful Pacific storms during the winter and spring can create high-water episodes that send rivers and streams over their natural levees, with cold, surging flows that sweep away everything before them. Most hazardous is a warm, early spring storm from the South Pacific, locally known as a "Pineapple Express," which will rapidly accelerate runoff from the mountain snowpack. No one can predict exactly when the floods will come, but everyone understands that at some not-too-distant date, come they will.

Before the Rush

Nature did not fashion in the Sacramento region a place congenial for the development of urban life. Centered geographically on the confluence of the American River and the Sacramento River, this area entered history with a reputation for extreme physical isolation. Neither river led anywhere that was inviting or, as late as the mid-1840s, seemed likely to become commercially profitable. The Sacramento Valley itself was a frequently flooded basin, lacking timber, with overflow lands and natural pastures that went yellow and dry during the hot summer months, when waterways dwindled or disappeared. To the west and south, the Sacramento–San Joaquin Delta completed the area's isolation. A trip toward the San Francisco Bay region by foot or horseback required a great detour to the south. River crossings and boggy marshlands choked with tule reeds might halt the traveler indefinitely during periods of high water. Experienced boatmen in small craft could navigate through the delta's maze of channels, but these waterways lacked the leeway for efficient wind-powered sailing, making the voyage tedious and wearing. In the 1840s, under the best conditions, it required an uncomfortable, intensely insect-aggravated week or more to travel by water between the small trading town of Yerba Buena, later renamed San Francisco, and the mouth of the American River. Ship navigation, never possible on the American River, became difficult on the Sacramento above its confluence with the Feather River during low-water years. In short, the Sacramento area before the gold rush was halfway to nowhere.

Commodore Charles Wilkes was commander of the official US naval exploring expedition that visited the valley in 1841. His report summed up his men's view of the region's environment in decisive language. A large part of the area, he wrote, "is undoubtedly barren and unproductive, and must for ever remain so. The part that is deemed good soil," he continued, "is inundated annually, not for any great length of time, yet sufficiently to make it unfit for advantageous settlements." At the edges of the valley, reported Wilkes, "the high prairie is spoken of as being in general barren, and as affording but little good pasture."[1] Even allowing for the fact that Wilkes's men carried out their reconnaissance in mid-August during a drought year, his judgment did no more than reflect a widespread impression of the inland region that held constant through the mid-1840s.

At the time of the visit by Wilkes's command, the Swiss émigré John Sutter was attempting to build a personal empire by trade, stock raising, and farming on land provisionally granted to him by California's Mexican governor. Sutter's varied enterprises, as the historian Richard White has pointed out, rested on two separate but allied processes, each with long-term environmental effects. One was a process of extraction—removing from the natural system anything that might be sold or bartered for profit. Sutter's men killed beaver for their pelts, spawning king salmon for their flesh, and valley elk both for their hides and for the fat used to make candles and lubricate wagon wheels. The other process was that of addition—bringing into the region herds of horses, cattle, and sheep, along with a few swine. These species all multiplied rapidly as they fed on the valley's bunch grasses and, for the hogs, the abundant acorns. While Sutter's herds—and those soon built up by his neighbors with his assistance—prospered, he also introduced grain crops that would, he hoped, become the basis for an agricultural colony in the vicinity of Sutter's Fort, the colony that he promoted with the name New Helvetia. Unwittingly, the addition of these herds and crops also introduced exotic annual grasses and weed species that began to remake the valley's diverse grasslands into something quite different: a uniformly degraded pasturage.[2]

All of these efforts brought Sutter only marginal success. He was not an adept businessman nor, despite all his grand talk, was he a skilled promoter. Even after he purchased on credit all the equipment, animals, and structures at the Russian-American Company's coastal establishment at Fort Ross and Bodega Bay, thereby plunging himself deeply in debt, the environmental realities of his situation limited what he could accomplish with the abundant land and very limited labor force he controlled in the interior. Prior to 1848, the area around Sutter's Fort remained an isolated frontier district, commercially marginal and culturally a borderland where a few score whites lived in large part by their skill in exploiting the labor of native peoples.[3] Some easterners could identify Sutter's Fort as the western end of the California overland trail. Otherwise, this district was still all but unknown to the world outside of northern California. Samuel Brannan, the leader of a substantial Mormon colony in San Francisco and the most ambitious would-be civic promoter in northern California, twice passed through Sutter's Fort in the spring and late summer of 1847. At that time, he found nothing to make him linger.[4]

Gold Country

The gold of the northern California Mother Lode changed these conditions virtually overnight, transforming the Sacramento region physically and socially with dramatic speed. On the way downstream from Sierra peaks, rain and snow-melt flows into an intricate network of waterways that merge into ten major rivers descending into the Central Valley. During the runoff seasons, water tumbles and roars downhill all along the western slope. It cascades over rocks and through narrow canyons, overflows stream banks, widens through mountain meadows, then deepens and shapes natural levees as it reaches the soft soil overlay of the valley. All along the way, moving water continues its eons-long work, cutting into the Sierra and carrying it downstream piece by piece. Endlessly repeated episodes of freezing and thawing accelerate the erosion process, weathering and cracking the granite surface rock to make it more pervious to water's powerful action. Through successive geological epochs, this erosion process exposed, shattered, and ground the gold-bearing granites of the Mother Lode into gravel and fine, heavy black sands. Coming from rock that is uniquely free of other mineral and chemical admixtures, the Sierra's placer gold is in constant motion, brought to temporary resting places nugget by nugget, flake by flake, with the force of gravity and flowing water.[5]

In 1848 and 1849, the gold first located and mined came from surface deposits that contained unalloyed flakes and larger pieces mixed in a matrix of rocks, gravel, and heavy black sand. These deposits could be discovered within shallow streambeds, in gravel bars alongside the waterways, or simply lodged in the crevices of river rocks. As recalled later by Henry Bigler, the first person after James Marshall to make a gold discovery on the south fork of the American River, "I could see the yellow pieces lying as if they were looking at me saying, pick me up if you can."[6] Nowhere else on earth had geological processes created such extensive placer gold deposits. They were unique in that unskilled workers, by digging and washing the gold-bearing gravels and sands, at first could make astounding wages using only the most basic hand tools and rudimentary, self-constructed machines to process and separate out the gold.[7]

These surface placer diggings led miners toward larger deposits, reached with greater difficulty. Riverbed mining became popular in 1849 and 1850. Miners formed companies of a dozen or more men to dig channels and then build diversion dams that would expose the riverbed at promising sites. Then all hands would rush to shovel out as much as they could of the riverbed's rocky overlay before the onset of fall rains washed out the whole operation. By 1850, a second series of discoveries focused on placer deposits found in dry gravel beds at deeper levels beneath the surface, the geological artifacts of earlier river flows that in many places extended for miles and miles. The oldest, deepest, and richest were the so-called blue gravels, marking the course of extinct rivers more than forty million

FIGURE 2.1. *The War against Nature.* Photograph of an early, small-scale hydraulic mining operation, ca. 1857, most likely in the Yuba River drainage. Courtesy Center for Sacramento History, Gifts to Share Collection.

years old. They were worked underground by drift mining that ran tunnels into mountainsides to reach these hidden deposits.[8] A third group of discoveries came from prospectors searching for gold veins still embedded in the Sierra's granite rock, the ultimate source of placer gold. These discoveries from the mid-1850s onward opened a new phase in California's mining history, a phase of increasingly industrialized underground hard rock mining, carried out mainly by wage workers in the employment of mining corporations.

A War against Nature

Calling on the familiar rhetoric of their age, placer miners often described their activities as a development of northern California's natural resources. They were accurate in one sense: like fur trappers or salmon packers, they were extracting from the natural system something with commercial value and bringing it to market. In a process similar to the sale of beaver pelts or salt-preserved salmon filets, the earth's gold became a commodity. But in another sense, such descriptions were totally deceptive. By late 1849, thousands and thousands of people were arriving in the Sierra Nevada gold country as invaders, an army of wealth seekers enlisting in an all-out war against nature. Their weapons were hand tools—picks, shovels, axes, crosscut saws, hammers, drills—deployed by companies of recruits with strong backs, callused hands, and the know-how for using these implements of destruction. Black powder and blasting caps soon added to their armory. Within a few years, heavy equipment manufacturing firms in Sacramento, San Francisco, Oakland, and elsewhere were able to meet the miners' demand for advanced weaponry: iron monitor nozzles and canvas hose for high-pressure hydraulic mining; steam engines; huge iron buckets and steel girders for the construction of river dredges; stamp mills for crushing hard rock ore; and rail-mounted iron trams that brought ore out of deep mines.[9]

The skirmishes and battles in this war took place everywhere in the gold region. They were fought with greatest intensity during the summer months, when water flow and weather conditions were most conducive to the miners' assaults on the countryside. With the possibility that gold might be anywhere, no watercourse escaped attack, no hillside was safe from danger. Virtually every Mother Lode river and stream was ransacked for its hidden minerals, dammed, diverted, and often carried elsewhere in miles-long wooden sluices hammered together to bring water to dry diggings or hydraulic mining sites. Amateurs when they arrived in northern California, these newcomers quickly became expert in every sort of engineering skill that could aid them in their battles for gold. Whether or not they were rewarded with wealth, the miners' campaign of hard work, ingenuity, and skills completely altered the face of the land.

When they retreated from the scenes of hostilities, they left behind a landscape ravaged by their digging, stripped bare of timber, with erosion washing away the gold country's thin soils. Placer mining uprooted streambed vegetation and deposited enormous piles of gravel rubble and expanses of barren stone cobble where nothing could grow and where not even a rattlesnake could find suitable habitat. The most dramatically visible environmental impact came from hydraulic mining operations, especially in the Feather River and Yuba River drainages. From operations like the Malakoff Diggins near North San Juan, floods of muddy clay and gravel, called slickens, were swept downstream, overtopping natural levees, spreading out across cultivated fields at lower elevations, destroying croplands, and forcing valley towns to build their own protective levee systems at public expense. Not until 1884, in the historic Sawyer Decision, did the Ninth US Circuit Court compel hydraulic operators to cease and desist unless they could protect downstream farmers and urban residents from the irremediable property damage caused by their operations, "a general, far-reaching, and most destructive public and private nuisance." Even then, some small operators risked violating the court injunction, keeping shadowy, illegal operations going at least until the 1890s.[10]

Less obvious damage resulted from the addition of huge amounts of mercury to the Sierra's environment. Readily available at the New Almaden mines near San Jose, mercury came into use in placer operations for separating fine gold dust from heavy black sands by means of amalgamation. When the compound was heated to gasify the mercury, the gold remained behind. Tried as early as 1848 at Mormon Island, mercury amalgamation techniques became particularly significant in hydraulic mining and drift mining operations during the 1850s and later, as well as in milling the crushed ore from granite veins. No accounting can be made of the damage to the men who handled the mercury and thus risked danger to the central nervous system. Yet, once dumped into nature, mercury flowed downstream with other mining debris, becoming a permanent hazard at the lower end of the aquatic food chain.

Today, like battlefields long after a violent siege, Sierra gold districts still contain areas pitted and cratered by the digging, damming, tunneling, and blasting efforts of the miners. Abandoned wooden flumes stand as rickety remnants of the vast labor needed put them in place. Stone foundations that once supported shanties and store buildings in short-lived mining towns can still be seen. At other locations, floods have silted over the sites of once flourishing gold camps. Sturdy-appearing structures fashioned from hewn stone, often with iron doors, stand here and there like abandoned forts, vacant relics of banking houses and express offices that once served these transitory communities.

Collateral damage from the miners' gold rush combat against the countryside is less easy to discern but no less severe and enduring. Native peoples throughout northern California suffered grievously. They faced perils from murderous assault by newcomers who wanted to drive all natives out of their Sierra Nevada homelands. They were exposed to newly introduced diseases, including pneumonia and tuberculosis, venereal diseases, measles, smallpox, diphtheria, and whooping cough, touching off so-called virgin soil epidemics among populations that lacked any acquired immunities. These disastrous disease episodes severely thinned the native population and disrupted their cultural and community life. Adding to these risks was the very real danger of starvation caused by the destruction or disappearance of staple foods in the domestic economy of northern California's indigenous people. Mining operations destroyed the annual salmon runs by obliterating spawning beds. Miners hunted deer and elk to extinction. Inexplicably, at the height of the gold rush, the acorn crop failed entirely throughout northern California. Lashed by starvation, the small, severely depleted communities of California natives were easily driven to accept relocation in refuge areas outside the gold country, so-called rancherias or reservations, where they might be able to survive by the uncertain charity of state or federal authorities. As another lasting heritage of the gold rush social environment, these surviving natives and their descendants would for generations be labeled with the derogatory, racist appellation "Digger Indians," a term that Mark Twain helped popularize through his widely read stories of the gold rush era.[11]

Free Gold, Free Water

California's governmental situation from 1848 through the 1850s aided and abetted the miners' war against nature. Because of peculiar circumstances, northern California's gold was entirely free to the finder. Until the Sawyer Decision, no governmental entity provided the least check upon the unprecedented rush to attack the gold country's environment. No agency had the power to regulate mining practices or protect the property rights of non-miners. The US Congress had formerly managed the nation's mineral lands by reserving them from sale and leasing mining rights to private citizens, a system applied mainly to lead-mining regions in eastern Missouri and a tri-state district along the upper Mississippi River. Lax administration and local resistance led to the breakdown of this mineral leasing system by the 1840s. Consequently, Congress abolished the system in 1846 and put nothing in its place, allowing lands known to contain mineral deposits to be sold by the General Land Office on the same basis as agricultural lands.[12]

Federal administrative authority over California's public lands was not yet established when the gold rush began. The Treaty of Guadalupe Hidalgo brought an end to the war between the United States and Mexico less than two weeks after James Marshall's Coloma gold discovery. According to this treaty, the United States agreed to recognize all valid land titles under previous Spanish or Mexican land grants. US law of long standing also required federal authorities to settle the aboriginal title claims of California's native peoples before the customary process of federal land survey and sale could be carried out.

The nation's officials knew very little about California at the beginning of 1848. Any intent by either President Polk's administration or Congress to move forward with these legal requirements in an orderly way was swept aside during the excitement that followed the first gold discoveries. Consideration of California's political status was further complicated and delayed by the rancorous sectional debate over the extension of black racial slavery, a debate raised by the US-Mexico War and only quieted temporarily in Congress by the Compromise of 1850. While the nation's representatives wrangled, California remained technically a conquered province under a makeshift form of military rule. In 1850, the military governor at Monterey encouraged local leaders to bypass established procedures, form a state constitution, and petition for direct admission to the federal union. Meanwhile, no army commander dared send his troops close to the gold country for fear that every last recruit would desert and join the unnumbered thousands digging for wealth. Outside of Monterey and perhaps San Francisco, where small cadres of military and civilian officials dutifully carried out their assignments, federal authority in any form remained largely illusory until well after statehood.[13]

Throughout the gold rush era, miners enjoyed title-free, regulation-free, tax-free access to the land's mineral treasure.

With respect to legal order, California's geographical interior during the gold rush was ungoverned, existing in a virtual state of nature. This condition of affairs also applied to the determination of water rights, critical both to mining operations and to agriculture. Unlike mineral rights, always within federal purview, water rights were constitutionally a matter for determination by territorial and state governments. The military government entirely ignored water rights issues, leaving this matter also to local self-determination. After statehood, it took decades for state courts and the legislature, drawing on both Hispanic and Anglo American precedents, to cobble together a rudimentary, hybrid code of water rights.[14]

This legal lacuna left disputes over water to be settled among rival claimants by self-constituted local bodies such as miners' courts or, failing that, by force of numbers and force of arms. Such was the case when Jared Sheldon in 1851 constructed a dam for a gristmill on his ranch along the Cosumnes River, a short distance southeast of Sacramento. His dam flooded the claims of placer miners working upstream. Threatened by these men, Sheldon built a small fort equipped with a cannon. Taking up the challenge, in mid-July the well-armed miners captured the fort. Two hours later, Sheldon arrived with reinforcements. The ensuing battle ended with the death of Sheldon and two of his employees. But the miners gained no victory. The dam remained in place until it was swept away by high water the following winter.[15]

Perhaps surprisingly, however, armed combat for control of the environment was a rarity in northern California's mining country. So long as placer gold remained plentiful, serious disputes over mineral and water claims were usually settled by miners' courts, which were locally self-constituted bodies in the mining camps. Although they varied widely in composition and efficiency, these temporary governments in general acted to establish rules of property rights and mining rights that ideally would be upheld by community consensus. Based in part on precedents both in Hispanic gold fields and in the upper Mississippi lead mines, where a similar lack of authority had prompted experiments in miners' self-rule, the creation of well-defined gold districts, each with its own miners' court, served in rough fashion to maintain a reasonable semblance of security and good order in the gold region.[16]

Sacramento's Hasty Beginning

Sacramento's civic birth was tightly linked to the first gold discoveries and the start of the gold rush in 1848. Although a few people—including the mystically inclined James Marshall—later claimed they had previously suspected the existence of gold in northern California, these speculations had no public credence prior to Marshall's accidental discovery in January 1848. He found small chunks of gold in the millrace of a sawmill that he and a small, mostly Mormon work crew

FIGURE 2.2. Samuel Brannan. Leader of the San Francisco Latter-day Saints colony, Brannan became the foremost promoter of the Sacramento townsite at Sutter's Embarcadero. This photograph dates from ca. 1870. Courtesy Center for Sacramento History, Eleanor McClatchy Collection.

were building in partnership with John Sutter at the Coloma Indian village. The location was in a foothill valley some fifty miles east of Sutter's Fort on the American River's south fork, high enough to be in the yellow pine belt.[17] Believing at first that this discovery was a freak of nature, a single outcropping of gold confined to a small area, Marshall and Sutter made a pact to keep it secret at least until they could secure some color of legal title to the mill site. But the Mormon Battalion veterans working under Marshall's direction soon spread the news to some of their comrades employed at the fort. They in turn made a richer, far more productive strike at the confluence of the south and middle forks of the American River halfway between Coloma and Sutter's Fort, a site immediately named Mormon Island.[18]

Hearing stories about these first discoveries, Samuel Brannan returned from San Francisco to Sutter's Fort in early May and toured the Mormon Island diggings for two days. His inspection convinced him that, as he later stated, "there was more gold [here] than all the people of California could take out in five years."[19] Rapidly heading back to the Bay Area, he paused briefly at Sutter's Fort and, according to one account, "visited the new town where he intend[s] to build a Warehouse & a store."[20] He then rushed on to San Francisco, carrying along a sample of Mormon Island's placer gold in a quinine bottle. This small bottle he famously waved in the air a few days later at the corner of Portsmouth Square, proclaiming, "Gold, gold from the American River!" After taking the first step toward forming a new town, Brannan meant to begin a gold rush that he expected would make him wealthy—without ever turning over a single shovelful of gravel himself.

Brannan's decisive action marked the genesis of Sacramento. The site of his "new town" was Sutter's Embarcadero, a crude ship landing on the low bank of the Sacramento River a few hundred yards south of the mouth of the American River. From the very first, its location and its location alone made this place a valuable piece of real estate. The embarcadero immediately became the key exchange point for cargo and people heading from the Bay Area toward the gold diggings. Here, Brannan and a few other merchants and land speculators began promoting the hasty construction of a commercial hub, building it atop the shambles of John Sutter's failed New Helvetia colony.

Civic Challenges

This prime location had a great many drawbacks. Along with its isolation and the tenuous, easily tipped balance between flood and drought throughout the region, the riverside environment in many ways made the place perilous for settlement. River cities in the mid-nineteenth century were notoriously unhealthy. In that pre-Pasteur age, before discovery of the microorganisms that cause human disease, medical practitioners would customarily blame health problems on various combinations of climatic, genetic, and psychic or spiritual causes that today may seem quite bizarre. But experience had taught everyone that serious illness was extremely prevalent in towns and cities situated alongside rivers. We should not wonder why. In river cities, residents customarily drew their drinking water downstream from other people's sewage and waste disposal sites. Floods and seasonal overflows readily contaminated shallow wells. Streamside sloughs and low-lying, swampy areas were breeding grounds for disease-carrying insects. Without well-enforced regulations, public streets and vacant lots became dumping sites for all kinds of waste, including dead animals and piles of household garbage that frequently were left to rot in the summer heat or to molder alongside walkways that turned into putrid, muddy bogs during the rainy season. Sacramento's mud earned a particular reputation for its depth and clinging density. In November 1849, according to one visitor, "the town was submerged in mud, the streets almost impassable. Flour, Pork, bread &c. were piled up along the sides of the streets, without protection."[21]

In the eastern states and especially in the Midwest, inhabitants of river towns were accustomed to seasonal episodes of the ague, a severe, sometimes fatal disease marked by episodes of high fever alternating with chills, shaking, and delirium. This disease we identify today as malaria. It first reached the Sacramento Valley in 1832–33, unwittingly brought south from the lower Columbia River basin by a Hudson's Bay Company fur-trapping brigade led by John Work. With mosquitoes of the *Anopheles* genus already present in abundance, the arrival of a few dozen infected individuals, unknowingly carrying the malaria protozoa in their bloodstreams, set off an epidemic that fatally struck down an estimated 70 percent of the Indian people in the Sacramento Valley and the delta, perhaps as many as eighty thousand individuals.[22] Following this immense demographic and cultural disaster, malaria became endemic throughout the region, always present, always a danger, especially to newcomers not previously infected and to the young. Moreover, that danger increased with each group of immigrants that arrived, in particular those who came overland from the river towns of the Midwest. These newcomers brought additional strains of malarial microbes to enter the local disease pool, thus setting off fresh cycles of infection, even among those previously stricken.

Worldwide, great cities in the nineteenth century were enormous killing machines. City conditions everywhere destroyed far more lives than could be replaced by residential births. To survive and grow, every city depended on a constant recruitment of newcomers from the adjacent countryside or more distant places. The severe death toll in river cities, whether European capitals like Paris, Vienna, London, and Saint Petersburg, an Asian metropolis like Canton, China, or American centers of trade like New York City, New Orleans, or Saint Louis, meant that this type of urban concentration had to attract great numbers of immigrants year after year if they were to endure and grow.[23] To develop a settled, permanent population, the influx would need to include a significant proportion of respectable females: wives, sweethearts, daughters, sisters, cousins, and maiden aunts who would provide a domestic anchor to restrain the roving impulses of solitary, unattached men. Everywhere and in every class, the family-based household was the normal unit of community building. No cities survived and prospered with a primary residential population of men living in tents or shanties, in bunkhouses or company-run barracks, in residential hotels or boardinghouses. No cities could be built by men alone trying to look after their own well-being. This was particularly true in nineteenth century Euro-American society, which inculcated a strongly defined separation of gender roles that trained adult males to be virtually helpless in any and all domestic tasks.

Location, Location

The northern California gold rush set in motion a new order of population dynamics: the largest voluntary, self-financed mass migration the world had ever seen. A trickle of immigrants arrived in 1848, coming mainly from southern California, Oregon, northern Mexico, Chile, and Hawaii. This trickle reached flood tide by the late summer of 1849, drawing tens of thousands of people from the eastern United States, Canada, and all of Latin America, both northern and southern Europe, and with a pioneer few traveling from southern China. The immigrant wave crested in 1857. By that time, an estimated three hundred thousand newcomers had reached northern California, coming about equally by sea and overland. For most of them, the Sierra gold fields were their first objective.

This unprecedented flow of people heading for gold country was more than enough to launch a speculative boom in city building up and down the Central Valley. For all of its disabilities, Sacramento's location could not be bettered. Within a few months after the mining excitement began, Sacramento was emerging as the commercial and social capital of the northern California gold country, its growth promoted by the nearly incredible returns from the Sierra's placer diggings. As Samuel Brannan first perceived, Sutter's Embarcadero was ideally situated at a trading crossroads, commanding the most convenient routes to and from the northern California gold fields. The city's early businessmen made the adjacent district a central outfitting and supply depot, a transportation hub, and the key inland location for managing the commerce of the northern Mother Lode mining towns. Not least important, this area became the rowdy, raucous center of sinful recreation for all who passed through the area. While San Francisco, with its unequaled seaport facilities, developed into the great emporium of the Pacific, Sacramento—California's second city—sprang up as the prototypical example, the poster child of gold rush boomtowns.

By the fall of 1848, the embarcadero riverfront had become the site of a lively trade, some of it conducted aboard ships tied to the bank, some in frame buildings and tents that crowded the area, some of it simply conducted in the open, on the river levee. This site was part of the provisional Mexican land grant that John Sutter had received eight years earlier. Its ownership, however, remained questionable under US law. Already heavily entangled in debt, Sutter was proving unable to cope with prosperity by the winter of 1848. He starred in the role of a sot and spendthrift, incapable of managing his own business affairs. His oldest son, John A. Sutter Jr., arrived unexpectedly from Switzerland in mid-September. To escape his creditors and, he must have hoped, to put his finances in better order, the elder Sutter signed a power of attorney and transferred his landholdings to the younger Sutter, although the son communicated in awkward English, had little experience in business, and possessed only a rudimentary knowledge of American ways.

In short order, while his father was disporting himself scandalously in the mining camp named Sutter Creek, Sutter junior heeded the advice of Sam Brannan, who by now had turned away from promoting Mormon colonization and had resolved to build his worldly wealth by gold rush trade and real estate speculation. In December, anxious to get the Sutter lands onto the market, young Sutter hired an army engineer, Capt. William Warner, to survey and lay out a city plan along the riverfront. Captain Warner, with his assistant (and business partner) Lt. William Tecumseh Sherman, finished the job quickly. Within a month, young Sutter's agent and lawyer, Oregonian Peter Burnett, began selling the hastily surveyed town lots.[24]

With their hurried work, Warner and Sherman created a city without a center. They imposed on the terrain the simplest, most mathematically rigid, least imaginative urban design imaginable. Every resident can describe the original plan's rectangular grid of evenly spaced blocks. From Front Street, edging the embarcadero, the north-south streets are consecutively numbered eastward, the east-west streets identified by consecutive letters of the alphabet from the American River southward.[25] Utterly simple, instantly self-evident, lacking any hint of adaptation to the physical setting, this plan is remarkably convenient for newcomers. Anyone can find a downtown Sacramento address with only a moment's orientation. But this convenience has always been offset by the lack of a central physical focus for the city. The opportune product of speculative mania in 1848 and 1849, Sacramento's design set aside no land for a civic plaza or courthouse square; it provided no public space that could be identified as the geographical core of Sacramento's official life; it gave the town no commercial or social focus.

Before he fled Sacramento for Mexico, filled with anger toward his dishonest former business colleagues, Sutter junior made the city a gift of twelve square blocks dispersed evenly within the undeveloped survey grid.[26] This generous benefaction included what would later become the site of the state capitol, and it included also a square in front of city hall now called Cesar Chavez Plaza. Though pleasant as urban amenities, whether as small urban parks or later as sites for public elementary schools, these blocks did little to bring Sacramentans together. For a few years, a tall oak tree on K Street near Sixth became a convenient civic gathering place. As one resident described it, the site served as the commercial exchange, board of trade, and chamber of commerce, all in one. It was an open-air horse market and a place of public debate. Here occurred Sacramento's best-known public lynching, in 1851, with the oak tree serving as an improvised gallows.[27] Such ad hoc social contrivances only emphasized early Sacramento's shortcomings in urban design.

Away from Isolation

On his return to San Francisco, Samuel Brannan urged his fellow Latter-day Saints colonists to go gold digging at Mormon Island. Most made the inland journey on foot or horseback, traveling by land around the delta's tule marshes. Other early gold seekers who came south from Oregon or north from the Los Angeles region walked or rode through the Central Valley. But as the excitement spread during the spring and summer of 1849, river travel became the most convenient and popular means of transport for the masses of people and heavy cargoes of supplies coming from the Bay Area.

A mismatched fleet of steam-powered riverboats, most of them built in Sacramento River boat yards or along the shores of San Francisco Bay, carried gold seekers and freight through the delta for tidy sums. The first to enter regular service was John Sutter's schooner, the *Sacramento,* led by Capt. John Van Pelt, which was making regular trips between the embarcadero and a speculative Bay Area townsite east of San Francisco, called New York on the Pacific, by the time Sutter's son arrived in September 1849.[28] For the freight trade, local boat makers designed a flat-bottomed, blunt-ended scow schooner with a high "pulpit" wheelhouse on the stern. These powerful, graceless craft became the all-purpose work boats of the 1850s and later decades. They shared the waterways by the close of the 1850 season with about fifty steamboats—side-wheelers and stern-wheelers—that moved passengers and supplies back and forth between bayside docks and landings on the Sacramento and San Joaquin Rivers.

While Sacramento's embarcadero became the major riverport, these small, broad-beamed steamers, some drawing only two feet of water, traveled as far north as Marysville and Red Bluff before river shoaling, caused by hydraulic mining debris in the 1870s, limited their upstream range. During the flood of 1852–53, four steamboats a day made the trip upstream from the embarcadero to a temporary trading center on the American River named Hoboken, located just east of the present campus of California State University, Sacramento. This arrangement and the town ended when river flow returned to normal. In 1854, a regional consortium of steamboat owners formed the California Steam Navigation Company, with capital fixed at $1.25 million and stock selling for $1,000 a share. The firm succeeded in bringing a large measure of stability to a highly competitive, sometimes recklessly run business by stifling competition and controlling passenger and freight rates. The company's premier boats, fast, trim, and elegantly appointed, could make the daily trip between Sacramento and San Francisco in as little as six hours under exceptional conditions, though nine or ten hours was the more usual running time.[29]

According to one well-informed estimate, Sacramento received at least 165,000 tons of river freight in 1852. Of this total, perhaps 10 percent was for local use, 15 percent was carried farther up the Sacramento River, and the remaining 75 percent was transshipped to the Mother Lode mining camps and gold rush towns. At their summertime peak, these wagon cargoes amounted to three hundred to four hundred tons a day.[30]

Once unloaded on the embarcadero, everything needed to be moved out quickly. Strings of pack mules, with each mule carrying two hundred to more than three hundred pounds, took some of the load. Usually managed by experienced Mexican muleteers, these pack strings could reach isolated gold camps deep in the Sierra that were served only by trace trails. From an early period, however, the great bulk of freight left Sacramento in mule-drawn wagons, locally constructed. The city's pioneer wagon makers built tall, sturdy, long and narrow freight wagons with rear wheels six feet high and iron tires as much as four inches wide—"California Wagons" they came to be called. With an empty weight of nearly two tons, they commonly held six to eight tons of cargo, often stacked and cinched tight far above the wooden wagon sides. The whole rig, which might include a smaller wheeled trailer, was pulled by six to ten spans of mules, controlled by a single jerk line rein.[31]

In the summer of 1849, one witness declared that at the embarcadero "all was confusion and dust, each generating the other. This is the point from which the first move [of cargo] is made by land, and every man was on the run; mule-teams were moving in every direction, some loading, some preparing to load, each surrounded by a halo of dust which rendered mules and driver invisible."[32] Once on their way, the mules and their wagons headed up J Street, the city's central thoroughfare, rolled eastward past the crumbling walls of Sutter's Fort, and turned into a swiftly growing network of wagon roads that led toward the Sierra gold country.[33] Their progress could be tracked by the shouts of the wagon masters, decorating the air with colorful profanities.

While thousands of gold seekers arrived by water from San Francisco Bay, other thousands came to northern California from the eastern states and Midwest by way of overland trails. In 1848, the only established trail into northern

California was the Truckee River–Donner Pass route, which led from the northern Nevada desert upstream along the Truckee River (making twenty-three forced crossings), skirted Donner Lake's north shore, wound through the challenges of the Sierra's high ridges, and found its way down the Bear River before reaching Sutter's Fort. It was a hazardous, arduous way to approach the gold country.[34]

During the summer of 1848, a party of Mormon Battalion veterans—forty-five men and the determined wife of one these former soldiers—left the Mormon Island diggings and started eastward, anxious to rejoin their families and friends who had recently settled in the Salt Lake region under Brigham Young's direction. Following President Young's instructions, these men had worked for John Sutter over the winter months, then made good returns mining at Mormon Island while waiting for the snowpack to clear from Sierra passes. Turning their back on the gold fields, in late June they set out with seventeen ox-drawn wagons loaded with supplies, farm tools, seeds, and two brass cannons they had obtained from Captain Sutter, accompanied by substantial herds of cattle and horses. Confident they could make a new and better road, they traveled slowly up the ridge dividing the American River and Cosumnes River drainages, pulled their wagons through snowbanks over West Pass summit, then eased across Carson Pass and down the rugged terrain of the Carson River's west fork. From that point they headed north and joined the established overland route along the Truckee River at Immigrant Meadows, the site of modern Reno, Nevada. Their work established what came to be called the Mormon Emigrant Trail or, more accurately, the Mormon–Carson Pass Wagon Road. For the next three seasons, during the heaviest flow of overland immigration into northern California, this route was the favored way to reach the gold country from the western border of Missouri.[35]

Midway in the 1852 season, a shorter, more convenient alternative—the Johnson Cutoff Wagon Road—began to divert arriving immigrants by way of Lake Tahoe's south shore and the American River's south fork, the general alignment taken today by US Highway 50. After securing a toll road franchise from the state legislature, Placerville's business leaders financed impressive improvements on this route, making it the new preferred route for the California overland trail's final section, which led to Sacramento. Although other towns, including Marysville, Stockton, and Sonora, made attempts to redirect the incoming overland migration toward their own business districts, through the 1850s Sacramento continued to enjoy the benefits of its location as the natural, obvious transportation hub, supply center, and commercial capital for northern California's gold country.

This advantage increased with the construction of western America's first railroad line, the Sacramento Valley Railroad (SVRR), which ran twenty-two miles between the Sacramento waterfront and the town of Folsom, close to the Mormon Island diggings and other American River mining sites. Incorporated in 1852 by Col. Charles L. Wilson, who brought from the East a young engineer named Theodore Judah, the line experienced many hardships during its early years. These included Wilson's bankruptcy and resignation, then the death of Capt. James Folsom, Wilson's successor as SVRR president. Under Judah's direction as chief engineer, construction finally began in February 1855. The first train reached its Folsom terminus a year later. This project changed Sacramento's urban geography in two ways. First, it called into existence a warehouse and manufacturing district along the railroad's right of way, the R Street corridor at the city's southern edge. Second, it shifted the bulk of the long-distance wagon freighting business away from the embarcadero district to Folsom.

By bringing down freight rates for delivery to the Mother Lode towns and mining camps, the SVRR gave Sacramento merchants a tighter hold on the commercial life of the gold country. Locally based stage lines and express companies added to Sacramento's prime role in managing northern California's gold rush trade. While San Francisco eventually became the headquarters for the largest of these firms, all roads to and from the mines led first through the River City.

For Sacramento's future as a transportation hub, the most significant development came at the end of the 1850s, when four Sacramento merchants guided by Theodore Judah joined together to form the Central Pacific Railroad and began a quest for federal funding to complete the western portion of the nation's first transcontinental rail line. Incorporated in June 1861 with Gov. Leland Stanford as president, the Central Pacific (CP)—and in time its offshoot organization, the Southern Pacific (SP)—would give Sacramento a new economic base that reached into farmlands up and down the state. The grand success of the CP/SP conglomerate, based in Sacramento, and the agricultural boom that came with rail connections continued well into the twentieth century. Together, farming and railroading underwrote Sacramento's prosperity as a business center long after gold mining's decline.

Lagging Population Growth

During northern California's gold rush years, to repeat J. S. Holliday's memorable phrase, the world rushed in. According to early census records—a federal census in 1850 and a state census in 1852, both produced by imperfect administrative procedures in chaotic times—Sacramento's founding population included quite varied American and immigrant groups: at least as much as San Francisco, Sacramento filled with sundry peoples who were strangers to one other. Each newcomer, as the journalists, diary keepers, and letter writers among them uniformly attested, gained an instant education in cultural diversity if not in social tolerance.[36]

According to Sacramento's first historian, Dr. John Morse, at the start "the whole fabric of society was little less than chaos, and still there was a oneness and harmony in its movements which can scarcely be paralleled in the annals of the world. . . . There was no moral restraint, and yet for months there never was a community more perfectly exempt from violence and immorality."[37] Luzena Stanley Wilson, another eyewitness to Sacramento's first months, offered in retrospect an even more complimentary testimonial to the city's founding population: "They were, as a rule, upright, energetic, and hard-working, many of them men of education and culture whom the misfortune of poverty had forced into the ranks of labor in this strange country. The rough days which earned for California its name for recklessness had not begun. There was no shooting, little gambling, and less theft in those first months. The necessities of hard work left no leisure for the indulgence of one's temper, and the 'rough' element which comes to every mining country with the first flush times had not yet begun to crowd the West."[38]

But after the world rushed in, we should add, with scarcely a pause most of the world rushed right out again. Luzena Wilson also summed up the transient quality of Sacramento's life in 1849: "The population in Sacramento was largely a floating one. Today there might be ten thousand people in the town, and tomorrow four thousand of them might be on their way to the gold fields. The immigrants came pouring in every day from the plains, and the schooners from San Francisco brought a living freight, eager to be away to the mountains."[39]

A small cadre of merchants, along with other business people, tradesmen, and service workers, positioned themselves to turn a profit from the thousands of people who flowed through. But these early figures in the city's history seldom stayed long themselves. It is an amazing experience to go through the historical records of gold rush Sacramento, to look at documents of land ownership, to view the earliest city directories, to read the newspaper stories and advertisements, to scan the minutes of city government meetings, and to see in all these materials scarcely one name that would be familiar in later times. The gold rush city was largely a population of sojourners, some who stayed for a day or two, some who remained a week or a month, and others who found it worth their while to remain in place for a short span of years, making their fortune. Although we lack exact statistics, Sacramento's rate of population turnover was huge. This phenomenon is especially striking compared with other western cities of the same era, such as Portland or Salt Lake City, where the founding generation established long-lived dynasties

TABLE 2.1. Comparison of population growth between Sacramento and the state of California, 1850–1900

Year	City population	Rate of increase (%)	State population	Rate of increase (%)
1850	6,820		92,597	
1860	13,785	101.1	379,994	310.4
1870	16,283	18.1	580,247	47.4
1880	21,420	31.5	864,894	54.3
1890	26,386	23.2	1,213,398	40.3
1900	29,282	11.0	1,485,053	22.4

Source: Residential population data, 2010 US Census.

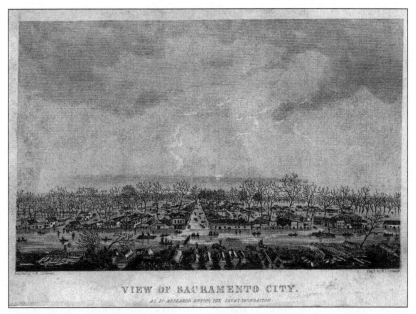

FIGURE 2.3. *River City Submerged.* In January 1850, Sacramento's first great flood covered the city's embryonic business district. This lithographic view shows the scene from the west bank, looking across the river up J Street, the main thoroughfare that led toward Sutter's Fort and the placer mining districts beyond. Courtesy Center for Sacramento History, Eleanor McClatchy Collection.

that remained prominent and influential decade after decade. Most of Sacramento's leading figures seemed to change virtually from season to season.

With this high turnover, the city's nineteenth-century population growth rate was quite modest. Even during the 1850s gold rush decade, Sacramento's net population just barely doubled while the state's grew more than 310 percent. For the next four decades, Sacramento's population growth consistently lagged behind the overall state growth rate by nearly half.

Calamities, Sickness, and Discontent

Some major reasons for the city's slow growth can be identified quickly, for they were inherent in Sacramento's location and the character of its environment. Floods and fires repeatedly destroyed property, wiped out businesses and personal savings, and prompted instantly impoverished, shocked residents to move elsewhere. Luzena Wilson and her husband, for example, were operating a rooming house and restaurant close to the riverfront embarcadero in late 1849. They invested their gains in sacks of seed barley, which they stacked up alongside the small frame building they had leased. Then in January 1850 the entire area was submerged by the first great flood in the city's history. When the water finally receded, the couple had to face the worst. "Our little fortune was gone," Luzena Wilson recalled, "the sacks had burst and the barley sprouted—and ruin stared us again in the face. We were terrified at the awful termination of winter, and I felt that I should never again be safe unless high in the Sierra."[40] The Wilsons departed the city, moving up to the foothill boomtown of Auburn, later returned briefly to Sacramento, and then established themselves for the rest of their lives on drier, safer ranch lands near modern Vacaville.

In a hastily built city of tents and frame structures covered by canvas, fire was a great and persistently worrisome danger to property and lives. The city's bustling business district went up in flames the first time in September 1849. A smaller conflagration in April 1850 destroyed one block along Front Street. In October, another fire spread widely through Sacramento's commercial district adjacent to the embarcadero. These disasters, foreseeable but unpreventable in the circumstances, encouraged a few property owners to erect substantial buildings of stone or brick, yet the speculative, transient character of the city's booming business life argued against such long-term capital investment. In early November 1852, Sacramento experienced its most devastating fire. An inferno fanned by north winds spread through the entire business section, the flames raging so fiercely that the glow at night could be seen in San Francisco, a hundred miles away. Fifty-five blocks were left in ashes. This disaster became legendary in local chronicles as the "Great Holocaust."

Business people who remained after the 1852 calamity began to rebuild, this time making brick the construction material of choice. During the next few years, Sacramento gained a measure of protection with the organization of volunteer fire companies. Another fire, however, leveled twelve business blocks in 1854, proving that Sacramento remained combustible and vulnerable.[41]

The fairy-tale mythology of frontier towns, the sort of story that well-meaning boosters everywhere make up about their civic past, would have us believe that after every major disaster—fire, flood, disease epidemic, or earthquake—the brave, resourceful, intrepid, and wonderfully plucky residents quickly began to rebuild and improve their fair city. The same mythology assures us that the pioneer generation at once become devoted to their new home country, determined to settle, and quickly began to organize institutions of community permanency: churches, schools, hospitals, orphanages, debating and literary societies, and other forms of voluntary association that would provide for the cultural needs of society. But this Pollyanna-like version of history, however attractive to the sentimental among us, does not fit the facts in Sacramento's case. Natural disasters and dangers, the constant disease problems, and a substantial degree of social fragmentation all contributed to a high population turnover. And with this turnover, Sacramentans—a predominantly male aggregation of newcomers—were too preoccupied with making money to invest substantial time and energy in projects for civic improvement.

Along with its calamities, Sacramento's weather, summer and winter, persuaded many to look for more pleasant surroundings. Mary Crocker, a recent arrival in

March 1853, succinctly described her impressions of the spring weather in a letter home: "Storms arise, the rain comes down, the wind blows, the mud is deep, yes, deeper than you ever saw."[42] Because men and women alike tended to dress in layers of heavy fabric, the extreme heat of the summer months brought its own distinctive forms of suffering. Some enterprising souls made a successful business of cutting ice in high Sierra lakes and freighting it into town, protecting their frozen merchandise with layers of sawdust.[43] In time, moderately affluent families founded a virtual Sacramento summer colony by the ocean in Santa Cruz, where wives and children could enjoy the sea breezes—and avoid Sacramento's summer-time disease dangers—while husbands and brothers remained at work in the hot, hazardous interior.

For many whose personal correspondence has been preserved, the disease problems in Sacramento were an ever-present concern. The story of the cholera epidemic that struck in October 1850 has frequently been told.[44] Spreading in ways that no one then understood, though we now know that contaminated water sources carried the disease organism, this outbreak killed an officially reported 364 people. (Some estimates ran as high as 600 deaths.) A disease with horrifying symptoms, cholera struck and killed quickly, often within twelve to twenty-four hours. Its appearance created panic, causing Sacramento's residents to flee the town in great numbers until the danger passed. More than a few never returned.

Among other disease problems, malaria was the most persistent, the most dangerous over the long run, and the most likely to discourage newcomers from making Sacramento their permanent home. Everyone was exposed; virtually everyone went through disease attacks of greater or lesser severity that might recur again and again. As a precaution after being stricken repeatedly, to take one example, the prominent banker D. O. Mills began to spend part of his summers living with a congenial family on their farm near San Jose, far from the algae-covered, mosquito-breeding sloughs and backwaters of the Sacramento area. As soon as he could reasonably afford it, no one should be surprised to learn, Mills took his Sacramento-created fortune and built a red sandstone mansion on East Fifty-Seventh Street in New York City.[45]

Scurvy, a debilitating, life-threatening result of vitamin C deficiency, also had a public impact that discouraged transients from lingering in the area during the early years. Scurvy commonly occurred among overland travelers and those who had come great distances by sea. On the trail, aboard ship, and in the mining camps as well, a customary diet of beans, bacon, and hard bread could produce scurvy symptoms within a few months. Fresh vegetables and fruit, particularly oranges and limes, offered a simple, effective cure. But this dietary advice was also not part of the medical profession's general knowledge in the 1850s. Sacramento received an enormous number of people suffering more or less seriously from scurvy, prompting physicians briefly to utilize Sutter's east adobe, built next to Sutter's Fort to house his Indian soldiers, as a "pest house" to provide beds and minimal care to scurvy victims.[46] Weakened by this ailment, such sufferers were also more vulnerable to malaria and other infectious diseases. Though scurvy victims had not originally become ill in the gold rush capital, the presence of so many sick people contributed to the impression that Sacramento was not a healthy place to live.

The shortcomings of Sacramento society during the gold rush era, particularly as perceived by the small number of women residents, became another reason for high population turnover. Respectable women, few in numbers, found themselves accorded the utmost consideration. "It was a motley crowd that gathered every day at my table," Luzena Wilson declared, "but always at my coming the loud voices were hushed, the swearing ceased, the quarrels stopped, and deference and respect were as readily and as heartily rendered to me as if I had been a queen. I was a queen," she recalled. "Any woman who had a womanly heart, who spoke a kindly, sympathetic word to the lonely, homesick men, was a queen, and lacked no honor which a subject could bestow."[47]

This honor did not fully compensate for the absence of female society and for the hard labor it took for non-elite women to survive. During the earliest period of its growth, Sacramento, even more than San Francisco, was almost entirely a male city. Armies marched to war during the nineteenth century with a larger contingent of female camp followers, cooks, washerwomen, and prostitutes than appeared in Sacramento in 1849. "Women were scarce in those days," Mrs. Wilson remarked. She continued,

I lived six months in Sacramento and saw only two. There may [have] been others, but I never saw them. There was no time for visiting or gossiping; it was hard work from daylight until dark, and sometimes long after, and I nodded to my neighbor and called out "Good morning" as each of us hung the clothes out to dry on the lines. Yes, we worked; we did things that our high-toned servants would now look at aghast, and say it was impossible for a woman to do. But the one who did not work in '49 went to the wall. It was a hand to hand fight with starvation at the first.[48]

Four years later, well after Luzena Wilson had moved elsewhere, the output from the mines had brought flush times to the city and Sacramento had more women residents. The work of these female newcomers may have been less arduous than in 1849, but one of them, Mary Crocker, thought the lack of polite society a heavy emotional burden. "I have found it almost impossible," she wrote home, "for a perfect stranger to make acquaintants. Several that I have met say they have been here a year or two & only know two or three families." Neither the social life nor the living conditions, she believed, made Sacramento an attractive place to settle. "Any person had better take what [money] they can get for three or four years hard work," she advised one of her friends, "& go to the 'States' to enjoy it. Money slips away here about as fast as it is made if one indulges in the common comforts of life; what would last years at home would here disappear in as many months [if one were] living here as they would there. I have not given up the hope of having my final home somewhere East. The wish grows stronger," she concluded, "the more I think of it & the more I become familiar with this country."[49]

There are many departure stories. John Sutter left right away, of course, relocating with his newly arrived Swiss family first to his Hock Farm property on the Feather River, then to the Swiss-German community in Lititz, Pennsylvania, where he and Mrs. Sutter lived out their lives aided by a small pension from the California state legislature. John Sutter Jr., declaring that he never wanted to see Sacramento again, moved first to Sonora, Mexico, then to Acapulco, acquired a substantial plantation, married a pleasant, amiable woman of good family, and began raising a family—though he and his wife would later separate and he then set up housekeeping with a younger woman who eventually presented him with nine additional children.[50] Among many others, John Bidwell, Pierson Reading, Samuel Hensley, and Sam Brannan each soon moved on, along with virtually all their business colleagues of 1848 and 1849. The January 1850 flood that drove away Luzena Wilson also sent fleeing Sacramento's first acting troupe, the Atwater Company, which had opened the Eagle Theater in the fall of 1849.[51] Hardin Bigelow, the city's first mayor, died in San Francisco after being badly wounded in Sacramento's violent squatters' rebellion, a civil disturbance in August 1850 that also resulted in the death of the city assessor, the county sheriff, and six others.[52] The cholera epidemic that same year killed seventeen members of the local medical profession. Fire convinced the immigrant German artist Charles C. Nahl to relocate to San Francisco, where he would later paint his immense, romantically idealized depictions of gold rush scenes.[53] Rosanna Hughes, the most prosperous of Sacramento's early brothel owners, was relocating her business interests to Vancouver, British Columbia, during the Fraser River gold rush when she lost her life in the shipwreck of the *Brother Jonathan* off the northern California coast.[54]

Some early pioneers, to be sure, did remain. Mary Crocker was still present in 1860, along with her husband, Charles, who had become a successful Sacramento merchant and would achieve greater fortune as one of the "Big Four" founders of the Central Pacific Railroad. So, too, was James McClatchy, a newspaperman prominent as a squatter spokesman during the 1850 squatters' rebellion and by 1860 the owner and editor of the *Sacramento Bee*.[55] Also still resident was Dr. John Morse, a leader among Sacramento's medical doctors and the city's first historian.[56]

A Middling Sort of Social Order

As these few examples suggest, the city's social order was not shaped by the tens of thousands who came for a short while but rather by the few thousand during each decade who remained. Although we lack the data for a full-scale statistical investigation, census records, property records, business directories, and detailed biographical information for some residents suggest a general pattern, a few common traits to explain the development of Sacramento's pioneer society. Those who preserved their health and made a stake, stayed. Those who did not, those who suffered excessively from disease or were wiped out and lacked the capital or confidence to rebuild after fire or flood, those whose businesses failed to prosper—these people moved on. Either they returned "back home," ready to admit that California had brought them no great fortune, or they searched for other, better places where fortune might be found. It is understandable that not only miners but merchants and professionals with California experience, often Sacramento experience, were among the first to open new mining frontiers in southern Oregon, British Columbia, throughout the Rocky Mountain West, and Australia and New Zealand.[57] The region and its opportunities had attracted countless men and women with an entrepreneurial spirit. Apparently that same spirit in due time led many of them elsewhere.

One other group also departed virtually without fail: those who hit it big, those whose great financial success allowed them to live wherever they might like. In case after case, Sacramento's newly rich, Charles and Mary Crocker soon among them, abandoned the city. They took their wealth elsewhere. This flight of great fortunes from Sacramento had striking consequences over the years. For better or worse, city boosters could point to few monuments to wealth of the type that added distinction to many other western urban centers. Sacramento-created money built magnificent mansions—but they were mostly found in New York City, in Mill Valley, on Nob Hill in San Francisco, and in other more interesting, cooler, less disease-ridden places than Sacramento. Sacramento-created money founded a distinguished private institution of higher education—but it is located in Palo Alto, not in Sacramento. Sacramento-created money endowed a magnificent cathedral in San Francisco, bred champion racehorses in Kentucky, hired workers to excavate the ancient ruins of Troy, and established in Rome a foundation meant to benefit rural farm populations all over the world.

A Magnet for Immigrants

While the Sacramento region was becoming a living paradigm for evolving Anglo American middle-class social aspirations, it proved also a locality with strong attractions for refugees emigrating from distressed societies elsewhere. The most prominent examples during the gold rush era were the large numbers of working people who arrived from Ireland, from the German states, and from the Portuguese Azores. Also among the immigrants was a small but influential contingent of Jews from Russia, the German states, and the Austro-Hungarian Empire who would achieve early success in commerce and banking.

These newcomers arrived mostly in multigenerational family units of men, women, and children—though with young adults in the majority. They were refugees from natural disasters and famine, from political upheavals and repression, from social distress and economic hardships of many types. Cut off from their homelands, most planned from the start to resettle in northern California. Though certainly not every Irish or German or Portuguese or Jewish family that reached Sacramento remained for all time, these groups constituted distinctive and enduring elements in the pioneer population. Without exception they established many familiar, ethnically based cultural institutions that mediated the stress of migration and the problems of raising a new generation isolated from the parents' homeland. To find documentation of their presence, one only needs to look to Sacramento's religious history, at the houses of worship they founded—where some of their descendants are members today—and to their religiously affiliated organizations.[58]

Chinese immigrant gold seekers, a preponderantly male population, also reached northern California in large numbers during the gold rush era. Through the 1850s, most Chinese were dispersed in placer mining camps throughout the gold country. San Francisco, their port of entry, quickly became the metropolitan center for Chinese business and social affairs. Sacramento and other interior towns served only as staging areas and service centers for Chinese working in the mining regions. A few Chinese boardinghouses, small-scale groceries, and herb shops in Sacramento operated as satellite enterprises, usually linked to the great Chinese merchant houses of San Francisco. Federal census takers in 1860, recording another service industry, counted nearly one hundred Chinese women residents in Sacramento, apparently all located in one or another of the small Chinese brothels clustered close to the embarcadero in the West End.[59] By 1870, these women were gone, another sign of a continued concentration of Chinese urban enterprise and social life in San Francisco, a tendency encouraged by growing anti-Chinese agitation throughout northern California. Only after passage of the federal Chinese Exclusion Act in 1882, which banned immigration by single males, did demographic patterns begin to shift among northern California's Chinese, leading toward the twentieth-century development of family-centered communities and fixed, long-term settlement in Sacramento and other localities outside San Francisco.[60]

While the shortage of respectable women remained a complaint throughout the gold rush era, to some extent Irish, German, Chinese, and other immigrant males found work in domestic service occupations normally taken by women in Anglo American society. They became cooks and waiters, laundry workers, house servants, hotel attendants, and boardinghouse keepers. But the educational and humanitarian roles also customarily filled by women—providing schools, orphanages, and health care—generally suffered neglect, even after the demographics began to change somewhat during the 1860s. It remained, for instance, for the Sisters of Mercy, a contingent of Roman Catholic nuns just arrived from Ireland, to open Sacramento's first school and first orphanage in 1857. Other newly arrived women led the struggle for public-funded common school education in Sacramento through the decades of slow growth that followed the gold rush.[61]

In time, all foreign-born immigrant groups in the Sacramento region would measure their success by their acculturation and emulation of an Anglo American middle-class lifestyle. The massive transfer of population from rural villages and small towns to urban centers, with the accompanying transformation in lifestyles, family patterns, cultural horizons, and generational ambitions, was the central demographic and social phenomenon of this age—termed by historian Eric Hobsbawm the "Age of Capital."[62] This dual process of demographic transfer and social transformation had a worldwide sweep, as seen in the immigration history of the western United States but nowhere more clearly than in northern California during the gold rush era.

Saving Sacramento

The city's leadership during the gold rush era—even with a high turnover rate—followed a typical pattern for frontier America. Dominated from the beginning by merchants and professionals, these self-anointed leaders showed a high degree of entrepreneurial energy decade after decade. Although they quarreled over the city's governing charter and awarded themselves scandalously high salaries, they also made sincere efforts to enhance property values, to improve Sacramento's attractiveness to newcomers—excepting for many years Chinese, Japanese, and other Asian-born immigrants—and to keep it prosperous and growing.[63]

After the disastrous 1850 flood, construction of a rudimentary flood protection levee on the American River was the city government's first major project. City officials and private property owners cooperated a few years later, after more floods, in an ingenious, hugely ambitious scheme to haul in landfill and raise the level of the downtown streets a full nine feet, converting the first floor of older buildings into basements.[64] Just as ambitious was a city project to alter the lower course of the American River, moving it away from the embarcadero business district by redirecting its flow to meet the Sacramento River a half mile farther north, and then filling in a large swampy overflow—called Sutter Lake or China Lake—that was bordered by small laundry businesses and had become a malodorous public nuisance. This area soon became part of the Central Pacific/Southern Pacific railroad yards, with machine shops that built great steam engines and rolling stock.

Many other city-funded projects sought to improve Sacramento's quality of life during the 1850s. In 1853, the city council authorized an appropriation of $185,000 to plank the streets in the business district and install a sewer system, both temporary expedients at best. Drinking water also received attention. Sacramento River water, muddy and contaminated by mining debris, gained the sarcastic label "Sacramento Straight." Household wells were not a satisfactory substitute, since they produced water that had a high iron content and smelled and tasted of sulfur. With a voter-approved levy, the city government constructed a crude water distribution system. It served the business district, giving it some level of fire protection. The system transported water in underground wooden pipes from a reservoir atop a newly built brick city hall at the foot of I Street. Residents paid a flat water fee of two dollars a month per family, with a guarantee fixed in the city charter that no meters would ever be installed to measure water usage. City officials also took the initiative to construct a gas works near the I Street city hall and waterworks, completing the plant in time to illuminate the first streetlights just before Christmas 1855.

The city's waste disposal issues did not receive attention until the mid-1860s. Householders and businesses at first depended on open cesspools, septic tanks, and drainage ditches. Beginning in 1864, the city government built a sewage and drainage canal system that placed sewer pipes underground, all emptying into a canal at Sixth and R Streets. From this point the effluent flowed in a large cement pipe to Sutterville Road, where it went into an open ditch that carried the city's wastes southward more than twenty miles to Snodgrass Slough. The slough emptied into the Sacramento River, so the city's waste became someone else's problem.[65]

As the gold rush was ending, Sacramento's leaders put together a political deal that brought their city the permanent state capital.[66] Even though Leland Stanford, newly elected to the governorship, had to reach his inaugural ceremony in January 1862 by rowboat, this businessmen's coup assured the town a population of state workers who in later years would strongly reinforce the city's middle-class ethos.

Sacramento's middle-class heritage, it should be noted, has frequently been in an uneasy balance with a rowdier spirit. The gold rush era, with its mostly male society, bolstered a male-oriented popular culture that became another enduring legacy of Sacramento's formative period. By the choice of Sacramento's earliest civic policy makers, the town was wide open. Its waterfront entertainment district, catering to transient men toting gold pouches, helped in no small way to define the character of the infant metropolis. Even after the gender balance began to shift toward parity, there long remained embedded in the city's social life a male saloon and brothel subculture that had its geographic center in the West End near the Sacramento River. Urged by US military officials, Sacramento's city government adopted a red light abatement ordinance to abolish brothels shortly after World War I, following an exceedingly divisive public controversy.[67] Yet, some will argue that this subculture still thrives, only slightly tamed, close to the state capitol complex, where mostly male, mostly transient legislative members and lobbyists gather to attend boozily to the public's business.

Absent old money and major private investment in community institutions, over the years the city's leaders have taken many other steps to overcome Sacramento's environmental problems by using public authority and public funding. The city can now boast, for example, highly effective municipal systems for waste disposal, for supplying low-cost, unmetered, high-quality water, and for mosquito eradication.[68] Late in the nineteenth century, the McClatchy family's *Sacramento Bee,* the city's popular morning newspaper, promoted a tree-planting campaign that immensely helped to beautify city neighborhoods and moderate the harsh impact of the summer climate. This arboreal ardor resulted in an urban forest that gives Sac-

FIGURE 2.4. *Flood Plain Architecture.* This example of Sacramento's Victorian architecture illustrates the typical practice of locating a home's living area one flight above ground level, a characteristic still generally found in midtown Sacramento homes and apartments, large and small, built prior to the 1950s. Courtesy Center for Sacramento History, Schroth-Beauchamp Collection.

ramentans currently a reason to challenge the reputation of Paris as a city of trees.

From an early date, the city's architects and contractors accommodated to flood danger by adopting a style of architecture that allowed ten or twelve feet of water to immerse a ground-level garage or shop temporarily, with no great loss, while the residential or business first story was situated above flood level. Throughout the older districts of the city can be seen block after block of frame homes in which long flights of stairs lead upward from the street, usually to an unenclosed front porch and the front door, well above the expected high water line.[69] This type of floodplain architecture appears even in the trophy mansions built by a few of Sacramento's wealthiest families in the 1870s. The Stanford mansion at Eighth and L Streets, now refurbished as a state historical park, the Third and O Street mansion constructed by Judge E. B. Crocker, Charles Crocker's nephew, that is preserved as the Crocker Art Museum's core building, and the former Governor's Mansion at Fifteenth and H Streets, also now included in the state park system, are all monuments of Victorian residential taste that display the same key feature to ensure that the family's first floor would remain safely dry during the unavoidable sporadic episodes of flooding. Strikingly different in design from more recent construction, these structures all testify to their builders' success in adjusting to the major environmental peril of life in Sacramento prior to the dam and levee construction projects of the mid-twentieth century.

There's No Place Like Home

Before 1848, city growth throughout world history was a gradual, organic process built economically on trade in the natural resources of productive hinterlands, most frequently farm lands and livestock pasturage. During the westward movement of settlers into the American Midwest, experienced townsite speculators led the way in creating an urban frontier, platting commercial towns at strategic points to serve the needs of an expanding rural population.[70] But with rare exceptions—Peter the Great's creation of Saint Petersburg may be the single familiar case—rising metropolitan centers only gradually gained the success that made them prominent cities. In the typical American scenario, the natural leaders of aspiring urban centers were merchants, bankers, and newspaper editors, perhaps augmented by local politicians and clergy, who all happily served as local boosters. They claimed leadership in a traditional system based on the expectation that, despite occasional speculative excesses, economic growth would be steady and that it would reward hard work, sound judgment, sober habits, and careful stewardship, bringing in due time a secure modicum of wealth and comfort.

At the same time as the northern California gold discoveries, in 1848, Karl Marx and Friedrich Engels published the *Communist Manifesto,* urging the workers of the world to overthrow this system by revolutionary action. Four years later, trying to assess the failure of their call to action, Engels took notice of the gold rushes in California and Australia. These discoveries, he remarked ruefully to Marx, had created large new markets "out of nothing," a development the two radical socialist theorists had not at all anticipated.[71]

In Sacramento and similarly situated places adjacent to gold country, the same discoveries also created new cities out of nothing. The unanticipated consequences of the invasion of once peripheral regions by capitalist commerce and industry, these hastily located gold rush business centers and the societies they fostered were significantly different than any previously known. Built on the energy and ambitions of a great many speculative, venturesome men and women coming in a short time from a great many different places, they were unique in their cultural diversity, their singular dedication to commercial profit, and their resolutely middle-class character.

These upstart places, the "River City" of Sacramento foremost among them, often had precarious beginnings due to the environmental and social circumstances of their early years. Their emergence on the world scene out of nothing was indeed remarkable. More remarkable still has been their survival and growth after the gold rush excitement diminished. They have lasted into the twenty-first century because of neither the grand schemes of a princely few aristocratic leaders nor the revolutionary ardor of a proletarian underclass. Sacramento and similar cities have succeeded mainly because of the usually unheralded, quiet accomplishments of ordinary people who decided to stay and make this place a home—a pleasant and comfortable home—for themselves and their families. The city's history has been guided throughout by a commitment to the commonplace, an embrace of middle-class, bourgeois joys as the basis for a good life.

CHAPTER 3

"We Must Give the World
Confidence in the Stability and
Permanence of the Place"
PLANNING SACRAMENTO'S TOWNSITE,
1853–1870

Nathan Hallam

C apt. William Dane Phelps of Gloucester, Massachusetts, arrived in the Sacramento Valley in July 1841. A merchant in the California hide and tallow trade,
Phelps had taken leave from his business along the coast to visit John Sutter at
New Helvetia, where a team of Indian laborers put the final touches on Sutter's
adobe fort overlooking the American River. While touring the grounds, Phelps
also met John Sinclair, a Scottish immigrant who settled lands north of Sutter.
Over dinner, Sinclair proposed a hunting expedition to the Feather River, sixteen
miles to the north, where herds of tule elk grazed along the riverbanks. Departing
the following morning, Phelps marveled at the Sacramento Valley countryside.
"After crossing the American Fork," he observed, "our route lay over a beautiful
country of plains and gently rising hills all well covered with oats, with here and
there groves of trees, presenting a fine landscape to the eye." Returning to the fort
the following day, however, Phelps encountered a different landscape. "On our way
back," he wrote in his journal, "we passed the remains of Indian villages, long since
abandoned." Through his hosts, Phelps learned that some of the valley's "gently
rising hills" were in fact living quarters built by Indians for the flood season. "Their
villages," he remarked, "were on a mound which they had raised about 18 feet
high with the earth taken from the plain on which they built, and the plain being
overflown with water in the winter, puzzled me to imagine why they should select
such a location."[1]

Perhaps it would have further puzzled Phelps to know that, within twenty-five years, thousands of Americans would undertake a very similar project in very nearly the same location, raising the streets and buildings of Sacramento twelve feet above the surrounding American River flood basin. Today, most residents of Sacramento are familiar with the city's gold rush origins, but few recall the twenty-year effort to build the foundations of a stable, permanent city. For all that Sacramento offered merchants and miners in 1849—a natural river landing, a marketplace for goods and supplies, ample space for squatters—its physical location posed problems. Between 1850 and 1862, Sacramento endured four major floods and scores of smaller inundations, costing residents millions in property damage. "We all admit that this is no place for a city," remarked J Street iron dealer Isaac Van Winkle in 1862. "The ground is like a sponge. The water comes in from the river, and overflows the lower part of the city, even when there is no flood."[2]

For merchants like Van Winkle and others who stayed in Sacramento after the gold rush, flooding posed an acute dilemma: abandon the city and relinquish the time, money, and effort invested in building homes and businesses, or stay on and help shoulder the considerable burden of making the townsite tenable. Some left, but many remained; staying on in Sacramento had its advantages, too. Situated at the crossroads of California and surrounded by rich farmland, the city lay at the foot of some of the richest gold and silver mines in the world. "Whether we stayed here or left and sacrificed our property," reasoned one K Street business owner, "this was destined to be a great point for trade, and we should not allow others to reap the benefits we might enjoy."[3] Nor would they. During the 1850s and 1860s, Sacramento's residents graded and planked streets, raised the city twelve feet above the flood basin, opened new channels for the American River, and altered their street grid to accommodate prominent public institutions. All of this came at great expense to property owners, who levied taxes upon themselves and complied with condemnation proceedings to ensure the stability and permanence of their city. "Planning," as Robert Fishman writes, involves "collective action for the common good, but particularly action that concentrates on building and shaping the physical infrastructure for present needs and future growth."[4] One can read the early history of Sacramento as a turn toward such collective action, as property owners came to perceive their individual fortunes as bound together in a shared investment in the townsite—a townsite planned not for long-term growth but short-term speculation.

Planning Sacramento's Townsite

Sacramento's "townsite" refers to the streets, blocks, and lots comprising what is now known as the central city, or simply "the grid." Built at the base of the American River flood basin, the grid occupies a landscape that for millennia absorbed floodwaters caused by winter rains and Sierra Nevada snow-melt; regularly these floodwaters converted valley flood basins into "huge, shallow, temporary lakes."[5] The story of how Sacramento came to occupy one of these basins begins with its survey, commissioned by John "August" Sutter Jr. in 1848. Unlike his more famous father, August came to perceive the land fronting the Sacramento and American Rivers as real equity and a convenient solution to his father's overwhelming debt. Though John Sutter Sr. is popularly celebrated as Sacramento's "founder," it was actually his business failures, and his son's efforts to resolve them, that prompted Sacramento's founding. Deeded his father's estate in September 1848, August also inherited a twenty-thousand-dollar balance owed to the Russian-American Company, whose officials moved to foreclose on Sutter's forty-eight-thousand-acre rancho, New Helvetia, that fall.[6] Transferring ownership of the estate stalled foreclosure, but August soon discovered other debts totaling tens of thousands of dollars in excess of the Russian obligation. "I am sure," he later recalled, "there was not a man in the fort or in San Francisco, not a man, I may say so, in the whole country, with whom my father had not unsettled accounts."[7] With a limited command of English and an even lesser familiarity with the Sacramento Valley, August began searching for ways to raise revenue and retain his father's rancho.

The answer came from Samuel Brannan, a mining supply merchant who had taken to squatting along the embarcadero, a natural landing on the Sacramento River just south of the American River confluence. Peddling picks and pans to the few fortunate gold seekers who arrived before 1849, Brannan anticipated the forthcoming gold rush and wanted to acquire town lots at Sutterville, John Sutter's townsite laid out on higher ground three miles upstream.[8] Sutterville's land agent, Lansford Hastings, could not reach an agreement with Brannan, so upon hearing news of New Helvetia's transfer, Brannan approached August with an idea: why not lay out streets and lots between the fort and the embarcadero, where ships already docked and where squatter merchants like Brannan himself reaped sizable profits? Through the sale of town lots, August might raise enough revenue to pay his father's creditors. As August later recalled, "Mr. Brannan and others had suggested to me . . . the propriety of having the fort and the surrounding plain until to the river laid out in a city."[9] Heinrich Lienhard, an employee at the fort, recalled the episode more vividly:

Not long after my return to the fort, young Sutter came to see me and asked me what I thought about some advice he had received from a former elder of the Mormon church, Mr. Brannan, who had told him that it would be unwise to build a city on the site where Sutterville had been laid out, because no one could disembark there until a canal half a mile long had been built, and at that time wages were so high—workmen received at least an ounce of gold a day—that it would cost an immense sum. At the landing place, on the other hand, lots could be sold without delay at good prices. People would build immediately, and the place, although low, would become a great metropolis.[10]

Despite its suspect topography, therefore, the embarcadero's river landing made it a more accessible place than the high ground at Sutterville. "The attention of everybody," August later insisted, "was drawn upon this place and not upon Sutter-ville; even if I had wanted to do so, I could not have stemmed the current. Nobody would go to Sutterville and if I had not commenced selling lots at Sacramento, everybody would have gone to squatting."[11]

Before he could sell lots, however, August needed a surveyor to lay out the townsite. "Brannan," Lienhard wrote, "advised young Sutter to make his plans im-mediately, because a United States engineer was temporarily available to lay out and survey the site."[12] The engineer was Capt. William H. Warner of the US Army Corps of Topographic Engineers, a veteran of the US-Mexico War, and a West Point trained surveyor. With commission in hand from August, Warner obtained leave of absence and recruited fellow officers William Tecumseh Sherman and Ed-ward Ord to serve as draftsmen. The party camped along the American River north of the fort and completed their work in December.[13] Grateful for the commission, Warner, Sherman, and Ord may have also privately questioned the propriety of laying out a city at the bottom of a flood basin. "At Sutterville," reflected Sherman years later, "the plateau of the Sacramento approached quite near the river, and it would have made a better site for a town than the low, submerged land where the city now stands; but it seems to be a law of growth that all natural advantages are disregarded wherever once business chooses a location."[14]

For Sacramento, Warner, Sherman, and Ord laid out a five-square-mile town-site. Reflecting on the size and symmetry of the layout, John Reps calls Sacramento "the standardized grid town *par excellence*."[15] From the Sacramento and American Rivers, the city extended two miles east and south. Warner named roads running east and west for the letters of the alphabet and roads running north and south for numbers ranging from two to thirty-one. Evoking Philadelphia, he named the road along the waterfront Front Street. Each street measured 80 feet wide with the exceptions of Front Street, which equaled the width of the waterfront, and M Street, which Warner set at 100 feet wide. Individual blocks measured 340 by 320 feet, bisected into northern and southern halves by 20-foot-wide alleys. Each block contained eight lots that measured 40 feet wide by 160 feet deep. Only a handful of blocks deviated from this configuration: the alley between Front and Second Streets ran in a north-south direction to accommodate preexisting structures, while the alley between J and K Streets from Fourth to Eighth Streets, a stretch called Oak Street (now Merchant Street), measured much wider than 20 feet, perhaps because it followed the original footpath from the embarcadero to the fort. Warner also set blocks between Twelfth and Thirteenth Streets at 340 by 400 feet. These blocks contained ten lots apiece. At the layout's western and northern ends, Warner created short, irregular streets to fill in pockets of land created by bends and curves in the Sacramento and American Rivers; Samuel Brannan himself completed this work in May 1851, extending the grid to the banks of the Sacramento River below Q Street in a section called Brannan's Addition.[16]

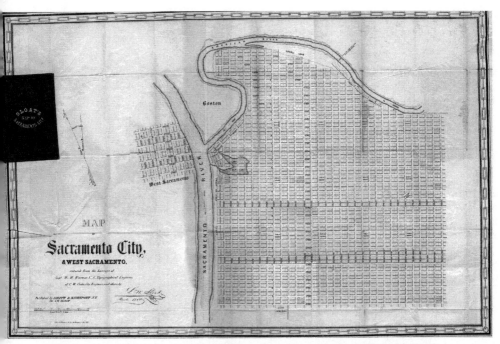

FIGURE 3.1. This 1850 reproduction of William H. Warner's 1848 plat map for Sacramento shows the original parceling of the city's townsite: a vast, uniform layout of streets, blocks, and lots. Courtesy Center for Sacramento History, Eleanor McClatchy Collection.

On January 2, 1849, six days before he commenced the sale of lots, August decreed that all streets and alleys must "remain at all times open for Public use," with the exception of Front Street, which he reserved for the privilege of Front Street property owners. August also made a gift to the city, reserving ten city blocks "for the public use of the inhabitance of said City to be applyed to such public purposes as the future incorperated authoritys of said City from time to time declare and determin."[17] These blocks became city parks; many remain in use today. With the city parceled, August hired Peter Burnett, an itinerant lawyer, to manage the sale of lots, which Burnett priced at $250 near the fort and $500 near the embarcadero. As Burnett later recalled, "Nearly all the first sales were of lots near the fort; but toward the end of January the lots near the river began to sell most rapidly."[18] That month, an agent of the Russian-American Company arrived at the fort demanding full repayment of John Sutter's debts, and Burnett settled the matter on the spot with a payment of gold dust and promissory notes furnished by lot buyers.

Platted at the bottom of the American River flood basin, Sacramento took shape within a dense riparian landscape. In their travelogues and memoirs, many of the "forty-niners" who arrived in the summer and fall of 1849 noted with curiosity the contrast of rough wood-frame buildings, white canvas tents, and "the original forest-trees," as Bayard Taylor called them, "standing in all parts of town." Trees served as Sacramento's public infrastructure during the gold rush. An "immense evergreen oak" at the base of K Street became the site of a horse market, while incoming ships fastened cables "to the trunks and sinewy roots of the trees" along the waterfront.[19] Trees also suggested latent hazards. "A close observer, even in dry season," noted J. Horace Culver, the city's first historian, "could not fail to notice the evidence of former overflows, as exhibited by the marks on the bark of the trees. . . . There were wooden pins shown, also, driven into trees, five, eight and ten feet from the ground, said to indicate the height of previous floods."[20]

Rumors of flooding were substantiated on January 9, 1850, as lingering rain caused the Sacramento River to spill over its banks and into Sutter Lake, a slough on the north side of I Street between Front and Sixth Streets. Before nightfall, the slough's waters breached I Street and began creeping down Second and Third Streets. In her canvas tent, Sarah Royce had put her infant daughter to bed when she heard a man "saying hastily to my husband who stood at the door, 'The water's coming in . . . come this way—to this low spot—and you will soon find yourself stepping in water . . . don't you see it rising on your boot?'"[21] Taking shelter in a nearby house, Royce awoke the following morning to the sound of boats outside her second-story window. "For miles north and south," she later recalled, "I could see nothing but water."[22] Almost all of Sacramento's buildings suffered first-floor flooding, while several rose off their foundations and floated away. "The damage to merchandise and to buildings," reported the *Placer Times*, "and the losses sustained by persons engaged in trade is very great—vast quantities of provisions and goods having been swept away by the rushing waters."[23]

The flood made plain to everyone the hazards of Sacramento's townsite. It is easy to imagine nineteenth-century "instant cities" such as Sacramento as rude disruptors of natural landscapes, but in early Sacramento the opposite was also true, as floodwaters played havoc with the fledgling city. In the fall of 1850, Sacramento's newly chartered city government arranged for the construction of a levee along the south bank of the American River—the first instance of collective action to improve the townsite. Yet, as Andrew Isenberg shows, the levee did more to legitimize city government than to protect the city.[24] In March 1852, heavy rains again lingered over the lower Sacramento Valley, and, on March 8, 1852, residents of the city awoke at 1:00 a.m. to the sound of an alarm; by morning the city had flooded again. New flood control measures followed. During the fall of 1852, the city government oversaw construction of an I Street levee that shielded the city from Sutter Lake. As if to mock these efforts, another flood, the largest yet, greeted Sacramento on New Year's Day, 1853. On K Street the water stood three to six feet deep, while on J Street hundreds of small boats plied waist-deep waters.[25] Clearly, more aggressive measures were needed if Sacramento was to survive in this location.

Grading and Planking the Streets

Skepticism of the levees widened in the wake of the New Year's Day flood. "Our city government," lamented an anonymous contributor to the *Sacramento Daily Union* in January 1853, "has been in operation nearly three years, has expended more than two hundred thousand dollars upon the levee . . . [but] after all this taxation and expenditure, the city has not received a benefit commensurate with the costs." Some were willing to try a new approach: "I am well satisfied," continued the contributor, "from my own observation during the last four years at this point, that the only safe and certain remedy against high water and muddy streets, is to raise the site of the city." Better to lift Sacramento out of the flood basin than confine it within. Improbable as it seemed, raising the townsite involved a fairly straightforward process: "a stratum of sand at the bottom, and a stratum of course [*sic*] gravel at the top, about a foot thick." Property owners would then raise the first floors of their own buildings to meet the new grade. With even one foot of fill, Sacramento could be made to slope imperceptibly to the south to allow for better drainage. Improved drainage might, in turn, reassure the city's skeptics. "We must," the contributor pleaded, "give the world confidence in the stability and permanence of the place."[26]

The idea gained traction with Sacramento voters. Within two weeks of the New Year's Day flood, the *Sacramento Daily Union* spotted "several public spirited gentlemen" canvassing the city for signatures in favor of a grade ordinance.[27] It was a scene almost unimaginable four years earlier, when speculative interests outweighed concerns for public order. By 1853, however, those interests had given way to what the historian Mark Eifler describes as "the greater transformation of miners to businessmen," the tendency of gold seekers after 1850 to abandon the "diggings" and trade picks and pans for stable livelihoods in Sacramento and other California towns and cities.[28] A stable livelihood, however, required a secure urban environment. In February 1853, the Sacramento Common Council instructed its surveyor, Edward Suffern, to determine the New Year's Day high-water mark and make recommendations for grading the city's built-out area. Suffern issued his report in late March: workers would raise I, J, K, and L Streets and their numbered cross streets between twenty and thirty inches. The grade on I and L Streets would extend from the Sacramento River to Eleventh Street, while on J Street it would extend to the city's eastern boundary at Thirty-First Street. The city would be made to drain excess water into a slough behind R Street. Suffern also recommended surfacing Front, J, and K Streets with wood planks to improve ground transportation through the business section of town; that costly procedure would require more than two million board feet of Oregon pine.[29]

In early March 1853, the city modified its charter, allowing property owners fronting streets assigned Suffern's grade to petition the common council to begin work. In late April, the city added an amendment requiring that property owners bear two-thirds of the costs.[30] At that point, the whole matter came up for discussion among council members. Peter Burnett, the former land agent of August Sutter, the former governor of California, and now chair of the Committee on Streets, issued a report echoing Suffern's recommendations. Thomas Youngs, however, spoke in favor of a much higher grade, perhaps five or six feet: "high enough," explained Youngs, "to place the city above such high water as we have had the past season."[31] Though foresighted, Youngs's proposal found little support among council members, who went forward with Suffern's more modest two-foot grade. Much to the pleasure of teamsters who freighted goods between Sacramento and Sierra Nevada mining communities, the council also agreed to grade and plank J Street to the city's eastern limits, where it bridged a slough near Sutter's Fort and met a private plank road extending to Patterson's Hotel, twelve miles distant.[32] Merchants were especially pleased with the work. "The filling & planking of the streets goes on well," wrote K Street hardware retailer Mark Hopkins in September 1853. "The filling in of Front Street is in appearance the greatest improvement in town."[33]

Hopkins's sense of optimism epitomized the general outlook of Sacramento residents through the mid-late 1850s. Real estate values remained constant, but the value of the city's improvements—its built environment—nearly doubled, a sign that those who owned city lots reinvested in the townsite by constructing permanent buildings.[34] Sacramento also welcomed a host of public infrastructural improvements that signaled a turn toward stability: a new levee along R Street at the southern edge of the city's built-out area, a municipal waterworks that pumped water from the Sacramento River and distributed it to homes and businesses through iron pipes, a public school system and county hospital, and a stately neoclassical county courthouse built at the corner of Seventh and I Streets. Also during these years, a special committee appointed by the common council discussed the possibility of re-routing the American River, but council members dismissed the plan, reaffirming their confidence in the levees and the street grade, which seemed to provide sufficient flood control. Sacramento's leaders now turned their attention to attracting prominent public institutions, though again the townsite would prove problematic.

The Grid Interferes

The new courthouse at the corner of Seventh and I Streets marked a turning point in the development of Sacramento, as city leaders, confident in the tenability of their townsite, leased the building to the State of California as a temporary statehouse. For any fledgling western city, attaining the state capital paid immediate dividends. It signaled, as John Reps suggests, "that the town was destined for permanency."[35] For this reason the capital was also a hotly contested commodity in early California, and despite its recent floods, Sacramento emerged a strong candidate. Centrally located, accessible by steamship, and substantially developed, the city had inherent advantages over San Jose and Benicia, its main rivals. To enhance the city's chances, Sacramento's common council also offered the state legislature one of August Sutter's public squares as a building site for a future statehouse. Though some questioned the wisdom of locating the capital at the bottom of a flood basin, Sacramento County's state senator, Amos P. Catlin, argued persuasively that recent public infrastructural improvements reflected the "confidence of the citizens in the permanence of their location."[36] The legislature agreed. In February 1854, Gov. John Bigler signed an enabling act removing the state capital from Benicia to Sacramento.

By 1859, however, Sacramento's hold on the capital had become tenuous, as lawmakers struggled to arrange for the construction of a permanent capitol building. Three years earlier, the legislature had authorized $300,000 in bonds to build on the public square, but the California Supreme Court declared the bond measure unconstitutional and returned the public square to the City of Sacramento.[37] Then, in March 1859, rumors surfaced of the legislature's impending move. Assemblyman William Rodgers of Alameda County substantiated those rumors by announcing Oakland's intentions to raise $200,000 and provide ten acres of land near the center of town. Lawmakers delayed the matter until the following session, but, upon reconvening in January 1860, they were greeted with a second proposal: San Francisco now offered $150,000 and four blocks in the city's soon-to-be-developed Western Addition.[38]

This situation presented Sacramento with a problem. Oakland offered ten acres while San Francisco's proposal totaled more than thirteen acres. By comparison, Sacramento's public square totaled just over three acres. If Sacramento wanted to keep the capital, it would have to put together a commensurate gift of land. The city's street grid now stood as an obstacle. By overlaying the townsite with thousands of small, indistinguishable lots, the grid had suited August Sutter admirably in his rushed attempt to raise revenue, but now the layout frustrated those who sought to combine multiple lots and blocks into a single multiblock parcel. Creating such a parcel would require purchasing lots one at a time, block by block, and although the city and state possessed the power of condemnation, that process was time consuming and often politically perilous.

But some institutions were worth the trouble. In 1860, city leaders set about altering Sacramento's street grid to retain the state capital. In January, a delegation of Sacramento-area legislators led by State Sen. Robert Clark prepared new bills providing for the construction of a statehouse; this legislation closely resembled the 1856 bill, with one key exception. The building would be located not in a public square but in the center of a four-block parcel between L, Twelfth, N, and Tenth Streets.[39] "After the adjournment last evening," explained Clark, "I consulted with many of the citizens of Sacramento in relation to the proper location of the Capitol building. I also consulted with several Senators upon the same subject, and I found some little diversity of opinion as to the proper location on the part of both Senators and citizens." The four-block parcel sat two blocks from Sacramento's business district and centered on M Street, the city's widest street. "It is," promised Clark, "good ground—not as high as the public square by perhaps two or three feet, but it could be easily filled; would but cost little; and the ground, if condemned, could be procured for much less money."[40] Clark also indicated that Sacramento taxpayers would assist with the costs of condemnation. His colleague from Sacramento, James McDougal, reiterated that "the citizens of this city are willing to pay for this ground; and in good faith they desired this amendment to pass, and were willing to be taxed for the value of the land."[41] With no opposition from the state's high court, on March 29, 1860, Gov. John Downey signed a bill providing $500,000 for a new statehouse at the M Street site. The bill also created a five-member Board of State Capitol Commissioners to oversee condemnation hearings and manage the construction of the building. A week later the city's board of supervisors passed an ordinance by unanimous vote to vacate the parcel's streets and alleys.[42]

The commissioners did not stop with the initial four-block parcel, however. As California's white domed statehouse took shape during the 1860s, the commissioners eyed land suitable for a park that would complement the building. In his 1863 message to the legislature, Gov. Leland Stanford described his vision of "a State Capitol of California that is to endure for generations . . . a structure that the future will be proud of, and surrounded by grounds that should extend into the dimensions of an ample park."[43] Seven years later, the commissioners began fulfilling this vision, beginning with the acquisition of a single square block bounded by L, Fifteenth, M, and Fourteenth Streets to serve as the site of a future governor's mansion. Two years later, they acquired the remaining five square blocks in between with the intention of combining the three acquisitions into a single ten-square-block parcel bounded by L, Fifteenth, N, and Tenth Streets. Sacramento voters assisted the acquisition by levying a 0.20 percent property tax upon themselves to cover more than 30 percent of the condemnation costs.[44] The landscaping of Capitol Park proceeded through the 1870s, and, when finished, the entire ten-block property added considerable grandeur to Sacramento: "The beauty of the whole is equaled in but few of the public buildings in the country," noted a travel writer in 1876. "The extended landscape is incomparably lovely."[45]

While working to retain the state capital in 1860, Sacramento leaders also pursued the California state fair, an equally hotly contested public institution. As the annual exposition of the California State Agricultural Society, the fair ranked among the largest social gatherings in the state.[46] San Francisco hosted the inaugural fair, followed by Sacramento in 1855. Described as a "triumphant exhibition for young California," the 1855 fair proved equally triumphant for Sacramento merchants, who for three days enjoyed a volume of trade unseen since the gold rush. "Never," reported the *Union,* "in the annals of this juvenile city of the plains have there been congregated here so many human beings as the place contained yesterday."[47] The fair went to San Jose in 1856, to Stockton in 1857, and to Marysville in

1858 before returning to Sacramento in 1859, when city leaders resolved to keep it there permanently.

Retaining the fair, like retaining the capital, required public expenditure. In February 1859, Sacramento city and county voters levied a 0.25 percent property tax for the purposes of building the Agricultural Pavilion, a two-story exhibition hall designed by Miner Frederic Butler, architect of the future state capitol building. Located at the corner of Sixth and M Streets in what would become Capitol Park, the Agricultural Pavilion, by contemporary account, ranked among the finest meeting halls in the United States, "a superior specimen of workmanship and finish."[48] Due, in part, to these new accommodations, the 1859 state fair in Sacramento ranked "much larger than any of its predecessors," compelling the State Agricultural Society board to keep the fair in Sacramento a second consecutive year. This prompted loud protest from society members in San Francisco and elsewhere, who preferred that the fair remain itinerant.[49] Yet, two-thirds of the society's membership lived in Sacramento County, and when the board put the matter up to a vote of its members, Sacramento received 190 votes to San Francisco's 44. "The Sacramentans," remarked editors of the San Francisco–based *Daily Alta California*, "have been berated severely by many members of the Society, for insisting on having the next State Fair held in their city. It is due them, however, to state that they have given greater evidence of their interest in the welfare of the association than any other section of the state."[50]

Keeping the fair in Sacramento, however, also required a gift of land comparable to Capitol Park. At the society's January 1861 board of directors meeting, a group of Sacramento residents calling themselves the Sacramento Park Association announced they had pooled money to purchase six blocks between E, Twenty-Second, H, and Twentieth Streets. Situated in the northeast corner of the city, the blocks were to be enclosed within a brick wall and made into a venue for cattle shows and horse races. A year later, the same group of residents, now calling themselves the Union Park Association, announced another purchase of six blocks directly north, between B, Twenty-Second, E, and Twentieth Streets. When conjoined, the State Agricultural Society's two parcels formed a single twelve-block park large enough to accommodate a mile-long racetrack, where horse races entertained fairgoers.[51] "It has gone abroad that Sacramento desired to have a monopoly of all the public buildings and institutions," quipped E. B. Crocker in 1860.[52] Those buildings and institutions, however, represented a larger effort on the part of city leaders to reconcile their townsite layout with the needs of prominent public institutions.

Re-routing the American River

After the New Year's Day flood of 1853, northern California entered a drought cycle lasting seven years, a period of time long enough for many Sacramento residents to assume levee building and street grading had made the city impenetrable to floods. Then, in March 1861, the rains returned, hovering over the Sierra Nevada's deep winter snowpack and releasing a surge down the American River that ruptured the levee on the American River at a weak point on the bend above Twenty-Eighth Street. This relatively minor flood, however, was only a prelude to the "Great Calamity" the following winter, when nearly twenty-four inches of rain fell upon Sacramento, swelling the American River's flow to an astonishing 318,000 cubic feet per second, more than thirty-seven times its winter-spring average.[53] On December 9, 1861, the levee above Twenty-Eighth Street broke again, but water did not enter the city at first, pooling instead behind the R Street levee southeast of R and Sixteenth Streets. Then, all at once, the levee failed and the lake spilled into the city with incredible force. From high ground at Poverty Ridge, George Bromley and others watched the scene unfold as thousands fought for their lives: "We only knew that between us and them was a raging torrent carrying death, devastation and ruin in its course, and that from a distance beyond the reach of our assistance we could distinctly hear the despairing cries of men, women, and children who were expecting any moment that their homes would be afloat and themselves borne with them."[54] A month later, the levee gave way again above Twenty-Eighth Street. This time, however, the water eased into the city more gradually, creeping up the sides of buildings an inch every five minutes. Onlookers recalled the "extraordinary bustle among merchants and businessmen to prepare their houses for inundation."[55] This third flood set the new high-water mark for Sacramento. The city had eluded flooding for seven years, but the floods of 1861–62—an inordinately wet year in California—revealed again the hazards of the city's townsite at the bottom of the American River flood basin.

Clearly, the Sacramento city council should have enforced the higher grade ordinance Thomas Youngs lobbied for in 1853. For that matter, the city also should have followed through with discussions in 1854 to re-route the American River through dry slough beds a mile north of town. These slough beds, as evidence suggested, had once served as the river's main channel; perhaps they could be cleared of trees and brush and made to serve the river once again. Talk of this plan resurfaced in 1859, when a sandbar at the mouth of the American River threatened to silt up the embarcadero landing.[56] The floods of 1861–62, however, made the situation far more urgent. In April 1862, the state legislature passed levee repair legislation, creating the five-member Board of City Levee Commissioners to oversee city flood control efforts in Sacramento County; the bill also gave levee commissioners the "power and authority to turn or straighten the channel of any portion of the American River deemed necessary for the protection of the city."[57]

This task fell to Andrew R. Jackson, a Sacramento schoolteacher who served a term in the state assembly in 1859.[58] After studying the riverbed through the summer of 1862, Jackson issued his recommendations in September. Workers would clear trees, brush, and other debris from a dry slough above Twenty-Eighth Street. Called the American River Cut-Off, this new channel would take significant pres-

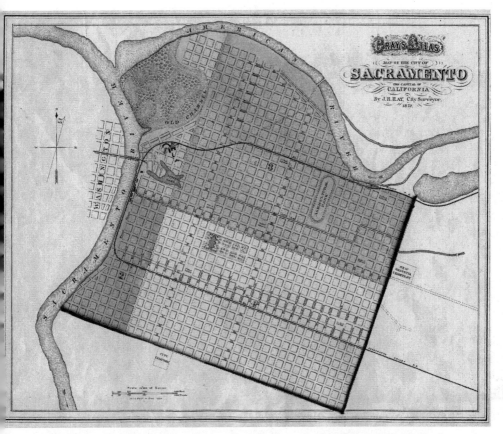

FIGURE 3.2. This 1874 map shows the new channel and mouth of the American River opened northwest of the city. The bend above Twenty-Eighth Street is erroneously shown to carry the main stream; it had since been channeled along the narrow line shown above the bend. Modifications to the street grid are also evident, as Sacramento accommodated the state capitol building and state fairgrounds. Courtesy Center for Sacramento History, City of Sacramento Collection.

sure off the weak point where the levee had repeatedly failed. Farther downstream, at an S-shaped bend near the American River's confluence with the Sacramento River, Jackson ordered a second slough cleared and a new confluence excavated through the firm clay separating the slough from the main channel of the Sacramento River. This new confluence would divert the American River a mile north of Sutter Lake and also wash away the sandbar that threatened to silt up the embarcadero.[59] Work began in September, as woodcutters set about clearing the slough north of the S-shaped bend near the confluence while others hacked away at the clay embankment. In early November, a side stream of the American River spilled into the new channel and then flowed through the cut; by the middle of the month, the entire river occupied its new channel and confluence.[60]

Upstream, however, the project suffered a major setback in early November when the levee commissioners ran out of project funds. Work on the American River Cut-Off above Twenty-Eighth Street stalled for six years. Meanwhile, unexpected maintenance issues on the confluence emerged. In April 1864, a surge sent the American River spilling into its old channel, forcing workers to dredge the new channel deeper. Around this time engineers also discovered that the river flowed through its new confluence with too much force, causing the American River's current to ricochet off the Sacramento River's west banks and scour the Front Street levee. In the fall of 1868, workers solved this problem by cutting a new, more angular confluence. They then turned their attention back upstream to the American River Cut-Off. The American River now took a dramatically straighter and safer course. Though the cut-off required alterations, by December 1868 residents could take solace knowing that the American River no longer placed such enormous pressure on the levees north of town.[61]

The High Grade

Dramatic as it was to alter the course of the American River during the 1860s, this work was but a backdrop to the "high grade," a Sacramento street-raising effort twice as ambitious as the plan lobbied for by Thomas Youngs in 1853. Ironically, city officials had passed a grade ordinance mere weeks before the December 1861 flood; the ordinance called for raising I Street to a point eighteen inches above the high-water mark of 1853. There was no way, however, that workers could have brought streets up to grade before the December flood. Even if they had, the high water of 1861–62 would have twice inundated the city. The new high grade would leave nothing to chance: Front and I Streets would be raised four feet above the 1861–62 high-water mark, with streets east and south descending six inches with every block. The crowns of streets would rise to an elevation sixteen inches above the grade and round down to gutters fronting the sidewalks, facilitating more orderly drainage.[62] The high grade, one of the more ambitious urban infrastructural projects of nineteenth-century California, would lift Sacramento out of the flood basin so as to reach the height of Sutterville, the abandoned townsite on high ground three miles upstream.

Work on the high grade began in January 1864 and proceeded, block by block, through the remainder of the decade. Because the high grade reached ten to twelve feet above the city's natural topography, property owners built brick bulkheads, or walls, along the sides of streets to contain fill piled up in the roadways. Workers excavated much of the fill from the rerouted American River channels north of town. As grading proceeded, the newly chartered Sacramento Board of Trustees levied assessments against property owners to pay for the work, while property owners themselves arranged for the raising of their own buildings. Raising buildings typically involved a team of workers turning jackscrews in unison

FIGURE 3.3. Workers use jack screws to lift the Sacramento County courthouse up to the higher grade in 1870; I Street in the foreground has not yet been filled. Courtesy of the California History Room, California State Library, Sacramento.

to lift a building up while masons scurried underneath to lay new foundations. Other property owners added second or third stories to their buildings, converting first floors into basements. With streets and buildings raised to grade, all that remained were sidewalks in between. Most property owners bridged these fourteen-foot gaps with two-inch thick planks, leaving hollow spaces below. Though city leaders had expected all city streets to adhere to the high grade, grading never reached east of Eleventh or south of L Street, as M Street property owners refused to authorize the work.[63]

Because grading proceeded one block at a time, Sacramento's streets remained maddeningly uneven during the 1860s. Some pedestrians sustained serious injuries falling from graded sidewalks onto ungraded streets, lots, and blocks. Everyone shared the burden of trudging up and down slopes and steps. "The grade has proved of high sanitary importance to Sacramento," joked Mark Twain in the *San Francisco Bulletin*. "What the people there needed was a chance for up-hill and down-hill exercise, and now they have got it."[64] What Sacramento really needed, of course, was a sense of security in the wake of the 1861–62 floods, and this too they obtained. "The city looks better than it has at any time since the flood," reported the *Daily Alta California* in September 1866. "A good deal of work has been done in the way of grading and repairing the streets, putting up new buildings, etc. . . . To raise the buildings and fill the streets require immense outlay, compared with the value of the real estate, yet, when completed, will give a feeling of security and add greatly to the appearance of the city."[65]

In his 1875 memoirs, William Tecumseh Sherman offered a first-hand account of Sacramento's tumultuous first two decades: "For several years," he wrote, "the site was annually flooded; but the people have persevered in building the levees, and afterwards in raising all the streets, so that Sacramento is now a fine city, the capital of the State, and stands where, in 1848, was nothing but a dense mass of bushes, vines, and submerged land."[66] It was within this untenable landscape, in a townsite planned for speculation, that the city's first generation built the foundations of a stable and permanent city.

CHAPTER 4   # Railroads and the Urban Environment
SACRAMENTO'S STORY

Richard J. Orsi

Sacramento's railroad era dawned on January 8, 1863, on Front and K Streets at the downtown edge of the Sacramento River. City leaders, railway officials, and practically all the citizenry had gathered to celebrate the "groundbreaking" on the Central Pacific Railroad (CPRR), the Pacific link of the nation's first transcontinental line. Unknown to the joyous throng, the natural setting and the event's program foretold railroads' central environmental influence on the struggling city. After days of winter rains, the rising river already lapped over shipping docks and a low levee, converting the bank and adjacent Front Street into hub-deep quagmires and threatening to flow eastward onto low-lying downtown streets, just as flooding had nearly destroyed the city the year before and several other times over its first decade. But this morning, clouds and spirits had lifted a bit, hazy sunbeams broke through, and workers had packed hay bales into the mud to lay a slippery footing for those attending the festivities. Nevertheless, fastidious women escaped "the sea of mud and bobbing bales" to surrounding second-floor verandas. After appropriate prayers, band serenades, and speechifying by dignitaries about prosperous days ahead for city and nation, festooned horses hauled in two flag-draped wagons of dirt. Central Pacific president and state governor Leland Stanford "seized the shovel and amid the lusty cheering of the crowd deposited the first earth" on the railroad's elevated embankment, the eventual platform for ties and steel rails and a high bulwark against future floods. By some accounts, Stanford became so caught up in the excitement that he emptied the entire wagon onto the embankment. Commemorated as the CPRR's official groundbreaking, it was actually more of a "ground-making."[1] And in the next century and a half, Sacramento would come to depend on the railroad's new ground.

Sacramento provides an excellent case study for railroads' environmental influences on cities. Although not technically a "railroad town" in the sense of having been founded by and for a railroad, Sacramento quickly became a railroad town in a deeper sense, as one of the West's preeminent railroad centers, its urban existence and environment transformed thereby. After 1863, railroads, particularly the Central Pacific (renamed Southern Pacific [SP] in 1884), revived the city's languishing economy, multiplied its population and land area, dominated its workforce, and obliterated its fading gold rush character, doing so in large part by reshaping the city's relationship with nature.[2] What's more, railroads' pivotal influence lasted into the early twentieth century and echoes into the present, though railroads have long since ceased to dominate transportation.

The Central/Southern Pacific completed its first transcontinental connection from Sacramento to the east in May 1869, and, in the fall of that year, it completed a line west to Oakland, on San Francisco Bay. Its network kept expanding for decades thereafter, through much of the far West and Southwest, with Sacramento remaining the most important inland, northern California hub. That company, however, was not the city's only, or even its first, steam railroad. In 1856, the Sacramento Valley Railroad (SVRR) had completed a twenty-three-mile track from the city to Folsom, a Sierra foothill gateway to California and Nevada gold and silver mines. That seminal railroad, the first in the state, provided Sacramentans with glimpses of the economic benefits that could come from railroad service, in this case access to the mining trade. However, the underfunded, poorly built, mismanaged company, soon controlled by San Francisco financiers, never fulfilled its potential. Prone to self-destructive business and political strategies, it fought a decade-long losing battle against city and state authorities, finally removing its terminus from Sacramento. Defeated in Congress by the CPRR for the all-important transcontinental charter and subsidy, the bankrupt SVRR sold out to the Central in 1865, leaving little in its wake.[3] Another would-be rival, the California Pacific, opened a line from San Francisco Bay to the Sacramento River bank opposite the city in 1868. Overcoming the Central Pacific's opposition, the Cal-Pacific bridged the river and crossed CPRR tracks into Sacramento in 1869, only to have the CPRR also take it over in 1871.[4] Finally, the Western Pacific Railroad (WP), founded in 1903 to rival the Southern Pacific's near traffic monopoly in northern California, started building east from San Francisco Bay, completing its line through Sacramento to Salt Lake City and transcontinental connections in 1909. The WP, though financially shaky, did build substantial facilities in Sacramento, including repair shops southeast of downtown. Like other railroads, however, its influence was dwarfed by the SP, and, especially because it arrived late on the scene, the WP remained a minor player in the city's environmental transformation.[5]

Other railways—horse-drawn and electric streetcars, as well as electric interurbans, particularly the Sacramento Northern Railway—played relatively small environmental roles in the city, primarily echoing the larger steam railroads' influences. A distinctive legacy of streetcars and interurbans, particularly after 1890, was the outlying land they opened to Sacramento's urban expansion into the countryside, with predictable, contradictory environmental results: urbanites' access to more space for homes, businesses, recreation, and, in many ways, a more sanitary environment, while on the other hand increased sprawl and destruction of farmland and natural lands, wetlands, and their species.[6] This chapter, however, focuses on steam railroads, and particularly the Central/Southern Pacific, which dominated into the late twentieth century.

Railroads and the Urban Environment

Historians of cities, particularly earlier writers, have tended to minimize, or overlook entirely, railroads' shaping influences on the fundamental structures of city environments and the relationships between city dwellers and nature.[7] Distinguished urban history scholars Joel Tarr and Gabriel Dupuy, for example, have concluded that, with few exceptions, railroads and other technological infrastructures "were unevenly inserted into existing urban environments without drastically altering the uses of space."[8] To the extent that steam railways have entered into the analysis at all, most attention has been confined to general discussion of railroads' expansion of urban markets and economic and population growth. Such studies have tended to dwell on railroads' negative effects: pollution, congestion, sprawl, decline of open space, and destruction of natural landscapes, species, and ecological patterns. Primarily, historians have stressed the effects of streetcar expansion of internal rail systems.[9] Some important studies, however, have examined the environmental impact of urban steam railroads in industrializing outlying and distant natural and rural landscapes.[10]

Recently, as environmental historians have advanced beyond their initial focus on "wilderness," some have turned their attention to cities. Closer examination of railroads' influences within broader, more complex definitions of "environment" has disclosed that, far from being peripheral to cities' internal environments, rail technology fundamentally reorganized urban space, people's access to it, and the citizenry's relationships to resources and nature generally. Particularly suggestive are such innovative studies as those of Blake Gumprecht (of Los Angeles), Ari Kelman (of New Orleans), Matthew Klingle (of Seattle), and David Young (of Chicago). Central to the environmental history of cities generally, railroads' effects, these studies show, proved especially intense and long lasting in so-called "port cities" along rivers, lakes, and oceans, where nineteenth-century urban railroads controlled and revolutionized water and waterscapes, with legacies that reverberate today. Rail embankments inhibited drainage and exacerbated flooding, and the companies polluted flowing and ground waters, filled in wetlands, diverted or obliterated streams, occupied, closed off, industrialized, and degraded shorelines, and soured citizens' very perceptions of their waterways.[11]

The following study of railroads' influences in Sacramento, another riverside city, validates and expands on the findings of these recent authors. Railroads, particularly the Central/Southern Pacific, were indeed central to the city's and its residents' changing relationships to nature, and the legacy lasts into the present and future. In the process of building, operating, and encouraging multitudes of large-scale industrial and commercial ventures in Sacramento, railroads created and aggravated problems of pollution, congestion, landscape degradation, and space allocation. Those problems had particularly strong impacts on the city's relationships to its rivers. Sacramento's experience, on the other hand, also demonstrates that railroads' influences on human-nature relationships in cities were more complex and ambiguous than outlined in earlier studies.[12] Certainly, railroads disordered environmental patterns, but, when viewed in a larger and longer-term context, the technology was also constructive, in the sense of having created or encouraged more balanced, sustainable human-nature relationships. In fact, Sacramento came to depend for its very survival, including as the state's capital, on the new equilibrium with nature that railroads forged.

Sacramento, Rivers, and Railroads

Local civic and corporate geopolitics governed the inception and character of Sacramento railroads and their influences on the city and its transformation of nature. Clouding Sacramento's future in the mid-nineteenth century was the complex flood problem. Only a few feet above sea and river levels and at the outlet of immense high-mountain watersheds, the city lay just south of the confluence of the two mightiest Sacramento Valley rivers—the Sacramento and the American. The site sloped to an even greater degree east and south from the rivers. A natural levee on the eastern bank of the Sacramento provided minor protection from that river's regular winter and spring floods, but not so with the American. Two sharp, S-shaped bends just east of its joining with the Sacramento backed up the American's floods east and south into Sutter Lake, a muddy Sacramento River slough in modern times but prehistorically the American River's older channel into the Sacramento.[13] Easily overtopping shallow Sutter Lake just north of downtown, deep floodwaters in many years poured over the city's site. Local natives and Mexican-era settlers like John Sutter were well aware of the inevitable floods and had established themselves on higher, inland ground, but gold rush economic pressures dictated that the unfortunate city be founded in 1849 on the Sacramento River's east bank, with direct shipping access to San Francisco Bay. Floods followed immediately in 1850 and several more winters over the next decade.[14]

The city's leaders groped for solutions against long odds: imperfect information, financial constraints, opposition from many interests (particularly to paying taxes and inhibiting property use), and the transience of leaders and residents. Low, hastily constructed levees broke down or worsened flooding elsewhere. In the 1850s, more substantial, longer-term plans emerged: deep-dredging the Sacramento River to accommodate larger floods, straightening the American River's bends and relocating the river's confluence with the Sacramento farther north, ac-

FIGURE 4.1. *1870 Birds-eye View of Early Central Pacific Railroad's Facilities and Old Sacramento.*
Looking northeastward, this 1870 bird's-eye view can serve as a map of the Central Pacific
Railroad's early facilities in Sacramento. Visible are the Sacramento River, flowing from
north to south, as well as multiple tracks, a depot, freight sheds, and wharves resting on
mostly filled land and cribbed trestles over the former river shallows from Front Street west
to the new deep river channel. North of the downtown lies mostly unfilled Sutter Lake, the
railroad's growing shops on filled lakebed, and, farther north, the now-dry bypassed old
bed of the American River. The California Pacific's combined rail and wagon bridge over the
Sacramento from the west is at lower left. Courtesy of the California State Railroad Museum
and Center for Sacramento History.

quiring title from the state to Sutter Lake and filling it, raising levees much higher
and wider along the Sacramento's east bank and especially between the American
River (and Sutter Lake) and the downtown to the south, and finally, and perhaps
most ambitiously, raising the city itself above flood levels. Eventually, a low northern levee along I Street was built in the vain hope of separating Sutter Lake from
the downtown. An ill-conceived southern levee built along R Street from the east
to the Sacramento River did little more than worsen flood damage by retaining
water longer in the downtown. The state did transfer title to Sutter Lake in early
1857 on the condition that the city fill it within six months, which Sacramento was
unable to do.[15] Throughout the 1850s, opposition and scant resources blocked more
substantial improvements, and the floods recurred, indeed worsened, as debris
from upriver hydraulic mines filled in riverbeds and reduced their flow capacities.[16]

Enter the railroads. In the mid-1850s, when serious rail projects first began to be mounted, city leaders immediately sought to draft railroads—their capital resources, workforces, engineering expertise, and corporate self-interests—into the war against the water. The nascent Sacramento Valley Railroad's petition to the city in early January 1855 for a charter and right-of-way directly from the east to the Sacramento River port proved controversial from the beginning. Some council members supported quick acquiescence to the railroad's plans to run their embankment to the river along the top of the R Street levee, the southern boundary of the city. Other officials, however, including Mayor R. P. Johnson, who vetoed an early charter draft, tried to get the company to veer north and enter the city along the northern, I Street levee, between downtown and Sutter Lake overflows, and then turn south along the levee between the Sacramento River and the downtown, thereby raising both levees with rail embankments. The dangerous northern levee, the mayor argued, would "need to be strengthened in the near future," and running the railroad's embankment on top of it would "answer the double purpose for a Railroad track and offer the city perfect and permanent protection," a "great service to the city [yet] would add little (if anything) to the expense of the company."[17] Unwilling to bear the extra costs of lengthening their line and especially of bridging the American River, company leaders refused to change their plan. Eager for a railroad under any conditions, especially as a more reliable, flood-proof conveyance, the city council in February agreed to a charter granting the company's original request for an approach to the river atop the R Street levee. The council did require the company to terminate several blocks from the riverport and to install and maintain wide bridges over drainage channels to allow south-flowing floodwaters to escape the city.[18]

As it turned out, the anticipated flood protection of the SVRR's strengthened R Street levee proved worse than useless. Violating many provisions of its charter, the company built flimsy, poorly maintained trestles that easily clogged and were too narrow to allow floods to evacuate south. In the record-setting deluge from December 1861 through the early spring of 1862, with four major floods powered by more than forty inches of rain, the SVRR's embankment blocked drainage, repeatedly backing up and deepening water over the entire downtown, up to the roofs of some single-story structures, causing the worst of the flood's damage.[19] Most ominously, the inundation carved deep, potentially permanent channels from the American, extending south through Sutter Lake and from farther east over downtown and creating new pathways to yearly crises.[20]

As early as the flood's first peak in December 1861, desperate city leaders pleaded for the company to breach its embankment and relocate the rail line to the northern levee. Having been taken over by San Francisco investors, the company refused.[21] "We have built our own road, we paid for it, work it to suit ourselves," announced company official Lester Robinson.[22] The SVRR's intransigence in the face of looming disaster converted the company into a civic pariah. The board of supervisors revoked the railroad's charter, right-of-way, and right to run trains in the city. When the company refused to cease operations, the city sued it for charter violations and, in early 1862, sent the sheriff with a gang of convict laborers to tear up the railroad's tracks and breach the embankment to release floodwaters. The force of escaping water destroyed twenty-five homes. In March, the supervisors also formed a committee to plan and raise funds for "building a levee and improving the City front" more permanently.[23] The SVRR's response was to abandon the city and, in October 1862, move its terminus downriver a few miles to Freeport, where it could also reach the river itself and escape Sacramento's port fees.[24]

The Central Pacific Railroad

Incorporated by longtime Sacramentans as a speculative enterprise in June 1861, the Central Pacific Railroad took actual form during a propitious time, while Sacramento was still drying out from the great flood and the battle between the city and the SVRR was climaxing. Other than its founders' small investments, the Central Pacific had no assets until the summer of 1862, when its lobbyists in Washington outmaneuvered rivals to win the charter and subsidy from Congress to build the western segment of the first transcontinental line from Sacramento eastward. The CPRR's second strategic victory, securing a right-of-way, terminus, and riverport in Sacramento, proved critical for both company and city. Five city business and civic leaders—Leland Stanford (also governor from 1862 to 1863), Collis P. Huntington, Mark Hopkins, Charles Crocker, and Charles's brother, attorney and former judge Edwin Crocker—emerged quickly as the Central Pacific's most powerful leaders, or "Associates." Their stature, connections, and previous activities eased negotiations with the city. Not only had the men invested in previous flood control and other infrastructure improvements, they had also promoted raising the city's grade.[25] They understood the city's problems and how the railroad, in its own interest, could help create solutions. Their new venture thus became the instrument of both personal fortune-building and civic progress.

The Central Pacific preempted potential opposition by offering to build a right-of-way and port facility that would become an essential northern and western bulwark protecting the city from future floods. At an amicable, one-day meeting in early October 1862, while the SVRR was in the midst of pulling up stakes from the city, Hopkins, Charles Crocker, company engineer Theodore Judah, and a board of supervisors committee reached an agreement for the new railroad to fulfill the city's long-range plan to shore up its flood defenses.[26] Details were worked out by give-and-take during a series of board meetings over the next two months. Finally passed on December 1, 1862, the CPRR's charter and right-of-way avoided earlier mistakes made with the SVRR and satisfied many needs of the city, thereby also gaining the new railroad initial public support and a large, ideal urban center for its operations. The railroad agreed to enter from the east to the Sacramento River along a new northern levee, which the company would build across Sutter Lake, then south along the river levee on Front Street to K Street (later extended south to M Street). The company also gained the right to fill land and marshes to reach deep water, and it assumed the responsibility of raising, widening, and maintaining both levees. For its part, the city also ceded its rights to Sutter Lake and the land west from Front Street to the river, with the requirements that the company fill and raise the lakebed to the level of its elevated embankment to house its planned shops and depot. To the south, the company agreed to build its wharves, warehouses, and other buildings and facilities on the strengthened river levee directly west of downtown. The railroad was required to build and maintain grade crossings over its tracks for the passage of wagons on streets and to allow free access for all to the waterfront.[27] To avert possible litigation, in early 1863 CPRR president Leland Stanford used his power as governor to press the legislature to ratify the city's agreement with the company and the state's original grant to the city of Sutter Lake, which had expired.[28]

The board of supervisors did not adopt the agreement without controversy, however, especially because of concern some provisions would later create new environmental problems. The supervisors and the railroad agreed to charter revisions, tightening the railroad's requirements to raise streets at grade crossings to allow traffic to pass and strengthening the city's legal power to force the company to abide by charter requirements or forfeit its rights and grants. More importantly, many, including the mayor, who twice vetoed drafts of the charter, objected that the waterfront grant would hand the Central Pacific too much prime downtown land and virtual monopoly over river access, which was critical to the well-being of the city and its business. A majority of supervisors, however, with vivid memories of the previous year's flood, was willing to settle for the city's remarkable victories, and, on December 1, 1862, they easily overrode the mayor's veto, barely a month before the CPRR's groundbreaking.[29] Although coming at a high price, Sacramento's bold move had secured the transcontinental terminus and, at the same time, a more substantial riverport and protection from both its angry rivers.

The Central Pacific Railroad and Sacramento's Second Nature

Before, during, and after its critical fall 1862 negotiations with the Central Pacific, Sacramento simultaneously advanced other plans for creating a "second nature"—a higher topographical platform assuring the city a more secure future.[30] The catalyst was the 1861–62 inundation, which had finally exposed the city's dire situation and silenced opponents of comprehensive flood control. In the spring of 1862, the city got the state legislature to authorize a Sacramento City Board of Levee Commissioners to straighten the American River's bends, move its confluence with the Sacramento north, and fill the bypassed riverbed. Engineering plans were completed September 11 and work commenced a week later. In November, American River water started running down the straightened channel directly out its new mouth, three-fourths of a mile farther north up the Sacramento, and the entire diversion was completed in 1864. As an added benefit, the stronger current of the two combined streams cleared silt and deepened the Sacramento's channel off the downtown, unclogging the port and increasing the river's flood capacity, although ironically heightening danger for Yolo County on the opposite bank.[31] California's fickle climate, which had impelled Sacramento's monumental flood projects, wound up also aiding the earthworks of both city and railroad. The state and region's rainiest winter, 1861–62, was succeeded by three years, 1862–65, of the worst drought, when virtually no rain fell. Many streams ran dry and wetlands receded, reducing inundation and speeding up flood control improvements.

With the American River somewhat tamed and the CPRR's massive embankment starting to rise around the western and northern edges of downtown, Sacramento finally began the long-debated grade elevation essential to its new second nature. In February 1863, after years of indecision, supervisors finally adopted an ordinance to elevate the city. Streets and buildings would be raised to the railroad's new grade, commencing with a twelve-foot rise at the tracks, with the new level descending no more than twelve inches block by block to the east and south to provide drainage. Sacramento's new foundation above the floods was substantially in place ten years later. In 1868, the city granted the Central Pacific title to the abandoned American riverbed north of Sutter Lake, on condition that the company also fill it to the city's new grade.[32]

Not only was the Central Pacific's fulfillment of its contract with the city integral to Sacramento's reengineering of its site, the company also had its own incentives to move aggressively. Facing federal deadlines for starting its line eastward to qualify for congressional subsidies and desperate to build investor confidence in its unproven venture, the CPRR commenced grading its embankment even before January 8, 1863, when Leland Stanford shoveled the ceremonial first wagonload onto the waterfront. The route was to proceed north along Front Street to a point north of J Street, where it would curve northeastward around the city hall and waterworks building, across and then north of Sutter Lake, south of the American River, and onto higher ground east of downtown and an eventual bridge over the American River. As it built, the railroad widened levees, reinforced them with granite blocks, gravel, and log pilings, and raised them and Front Street at least six to twelve feet, so as to stay five feet above the benchmark of the 1861–62 flood. Where no levee existed, as across Sutter Lake, the railroad built one, or if it was safe and necessary, a trestle, as across the outlet that drained Sutter Lake. Between the railroad's new Front Street grade and the Sacramento River, the company raised and leveled the riverbank and the railroad's new operating facilities, as well as docks and structures of the California Steam Navigation Company. The railroad filled and strengthened the elevated riverbank with soil and granite blocks from the Sierra foothills, lining the bank with gravel to reduce erosion. Within a year, twenty wagons were hauling gravel around the clock from the abandoned American riverbed, and CPRR river dredges deepening the Sacramento River were also depositing silt onto the rising shoreline. To level several tracks and numerous

FIGURE 4.2. *Central Pacific Railroad Embankment over Sutter Lake under Construction.* The CPRR's embankment curving northeast from the Sacramento River over Sutter Lake and wetlands to the north, shown here under construction in the mid-1860s, served as the city's northern perimeter levee, raised by the company as much as twenty feet higher than the lake level so the tracks and embankment matched the city's new, higher grade. Also visible in this Lawrence & Houseworth stereoview (no. 1203) are the older stilt-houses and shacks then still found on the lake, unfinished rail sidings, some of the early "islands" the company was filling to house its maintenance buildings, and some of the half-finished structures. Soon to arise on these waters and surrounding quagmire would be the railroad's famous Sacramento Shops. Courtesy of the California State Railroad Museum Library, neg. 19017.

structures, the railroad erected a long, timber-cribbed platform, elevated above bank and water, west to the new deep channel.[33]

By October 1865, the *Sacramento Union* was already boasting that the "city front has undergone a marvelous transformation in the last two years. Instead of the old levee, clouded with dust in Summer and occasionally hub-deep with mud in the season of softening showers, Sacramento will soon have a spacious esplanade, graveled, kept free from dust by sprinkling in the dry season and easily drained in Winter, substantially side-walked, adorned with shade trees, tracked for railway travel and fronted with wharves for accommodation of the river fleet. The transformation . . . has been . . . to a great degree, effected by the Central Pacific Railroad

FIGURE 4.3. *Central Pacific Railroad Cars, Sidings, and Cribbed Platform under Construction, Mid-1860s.* Beginning with its groundbreaking in early 1863, along the Sacramento River west of Front Street and downtown, the CPRR built its initial mainline terminus, depot, wharves, other structures, and several sidings all on filled land and a cribbed platform stretching over the sloping bank and mudflats out to the deep channel. Visible in this photograph are the partially filled bank and materials and methods used in constructing the platform. Courtesy Center for Sacramento History, Eugene Hepting Collection.

Company."[34] As corporate needs and construction innovations dictated over the next half-century, the railroad periodically improved and expanded its riverfront earthworks. Gradually, the company filled the cribbed platforms with rock and soil. In 1881, it replaced the remaining platforms with a solid earth embankment along the Sacramento riverfront, and, after 1910, it installed the tall concrete sea-wall that lines the riverbank today.[35]

Filling Sutter Lake, the surface of which lay twenty feet below the city's new grade, turned out to be an even more monumental, complex, conflict-ridden, and time-consuming project than originally expected. Early during construction of the first right-of-way's embankment curving over the lake, in 1866, crews started filling "islands" along the mainline to eventually hold the large buildings the company would need. Thirty feet under the surface, the lake bottom was soggy, so footings had to be laid to support the giant masonry structures and heavy machinery. These footings consisted of multiple layers of cobblestones, sand, riprap, and granite blocks, supported by tens of thousands of feet of sixty-foot creosoted cedar pilings driven through the muddy bottom to bedrock. The first structures, including a huge roundhouse, had begun taking shape by 1867. The ongoing work fused the islands together on the northern part of the lake, and, by 1869, the railroad had reclaimed about twenty acres and maintenance and manufacturing work was already centered there. Over the years, more powerful technologies enlarged the new land mass, which came to house the railroad's famed Sacramento Shops, one of the West's largest industrial complexes. Wagons hauling fill around the clock were joined by steam shovels and company-designed steam dredges anchored in the Sacramento River. Movable metal pipelines ultimately dumped many millions of cubic yards of river bottom debris to level the new tract immediately north of downtown. By century's end, the railroad shops encompassed more than eighty acres of former lake and wetlands north to the new bed of the American River. Often occasioned by arguments with the city over the company's slow progress, spurts of activity occurred from 1879 into the late 1880s and from 1904 to 1907, with the project completed in time to open the present railroad depot in 1926 on the last piece of reclaimed land.[36]

Railroads and Environmental Disturbance

Over the months and years following 1863, the CPRR's new ground, including the new shoreline and the Sacramento Shops, provided a base for its burgeoning rail operations and its powerful influence on the city, as well as Sacramento's growing population, business, and altered relationships with nature. By the end of the 1860s, the railroad's expanding workforce—more than a thousand management, operations, maintenance, and shops employees—was by far the city's largest, and it would remain so until the state government's number of workers increased in the twentieth century. By 1870, the company's wages alone were injecting more than $500,000 per month into the city's economy. Well into the twentieth century, whenever labor strikes shut down the trains, about one-quarter of Sacramento families went without incomes. The railroad's huge infrastructure dominated much of the city, particularly the downtown area, the northern and central Sacramento riverfront, and the city's northern perimeter. From Front Street west to the river, almost all buildings and wharves, and several busy tracks that lined them, belonged to the company, especially after the late 1860s, when the Central Pacific took over the California Steam Navigation Company. Renamed Southern Pacific in the mid-1880s, the railroad continued to expand its presence, adding tracks through other Sacramento neighborhoods, filling more of Sutter Lake and the old American riverbed, and acquiring additional waterfront property.[37] Networks of streetcars, at first horse-drawn, then electric-powered after 1890, radiated across the city and into surrounding open and farmed land, all converging at the Southern Pacific's succession of passenger and freight depots on reclaimed land near the river. By the 1870s, dozens of trains—soon to be hundreds—left the depots daily.

Unsurprisingly, the Central/Southern Pacific's new and rapidly expanding human, spatial, and technological structure made a substantial environmental imprint. Most obvious, rail transportation, by opening up new markets, stimulated new and expanded old industries in Sacramento, bringing with them incalculable development and spin-off disturbances. Moreover, specific ecological strains caused or aggravated by urban railroads, which other historians have documented, also quickly troubled the city. Wherever they went in towns and cities, including in Sacramento, railroads spread congestion, noise, fire, crime, noxious and toxic pollution, and neighborhood blight.[38] For decades in the city, trains did not run on isolated rights-of-way but hurtled directly down or adjacent to streets, with Front Street as the prime example, as well as across backyards and between house and business lots, within a few feet of people and their properties. Dense, black smoke choked city dwellers and coated everything indoors and out with soot, oil, and untold other chemical agents. Rumbling locomotives and screeching steam whistles hounded residents day and night, and vibrations from heavy rolling stock barreling through even broke down the mortar holding masonry together.[39]

One notorious example in Sacramento was the sad fate of the three-story city hall and waterworks building, erected in 1854 at the north end of Front Street. After early 1863, the CPRR's main line eastward and multiple sidings pressed the structure on its western and northern flanks, and the California Pacific rail bridge across the river disgorged its trains from the west immediately adjacent to the city hall. By 1880, frequent trains had so fractured the building's thick brick walls and weakened its leaky, heavy rooftop wooden reservoir that almost all city offices had to move out, the water tank had to be reinforced, and the entire western forty feet of the building had to be torn down. Still the crumbling continued. By century's end, the building served only as a jail. In 1906, the deteriorating reservoir was shut down and the city sold the building and its prime site to the Southern Pacific, removing a last vestige of public presence and solidifying even more the railroad's hold on the waterfront. The company demolished the structure in 1913 to make way for still more freight facilities.[40] By the turn of the century, Sacramento's riverscape had become completely industrialized, a major impetus for the downtown to move east, around the state capitol and associated public buildings after 1900, and for many citizens to abandon the original western blocks, which decayed into the skid row of "Old Sacramento."

Southern Pacific trains opened the city to not only the world's commerce but also its exotic species, including contagious diseases hitching rides on the cars. The worldwide influenza epidemic of 1918–19, for example, spread by rail around the state and nation and first invaded the city in force in October 1918, when the Southern Pacific transferred ill employees and dependents from Dunsmuir, California, to the company's hospital near the Sacramento Shops.[41] The city's railroad yards and environs in general became congested, smoky, polluted, noise-plagued, hobo-infested, dangerous neighborhoods, shunned by all except those on business, legitimate or nefarious.[42]

The trains also exacerbated conflict over urban space. Even before the first railroad, the Sacramento Valley line, had started construction, the *Sacramento Union,* in reporting on mass meetings in which citizens protested the city's granting of track rights down the streets, observed with undisguised irony that "although many are desirous that their property may be benefited by the proposed enterprise, few, if any, are willing that the track should pass their doors."[43] Like the earlier Sacramento Valley Railroad, Southern Pacific embankments and tracks created new safety problems, impeded foot and especially wagon traffic, and isolated some neighborhoods, unleashing periodic complaints from citizens exasperated by railroad-caused neighborhood blight and the company's slow pace of leveling its street crossings. Many, often deadly, collisions between locomotives and draft animals, wagons, and pedestrians, particularly children, now unable to hear approaching trains because of the constant, railroad-produced din, also provoked demands to remove tracks from the street.[44] Frequent altercations between railroad police and citizen intruders on company property, especially shops and yards, brought more denunciations and lawsuits for false arrest.[45] As had happened earlier with the SVRR, shopkeepers and other persons having business along Front Street charged that Southern Pacific's trains and long lines of empty cars idling along the street blocked access to stores and the port and that the railroad's own eateries created unfair competition for travelers' spending. In general, bearing out some early critics' warnings about the city's original land grants to the Central Pacific, citizens soon wearied of the railroad's monopolized access to the waterfront and profits derived from it, causing numerous attempts by the city and state over the next century to recapture control of the riverbank.[46]

Southern Pacific Shops

Southern Pacific Shops was responsible for many of the railroads' negative environmental influences in Sacramento, including some of the most visible, dangerous, and tenacious. The rapid growth of the facility into one of the largest, most technologically and chemically intensive industrial centers in the American West created what would a century later be called a "Superfund" site. Not only was the work, like all railroad employment, incredibly dangerous to life and limb, but the many acres housed numerous smelters, foundries, paint shops, and powerhouses, replete with piles of surplus lumber, sawdust, metal shavings, and decaying equipment, as well as often-leaky tanks and buildings storing fuels, acids, solvents, and myriad toxic and flammable chemicals. The huge complex generated pollution on a scale never before faced by the city, poisoning the soil, air, and water, including the rivers, Sutter Lake, runoff, and groundwater, not only saturating the site itself but also spreading plumes of contaminants underground and into the surrounding

FIGURE 4.4. *Southern Pacific Railroad Sacramento Riverfront Facilities, ca. 1925.* Looking northeast, this aerial photograph captures the Southern Pacific Railroad's major Sacramento facilities near their peak shortly before 1926. Extensive railroad trackage, buildings, and wharves isolate the original Sacramento downtown from the river. Just north of the city, toward the upper-left corner of the photo, is the open, recently filled portion of Sutter Lake prepared to hold the present depot, which would open in early 1926. Farther north is the huge Sacramento Shops facility, with numerous tracks and structures, occupying the rest of filled Sutter Lake and wetlands originally north of that. A new railroad and auto bridge, lower left, carries the SP mainline westward toward Oakland. Courtesy of the California State Railroad Museum Library.

wetlands and downtown and plaguing the city for more than a century, until clean-ups began after the 1980s.[47] Nor did the Southern Pacific's "reclamation" negate all of the lake's natural liabilities. Though the railroad dumped mountains of fill into the water, the dampness remained for decades, repeatedly rotting out building timbers as well as floor planks until they were eventually replaced by concrete pads. Old-time denizens of the marshy area, rats proliferated and ran freely under floors and in the rafters and masonry walls, feasting on the railroad's sewage, garbage, and thousands of leather belts used to drive machines, creating one of the most frequently encountered safety hazards. From their base at the facility, the rat hordes invaded the city.[48]

The railroad's effluent discharged into Sutter Lake, along with chemicals, metal shavings, sawdust, and coal dust, and, even worse, petroleum spilled from huge fuel storage tanks after the railroad converted to oil-burning locomotives in the late 1890s. Sacramentans continued doing what they had always done before the railroad arrived: dump into the lake their sewage, trash, laundry water, and thousands of animal carcasses annually. Especially in summer and fall, Sutter Lake became a shrinking, stinking, open sewer, a diseased, rat- and mosquito-plagued brew ironically made more concentrated and deadly as the Southern Pacific filled it in. Its fumes sickened people on hot days; on several occasions, the lake caught fire.[49] Even the railroad's well-intentioned attempts to mitigate perceived environmental dangers often proved counterproductive. To shade and cool the hot location of the shops and, naïvely believing, like most others, that vapors from imported eucalyptus trees would cleanse the air and kill disease "miasmas" emanating from polluted Sutter Lake, railroad leaders ordered plantings of acres of fast-growing, fire-prone eucalyptus groves interspersed among the buildings. Quickly covering the ground with a thick, oil-absorbing mulch of shredded bark and dry leaves, the trees could explode into immense fireballs at even a chance spark.[50]

Indeed, fire proved to be the most immediate and dramatic environmental product of the Sacramento Shops. Conflagrations erupted frequently, with major ones in 1879, 1898, 1916, and the especially terrifying April 1905 blaze, which threatened both the shops and the city. A red-hot rivet accidentally dropped by electric utility workers atop a transmission pole ignited ground covered with sawdust and saturated with spilled fuel oil, and a strong northwesterly wind drove the flames through eucalyptus groves, buildings, and piled scrap toward Sutter Lake and three tanks holding 120,000 gallons of locomotive fuel. Black smoke enveloped the shops and surrounding neighborhoods as far as Stockton, forty miles south. Quickly, several thousand Southern Pacific employees and city firefighters massed to combat the blaze, but, unorganized and forced to work in choking darkness, they could make no headway. Only a fluke, last-minute change in the weather saved the city. As flames moved south into the lake, about to ignite the oil tanks and the whole body of water, shoreline, and the downtown blocks stretching from the southern bank into the capitol district, the gale suddenly reversed, turning the fire back onto itself and giving the fire crews their first momentum. Control followed, but damage to the shops was extensive. The close call, however, had highlighted the unacceptable danger the shops posed for the city. The railroad immediately relocated all large fuel tanks into unpopulated areas outside Sacramento, cut down all eucalyptus trees within a year, worked with the city to install better fire-fighting equipment and coordinated procedures by both agencies to fight each others' fires together, and mounted its final push over the next several years to fill the lake once and for all.[51]

Railroads as Contradictory Environmental Agents

Though significant, disturbances such as fire, noise, disease, congestion, pollution, heightened conflict over urban space, a decayed original downtown, and an industrialized, monopolized riverscape remote from citizens, even when considered as a whole, did not completely define railroads' complex environmental influences in

Sacramento. The Central Pacific's participation in Sacramento's creation of a second nature in the 1860s, for example, contributed to all those problems and others, particularly injury to riverine and wetlands zones and their species, but it also provided critical flood protection, enhanced public safety and health, and was an essential ingredient in a vulnerable city's forging of a more balanced, reliable, and lasting rapprochement with nature. Sacramento's site was no longer "natural" after railroads arrived, but it had ceased being so decades, if not centuries, earlier, and given the gold rush and the city's founding in that particular place, preservation of a completely pristine order was no longer feasible.[52] Environmental "progress" for the city and the railroad, then, consisted of devising ways to live with natural conditions in the long term, reliably using resources without disorganizing or depleting them. Thus, the city and railroad built a flood control perimeter, relocated the American River, and elevated the city and the railroad tracks, while leaving much about the rivers basically intact. Similarly, railroads' environmental influences in other ways were complex and ambiguous, causing damage even while the railroad also introduced, or paved the way for others to introduce, more balanced relationships between humans and nature.

Potential environmental benefits from urban railroads were evident from the earliest days. One of the first major cargoes the SVRR imported from the Sierra foothills in the mid-1850s was countless tons of cobblestones called "Folsom potatoes," making possible the first major street-paving effort. Hitherto an unhealthy quagmire for much of the winter and spring, Sacramento's network of thoroughfares began to offer citizens greater safety, sanitation, and freedom of movement. Starting in the next decade, the CPRR continued and expanded the trade, adding blocks of building granite.[53] Over time, railroads, including the CP/SP and especially the streetcar lines, did some of the paving themselves, either finding the effort a more convenient, cost-effective way to raise the streets over their tracks, especially at intersections, or after having been required by the city to do it as a condition of their charters.

In general, railroads promoted modernization of the urban infrastructure, again with many positive environmental implications. Here, as elsewhere, railroads increased population and business activity, expanding both tax revenues for civic improvements and demand for more plentiful and cheaper utilities. Modern, safer, less polluting energy was one example. As by far the city's principal business and using the most sophisticated and modern technology, the Central/Southern Pacific itself, just by its potential buying power, provided a critical market that made utility development feasible.[54] The railroad's Sacramento Shops had from the beginning stressed energy efficiency, relying on economies of scale and the inventiveness of its skilled engineers and mechanics. To replace its many original small boilers that generated steam to drive machines for each building, the shops installed twenty-five larger boilers, all connected to the same piping network extending to most of its facilities; higher, more consistent steam pressures resulted, for much less fuel and cost.[55] For better and safer lighting, the Sacramento Shops began to replace open flames with electricity earlier than other enterprises, experimenting with the new technology as early as the late 1870s and converting a few machines to electric motors. In 1890, mechanics rigged two generators to a large, coal-fired Corliss steam engine to produce steam to operate machinery by day and generate electricity by night. Workers continuously experimented with higher-output generators, more powerful motors, greater conductivity, and new uses for electricity. Many improvements quickly followed, additional generators were installed, and electric motors began replacing even more steam-driven belts and animal power, with horses giving way to electricity to drive the turntable in 1895. Soon, veritable rats' nests of electric wires spread a chaotic aerial net over the shops.[56]

Electricity and Other Utilities

As it had done with modern water systems throughout the West, the railroad also stimulated electrification and development of other utilities in the broader city.[57] Beginning in the late 1870s, the leading advocate of electric lights was the daily *Record-Union,* co-owned by its editor, William H. Mills, and the Pacific Improvement Company, a Central/Southern Pacific Railroad subsidiary. Mills, a leading western conservationist who after 1882 also became chief land executive and a vice president of the railroad, promoted electricity in editorials, news coverage, and civic actions. To celebrate the annual state fair in 1879, the *Record-Union* furnished steam from its press and engine room to the pioneering California Electric Light Company to power its electrical dynamo. Wires strung across rooftops carried the current to the façade of the Mechanics' Store at Fourth and K Streets, where, on September 9, five thousand cheered the city's first electric light display.[58] In the late nineteenth and early twentieth centuries, Southern Pacific mechanics, including the famous William Trapper, invented many devices furthering electrification, not only of the shops but of Sacramento at large. By the mid-nineties, the shops' generators also were powering arc lights in some city neighborhoods, the downtown having been the first to be illuminated.[59] When Sacramento's famous annual Carnival of Lights celebration and nighttime parade debuted in 1895 to promote electrification, the shops contributed the most popular floats—a dozen kinetic exhibits of new uses for electricity, built in a competition by shops' departments to sit atop special motorized flatcars operating on streetcar tracks and illuminated and powered by overhead trolley wires.[60]

After the early 1890s, it was new electric streetcar lines, with multiple links to the Southern Pacific, that led the push for the complete electrification of Sacramento. At first, the high price of imported coal to fire steam-powered generators had limited the use of electricity in the city. The Southern Pacific's ability to import coal cheaply, some of it from its own Sierra and Vancouver Island mines, carried by its own ships and trains, had allowed the railroad to electrify first and most extensively among city businesses. After 1890, several new electric streetcar companies, at first generating their own power, turned to additional markets to lower unit production costs by selling electricity to the public. Electric wires, thus, tended to move into Sacramento neighborhoods first alongside streetcar and steam rails.[61]

Rapid consolidations ensued, resulting in 1892 in the creation of the Sacramento Electric Power and Light Company, a streetcar and electric combination under the leadership of the major investor, Albert Gallatin. An associate of Southern Pacific president Collis P. Huntington, longtime manager of Sacramento's Huntington-Hopkins Hardware firm, and periodically a minor official or board director of various Southern Pacific Company subsidiaries, Gallatin was an entrepreneur with steam railroad connections who began diversifying into streetcar operation. In 1894, streetcar operations were transferred to yet another, larger company, the Central Electric Railway Power and Light Company, again under Gallatin's control. Now with size and capital backing, the new company converted to cheaper hydroelectric power and expanded its operations. In July 1895, preparatory to the first Carnival of Lights, the new streetcar/electric company, in part using equipment invented or remodeled at the SP shops, finished a new hydroelectric powerhouse on the American River near Folsom, twenty miles northeast. The suddenly plentiful supply of cheaper electricity paved the way for a boom in streetcar construction, with the expanding lines all radiating outward from the Southern Pacific passenger depot and shops, in part by design, to tap the commuting market of thousands of Southern Pacific workers residing throughout the city and suburbs. Diversifying into water and gas utilities, the streetcar company was purchased in 1906 by the emerging northern California utility monopoly, Pacific Gas & Electric, which continued to operate the streetcars for several decades. Preferring to buy electricity, as well as water and gas, from outside utilities, the Southern Pacific in the 1890s shifted to purchased power and turned off its shops' steam and electrical generators, the last ones going cold in 1901.[62]

The Southern Pacific was an important stimulus for the improvement of other Sacramento utilities, not only, as in the case of electricity, because its large purchases constituted a concentrated market for better services, which were critical to profitable investments for fledgling utility companies, but also through the railroad's direct involvement. In 1882, for example, when the city refused to approve funding for police department telephones, editor Mills of the railroad's *Record-Union* personally paid for the department to be connected into the Central Telephone Company's system, which delivered dividends when police immediately began to make quicker arrests aided by telephone use.[63] Needing more water of higher quality even than the city's, the shops at first bored many deep wells and developed its own pumping, filtration, and purification devices. Engineers and mechanics, most notably the legendary A. J. Stevens, invented a succession of better pumps and sanitation technologies that the railroad not only put to its own use but also gave to the city to increase the volume and safety of the public water supply. As it had done with electricity, when adequate outside supplies became available, the railroad shut down its own system and started buying water from the city.[64]

Railroads and Modernization

In many other ways, railroads, particularly the dominant Southern Pacific and its shops, fostered modernization in Sacramento, with many changes benefiting the relationship between people and their environment. Over the years, the shops invented countless devices improving safety for moving trains as well as surrounding neighborhoods and their residents: electrical fences along vulnerable tracks to warn of debris or floods; brighter, more focused locomotive headlights that allowed approaching trains to be seen earlier but did not shine into nearby houses; safety valves to help prevent boiler explosions at the shops and aboard locomotives; stronger car couplings, bridge supports, and guard rails for passenger cars and stations; improved crossing gates and train brakes; oil-fueled locomotives to reduce smoke, cinders, and train-caused fires; railroad fire-fighting equipment, and more.[65]

Facilitated by its size, capital, economies of scale, and diverse skills concentrated in its shops, the railroad also pioneered in large-scale recycling and resource conservation in Sacramento. By the mid-1870s, the Sacramento Shops operation was, in the words of its principal historian, generating "mountains of scrap," which multiplied geometrically as the railroad began sending regular trains around its far-western empire to bring cast-offs into Sacramento for sorting. Usable materials were reissued; recoverable materials (such as bolts, spikes, rails, and wheels) were repaired, straightened, or retooled; metals were melted and recast for new, often completely different, lives; assorted used parts were reassembled into "new" locomotives, cars, and machines; surplus materials were resold to outsiders; and true junk was discarded. By the early 1900s, the company's recycling systems, led by Sacramento Shops, annually produced more than a million dollars in surplus sold to others, as well as many more millions in reused material. The company was saving incalculable money and resources.[66]

Reflecting William Cronon's conclusions about railroads generally in *Nature's Metropolis,* the Southern Pacific also altered some fundamental relationships between Sacramentans and nature, in this case by mitigating the effects of climate. By the early 1870s, many middle- and upper-class Sacramentans were already regularly seeking relief from sweltering summers by taking the train to the breezy Santa Cruz and Monterey oceanside resorts and the cool Sierra forests of the Truckee–Lake Tahoe valleys. Investing heavily in Truckee River and Donner Pass ice companies as early as the late 1860s, the railroad stored and imported a vast tonnage of winter-produced, low-cost natural ice, breaking the previous monopoly of Alaskan producers and for the first time allowing masses of ordinary Sacramentans and other low-elevation westerners to sip cool drinks and preserve foods in all seasons. By the early twentieth century, the railroad's Pacific Fruit Express subsidiary, with its giant ice plant, the largest in the world, located at nearby Roseville, transformed Sacramento into a major center for growing and shipping perishable produce, from which the city's dwellers also gained the benefit of healthier diets year round.[67]

Although certainly a major polluter, cause of injury, and vector of communicable disease, the railroad also had compensating positive influences on public health in Sacramento beyond the safer, fresher foods. Important was the Central Pacific's employee health-care program, which the company began in the mid-1860s to cope with its many worker injuries, reduce its high turnover of skilled and unskilled labor, and compensate for poor medical services in its generally thinly populated territory. Having appointed or contracted for "railroad surgeons" in many of its towns as soon as construction began, the railroad instituted a low-cost, mandatory payroll deduction, health-insurance system for all employees and, in 1867, opened its first, albeit temporary, employee hospital in Sacramento. Made possible by concentration of its early management and operations in one city, Sacramento, the railroad two years later moved the hospital to a larger, specially built facility, one of the most modern in the West, adjacent to the shops. Sacramento's hospital served as headquarters of the network of more than fifty hospitals the company owned, managed, or contracted with other agencies for its employees, until network management was shifted to San Francisco's railroad hospital, reflecting the company headquarters' earlier move to the Bay City in the 1870s. Sacramento's facility, however, remained active into the mid-twentieth century. In the twentieth century, the Southern Pacific extended the health program to dependents and retirees. The railroad staffed its Sacramento hospital and later its other health-care centers with leading, scientifically trained, research-oriented general practitioners, as well as more trained nurses and specialists, particularly surgeons and orthopedists, than found in other hospitals. Patients needing greater care than the company could provide at remote sites were transferred quickly by rail ambulance to the hospitals. Faced with healing a flood of employee injuries, many resulting in deadly infections and major surgery, sometimes amputations, Sacramento's railroad physicians conducted long-range studies of effective procedures, especially under chief surgeon Thomas Huntington, whom the company transferred to the city in 1882 from his work with employees in Nevada.

By the early 1880s, the railroad's Sacramento physicians, proponents of Louis Pasteur's germ theory, were developing pioneering techniques for reducing infections and amputations, conducting antiseptic surgery, using new types of sterile sutures, and operating on patients for hernia, arthritis in knees and ankles, and appendicitis, in fact performing the first appendectomy in California in 1891. New procedures proving successful were instituted throughout the railroad's health-care system. Thousands of Sacramentans who had a connection with the railroad, as well as many others across the company's western territory, immediately began receiving the best in modern health care, at practically no cost. More significantly for the city, however, the railroad's physicians achieved wider community acceptance of their methods. Overcoming opposition from entrenched traditionalists dominating the medical establishment, Huntington and colleagues publicized their research in papers and lectures, debated at physicians' meetings, assisted others in incorporating new methods, and made use of personal networks and growing prestige in the state's capital, especially after Huntington won election as president of the city medical association. The railroad's Sacramento facility became the prototype for American industrial hospitals and the major force converting the city into a western center of modern medical practice.[68]

Railroad Legacies and Placeholders of Public Space

Railroads' environmental significance in Sacramento peaked in the late nineteenth and early twentieth centuries. As elsewhere after the 1940s, social, economic, and technological change and emergence of new transportation systems diminished railroads' importance, companies' traffic and profits plummeted, new-generation diesel-electric locomotives and modern rail cars required less maintenance, and many tracks were torn up and once-massive property holdings vacated. Sacramento was a prime example. Few other cities had such a large percentage of downtown land held by one private owner and suddenly idled. Wide, multitrack SP rights-of-way flanked Old Sacramento west to the Sacramento River; the right-of-way along the central city's north side was much wider, bulging as it neared the river from the east to accommodate the several-hundred-acre shops tract. After the 1940s, the Southern Pacific deactivated most of this land, with all but a few of the most historic structures torn down by 1999, when the shops finally closed. By the 1990s, the railroad retained operations only on the northern main line, small yards farther east, and in the 1926 passenger depot, now occupied by Amtrak. With riverboat traffic decreased even more than rail, the railroad also stopped using the entire shoreline and demolished its port facilities. The Western Pacific also abandoned its yard and shops southeast of downtown. By the 1960s and 1970s, great tracts of prime, close-in land were opening up, much of it with precious river access.

For many years, anxious to reclaim public ownership and access to the waterfront and river, the city and state moved to acquire the abandoned land, finding a willing seller in the Southern Pacific, and after 1990 the Union Pacific, the rival company that took over both the SP and the WP. Made easier by the fact that only one owner had to be bargained with, land transfers in the early 1970s provided waterfront space to the state for the creation of Old Sacramento State Historic Park, anchored by several blocks of restored gold rush era buildings, small museums, reconstructed original railroad facilities, public plazas and promenades along the river, and especially the California State Railroad Museum. Opening in 1981, the acclaimed railroad museum stamped a railroad-history identity on the preservation district.[69]

To the north and east, the shops' tract took longer to return to some level of public control. Eventually, in the early 2000s, it passed to a complicated "part-

FIGURE 4.5. *Sacramento Shops, 2001.* Using an aerial camera, CalTrans photographers captured the site of the former SPRR Sacramento Shops in March 2001. Westward toward the Sacramento River, with portions of downtown in the foreground, evident to the far left is the last SP depot, currently used by Amtrak. In the middle of the now-vacant shops' site stand the few remaining original buildings, which may ultimately house a new Museum of Railroad Technology, a branch of the current California State Railroad Museum, whose irregular footprint and roofline appear between the freeway interchange and the river, upper left. The riverfront and shops' site, abandoned by the railroad after the 1940s, gave the city and state the opportunity to redevelop the riverfront in Old Sacramento State Historic Park and, perhaps in the future, most of the shops' site into the Railyard, a large, multipurpose, planned, in-fill community. Courtesy of the California State Railroad Museum Library.

nership" of the city, state, and a private developer. With outcomes still uncertain because of turmoil in the economy and the real estate market since the beginning of the twenty-first century, the goal is that the former shops' land would host Sacramento's Railyard, the largest urban in-fill project in the nation. Work had barely begun by 2012, but the completed Railyard is slated to become a mixed-use, high-rise, self-contained neighborhood, not reliant on automobiles, containing professional, commercial, and residential buildings, cultural and recreational facilities, and the city's transportation hub, all near downtown, the capitol, open space, and the rivers. A planned Museum of Railroad Technology, a new branch of the nearby California State Railroad Museum, is to occupy some of the remaining shops' buildings. In April 2010, the city council also approved redevelopment of the Western Pacific Railroad's vacant railyard site in the Curtis Park district into a mixed commercial/residential neighborhood, although the project's future is still clouded by incomplete cleanup of toxic residues and possible disagreements with the current owner, the Union Pacific Railroad, which has other plans for the land.[70] In Sacramento, as in major rail centers like Chicago, Seattle, Portland, San Francisco, and Los Angeles, and even in small towns such as the Southern Pacific's Sierra town of Truckee, one of the principal long-term legacies of railroads has been to serve as inadvertent environmental placeholders, vital reservoirs of new urban space offering city dwellers new opportunities to rebuild parts of their communities and recapture some contact with nature.[71]

Railroads' environmental influences in Sacramento proved destructive in ways historians have hitherto emphasized in researching other cities. In the long run and within broad definitions of "environment" and "ecology," however, railroads, particularly the dominant Central/Southern Pacific, were also constructive, in the sense of having adopted or encouraged others to adopt more balanced, more sustainable relationships with nature. The Central/Southern Pacific, with city approval, devised and built the flood control perimeter essential in shielding the city from the rivers, thus participating directly in the city's creation of a new, higher topography that assured Sacramento's survival, indeed thriving, as an inland Pacific Coast transportation, manufacturing, commercial, and governmental center. Railroads also promoted modernization of environmental practices, from street paving and electrical energy to early industrial recycling, improved public health, and the scientific practice of medicine. Into current times, by withdrawing after the 1940s from their landed empires dominating the riverscape and circling the city's downtown, railroads, especially the Southern Pacific, unintentionally handed Sacramento a second chance not only to regain much-needed development space but also to ensure that this close-in land could now be subject to planning for diverse public uses: renewed river access, shoreline restoration, parks, trails, cultural facilities, historic preservation, education about the city's gold rush and railroading past, and creation of new, more environmentally sensible mixed residential, employment, and transportation cores. Beyond just clarifying railroads' local impact on this city, studying Sacramento demonstrates the importance of reexamining railroads' contradictory environmental effects in other cities, as well as in rural and still-wild regions.[72]

PART II

Valley Reclamation

The Perils of Agriculture in Sacramento's Untamed Hinterland

David Vaught

In the decade after the gold rush, few areas in the Sacramento Valley seemed less hospitable to prospective farmers than Putah Sink. This grizzly-infested, swamp-ridden region of several thousand acres in Yolo County, twelve miles west of the city of Sacramento, had discouraged all previous settlement, from Patwin Indians, to Spanish and Mexican rancheros, to Anglo explorers. As late as 1862, a federal surveyor deemed the land "unfit for cultivation" for its "impenetrable thickets of underbrush."[1]

Yet, between 1855 and 1860, a new state law sparked a small-scale land rush on Putah Sink. More than one hundred settlers purchased "swamp and overflowed land" in tracts of up to 320 acres, determined to reclaim the land for grain and stock farming. They called themselves "swamplanders" to distinguish themselves from, in their minds, less-hardy "drylanders." Ignorant of the region's volatile environment yet seduced by its "natural advantages," confident in their ability to tame nature yet lacking due respect for its power, swamplanders were utterly unaware of the enormity of what lay ahead of them.[2]

The historical *outcome* of the struggles of this first generation of Anglo settlers—not just in Putah Sink but throughout much of the Sacramento Valley—will surprise few readers of this volume. These farmers helped transform the landscape into one of the most productive agricultural regions in the world. They began by supplying miners in the gold country and residents of the booming cities of Sacramento and San Francisco with their grain and beef. As wheat production skyrocketed toward the end of the 1860s, they helped California earn its reputation as the "granary of the world." And as the state's great wheat bonanza began to wane in the late 1880s, many of them (or their sons) participated in the Golden State's extraordinary transformation to the production of specialty crops. Increasingly, the

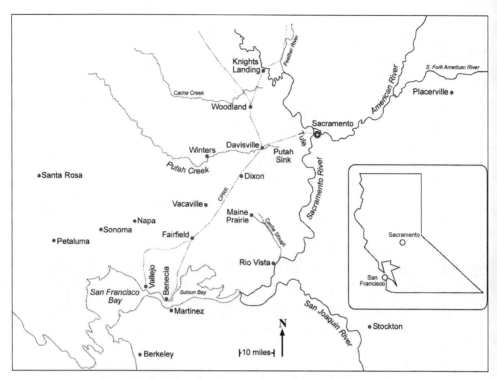

FIGURE 5.1. Map of Putah Sink and vicinity, northern California, in the second half of the nineteenth century. Drawn by Ethel Vaught.

city of Sacramento became not just the state's seat of government but the economic capital of this immensely rich farm belt. By the early twentieth century, enormous quantities of grain and rice, fruit, produce, and meat, dairy products, and nuts rolled into the urban marketplace by water, road, and rail to be stored, processed, refined, and packaged in the city's silos, warehouses, canneries, stockyards, and tanneries. Sacramento, one might argue, became the "nature's metropolis" of the region.[3]

The historical *process* of the growth of agriculture in the Sacramento Valley remains less well known, however. A fresh starting point might best be achieved here through an intensive, if suggestive, case study—which brings us back to the swamplanders of Putah Sink. Their struggle to reclaim the region would be mighty indeed. More than a few—roughly 30 percent of the original purchasers—would battle the forces of nature for decades to come with a resolve and, indeed, a vengeance that can only be described as remarkable—as revealed with special clarity in the trials and tribulations of one of these early settlers in particular, Ransom S. Carey.[4]

The vast majority of Putah Sink swamplanders migrated to California from the Midwest; Carey came from Missouri, in 1852. Swept westward, in the prime of their lives, by the intense excitement of the gold rush, they had come not to farm but to seek riches in the diggings. Those unfortunate to arrive after 1850 found that surface deposits had been depleted by the one hundred thousand forty-niners who had gotten there before them. The late arrivals brought with them a belief that had long been a staple of rural America—that hard work and right values would be rewarded by success. That faith left them with a sense of personal failure in the gold fields. Too ashamed to return home, they turned to what they knew best—farming—and with the same intensity of expectation that had brought them to California in the first place. The pressure to succeed *after* the gold rush both motivated and haunted them for the rest of their lives. Admitting failure again would simply not be an option.[5]

Their experience proved tantalizing from the outset. With much of the land in the Sacramento Valley tied up in court battles over Mexican land grants, swamp-landers found the terms set by the California state legislature in 1855 irresistible. A settler could purchase a maximum of 320 acres for one dollar per acre with a down payment of just 10 percent and the balance, with no interest, due in five years. If half the land was reclaimed by that time, the state would grant title. Carey and other stock raisers learned quickly that burning off the mass of "thickets" in the fall created lush pastureland the following spring, and grain farmers who undertook the arduous task of clearing and draining the land discovered rich, porous soil. The latter reported with glee that yields of fifty, even sixty, bushels per acre of wheat and barley were not uncommon.[6]

Putah Sink settlers also did not have to worry much about the legal turmoil that consumed many other swamplanders. Federal and state surveyors often argued over where to draw the line between swamp and dry land. The federal Swamp Land Act of 1850, which ceded these lands to the state, required federal surveyors to decide, but, after waiting five years, the state legislature authorized its own survey and, in the process, classified a much greater amount of land as subject to the law. Most buyers lived in fear that the swampland they purchased from the state might later be declared public land. But Putah Sink was "really and truly swampy," as one federal official put it—so much so that Carey and his neighbors never gave the status of their land a second thought.[7]

Even the weather seemed to cooperate. By coincidence, the Sacramento Valley was in the midst of an exceptionally mild cycle, with no serious flooding occurring between 1854 and 1861. Settlers in Putah Sink experienced occasional winter overflows but came not to fear them but to depend on them to deposit fresh soil on their land and to provide a cost-free form of irrigation. The overflows also shaped the landscape to their liking. Putah Sink consisted of a maze of sloughs, channels, and the so-called "islands" they formed. The first purchasers snatched the largest of these islands. Not wanting to waste a single acre, they insisted that the county surveyor include only "dry" land in their official plats. The resulting field notes often resembled those of Mexican land grants—"commencing at a stake standing in the timber about twenty five or thirty feet from a large Cottonwood," as the description of Carey's 320-acre tract began. Everything seemed under control. As long as the mild cycle held, it looked for all the world that these farmers had been given a second chance to strike it rich in California.[8]

In fact, they had been lulled into a false sense of security. Putah Sink owed its very existence to annual flooding from both the Sacramento River and Putah Creek. Fed by several large rivers cascading down from the high Sierra, the Sacramento's normal flow was large—about five thousand cubic feet per second—but in flood could swell to an astounding six hundred thousand cubic feet per second. Rarely a winter went by when the river did not pour out of its channel and create a vast inland sea over much of the valley floor. Over the centuries, in the lowlands beyond the natural levee across from the confluence of the American River, the overflow left more than one hundred thousand acres of sloughs, swamps, and marshes of immense bulrushes fifteen to twenty feet high—a region then known as "the Tule" (and today as the Yolo Basin). Putah Creek flowed eastward out of the much drier coastal mountains for about twenty-five miles across its alluvial fan straight toward the Sacramento River. The Tule, however, prevented it from reaching its destination (except through a maze of tiny distributaries) and instead caused the creek to back up into a large sink that was every bit as dense and foreboding as the Tule itself. Often bone dry in the summer, Putah Creek routinely jumped its channel during heavy winter rains—but only rarely, and with little force even then, in the late 1850s. Mischievous and deceptive, both rivers seemed to mock the settlers, revealing to them only a fraction of their collective power.[9]

Then, in the winter of 1861–62, a flood of enormous, almost biblical, proportions hit the Sacramento Valley. It began in early December, when a series of warm, tropical rains melted several feet of snow that had accumulated in the Sierra. Rampaging rivers poured out of their channels, filling much of the valley like a bathtub and in less than three days' time. Cattle died by the tens of thousands, much of Sacramento was buried deep in water and mud, farms and ranches were destroyed, and hundreds of people were swept away to their deaths. Putah Sink was hit especially hard. From east to west, the waters of the Sacramento River spread well beyond the Tule, drowning the region in a torrent twelve miles wide and ten feet deep. From there to near the western rim of the valley, Putah Creek created a lake so deep and so vast that sloops were seen sailing across it. Putah Sink, where the two overflows overlapped, was completely under water. "There is nothing to indicate the locality of the ranches but a windmill," observed one stunned swamplander. When the water eventually receded, swamplanders barely recognized the landscape. The meandering sloughs and channels had abruptly altered their courses, making new islands without regard to the once carefully surveyed and productive farms.[10]

The "flood of the century" spread shock, fear, and devastation but not defeat—at least not in R. S. Carey. While most of his neighbors faced foreclosure and many simply fled the scene, Carey managed to put the fury of the flood behind him.

With the stigma of having failed in the gold rush still tormenting him, and having witnessed, with his own eyes, the great productive powers of Putah Sink, Carey felt that he could and indeed *had* to succeed. Then, in what must have seemed like a cruel hoax, the most severe and prolonged drought in the state's history hit the following year. Hundreds of thousands of cattle perished, including most of Carey's. At that point, Carey's speculative instincts took over. He began buying up surrounding swampland, quarter section by quarter section, for pennies on the dollar. By the time the drought broke in 1865, he had not only tripled the size of his ranch in Putah Sink but purchased another twenty-five hundred acres of tule land—none of which would amount to much unless he could contain the region's raging waters.[11]

Carey's hopes to do just that hinged on the success of an extraordinarily ambitious reclamation project launched by the state legislature in Sacramento in 1861. Even before the great flood of 1861–62, settlers—especially those along the ever-dangerous Sacramento River—had come to realize that swamp and overflowed land would never be reclaimed if left in the hands of each individual farmer, as previous legislation had intended. Even small-scale floods often overwhelmed the levees and ditches that most property owners could afford to build themselves. Seeking a more systematic, centralized approach, the Republican-dominated legislature created the Board of Swampland Commissioners, the first in a long line of independent agencies in California charged with managing the state's natural resources. The board intended to build a series of flood control works aligned not with property ownership but with natural drainage patterns—which in the Sacramento Valley often meant entire basins encompassing more than a hundred thousand acres.[12]

The key to the law was a new legal entity called the swampland district. Upon receiving a petition from one-third of the landowners in any geographic region "susceptible of one mode or system of reclamation," the state board proceeded to establish the district, which was designed to essentially pay for itself. Drawing on the money held in the "swamp land fund" created from the sales of swampland in the district, the board hired engineers and workers to construct a single system of levees, canals, and drainage ditches to protect all the land in common. "In no case," the law stipulated, "shall an account be certified, or a warrant drawn, in payment for the reclamation of a particular district, for a greater sum than has been paid into the Swamp Land Fund for the district." That clause, designed to impose fiscal responsibility, handcuffed the board from the start. The one-dollar-per-acre selling price did not produce nearly enough money, especially when a substantial part of the swamplands remained unsold. Any hopes that landowners would contribute more in any of the twenty-eight districts scattered throughout northern California by the end of 1861 were wiped out by the great winter flood of 1861–62. The following spring, the board secured remedial legislation, in which the county boards of supervisors were authorized to levy reclamation taxes on those districts where one-third of the landowners supported such action. All but one district, however, ran out of money and ceased operations far short of completing their planned works.[13]

Only Swampland District 18, which embraced 164,318 acres west of the Sacramento River in Yolo County (i.e., the Tule), accomplished most of its objectives. Plans for the district included a twenty-five-mile drainage canal running north-south through the middle of the Tule from Knights Landing to Cache Slough, along with a lateral that tapped the sink of Putah Creek, and a continuous levee along the Sacramento River seventy-eight miles in length. "It is believed," wrote the chief engineer of the project, "that if the waters of [Putah Creek] are prevented from accumulating in the Tule that it can be so thoroughly drained as to make the best grass land in the State." Farmers who had previously cleared small portions of their own knew that to be true firsthand. They eagerly submitted to a special reclamation tax that nearly doubled their existing swampland fund to more than twenty-five thousand dollars. By the summer of 1865, the main canal and levee were in place and detailed plans for the Putah Creek lateral were ready to proceed, there being almost seven thousand dollars left in the district's account. The board trumpeted the success of district 18 in its annual reports and in northern California newspapers, hoping that others would follow its example.[14]

Another powerful flood in the winter of 1867–68 exposed these best-laid plans as folly. The Sacramento River, flowing at fifty to one hundred times its normal capacity, breached the levee in dozens of places, the largest of which lay directly across from the confluence with the American River. A rampaging Putah Creek washed away the branch canal still under construction—the very canal designed to carry its floodwaters around the farms of Putah Sink and redeposit them out of harm's way. As for the main canal itself, the thirty-foot-wide, nine-foot-deep ditch lay submerged under a vast inland sea ten to fifteen feet deep. The engineers were dumbfounded. Their bold project, a seemingly foolproof plan to "drain the Tule," proved utterly powerless against the forces of nature. In a rare moment of humility, one engineer finally admitted, "The average rainfall of the country is doubtless greater than formerly believed. . . . By observation, I am forced to the conclusion that the system of reclamation adopted for this district is insufficient."[15]

Historical hindsight tells us that district 18, not to mention the valley-wide flood control system envisioned by the board, was simply too big a task and way beyond what was remotely possible at the time. Indeed, generations would pass before engineers would develop the knowledge, expertise, and technology to tame the Sacramento River and its tributaries. Yet, almost before the water receded, engineers and farmers were back at it with a collective exuberance that was exceeded only by their collective amnesia. Legislators, on the other hand, absolved themselves and the state of the burden of reclamation with two new laws. The first, passed on March 22, 1866, abolished the Board of Swampland Commissioners and turned their job over to the county governments, while the second, two years later, placed the responsibility for swampland management squarely back on the shoulders of the swamplanders themselves.[16]

In Putah Sink, R. S. Carey emerged as the key figure during these developments. Determined to increase his landholdings and protect them from future inundation, he regularly attended district 18 meetings, learning the basics of levee building and dredging and contributing his own knowledge of Putah Sink's complicated geography. Engineers relied heavily on his input when planning the branch canal. When the Yolo County Board of Supervisors assumed control of district 18 in accordance with the March 1866 state law, Carey dominated its meetings even more. The new law placed the county surveyor in charge of supervising all reclamation projects, but Carey was not about to leave the fate of his ranch in the hands of someone who, in his mind, had nothing more serious to do than survey straight lines. By the fall of 1866, Carey had not only greatly increased his ranch's acreage and restocked it with more than twelve hundred cattle; he had also seized control of the construction of the Putah Sink lateral.[17]

When heavy rains flooded his ranch the following winter and washed away the canal, Carey was beside himself. Unable and unwilling to comprehend the scale and scope of the disaster, he became all the more convinced that more canals and more levees, properly built and situated, would remedy the situation. Others in the Sacramento Valley shared his consuming obsession, most notably Will S. Green of Colusa County, himself a gold rush migrant (from Kentucky) and self-taught engineer. After consulting with Carey and other likeminded swamplanders, Green, who had just been elected to the state assembly, sponsored a bill that changed the face of the state's swampland system.[18]

Its underlying premise maintained that only those with the most at stake—the swamplanders themselves—could do the job right. Green had no intention of reverting to the practices of the 1850s, when individuals reclaimed their land 320 acres at a time. Instead, the 1868 law (the "Green Act") allowed individuals to buy as much swampland as they could afford at one dollar an acre, provided that title to the property would be withheld until it was adjudged to be reclaimed. The act retained the idea of the "district," in that any group of landholders could create one of their own and tax themselves when "half or more" gave their approval. But no public authority—commission, board of supervisors, or otherwise—could intervene in the affairs of the district for any reason. If, moreover, the owners of a given district could prove that the land had been cultivated for three years, they would receive a full refund on their purchase. Incentive had always been part of swampland policy, but now the carrot at the end of the stick was larger and more tantalizing than ever. Green's fellow legislators, delighted to be relieved of the responsibility for reclamation, approved the bill unanimously.[19]

When the Green Act went into effect late in May 1868, swamplanders and prospective swamplanders lined up outside the Yolo County courthouse in Woodland to file their applications. At the front of the line, metaphorically and perhaps even literally, stood R. S. Carey. He had persisted through rough times in the gold fields, two major floods, a devastating drought, and almost two decades of economic uncertainty and now had the opportunity to purchase as much land as he wanted for one dollar an acre. In just a few months' time, he more than doubled his already large holdings to more than ten thousand acres. Virtually every acre of swampland in Putah Sink, in fact, much of it deemed fit only for grizzly bears less than two decades earlier, passed into private hands. Carey had already made known his plan for reclaiming the region and had full confidence in his expertise. His dream of striking it rich, as vivid as ever, could not be realized otherwise.[20]

The impetus behind this revived dream was the beginning of one of the most extraordinary episodes in American agricultural history—California's wheat bonanza. By coincidence, after the drought broke in 1865, California produced three straight bumper crops at the same time that Great Britain and other European nations suffered dangerously deficient harvests. Enterprising grain merchants in dozens of new railroad towns (including Davisville, just upstream from Carey's ranch), in San Francisco, and in Liverpool, England, exploited the opportunity to the fullest, as did the farmers themselves. The wheat that they grew on their farms moved in greater volume over greater distances than any product ever before in human history. Carey knew that if he could protect even a small portion of his holdings and plant them with wheat, he stood to be a wealthy man.[21]

With that motivation, and with the 1867–68 flood still fresh in their minds, farmers in Swampland District 18 doubled their efforts to reclaim Putah Sink. Employing gangs of Chinese laborers, they not only rebuilt the branch canal that had washed away but dug it deeper and wider and actually made it *the* creek by raising a levee across the mouth of the old channel to redirect the flow. That, along with ten miles of levees along the tule line on the east side of the sink, created three thousand acres of new farmland, half of which belonged to Carey and the rest to a dozen other swamplanders. Carey considered this engineering triumph to be his alone, and not without good reason. When the district's swampland fund dried up toward the end of 1869, he contributed several thousand dollars of his own money to finish the job. The first crop of wheat in 1870 seemed to make it all worthwhile. Everyone knew that the reclaimed swampland would be fertile, but reports of seventy bushels per acre exceeded all expectations.[22]

This time, just one storm was all it took to burst their bubble. Twelve inches fell in four days in December 1871—almost half the total rainfall for the season. Though nothing compared to the rains prompting the floods of the 1860s, the deluge was enough for Putah Creek to rise eighteen feet and "fill the Sink," as one newspaper put it. Gathering force in the coastal mountains to the west and roaring across the valley, a raging torrent rushed toward the constructed barrier standing in its way across the "old" channel. Rather than veering northeastwardly into the branch canal, the creek, on the morning of December 17, slammed into the levee, burst through, and "spread out" over the freshly plowed land, "playing havoc" with

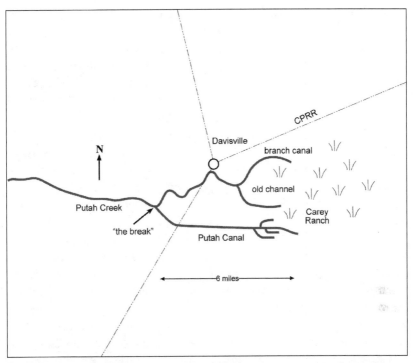

FIGURE 5.2. Putah Creek reclamation, 1870s. Based primarily on maps and information in *S. H. Cowell v. Lydia T. Armstrong* (1930), California State Supreme Court, no. 4341 (SAC), California State Archives, Sacramento; and Yolo County, "Board of Supervisors, Swampland District No. 18, Supervisors' Record, 1866–1873," Yolo County Archives, Woodland, California. Drawn by Ethel Vaught.

the farms that stood in its way. Putah Sink, the newspaper report continued, "is, to use an expressive phrase, afloat." Just what expressive phrases Carey must have uttered that day one can only imagine. Judging from his subsequent actions, his vendetta reached Ahab-like proportions, with Putah Creek becoming his great white whale.[23]

Indeed, Carey did not give up, even for a moment. Two days after Putah Creek drowned his wheat fields, he resumed his offensive with a plan that dwarfed all previous ones in scope and ambition. Another break in a levee farther upstream inspired him. Putah Creek flowed across the valley floor without any sharp meanders until it reached a point about six miles west of Carey's ranch, where it veered roughly forty-five degrees to the southeast for half a mile before making a full right-angled turn northward. In flood, the creek often spilled over at both bends, prompting landowners to construct two huge levees. On the fateful morning of December 17, the creek exploded through the second levee with a roar that woke farmers out of their sleep two miles away. The full force of the creek then maintained its southeasterly course for half a mile before running up against the railroad, where it spread along the banks of the tracks for miles in both directions. Eventually, a crevasse opened up, through which a narrow stream of water began flowing straight eastward down an old farm road right along the section lines. It ran all the way to the Tule, six miles from "the break," as locals called the breach in the levee for years to come. Carey surveyed the situation intently. Putah Creek, he believed, had just provided him a blueprint for a much more effective flood control system.[24]

When Carey soon thereafter proposed excavating a canal from the break to the Tule, many of his neighbors supported the idea enthusiastically. Other Putah Sink farmers, whose land was two feet under water at the time, did not need much encouragement. If successful, the proposed canal would steer future floodwaters to the far southern reaches of the sink, past their farms and out of harm's way. Those whose land would border the canal were pleased that it would run along the section lines and thus not burden any one of them excessively. Davisville merchants, who watched their town get inundated, liked the idea of rerouting the creek a mile to the south. And a number of farmers upstream from the break observed that they, too, might benefit. When the levee broke early that fateful morning, "the water," one wrote, "did not raise anymore" in front of his ranch. By straightening out the creek's channel, the proposed canal promised to have the same effect. It would eliminate a major pressure point, prevent the creek from backing up, and thus reduce the chance of overflow. Constructing the canal would not be simple, its advocates knew, but it would be well worth the try.[25]

The initial problem was how to pay for the project. No one knew what the work might cost, only that it would be much more than the fourteen thousand dollars it took to build the previous branch canal. And because district 18 had been drained of all its funds, they would have to start from scratch. Carey's first inclination was to organize a new swampland district, and, on February 7, 1872, he presented a petition to the Yolo County Board of Supervisors to do just that. The board's collective hands were tied, however. While most of the farmers who would benefit from this project resided in Yolo County (i.e., north of Putah Creek), the proposed canal itself lay almost entirely in Solano County (south of the creek). Neither the swampland law of 1866 nor the Green Act of 1868 accounted for such a scenario. Who would authorize it, who would pay for it, and who would even survey it? When the bewildered board members tabled the issue, Carey turned to Frank S. Freeman, his state assemblyman, who recommended legislative action.[26]

Carey and Freeman moved quickly—Carey because he wanted construction to commence as soon as possible and Freeman because Carey was among the biggest taxpayers in Yolo County. In less than a month, they drafted "An Act to provide for the protection from overflow by Putah Creek of certain lands in the Counties of Yolo and Solano." In the process of trying to please one another, Carey and Freeman made promises that neither could keep. In particular, Carey assured Freeman that landowners in the proposed "Yolo and Solano Canal District" would approve the bill's provisions, while Freeman insisted that nothing in the bill was unconstitutional. Freeman introduced it at the end of the legislative session, persuaded his fellow lawmakers to suspend the rules of deliberation, and presided over its passage on April 1—all in just four days.[27]

Had they simply created a new swampland district across the two counties with the usual provisions—especially the "half or more" approval clause—the canal act might have flowed smoothly. Instead, the new law created almost as much disruption as the flooding itself. It was bad enough that the rectangular-shaped district encompassed much too large an area—fifty thousand acres, starting well west of the break, extending well east of Carey's ranch, and covering five to six miles both north and south of Putah Creek. Landowners on the outer portions of the district stood to benefit far less from the canal than the canal would from their tax dollars. Worse yet, no landowner would get a say in the matter. The law forced the district upon them. It gave a three-member board of trustees (two appointed by Yolo County's board of supervisors, one by Solano's) full power to "levy assessments anytime they deem necessary," to rule on appeals, and to bring suit in the name of the district against delinquent taxpayers—"the same power," the law proclaimed, "as is possessed by County Courts."[28]

Opposition to the district emerged slowly, but when the Yolo board appointed Carey as one of the trustees on April 22, cries of "inquisition" and "swindle" filled the air. On May 4, 150 landowners met in Davisville to band together against the law. They found it "odious and oppressive," especially the implied power of the trustees to seize their farms if they refused to pay what they were told. "Had the Act been entitled 'An Act to confer the property of all parties within a radius of ten miles to the Trustees of said Land District,' the meaning would have been plain and explicit," one of them declared. Many in the crowd very much wanted the canal, but not on these terms. When someone made known that just a few days earlier Carey had been spotted at the meeting held by the Solano board to appoint its trustee, talk changed to action. Pledging to "use all honorable means at our command to prevent any of the provisions of said act from going into effect," they adopted their own code of by-laws, elected officers, and subscribed "several thousand dollars to fight the infamous bill in the several Courts of the State."[29]

The Solano board, they soon learned, had already sealed the fate of the law by refusing to appoint a trustee. Board members could not have been too happy to be called to a special meeting on April 30 with just this one item on the agenda. They took all of ten minutes to denounce the canal act. Already burdened with several other swampland districts in their jurisdiction, they did not want to take on another one. When they discovered that the canal would serve farmers primarily in Yolo County, that the Solano board would appoint only one of the trustees, and that the law itself was undoubtedly unconstitutional, they declared it a "gigantic fraud" and dared its supporters to take legal action. When Carey tried to persuade them otherwise, he quickly found that he had nowhere near the pull that he had in his home county. Though the law would not be officially repealed for another two years, Carey knew that day that it was a dead letter.[30]

Furious but all the more determined, Carey called his own meeting. Most of the attendees were Putah Sink farmers—those most vulnerable to floods. If the Solano board and a few wayward farmers insisted on being obstinate, Carey told them, then they would simply have to build the canal themselves. Exactly how much they subscribed to the cause that day was not disclosed, but it was enough, apparently, to get started. And exactly how this informal group financed the canal thereafter remains even more of a mystery. No records have survived, if indeed any were kept. The available evidence suggests, however, that whenever funds were tight, Carey stepped in to make up the difference. He had already invested too much of his money and too much of himself to do otherwise. Carey's detractors could have taken him to court to stop the project but chose instead to take a wait-and-see attitude. Few were against the canal; they just did not want to pay for it. And no one wanted to actually stop the annual overflows that replenished their fields; they just wanted to control them.[31]

Construction began that summer. The first step was to block the break to prevent the creek's floodwaters from interfering with their work on the new channel. Hoping to make a stronger barrier, they built a bulkhead with boards and lumber and reinforced it with earthwork. Work on the canal was then divided into segments, with the adjacent landowners themselves serving as "contractors." Starting at the break and heading eastward, the owner on each side of the section line agreed to remove a one-hundred-foot strip of ground to a depth of six feet, thus making a two-hundred-foot-wide channel—the widest, to date, of any canal built in the Sacramento Valley. Contractors did most of this work with horse teams pulling slip scrapers. They then employed Chinese laborers to raise levees with the earth from the dug-out channel. The heavy, tedious work progressed slowly but surely over the next two years, with few interruptions or problems.[32]

The calm before the storm ended on December 30, 1873. That evening, Putah Creek, in full flood, ripped through the bulkhead. This time, it did not back up at the railroad but instead rushed under a newly built trestle and down the unfinished canal, "taking out fences and everything as it went," an eyewitness recalled. "Everything" included a good portion of the levees and much of the heavy excavation equipment. Worse yet, the floodwaters deposited thick layers of sediment and debris in the channel, literally washing away several months' work. Frustrated but not discouraged, farmers built a bigger bulkhead across the break and resumed the scraping. The same cycle of events occurred again the following winter, in January 1875, and then again one year later, in November 1876. The rebuilt (and still bigger) bulkhead held for the next two years before being obliterated in January 1878 by "a torrent that roared by like the Amazon," as one exasperated farmer put it. The canal levees, wrote another observer, were "destroyed on both sides, the channel was filled with sand, and farms for miles were entirely under water." The work resumed, only to be wiped out once again by heavy rains the following year.[33]

The sequence repeated itself, though not always every year or with such force, for the rest of the century and beyond. In the end, Putah Creek—not Carey, not the boards of supervisors, not other farmers—decided where it wanted to go. The more often the creek burst through the break, the more the new channel gradually deepened. By 1880, the two channels were more or less the same depth, which allowed Putah Creek to flow "naturally" in either direction. By the turn of the century, the new channel, observed one farmer, "has to be half full before it goes into the old channel." Recalled another, "Nothing had to be done to turn the water out of the old channel and into the new. It turned itself out." It is little wonder, then, why mapmakers since 1878 (and even today) could not reach a consensus on what to call the new channel—some labeling it a ditch or a canal, others insisting on South Fork Putah Creek or simply Putah Creek. Part natural and part manmade, the new channel proved just as confounding as the old.[34]

All along, no one battled Putah Creek longer, harder, and with greater futility than R. S. Carey. At least five times over the course of his life, flooding forced Carey to reconstruct the ten miles of levees designed to protect his fifteen-hundred-acre Putah Sink ranch. A third of them bordered the tule margin on the east, while the other two-thirds held back the waters of the "old Putah Creek" to the north and the canal to the south. Carey was never sure just how to utilize this productive land—whether for cultivating wheat or raising stock. He was, moreover, "a poor guesser," as one neighbor put it, saying, "If he sowed, the flood came; if he failed to sow[,] the flood failed to come and a favorable season was lost." His luck was never worse than in 1895. Hoping to ride out the slumping economy with a huge crop of wheat, Carey instead met his nemesis once again. On January 5, the raging waters of Putah Creek, with virtually no warning, roared through the break and poured into the canal on a collision course toward Carey's ranch. Their destructive impact, mighty enough already, was made even greater by the fact that landowners upstream had not been maintaining the canal very well, allowing its width to narrow to one hundred feet. The "ocean of water" that came down from the mountains burst through the narrow channel and shot forward onto Carey's land, exploding over the top of his levees, which then "merely served to keep in the water," one of his hands recalled. "You could not see the fences, which were at least four feet high."[35]

This time, Carey would not recover. In this season as never before, he was in dire need of a big crop and a big payoff. Back in 1886, embarking on yet another effort to reclaim Putah Sink, Carey had borrowed fifty thousand dollars from Henry Cowell, a San Francisco financier. The terms were steep—8 percent interest, compounded yearly, with one-third of the principal due in three years, another third after five, and the last third in seven. To secure the loan, Carey had mortgaged much of his land—not only the fifteen hundred acres he intended to levy off, but another forty-five hundred of surrounding swampland. Another flood in 1889 and rapidly falling grain prices prevented him from making even one payment. In July 1893, with Carey owing him sixty-six thousand dollars, Cowell decided he could wait no longer and filed suit in the Yolo County Superior Court. Though his lawyers managed to delay attachment for a couple of years, the flood of 1895 spelled certain doom for Carey. On the afternoon of June 18, while sitting in his favorite chair on the rear porch of his home, overlooking his swamp-ridden ranch, he drew a pistol from his pocket and, placing the muzzle just beneath his right ear, sent a bullet crashing through his head.[36]

Carey had fought a losing battle from the very start. He would have marveled at the soaring dams, many hundreds of miles of high levees, numerous bypass channels, and maze of canals that now protect the Sacramento Valley from the terrifying floods that so tormented him. The Sacramento Flood Control Project, constructed over the first half of the twentieth century, still stands as one of the most complex and massive systems of its kind ever built. Carey would have marveled further still at the agricultural empire that this engineering wonder helps sustain and protect. He died unaware that California's farm economy was about to experience, in the words of one economist, "one of the most rapid and complete transformations ever witnessed in American agricultural history" and that one of his neighbors a few miles upstream on Putah Creek, George W. Pierce Jr., would personify that transformation. A second-generation gold rush migrant, longtime wheat farmer, and one of the region's pioneer specialty-crop growers, Pierce proved instrumental in forming California's first nut cooperative, the Davisville Almond Growers' Association, in 1897, and again in organizing the statewide California Almond Growers' Exchange, for which he served as president in 1913. The home-grown exchange, forerunner to the corporate powerhouse Blue Diamond Growers, epitomized the historical interplay between city and country in the Sacramento Valley.[37]

Carey's demons have not been washed away entirely, however. While all the dams, levees, bypass channels, and canals prevent the valley from routinely filling up and becoming an inland sea, the system remains by no means foolproof—witness the immense devastation caused by the floods of 1986 and 1997. Even the "old Putah Creek," sealed off at "the break" by the US Army Corps of Engineers in 1948 (making Carey's canal the only through channel), continued to flood during heavy rains as late as 1973. But should any of us succumb to the temptation to chide Carey and his fellow swamplanders for their arrogant and ultimately futile quest to control nature, we need only look at the huge new housing developments that now spread across the expansive American River floodplain north of Sacramento, where for almost 150 years, no one dared build at all. Another "flood of the century" awaits only a break or two in the levee.[38]

CHAPTER 6   Rivers of Gold, Valley
of Conquest
THE BUSINESS OF LEVEES AND DAMS
IN THE CAPITAL CITY

Todd Holmes

Steamboats slowly made their way up the streets of Sacramento on the night of January 9, 1850, rescuing the wet and stranded from floodwaters that had quickly turned a riverport town into a sea of death and destruction. Days earlier, blue skies had greeted the residents of Sacramento, no doubt strumming the same chord of optimism that had driven these gold seekers to the surrounding mines the previous year. Many believed they had seen and survived the worst a northern California winter could muster, as heavy November and December rains resulted in only minor flooding throughout the town. The storm clouds of January 8, however, proved them wrong. Within twenty-four hours, a torrent of floodwaters surged through Sacramento, carrying away most anything in their path, from tents and small buildings to wagons and livestock. Just as daunting was the human toll. "There was no adequate means of escape for life or property," one resident observed. "Consequently many were drowned, some in their beds, some in their feeble efforts at escape." Boats ferried survivors to the safety of second-story windows amid the helpless cries of the sick, who, miraculously buoyed by their cots, floated among debris and the dead in the flooded streets. The Great Inundation, as the floods of 1849–50 came to be known, provided the California argonauts their first lesson in the environment of the Sacramento Valley—"like a thief in the night" fortunes of gold could quickly turn to the misfortune of floods.[1]

Over the next 150 years, struggling to control the floodwaters of the Sacramento Valley would stand at the heart of settling northern California. In no other place was this battle more clearly seen than in the city of Sacramento. In fact, the business of levee building and flood control began just weeks after the floodwaters receded in January 1850, as a group of Sacramentans led by Hardin Bigelow built up and reinforced the surrounding riverbanks. Bigelow's makeshift levees may have saved the town from disaster during the spring runoff and secured his election as mayor later that year, but ultimately Sacramento's fortification against the valley's water—no matter how sophisticated and costly over the decades—would prove in vain. As one native *californio* observed in 1852 regarding Sacramento's Anglo settlers, "the Yankees . . . no doubt are a very smart race of people, but not quite so smart as God almighty."[2]

The process of flood control and reclamation remains overlooked in the literature of the American West and, more specifically, California. Indeed, the grand irrigation projects of the Golden State, which reign as the most complex in the world, have taken center stage within the historical discourse. From rivers of empire to Cadillac deserts, scholarly attention has rarely diverged from, in William Smythe's words, "the conquest of arid America." Yet, in upstreaming the irrigation canals of the state, it becomes clear that the Sacramento Valley does not fit within this paradigm of the West—an important omission since it was the floodplains of Sacramento that largely gave life to California's famous hydraulic society. The business of levees and dams not only made the desert bloom but also enabled the capital city of the Golden State to exist.[3]

Divided into three sections, this chapter traces the reclamation and flood control efforts of Sacramento over a century, from the rise of the city during the gold rush to the 1955 construction of its most formidable protector, Folsom Dam. The first section offers a brief look at the environment of Sacramento and larger Sacramento Valley, highlighting the region's unique geography while also detailing the industrious—and frequently helpless—attempts of settlers to tame the valley's waters in the late nineteenth century. The chapter then discusses the Natomas Water Company, which stood as one of the earliest business ventures of reclamation at the turn of the century. As one of the largest landholders in the region and builder of the original 1893 earth dam at Folsom, Natomas provides valuable insight into the range of economic activity that arose around the river environment of Sacramento after the company's incorporation in 1851—from gold, domestic water, and irrigation to the reclamation-driven endeavors of electricity, agriculture, and real estate. Moreover, the activities of Natomas clearly highlight the developing merger between the public and private, with flood control around the capital city resting as much in the hands of businessmen as those of engineers. The final section details Natomas's replacement by the larger interests of state capitalism, as the business of levees and dams moved firmly under the auspices of federal contractors. The opening of the 340-foot concrete dam at Folsom in 1955 stood as a testament to both the changing industry and the necessity of flood control in Sacramento.

Rivers of gold brought people from all over the world to Sacramento. To stay, these settlers of the capital city had to conquer the valley. In doing so, they laid the foundation for California's hydraulic society and made the Sacramento Valley the most populated and altered floodplain environment in America.

Gold Rush Levees

Stretching 150 miles long and an average of 30 miles wide, the Sacramento Valley comprises the northern third of California's 400-mile-long Great Central Valley, encompassing 5,000 square miles from present-day Red Bluff to the delta at San Francisco Bay. The valley is bordered by four mountain ranges: the Coastal Ranges on the west, the Klamath Mountains on the north, and the southern Cascade Range and northern Sierra Nevada on the east. Dominating the valley's center is the mighty Sacramento River, running more than 400 miles from its headwaters in the Klamath Mountains to the Suisun arm of San Francisco Bay. The Sacramento is California's largest river, with a drainage basin of 26,150 square miles and an average flow of 5,000 cubic feet per second. Yet, its size is equally matched by its seasonal variability and destruction. The river flows gently through the valley during summer months, yet, in winter and spring, rain and snow-melt increase its volume to an astounding 600,000 cubic feet per second. Geography explains this dramatic seasonal flux. While the Sacramento Valley represents only a third of the state's long Central Valley, it receives more than two-thirds of California's precipitation, much of it in the Sierra Nevada snowpack—the deepest in the nation. To handle this influx, the Sacramento River would overflow annually, transforming much of the valley floor into an inland sea more than 100 miles long that persisted well into summer.[4]

It would be at the southern tip of this inland sea, at the confluence of the Sacramento and American Rivers, where settlers staked out the site for Sacramento City. In many respects, the location seemed logical. The Sacramento River was the main transportation route up the valley from San Francisco, and the American offered easy access to the foothill mines of the Mother Lode. Moreover, both rivers afforded necessary resources, such as drinking water, fish, game, and lumber ready to be cut from trees along their banks. Such advantages notwithstanding, geography once again dealt a hefty blow. Exacerbating the annual flooding of the valley were two large basins that surrounded the site of Sacramento City. Both the American basin in the north and the Yolo basin in the west represented two of the lowest points in the valley—saucerlike depressions that naturally pooled floodwater and offered no outlet for drainage. Such precarious geography was not lost on pre–gold rush settlers. As John Sutter recalled in his autobiography, "I had always been opposed to the plan of establishing the metropolis of the valley at New Helvetia [present-day Sacramento and environs]. The location was favorable enough, to be sure, but the land was so low that a rise of the river above normal would cause a flood . . . with heavy loss of life and property." In blunter fashion, Sutter derided the decision to erect a settlement at the confluence of the Sacramento and American Rivers: "Had I not been snowed in at Coloma, Sacramento never, never, would have been built." Lt. Charles Wilkes expressed similar observations in his 1841 report on the Sacramento Valley, stating, "According to the testimony of the

Indians, the whole country was annually inundated," which made the region "unfit for advantageous settlement."⁵

The death and destruction experienced in Sacramento during the Great Inundation of 1849–50 underscored how such warnings were neither heeded nor remembered. After the floodwaters receded and residents narrowly escaped another inundation during an early spring snow-melt, the city approved $250,000 for levee construction in September 1850. Sacramento's first levee system stretched a total of nine miles and ranged from heights of three feet along the American River to six and even twenty feet along the Sacramento. All told, 120,000 cubic feet of earth was used to fortify the city—a bulwark that proved no match for valley floodwaters two years later. On March 7, 1852, a breach in the levee once more left Sacramento under water. The levees gave way again in January 1853, as floodwaters twenty-two feet above the low-water mark engulfed the city. According to Lt. R. S. Williamson, who sailed down the Sacramento River in the winter of 1852–53, the valley's inland sea had returned with a "sheet of water covering the country . . . fifty miles broad." City residents remained undeterred in their aspirations to settle Sacramento, however, and, in the wake of the January floods, they embarked on a range of flood control projects, from fortifying levees to raising city streets. By 1854, these efforts had restored confidence in the city's protection, and Sacramento, after a hard-won political battle in the legislature, became California's fifth and final capital city. Yet, such assurance was quickly put to question, as winter rains caused another deluge and forced the legislature to flee to drier ground some sixty miles south, in the town of Benicia.⁶

The outbreak of the Civil War opened up new opportunities and ambitions for flood control in the Sacramento Valley. Taking advantage of a weakened Democratic Party, California Republicans, who more eagerly embraced state projects, pushed through the Reclamation and Swampland Act of 1861. The act called for a valley-wide flood control plan and created the Board of Swampland Commissioners—the state's first independent agency. Bold as the 1861 act was, however, it was too little too late, as the winter of 1861–62 ushered in the worst floods to hit the Sacramento Valley. The floods began in early December, when tropical rains melted several feet of snow in the Sierra Nevada, covering much of the valley floor with water in less than three days. By the morning of December 9, floodwaters had pushed through the levee along the American River and engulfed Sacramento. Since the levee along the Sacramento River remained intact, it provided no outlet for floodwaters to escape. Soon the capital city stood in a lake of its own creation, forcing crews to blast out a section of the Sacramento levee to drain the waters. As residents began to recover from the first inundation, another storm hit the valley in January 1862, claiming the lives of hundreds and burying Sacramento deep in water and debris for almost three months. The torrent of water was so strong that it even washed away Indian mounds of great antiquity from the valley's floor in neighboring Yolo County. To reaffirm the necessity of the Swampland Commis-

FIGURE 6.1. Sacramento, January 1862. Courtesy Center for Sacramento History, David Joslyn Collection.

sion just enacted, the legislature was once again forced to flee to drier land in the face of a disaster that, according to one newspaper, only "an Angry God" could have produced.[7]

While some pointed to an "Angry God" for explanations of the floods, many others began to look toward geography—a source of causation that Sacramento began to address in serious ways during the 1860s and 1870s. In the storm's aftermath, the city set out to repair and raise not only its nine-mile levee system but also a large number of its streets, elevating twelve blocks along the Sacramento River upwards of fifteen feet above their original level. By 1873, much of the city stood a story taller than it had a decade before. Most importantly, crews redirected and straightened the American River on the northern edge of the city in order to eliminate a natural bend that was a frequent entry point for floodwaters. The city enjoyed a new level of protection by the late 1870s, for just as canal works removed

FIGURE 6.2. *What Hydraulic Mining Is Doing for the Country. Sacramento Bee* political cartoon, ca. 1880s. Courtesy Center for Sacramento History, Eleanor McClatchy Collection.

"the American River floodgate," levee improvements, along with a southern addition in 1878, ultimately secured the city in a triangle that spanned a total of twelve and a half miles at a height of twenty-eight feet above the low-water mark.[8]

Yet, every step forward Sacramento took in its battle to control the valley's inland sea resulted in two steps back for overall flood control in the Sacramento Valley itself. The first of these setbacks occurred in 1868 with the passage of the Green Act, which reversed the 1861 Swampland Act discussed above. The Board of Swampland Commissioners and the agenda of a centralized, valley-wide plan for flood control gave way to the more laissez-faire model favored by the returning Democratic majority; it largely abolished any kind of state planning and intervention. Increased flooding and local levee wars resulted. With the valley floor divided under the Green Act into private districts whose owners built their own levee systems, the lands of the wealthy were often fortified at the expense of the poorer farmers both on the other side of the river and downstream. Amid the anarchy that followed, a masked party rowing to a disputed high embankment with dynamite in hand attempting to save their lands from flood was not an uncommon sight along the Sacramento and its tributaries. As one newspaper averred in 1890, "Under the present reclamation system the residents of one bank of the river are thus frequently pitted against those of the other bank," with all ascribing to a philosophy that "if the levee must break let it be on some other man's land."[9]

Even more of a setback for flood control in the valley was the continued onslaught of hydraulic mining. As Kenneth Owens and David Vaught detail elsewhere in this volume, the washing away of hillsides between 1850 and 1885 dumped 885 million cubic yards of debris into the valley's waterways—a volume more than three times greater than that excavated for the Panama Canal. As early as the 1860s, the pollution in the rivers from hydraulic activity became so extensive that, in Sacramento, residents jokingly referred to their drinking water as "Sacramento Straight" due to its brown, whiskeylike tint. The severest consequence of hydraulic mining for valley residents, however, was not its effect on the water they drank as much as how the water around them flowed. To be sure, depositing millions of cubic yards of debris into the waterways annually raised the riverbeds faster than many towns and cities like Sacramento could raise their levees. By the 1870s, reports circulated that mining operations had raised the riverbeds of some of the Sacramento's tributaries as much as eighty feet, placing the bottom of the water-ways in certain areas above the surrounding countryside. The capital city no doubt experienced these same consequences, as the city's heightened levees and other flood control improvements still failed to stem inundations in 1871, 1875, 1878, and 1892. Thus, in a landscape whose rivers were already prone to overflow their banks and form the great inland sea of northern California, the effects of hydraulic mining could not have been worse, as they largely undermined any progress made against flooding in the Sacramento Valley.[10]

Progressive Reclamation

The turn of the century offered new hope for Sacramento Valley residents in their battle against floods, as the political currents of Progressivism underwrote a more active role for state and federal authorities in, above all, resource management. On the federal level, this more active role was seen in the creation of national forests, as well as the Newlands Reclamation Act (1902). Although often associated with irrigating the West, the act also established one of the primary foundations for future federal involvement in "reclaiming" the floodplain of the Sacramento Valley. The first use of this foundation, however, was on the state level, as the father of California Progressivism, Hiram Johnson, championed flood control as one of his top environmental priorities during the 1910 gubernatorial race. Once in office, the Johnson administration advanced an agenda of centralized planning and modern engineering to solve the valley's flood problem. His administration created the California Reclamation Board, charged with regulating and approving all levees in the state, as well as pushed through the Flood Control Act of 1911, which offi-cially adopted a valley-wide plan for the Sacramento Valley. In doing so, Governor Johnson not only entrenched a more active role for the state in battling northern California's inland sea but also forged long-lasting avenues between the public and private sectors within the burgeoning business of levees and dams. Around the flood basin of the capital city, no company proved more adept in traveling upon these fledgling avenues in the first few decades of the twentieth century than the Natomas Company.[11]

Founded in 1851 by Amos P. Catlin and A. T. Arrowsmith, the Natoma Water and Mining Company, as it was originally called, began as just one of many mining corporations that dotted the Mother Lode region around Sacramento. Over the next century, however, the company came to play perhaps one of the most important roles in developing both the waterways and floodplain around the city. Natomas embodied the full economic evolution from rivers of gold to the conquest of the Sacramento Valley, as the company's mining and irrigation operations in the nineteenth century gave way to the reclamation-driven ventures of agriculture and electricity in the twentieth. Moreover, through the company's history, we can see how the business of levees and dams in Sacramento arose amid the confluence of interests. Just as Natomas found new ways over the decades to profit from the valley's waterways, so too did the capital city seek new ways to protect itself and surrounding communities from those same waters.[12]

Water stood at the center of Natomas's business ventures from the beginning. By the time the company incorporated in 1851, the days of the individual miner panning for gold in one of the Sacramento River's tributaries had been replaced by the more capital-intensive forms of hydraulic and riverbed mining. To be sure, Natomas stood in a prime position to profit from both. Within two years, Natomas had secured a near monopoly on the south fork of the American River under California's business-friendly water law ("first in time, first in right"), and from its sixteen-mile canal and fifty miles of branch ditches it supplied more than two thousand miners with water. While the company's extensive rights on the American allowed it to supply much of the needed water for hydraulic mining operations and drinking water for several communities, these rights also enabled Natomas to become one of the largest operators of riverbed-mining activities in the valley. Unlike hydraulic mining, which used high-pressure nozzles and river water to wash away mountainsides into large wooden sluices, riverbed mining diverted and dammed the river itself, allowing the bed of the stream to be excavated for gold. Natomas perfected the diversion, damming, and storage of river water within just a few years, supplementing the company's canals and other water systems with twelve reservoirs. As one newspaper trumpeted, its mastery of the water and mining business made "the Natoma Water and Mining Company . . . one of the most profitable investments in California." Just three years after its founding, Natomas fulfilled such expectations with a gross profit of $196,000 (some $5.3 million in twenty-first-century terms).[13]

The company's mastery of Sacramento's waterways was best seen in the dam it constructed on the American River, twenty-two miles east of the capital city. While the dam, upon completion, stood at the cutting edge of American engineering, its construction also represented one of the first business contracts between the state of California and Natomas. The company had long benefited from friendly relations with the state, notably seen in California's favorable water and land laws that afforded Natomas a monopoly on much of the American River and, as discussed below, the countryside surrounding Sacramento. The construction of Folsom Dam proved no different. In 1866, the state agreed to furnish Natomas with convict labor to build the dam in exchange for 350 acres, which would be used for a penitentiary known today as Folsom Prison. After twenty years of delays and further negotiations, Natomas completed the 290-foot-long dam in 1892 and added four hydroelectric stations three years later. The company's powerhouse at Folsom Dam, under its subsidiary, the Sacramento Electric Power Company, would light the streets of Sacramento for the next fifty years. The twenty-two-mile transmission ranked as America's first long-distance use of hydroelectric power.[14]

While Natomas was finding new ways to profit from the valley's waterways, the company also began to develop its other large asset amid the wane of California's mining boom—land. In 1857, Natomas purchased 11,000 acres of the Rancho Rio de los Americanos, a Mexican land grant composed largely of present-day Sacramento County. Within a decade, these lands provided an important source of diversification for the company, as mining soon gave way to the development of industrial agriculture. Fed by the company's ever-expanding system of canals and waterlines, Natomas's lands soon led the valley in irrigated horticulture and viticulture. By the late 1880s, the company maintained 350 acres in orchards, 80 acres in grain, and more than 2,000 acres in grapes, which at the time gave Natomas ownership of the world's largest vineyard. The company's agricultural lands continued to claim a host of notable achievements: the state's first raisin operation and the state's largest winery, as well as one of California's most sizable plants for the drying and shipping of raisins and various types of orchard fruit. Outside of land management, Natomas's nursery operations stood at the heart of the company's agricultural success, developing sixteen hundred varieties of plum and pear trees, while also importing cuttings from some of the finest grape varieties in France, Spain, and Germany. By the time of Folsom Dam's completion, Natomas ranked as both master of Sacramento's waterways and one of the leaders of specialized agriculture in the valley, as the company sold wine, table grapes, and raisins in eastern markets as far off as Chicago, Saint Louis, and New Orleans. Mining and agriculture are often placed at odds in the historical discourse on the Sacramento Valley, as the destruction of waterways frequently spelled disaster for valley farmers. That Natomas successfully operated in both industries underscores an important anomaly in valley history, as well as the diverse reach of California capitalism.[15]

Land and water provided the economic basis from which Natomas rose to prominence in the nineteenth century, and it would be these two assets in the twentieth that gave the company both the investment wherewithal and expertise to answer Gov. Hiram Johnson's call for flood control in Sacramento. In many respects, Natomas looked very much the same at the turn of the century, only larger. By 1911, the company's land assets totaled almost one hundred thousand acres around Sacramento, a third of which were irrigated by a waterworks system that stretched some fifty miles. The company also maintained its controlling stake

FIGURE 6.3. *Capitol Building during Sacramento's Electric Carnival, September 1895.* Courtesy Center for Sacramento History, Robert and Marlene Calbo Collection.

in the Sacramento Electric Power Company and continued in the mining business, operating seven thousand acres of gold gravel lands near Folsom and Oroville, with excavation carried out by eleven large dredges and two rock-crushing plants serving them. Absorbing a number of land and development firms throughout the valley, Natomas even extended its reach within California's corporate world as its board of directors forged links to more than fifty different companies, ranging from banks and land operations to electric power companies and agricultural enterprises. Thus, as Natomas touted to investors a mission statement of "extending its operations in the Sacramento Valley," in the years to come this mission would mean placing flood control and reclamation in the hands of as many business leaders as engineers.[16]

Natomas began acquiring large tracts of land north of Sacramento around the turn of the century. By 1911, it claimed more than sixty thousand acres in the heavily flood-prone area known as the American basin. As in most aspects of the company, business drove the decision. With California's population increasing at a rate of one hundred thousand per year, and Sacramento's number of residents doubling between 1903 and 1907, the need for suburbs and farmland close to the capital city was not lost on Natomas. The company also envisioned an array of transportation networks—five railroad lines and three steamship companies—that placed the southern portion of the basin within a downtown commute time of fifteen minutes. The area seemed to offer a profitable investment for the company: location, transportation, and some of the richest soil in the Sacramento Valley. Yet,

FIGURE 6.4. *Natomas Dredge and Levee Construction in Reclamation District 1001, ca. 1911.*
Courtesy Center for Sacramento History, James E. Henley Collection.

like Sacramento and much of the valley itself, the American basin also suffered from the annual onslaught of floodwaters. On one hand, this situation offered a boon for the company, as it made Natomas's land grab rather easy among many basin farmers who were more than willing to surrender to the valley's inland sea and sell their land, especially after enduring five horrendous floods between 1902 and 1909. Moreover, under California's new reclamation laws, the company received an array of benefits, such as tax breaks and the ability to levy local taxes on their lands. On the other hand, the waterlogged lands placed Natomas at center stage in the fight against floods, offering the biggest test for the company that throughout the decades had trumpeted its mastery over Sacramento's waterways. Christened Reclamation Districts 1000 and 1001 in April 1911, the lands of the American basin now officially put their owner, Natomas, in the business of levees and dams—a project touted as "the largest reclamation work of its kind to be undertaken in the United States."[17]

Natomas began its reclamation work in the northernmost end of its basin landholdings (labeled Reclamation District 1001), which lay more than thirty miles from the capital city and encompassed sections of the Feather and Bear Rivers in the north and the Sacramento River on its western flank. Geographically, the district was a logical starting place for the company's project, considering the valley's north-south drainage. This situation highlighted the fact that even corporations like Natomas were, by 1911, beginning to look at flood control through a larger—if not valley-wide—lens of prevention. The company's work in the northern district first focused on the Bear River, where a dragline excavator helped strengthen and raise the levees, while also retrenching more than two miles of the river itself. Farther south in the district, along the Feather and Sacramento Rivers, Natomas continued the same process, using two dragline excavators and a clamshell dredge. The dredge, nicknamed Thor, was one of eleven in the fleet the company maintained for its gold-dredging operations. And just as the dredges took riverbed mining to new levels for the company between 1900 and 1940, they also revolutionized the building of levees, with each machine's massive bucket scooping up sand and mud from the river bottom and transferring the materials to the new embankments. As Thor raised the levees along the Feather River six feet and the company's Hercules dredge did the same on the Sacramento portion of the district, more than forty horse-drawn scrapers shaped the new embankments into final form with crowns of twelve feet. Once the levees were complete, Natomas proceeded to clear and plant the land, bringing to plow many portions of the flood-ravaged district for the first time in more than a decade.[18]

The company successfully tamed the valley waterways and brought the land in district 1001 to plow, but at a large environmental cost. Indeed, reclamation sounded the final death knell for the Sacramento Valley's riparian forests. Composed of a rich variety of vegetation, these forests stretched more than five miles from the riverbanks before giving way to the more recognizable grasslands of the Sierra foothills. Oak, ash, cottonwoods, willow, and sycamore trees lined the rivers, helping to create vegetation so thick that many early ecologists in the region often used the term "jungle" to describe it. As one observer reported in 1868, "The timber belt along the Sacramento was at one time so broad and dense as to render the navigation of that stream difficult by sail vessels." An abundance of wildlife flourished in these riparian habitats, giving rise to both a diversity and density of fauna that, in the words of one historian, "was unsurpassed in any region in North America." What remained of the valley's riparian forests by the time the dredges and excavators of Natomas worked the riverbanks would soon be lost to the company's march of reclamation. As scores of trees were felled and other vegetation erased through "slash and burn" techniques and often replaced with small groves of highly absorbent eucalyptus trees, the company's reclamation proved but just another phase of Anglo conquest in the valley.[19]

Completing its work in the northern portion of the American basin, Natomas moved south in 1912 to begin reclamation work in district 1000, which ran roughly fifteen miles north from the American-Sacramento confluence. As discussed before, this section of the basin represented the pearl of Natomas's investment due to its proximity to the capital city. Its reclamation, however, would also prove the most difficult and costly. Situated at the southern end of the basin and thus exposed

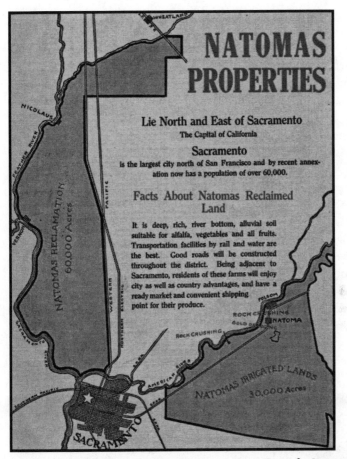

FIGURE 6.5. Map of Natomas properties, ca. 1911. Courtesy Center for Sacramento History, Natomas Company Collection.

to some of the harshest floodwaters, district 1000 required levees much greater in height and width than its northern counterpart, and many of them had to be built anew. To accomplish this effort, the company used two dragline excavators to amass along the Sacramento River two parallel levees, each nine feet high and with a thirty-two-foot base. A suction dredge, capable of digging some thirty feet below water, then transferred the mud and gravel of the riverbed through a pipe to fill in the trench left by the excavators. As in district 1001, horse-drawn scrapers gave the new embankments their final form, smoothing off a crown of some twenty-four feet. Work on the American River levees proceeded in similar fashion, with clamshell dredges amassing new and heightened fortifications along the basin's southern perimeter. By October 1912, Natomas had completed forty-eight miles of levees in the American basin and another twenty miles of back levees along partic-ular sections of the Sacramento River. The company would continue work in the two districts over the years, constructing additional drainage canals and clearing land for both agricultural and suburban real estate, which it sold in five-, ten-, and twenty-acre lots. By the end of 1912, however, it was clear that Natomas had successfully reclaimed the basin and pioneered the techniques that, over the next three decades, would make "a Holland of the Sacramento Valley."[20]

Just as Natomas succeeded in fortifying Sacramento and its adjacent American basin from floodwaters, progressives and other California activists began making headway in their effort to garner federal support in conquering the valley and its inland sea. Both national parties pledged "unequivocal" support for the "improvement of the nation's great waterways" at their respective conventions in 1912, which undoubtedly incited levels of optimism and relief among northern California residents. Even Democrats, who had long opposed centralized planning and state projects, favored "the co-operation of the United States and the respective states in plans for the comprehensive treatment of all waterways" and included "swamp and overflowed lands" in such plans. Thus, as Natomas put the final grade on the outer levees of the American basin, the issue of flood control in the Sacramento valley began to encounter favorable political waters on the national level. In the years to come, these waters would usher in new levels of state capitalism into the Golden State, which would both build upon and dwarf the work of Natomas in the business of levees and dams.[21]

Federal Reclamation

Five years after the 1912 Republican and Democratic national conventions, rhetoric finally met reality in crafting a flood control policy on the federal level. As Anthony Carlson details later in this volume, in 1917 congressional representatives from California and the Mississippi valley mustered enough votes to pass the Flood Control Act, the first such official act at the federal level. Covering the Sacramento and Mississippi Rivers, the bill established a rubric in which the cost of flood control projects would be split between federal, state, and local governments, while requiring states to assume the full costs of maintenance. For Sacramento, the legislation provided more than $5.6 million to fortify the valley's waterways and placed additional federal financial backing behind the Sacramento Flood Control System—the valley-wide plan of levees, weirs, and bypasses enacted under Hiram Johnson in 1911. The new act gave the federal government an unprecedented level of responsibility over the nation's river lands, while further institutionalizing the public-private partnership in flood control.[22]

A decade later, both this federal responsibility and the practice of public-private partnership were heightened once more with the passage of the Flood Control Act of 1928. Spurred by the massive floods of the Mississippi in 1927 and those along the Sacramento the following year, which ended two decades of perceived security in the valley, the new act largely made the federal government the sole source of financing for levees and other flood control projects along both the

Mississippi and Sacramento, as well as other major rivers in the country. Moreover, construction and maintenance of the nation's levees now fell under the purview of the Army Corps of Engineers. Thus, in the stroke of a pen, Natomas was forced to share the waterways of the Sacramento Valley with the federal government and its contractors.[23]

As California advanced the famous Central Valley Project (CVP) in the 1930s, the business of flood control for the federal government and its contractors came to extend beyond levees to include dams. Proposed statewide in 1933, the CVP was not originally pitched within the tones of California agrarianism, as much of the historical literature focuses on and implies. In fact, flood control, not irrigation, topped the list of reasons justifying the undertaking of such a colossal project, as many a proponent referenced the "yearly damage done by floods in the Sacramento River Valley." Even the California Chamber of Commerce—an entity dominated by the state's agribusiness community—pointed to the need for flood control in the Sacramento Valley before turning to irrigating the vast, arid tracts of the San Joaquin Valley in their promotion of the project. As if to assert their own voice in the discussion, the valley's floodwaters once again reclaimed the land in spring 1935, taking the lives of twenty-one people and forcing government officials to flee the capitol in Sacramento. The model levees of Natomas also proved no match, as the American River broke through and inundated the southern portion of the company's American basin. Within months, calls for the federal government to take over the CVP and all major waterway and dam projects echoed in the halls of Congress—calls that were answered with the Flood Control Act of 1936. Yet, amid federal plans to commence the construction of Shasta Dam at the headwaters of the Sacramento River, the first phase of the CVP, the valley's waterways continued to reassert their power. In December 1937, more than thirty towns stood under water when the Sacramento and a few of its tributaries breached their levees, leaving some five thousand residents homeless. A few months later, the inland sea returned when a series of ferocious storms ravaged the valley for nineteen days, claiming the lives of sixteen people and inundating more than twenty-five thousand acres. Floodwaters surged through the capital city and other towns again in 1940, leaving six thousand homeless and many more looking to the government for help.[24]

The completion of Shasta Dam in 1945 answered the pleas of many northern California residents, and, more importantly, it marked the true beginning of the federal government's involvement in conquering the Sacramento Valley. Standing 602 feet high, with a base width of 543 feet, Shasta ranked as the world's second-largest concrete dam at the time of its completion, making the Sacramento River into a lake that covered thirty thousand acres. In the words of the Bureau of Reclamation, Shasta was the "mighty monitor of the Sacramento River." To native communities like the Winnemem Wintu tribe, who saw more than 90 percent of their ancestral land flooded by the new lake, the dam stood as quite another symbol of conquest. With the first cornerstone of the CVP complete, government contractors and engineers sought to move farther south in the valley and build a bulwark that would finally secure the capital city.[25]

Congress approved the construction of a new Folsom Dam in 1944, reaffirming the need for a more permanent flood control structure for Sacramento and the adjacent American and Yolo basins. Not originally included in the plans for the CVP, Folsom came to be seen as a natural addition. As Ben Glaha of the Bureau of Reclamation asserted, "God picks the dam sites. All we do is go out and find them." Yet, the location of the new dam, just downstream from the original structure completed by Natomas in 1892, did not prove as much a source of debate as the question of who would control the construction. Advocating for a low dam, the Army Corps of Engineers argued that 355,000 acre-feet of storage capacity was more than enough to regulate the waters of the American River and protect the communities of the Sacramento region. The Bureau of Reclamation, however, pushed for the building of a large, multipurpose dam that would store 1.0 million acre-feet of water. In fact, money lay at the heart of the problem. By 1947, federal and state spending on California flood control exceeded $500 million, with millions more earmarked for future projects. With Washington tightening its fiscal belt, the smaller structure proposed by the Army Corps of Engineers more readily fit the bill. Advocates in California, like Gov. Earl Warren, refused to settle, however. Urging construction of the larger dam, Warren reminded Washington, "We [Californians] have for too long witnessed the spectacle during wet years of destructive floods . . . sweeping over our lands, and leaving death and destruction in their wake." Fortunately for Sacramento, the efforts of Warren and the state Board of Water Resources paid off and secured the approval of the larger dam proposed by the Bureau of Reclamation. Completed in 1955, the new Folsom Dam wasted no time in validating its increased capacity, as floodwaters raging down the American River filled the entire reservoir. It would be the first of many times the dam would save the capital city.[26]

The 340-foot Folsom Dam, with Natomas's original structure resting at the bottom of its reservoir, stood as a testament to how the business of levees and dams, as well as the effort to conquer the Sacramento Valley, dramatically changed over the twentieth century. To be sure, the company's earlier works offered a model that its successors built upon in harnessing and mastering the valley's waterways, from dams and levees to hydroelectricity and reclamation. The Natomas dam, generators, and transmission lines lit up the capitol building in Sacramento as early as 1895, just as its pioneering levee system allowed "the sea of flood waters [to be] replaced by a sea of waving grain" in the American basin by 1916. Yet, at the completion of the new Folsom Dam in 1955, larger corporate entities funded by robust state capitalism replaced Natomas as master of the valley's waterways. The simple structure first built on the American River by prison labor in the late nineteenth century gave way to a host of engineering marvels constructed by Kaiser

Industries—a multibillion-dollar corporate giant whose business ventures ranged from cement, steel, and aluminum to construction, shipbuilding, and health care. Similarly, Natomas's fifty-year control of Sacramento's electricity became part of the vast domain of the Pacific Gas & Electric Company, which, by 1965, ranked as the largest utility company in the United States.[27]

Paralleling this change of the corporate guard was the increase and shift in population around the capital city. From a growth of 181 percent between 1860 and 1910, Sacramento County's population increased 309 percent between 1910 and 1950, and it skyrocketed an additional 746 percent by 1980. Similarly, the settlement patterns of this growing populace shifted from rural to urban. The irrigated orchards, vineyards, and homesteads Natomas promoted in the company's monthly news pamphlets throughout the early decades of the century represented an agrarianism of the past as the urban subdivisions and strip malls of Sacramento suburbia came to dominate the landscape.[28]

Folsom Dam towers as one of the southern cornerstones of the Sacramento Flood Control Project—the engineering marvel that today tames the valley's waterways through a matrix of more than thirty-five dams, six weirs and bypasses, 980 miles of levees, and numerous pumping stations and canals. In the words of historian David Vaught, without question the project "stands today as one of the most complex and massive systems of its kind ever built." To be sure, the devastating floods of 1986 underscored the limits of this system in conquering the valley's waterways. Yet, at the same time, the floods demonstrated the level of security the capital city and its surrounding communities enjoyed, as the $17 million in damage accrued in the American basin would have been closer to $5 billion without the protection of Folsom Dam, which held back floodwaters exceeding an unprecedented one million acre-feet per second. By the early years of the twenty-first century, however, the threads of security offered by the Sacramento Flood Control Project had woven a fleece of greed and neglect that shrouded the valley's geography. In the wake of California's housing boom, some twenty-five thousand residents of a Sacramento suburb stood aghast at the news in 2007 that the newly paved streets, fancy strip malls, and luxurious tract homes of their community rested on a dangerous floodplain and that they thus needed to buy additional insurance. The location of the suburb was the American basin and the name of the community, Natomas.[29]

During the last 150 years, residents of northern California claimed many successes in their efforts to conquer the Sacramento Valley. Yet, as the devastating floods of 1986 and 1997, as well as the continued risk to communities like Natomas, reveal, that conquest remains neither final nor complete. The tremendous success in mastering California's northern waterscape, first by Natomas and later by the federal government and its corporate contractors, helped develop not only the valley but the rest of the state as well. Sacramento water played a significant—and overlooked—role in the rise of the agricultural kingdoms and "Cadillac deserts" of the Southland. The hundreds of miles of canals irrigating the arid landscapes of the Golden State, however, are not the only crowning achievement of California's hydraulic society. That the capital city and its surrounding urban metropolis still rest on the southern edge of what was, and is, the inland sea of the Sacramento Valley floodplain points to a legacy of conquest all too easily forgotten.

CHAPTER 7   Forging Transcontinental
Alliances
THE SACRAMENTO RIVER VALLEY
IN NATIONAL DRAINAGE AND FLOOD
CONTROL POLITICS, 1900–1917

Anthony E. Carlson

In August 1903, the Trans-Mississippi Commercial Congress met in Seattle, Washington. Dedicated to promoting economic growth in the western United States, the congress adopted resolutions pertaining to water, forest, mineral, and rangeland conservation. One of the most strongly worded resolutions implored the federal government to develop the Sacramento River valley. Decades of ineffective local policies and conflicting water laws delayed flood control, irrigation, and wetlands drainage, causing the valley to languish as the country's biggest untapped source of wealth. The sheer scale of the valley's environmental problems, the congress concluded, justified intervention by the embryonic administrative and regulatory state. Once drained and irrigated, the valley would serve as an emblem of national power, progress, and prosperity. The resolution stated,

In the great interior central valley of California the problem of the control of the floods of the Sacramento River, which would furnish water enough to irrigate 10,000,000 acres of land, if conserved and utilized, should be treated as a single problem involving arid-land reclamation, flood control, navigation, and drainage, and while the improvements of the Sacramento and San Joaquin Rivers should be continued and extended by the National Government to fully develop the navigability of those rivers, the necessity of coping with the problem in its broadest aspects should be . . . prepared without delay by the engineers of the Reclamation Service and of the War Department.[1]

The Sacramento River valley's ensemble of water resource problems and status as an intrastate navigable river captivated early twentieth-century federal conservationists, hydrologists, and members of Congress. Aside from the Columbia River, the Sacramento River was the far West's only navigable watercourse. All of its tributaries were intrastate, meaning that federal agencies dealt only with the California state government regarding water rights. In the early 1900s, the Sacramento Valley emerged as the centerpiece of the US Geological Service's (USGS) strategy of institutional aggrandizement, which emphasized exporting its land reclamation program outside of the arid American West. The USGS sought to curry favor with midwestern and southern policy makers, build a national constituency, and supplant the US Army Corps of Engineers (USACE) and US Department of Agriculture (USDA) in drainage and flood control by using the Sacramento Valley as a staging area to showcase its managerial capabilities. Seeking to unify the arid and humid halves of the United States under a single water program, the USGS transformed the valley into a political battleground where it could seize power and funding from rival agencies.

In order to carry out the USGS's institutional power grab, a handful of little-known USGS engineers and topographers with experience in California water politics encouraged Sacramento Valley booster organizations and Congress members to forge alliances with southern communities. They argued that comprehensive drainage and flood control legislation would never be possible without robust regional political alliances. The Sacramento Valley's broader significance in Progressive era water politics was its budding, and uneasy, relationship with the Mississippi River valley, which was sealed during a string of catastrophic floods in 1912–13 in the lower Mississippi and Ohio River valleys. Natural disasters cemented the marriage of convenience between both valleys that the USGS initially cultivated and fostered. This essay takes a fresh look at national flood and drainage policies from the perspective of the Sacramento Valley. It argues that the Sacramento-Mississippi valley alliance revolutionized and accelerated the federal state's role in national water resource planning by paving the way for the passage of the Flood Control Acts of 1917 and 1928.[2]

Progressive Era National Water Politics

The federal government acquired new administrative and regulatory powers around the turn of the twentieth century. In response to urbanization, unprecedented immigration, the excesses of industrial capitalism, and growing disparities in the distribution of wealth, federal agencies intervened more forcefully in economic, environmental, and social affairs. Attempting to expand the federal government's managerial powers over the nation's waters, forests, and public lands, a group of university-trained engineers and scientists rose to power in Washington in the 1890s. Harnessing the authority of the emergent administrative and regulatory state, these conservationists linked efficient natural resource management to solving environmental problems through the application of scientific principles. By casting localism, legislative compromise, laissez-faire economics, and limited government as the enemies of enlightened environmental stewardship, conservationists championed bureaucratization as the best policy for achieving "efficient" natural resource administration.[3]

The Reclamation Act of 1902 was the crowning achievement of Progressive era conservationists. The law created the Reclamation Service in the Department of the Interior's USGS to build irrigation projects in the arid western states and territories using public lands revenue. The terms of the Reclamation Act were liberal and straightforward. Settlers on government reclamation projects received up to 160 acres at no cost. They were required to repay only their share of the construction costs associated with building canals, storage reservoirs, and dams over a ten-year period. Revenue collected from public land sales and individual repayments were deposited into a "reclamation fund," which supporters envisioned would provide a perpetual source of money. In order to promote an equitable distribution of government irrigation aid, the law stipulated that 51 percent of the revenue generated by any state's public lands be spent on projects within its boundaries. Framers of the law expected federal irrigation projects to lure urban tenement occupants and slum dwellers to the West, revive rural America, liberate the western economy from its dependence on range and extractive industries, and moderate the ravages of the corporate business cycle. In 1902, Frederick H. Newell, the first chief engineer of the Reclamation Service, wildly boasted that federal reclamation promised to transform 60 million to 100 million acres of desert wastelands—an area almost as large as California—into irrigated sanctuaries for immigrants and displaced factory workers.[4]

The Reclamation Act owed itself to a transcontinental political coalition of western policy makers and southern Democrats. Supporting federal reclamation by a margin of four to one, states' rights southerners anticipated that the law symbolized Congress's eagerness to subsidize a broader reclamation program that included southern wetlands, western deserts, and cut-over forests in the Great Lakes region. The ink was barely dry on the Reclamation Act when southern politicians clamored for westerners to share reclamation funding for drainage. In early 1905, for instance, South Carolina representatives asked Massachusetts representative Charles Q. Tirrell, the powerful chair of the House Committee on Irrigation of Arid Lands, to borrow money from the reclamation fund to drain southern swamps. South Carolinians insisted that drainage constituted a form of land conservation no less important than irrigation. Although the request attracted little political support, it demonstrated a collective aspiration for the improvement of all "wastelands."[5]

Historians of federal water policy have not pointed out that Progressive era conservationists celebrated wetlands drainage as much as irrigation, forestry management, and the regulation of grazing and mineral extraction on public lands. Since the settlement of North America, colonists and, later, Americans stigmatized wetlands as a menace to progress and prosperity. Wetlands inhibited travel, isolated land from agricultural production, drove down property values, provided refuge to dangerous predators and runaway slaves, and were believed to discharge into the atmosphere "miasmas" and other poisonous gases that people blamed for the onset of febrile illnesses. The only useful wetland, Americans believed, was one that had been drained, filled, and cultivated. After 1900, reform-oriented policy makers, farmers, and public health advocates tapped into the historical antipathy toward wetlands and extolled drainage as a paramount public policy objective. Preoccupied with agricultural progress and eliminating the social turmoil associated with urbanization, Reclamation Service administrators publicized federalized drainage as a natural counterpart to irrigation. Since federal administrators recognized wetlands and flooded lands as anomalous landscapes, they interchangeably described conservation acts that eliminated surface water concentrations as "drainage" or "flood control."[6]

Despite favorable public opinion in the South, federal aid for drainage work was a tough sell in Congress. Federalism and constitutional obstacles hampered Congress's sponsorship of water projects that did not directly improve waterway navigability. Since 1824, courts had recognized the constitutionality of removing snags, ice chunks, submerged steamboat vessels, and sandbars from navigable watercourses. In addition, Congress funded levee construction in order to increase a river's velocity in the hopes of "scouring" its bottom, supposedly achieving a more even stream flow for enhanced steamboat navigability. Nevertheless, confusion dominated Congress's role in draining swamps or protecting private lands from floods. In 1849, 1850, and 1860, Congress had passed swampland acts that ceded federal "swamp and overflowed" lands to fifteen states on the condition that their legislatures sell the lands and invest the revenue in building drainage and flood control works. Many policy makers and jurists interpreted these laws as evidence that Congress expected states to exercise drainage and flood control responsibilities. In 1881, Congress formalized this division of authority by specifying that federal monies could not be expended to shield riparian lands from floods. Simply put, federal authority ended at a navigable watercourse's banks.[7]

The USGS and Water Imperialism

In the ebullient era of social, political, and environmental reform ushered in by the Progressive era, long-standing assumptions about the limitations of federal power came under attack. Perceiving federalism as a curse rather than a blessing, reform-minded USGS conservationists celebrated the federal state's ability to transform flooded lands and wetlands into thriving farms. Although southerners anticipated that the agency would quickly expand into their region, the USGS initially touted the Sacramento Valley as the appropriate venue for demonstrating the benefits of top-down intervention. If the agency solved the Sacramento Valley's multitude of water problems, it might be invited to build drainage and flood control structures in the South or Midwest at the expense of its institutional rivals, the USACE and USDA.

Encompassing the northern third of California's Central Valley, the Sacramento Valley extends 150 miles along a north-south axis from the flatlands below Red Bluff to the Sacramento River's mouth. The broad, flat, and fertile valley claims an average width of 40 miles and serves as the mighty Sacramento River's natural floodplain. Rising in northern California's Trinity Mountains, the Sacramento River, a navigable stream measuring several hundred feet across, boasts a substantial velocity and volume. The river's normal flow is five thousand cubic feet per second, but during high-water stages it can reach as high as six hundred thousand cubic feet per second. Unable to contain such immense volumes, the Sacramento River would regularly overflow and inundate the valley, creating a sprawling "inland sea." Lingering floodwaters pooled together in the lower sections of the valley in impenetrable marshes of tule (large bulrushes) fifteen feet high. In the early 1900s, the USGS estimated that the valley contained at least six hundred thousand acres of tule swamps.[8]

The collapse of the Sacramento Valley's wheat industry in the 1890s provided an opportunity for federal administrators to encourage diversified agriculture. During the 1880s, California emerged as the United States' second-largest wheat-producing state. In 1885, Californians cultivated nearly 3.8 million acres of wheat—two-thirds of the state's agricultural output—which fetched a dollar per bushel. Nevertheless, the depression of 1893, drought, widespread soil exhaustion, declining yields, and the soaring costs of farm machinery ruined many small farmers during the "terrible nineties" and promoted land monopolization. In early 1901, Elwood Mead, the head of the USDA's Office of Irrigation Investigations (OII), reported to Congress that irrigation promised to revitalize the valley's moribund economy by accelerating the shift to diversified agriculture, encouraging crop rotation, and increasing yields. "Enough water leaves the valleys of the Sacramento and San Joaquin to irrigate between ten and fifteen millions acres of land," the report to Congress indicated. The report trumpeted the abundance and diversity of valley crops. Apples, oranges, almonds, olives, dates, figs, grapes, and barley thrived thanks to the valley's moderate climate and fertile soils. Mead predicted that, if the valley's surplus floodwaters were captured, stored, and diverted onto nearby arid lands, the area might again evolve into the Western Hemisphere's breadbasket.[9]

The OII's investigations in the Sacramento Valley caused tension with the USGS. The USGS's Hydrographic Division and the OII, organized in 1895 and 1898, respectively, often sparred over irrigation duties. The personal animosity between Newell and Mead intensified the institutional rivalry. For the USGS in the late 1890s, Newell supervised more than one hundred gauging stations on the Arkansas, Colorado, Columbia, Platte, Sacramento, San Joaquin, and upper Missouri Rivers, as well as the Rio Grande and various eastern waterways. He identified

Mead as an interloper whose agency duplicated the USGS's work, promoted states' water rights at the expense of the federal government, and sought to take over responsibilities for irrigating the West after 1902. In response, Mead criticized Newell as a dilettante who knew nothing about western soils, water rights, agricultural techniques, and siltation problems and who exaggerated the amount of irrigable public land in the western United States. When Congress in 1903 changed the OII's name to the Office of Irrigation and Drainage Investigations, Mead concluded that the USDA was the appropriate agency to drain southern and eastern wetlands. It was no wonder that the USGS scrambled to launch drainage ventures in northern California.[10]

USGS director Charles D. Walcott, Newell, and supervising engineer J. B. Lippincott touted the Sacramento Valley as a testing ground for "multiple-use" conservation, which was a holistic and comprehensive approach to managing the hydrological cycle. Fulfilling Progressive conservationists' rationalist and managerial worldview, the multiple-use philosophy envisioned equalizing the distribution of water on the earth's surface by building integrated water resource projects. According to the theory, the selective placement of forest reserves at river headwaters stabilized stream flow, moderated runoff, prevented soil erosion, and countered river sedimentation. In combination with forest reserves, storage reservoirs promised to sequester floodwaters, supply water for irrigation, and reduce the frequency and severity of floods. By minimizing seasonal overflows, storage reservoirs would theoretically starve the tule marshes of water and prepare them for settlement. The multiple-use idea also served a political function. As historian Donald J. Pisani argues, the USGS's Reclamation Service used the concept as an "advertising technique" and "weapon" to repudiate USACE's "levees-only" solution to flood control and to challenge their predominance in the development of western river basins. The Reclamation Service also resented that the USACE could improve rivers without charging local water users, especially since the Sacramento Valley by 1900 contained so little public land available for federal irrigation.[11]

The USGS and California State Board of Examiners agreed in 1903 to establish gauging stations on the Sacramento River watershed. Jointly funded by the USGS and the State of California, the work commenced under Lippincott's supervision. Lippincott's past experiences in California uniquely qualified him for the job. Born in Scranton, Pennsylvania, in 1864, he attended Dickinson College in Pennsylvania before moving to Kansas, where his father later became chancellor of the University of Kansas. In 1887, he graduated from the University of Kansas with a civil engineering degree and went to work for the Santa Fe railway. Two years later, he joined the USGS as a topographer in New Mexico and California. During his initial USGS stint, Lippincott acquainted himself with other young professional engineers, including Arthur P. Davis, the nephew of John Wesley Powell, the USGS director. After briefly leaving the agency in 1892, he returned in 1895 and became the chief hydrographer of California. In 1902, after the passage of the

Reclamation Act, he used his professional connections to secure an appointment as the Reclamation Service's supervising engineer for California. Under the 1903 cooperative agreement, Lippincott expanded the number of gauging stations on the Sacramento River to fifteen. By summer 1905, the stations monitored 82 percent of the Sacramento basin.[12]

The gauging program galvanized a partnership between the USGS and California's political class. In January 1905, S. G. Bennett, a USGS engineer, submitted a preliminary report on the progress of hydrographic investigations to California governor George C. Pardee, a leading Republican conservationist. Stream flow measurements indicated that 1.5 million acre-feet could be stored at upstream reservoirs for a total cost of $5.6 million (one acre-foot of water covers an acre to a depth of one foot). Favoring a multiple-use approach, Bennett promoted expanding forested areas in order to ensure "a more constant stream flow and lessen the liability of great floods." Forest reserves and storage reservoirs, he continued, also promoted navigation. "Even in years of low rainfall," he wrote, "[the flow] of the Sacramento River would be greater than that required for navigation and the irrigation of the entire valley." As Bennett explained, deepwater ships at one time could dock at Marysville, but the rapid accumulation of debris from destructive nineteenth-century hydraulic mining operations ended that. "In planning for irrigation," Bennett reported to the governor, the Reclamation Service "has kept in mind the possibilities of the navigability of the river. The economic importance of a navigable stream cannot be readily over-estimated" because waterborne transportation "regulate[d] the railroad rates to the market. . . . If these reservoirs were built under the 'Reclamation Act' and paid for in ten equal payments, the cost would be $0.363 per acre-foot per annum and the reservoirs would then become the property of the irrigators." In an article in *Forestry and Irrigation,* Lippincott boasted that the Sacramento Valley's annual runoff of 26 million acre-feet was enough water to cover the valley's entire floor to a depth of nine feet.[13]

Bennett's preliminary report represented an early example of the USGS's commitment to water imperialism—its goal of taking over the work of other agencies. California's congressional delegation applauded the agency's power grab and commitment to multiple-use planning. In January 1905, Rep. Theodore A. Bell, a one-term Democrat, introduced legislation authorizing the secretary of interior to "include swamp and overflowed lands in any [federal] irrigation project." "It is not my intention," Bell told the House Committee on Irrigation of Arid Lands, "to have the reclamation service branch out and go into the reclamation of swamp and overflow lands; but very often in these different [irrigation] projects the reclamation of swamp lands is incidental, and in some cases it may often become an integral part of an irrigation project, and will probably [be] so in the Sacramento Valley." Bell's legislation intended to bypass thorny constitutional issues associated with flood control and drainage by establishing a nexus among navigation, flood control, and wetlands drainage. Valley newspapers endorsed the prevailing ecological wisdom.

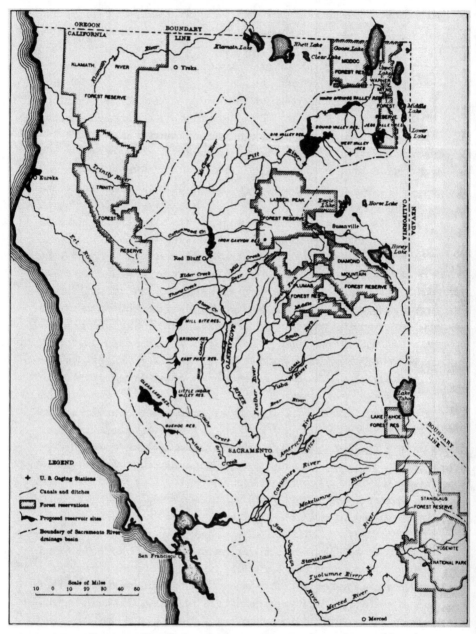

FIGURE 7.1. Sacramento River drainage basin, 1905. From *Fourth Annual Report of the Reclamation Service, 1904–1905* (Washington, DC: Government Printing Office, 1906).

In September 1905, editors of the *Oakland Tribune* expounded on the interrelation-ship: "When you have prevented the overflow of the Sacramento and its tributar-ies[,] you have reclaimed the overflow lands. Their swamp condition ceases as soon as the flood maximums receded." The *San Francisco Chronicle* editorialized that the federal government had "a duty in respect to the control of the Sacramento river[,] without which the reclamation of the swamp and overflowed lands of the valley is impossible." Unless navigation, flood control, and drainage were combined under a single program, the valley would never reach its agricultural potential.[14]

Sacramento Valley booster organizations were at first hesitant to embrace the USGS's water imperialism. Following disastrous flooding in 1904, a group of wealthy valley farmers, absentee landowners, bankers, and journalists organized the River Improvement and Drainage Association of California (RIDA). A powerful and well-connected lobbying organization, RIDA persuaded Governor Pardee to appoint a commission of prominent civil engineers, led by the USACE's Maj. T. G. Dabney, to study the valley's flooding problems. Wedded to USACE's levee-only approach, the Dabney commission recommended confining the entire Sacramento River between the levees in order to intensify the river's velocity and scour its bot-tom to a depth that would enable floodwaters to reach the sea without overflowing the riverbanks. RIDA applauded Dabney's report and asked the state legislature to establish an autonomous commission to coordinate levee construction. The costs of the project, the organization contended, should be evenly divided between the valley's landowners, the State of California, and the federal government. In March 1905, the legislature buckled under the political pressure and created the Sacra-mento Drainage District to oversee levee building in the Sacramento and lower San Joaquin Valleys. The enabling legislation required either California or Congress to put up the requisite funds before the district could become operational. Yet, since funding from Congress did not initially materialize, RIDA elicited support direct from USACE.[15]

On September 28, 1905, RIDA invited Secretary of War William Howard Taft to ride a boat up the Sacramento River. During the journey, RIDA's leaders cel-ebrated the valley's rich alluvial soils, healthy climate, and proximity to urban markets. Taft recognized the array of interconnected water problems that hindered intensive monoculture, but he rejected a role for USACE because its institutional culture emphasized levee building and navigation, not reclamation. "The matters of reclamation, of the prevention of floods and of the preservation of the depth of the channel," Taft told reporters, "are not under the war office at all." Although he hinted that the federal government had betrayed its constitutional duties by turning a blind eye to hydraulic mining practices that choked upstream tributaries with mining debris and disrupted navigation, he argued that federalism buffered flood control and drainage from a federal takeover. "It is a question," he concluded, of "how far the Government may go without taking up the work that belongs to the State or private owners."[16]

Spurned by Taft, RIDA in late November 1905 convened a meeting with nine California senators and Congress members at San Francisco's Palace Hotel. Among the most knowledgeable participants was Republican senator Frank P. Flint. Born in 1862 in Massachusetts, Flint and his family settled in San Francisco in 1869. After finishing public school, he moved to Los Angeles, served as a US marshal from 1888 to 1892, studied law, and took a position as US district attorney for the Southern District of California from 1897 to 1901. Elected to the Senate in 1905, Flint served a single term before returning to law practice. Nevertheless, his position as chair of the Committee on the Geological Survey in the 59th and 60th Congresses and close friendship with USGS director Walcott uniquely positioned him to influence the course of national drainage and flood control policies. At the Palace Hotel, Flint proposed three solutions to the Sacramento Valley's water problems: first, the construction of storage basins in the Sacramento's upper watersheds to reduce flooding and store water for irrigation; second, the reclamation of swamp and overflowed lands; and third, the removal of mining debris from the lower river's bed to improve navigation. Despite the advantages of pursuing all three courses of action at once, Flint doubted that Congress would ever appropriate money for projects that did not primarily promote navigation. Multiple-use planning was a noble but unattainable goal.[17]

Undeterred, hydraulic mining groups bypassed the USACE, dismissed constitutional scruples, and directly enlisted assistance from the USGS. In November 1905, the California Mining Association (CMA) convened its annual meeting at Nevada City. Committed to reviving hydraulic mining in the Sacramento and San Joaquin watersheds, the CMA concluded that the California Debris Commission, a federal agency created in 1893 to regulate new hydraulic mining operations and promote river navigation, was negligent in fulfilling its responsibilities. Rejecting the notion that hydraulic mining, farming, and navigation were incompatible, the CMA insisted that hydraulic mining, if properly regulated, *benefited* agriculture. In support of this assertion, the association cited the work of University of California professor Eugene W. Hilgard, a world renowned soil chemistry expert. Hilgard argued that fine mining debris particles, once evenly distributed over and tilled into the ground, enriched the soil. He urged that mining slickens be collected, stored, and used to fill the Sacramento Valley's "peaty tule lands." In a strongly worded resolution, the CMA cited Hilgard's dubious thesis when it implored the USGS to expand into wetlands drainage and resurrect northern California's stagnant hydraulic mining industry, which by 1908 annually produced only $1 million in gold revenue:

It was resolved that the President of the United States be urged to recommend to Congress that it take such action as shall extend the scope of the reclamation service of the United States Geological Survey so that it shall be confined no longer merely to the storage of flood waters and to the irrigation of arid lands, but that it may also include the reclamation of swamp and overflowed lands by the deposition of sediment upon them from sediment bearing streams in such manner as to reclaim them for the purpose of agriculture and enable the resumption, without injury to others, of that great industry of hydraulic mining, to which California owes so much, under conditions similar to those in force for the reclamation of arid lands.[18]

C. E. Grunsky and the Advent of a Second Reclamation Program

The CMA's resolution afforded the USGS and the Reclamation Service a cherished political opportunity. Eager to compete with rival agencies for power and funding, opportunistic water bureaus forged self-serving relationships with local booster organizations. Although USGS director Walcott never doubted his agency's authority to drain public swamps on western reclamation projects and he criticized Bell's 1905 legislation as unnecessary and superfluous, he asked consulting engineer C. E. Grunsky to study the CMA's petition and submit a report.

Walcott's selection of Grunsky was thoughtful and shrewd. Born in San Joaquin County in 1855, Grunsky studied at German universities in the 1870s and later received an engineering doctorate from New York's Rensselaer Polytechnic Institute. In 1878, he took a position as topographer on William H. Hall's river surveying party with the California State Engineering Department. Over the next decade, Grunsky stayed on with that department, specializing in irrigation and flood control, before entering private practice. In 1894, he teamed with San Francisco engineer Marsden Manson to write a brilliant, richly detailed, and seminal report about comprehensive flood control in the Sacramento Valley for the commissioner of public works. Continuing in private practice, Grunsky assisted Manson and in 1904 was appointed by Pres. Theodore Roosevelt to the Isthmian Canal Commission. A year later, Grunsky joined the Reclamation Service.[19]

In January 1906, Grunsky reported on the connection between the Sacramento Valley and federal drainage and flood control policy. In 1849, 1850, and 1860, Congress had passed "swampland" acts that ceded public "swamp and overflowed" lands to fifteen states on the condition that the states sell the lands and invest the revenue in building drainage projects. With few exceptions, the states—including California—blatantly violated the terms and the spirit of the law, selling or giving away the lands to speculators, railway corporations, and county governments. The legacy of failure led state legislatures to authorize local levee or drainage districts to incur bonded indebtedness in order to raise revenue for water projects. The results were unimpressive. Extensive tracts of unreclaimed wetlands and overflow lands, scattered throughout the United States, revealed the futility of localism. Like most Progressive era conservationists, Grunsky believed that uncoordinated, unfocused, and piecemeal efforts produced uneven results because levee districts engaged in counterproductive practices such as raising levees without regard for downstream communities. The Sacramento Valley was a case in point. "Harmonious action by the [valley's] landowners," Grunsky explained, "has in the past been out of the question, mainly due to the vastness of the areas which should be included in single drainage projects. [Farmers] who believe themselves favorably located prefer a partial protection, according to their own ideas and at their own expense, to a participation in one comprehensive project. Disasters have been so frequent under this system that efforts are being constantly put forth for relief." Localism was a colossal failure.[20]

The solution was the passage of a second reclamation act. As the intellectual architect of a federal drainage and flood control program, Grunsky argued that valley farmers needed to ally with other communities across the country to push through comprehensive legislation to free up money for wetlands reclamation and flood control, thus enabling the USGS to pursue multiple-use projects through separate funding sources. During an interview with San Francisco newspaper reporters, Grunsky bemoaned the scarcity of available money that forestalled the expansion of federal reclamation into wetlands. *Irrigation Age,* the foremost American irrigation periodical, reprinted the interview in April 1906 under the ominous title "Reclamation Fund Exhausted." Grunsky explained that the Reclamation Service had invested $28 million building irrigation projects encompassing six million acres, in thirteen states and three territories, which pushed the reclamation fund to the brink of insolvency. Unless Congress replenished the reclamation fund, the agency would be forced to scale back its ambitious mission of transforming uncultivated landscapes into sanctuaries for displaced factory workers, tenement dwellers, and immigrants. Grunsky was particularly troubled about the revenue shortfall's dire consequences for the Sacramento River valley. "Projects of the magnitude of that of the Sacramento valley, where drainage and irrigation might well be united in one great project," Grunsky concluded, "can not [*sic*] be undertaken in the near future unless Congress adds to the revolving fund which is now available for work."[21]

Grunsky's call for comprehensive reform fell on deaf ears. In early 1906, Republican representative Halvor Steenerson of Minnesota introduced legislation that deposited proceeds from the sale of Minnesota's public lands into a "Drainage Reclamation Fund" to be used by the secretary of interior to drain his state's public and ceded Indian wetlands. A few weeks later, North Dakota Republicans Henry C. Hansbrough and Asle Gronna introduced bills that redirected the next $1 million raised by their state's public land sales to draining wet prairie lands in the valley of the Red River of the North. In March, Democratic representative John Humphrey Small of North Carolina proposed transferring $3 million from the reclamation fund to drain the Dismal Swamp. Sen. Asbury Latimer of South Carolina intended to request reclamation fund loans to drain and clear his state's abandoned rice plantations if the other measures succeeded.[22]

Proposals to transfer money from irrigation to drainage invited intense opposition. First, western farmers, newspaper editors, and policy makers denounced reclamation fund "raids" because they jeopardized the completion of unfinished reclamation projects, redistributed public land proceeds outside of the West, threatened to lure home seekers to the Midwest and South, and delayed the diversification of the western economy. Second, Walcott opposed the measures because they interfered with unfinished reclamation projects, elevated the interests of some communities over others, and were too narrow in scope. Supporting Grunsky's call for a second reclamation act, Walcott concluded that "there was no apparent reason why one State should be selected from among those in which swampland reclamation is possible" when many states could participate in a broader program. Third, the General Land Office (GLO), the agency responsible for administering public swampland cessions, identified drainage as a local responsibility. In early 1906, GLO director W. A. Richards opposed any federal takeover because the Swamp Land Acts had already ceded 64 million acres of public swamp and overflowed wetlands to the states as drainage subsidies.[23]

The tepid response did not deter Senator Flint. Looking to curry favor with RIDA and CMA, promote the USGS's mission of water imperialism, and integrate irrigation and drainage planning, Flint in the spring of 1906 introduced twin bills seeking funding for the Sacramento Valley. An adept political tactician, Flint recognized that the interests of drainage and irrigation were irreconcilable as long as drainage diversions imperiled irrigation funding. Indeed, Governor Pardee, serving as president of the National Irrigation Congress during the summer, insisted that arid land reclamation was "much more important" than drainage and should not be "delayed or hampered" by diverting irrigation funds to southern drainage projects. The reclamation fund was off limits to southerners. As a result, Flint pursued money from independent sources. His first bill appropriated $200,000 from the general treasury for a federal agency, presumably the USGS, to conduct surveys and examinations to build "reclamation and irrigation works for the storage, diversion, and control of waters" in the San Joaquin and Sacramento River valleys. The second bill appropriated $5 million for the construction of a series of interconnected water projects in the two river valleys. Envisioning a federal-local partnership, this bill directed the USGS director to build irrigation, drainage, or flood control projects in the Sacramento and San Joaquin River valleys whenever three-fourths of the landowners of a tract formed a drainage or levee "association" under state law. At that point, the legislation empowered the USGS director to lend money to the association on the condition that landowners reimburse the government, in twenty annual installments, for the costs of building storage or drainage works.[24]

Because the USGS viewed the Sacramento Valley as a staging area for a broader drainage and flood control program, Walcott, Grunsky, and assistant USGS director H. C. Rizer extolled the virtues of Flint's proposal. "Questions of drainage, or land protection, of the improvement of the river channel, and the disposition of the debris from hydraulic mining," Walcott told the secretary of interior, were "essential features of any comprehensive system of development in these valleys[,] and additional legislation is therefore necessary for the construction of program works for reclamation." In recommending the swift approval of Flint's legislation, Grunsky argued that the importance of Flint's proposal transcended the Sacramento Valley. The bill constituted a "proper and wise" opportunity for the Reclamation Service to demonstrate that centralization offered a superior managerial and organizational form of organization than localism. According to Grunsky, it behooved Sacramento Valley residents to revive the grand cross-sectional alliance that contributed to the Reclamation Act's passage in order to attract political support for multiple-use projects in northern California.[25]

Establishing Tentative Alliances

Buoyed by the USGS's enthusiasm, Senator Flint traveled to Oklahoma City in late 1906 to attract support for a broader drainage and flood control proposal. From December 5 to 7, seventy-five people from seventeen states, local drainage associations, railroad corporations, the Reclamation Service, USDA, and various corporations congregated in Oklahoma City for the first national drainage convention. Organized by the Oklahoma City Chamber of Commerce, the convention got off to a rocky start. Thomas L. Cannon, the National Irrigation Association's (NIA) Saint Louis secretary, recommended making the reclamation fund available for irrigation and drainage projects in any state or territory. Delegates from the Reclamation Service harshly denounced the proposal, worked to secure its defeat, and rallied behind Flint's alternative proposal. Modeled after the Reclamation Act, his bill appropriated $2 million and retroactively, beginning on June 30, 1905, dedicated revenue generated by public land sales in nonwestern states to a "drainage fund." The legislation empowered the secretary of interior to build projects for "drainage or reclamation of swamp and overflowed lands" on public or ceded Indian lands. Settlers could receive up to 160 acres of land and were required to repay their share of construction costs in ten annual payments. Eager to unify the nation's water policy, delegates voted to approve Flint's bill and created the National Drainage Association (NDA) to lobby on behalf of its passage.[26]

California newspapers praised Flint's deliberative leadership. The *San Francisco Call* editorialized that his bill "touches California closely. This state has in the delta of the Sacramento and San Joaquin rivers the most fertile body of land to be found out of doors, which for want of reclamation suffers from overflow." Reducing floods and draining swamps was no less important to western communities than irrigating deserts. "The job of restraining the overflow is too big for private enterprise," the newspaper editors later concluded, so the job fell to Congress. The *Pacific Monthly* rallied westerners behind Flint. "While the bulk of the swamp lands are in the East and South," Ira E. Bennett lectured, "the West cannot afford to ignore the drainage question." Vast tracts of tule swamps near Oregon's Klamath Lake, North Dakota's prairie potholes, and especially the Sacramento Valley's inland sea repudiated the myth that the western environment was an uninterrupted desert. "The lower reaches of the Sacramento and San Joaquin," Bennett stated, "are reckoned among the richest lands of the world. Over $17,000,000 has been expended by the state, counties and individuals in associations in the attempt to control the flood waters of the two rivers and reclaim the lands. The money has been practically thrown away on account of the lack of any comprehensive plan of action." Academics also lent their support. S. Fortier, a professor in the University of California's Department of Irrigation, implored Congress to drain, collect, and then divert surface waters from the Sacramento Valley's floor onto adjoining arid lands. "The problem in California is not so much the need of irrigation as it is the question of drainage," Fortier insisted. "The [Sacramento and San Joaquin] valleys are full of pools of water, and the task before the engineer is to get rid of this water and use it to irrigate the sections that are in need of it."[27]

Unprecedented Sacramento Valley flooding in 1907 prompted Flint to redouble his efforts. From November 26 to 27, 1907, the NDA hosted the second national drainage convention in Baltimore, Maryland. Attended by hundreds of federal agency administrators, members of Congress, governors, entomologists, and mosquito control advocates, the convention aimed to overcome the provincialism that hindered comprehensive drainage planning. Southern and Californian politicians dominated the proceedings. Rep. Joseph Taylor Robinson, an Arkansas Democrat, complained that the legacy of plantation agriculture retarded southern drainage and floodplain reclamation because plantation owners had put slaves to work growing cash crops rather than building levees. Napoleon Bonaparte Broward, the Democratic governor of Florida and NDA president, insisted that his home state was incapable of draining the Everglades without federal assistance. South Carolina's Senator Latimer endorsed a second reclamation act as the best strategy for coordinating the resettlement of his state's abandoned rice fields. James Norris Gillett, the new governor of California (1907–11), read a paper supporting the federal government's drainage of his state's tule marshes. Recognizing the collective benefits of national drainage and flood control legislation, delegates endorsed Flint's national bill and demanded its immediate enactment. Due to Flint's tireless coalition building, Latimer boasted to the *Charlotte Observer* that the convention "g[o]t all of the friends of swamp drainage behind one bill."[28]

The daunting task of holding the fragile coalition together fell to Flint, Newell of the Reclamation Service, and Secretary of Interior James R. Garfield. Seeking to revive the bipartisan and transcontinental coalition that pushed through the Reclamation Act, Newell and Garfield in January 1908 invited a large contingent of southern Democrats to a meeting in the secretary of interior's office. Although conferees agreed that local reclamation efforts regularly ended in "confusion" and "delay," Flint's actions turned the January 25 meeting into a contentious, confrontational, and counterproductive affair. At his recommendation, Garfield requested that all of the attorneys form a special committee to write a bill capable of attracting bipartisan support. Latimer perceived the move as partisan brinkmanship. Flint's move "eliminated me as a layman from helping to revise the bill," Latimer confided to Broward. "They are determined to have the bill that passes the Senate go to the country as a [R]epublican measure." After the meeting adjourned on a sour note, Garfield called another meeting on February 1 and made several concessions to southern delegates. The bill that emerged from the negotiations retroactively dedicated, starting on June 30, 1901, the revenue generated by the sale of public lands in states not covered under the reclamation act (Alabama, Arkansas, Florida, Illinois, Indiana, Iowa, Louisiana, Michigan, Minnesota, Mississippi, Missouri, Ohio, and Wisconsin) to a "drainage fund" that the secretary of interior would use to reclaim public wetlands in any state. In order to solidify support from Alabama and North Carolina—states that had not authorized the creation of drainage districts or the sale of drainage bonds—conferees wrote two specific sections into the legislation. The fifth and sixth sections authorized the secretary of interior to purchase bonds or lend money to municipalities, drainage districts, levee districts, or corporations using the drainage fund. Pleased with the legislation's final form, Flint believed that the proposal cemented a transcontinental water resource alliance. He introduced the bill in the Senate on behalf of the Reclamation Service.[29]

In April 1908, the fateful moment arrived when the bill reached the Senate floor. Southern Democrats immediately assailed the proposal as an unbridled, unconstitutional, and unprecedented expansion of federal power. Georgia's Augustus O. Bacon lambasted section 5 of the bill as "one of the most stupendous and unlimited projects for emptying the Treasury that I have ever heard of." Alexander Clay, Georgia's junior senator, argued that the bill established a bad precedent by enlarging the powers of the federal government far beyond those conferred in the Reclamation Act of 1902: "the reclamation act did not contemplate that the Government funds should be utilized for the purpose of loaning money to private individuals to develop and reclaim their lands." James Clarke of Arkansas balked at the "manifestly unjust" method in which Flint's bill redistributed public land revenues. He bemoaned that the measure violated a respective legislative precedent by collecting public lands revenue in nonwestern states and, unlike the Reclamation Act, permitting the secretary of interior to initiate the construction of drainage projects in *any* locality. Concluding his remarks, Clarke asserted that the redistribution of southern public land revenues to the upper Midwest or the Sacramento Valley was unjust, inappropriate, and inconsistent with the spirit of federal conservation.[30]

Southern Democrats' unexpected opposition enraged Flint. Eager to salvage the fragile coalition, he angrily accused Bacon, Clay, and Clarke of obstructionism and naked partisanship. The California senator explained that southern policy makers had attended the Oklahoma and Baltimore drainage congresses, introduced several drainage measures, and participated in the conferences with Garfield. "It is my understanding that all the Southern States which had swamp and overflowed lands were represented at [Garfield's] conference, and that invitations had been sent to the Senators and Members of the House from those States, and that this bill was the result of the conference." In concluding his remarks, Flint lamented that, prior to the floor debate, "this bill met with the approval of practically all the senators on that side of the chamber." Last-minute efforts to revive the alliance proved futile. In late April, senators agreed to strip out sections 5 and 6 so that the legislation would apply only to public lands. At that point, Bacon floated an amendment to kill the bill, which was voted down by a party-line tally of 15 to 37. Nevertheless, Flint never called the amended bill up for another vote.[31]

Torrents and Transcontinental Cooperation

The rejection of Flint's bill delivered a temporary knockout to the Sacramento-Mississippi valley water resource alliance. Chronic problems with the western reclamation program and the election of Republican president William Howard Taft, a vigorous opponent of expanding federal reclamation into southern swamps and a harsh critic of the western irrigation program, eliminated any possibility that Congress would underwrite another public water works program. By early 1909, the Reclamation Service was in serious trouble because public land sales had not met expectations, construction costs exceeded initial estimates by a factor of six, migration from eastern cities failed to materialize, the price of private property on reclamation projects jumped 759 percent by 1913, and the reclamation fund was broke. In 1910, Congress was forced to authorize a $20 million bailout to rescue the faltering program. Furthermore, southern opposition to Flint's bill revealed that the Democrats' states' rights philosophy remained unwavering and uncompromising.[32]

It was left to former California attorney George H. Maxwell to piece the coalition back together. Maxwell had been involved in national water politics since the 1890s. In 1897, he had founded the NIA, a consortium of western railway corporations, social reformers, chambers of commerce, and politicians, to lobby on behalf of a federal irrigation program. While serving as a California irrigation district and water rights attorney during the 1890s, Maxwell grew to despise districts' corruption, injustice, greed, inefficiency, incompetence, and self-interestedness. As the NIA's leader and chief propagandist, he argued that the comprehensive reclamation of western deserts awaited the implementation of a vigorous federal program staffed by disinterested experts and scientists. The Reclamation Act of 1902 largely owed itself to Maxwell's tireless and adept consensus-building efforts. Although his power and influence waned as the Reclamation Service sputtered along, he reemerged in national water politics shortly after the defeat of Flint's drainage legislation.[33]

When massive flooding in 1907 submerged Pittsburgh's business and industrial districts, the city's chamber of commerce hired Maxwell as executive director of the Pittsburgh Flood Commission. Maxwell used his position of authority to spearhead a crusade against piecemeal, unfocused, and uncoordinated drainage and flood control efforts. By the early 1910s, Maxwell had endorsed Nevada senator Francis Newlands's proposal to create a permanent Inland Waterways Commission (IWC) to oversee and direct the planning of natural resource agencies. The systematic and coordinated development of water basins from their headwaters to outlets, including irrigation, hydropower, drainage, reforestation, and flood control, through an autonomous board of experts constituted the proposal's core objective. Rejecting the idea that levees alone reduced flooding, Maxwell championed building an ambitious chain of multiple-use projects in the Mississippi River watershed, from New Orleans to the headwaters of the Allegheny and Monongahela Rivers, whose confluence at Pittsburgh forms the Ohio River. On April 11, 1911, the Pittsburgh Chamber of Commerce formally asked Congress to adopt the IWC.[34]

A masterful coalition builder, Maxwell assembled a broad consensus in favor of Newlands's legislation. In early 1912, he spearheaded the organization of the Louisiana Reclamation Club (LRC). Funded by New Orleans land companies, real estate speculators, manufacturers, bankers, dredging companies, and rice millers, the LRC lobbied for the federally funded drainage of Louisiana's wetlands and flood control aid. According to Maxwell, "Floods in the Mississippi River must be prevented by irrigating millions of acres of arid lands from great flood water canals, and floods in the Ohio River must be prevented by the reservoir system advocated by the Flood Commission of Pittsburgh." In December 1911, the Louisiana Development Corporation (LDC), a consortium of southern real estate developers, orchestrated the breakup of the National Irrigation Congress into rival irrigation and drainage factions at the latter organization's annual meeting in Chicago. Since the passage of the Reclamation Act of 1902, the irrigation congresses had generally been supportive of federal drainage and flood control initiatives that did not imperil western irrigation funding. Benjamin Fowler, president of the Chicago Irrigation Congress, welcomed the breakup since the interests of drainage and irrigation "can never be satisfactorily merged." Soon thereafter, Louisianans formed the powerful and aggressive National Drainage Congress (NDC) to lobby for federal flood and drainage aid. Disturbed by the LDC's hostility toward western irrigation, Maxwell used the LRC to coordinate a rapprochement between southerners and westerners, whose support was crucial to securing the IWC's passage. "The West will work hand in hand in hearty co-operation with the South," he optimistically told Louisianans, "and if the West and South combined cannot get enough votes in congress to carry out [the IWC,] we all deserve to be submerged beneath the great Father of Waters (the Mississippi River)."[35]

Calamities on the Mississippi and Ohio Rivers lent urgency to Maxwell's crusade. In April 1912, catastrophic flooding on the lower Mississippi displaced thirty thousand people from their homes, ruined countless farms, disrupted navigation, and killed untold numbers of livestock. Additional flooding on the Ohio River throughout 1912 and January 1913 killed two thousand Americans and submerged much of Louisville and Cincinnati. The series of floods paved the way for a new era in water resource administration by breaking down the predominant states' rights philosophy in the Democratic South, eroding confidence in local government's ability to solve interstate water problems, awakening the public and eastern media outlets to flooding tragedies, and eliciting sympathy from newly elected Democratic president Woodrow Wilson. Unlike his predecessor, Wilson concluded that the federal government had a moral obligation to protect people and property from natural disasters. Writing in March 1913 to Edmund T. Perkins, chair of the NDC's executive committee, Wilson explained that "the calamity in Ohio and Indiana makes clearer than ever before the imperative and immediate necessity for a comprehensive and systematic plan for drainage and flood control. I earnestly hope that [the NDC's] deliberations may mark a long step forward in this direction." Significantly, the 1912–13 floods shifted the NDC's programmatic emphasis from drainage to flood control. This change was a crucial ideological shift. While federalism impeded Congress's authority to drain private wetlands, resistance to federal flood control initiatives faded as floods killed people and livestock, ruined private property, and disrupted waterborne commerce. Sensational media reports about the human suffering due to flooding captured the public's empathy far more readily than stories about wetlands' baneful impact on rural communities. Saving lives and protecting private property in populous major river basins now trumped transforming isolated swamps into farms.[36]

Sectional politics fortified support for comprehensive drainage and flood control legislation. Irritated by the inequitable distribution of public lands revenue for water projects, Southern Democrats conceded that their party's rigid states' rights philosophy widened the gap in federal water expenditures between the arid West and the rest of the United States. As torrents ravaged the Ohio and Mississippi River basins, Sen. John Sharp Williams, a Mississippi Democrat, revived Flint's abortive campaign for a second reclamation program. "I have a specific purpose in view," Williams told Secretary of Interior Walter L. Fisher in 1912. His goal, he wrote, was "the reclamation of swamp and overflowed lands as a counterpoise in appropriations to the immense sums which have been spent for irrigation." From 1912 to 1917, Williams introduced bills in every congressional session to create a swampland reclamation fund using public lands revenue from nonwestern states. Along with unprecedented flooding calamities, Congress's perceived favoritism toward irrigation was the catalyst for cross-sectional and bipartisan political cooperation in communities not primarily benefited by federal irrigation projects.[37]

In northern California, Sacramento booster organizations and landowners capitalized on the favorable political climate. Natural disasters and the tension between irrigation and drainage boosters constituted a more urgent catalyst for political mobilization than the USGS's limited agenda of institutional aggrandizement. Riding the wave of momentum, the San Francisco Call was pleased that the series of floods "directed public attention to the subject [of flooding]" and broadened interest in flooding beyond "riparian communities." Praising President Wilson's "cordial attitude" toward federal flood control aid, another northern California editor reminded southerners that "California is keenly interested in the adoption by the drainage congress of a policy broad enough to include the entire country." On July 5, 1913, California Republican George Perkins introduced a petition in the US Senate from the California legislature asking the federal government to appropriate money to carry out the so-called "Jackson Report." Written in August 1910 by Capt. Thomas H. Jackson, a young USACE engineer, the report compiled several years of stream flow measurements and hydrological investigations conducted by the California Debris Commission. The Jackson Report asked Congress to appropriate $11 million to launch the Sacramento Flood Control Project, a comprehensive flood control program including levees, bypasses, dredging, and channel improvements (with California and local landowners responsible for the remaining $22 million).[38]

When the NDC convened its 1913 annual meeting in Saint Louis, J. L. Craig, president of the Stockton (California) River Regulation Commission, secured a position on the NDC's prestigious Committee on Federal Action, which was responsible for cooperating with the secretary of interior and secretary of agriculture to draft a national flood control and drainage bill. Craig, the only member of the ten-person committee from the trans-Mississippi West, anticipated that any form of comprehensive flood control legislation would free up money to launch the Sacramento Flood Control Project. That summer, the Committee on Federal Action convened meetings with the Department of the Interior, USDA, USACE, and Forest Service that resulted in a prospective bill. Speaker of the House Champ Clark, a Democrat from Missouri, introduced the legislation on September 16. Rivaling Newlands's IWC legislation, the bill created a "flood protection and drainage fund" made up of public lands revenue collected from nonwestern states *as well as* Alaska since June 30, 1901, and provided an initial installment of $20 million from the general treasury. It empowered the secretary of interior to order examinations, select project locations, withdraw public lands, create the terms under which settlers could purchase reclaimed tracts (not exceeding 160 acres), and enter into contracts. Supporting the federal government's constitutional right to improve private lands, the NDC pointed out that many western reclamation projects included private property: the Garden City, Kansas, project encompassed 10,677 acres (all private); the Hondo project in New Mexico included 10,000 acres (all private except 240 acres); the Orland project in the Sacramento Valley covered 14,000 acres (all private except 200 acres); and the Strawberry valley project in Utah included 60,000 acres (all private). "If it is constitutional and right and good for the Government to reclaim private arid land," an NDC circular proclaimed, "it is just as constitutional, right, and good for it to reclaim private overflowed and swamp lands."[39]

Emboldened by the resurgence of political support, Maxwell went to an irrigation conference in Denver in 1914. Sixteen western governors attended the meeting, which was hosted by Secretary of Interior Franklin Lane. During the proceedings, Maxwell pushed through a resolution that called for the enactment of the IWC, which he claimed would provide $25 million for western river basin development. Nevertheless, his attendance triggered feelings of resentment. Wyoming Republican governor Joseph M. Carey, a former territorial delegate to Congress and one-term senator, attacked Maxwell on the conference's second day and urged his counterparts to reconsider the favorable resolution. Long-standing regional grievances fueled the governor's anger and skepticism:

I do not care how much money they spend for the drainage of these lands in the South, but I beg Mr. Maxwell not to inflict upon us the burden of saying that we have endorsed this great proposition and tangled up our reclamation business. . . . [T]he passage of this resolution through this convention last night was a great outrage on this western country. The river and harbor men did all they could to keep the reclamation act from getting through. Don't you know that during the last days of the McKinley Administration the late Thomas Carter stood on his feet and spoke day and day in the Senate to defeat the river and harbor bill because the river and harbor people would not let us have anything in the West. . . . I am for my country, I am for my State, I am for the States in this western country.

Like Carey, Utah governor William Spry denounced Maxwell as a pawn of the New Orleans business community. "I do not believe that this convention should be asked to wash the linen of any other part of the United States," he declared. The fresh wave of opposition led the convention, by a vote of 9–6, to table the resolution, a largely symbolic gesture revealing how sectionalism inhibited the rapprochement of western and southern communities.[40]

The alienation of western governors thrust the Sacramento and Mississippi valleys into a political union. Indeed, the fusing of the alliance occurred January 19–21, 1916, at the NDC's sixth annual meeting, held in Cairo, Illinois. The lineup of speakers was dominated by residents, public administrators, and drainage engineers from both valleys. Speakers articulated a common theme: the federal government had neglected both river basins to the detriment of progress, prosperity, navigation, and public health. Sacramento's V. S. McClatchy, president of the State Reclamation Board of California, a state agency created in 1911 to coordinate the work of the valley's forty-eight independent reclamation districts, argued that the Sacramento Valley's interrelated water resource problems and legacy of hydraulic mining made it uniquely qualified for federal assistance. "The Sacramento river, which is, in flood volume, the fourth greatest river in the United States," McClatchy emphasized, "is the greatest [flood control] project in being or in contemplation in the west and one of the greatest in the United States, involving an estimated cost of about $42,000,000." Federal flood control aid, he insisted, constituted a form of reparation payments intended to make up for Congress's "tolerance" of the nineteenth-century hydraulic mining industry, which intensified the frequency and severity of valley floods and compromised navigation. Spectacular local economic growth lent urgency to McClatchy's pleas. During the second decade of century, the Sacramento Valley witnessed heavy investment in private reclamation schemes (the number of reclaimed acres jumped from 300,000 in 1910 to 700,000 in 1918), soaring land prices (values tripled between 1910 and 1920), population growth, and a surge in rice cultivation (in 1910, a scant 160 acres were planted in rice, but six years later valley farmers produced 2.5 million sacks of rice, worth $5 million). Traffic on the Sacramento River skyrocketed. In 1910, the river carried 496,147 tons of freight, but, by 1918, that number had doubled, to 1,053,510 tons. According to McClatchy, it behooved Congress to maintain the economic momentum by appropriating money for levees, bypasses, and weirs.[41]

Mississippi River valley residents and boosters also blamed Congress's stubborn parsimony for recurrent flooding and substandard navigation. Furthermore, as NDC president Perkins lamented, swamplands and overflow tracts were "disease breeder[s]" that sickened and killed untold residents every year. Private enterprise was not up to the task and the interstate nature of flood control demanded federal oversight. In an unexpected turn of events, Newell, who had resigned the previous year from the Reclamation Service, provided the most vocal support for comprehensive flood control legislation. By the end of his directorship, Newell had concluded that the federal reclamation should have started with drainage in the southern United States and then proceeded to western irrigation as the program succeeded. He maintained that the reason arid lands reclamation preceded comprehensive flood control and drainage was that western communities, railways, and booster organizations had produced a "unified effort" to pass such legislation. The 1916 Cairo conference, in which the interests of Sacramento and Mississippi valley landowners merged, was evidence of the kind of "concerted action" needed to pass sweeping legislation. "It is obvious that little or nothing can be accomplished except by concerted action of this kind," he explained. "Where there is a diffusion of strength and lack of agreement upon details[,] it is impossible to accomplish large results."[42]

The Cairo meeting acted as a springboard for the Flood Control Act of 1917. In 1916, Republican representative Charles Curry of California and Democratic representative Benjamin Humphreys of Mississippi convinced Speaker Clark to create a new Flood Control Committee for the purpose of "regulating and controlling the flood waters of the country by all practical means through levees to prevent overflow, through arid land reclamation, through swamp land reclamation, through storage for water power and other purposes." After months of exhaustive testimony and lengthy hearings, the committee cobbled together a bill that appropriated $45 million for flood control from the mouth of the Ohio River to the mouth of the Mississippi River, at a rate of $10 million per year. It also provided $5.6 million for the construction of bypasses, levees, and weirs on the Sacramento River. Enacted on March 1, 1917, the Flood Control Act cemented the Sacramento-Mississippi valley alliance, expanded the federal government's authority over waterways beyond navigation, and symbolized localism's failure to solve basin-wide water resource problems. A new era in water resource management had dawned.[43]

In conclusion, the Sacramento-Mississippi valley alliance demonstrated that the nationalizing reforms of Progressive era conservationists ironically elevated localism, pork barrel politics, and cross-sectional vote trading above "efficiency" and centralized management. The political partnership originated in 1902 and was revived in late 1905 as part of the USGS's institutional strategy of self-aggrandizement and water imperialism. Cultivating and fostering such alliances, the agency intended to export its land reclamation program to southern swamps and floodplains after first draining the Sacramento Valley and establishing the superiority of multiple-use water development projects, yet funding never materialized. In 1908, federalism, Democrats' states' rights philosophy, sectional rivalries, and disagreements about the inequitable distribution of public lands revenue led to the defeat of Senator Flint's general drainage bill, causing the alliance to crumble. Nevertheless, catastrophic flooding in the lower Mississippi valley and Ohio River watershed in 1912–13, which, unlike the 1904 and 1907 Sacramento floods, stirred the public's imagination and captured national media attention, sealed the alliance. The series of floods elicited broad public sympathy for flood victims, broke down the states' rights philosophy in the Democratic South, and shifted the focus of booster organizations from wetlands drainage to flood control. This ideological reorientation symbolized more than a subtle evolution in the lexicon of federal water conservation. By 1917, policy makers and grass-roots activists from the Sacramento and Mississippi River valleys were proving more than willing to sacrifice the social engineering fantasies of Washington bureaucrats in order to secure federal flood control aid and redistribute money and power from desert communities to populous, flood-prone river basins. Preserving lives and promoting navigation finally eclipsed reclaiming swamps for farms.

CHAPTER 8

Both "Country Town"
and "Bustling Metropolis"

HOW BOOSTERISM, SUBURBS, AND
NARRATIVE HELPED SHAPE
SACRAMENTO'S IDENTITY AND
ENVIRONMENTAL SENSIBILITIES

Paul J. P. Sandul

In 1808, well before Sacramento became a diverse multicultural metropolis (the twenty-seventh largest in the nation) housing about 1.4 million people by the start of the twenty-first century, Spanish army officer Gabriel Moraga reached the site of Sacramento by trekking upstream along a big river. Moraga's horseback expedition had already spent two years exploring the California Central Valley for Europeans, despite the fact that the land had already been discovered, explored, and even settled by native Americans for thousands of years. As one local historian wrote, "The air was like champagne, and the Spaniards drank deep of it, drank in the beauty around them." Moraga then exclaimed, "*Es como el sagrado Sacramento!*" (This river is like the Holy Sacrament!). Thus the river, then the metropolis later hunkering on its banks, got its name. The naming of Sacramento, while reflective of Spanish culture and Catholicism, comes from seeing a natural resource as a blessing (one compared to the blood of Christ).[1] In fact, during the 1950s, Sacramento's chamber of commerce offered a booster pamphlet (*Sacramento Facts*) with the tagline "The Land the Lord Remembered."[2] Moraga and the chamber offer snapshots of a mind-set characterizing a view of the environment as simultaneously something to exploit and something in which to find deep personal meaning. These worldviews have driven and defined Sacramento's suburban growth and metropolitan makeup.

Sacramentans' perception of and relationship with the environment, and hence their willingness to alter it or not, are largely the result of sustained urban boosterism, suburban development, and local historical narratives that tout Sacramento and its suburbs as an agrarian and industrial paradise (the proverbial "machine in the garden"). Put differently, the massive transformation of the land that accompanied the development of a sprawling metropolis both came about because of and influenced Sacramentans' view of the environment and themselves. Such a view is not an organic phenomenon, however, but rather a narrative invention first crafted by Sacramento's boosters to reap profits and later legitimated by local historical narratives and spectacles. Ultimately, the original and subsequent publicity campaigns of Sacramento area boosters have had long-lasting consequences because they have effectively crafted a sense of place that informs the construction of local identity, that conditions and shapes the lives of those who live there, and that moderates behavior and beliefs.[3] The sense of place the boosters and others have crafted has mandated that the environment is a blessed resource—one that can be used, however. Such a narrative exposes an identity for Sacramento that is ensconced within the exceptional paragons of the rural and the suburban, the traditional and the modern. The actual process of suburbanization in Sacramento bears this out. The promotional literature, actual design, and subsequent histories of suburban housing subdivisions in Sacramento reveal the striking extent to which developers, real estate firms, and later suburbanites constructing local histories employed the language of Sacramento's early urban boosters and, ultimately, contributed to the overall commercial packaging of a metropolis—a branding that has helped shape how many in Sacramento view the environment and, likewise, themselves. These views of the environment and self then guide how Sacramentans interact with, shape, and treat the actual environment.

Suburbia and the Transformation of an Environment

Much of the narrative construction concerning Sacramento is a result of local boosters and developers appropriating the popular imagery of the rural and suburban ideals that romantics began to spread in the early to mid-nineteenth century. Famously extolling a "rural virtue" and lamenting the effects of industrialization, romantics contributed to an early and growing hostility to the city and a romanticized celebration of nature.[4] In this view, the city emblematized a menace and lacked the means to support a moral life. According to romantics, a home in the countryside provided families a safe, simple gathering place in an environment of natural surroundings far from the oppressive modes of city life. The image of picturesque cottages and villas in a bucolic landscape subsequently became a commodity eagerly consumed by middle-class Americans.[5] This rural (and suburban) antidote to a growing urban disease celebrated an agrarian past, linked an egalitarian republic with rural life (with or without agriculture), and represented a place for experiencing what it meant to be an American.[6]

The exploitation of nature and its resources as fuel for the engine of industrialization stood in seeming contrast—or a contributing cause thereof—to the rise of the rural and suburban ideals in the nineteenth century and beyond. Nature, in this scenario, while as sacred as any rural ideal because it provided necessary resources, lay subject to human will and domination. It could either be put to use and service, or it could be circumvented altogether. In either case, this worldview claims nature must always be subject to humans. Materials mined from the earth helped feed the machinery of industry; wilderness, at best, provided a pretty and proper place for a house and family or, at worst, had to be tamed and conquered. Thus, both metaphorical and, by World War II, literal bulldozers transformed much of the countryside. Suburbia proliferated, forests fell.[7]

The rural ideal and the exploitation of nature were essentially two sides of the same coin. The price was the commodification of nature. As historians of suburbia point out, the rural ideal gave rise to the suburban ideal and turned land and nature into commodities of real estate capitalism and speculation.[8] Some theorists have even said it saved capitalism as a viable economic system at the end of the nineteenth century.[9] The irony is that the rural ideal sowed the seeds of nature's further exploitation. Transforming sacred nature into a fetish commodity helped turn nature into an object of use, not an object of adoration and conservation. Certainly more recent conservation efforts, environmentalism, and a concern with the misuse of the environment (to a catastrophic degree) underlie nearly any discussion concerning sustainability and, historically, any movement to retard environmental degradation. The rural ideal, or, more accurately, the suburban ideal, along with a fabricated disposition to view nature as subservient to the needs of a modern industrial world, have deep roots and long histories.

Sacramento's boosters and local histories, all promoting rural and suburban ideals, have characterized and defined Sacramento's urban and suburban growth. They also help reveal how Sacramentans view their relationship with, and responsibility for, the environment within a historical context. In short, Sacramento's relationship with the environment is a historical creation, one deeply rooted in the suburbs, local boosterism, and purposeful history making. To understand better how Sacramentans have come to view the environment as a blessing is to understand the suburban side of Sacramento's growth. To better comprehend why Sacramentans embrace a rural-like image, even to the point of calling their city Cowtown, is, likewise, to realize the suburban side of the story. Further, in the other pages of this book are tales of Sacramento's alteration of the environment, sometimes to a depressing degree. To better appreciate how an environment that once featured vast wetland valleys of marshes, cattails, and other water plants became a testing ground for lunar rockets whose manufacturer let its by-products seep into the soil is to understand the suburbanization process in Sacramento. To ask "Where Have All the Flowers Gone," along with vast acres of grass, giant oaks, sycamores, cottonwoods, willows, and ash and why wild oats have all been replaced by "Little Boxes on the Hillside" is to ask about the suburban side of the story yet again. It is no surprise that prehistoric creatures such as mastodons, horses, camels, huge bears, wolves, and fearsome saber-toothed tigers are long gone, but also gone are the flocks of waterfowl that clouded the skies on the Pacific Flyway only a hundred or so years ago, as are the large herds of elk, deer, and antelope. Even the grizzlies are gone, except for the golden bear that still graces the state flag. Equally depressing is the depletion of salmon that, before Sacramentans altered the river system and built dams, annually had runs of 130,000.

Native Americans lived harmoniously on the land for centuries. As environmental historian Raymond F. Dasmann has written, "They did not become oriented toward slaughter or commercialization of wild animal life." When Europeans and Americans entered the regional picture in the 1800s, the "period of wildlife slaughter and commercialization began, which continued into the twentieth century."[10] Sacramentans straightening a river to eliminate a curve and actually proceeding in 1862 to raise the city itself because of devastating floods (in its floodplain townsite) prompted a Nevada correspondent to ask, "Did you ever hear of the dementia that possesses Sacramentans?" He added, "They are what is called grade crazy."[11] The untold damage of mining and dredging also took their toll, as evidenced today by acres of tailings lying in parks along the American River. Sacramento, to be sure, seems to suffer from multiple personality disorder at times. On the one hand, it builds water treatment plants, more dams, and powerhouse substations and kills off unthinkable amounts of wildlife and plant life. On the other hand, it imports camellias, a non-native plant, and, with more than one million bushes in bloom, hosts a Camellia Festival, while it destroys many acres of wetlands to build suburban tract housing and then plants trees in these same suburbs so as to gain the designation "Tree City USA."

Sacramento's exploding population, particularly from the days of '49 forward but especially since suburbanization began, has unquestionably taken an environmental toll: pollution, air quality, land devastation, and so on. While the suburban history of Sacramento does not offer the type of detailed explanation of exactly how these damaging changes occurred (as most of the chapters in this book do), it does offer an explanation of why these changes were even possible. It also reveals something about the cultural and environmental dimensions of identity construction. The suburban side of Sacramento's story explains how residents have come to see the environment in which they live. It goes a long way toward explaining Rachel Carson's famous assertion, "'The control of nature' is a phrase conceived in arrogance, born of the Neanderthal age of biology and philosophy, when it was supposed that nature exists for the convenience of man."[12]

Sacramento established itself as an "agriopolis." The city embraces a country town image and, despite all metropolitan signs otherwise, views itself as an arcadia, embracing "rural virtue." Here, the rural ideal, which is at the core of the suburban ideal, has compelling appeal. The rural (and, to an extent, suburban) ideal cast those living in such presumably wholesome places as "real Americans," the backbone of the Republic and that for which it stands. This view is the familiar agrarian orthodoxy of farmers as society's heroes, imbued with moral superiority, and this aura then is applied to all rural people (real or imagined, farmers or not—the majority are categorically not farmers).[13] Rural Americans, however, are also seen as "country bumpkins," an uneducated, backward electorate (and national embarrassment) that ensures America's continuous, and destructive, stagnancy ("poor white trash," "yokels," and "rustic ignoramuses," decried satirist H. L. Mencken).[14] But Sacramentans appropriated this negative view and converted it into an endearing, kinder image (or what singer Randy Travis called "A Better Class of Losers"). They see this image as a way to mark themselves as different and, thus, somehow special and hence better than the Golden State's other metropolises—Los Angeles, Oakland, San Diego, San Francisco, and, to an extent, San Jose. These cities represent the "city as menace" or what Thomas Jefferson, speaking critically of cities in general, condemned "as pestilential to the morals, the health, and the liberties of man."[15] Sacramento thus embraces an agrestic image. If one sees such an image negatively, as Mencken did, and one can, Sacramentans see their rural but urban metropolis as distinctly *not* Los Angeles, San Francisco, or any other "big city." They are better, more American, and superior, or so they say.

Packaging a Rural Image

A long history of boasting about Sacramento and its suburbs has led to a dominant image of Sacramento as a country-town metropolis. Dating from the nineteenth century, civic promotions that sought to attract investment, spur business growth, and sell real estate made good business sense. Promoters over the years sought to spread the word about Sacramento's special qualities (real or imagined). This "packaging of place" has attempted to distinguish Sacramento from other places in order to secure actual growth. Sacramento's promoters, often labeled a "growth machine," helped secure the construction of bridges, transportation routes, factories, schoolhouses, churches, and much more.[16] This infrastructure, for business and for culture, confirmed Sacramento's seat atop one of those places best able to support industry and the needs of an expanding population. Promoting Sacramento also called for more than material benefits, social institutions, or watering holes. Promoters throughout the nation, whether in big cities or rural oases, have long crafted stories about their respective places—to create a "sense of place." That is a part of packaging place.[17] Places are more than physical environments. They are also spaces experienced in art, books, local histories, music, photographs, and TV. Primarily using booster literature, history, and photographs, Sacramento's promoters publicized their metropolitan landscape to ensure that a steady stream of profit flowed, through real estate sales, flourishing trade, and the inmigration of people who simply had more money, by volume (if not real wealth), to spend locally.

Local chamber of commerce and history publications are some of the most effective promotional tools a community can muster. Such publications, often called "booster" materials, are by design intended to lure new residents and investment to the area. Chamber of commerce motivations for issuing such materials are obvious: businesses and political leaders together thrive on the steady infusion of capital (investment) and new consumers (migrants). Local history books do much the same. Specifically, they are a means of disseminating information about past achievements. Disregarding the wholesale deracination of native peoples, the murder of a natural landscape, and the brutality of exploiting minorities, workers, and women, local histories have panache and romance and make present-day locals feel good about past locals and, ergo, themselves. Past locals are cast as innovative, intelligent, and exceptional pioneer founders. Sacramentans, by remembering the city's founders, entrepreneurs, early commerce, and social institutions, designate themselves as benefactors for maintaining that tradition, even if invented, in the present, and subsequently broadcast that image to the outside world, affirming local histories as booster literature writ large.[18] So, whether the booster materials are chamber publications or local histories, what is so dynamic about them is that they provide a snapshot of the dominant narrative themes of a region. The ways in which chamber and local histories tout locales show, first, what the region's movers and shakers think is most persuasive and, second, what those elite locals think make their place a good place—what defines them by actually defining them.

Sacramento's booster literature has long sought to brand the city and to entice investment and migration by celebrating its gold rush past, idyllic environment, industry, and middle-class lifestyle.[19] One hundred years of such literature has collectively molded a dominant image of Sacramento, which, according to one 1980s booster pamphlet, is both "a country town" and "bustling metropolis."[20] Publications like *Visiting the Mother Lode of California* (a 1940 item referencing the gold rush from nearly a century earlier) have figured prominently in booster literature and histories. Such literature referenced tales of not only actual riches but also John Sutter, who established his famed fort in 1839 and then saw the riches pass him by (though he was still a pioneer in this story). There were also references to tales of noble but rugged mining life, like those told in author Bret Harte's "The Luck of Roaring Camp."[21] One could still make money digging for gold, according to the publicity, for as late as 1904 boosters bragged of gold output at nearly half a million dollars.[22] But while Sutter did not find himself awash in riches and few miners struck gold in the twentieth century, the real hardships of this past and this rough lifestyle were downplayed in favor of casting Sacramento's soil as productive. The "Valley of Sacramento is a garden and Sacramento is the 'urbs in horto' [city in a garden] of it," wrote the boosters in 1888. "It is our first glimpse of the celestial flowering kingdom of the Christian world."[23]

The packaging of Sacramento placed emphasis on the region's "natural advantages" and "natural resources." *The Good Earth That Is Sacramento's*, as one 1940s chamber publication awkwardly put it, had both sacred, bountiful soil and perfect climate, superior even to idyllic Italy's average temperature of 60 degrees

FIGURE 8.1. *Resources of Sacramento County, California,* pamphlet. Courtesy of the Center for Sacramento History, Eleanor McClatchy Collection.

and 220 clear days with its own average temperature of 61 degrees and 238 clear days.[24] Sacramento enjoyed low humidity but few droughts, and any worries about flood or fire were met with assurances about the newly built levees, secure buildings, and municipal services. Even better, the "world's garden valley" had a beguiling smell: "the prevailing breezes come laden with ozone from the sea, or bearing balsamic piney odors from the forests of the Sierra Nevada."[25] In reality, mining, smelters, intensive agriculture, and subdivisions in turn were destroying the Sierra Nevada forests and the Sacramento Valley landscape, but in the booster literature Sacramento still had "the richest portion" of the Golden State, where "the major part . . . favorably rank[ed] with the best land in the Union." While "fruit growing is California's greatest industry," according to the title of one chamber publication issued in 1904, the pamphlet's subtitle proclaimed that "Sacramento County is the very heart of its greatest production." Time and again, decade after decade, even century after century, Sacramento's promoters and local histories cast Sacramento as an agricultural empire, a virtual Edenic paradise where even Adam and Eve would feel at home. This is the type of packaging of place that, while prevalent throughout California and even the nation via the rural ideal, has characterized Sacramento.[26]

The flip side of the "country town" coin is Sacramento the "bustling metropolis." The two views, however, should not be considered mutually exclusive. Even agricultural endeavors, epitomized by horticulture (i.e., intensive, small-scale, cash-crop farming) or what the boosters called the "scientific modes of cultivation," were trumpeted for their rural virtues, with the farming life being described as "an art that demands a rare combination of qualities for perfect success."[27] Farming in Sacramento was a modernistic business and helped to prop up the metropolis, which, in turn, propped up agriculture with trade and transportation. According to *Sacramento County and Its Resources,* "When you see a man obtaining, every year, phenomenal conditions, he has intelligence, judgment, practical experience, energy, executive ability, and business sagacity. . . . A community of fruit growers is a community of able men—often cultured men—as different from a community of purely grain-growing farmers as can be."[28] Sacramento's natural advantages and resources, such as two rivers, supported and augmented Sacramento's agricultural proficiency on the one hand and helped establish the region as a large, growing, and prosperous business sector through perceptive business intelligence on the other. The same natural resources that made agriculture so successful also provided commercial advantages in a number of economic ventures. Agriculture spurred urbanization and metropolitan growth. Sacramento enjoyed the benefits of a "bustling" site of business, as the chamber of commerce itself suggested, but banks, retail trades, factories and mills, and manufacturing also benefited, and transportation improved as a result, with railroads and interurban transit, followed by good roads, bridges, and freeways. Sacramento was thus, as the titles of booster pamphlets proclaimed, *The Commercial Metropolis* and *The Hub of Western Industry.* The chamber and local historians produced a legion of works with their titles referencing *Industrial Facts* and the high *Business Barometer,* and they claimed that "panics and speculative excitement never disturb the people of the city."[29] These were smart people who enjoyed the best parts of two worlds: rural and urban, country town and bustling metropolis.[30]

Sacramento's agriculture and commercial strengths sustained a vibrant social culture, which, in turn, according to the boosters, contributed to further agricultural and commercial growth. Sacramento's boosters incessantly spotlighted the region's bucolic landscape, including a plethora of trees, flowers, and parks. Also, in keeping with the rhetoric of the suburban ideal, the boosters further claimed that a "displacement of the old for the modern" had taken place. The boosters bragged of Sacramento's urban amenities, high cultural life, and infrastructure to prove the area's modernity and "civilization."[31] They highlighted schools, churches, hospitals, fire and police departments, numerous clubs and organizations, hotels, libraries, an art gallery, post offices, the water supply, sewer system, transportation, and lighting and heating. Sacramento also had homes, especially suburban homes, with a republican, civic-minded family living inside. It was "a city of homes and flowers, the residence portion being embraced by choice foliage, and the streets well shaded." "As a rule," said the boosters, "present the home life and surroundings of a people to the intelligent stranger, and you give him the master key to their civilization and character, social state and conditions of thrift." So Sacramento had suburban homes in a modern, yet pastoral, landscape that featured urban amenities, traditional values, or, as the boosters said, "rural conservatism," good business, and an agricultural industry that could support men of intelligence or, because Sacramento was that good, men of "average intelligence."[32]

Agricultural Suburbs

Sacramento's suburban development and cultural activities carried on the rural rhetoric of urban boosters and helped further cement the image of the region as an agricultural wonderland. Beginning with the development of suburbs on the northern and northeastern fringes across the American River at the turn of the twentieth century and continuing with the construction of suburban tract housing and the production of historical narratives in the post–World War II era, Sacramento's boosters, developers, and local historians successfully crafted a narrative sense of place that casts the region and its people as rural and thus noble. In the process, Sacramentans' views of the environment and alteration of it resulted in, and simultaneously reinforced, the view of Sacramento as a rural nirvana to be used (and abused) as locals saw fit.

Suburbanization in Sacramento did not limit itself to the familiar process of outward growth, adding a sequence of tiers like rings on an onion. While Sacramento certainly did grow outward from its core, several of its earliest subdivisions began on the north and northeast fringe across the American River: Orangevale, Fair Oaks, Carmichael, North Sacramento, Rancho Del Paso, Citrus Heights, and Arcade Park. I have elsewhere argued that these suburbs, often called agricultural colonies, were agricultural suburbs, or what I label "agriburbs," a unique suburban type.[33]

Agriburbs were consciously planned, developed, and promoted based on the drive for profit in emerging agricultural markets at the turn of the twentieth century and were advertised as the perfect mix of rural and urban. Agriburbs evoked the myths of agrarian security and virtue: a life on a farm in an environment good for both soil and soul. Agriburbs were also ideally urbane but not urban because of their many amenities that represented cultural symbols of modernity: good roads, shade trees, parks, houses, churches, schools, local businesses, social clubs, and commuter transportation. Agriburbs in California were common at the turn of the twentieth century, particularly in southern California, with Ontario and other so-called agricultural colonies along the San Gabriel Mountains being prime examples.[34] Prominent California historian and journalist Carey McWilliams created a neologism for them, too: *rurban,* which he defined as "neither city nor country but everywhere a mixture of both." Historian Kevin Starr called the inhabitants "bourgeois horticulturalists."[35] Sacramento's agriburbs appealed to middle-class dreams of success in horticulture coinciding with, and contributing to, the general Sacramento booster image of the region as a bulwark of rural virtue and modern urban niceties. Concluded Orangevale's promoters, "There is one especially great advantage to Sacramentans in the opening up and development of these suburban tracts, and that is the facilities afforded business men for enjoying the comforts and privileges of country homes, without interference with their business interests."[36] They were, according to Arcade Park's promoters, "ideal suburban home sites."[37]

Orangevale initiated the agriburb movement in Sacramento in 1887, and following it were Fair Oaks in 1895, Carmichael in 1909, North Sacramento and Citrus Heights in 1910, and Arcade Park in 1911. The Rancho Del Paso Land Company had obtained its tract in 1891, but more vigorous development took place after the Sacramento Valley Colonization Company bought it in 1910. Each community grew, developed, and received promotion as a suburban subdivision at the turn of the twentieth century as speculators sought to build up the communities for sale and promote the emerging metropolis. Businessmen like Harris Weinstock and Valentine S. McClatchy promoted Orangevale, while the Chicago-based real estate firm Howard & Wilson began work in Fair Oaks. Hardware magnate Marshall Diggs was behind the North Sacramento Land Company that developed North Sacramento, O. A. Robertson worked on Rancho Del Paso, Trainor & Desmond Realty built Citrus Heights, Ben Leonard (who became president of the Sacramento Real Estate Board in 1929) developed Arcade Park, and local businessman and politician Daniel W. Carmichael was the force behind Carmichael (he also had a hand in Rancho Del Paso). The direct correlation between these suburbs and the general boosterism of Sacramento lies in the claims of urban boosters in various promotional materials. These suburbs served as corroborating evidence for the larger packaging of place. They represented the agricultural richness and profitability of the region and places good for home, family, and middle-class lifestyles. They were also speculative ventures designed to profit the developers.

While all of Sacramento's agriburbs deserve discussion, to be sure, Carmichael exemplifies the way in which agriburbs were developed and promoted in Sacramento in general. Daniel Carmichael established Carmichael after purchasing land in 1909. Like agriburb developers elsewhere, he promoted his colony in two major ways: as a farmer's paradise and as the ideal suburb. Both promotional ploys were a part of the broader publicity campaign for the Sacramento area. Carmichael belonged to the Sacramento growth machine apparatus that tied politicians, businessmen, and others together in the pursuit of growth and profits. With a real estate firm established in 1895, Carmichael had already served a stint as city treasurer beginning in 1885, and he became county treasurer in 1903. He joined respected, well-connected social organizations, such as the Masons, Odd Fellows, and the local Sutter Club, and participated in the chamber of commerce and the State Realty Foundation of California. From 1917 to 1919, Carmichael served as mayor of Sacramento. This résumé placed Carmichael side by side with Sacramento's most powerful businessmen and politicians, including Harris Weinstock, David Lubin, and the McClatchys from the *Bee*. Together, these men sought the continuous growth of Sacramento so as to reap profit. Subdivisions were one route to riches.[38]

With iconic images of California as a land of wealth already in place thanks to California boosterism generally and the efforts in Sacramento for several decades, Carmichael drew from a deep well. He advertised his "Big Real Estate Deal" as "so located that its crops are sure and the quality of its products . . . unsurpassed."[39] In this land of "beautiful scenery" and "magic fertility" adjacent to the American River and in the shadow of the Sierra Nevada, the Carmichael colony had "the

Not a single Orange, Lemon or Pomeloe grown in Carmichael Colony lost its sweetness, color or exquisite flavor because of an unexpected and unusual visit of the Frost King to

California

D. W. CARMICHAEL
of Sacramento
Founder of Carmichael Colony

❡ Not a penny's worth of damage was done to the beautiful semi-tropical gardens of this magnificent, prosperous and productive section of the Sacramento Valley. Carmichael Colony is so located that its crops are sure and the quality of its products are unsurpassed.

Nothing in the way of a freak Winter ever occurred here to cause the settlers on **Carmichael Colony** a single hour of worry or disappointment. **Carmichael Colony** is absolutely beyond experiment as a place on which to build a home and achieve independence and contentment. Others have done it; others are doing it; why not you?

Land in **Carmichael Colony** will be sold on easy terms. A perpetual water right goes with every purchase. We help you to succeed and we locate you amid the best neighbors in the world who will also take an interest in your success.

We guarantee every inch of land to which we give you title. We place you in a neighborhood on the edge of Sacramento City, where the water is excellent, the roads are modern, schools are the best, churches are available and the environment is first-class in every particular.

Cut out the attached coupon and mail it to-day. We will be pleased to send you a beautiful illustrated booklet on **Carmichael Colony** and give all information regarding this attractive and productive settlement in the Heart of California.

THE CARMICHAEL

CARMICHAEL COMPANY
SACRAMENTO, CAL.
I am interested in your Colony. Forward literature and information.

Name ....
Address ....
State ....

COLONY

SACRAMENTO
CALIFORNIA

FIGURE 8.2. Advertisement for Carmichael Colony. Courtesy of the Center for Sacramento History, City of Sacramento Collection.

most notable of all for climate, fertility and productiveness" in not only Sacramento but "the whole world, excepting the Valley of the Nile."[40] The developers of Citrus Heights were actually a bit tamer, as they boasted only of being the best in the entire West.[41] Carmichael portrayed his colony's land as the most profitable for fruit production, citing nearly everything able to grow under the California sun and even bragging that oranges ripened about two months before those of southern California, thus giving growers in Carmichael and the Sacramento Valley a competitive edge in the rush to market.[42]

The promotion of agriculture went with the packaging of middle-class life-styles and the image of Sacramento as a modern and cultured metropolis. Harvesting fruit in Carmichael or any other suburb on the fringe promised "a large income" that would allow "you a better home."[43] In Carmichael you could "build a home and achieve independence and contentment."[44] "Here are homes," Carmichael wrote in his promotional materials, "that equal those of the city's wealthiest class, homes sheltered by oaks and surrounded by orange, lemon and olive orchards, avenues lined with palm, walnut and fig trees, vivid green lawns bordered with a profusion of flowers, the year round."[45] Rancho Del Paso promoters simplified to a plainspoken call their appeal to those intent on having a suburban farm capable of quick production for market: "Secure a Home in Park View."[46] Fittingly, the Sacramento Suburban Fruit Lands Company also promoted portions of Rancho Del Paso, such as Rio Linda—what the developers called the "Most Progressive Suburb" of Sacramento.[47] Still, "the growing of oranges is a gentlemanly occupation and requires none of the drudgery attached to farm life," Carmichael wrote.[48] In this light, suburban farming morphed into a middle-class occupation requiring as much brainpower as brawn, returned a good profit, promised a good home in natural surroundings, and even promised "plenty of leisure" time for meandering in the woods, dipping toes in the river, frolicking with (or shooting) deer and geese, and jumping a commuter train or (eventually) driving a car to Sacramento to enjoy city shopping or cultural activities.[49]

Promising "good neighbors," or rather, "the best neighbors in the world who will also take an interest in your success," Carmichael and Sacramento's other promoters explicitly utilized the language of the suburban ideal as laid out by romantic suburban image makers of the nineteenth century like Catherine E. Beecher, Andrew Jackson Downing, and Frederick Law Olmsted.[50] Life amid orchards and trees did not mean "a sacrifice of urban conveniences, but their combination with the special charms and substantial advantages of rural conditions of life," wrote Olmsted.[51] As the chief promoter of the suburbia concept, Olmsted described "the demands of suburban life with reference to civilized refinement," such as good roads and businesses, and believed them "not to be . . . retrogression from but an advance upon those which are characteristic of town."[52] Carmichael and Sacramento's other agriburbs were thus places where "the roads are modern, schools are the best, churches are available and the environment is first-class in every particular."[53] Even North Sacramento's developers promised that "there will be broad walks, attractive avenues, boulevards centered with parks, children's playgrounds, semi-tropical shrubbery and floriculture that will provide exquisite harmony for the vision of those who love the beauties of nature."[54] Fair Oaks, too, offered "all the conveniences of a developed and settled community, in fine residences, water piped under pressure to the door, educational facilities, postal delivery, suburban communication with a large city, etc."[55] Churches spoke to the moral fortitude of the community, schools, to the intelligence, and businesses, to entrepreneurship and modern goods and services. Suburban developers cited post offices, newspapers, social clubs, libraries, local shopping, good roads, and easy transportation to Sacramento City. Carmichael said of his colony, as if channeling Thomas Jefferson, "The struggle and strife for daily bread will become a work of pleasure, away from the eternal grind and greed of the heartless city."[56]

One of the most astonishing outcomes of the agricultural boosterism and clearly one of the more amazing alterations to the natural world in Sacramento was the Natomas Consolidated Company's land reclamation project to build suburban farm homes (i.e., agriburbs) from 1907 to 1915. North of Sacramento, along the east side of the Sacramento River, and west of North Sacramento and Rancho Del Paso, the Natomas basin, formerly known as the American basin, was an overflow floodplain and wetland teeming with diverse plant and animal wildlife. Natomas Consolidated Company "reclaimed" the land from its natural state. Natomas Consolidated had a long history, under various corporate names and functions, of radically altering the natural landscape of Sacramento since its origins in 1851 as a mining, dredging, and irrigation enterprise. But to say the land was "reclaimed" is a serious misnomer. No actual claim to the land existed as far as human habitation is concerned. Humans never lost it and then had to reclaim it. Still, land reclamation essentially refers to the vast alteration of land (as well as beaches and waterfronts) for human use. Examples of reclaimed land include parts of New Orleans (built largely on a swamp), San Francisco's waterfront, Boston's Back Bay, Battery Park in Lower Manhattan, and many more from all around the globe. By draining wetlands, building levees, plowing earth, or using fill consisting of rocks and even garbage, reclamation often severely modifies the natural environment. Promoted as a means of preventing flooding, transforming a deteriorated environment into a productive one, or relieving population concentration in dense, land-hungry cities such as New York, reclamation has many champions. It also means the modification of natural ecosystems that took thousands to millions of years to evolve and stabilize, thus, among other things, regulating a region's climate, flooding, nutrient balance and cycling, water filtration, food and mineral supply, and soil formation. So what Mother Nature directed through complex evolutionary processes for millennia to best support life in a region, humans, possessed with a narrative conceit that nature should serve their needs, reclaimed in a few short years.

Natomas Consolidated ultimately formed two "reclamation districts," numbered 1000 and 1001, thus establishing more than fifty thousand acres of new farmland advertised as ideal for suburban living. By 1911, the company was promising the "redemption from flood" of seventy thousand acres of land (of which it owned fifty-four thousand) and the "colonization" of five thousand families who could profitably farm alfalfa, beans, corn, rice, tomatoes, and row crops in the rich soils of reclaimed river bottom lands.[57] Like Sacramento's other agriburb developers, Natomas boasted of the area's ideal climate, fertile soil, potential to return "big profits to the growers," commercial and commuter transportation to Sacramento, good roads, and the general enjoyment of "city as well as country advantages."[58] To pull this off, the company launched a massive construction of drainage ditches, canals and levees, and roads and railbeds.

Natomas's reclamation was the largest project of its kind to that date. Because older levees already dotted the landscape but had recently been breached by floods, work began in the northern section of the land area, known as the Bear River Garden Tract of district 1001. Teams of horses and a dragline excavator, an earth mover atop skids, worked to repair, strengthen, and raise older levees, create a new, two-mile long river channel, and build new levees. Clearing crews ripped up cottonwoods and willows, pulled (or burned) stumps, and cleared underbrush. This same type of work was also undertaken southward and involved a clamshell dredge, called Thor, which scooped sand from the river bottom and deposited it at breaks in the levees while older levees were again raised. Another divinely named clamshell dredge, Hercules (the largest clamshell in the world at the time), ripped through the southern portion as well. More earth was moved and more levees went up. More of the same activity took place in district 1000 farther south as dragline excavators did their jobs and levees rose and were filled by a 120-ton suction dredge operating at 300 revolutions per minute and driven by a then mighty 700-horsepower engine. Also, while stump-pulling equipment operated effectively, away from the river where no danger of ruining river-bottom soil existed, dynamite proved preferable. As work progressed, alfalfa was planted to prevent a second growth of underbrush, create a showcase area, and provide feed crops to reduce expenses. Similar work took place on the east side, away from the river. To put it all in perspective, the amount of material moved by two pieces of machinery in a one-month time span captures the alterations to the environment taking place. In September 1912, dragline excavator no. 1, operating twelve hours a day, moved more than thirty-eight thousand cubic yards of earth while dragline excavator no. 2, operating twenty-four hours a day, moved more than fifty-four thousand cubic yards. Also, in the Bear River Garden Tract (a small portion of the overall project), 159 acres were stumped, 219 acres cleared, 202 acres yarded, and 100 acres grubbed. Ultimately, thousands of acres were transformed, more levees were raised, and Natomas had completed its work by 1915.[59]

Natomas Consolidated, which went through corporate reorganization and financial difficulties, pulled out of the development, but not before creating new farmland advertised as further proof of Sacramento's overall agricultural, rural, and suburban potency. The Natomas basin did yield crops for many a farmer, but, by the 1980s, following the postwar growth taking place in Sacramento, as well as the construction of Arco Arena, the area, along with the rest of the agriburbs, grew tremendously and became booming suburban housing districts.

The Early Community Builders of Sacramento
and the Continued Packaging of Place

Sacramento's northern and northeastern outer tiers were not the only early suburban subdivisions. Sacramento's interior expanded outward as well, as subdivisions began near the city's downtown. Sacramento sprawled outward, primarily east and south at first, but then even farther east and south, then west past the Sacramento River in West Sacramento, and, then, thanks to more road, bridge, and freeway construction, out across the entire region following World War II. The familiar rhetoric of the suburban ideal, of a home featuring modern technologies beneath trees and with good transportation, continued the packaging of Sacramento to further brand the metropolis with the country-town image.

To be clear, not all of Sacramento's first suburbs were actually speculative subdivisions; some were enclaves of ethnic Chinese, Japanese, Italian, Portuguese, Croatian, and Filipino residents. At first glance, such ethnic enclaves, themselves really suburbs of type (i.e., working-class and nonwhite suburbs), do not seem to have resulted from, or contributed to, a narrative relationship with the environment. Yet, such suburbs actually came about in large part because of the Sacramento packaging of place that, explicitly at times, excluded immigrants and ethnic or racial minorities. Put differently, these suburbs existed not as a part of the packaging of place but as a consequence of it (because agrarian paradise was generally intended only for white residents). Because of overt racism and restrictive covenants, most new arrivals who were not white or of northern or western European heritage either found quarters in the fields surrounding Sacramento or were packed into the west side from the Capitol Park area, below Alkali Flat to the north (Sacramento's first residential suburb for wealthy whites), and to the Sacramento River. China Slough and "Japantown" are but two examples of this deplorable ghettoization. The gold rush brought approximately six hundred Chinese to Sacramento City by 1860, more than thirteen hundred by 1870, and a peak of nearly eighteen hundred by 1880 before the racist Chinese Exclusion Act went into effect. The Chinese settled near Sutter's Slough (soon called China Slough) along I Street from Second to Sixth and built homes, restaurants, entertainment facilities, and businesses (before Central Pacific filled in the slough and freeway construction shot it asunder). Few whites lived there, as many thought the area a health hazard. The area and I Street, as a levee road, suffered from flooding. Local citizens dumped their personal waste and dirty water into their Chinese neighbors' backyards. Japantown also sprang up on the west side, south of China Slough, running from about Second to Fifth Streets, and from L to O Streets. In its segregated existence, Japantown was self-sufficient and self-contained, and the area featured more than two hundred Japanese-owned enterprises, including pool halls, banks, hospitals, mutual aid societies, and an array of churches. Japanese and Portuguese residents also established themselves south of the Y Street levee into the Freeport, Pocket, Florin, and Elk Grove areas. Following passage of a 1924 law that restricted southeastern European and Asian immigration, an increased number of Mexican arrivals packed into the west end, as well as around Alkali Flat (no longer a neighborhood for the wealthy) near the rail yards and, of course, closer to the agriburb farms in the north where they often found work.[60]

Spreading mostly east and south, Sacramento's other early suburban subdivisions followed trolley lines and avoided the rivers. Trolleys (or promises thereof) were the focus of boisterous claims from Sacramento's developers promising modern amenities within their garden neighborhoods. Trolleys even went west and fed the rise of West Sacramento across the Sacramento River and, again, north across the American to feed places like Rio Linda and Elverta in the early twentieth century. In 1887, Oak Park began the era of Sacramento's outward expansion directly from the city's core, with other "streetcar suburbs," including Midtown, East Sacramento, Land Park, Curtis Park, Elmhurst, and Colonial Heights, developing immediately behind it.

In 1887, real estate speculator Edwin K. Alsip subdivided 230 acres southeast of downtown Sacramento and christened the area Oak Park because of the 8-acre oak grove in its center that also served as the terminus of the Central Street Railway (also owned by Alsip). Alsip employed the suburban rhetoric of the era and of Sacramento by announcing the "grandest auction sale ever held in California," the allure of paying no city taxes, commuter transportation to downtown, and guarantees of perfect soil, beautiful climate for health, and the potential to make a handsome income as a "gentleman" and farmer cultivating "semi-tropical fruits and the choicest plants of the floral world."[61] To further entice new residents and tourists to Oak Park, local streetcar owners, in a trend also seen nationally, opened an amusement park—Joyland—there in 1894. Still, despite the allure of paying no city taxes and of enjoying good times at Joyland, no taxes also meant no water or sewer services. Amid the panic of 1893, few settled in Oak Park. It did grow after 1900, as the economy healed and the low price of lots attracted the working class, African Americans, and Mexican Americans suffering restrictive covenants elsewhere in Sacramento.

The story in Midtown, immediately to Sacramento's east (running north and south from Boulevard Park to about Newton Booth), is much the same. Streetcars, like those on C Street and J Street, fueled residential expansion into the area by 1905. Trolley lines extended farther east, to East Sacramento by the 1910s, spurring development there and then to the southeast in Elmhurst and Colonial Heights. Directly south of downtown, trolleys and sprawl transformed farmland into the suburban utopias of Highland Park in 1887, Curtis Park in the early twentieth century, and Land Park by the 1920s. The suburban planners repeated the Sacramento packaging of place, casting areas like Highland Park as idyllic country estates that

FIGURE 8.3. Oak Park Addition advertisement, from the *Sacramento Union,* September 13, 1887. Courtesy of the Center for Sacramento History, City of Sacramento Collection.

offered "healthfulness" among "ornamental trees" on "wide streets" but with "all the privileges of the city"—transportation, cheap homes, and water service—"without the burden of their cost."[62]

Continuing to exemplify the packaging of Sacramento from the turn of the twentieth century to the turn of the twenty-first, Sacramento's suburbs sprang up as developers utilized the narrative of a perfect and beautiful land for suburbs. Following the era in which large developers purchased and marketed entire suburban developments, smaller real estate firms and construction companies had begun building specific housing tracts within these suburbs by the 1920s. They were not shy in using the Sacramento-as-Eden narrative. While many small developers, including J. C. Carly (Curtis Oaks, South Curtis Oaks, Colonial Acres, Homeland, and Casita), Charles E. DeCuir, and Frank E. Williams, actually operated in Sacramento at the turn of the century, none was as prolific as Wright & Kimbrough.[63] They were not only inexhaustible community builders but also masters of the Sacramento metropolitan and suburban narrative that has come to dominate the region and influence its environmental sensibilities.

A 1931 history of Sacramento boasted of Wright & Kimbrough that "no other single agency has contributed in so large a measure to the material development, improvement and upbuilding of Sacramento."[64] By 1930, the firm had subdivided thirty-three tracts and built 453 homes, financing about 2,500 more. Starting in the 1890s, Wright & Kimbrough included Charles E. Wright and Howard Kimbrough, followed by Alfred Gallaway Jr. and Wright's son, William C. Wright, by the 1920s, and then Charles's grandson, William P. Wright, by the late 1930s. (The firm still operates today as an insurance agency.) Over the years, the company developed a vast area of suburban housing tracts in and around Sacramento, from farm homes near downtown to Arden Park, Boulevard Park, College Tract in Land Park, East Sacramento (including the so-called Fabulous Forties), Gerber Court in Elmhurst, Lakeridge, Lake Hills Estates, Tahoe Park, and Willow Rancho.[65] The firm was also prominent in the Sacramento growth machine. For example, the eldest Wright, Charles, rubbed elbows with the Masons, Elks, and Odd Fellows, his son William served as president of the California Fair Board, and, finally, grandson William P. Wright helped establish and then served as a member of the Sacramento Housing Authority for nearly thirty years, from 1939 to 1967, with twenty years as president, and he belonged to the Elks and the local Sutter Club as well.[66]

Projects spanning each generation of the Wright & Kimbrough firm highlight their role as Sacramento suburban moguls and premier Sacramento image makers. Below the American River, north of Folsom Boulevard, and stretching from Watt to Alhambra, suburban development began in East Sacramento during the 1890s with trolley expansion. Wright & Kimbrough advertised East Sacramento in 1914 as a country-suburban tract "fifteen minute[s] . . . from downtown" with "choice homesites" (so choice that the large craftsman- and Victorian-style houses, predominating in the area that included Fortieth to Forty-Sixth Streets, led to the area becoming known later as the "Fabulous Forties").[67] Wright & Kimbrough also advertised cheap prices and good investment values and featured pictures of homes set back from a tree-lined street, with aerial drawings of the proposed lots amid roads laid out upon a grid (suggesting order and urbanity) surrounded by trees and the Sierra Nevada in the background (suggesting rurality).[68] In the

FIGURE 8.4. Wright & Kimbrough brochure for the College Tract development. Courtesy of the Center for Sacramento History, Melvin Spink Collection.

"Old Golf Links" tract adjacent to the Fabulous Forties, the name itself (i.e., "old") hinted at naturalness in a modern age that unremittingly saw the new replace the (romanticized) old.[69] By the 1920s, a longing for a bygone past swept a nation going through the growing pains of consumerism and ever newer technologies.[70] The golf links placed one upon a landscape of green grass and trees, even if not natural to the area. Nature was literally a playground.

In the 1930s, south of downtown Sacramento, Wright & Kimbrough offered "beautiful homes and gardens" in their College Tract in Land Park. Promising "scenic beauty" and the "finest schools," College Tract featured a park with golf links, proximity to a junior college (hence the name), "bridle paths and recreational grounds," transportation, the "Coolest spot in Sacramento on Summer days," "wise building restrictions" (likely racist restrictive covenants), "shade trees," "rich soil," "harmony and beauty in architecture," "a perfect environment outside in sunshine and fresh air," and favoritism from the new Federal Housing Authority loan program. The images splashed on the advertisements featured homes surrounded by trees and flora, manicured lawns, maps of orderly streets on a grid flowing out of a curvilinear center, and aerial drawings featuring a landscape of trees, rambles and parks, the Sacramento River, and downtown Sacramento close by.[71]

To the southeast of North Sacramento and Rancho Del Paso, between Watt and Eastern Avenues and Arden Way and Fair Oaks Boulevard, Wright & Kimbrough initiated the postwar sprawl in Sacramento in 1945 with Arden Park Vista (Now Arden Park). Formulaically (by now) citing good homes, superior architecture, amenities like schools, water, sewer, gas, nearby shopping, and good roads,

Wright & Kimbrough added under one section ("Country Living a Revelation") that this "unique rural community" offered a "healthier, happier way in the fresh air of the country and away from the noise and hazards of traffic." The developers continued, "Today a large number of families who are now city dwellers are looking forward to a permanent country home on a site which offers all the conveniences and utilities of the City." Once more images of trees, grid pattern roads mixed with curvilinear streets, groomed yards, and aerial drawings of a sylvan Shangri-la further promoted the dominant booster image of Sacramento as a country village for suburban homes.[72]

Postwar Sacramento and the Legacies of Local Boosterism

Like most of the nation, Sacramento experienced a postwar boom that featured population growth (aided by the McClellan and Mather airfields, the US Army Signal Corps depot, and a defense company, Aerojet) and suburban sprawl, primarily led by local builders like Wright & Kimbrough. Local builder Jere Strizek, for example, worked in the area surrounding McClellan (North Highlands). Manuel Jacinto built suburban homes near McClellan Field, Mather Field (Wherry Homes), North Sacramento, Fruitridge Vista, Roseville, and Folsom. The ranch-style houses of Larchmont Homes, courtesy Milton J. Brock & Sons, sprang up all over the city and its suburbs, while Mary Barden built suburbia in Sierra Oaks, Sierra Oaks Vista, South Land Park, and in College Tract. In the 1960s, builders like James and William Streng built Evergreen Estates on Winding Way near Auburn Boulevard, while Robert C. Powell and the Lincoln Parker firm built Greenhaven in the Pocket area south of downtown. After disco died, suburban home building from the 1980s to the present reached even farther out, though it also accompanied the population explosion in older suburbs like Fair Oaks, Orangevale, Citrus Heights, and Carmichael. It spread to the east: Antelope and areas around Roseville, Granite Bay, and Rocklin; to the northeast: Wineries Homes in northeastern Sacramento, El Dorado Hills, and Folsom; to the south: Laguna near Elk Grove, as well as North Natomas. Robert C. Powell continued work in the Pocket area, building the Riverlake gated community in the 1990s and developing planned communities like Serrano in El Dorado Hills.[73]

Like their predecessors, Sacramento's postwar suburban builders pushed their developments as idyllic homesites for those wishing to escape the urban jungle and settle in the suburban "countryside" without sacrificing nearby schools, shopping, jobs, easy transportation, and plenty of trees. In Sierra Oaks, a 1950s subdivision in Arden-Arcade directly east of California State University, Sacramento, and north of the American River, developers headlined an advertisement "Beautiful Country Homesites with City Conveniences," splashing their brochures' pages with pictures of large ranch-style houses surrounded by trees on curvilinear, but organized, streets. Powell's Greenhaven in the Pocket area in the 1960s, "the perfect place to live," centered on a park in which "tree-lined pathways will lead to school, shopping and recreation without ever crossing a street." In 1991, designer Peter Calthrope helped transform Laguna West (now part of Elk Grove) with a plan that called for "pedestrian pockets," a nature and riparian zone, and narrow streets lined with trees (also meant to slow traffic): "each house is to have two trees—there will be 20 species of disease- and drought- resistant trees, one species to each block." More recently, luxury real estate developers operating in Sacramento's more distant eastern El Dorado Hills, Serrano, and Cameron Park areas have enticed potential buyers with pictures of large, rustic-looking homes in rural landscapes with "breathtaking views of the Sierras," "equestrian friendly communities," shopping, commerce, and historic districts with "old town" centers.[74]

Population pressures sparked another phenomenon in Sacramento: the production of history. Historical societies, history books, and history-themed pageants sprang up around the city. The suburbs were no exception and, sometimes, led the way. What is significant about this explosion in historical remembering in the suburbs, however, is not that it occurred but rather what has been remembered. The legacies of Sacramento's boosterism—its consequences—can clearly be seen in what suburbanites choose to commemorate in their communities and not just in how they have decided to alter their environment. Still, with that said, it would be a gross error not to connect such historical remembering, often called "public memory" (i.e., public narratives about the past meant for popular consumption), with how Sacramentans have come to view their relationship with the environment.[75] Specifically, local history and historical remembering are, in fact, types of boosterism, as they are both an outcome of the packaging of place and a medium in which that packaging is further propagated. Put differently, looking at the ways in which suburban Sacramentans have remembered the past in the postwar era reveals the major extent to which the original urban and early suburban booster packaging of place pervades, and subsequently guides, the production of history in Sacramento. Again, such historical narratives are themselves booster materials helping to further shape, and legitimate by virtue of being authoritatively labeled "history," Sacramentans' relationship with, and understanding of, the environment.

Like the promotional narratives of the early urban boosters and suburban real estate developers in Sacramento, the dominant historical narrative concerning most Sacramento suburbs in the postwar era, including the fast-growing communities of Elk Grove and Roseville (so-called "supersuburbs"), is the celebration of agriculture and the rural ideal along with a celebration of innovation, modernity, and pioneer entrepreneurs as settlers, particularly impressive for rural-like communities at the turn of the twentieth century. This lionization of the rural, quintessential small-town past constitutes a dominant narrative that guides most attempts at remembering and representing the past in Sacramento's suburbs. These themes, originally set forth by Sacramento's promoters in the 1880s, have been repeated continuously in historical texts involving most Sacramento suburbs throughout their existence (but heightened by population pressures following World War II). In the process, these themes were further established and then given legitimacy and strength through repetition.[76]

Fair Oaks is emblematic of the type of historical remembering that is common in Sacramento's suburbs. Fair Oaks has been active in the (re)production of historical narratives. As the growth rate in Fair Oaks soared between 1960 and 1980 (with the population increasing from 1,622 to 22,602), residents published the most circulated and cited historical narrative (*Fair Oaks and San Juan Area Memories,* in 1960) and formed the most potent organization devoted to producing narratives concerning the past: the Fair Oaks Historical Society, in 1975.[77] Besides overseeing its History Center (a repository and museum), the society published a book, *Fair Oaks: The Early Years,* organized a walking tour, and updated the organization with collections management policies and training. It also created and maintained a vibrant website (www.fairoakshistory.org). The website's "History of Fair Oaks," the walking tour, and the "Old Homes of Fair Oaks" section in the society's newsletter (published online) reveal what the society considers "historical." In the "History of Fair Oaks," the community's "history," as with the walking tour and "Old Homes of Fair Oaks" newsletter piece, is distinctly limited in both time, roughly the 1890s to 1930s, and in scope—it is a celebration of agriculture, local pioneers, and early infrastructure and buildings. The "History of Fair Oaks" does begin with a sentence on the Maidu, who occupied the land "for at least 10,000 years we are told." While Maidu use of the land is acknowledged, it is trivialized by such a scant reference. The "History of Fair Oaks" is largely devoted to the "colonization" story, the establishment of farms, the construction of houses, and the creation of the "physical and cultural needs" of the community, such as a merchant store, churches, and schools. "History" ends with "a devastating freeze" that, in 1932, destroyed most of the crops and agricultural productivity in Fair Oaks. In other words, "History of Fair Oaks" portrays the suburb as a quaint semirural community steeped in a past of agriculture. There is little mention of nonrural or agricultural postwar life. The piece further works to cement the image of the Sacramento area as rural.[78]

The walking tour, which is a self-guided tour, and the "Old Homes of Fair Oaks" section of the newsletter also reveal a bit about what the society considers to be not only "historical" but also "architecture." For example, the walking tour consists of forty-seven "places of interest," all of which are located primarily, though not entirely, in the Fair Oaks "Village" area (renovated in the 1970s and 1980s to resemble a rural Dutch village). Sites include a cemetery, businesses, schools, churches, and houses. Noticeably absent is any potential site important to minorities, particularly those who picked crops in the fields, worked in packing sheds, and served in domestic roles. Admittedly, the society may not know of any sites. It is also likely that no such sites remain. Nevertheless, the society, through its walking tour, still managed to demarcate buildings, houses, and even a tennis court that are no longer there. It may seem striking that the walking tour memorializes a tennis court while no ethnoracial site, or even presence, is mentioned. Yet, when we consider the power of a dominant narrative that celebrates Fair Oaks and Sacramento as cutting edge in an otherwise rural landscape, the celebration of a departed tennis court is not at all that striking.[79]

The Consequences and Promises of Narrative

Sacramento's urban boosterism, suburban development, and public memory have helped construct a view of the region, and of the people living there, as rural-like despite the size of the city and the metropolitan character of it and its residents. Sacramentans, for their part, revel in this concept of themselves and their region. Being a "Cowtown," then, is not an epithet but a badge of honor. While other California areas like Los Angeles and San Francisco also share a rural past and have overtly celebrated agriculture and country living, they have also embraced other narratives over time, such as Los Angeles's role as the home of Hollywood or San Francisco's architecture and multicultural diversity. Sacramento thus embraces the rural image as a way to distinguish itself from places like Los Angeles and San Francisco, which are often portrayed as archetypes of the urban menace and thus presumably lack virtue and morals—that is, rural values.

The embrace of a rural, country town identity has been sustained by a pro-longed packaging of place. Boosters, developers, and local histories crafted an agrestic sense of place. This narrative image has come to dominate how Sacramentans view themselves, each other, their communities, and their relationship with the environment. The natural world, said the boosters and local histories, was both a unique blessing of the Lord and one that could be altered however humans saw fit (another blessing). So Sacramentans saw no irony when they plowed earth, reclaimed land, bulldozed farms, altered rivers, or built dams. It was their blessing and their heritage. Similar to how historian William Deverell explained the power of historical narrative in Los Angeles, one can say that Sacramento "is not so much a city that got what it wished for. It is a city that wished for what it worked diligently to invent."[80] Put differently, narrative construction has a real power to affect.

As early as 1873, the Italian geologist Antonio Stoppani acknowledged the increasing power and impact of humanity on the earth and referred to the "anthropozoic era." By 2000, scientists, including the Nobel Prize–winning Paul J. Crutzen, were using the term "Anthropocene": the age of man.[81] Certainly what geologists and other scientists choose to call a period of the earth's history matters little to the rest of humankind—unless it is to go snack on buttered popcorn and watch *Jurassic Park*. But the Anthropocene seems different. It is a moment much like when Copernicus realized the earth revolved around the sun, Newton comprehended gravity, or when Darwin grasped evolution by natural selection and changed how many people looked at the world. More than a call to rewrite the books, then, this discovery is a call to change humankind's relationship with the earth.[82] Humans have had so great an impact on the natural processes of the world's environment that we now get our own geological age to celebrate the damned occasion.

Sacramento's relationship with and view of the environment are a narrative construction. The way that Sacramentans, as well as many in the world today, view the environment, make decisions to alter it, or even unconsciously look away or even deny a problem exists is not an organic phenomenon. Neither is the narrative image of Sacramento as a rural paradise. These things are creations. A narrative that nature is subject to humankind's dominance has a long history. That we now live in the Anthropocene makes it a deplorable scientific fact. The redeeming thing about narrative, however, is that it can be challenged and, often ideally, changed.

Rather than being a force of ruinous environmental damage in the age of humans, Sacramentans can heed empirical science, recognize the narrative construction of their relationship with the environment as a historical phenomenon, and seek to remake their narrative relationship with the land no matter what any politician or talking head on television or radio says to the contrary. As seen with Sacramento's history, narrative is not only something written after the fact; it can also be self-fulfilling. So Sacramentans can choose to write a new narrative. Embracing a so-called rural virtue, reveling in an arcadian country image, and viewing nature as a blessing of the Lord can be fine narratives, but they should not come at the expense of nature. They should not cost us a livable world. Finding a new narrative, both in Sacramento and throughout the rest of the world, is imperative. Unsatisfactorily, no consensus exists for what a new narrative could actually be. With that said, scientists, psychologists, and many others have revealed how narrative construction is a peculiarly human way of doing things.[83] Moreover, human beings have evolved over thousands of years to possess a creative and critical intelligence the likes of which the planet has never seen. Sacramentans can thus choose to create a different narrative. It would be a very human thing to do. So as humankind has tipped the planet into instability, humankind can tip it back to stability.

PART III

Government Town

CHAPTER 9   Unseen Investment

NEW DEAL SACRAMENTO

Gray Brechin and Lee M. A. Simpson

In a letter published in the *Fresno Bee* on May 19, 1940, W. H. McConnell of the small Central Valley town of Parlier urged others not to take their city parks for granted: "No doubt few of us know how much the young children, tired mothers, and older men seen daily in the city parks and playgrounds enjoy what the New Deal under President Roosevelt has made possible. . . . Few realize what the [Works Progress Administration, or WPA] through the recreation department is trying to do and has done in establishing park playgrounds for children. Show your appreciation by paying the parks a visit and remember a beautiful park is a drawing card for visitors and one of the outstanding assets of a community."[1]

The ingratitude or lack of awareness of which McConnell spoke remains truer today than when he wrote his letter to the *Bee,* for at that time WPA signs identified the innumerable public works that—along with those of the Public Works Administration (PWA) and Civilian Conservation Corps (CCC)—were so rapidly vaulting California's Central Valley, as well as the rest of the nation, from the nineteenth into the twentieth century in order to combat the Great Depression.[2] McConnell echoed on a local level what Interior Secretary Harold Ickes had so recently told a crowd gathered for the groundbreaking of Friant Dam on the San Joaquin River above Fresno: "I wonder if the people of California have not come to take the Federal Government too much for granted. . . . Even those of us in Washington who are responsible for carrying out orders sometimes lack comprehension of the mighty sweep of this program. It may safely be said that no Administration in our history, perhaps even no two or three Administrations, has wrought in our land physical improvements comparable in worth, variety, and magnitude to those that have been and are being done under the present one."[3]

President Franklin D. Roosevelt's public works agencies left relatively few permanent markers: once the construction signs came down and workers mobilized for World War II, amnesia about what they had done quickly set in and flourished with succeeding generations. No one after the war undertook the task of inventorying the vast "worth, variety, and magnitude" of those public works. After decades of drumbeat insistence by neoliberals and libertarians that government's inherent inefficiency and venality only squanders tax revenues, far fewer citizens realize that they are living among and daily using public investments that have paid back dividends for nearly eighty years. Indeed, much of their health, safety, and enjoyment depend upon those projects.

Relics of the New Deal abound in California's capital city, as they do in Sacramento County and beyond. Their memory is fragmentally preserved in WPA and PWA microfilm, in yellowing scrapbooks and archival photographs, and in newspaper articles only partially indexed by clerical workers employed by the WPA. For those unwilling or unable to access these paper records, however, many of the remnants of this massive public works program remain in plain view. For Sacramentans, the Tower Bridge, McClellan Park, Sacramento City College, McClatchy and Grant High Schools, and a number of prominent water towers, all used daily by hundreds of visitors and residents today, are more than relics of the past. They stand in open testament to the continuing legacy of the New Deal.

Sacramento and the Great Depression

Just as the New Deal transformed the Sacramento landscape, so too did the early effects of the Great Depression. Less than a year after the October 1929 stock market crash, unemployment and homelessness began to stress the ability of the city to house its population. While new transient encampments sprang up along the American and Sacramento Rivers, new residential construction in the city's suburbs came to a near standstill. Perhaps no district felt the stress more than the city's historic West End, as it spiraled into a stagnant skid row that would not recover for nearly forty years.

Unemployment hit all of Sacramento's major employers: the agricultural sector, railroads, and government. Seasonal cannery workers were some of the first to lose their jobs, as demand for canned goods plummeted in 1930. The industry faced further decline in the winter of 1932, when a hard freeze destroyed the local citrus crop, bringing an end to Sacramento's dreams of being a northern citrus empire and rival to southern California. The freeze also affected the growth model for the suburbs of Fair Oaks, Orangevale, and Citrus Heights, all of which predicated their growth on the development of small horticultural properties engaged in the propagation of citrus.[4]

Unemployment spread quickly throughout the population. By 1931, workers at the city's two major rail yards were experiencing massive layoffs and reduced work weeks. As a result of unemployment, tax revenues began a precipitate decline and government employees at all levels were forced to accept delayed pay warrants and layoffs. Local unemployment intensified when a large transient population arrived to seek work in California's agricultural sector. By 1932, there were some twenty-seven thousand unemployed workers in Sacramento. Unable to afford housing, about four hundred of these unemployed persons ended up in a squalid Hooverville shantytown below the levees north of Sacramento's downtown.[5] By 1935, that population had grown to nearly three thousand, spread among a series of Hoovervilles mostly along the railroad tracks and along the American River.[6]

The size and duration of these homeless encampments led several of them to become identifiable communities. Reflecting the unsanitary and unhygienic conditions of the camps, they took on such monikers as Skunk Hollow and Rattlesnake District. In the Alkali Flat neighborhood, a Hooverville built near the city incinerator took on the name of Shooksville after its unofficial "mayor," Samuel Shooks. Shooksville served as home to nearly one thousand persons, from all races, age groups, and nationalities. Living among the city's refuse, from which transients scavenged food and reusable junk, residents contended with rodents, flies, and other assorted vermin drawn to the rotting garbage. The health risks would add to the pressures already straining state and local resources.[7]

Like most cities across the nation, Sacramento was unprepared to respond to the depth and duration of the economic downturn. Historically, city leaders embraced laissez-faire policies, turning a blind eye to vice and relying on charitable organizations such as the Salvation Army and the Community Chest to provide for the city's poor. Lacking a strong mayor, the city government vested the only real power in the city manager, local architect James S. Dean. With no city agencies to oversee relief, Dean had few options for responding to the crisis. Following the lead of President Herbert Hoover, city leaders in both government and the private sector sought to end the crisis by seeking to curb the "psychology" of the depression. They followed Hoover's fear of deficit spending and, lacking a strong revenue base, were unable or unwilling to initiate the local public works projects that Hoover championed as a means of generating employment.[8]

The inadequacies of private initiatives for dealing with poverty soon manifested themselves on the landscape, as an increasing number of families joined the single men looking for shelter in the city's dilapidated West End. In November 1930, the Community Chest, the traditional source of poor relief, announced it was $32,000 short of its fundraising goal. Donations failed to rebound, and, by 1932, the appeal fell short by a staggering $100,000. At the same time, the number of families seeking relief continued to rise. In only a brief month, from December 1931 to January 1932, the number of such families grew from 495 to 1,011. Running out of money in May 1932, the Community Chest turned over all of its cases to the county. Facing the same budget shortfalls as the city, the county proved no more able to provide relief to the homeless than the private sector, and the West End continued its downward slide.[9]

A New Deal for Sacramento

Although traditionally a Republican stronghold, the Central Valley in 1932 voted strongly for presidential candidate Franklin Roosevelt, by a margin of 82,000 to President Hoover's 33,000. Voters did so at the urging of the McClatchy family newspapers in Sacramento, Modesto, and Fresno, as well as because of the catastrophic decline in farm prices that cascaded through the local economy even as migrants from the Dust Bowl poured in, seeking often nonexistent work while Central Valley banks collapsed. Although a grandiose new post office building funded by Hoover's Reconstruction Finance Corporation pumped $1.3 million in federal money into the city's economy as part of Hoover's last-ditch effort to buoy a foundering economy, it—like his other public works—was too little and too late to save his own popularity and administration. The Roosevelt landslide of 1932 came as little surprise to the people of Sacramento.

Franklin Roosevelt first coined the term "New Deal" in his 1932 nomination address. While the speech did not lay out a specific plan for what this new deal would include, Roosevelt clearly expressed a vision of a massive public works program "as a further emergency means of stimulating employment." But, he continued, this would not be a scattered and random program of building; it must serve the public good. "[N]o economic end is served if we merely build without building for a necessary purpose," Roosevelt argued. "Such works . . . should insofar as possible be self-sustaining if they are to be financed by the issue of bonds."[10]

Once in office the new Roosevelt administration sought to turn the rhetoric of the campaign trail into a cohesive and effective program. That spring, a solidly Democratic Congress appropriated a staggering $3.3 billion (about $55 billion in 2012) to the Public Works Administration for grants and loans to contractors for construction projects. Across the nation, between 1933 and 1938, the PWA alone ultimately financed 15,976 federal and 10,498 state projects, erecting 17,300 buildings, "of which 2,200 were accessory to projects for sewers, gas, power, and water supply."[11]

PWA secretary Harold Ickes, however, was slow to initiate expenditures of PWA monies, so Roosevelt created a new work relief agency by executive order on November 8, 1933, to provide emergency jobs during the winter. His choice of social worker Harry Hopkins to head the Civil Works Administration (CWA) proved astute: within a month, Hopkins put two million of the jobless to work doing everything from digging ditches to painting murals and teaching in rural school districts. He more than doubled that figure in two months.[12]

The CWA speedily pumped into Sacramento County $355,000, a sum that in two months exceeded county relief for two years.[13] In Sacramento, CWA workers painted and repaired buildings and parks throughout the city. They constructed a $4,000 dog pound at Front and U Streets. County Executive Charles W. Deterding visited CWA regional headquarters in San Francisco to get funds needed to employ one thousand men to grade roads and sidewalks in the developing Rancho Del Paso district north of the capital city.[14] Relief workers improved the municipal airport, paved roads throughout the county, and conducted extensive mosquito abatement. A CWA grant and private subscriptions erected a concrete art deco stage and bandstand still in use in Southside Park.[15]

Having helped millions survive the winter of 1933–34, the CWA came to an end on March 31. The depression had not, however, so slightly more than a year later, on April 8, 1935, Roosevelt created the more famous Works Progress Administration with funds provided by the Emergency Relief Appropriation Act of 1935. He again put Hopkins in charge of a vast and varied work relief program that, before its termination in 1942, provided more than eight million people with jobs.

Together, the WPA and PWA transformed the Central Valley, its cities, and towns. In just the four years between July 1935 and 1939, it invested nearly $8 million in the Sacramento Valley. By September 30, 1938, it had spent $3,355,658 in Sacramento County alone, more than four times what local sponsors contributed.[16] Although reactionaries opposed the WPA on principle as socialism or worse, they often welcomed the improvements it brought to their own communities.[17] City Manager James S. Dean spoke of the multiplier effect the federal money had had on the local economy when he said that "with these New Deal activities have come reductions of delinquencies, an upswing of real estate prices, and a huge building campaign of private homes made possible by New Deal legislation reducing interest rates and encouraging home building."[18]

Harry Hopkins again wasted no time putting people to work at jobs that benefited the Sacramento Valley and Sierra foothills. Sacramento saw the first WPA project in California initiated by a nonfederal sponsor when twenty-two men paved the city's corporation yard.[19] By June 1936, the director of district 2 had reported that single transient and homeless men mostly over the age of fifty had "in less than five months . . . completed a $213,625 building and construction program for the state divisions of fish and game and forestry" that included "the largest bass-rearing plant in the world" at Elk Grove, south of Sacramento. They had built modern houses, offices, and maintenance buildings for the State Division of Forestry at Nevada City, Shady Creek, Auburn, Colfax, Camino, and Garden Valley, as well as at Davis. Most remain in use, though no markers identify them as WPA projects.[20]

An article published in the *Sacramento Bee* toward the end of 1940 gave a sketchy idea of what the WPA had done for Sacramento County in the five years since the program's creation.[21] It had constructed much of the California State Fairgrounds, giving the facility fourteen new exhibit and administration buildings, grandstand improvements, landscaping, roads, and water and electrical infrastructure. WPA workers had graded and paved 322 miles of highways and streets, including 183 miles of all-weather rural roads permitting farmers to get their produce speedily to market. Its workers built forty-six new public buildings and improved seventeen, of which ten were schools. It drained almost 40,000 acres of wetlands, built a new

FIGURE 9.1. Steel girders, erected in 1933 with a federal appropriation of $216,598 and a local contribution of $133,402, continue to support the I Street Bridge and the Jibboom Street Viaduct near Old Sacramento. Photograph by Lee M. A. Simpson.

pumping station and water treatment plant in Sacramento, constructed thirteen school playgrounds, and improved the county park swimming pool in Elk Grove.

WPA records transferred to microfilm after World War II provide a finer-grained but by no means complete picture of what the agency accomplished in Sacramento County. They specifically mention improvements and new school buildings at Antelope, Fair Oaks, and Franklin, but one card dated March 9, 1938, simply says that the sum of thirty-three thousand dollars was allotted to reconstruct and improve buildings and grounds at public schools throughout Sacramento County.

While WPA projects paid workers directly, those of the PWA did so through contractors allotted grants and loans channeled through Secretary Ickes's Interior Department. The former projects—focused on the welfare of often unskilled workers and the provision of a maximum number of jobs—tended to be more modest. Ickes intended the latter agency to stimulate the economy by putting the construction industry back into good health. With no apparent upper limit, PWA projects were often far more ambitious than those of the better-known WPA.[22]

The records for PWA public works are more complete than those of the WPA but more inaccessible because they are stored at a National Archives and Records Administration repository in the Midwest, from which they must be ordered from the NARA facility in Maryland. They are arranged and indexed by docket numbers: six dockets for Sacramento schools, for example, total an impressive $1,609,000, while one high school alone (McClatchy High School) accounts for another $781,000. Other dockets indicate that the PWA spent $131,000 on the city hall building and a new concrete annex to its rear, and $53,000 for an unnamed hospital.

A far greater sum was allotted to other city infrastructure: $225,000 went to reinforcing the levees protecting Sacramento from the rivers that bounded it to the north and west, $200,000 was spent on street improvements, $20,000 for traffic signals, $73,000 for bridges, and a further $271,000 for a modern citywide fire alarm system, which, the *Bee* editorialized, would "mean a substantial saving to the property owners of the city in fire insurance rates."[23]

In Sacramento, as in other California cities, the New Deal thoroughly modernized the water distribution and disposal systems, greatly improving the city's public health while aiding its expansion into previously undeveloped areas. Two dockets allocated $241,000 for sanitary sewers, and another provided $704,000 for waterworks in addition to work done by the WPA.[24] Prominent among the latter were massive twin landmarks that resembled fluted drums or classical columns. Hailed at the time as the "largest reinforced concrete elevated water tanks ever constructed," each tank holds three million gallons, ensuring a supply of clean, high-pressure water to the essentially flat city through mains largely financed by the PWA and at least partially laid by WPA workers.[25]

The Tower Bridge

One of the most stunning and important infrastructure improvements to come out of the New Deal for Sacramento was the iconic Tower Bridge, connecting West Sacramento to Sacramento over the Sacramento River. Requiring approval of the secretary of war since the structure would span a navigable river, the project also reflects the New Deal's significance in preparation for war and Sacramento's importance to any future war effort. Providing access to the San Francisco Bay and the Pacific Ocean, the bridge and the river could be used in times of war to move supplies and troops.[26]

Since the bridge would provide both auto and rail transportation, the Department of Agriculture's Bureau of Public Roads also played a role in its construction. The bureau laid out the regulations to be followed in connection with railroad grade separation work that involved funds made available for highway improvements through the National Industrial Recovery Act, the use of which stipulated that the private railroad companies and the government would share responsibility for maintenance and employment conditions.[27] District engineers also had to contend with regulations set forth in section 204 of Title II, Public Works and Construction Projects in the National Industrial Recovery Act, which "authorize[d] use of the funds appropriated to pay all or any part of the cost of improving safety at highway-railway crossings."[28] One of the purposes of this provision was to encourage improvements to traffic safety without prescribing involuntary contributions by the state or railway companies. However, so-called "incidental expenses" in connection with sustaining rail traffic, such as paying flagmen, were covered by the railroad.

Construction of the Tower Bridge was a major development for the city of Sacramento. Documents housed at the California Department of Transportation (Caltrans) and the California State Archives chronicle the construction of the bridge, from engineering proposals through the construction, opening, and operation. The information in these archives demonstrates the importance of the bridge as a source of pride for the community. Not only was it designed to improve transportation in and out of the city, the bridge was a conscious symbol of the city's status and stature. It beautified the entrance into the capital city of California and became the nexus of a multimodal transportation system that linked Sacramento to the world.

Before the contracts for the bridge construction could be advertised, the state first had to resolve the legal issues surrounding the unique ownership and operation of the bridge. The existing M Street Bridge had been built by the precursors of the Sacramento Northern Railway. The railway had a lease to operate the bridge, and replacing the existing span would require the state to enter into a unique partnership with the railroad. On May 3, 1933, the governor approved Assembly Bill 1343, amending the state Political Code to allow the director of public works "to enter into agreements for the construction, maintenance, and use of State highway bridges jointly by the public and private owners."[29] This action enabled the state to work out an agreement with the Sacramento Northern Railway. On March 8, 1934, an agreement was signed between Sacramento Northern Railway and the State of California in which the railway relinquished its rights to the old bridge in exchange for the right to continue to use the new span until its original franchise expired on March 21, 1960.[30]

The new bridge also had to accommodate a steady flow of traffic on the Sacramento River, and shipping concerns were among those that had to be considered. On September 19, 1933, those concerns were highlighted in a letter W. P. Dwyer, president of the River Lines, a riverboat company, wrote to F. H. Reynolds, of F. H. Reynolds & Company, a civil engineering firm in Sacramento. Dwyer raised concerns about river navigation should the newly proposed bridge opening be adopted. While the existing bridge opening crossed the natural channel, moving the opening 125 feet west, as proposed, would create navigational hazards. Dwyer recommended that the opening be moved no more than 50 feet west of its original location.[31] The state would eventually follow this recommendation.

Above and beyond practical concerns like traffic capacity and river navigation, the state clearly intended to build a beautiful bridge. Aesthetics were a regular part of the ongoing conversation between the state and Cortelyou and Harrington, the design engineers. California state highway engineer C. H. Purcell wrote, "While

FIGURE 9.2. The Tower Bridge, originally painted silver, remains an iconic structure for the city. While its date of construction is prominently displayed, one must look closely at the attached plaque to identify it as a product of the New Deal. Photograph by Lee M. A. Simpson.

we realize that it is difficult to make a lift span a beautiful structure, nevertheless we are anxious to do whatever we can to design a good looking bridge which will do credit to the city. We therefore [would] like for you to give the matter of appearance of the structure very considerable attention."[32] This bridge would not only be an entrance into the capital city but a landmark for all Sacramento residents to enjoy. Noting the symbolic importance of the bridge to the city and the state, the state agreed to absorb the added costs—an additional fourteen thousand dollars for tower construction.[33]

Eight contractors bid on the project, six from San Francisco, one from Oakland, and one from Sacramento. When the bids were opened in July, they ranged from a high of $1,025,224 to the low of $907,365, submitted by the winning hometown firm of George Pollock Company.[34] Work officially began July 16, 1934, but the old bridge would remain in service for another year while a railroad bypass bridge was completed.[35] Highway traffic was diverted on February 1, 1935, when dismantling of the old structure began.[36]

In May 1935, *California Highways and Public Works,* a publication of Caltrans, expressed the importance of the bridge to the city. No mere symbol, the bridge represented a fundamental shift in the city's transportation matrix. Henceforth, automobiles would become the dominant form of transit, forever altering the transportation infrastructure of the city. By default, this change altered the way in which visitors entered the city. No longer would the riverfront or the rail passenger station need to reflect the city's vision of itself. These places could be (and were) allowed to decay. An auto entry into the city was needed. "Civic pride, too, had a hand in hastening the obsolescence of the 1910 bridge. With the bulk of passenger travel switching from rail and water to highways," the Caltrans magazine reported, "it has become increasingly important that an attractive as well as adequate highway entrance to the State's capital city be provided."[37]

The January issue of *California Highways and Public Works* reiterated the need for the new bridge: "During the twenty-five years that the original M street bridge was in use, Sacramento's population expanded from 45,000 to approximately 100,000 and traffic increased 700 per cent in volume and 500 per cent in speed, making the old bridge with its nine-foot roadway cantilevered out from the trusses on either side of the structure not only entirely inadequate, but dangerous as well."[38] The new bridge was also touted for bringing the two sides of the river closer together: "Construction work on the Tower Bridge began in July, 1934 and was hailed by Sacramento and Yolo counties as the beginning of a new and greater bond between them."[39] In 1936, the Tower Bridge, already the darling of Sacramento, earned national acclaim, receiving an honorable mention from the American Institute of Steel Construction for "the most beautiful bridge built during 1935" for structures costing between $250,000 and $1 million.[40]

New Deal Preparations for War

While the Tower Bridge might be the city's most visible marker of the New Deal, monies funneled into Sacramento County's three military facilities profoundly altered the environment and the region's economy and laid the foundations for Sacramento's active and early participation in World War II. Funding for McClellan Field, Mather Field, and the Sacramento Army Depot developed out of the lobbying efforts of a chamber of commerce leader, Arthur S. Dudley. Seeking to reap the economic benefits of military installations like those found in San Diego and San Francisco, Dudley became an active promoter of air defense.[41]

Sacramento pioneered in air base construction with the opening of Mather Field in 1918. Closed in 1923, Mather essentially sat dormant and dismantled through the 1930s. Mather's closure spurred Dudley to begin an all-out lobbying assault on Congress and the War Department to reopen the base. He found willing allies among representatives of other regions also seeking defense projects and in the army leadership, among those who saw a need for development of West Coast air defenses to fight what they feared was an imminent war in the Pacific.[42]

In 1934, Dudley, along with Reginald Waters, his counterpart in the Miami Chamber of Commerce, founded the National Air Defense Frontier Association to organize chambers of commerce nationally and lobby for construction of air defense facilities on both coasts. They envisioned a ring of military airfields along the nation's coastlines. Sponsored in the House by J. Mark Wilcox of Florida and in the Senate by Hiram Johnson of California, the Wilcox National Air Defense Act of 1935 officially committed the United States to developing its air defenses, including constructing six air bases (although only four would actually be built).

Dudley initially hoped the bill would fund reopening of Mather Field. In 1935, the US Army began searching for a new facility to house its West Coast air and supply depot. Its current home, Rockwell Field in San Diego, shared with the US Navy, had limited space and potential for expansion. Officials took note of Mather Field as an excellent alternative. Mather's location, near a large and relatively stable community, close to well-developed water and rail transportation routes, available open space, and good landing terrain, all stood in its favor. But military officials in Washington eventually decided that Mather did not fit their needs as an air and supply depot. Dudley was given a choice: the military could reopen Mather as a traditional airfield or find another suitable location for a new depot that would repair and maintain military equipment. Anticipating Mather would eventually be reopened anyway, Dudley eagerly accepted the alternative repair base, and, often acting in secrecy, he shepherded the sale of nearly eleven hundred acres of marginal farmland northeast of Sacramento near the community of Ben Ali. Groundbreaking for the new facility took place in 1936.[43]

Environmental considerations proved critical in the awarding of the air base to Sacramento. As with Mather Field, the site chosen for the new McClellan Field sat close enough to the city to ensure a civilian workforce and residential housing and recreational opportunities for soldiers but far enough out on the open land to accommodate airplanes and equipment and to allow for future expansion. Proximity to the Sacramento River and established rail lines guaranteed relatively cheap and accessible transportation routes. Finally, the land's distance from Sacramento had protected it from the early rounds of subdivision that broke apart the region's other large Mexican land grants. In addition, those who owned the land had pursued sheep or cattle grazing rather than propagation of crops. They had less to lose with the sale of their land than did those in the more intensively worked agricultural areas surrounding Sacramento. Dudley thus had less resistance to overcome in his negotiations.[44]

Construction of what would become McClellan Field reflected the new sensibilities of the US Army. Unlike existing US Army Air Corps fields built as modifications to former cavalry posts, McClellan would be designed exclusively for the reality of air defense. With no stables or parade fields, the new depot would operate around large hangars, lengthy runways, and industrial repair shops. Built for the future, the site could grow as military aviation advanced.[45]

McClellan is unique not only for its status as one of the nation's first air depots but also for its architecture. Designed by the Quartermaster General's Office in Washington, the concrete structures in art deco, international, and minimalist pueblo styles reflect eastern conceptions of California's landscape and climate. The architect added pueblo stylistic elements to the structures to reflect the Hispanic influence in California and sun porches to residential buildings "in deference to the heat of the Sacramento Valley." The base historic district nomination notes, however, that "it was always too hot or too cold for their use except in the evenings." In addition, the international-style design elements, including steel-skeleton construction, concrete, long banks of windows, and aluminum sheeting for insulation, represent the innovative design approach of the Quartermaster General's Office architects.[46]

McClellan Field's planners designed a base that was both functional and livable. While the building architecture came from the East Coast, a University of California, Davis, professor of botany designed the residential and administrative area landscaping using plants that came to the base from a nursery that was shut down at Hamilton Field in Marin County. The landscaping plan proved to be an excellent fit for the base. Fifty years later, many of those plants were still alive and added to the integrity of the air force base as a historic district.

Despite the architectural and landscaping plans for McClellan, the airfield would not have been constructed without funding from the Works Progress Administration. WPA crews installed most of the base landscaping, planting vegetation, pouring sidewalks and streets, and installing tennis courts. The district's National Register of Historic Places nomination suggests that "the use of WPA crews during the construction phase resulted in a savings of over $200,000 below the estimated budget for the base."[47]

Legacy on the Land

The New Deal building programs did indeed leave a massive legacy on the land. Looking back on the work of the PWA in 1939, a survey of the agency's best structures captured the unique and visionary aspects of the program: "This vast building program presents us with a great vision, that of man building primarily

FIGURE 9.3. The auditorium at Sacramento City College served students and faculty for seventy years. In spring 2010, the campus began an ambitious restoration and upgrade of the structure that protects its historic features while ensuring its functionality into the future. Photograph by Lee M. A. Simpson.

for love of and to fulfill the needs of his fellowmen. Perhaps future generations will classify these years as one of the epoch-making periods of advancement in the civilization not only of our own country but also of the human race." For the first time in American history, the authors suggested, the American people had built "public works in unison, bettering the living conditions of all men." No longer focused on buildings that served a limited private sector, the New Deal–built structures "fit the needs of humanity in general. Hospitals are being built, floods are being controlled, new and humane prisons and asylums are replacing the old which were intended merely as places of confinement and not education, slums are being cleaned up, and in all building, as in town planning, sanitary and healthful conditions of life are being stressed."[48]

Sacramentans inhabit a city and region decisively shaped by men and women employed by New Deal agencies that built to better the conditions of all. Although such landmarks as Elk Grove's "largest bass-rearing plant in the world," the old California State Fairgrounds, and the WPA art center at 1422 Ninth Street have been redeveloped, leaving little trace of what those workers built there, much remains in daily use. Sacramentans receive and dispose of their water through systems built by the WPA and PWA. Their property is protected from floods by levees fortified by the PWA. They drive on roads and walk on sidewalks constructed

FIGURE 9.4. The WPA Rock Garden at Land Park is one of the few identifiable New Deal projects in Sacramento. The park's rock walls remain unmarked. Photograph by Lee M. A. Simpson.

by workers paid directly or indirectly by the federal government. Two enormous high schools and their athletic facilities—Grant Union in the northern part of the city and McClatchy in the south—were largely built by New Deal workers and with New Deal funds, as was Sacramento City College, whose auditorium features a WPA mural by Ralph Stackpole. Theodore Judah School was placed on the National Register of Historic Places in 1994 when a bronze plaque was affixed to its entrance with its PWA docket numbers; other schools throughout the region, either built or improved at that time, remain unmarked.

Rock walls and gutters throughout William Land Park testify to the efforts of WPA workers who literally left their mark on a pergola they built there, but few of the park's users know that its lakes, athletic fields, golf course, and mature trees are the legacy of that agency. As in San Francisco, records and articles in the *Bee* suggest that WPA workers improved every park in the city, including the arboretum on the grounds of the capitol whose tree labels were yet another WPA project. Noting in its application to Washington that "the shade trees of Sacramento are one of her greatest developed assets," the city park department got five hundred workers to plant 2,450 more along Sacramento's streets.[49]

From its inception, Sacramento's Tower Bridge was meant to be a landmark, a gateway befitting the entrance to the capital city of California. From its opening in 1935, the bridge rapidly became synonymous with Sacramento, and its image adorned everything from postcards to letterhead. Bypassed by new freeway construction in the 1960s, the bridge is still an integral part of the architectural landscape of the city and is enjoying a renaissance in popularity as the cities of Sacramento and West Sacramento redevelop the areas along the Sacramento River adjacent to the bridge and turn the once industrialized waterfront into a commercial and recreational center for the city.

The three great military facilities—McClellan Field, Mather Field, and the Sacramento Army Depot—were all built or greatly expanded by New Deal workers preparing for war, while the WPA-built Sacramento Municipal Airport was similarly justified for national defense.[50] Some projects that have left an indelible mark on the city were initiated under the New Deal but would have to wait until after the war for realization. Under the headline "Gateway to Capitol If Dream Comes True," the *Sacramento Bee* on May 1, 1935, published a bird's-eye view photograph, taken from a point high above Tower Bridge, of a formal park that would replace much of the older city between Second and Ninth Streets. Senator and former governor Hiram Johnson pledged his wholehearted support to obtain PWA funding to realize the extension of Capitol Park westward to the Sacramento River.[51] The Capitol Mall would have to wait for the statutory power and funding given it by the federal Housing Act of 1949, but those vastly enhanced powers—as well as plans—were set in motion by the New Deal prior to World War II.

In many respects, it is the lasting legacy of the New Deal that marks its significance more than what it did at the time to relieve the worst symptoms of the Great Depression. New Deal projects laid the groundwork for the growth and development of Sacramento and its suburbs in the immediate postwar years. Without the water and sewer improvements, the paved roads, and the connections made to the three military facilities, Sacramento would have been unprepared to develop its outer suburbs. The construction of the military facilities most clearly altered the city and its economy. Staying open in the cold war, they became significant employers and specifically led to the construction of the suburbs of Rancho Cordova (at the site of Mather Field) and North Highlands (at McClellan). For good or ill, this new identity, as a defense city, characterized the history of Sacramento in the second half of the twentieth century, fundamentally cleaving the city from its gold rush heritage. If nothing else, the New Deal needs to be seen as the single most important factor in reshaping the city and the county's urban environment for the twentieth century.

CHAPTER 10   The Legacy of War

SACRAMENTO'S MILITARY BASES

Rand Herbert

The military has played a dominant role in both the urban and environmental development of the greater Sacramento region. During World War II, Sacramento was home to three major military facilities that served and supported the war effort and persisted through the cold war era. A fourth had a much more limited period of activity before becoming an outpost for one of the three main facilities. Of the four, two served the US Army Air Corps and were created before World War II: Mather Field was a creation of the Great War, while the Sacramento Air Depot (later McClellan Air Force Base) was established in the 1930s. The US Army established the third, Sacramento Army Depot, in 1941, soon after the Japanese attack on Pearl Harbor. The fourth, Camp Kohler, began as an assembly point for Japanese American internees and was then converted to a Signal Corps depot. All had profound demographic and environmental impacts on the development of the city and region that exceeded their narrow initial purpose, although their effects were far more pronounced in the cold war era.

The Sacramento metropolitan area offered some unique advantages for the military. Unlike the San Francisco Bay Area, which was largely dominated by the US Navy and home to massive naval bases in Vallejo, Alameda, the South Bay, San Francisco, and on Yerba Buena and Treasure Islands, in the bay itself, the Sacramento region appeared to the army to be a congenial location for its facilities. Its suitability was the result of a combination of factors, including favorable weather conditions for aviation, availability of vacant lands near the city, proximity to major rail and river transportation hubs, and the general advantages of an urban center. The development of these military facilities, which occurred over the span of many years, had a significant effect on the urban and environmental condition of the region.

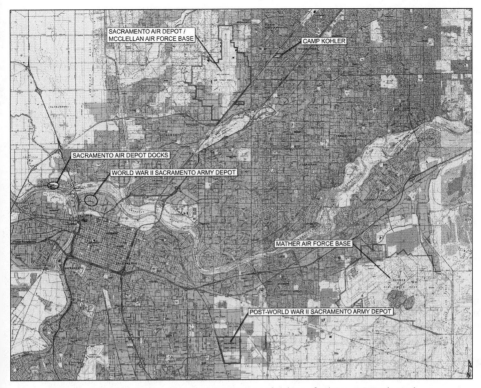

FIGURE 10.1. Map of Sacramento showing locations of military facilities. US Geological Survey quadrangles Sacramento and East Sacramento, annotated by JRP graphics technician Rebecca Flores.

In fact, as can be read elsewhere in this work, in the case of the development of the rail yards, these facilities, now closed, prefigured very different environmental developments. In the first instance, their establishment resulted in three massive properties that later became (and continue to be) areas of continued civilian use and redevelopment. The second was their role in helping stimulate development of large areas of residential properties in what are now known as Rio Linda, North Highlands, Fruitridge, Rancho Cordova, and other cities or neighborhoods within the Sacramento metropolitan area, a part of the population of which worked at the facilities. Finally, with closures came the realization that the vast military bases contained pollution that affected areas both in and outside their boundaries. These impacts became apparent only later, during the long era of the cold war, when the nation's military retained much of its size and strength to confront its enemies, real and perceived. During World War II, however, Sacramento's bases served the military in defense of the nation.

In the early 1960s, Pres. John F. Kennedy directed Secretary of Defense Robert S. McNamara to develop and implement a base realignment and closure program to downsize the military buildup that had occurred during World War II and the Korean War. After minimal consultation with the military departments or Congress, more than sixty major bases were closed. In 1965, Pres. Lyndon Johnson vetoed legislation that would have provided more congressional oversight, thus permitting the Department of Defense (DOD) to continue realigning and closing bases without consulting Congress or the military (and it did so throughout the rest of that decade).[1] The process changed in 1977, when Congress passed legislation requiring the DOD to notify Congress when an installation became a candidate for reduction or closure. In addition, the Department of Defense had to wait sixty days for congressional response. These stipulations, along with the requirements of the National Environmental Policy Act (NEPA), effectively put a stop to base closures for the time being.[2]

In 1988, the DOD budget had been in decline for three straight years and was expected to be reduced further. In response, Secretary of Defense Frank Carlucci chartered the Commission on Base Realignment and Closure (known as BRAC) to ensure that DOD resources would be devoted to the most important and pressing operational needs. Congress, in October 1988, established an independent, bipartisan commission to make recommendations to Congress and the secretary of defense on base closures and realignments. On December 28, 1988, the commission issued a report recommending closure of eighty-six installations, partial closure of five, and realignment of fifty-four others. The secretary of defense approved this recommendation on January 5, 1989.

Eventually, this program closed bases around the nation, while it expanded others. California, with its large number of facilities, was particularly affected by BRAC; virtually all of the naval facilities in the San Francisco Bay Area were closed, as were all major military facilities in Sacramento. With closure came the need to undertake environmental reviews for each facility, which included not only an assessment of whether or not each base contained historical resources under the National Historic Preservation Act but also, and more importantly, whether activities on the bases had resulted in generation of toxic wastes covered by the Comprehensive Environmental Response, Compensation, and Liability Act (CERCLA, or Superfund program).[3] McClellan Air Force Base, for example, not only contains two historic districts but also has a large number of contaminated areas within and beyond its boundaries. Mather Air Force Base and the Sacramento Army Depot have similar issues with toxic contamination, to a somewhat lesser extent. Such contamination has resulted in unique challenges for later reuse of the closed bases.[4]

Mather Air Force Base

Mather Air Force Base (originally Mather Field) was the earliest of the major military facilities established in the Sacramento region. The site, chosen for its good flying weather, available land, and adjacent rail connections, served the US Army Air Corps and US Air Force more or less continuously from 1918 through 1988.

The base's location, particularly during the cold war era, led to substantial suburban growth in the facility's environs. Likewise, defense activities at the base, particularly during World War II and the cold war, led to toxic contamination and the site's eventual placement on the nation's Superfund list in 1989.

The success of the Wright brothers' first powered flight in December 1903 and subsequent flight trials in the years that followed encouraged the US Army Signal Corps to establish an aeronautical division in 1907. This unit was the predecessor to the signal corps's Aviation Section, created in 1914, and the progenitor of the US Army Air Corps, US Army Air Force, and, eventually, the US Air Force.[5] Europeans were the first to utilize the airplane in critical combat situations. The Italian Royal Army was airborne during the Italo-Turkish War (1911–12), and, by 1914, nearly all of the Great Powers of Europe (Germany, Austria-Hungary, Russia, France, and Britain) had deployed aircraft in either intelligence-gathering or tactical capacities. When the United States entered into World War I in April 1917, the Aviation Section became the US Army Air Service and correspondingly began establishing airfields and training the first generation of modern air corps pilots.[6]

In 1918, the newly formed US Army Air Corps built a rude landing strip and scattering of hangars and support buildings east of Sacramento, along Folsom Boulevard, the main road leading out to the foothills, amid widely scattered farmsteads. The War Department chose this large, flat swath of undeveloped pasture and agricultural land east of Sacramento as the site of a new flight training facility. It was originally called Mills Field but was renamed Mather Field soon after its establishment, in honor of 2nd Lt. Carl Spencer Mather (1894–1918), who was killed during a flight-training accident near Ellington Field in Texas prior to his unit being deployed to Mills. The installation was first occupied at the end of April 1918, and construction was completed in June 1918. The end of the war in November of that year resulted in an abrupt cessation of training activities at Mather Field.[7]

Mather Field was lightly used during the period between the end of World War I and American preparations for entry into World War II. In March 1919, the War Department recognized an opportunity to provide military pilots with valuable flying experience and authorized the allocation of personnel, equipment, and facilities for forest fire patrols in California. Operations commenced in June 1919, and within three months of Mather's deactivation, service members piloting the Curtiss JN-4D ("Jenny") were taking off from its runways for flights over Tahoe, El Dorado, and Stanislaus National Forests. In May 1920, the 9th Corps Observation Squadron, the primary forest fire patrol unit, was deployed to Mather Field, among others. That year, US Army Air Service pilots spent almost four thousand hours flying the Jenny more than 476,000 miles in California and Oregon, covering more than 16 million square miles of forest and detecting more than sixteen hundred fires.[8]

Although aerial forestry patrols were successful in detecting fires, the US Army Air Service reduced these patrols after the 1920 fire season. A shortage of funds, personnel, fuel, and equipment prevented the Air Service from keeping up with the increased demands and expectations of the Forest Service. At Mather, the 9th Squadron could rarely obtain the high-test gasoline they needed to launch patrols safely and on schedule. In addition, aerial forestry patrols simply were not adequate military training. The Air Service gradually withdrew from its joint venture with the Forest Service and was out completely by the mid-1920s. The end of a fire patrol presence at Mather led to the Air Service placing the airfield on inactive status in June 1922. Less than a year later, Mather Field was closed.[9] The War Department retained the site.

Mather's closure was typical of the challenges the US Army faced in establishing a place for airplanes in the military during the interwar period. Specifically, securing funding was the biggest challenge. Though the airplane proved to be viable in combat during World War I, there was widespread belief that another war of such magnitude would not come again, at least anytime soon. There was a strong congressional push in the early 1920s to reduce the federal budget, which would leave the army with a significant reduction of funds to devote to aviation personnel, equipment, and facilities. Still, there was great support of aviation within the army. From 1923 to 1926, various investigations by the War Department, House of Representatives, and President Calvin Coolidge's administration determined that a minimally funded Air Service would be unstable and far less effective in the event of another large-scale conflict. In July 1926, after consideration of numerous bills that sought either to ensure that the Air Service remain an auxiliary branch of the US Army or to create a separate entity, Congress adopted legislation that effectively was a combination of the two proposals. The Army Air Corps Act established the US Army Air Corps as a subordinate organization of the US Army and authorized expansion and improvement of aviation units over the next five years. Command of these aviation units, however, was to remain with individual ground commanders, and thus the air corps was largely a logistics and administrative arm.[10]

The Army Air Corps Act was immediately found to have reached too far. It called for dramatic increases in the number of air corps officers, tactical units, enlisted personnel, and aircraft but provided insufficient funding. The newly formed US Army Air Corps was forced to return to Congress to secure the appropriations needed to accomplish the five-year improvement program. Lack of funds hindered the air corps's efforts throughout the remainder of the 1920s, and it failed to complete its goals. Funding was nearly eliminated altogether as a result of the Great Depression.[11]

Facilities such as Mather Field were consequently deactivated and reactivated as funding allowed. In April 1930, following a six-year deactivation period, Mather was reactivated as a sub-post of the Presidio of San Francisco. In November 1932, after the air corps's five-year program of improvement had failed, Mather was once again placed on inactive status. In May 1935, although still officially inactive, the airfield was made a sub-post of Hamilton Field, in Marin County. In February 1941,

FIGURE 10.2. Aerial view of Mather Field, 1930. Courtesy of the National Archives.

ten months before the nation entered into World War II, Mather Field became a sub-post of Stockton Field.[12] No buildings or structures related to World War I or the period prior to 1939 have survived; the runways, once short gravel or dirt airstrips or simply wide expanses of turf, have been completely replaced by modern surfaces.

A significant change in Mather Field's operational status occurred as a result of World War II. Although the United States did not formally enter the war until December 1941, the military had begun to increase preparedness in September 1938. Specifically, Pres. Franklin Roosevelt, greatly concerned about the growing militarism of Nazi Germany and the Empire of Japan, directed the War Department to expand aircraft production. In January 1939, he formally proposed to Congress that additional funds be allocated to aircraft procurement. The process became more urgent following Germany's attack on Poland in September 1939 and the subsequent escalation into a general war in Europe. Both the Nazi *blitzkrieg* against France in May and June 1940 and the subsequent Battle of Britain heavily featured aircraft, further pushing the Roosevelt administration to develop the nation's air power.[13]

In May 1941, Mather Field was reactivated as a separate army post. One month later, as Nazi Germany launched attacks on the Soviet Union, Gen. George C. Marshall, army chief of staff, reorganized the army, creating the US Army Air Forces as a distinct arm. At the same time, the army acquired additional land to expand Mather Field from 872 to 4,418 acres. In August 1941, the army opened a navigation school at the airfield. The army also renovated much of the installation, completely replacing the temporary World War I–era buildings. By March 1942, four months after Japan attacked the United States and Germany declared war on the nation, an entirely new facility had been constructed at Mather Field.[14]

Throughout the war, the size and scope of Mather Field steadily increased. In 1943, the new US Army Air Forces began stationing North American Aviation's B-25 Mitchell medium bombers at the facility.[15] Between 1944 and 1945, as the war in Europe was coming to a close and the military increasingly shifted its focus to fighting Japanese forces, Mather Field was designated the army's port of embarkation for the Pacific theater.[16] Beginning in 1944, Boeing B-29 Superfortresses, the most advanced World War II–era heavy bombers, were transported through Mather, on to Kwajalein, and finally Saipan.[17] One of these was *The Great Artiste,* the blast measurement instrumentation craft that accompanied both the *Enola Gay* and the *Bockscar* during their atomic bombing of Hiroshima and Nagasaki, respectively.[18] Those bombers returned to the United States through Mather Field in late 1945, following the surrender of Japan and the end of the war.[19]

Postwar development at Mather led to demolition of the vast majority of buildings erected before and during World War II. Only four remaining buildings at Mather relate to the period of preparedness and World War II. These four include two "portable hangars" and two small bombsight storage buildings; most of the remaining buildings on the base date to the cold war era. The base flight line currently operates primarily as an air cargo hub and general aviation facility of the Sacramento County Airport System. Land once devoted to military shops, offices, barracks, and housing is now being converted to civilian use, with offices, medical facilities, and other developments.

Mather Field was not closed or deactivated at the end of World War II as it was after World War I. The cold war followed directly on the heels of World War II, prompting the military to maintain and even expand its activities. In March 1946, the US Army Air Forces located its bombardment and flight engineer schools at Mather Field, and soon thereafter the US Air Force was an independent branch of the military. In June 1948, Mather Field officially became Mather Air Force Base (AFB).[20] By the late 1950s, the air force had selected Mather AFB as a home for a squadron of the Strategic Air Command's (SAC) Boeing B-52 Stratofortress.[21]

Prior to the development of intercontinental ballistic missiles (ICBMs), American nuclear capabilities were restricted to long-range bombers. Effectively, it was SAC that embodied American nuclear retaliation capabilities. Throughout the cold war, particularly in the late 1940s, 1950s, and early 1960s, SAC was entrusted with the primary responsibility of establishing the threat of "massive retaliation." This was seen as the foremost deterrent against nuclear attack on the United States, more so than the nation's efforts to develop defensive tools, such as the early warning system, air defense system, and, later, the antiballistic missile. As all SAC bases were connected with other facilities through a sophisticated series of communication links, the needs of each were relatively minimal. Very simply, they each required hangars for large intercontinental bombers and an area in which to store advanced weapons. Between 1956 and 1957, portions of Mather AFB were expanded specifically to accommodate B-52 bombers.[22] SAC's 4134th Strategic Wing was stationed at Mather AFB from 1958 to 1963 and was the base's major tenant unit during that time. SAC planned to disperse heavy bombers over a number of bases to make it more difficult for the Soviet Union to disable the entire fleet with a surprise attack. At Mather, SAC had one squadron of fifteen B-52s, half of which were on fifteen-minute alert (fueled, armed, and ready). The other half of the squadron was used for air refueling operations and training missions. From 1965 to 1966, and again from 1972 to 1973, the units serving at Mather were drastically reduced and the majority of support personnel, crews, and aircraft were lent to other SAC units for Southeast Asia operations. The base was eventually deactivated through BRAC in September 1989.[23] The majority of the buildings on Mather Air Force Base date to the cold war era, a period in which many new structures were added in support of an expanding air force. Many of these buildings were available for reuse after base deactivation.

After the BRAC commission recommended a major round of closings and realignments, all approved by the secretary of defense, Mather AFB's impending closure was announced. Immediately following this announcement, both Sacramento County and the Rancho Cordova Chamber of Commerce established commissions to plan for reuse of the base. The Sacramento County Board of Supervisors eventually approved a plan in 1991 focusing on retention of aviation use (representing a consolidation of proposals), and negotiations between the air force and the county began the next year. In March 1993, the air force issued a "record of decision" for the disposal of the base, and Mather was officially closed on September 30 of that year. On May 5, 1995, the former base was reopened as a general aviation airport with air cargo focus and made part of the Sacramento County Airport System. In September 1995, on the east side of the property, Mather Regional Park was established for recreational use, and, in the following year, 757 acres of the former base were transferred to Sacramento County for commercial development and redevelopment. In 1997, the air force approved the US Department of Veterans Affairs' request to use the Mather hospital; by the end of that year, the VA had moved the majority of its caseload from its downtown outpatient clinic to Mather. A new airport terminal opened in March 1998, with more than 40 percent of its space leased to Trajen Flight Support, the airport's fixed base operator. Sacramento Mather Airport was also developed, beginning in 1995, into an air cargo facility. Over the years, various air cargo operators have been located at the old field. There is now substantial urban development to the northwest of the field, and beginning in 2006 Mather has hosted the California Capital Airshow.[24]

At the time that Mather was being considered for closure, it was also being investigated for contamination under the CERCLA process. Investigations began in 1982, at which time investigators found eighty-two areas with contaminated soils, along with five groundwater plumes. According to the Environmental Protection Agency (EPA), the plume of greatest concern had migrated more than a mile beyond the old base boundaries. "Approximately 10,000 people live within a 1-mile radius of the site," the agency noted, "and approximately 60,000 people within a 3-mile radius of the site depend on groundwater for their main drinking water supplies." The EPA placed the entire base on the Superfund list in 1989. As of 2012, sixty-nine of the eighty-two sites with soil contamination had been cleaned up, with groundwater cleanup continuing. Concerns over contamination continued to affect the pace of reuse at Mather.[25]

McClellan Air Force Base

The other air corps facility in Sacramento, which ultimately became known as Mc-Clellan Air Force Base, started its life as the Pacific Air Depot.[26] It had a different purpose than Mather Field. Both before World War II and during the conflict, it served as a training, repair, and refitting base for aircraft either being readied for combat or being repaired after sustaining damage in combat. Like Mather Field, McClellan had the advantage of good weather, proximity to the center of the Sacramento metropolitan area, and easy rail access. Interestingly, McClellan also took advantage of its location near the Sacramento River and established a freight wharf at which it would take delivery of airframes carried on barges from San Francisco Bay. The airframes were then towed through city streets and county lanes to the airfield.

The base was established on lands that were once part of the Rancho Del Paso, a vast Mexican land grant that eventually came into the hands of James Ben Ali Haggin, the famous lawyer, land baron, and wealthy mining kingpin who owned major shares of the Kern County Land Company and the Anaconda Copper Mining Company. From the 1860s until Haggin's death in 1914, he had been the sole owner of Rancho Del Paso, which served as his horse farm; originally from Kentucky, Haggin remained a lover and breeder of racehorses throughout his life.[27] In the years after his death, his heirs sold the ranch to land developers, and it was from them that the government obtained a large portion of the land for the airfield.

McClellan Air Force Base played an important role during World War II as the principal supply depot and repair facility in the western United States. For years it was the only supply depot for the air corps on the West Coast. Later in the war, it was the principal training facility for staff that would operate newly created depots and subdepots elsewhere; McClellan was a major training facility for all western depots. It also retained authority for several subdepots that remained subordinate to the command at McClellan, and McClellan was at the heart of the air corps effort to repair and maintain aircraft for the Pacific theater.

A major portion of Sacramento Air Depot was developed prior to World War II, in the years between 1936 and June 1941. In 1938, the air corps renamed the base the Sacramento Air Depot. At first a repair and overhaul facility for prewar fighters, it was later adapted to provide service for bombers as well.[28] The Sacramento Air Depot was renamed McClellan Field in 1939. Increasing international tension and the outbreak of war in Europe in September 1939 led to an increase in activity on military bases around the nation. It was during this period that many of the buildings and structures still extant on the base were constructed. Construction commenced in 1936, and, by November 1938, staff at McClellan had begun work on aircraft, engines, and instruments.

At this time, the US Army Air Corps had four depots: San Antonio Air Depot (later Kelly Field), Middletown Air Depot in Pennsylvania, Fairfield Air Depot in Ohio, and McClellan. McClellan's main responsibilities included aircraft maintenance and supply for the West Coast, and, in the event of war, as noted by the military historian Maurice Miller, it "would become the hub of aircraft logistical support for the entire west coast." In May 1939, following President Roosevelt's signing of a law allowing the air corps 6,000 aircraft, McClellan began gradually expanding its workforce. By June 1939, there were 738 people at work. As Miller has observed, "one of the major tasks of the dept[.] was crating aircraft for sea shipment to Army Air Corps bases in the Pacific." With the onset of war in Europe, the expansion accelerated, particularly after the fall of France, Belgium, and the Netherlands in May 1940. The air corps increased by 4,000 aircraft, 187,000 enlisted men, and 15,000 aviation cadets. McClellan Field thereafter devoted an increasing amount of time and effort to training.[29]

McClellan supplied trained personnel to a new air corps depot at Ogden, Utah, but through 1941, McClellan remained the only air corps depot on the West Coast. In April 1941, its engineering department started operating three shifts, working twenty-four hours each day, to repair B-17D Flying Fortress bombers. By June 1941, McClellan had four thousand employees, and the air corps anticipated adding another fifteen hundred by mid-1942.[30]

In the summer of 1941, the air corps increased the pace of training, and, in June 1941, it established a radio mechanics' school at McClellan. The air corps was renamed the US Army Air Forces in June 1941. At this time, McClellan supported three Royal Air Force flying schools operating in the southwestern United States. By September 1941, there were 1,285 military personnel and 4,109 civilians working at the facility. During October, McClellan opened five additional subdepots, at Mather Field, Stockton, Mountain View, Taft, and Bakersfield. In November, additional subdepots opened in Merced, Lemoore, and Victorville. In June 1941, the air corps ordered construction of new school buildings to train the workers needed for repairing and maintaining aircraft; in a common expedient, the air corps converted standard design warehouses for the purpose. The base also leased space at the California State Fairgrounds in Sacramento for additional storage.[31]

The Japanese attack on Pearl Harbor and the US entry into the war led to a rapid expansion at the base. The workforce and aircraft traffic increased greatly. Between December 7 and December 28, 1941, the depot hired an additional twenty-five hundred employees. Because depots in the Philippines and Hawaii were damaged and new facilities at San Bernardino and Spokane were not completed, Mc-Clellan had to handle a great portion of their work until those locations were ready. Mandatory blackouts, begun in fear of Japanese attack, slowed production slightly during this period. McClellan received engine overhauls from the 13th Air Force, which was fighting the Japanese in the Pacific, especially after the fall of the Philippines resulted in the loss of important overseas facilities.[32]

During 1942, McClellan began adding taxiways and aprons to the original three runways to support the new aircraft traffic. The base also experienced difficulties in procuring warehouse space immediately after the attack on Pearl Harbor. Even before, by mid-April 1941, it had nearly $1 million worth of materiel stored in the open. For nearly the rest of the war, the base added warehouse space to accommodate the supplies and equipment it needed to undertake its assignments.[33]

McClellan also played a role in the Doolittle Raid on Japan in late March 1942, providing technical assistance and last-minute repairs and maintenance for the aircraft assigned to the mission. The aircraft were moved to the Alameda Naval Air Station, where they were placed on board the aircraft carrier that took them to their launch point east of Japan.[34] McClellan shipped most of its repaired aircraft from docks in Oakland and San Francisco to the Pacific theater. The base's personnel worked around the clock for most of the war, even after additional depots were opened in Spokane and San Bernardino. By 1943, the US Army Air Forces had eleven air depots in operation, including McClellan, along with 260 subdepots scattered around the nation. Although, by 1943, McClellan was no longer the sole major depot on the West Coast, high workloads remained a constant through the end of the war. This pace required a large workforce, and the base population grew from around 5,500 in September 1941 to 17,652 civilians and 4,250 military personnel by June 1943, an increase of about 500 new workers per month. Lack of space and limited equipment remained a constant source of complaint among the base's officers. The workers prepared or repaired fighter aircraft, such as the P-38 Lightning and P-47 Thunderbolt, as well as bombers such as B-24 Liberators and, later, engines for the B-29 Superfortress, along with a large variety of other aircraft. Through the use of sophisticated production methods and repair lines that increased productivity, the depot increased its workload by about 25 percent from December 1943 to June 1945, while reducing its civilian workforce from 17,652 to 11,680. The overall work level began to drop following the surrender of Germany in May 1945, and following the surrender of Japan on August 14, 1945, for the first time in five years the base was quiet and almost deserted. Workers shifted to storing surplus aircraft.[35]

McClellan had a number of outlying facilities and also had the use of Camp Kohler (discussed below). Another was the Sacramento River freight dock mentioned earlier, which comprised a wharf, crane, and small warehouse located on the left bank of the river just upstream of the confluence of the American and Sacramento Rivers. Barges laden with partially assembled aircraft would make their deliveries to the dock, where they would be met by runway tow equipment. The aircraft then made a slow procession from the river up to the air base. That dock facility, like portions of McClellan, is eligible for listing in the National Register of Historic Places.

After a period of quiet following the end of World War II, McClellan underwent a program of modernization, during which prewar and World War II–era buildings were adapted to modern needs (or, in the case of housing on base, remained in use) and new buildings were erected to serve more modern aircraft. The base serviced military aircraft throughout the cold war era, including those used in the Korean War and Vietnam War. The facility was later selected for closure in the BRAC process in 1995. The news that the base might close generated a substantial local effort aimed at keeping the base on the active list. The residents of the communities of North Highlands, which had grown up to the east of the base, and of the more sparsely populated suburban area of Rio Linda were particularly concerned over the proposed closure. BRAC records contain more than five hundred pages of letters from local government officials, citizens, workers, residents, and even schoolchildren, all urging the commission to keep the base open.[36] Nevertheless, the commission voted to close McClellan, a decision made official in July 2001.

Complicating the reuse of the facility is the existence of toxic contamination at the base, caused by spills and releases of solvents, industrial chemicals, and other materials. According to the Environmental Protection Agency, the sources of the contamination included "the use, storage, and disposal of hazardous materials including industrial solvents, caustic cleansers, paints, metal plating wastes, low-level radioactive wastes, and a variety of fuel oils and lubricants." The agency explained that "the Air Force has identified 326 waste areas of known and suspected contamination." Maps prepared by the EPA show that nearly the entire base has some level of contamination, from moderate to what is termed "complex and extreme." Cleanup efforts began in the mid-1980s, prior to the base being closed. At the time of this writing, most of the old base had been subject to remedial efforts, more than 60 percent of the usable building space had been leased to organizations and businesses, and other remediation projects continued.[37]

The base is now administered by the US Air Force Real Property Administration through McClellan Business Park, which is heading up the reuse and redevelopment process. Of course, the issue of contamination plays an important role in these plans. Recent studies, for example, showed that contamination from low-level radioactive materials related to luminous dial painting had migrated below a historic building within one of the National Register of Historic Places districts on McClellan. The contamination was too extensive to allow for reuse of the building.[38]

Sacramento Army Depot

Sacramento Army Depot during World War II was a different facility in a different location than the sprawling, now-closed facility known by that name today. During its life, it was located at three different sites within the city. The army chose Sacramento for the depot because of its proximity to the Pacific theater of operations and the ease of connections to major road, river, and rail transportation.[39]

During World War II, the depot was first established on the state fairgrounds on Stockton Boulevard (now primarily the location of the UC Davis's medical center), and soon thereafter it was relocated to a site just north of the great Central Pacific rail yards and on the left bank of the American River near downtown. The army obtained the site from the Bercut-Richards Cannery because it offered close and convenient access to the rail yards next door. The cannery property remained the home of the depot throughout the war. Only after the end of the war did the army move to permanent facilities south of the city.

The depot in the Bercut-Richards plant began its operations in the fall of 1942, when the US Army Signal Depot moved from the state fairgrounds to the commandeered cannery. Sacramento's inland location and access to major rail lines made it safe from Japanese air attack and ideal for shipping military goods on the West Coast for the war in the Pacific theater. The depot also served as a supply center for other army installations. The cannery's existing warehouses, available open space, and proximity to the rail depot made it an excellent location for this supply function. Although the military built many new facilities in California during the war, the use of existing industrial sites like the Bercut-Richards Cannery allowed vital supply operations to continue without the delay of waiting for acquisition and construction of a new site. The army used existing buildings at Bercut-Richards and left behind no permanent structures from its use of the property.[40]

As the war intensified, the need for military supplies grew, as did the workload at the signal depot. By the end of the war, hours worked had increased 650 percent, and shipments grew from 10,500 items in 1943 to 60,800 items in 1945. This workload translated into much-needed jobs for civilians, causing an increase in the number of employees, from 244 to 1,800. The army supplemented the Sacramento workforce by recruiting specialists from across the country, bringing new expertise to the area. The workforce also diversified as the depot hired more women and a few minorities. It also diversified after April 1944, when the army opened a prisoner-of-war camp at the cannery site. German prisoners from General Rommel's Afrika Korps lived in a tent city and worked in the depot's warehouses. The POW population peaked at 554.[41]

The Sacramento Army Signal Depot was valuable to the war effort, and from its success, it began to outgrow its space at the Bercut-Richards site as supply demands increased. The army began to lease other warehouses in the city to hold the surplus goods and started work on a larger permanent depot in Sacramento. The

FIGURE 10.3. Sacramento Army Signal Depot, located at Bercut-Richards Packing Company, ca. 1944. German POWs were housed in the tents seen in the background. Courtesy of the Department of Special Collections and University Archives, California State University, Sacramento, Sacramento Army Depot Collection.

war ended prior to the signal depot's departure from the Bercut-Richards plant, and the army moved the depot to a new location on Fruitridge Road, east of Power Inn Road, in late 1945.[42] The army gave the Bercut-Richards property back to its prewar owners once its new facility was operational. In 2012, the Bercut-Richards site was being redeveloped as an office and residential area served by a new light-rail station.

The Sacramento Army Depot known to most of the community is a cold war–era facility. The location, among what were then small truck farms and open fields, was near Polk Station, a Southern Pacific railroad stop. The army began construction just before the end of the war, in July 1945. Construction progressed far enough that the depot became operational a few weeks after the end of the war, on September 25, 1945. Known then as the Sacramento Signal Depot, it had massive warehouses, administrative offices, barracks, shops, and eventually eleven miles of railroad spurs. It eventually featured a small airstrip, called Reed Army Airfield, which was closed prior to the BRAC action to dissolve the entire depot.[43]

The army operated the depot in its current location throughout the cold war period, focusing on fabrication and repair of optical and electronic equipment, lasers, and other advanced military technologies.[44] Like Mather and McClellan, the depot experienced toxic contamination, which required federal cleanup. While the army had identified toxic contamination of soils and water in 1979, the EPA placed the site on the Superfund list in 1987. The agency reported that metal-plating and spray-booth operations and chemicals for degreasing and cleaning (the wastes from which were buried or disposed of on site in burn pits or waste lagoons) resulted in soil contamination and affected local groundwater supplies. Remediation efforts over the past decades have resulted in areas of the post having been successfully cleaned up; the groundwater treatment process is ongoing.[45]

The depot began to be affected by BRAC in 1991, when its industrial area was closed and tasks assigned to other facilities. Over the next three years, the army moved these functions, and this section of the depot was closed by the BRAC process in March 1995. A portion of the depot is still used by the California National Guard, US Army Reserves, and other military uses, including storage for the California State Military Museum.[46]

Camp Kohler

The most impermanent and short-lived military facility in the vicinity of Sacramento was the assembly center–turned–signal corps base known as Camp Kohler. Unlike Mather, McClellan, and the Sacramento Army Depot, it left little behind except for a radar installation serving the McClellan airfield, and it has since largely been swallowed up by suburban development.

Camp Kohler began its life as the Walerga Assembly Center, where Japanese nationals and Americans of Japanese ancestry were temporarily collected prior to being sent to more permanent internment camps. These Sacramento residents, some 4,739, were among the more than 120,000 people interned, as noted on the site's historical marker, "without charge or trial" during the war. The army converted the assembly center to military use in June 1942 and named it Camp Kohler. The Walerga Assembly Center is commemorated by California Historical Landmark No. 934, designated in May 1980.[47]

Camp Kohler originally encompassed some eight hundred acres during World War II, when it served as a basic and communication training facility for the army. After the war, most of its buildings were destroyed in a fire caused by a passing train. It later was the location of an industrial laundry serving McClellan Air Force Base, and it also housed an air force laboratory. After the war, the military sold most of the site. This area is now covered by suburban development within what is now the Foothill Farms-North Highlands subdivision; the camp's rifle range concrete wall serves as the back fence for a number of these houses. Today, the remaining thirty-five acres contain a radar facility used by McClellan Airport.[48]

Sacramento's Military Legacy

Sacramento entered World War II in much the same manner as did the rest of the nation—in the midst of a military buildup as hostilities in Europe and Asia became more likely—but with a relatively minor, but rapidly expanding, military plant. Its two major installations were aircraft related and on the periphery of the city; it was only when the war began that the army established bases in or near the city.

The installations grew rapidly in importance during the war, with expanding work forces of both military personnel and civilian workers. McClellan, Mather, and the Sacramento Army Depot were, during the cold war era, important economic drivers in the region, employing thousands of highly trained workers, with all the resultant economic activity generated by good jobs and good wages. The bases' continued use and expansion in the 1950s and later also contributed to the region's population growth. The county had a population of slightly more than 170,000 in 1940; this figure had grown by 61 percent, to more than 277,000, by 1950. The result was expansion of housing and building stock, local businesses, infrastructure, and other economic factors both around the military facilities and within the county in general.

These bases are now closed and are in the process of environmental remediation, reuse, and redevelopment. Historic buildings exist on McClellan Air Force Base and some of its outlying facilities and are reminders of the prewar and World War II periods; the other facilities lack historically significant structures. Perhaps fortuitously, the redevelopment of the bases—like the opportunities afforded by redevelopment of the Central Pacific rail yards in the heart of downtown Sacramento—has begun to stimulate a new, nonmilitary focus around them, in terms of commercial and industrial construction, housing, and new uses of land made available as military roles ceased.

CHAPTER 11   # Recalling Rancho Seco

VOICING A NUCLEAR PAST

Christopher J. Castaneda

On June 6, 1989, Sacramento County voters decided that the Rancho Seco Nuclear Generating Station (RSNGS) should be permanently closed. The initiative, known as Measure K, gave local citizens the opportunity to vote on whether or not the Sacramento Municipal Utility District (SMUD) should continue operating Rancho Seco or permanently decommission it. The ballots were counted, and while 97,945 voters (46.6 percent) wanted the plant to continue generating electric power for the region, 112,415 others (53.4 percent) cast ballots against the plant's continued operation. Soon after the vote count was officially reported, SMUD's general manager began the process of closing the plant. This was the first time in US history that an operating nuclear generating station would be shuttered by popular vote. While California's unique initiative process allowed for a successful public political movement to force SMUD to close Rancho Seco, this event cannot be viewed as simply an isolated case of radical environmentalists manipulating the political process to achieve their own ends. Indeed, the political process was carefully and even craftily used to that end, but Rancho Seco was a troubled plant and ratepayers were not pleased. Ultimately, the underlying and very real environmental, financial, and technological issues at Rancho Seco, and in the nuclear power industry generally, made Rancho Seco a victim, in a sense, of the tensions between nuclear power and the public. In this case, the public was given an opportunity to vote on the future of nuclear power. The decision? Close it down.

The Rancho Seco story is one that combines elements of environmental activism, grass-roots politics, a growing urban area, and pocketbook finance in an era of increasing environmental awareness intertwined with rising energy prices. When first conceived in the mid-1960s, SMUD's long-range plan to build and operate a nuclear power plant seemed like a great opportunity. The utility company's

FIGURE 11.1. Rancho Seco Nuclear Generating Station under construction. Courtesy of the Center for Sacramento History, Sacramento Bee Collection.

general counsel, David Kaplan, recalled that the "most informed opinion available at the time was [that] nuclear was clearly the best and cheapest alternative."[1] But years later, Rancho Seco's fifteen-year operating history had told a different story. By 1989, the plant had suffered through "more than 100 shutdowns, cost overruns, safety concerns, legal hassles and political maneuverings," and its annual average electric power output was less than 40 percent of capacity.[2] It is undoubtedly true that the operating, financial, and safety problems that had plagued Rancho Seco— within the larger context of an increasingly troubled nuclear power industry— provided many residents with more than enough justification to want the plant closed. The ultimately successful course of action taken by Rancho Seco's opponents provides a lesson in how a determined and persistent environmental coalition can achieve seemingly unattainable goals through the democratic political process.

Sacramento's Electric Power

To begin, one might ask why Sacramento needed a nuclear power generating station in the first place. The answer to that question has a lot to do with Sacramento's position geographically and its economic relationship with the San Francisco Bay Area. Located approximately equidistant between San Francisco and Lake Tahoe, Sacramento County in and of itself did not represent a huge electric power market.[3] But the region was unique in that its electric power was delivered by a municipal utility, the Sacramento Municipal Utility District (SMUD), whose service area was entirely surrounded by that of the much larger, investor-owned utility company, Pacific Gas & Electric (PG&E).

The Sacramento Municipal Utility District was established on July 2, 1923, when voters approved the creation of the municipal utility district. The newly created SMUD had authority to own and operate electric light, heat, water, and other utilities; it is noteworthy that only 28 percent of the electorate went to the polls on that day in 1923, and the deciding vote was 6,378 to 978.[4] The newly created district included the cities of Sacramento and North Sacramento, along with adjoining areas that initially included about seventy-five square miles. While SMUD had broader authority, it was most interested in developing and operating the electric power business within its boundaries, and that meant acquiring the electric power distribution facilities of PG&E, as well as the Great Western Power Company then operating within SMUD's new borders; neither of those companies was interested in selling.[5] A long-term struggle ensued between SMUD and PG&E over PG&E's properties, while SMUD sought authorization to issue bonds to finance the purchase of those facilities and otherwise finance its own future growth and development. SMUD's prospects to create an electric power system improved in 1934, when voters approved the issuance of general obligation bonds for the acquisition and/or construction of electric power facilities, but the conflict between SMUD and PG&E continued until 1946, when, after implementation of condemnation proceedings, SMUD took over PG&E's distribution system properties within SMUD's territory in exchange for $13,917,000. SMUD also agreed to buy all of its electric power from PG&E until June 30, 1954.[6]

SMUD was thus in business but as an electric power distribution company; it did not produce any of its own power. SMUD's service area was entirely encompassed by PG&E, and it purchased all of its electric power from PG&E. At the conclusion of the power-purchasing agreement with PG&E, however, SMUD moved forward with plans to develop its own power-producing properties by taking advantage of its geographical location near rivers flowing down the Sierra. The first of these was the Upper American River Project, for which SMUD received a license to begin construction from the Federal Power Commission in 1955; groundbreaking occurred in 1957. By its completion in 1971, this project, also known as the "Stairway of Power," included a forty-mile system of eleven dams and six hydroelectric powerhouses along the American River.[7]

Even before the Upper American River Project was completed, SMUD had been investigating what was then an exciting new technology for electricity generation: nuclear power. For SMUD, nuclear was a logical choice, and, most significantly, it would provide SMUD for the first time with its own base-load power. PG&E's service area surrounded SMUD, so the latter's management understandably sought alternatives to being solely dependent upon power purchases from PG&E and hydroelectric projects. With ongoing concerns about fossil fuels (particularly coal-fired plants) and increasing environmental concerns, nuclear energy at that time appeared to be both an efficient and clean source of power. After several years spent investigating the possibility of building and operating a nuclear power facility, SMUD announced plans in 1964 for a ten-year program to build its own nuclear-powered electricity generating plant.

In 1966, SMUD purchased the twenty-one-hundred-acre McConnell Ranch on the site of the Arroyo Seco Rancho Mexican land grant, about twenty-five miles southeast of downtown Sacramento. Then, in 1967, SMUD contracted Bechtel Corporation for plant design and construction supervision services. SMUD also decided to utilize a 913-megawatt Babcock & Wilcox (B&W) pressurized water nuclear reactor. George Pavia, an electrical engineer who later worked at Rancho Seco, reflected on the early planning for the plant and the decision to build one instead of two reactors. "Rather than build two 500-megawatt turbines," Pavia said, "they built one 900-megawatt turbine and that was problematic." In retrospect, he noted that "when it went down, the whole plant was shut down. If they had built two of them at least the output would have been reduced but the plant would have continued to function."[8] The Atomic Energy Commission (AEC) issued a construction permit in November 1967. Construction began in 1969, with an initial estimated cost of $180 million.[9] The AEC issued an operating license to SMUD for Rancho Seco in August 1974.

Nuclear plants require a constant water supply, and SMUD projected that Rancho Seco would need a flow of 35 cubic feet per second. SMUD contracted to obtain this water from the upper American River and Folsom Lake through the Bureau of Reclamation. In addition, the district expanded a small nearby pond into a 160-acre reservoir adjacent to Rancho Seco to serve as a backup water supply. The 2,750-acre-feet reservoir and surrounding 400 acres also served as a recreation area. Named the Rancho Seco Recreation Area, it has been used since its creation for picnics, swimming, fishing, and boating, all in the shadows of the Rancho Seco cooling towers.[10]

Rancho Seco began generating electric power for commercial consumption on April 18, 1975. However, the startup of Rancho Seco did not mean that SMUD was no longer dependent upon PG&E. In fact, Rancho Seco became an important linchpin in a new agreement between SMUD and PG&E that actually integrated the two systems more closely than before. The resulting integration agreement provided that SMUD would purchase backup power from PG&E during times when Rancho Seco was down for repairs or refueling, and SMUD would sell to PG&E excess power produced by Rancho Seco. This arrangement worked well for the first seven years of Rancho Seco's operation, particularly because PG&E was also producing electricity from its increasingly expensive oil-fired plants and dealing with delays in the construction of its own Diablo Canyon nuclear reactors.[11]

Early Protest

SMUD, several months before Rancho Seco began generating power, had officially dedicated the nuclear plant on October 20, 1974. The plant's electric power generation would replace twelve billion barrels of oil per year, according to a speaker at the event. One thousand spectators attended, along with a small group of pro-testers. Even before Rancho Seco began generating its first kilowatt of power, the small collection of individuals from diverse backgrounds who had organized an ad hoc protest group made it clear that they were intent on shutting down the plant.

Pat Macdonald was one of the protesters who attended the Rancho Seco ded-ication ceremony. "And there were a handful of us who were out there for that ceremony," she recalled. "Myself and two other women were out there and we were handing out leaflets about the hazards of nuclear power plants."[12] Macdonald had been following news about Rancho Seco for several years; she had been working as a draft counselor during the Vietnam War at a local draft help center to advise young men of their Selective Service rights. As the war was coming to an end, she and a cohort of her fellow counselors became increasingly concerned that "SMUD was considering a nuclear power plant. And this, although we had been busy with our draft help center, we decided that since the draft was winding down, we needed to become informed on this issue."[13] For Macdonald, making the transition from involvement in the antiwar effort to the environmental and the antinuclear movements was "kind of a natural thing to do."[14]

Well before the dedication ceremonies, Macdonald, along with several col-leagues from the draft help center and Homer Ibser, professor of physics at Califor-nia State University (CSU), Sacramento, who served as the group's science advisor, had voiced opposition to Rancho Seco. Ibser taught a course titled "Living with Nuclear Energy," although the course "didn't go for the nuclear energy," he recalled later.[15] Indeed, the course description on the syllabus noted that students would learn the "latest about our local nuclear lemon, Rancho Seco."[16] Ibser provided a persistent and aggressive voice against Rancho Seco in a variety of venues.

This small group of eight individuals earlier had intervened in the Atomic Energy Commission's hearings regarding the licensing of Rancho Seco. "We made public statements at these hearings," Macdonald said, adding that "we had to tes-tify. That was really our first involvement with an agency."[17] The initial group of "interveners," which included antinuclear activist Dick Gregory, found themselves frustrated by the hearings process, which restricted the interveners from discussing issues not directly related to Rancho Seco. They collectively wrote John B. Far-makides, chair of the AEC, that "we cannot, in good conscience, continue with the intervention proceedings in the licensing of the Rancho Seco Nuclear Generating Station, Unit 1 in Sacramento County. In the future we will be devoting our time and efforts to a nuclear power moratorium on a local, state and national level."[18] The AEC did approve Rancho Seco's operating license, but the small group of op-ponents continued their initially ineffectual but persistent efforts to close Rancho Seco.

After the AEC hearings, the interveners established their first formal organiza-tion, called Citizens to Stop Rancho Seco. They decided to attend SMUD's public board meetings in order to learn about the utility and the way it operated while expressing opposition to Rancho Seco. Most likely reflecting the thoughts of her compatriots, Macdonald later recalled that "I was surprised how very ignorant I was on my municipal utility district. . . . We started to attend our SMUD Board meetings. And [we] were very surprised to find out how those five board members operated. First meeting we were taken up on the fourth floor, to kind of an executive suite. And they didn't understand why we wanted to be at these meetings[;] . . . they asked if we were students, was this a project we were doing?" Until this time, few observers ever attended these meetings. The group explained to the board that "we were interested in our utility and we had never been to any of these public meetings and we would be attending in the future. They were a little disgruntled at that."[19] Macdonald observed that the board appeared to have the action items on its agenda predetermined before the public vote took place, and the board itself seemed to operate more like a club. The SMUD board was then known to be a very stable yet closed group. Prior to upcoming board elections, if there were board members who intended to retire, they would retire early so that the current board could appoint a "like-minded" interim member. The interim member was then the incumbent by election time and would invariably be elected to a permanent position on the board.[20]

David Kaplan, the SMUD general counsel at the time, also recalled the first appearance of what he termed the "environmentalist" group at the board meetings. Prior to the AEC's hearings on SMUD's operating license, "not only was there no public participation[,] though the public was perfectly [able] to come[,] they just were not interested, but reporters didn't even come at that time."[21] The board meetings took place in the general manager's office on the fourth floor of the SMUD building. It was at this point that the Citizens to Stop Rancho Seco group, according to Pat Macdonald, decided to change its name to Citizens for Safe Energy, in order to present a more positive image while regularly attending the board meetings.[22] With more public interest in their meetings, the SMUD board was compelled to move the meetings to the auditorium on the first floor of the building to make room for a larger audience.

The mid-1970s saw an increasingly active and influential antinuclear movement emerge throughout California and other states. While this movement's potential was likely mitigated by the energy crisis initiated by the 1973 oil embargo against the United States, it remained a potent force. A coalition of activists called People for Proof crafted an initiative proposal in California calling for a moratorium on new nuclear plant construction, as well as reduced operation for existing plants unless significant reform was made, particularly in the areas of waste disposal and reactor safety. The resulting Proposition 15 was ultimately defeated by a 2-to-1 margin in the June 1976 election, but the fallout from this and other antinuclear efforts in other states was to heighten the public's awareness of the goals and aims of the antinuclear movement. In California, the state legislature passed bills similar in many respects to the failed proposition.[23]

FIGURE 11.2. Rancho Seco control room. Courtesy Center for Sacramento History, Sacramento Bee Collection.

In Sacramento during the mid-1970s, SMUD had to deal with two significant setbacks to its own plans to maintain and develop its nuclear power ambitions. During 1974, SMUD announced plans for a second reactor, Rancho Seco Nuclear Generating Station, Unit No. 2. Expected to be a 1,100-megawatt unit located alongside Rancho Seco No. 1, SMUD planned for a $650-million bond issue that required voter approval. SMUD's plans received criticism in the press due to a perceived lack of public planning and public information.[24] But SMUD reasoned that the growing metropolitan area would need additional electrical generation capacity. In addition, if one generating station went down, the other could still operate and produce power. Eventually, during 1976, facing intense opposition, SMUD withdrew the application to build a second reactor.

Also in 1976, state senator Albert Rodda (D-Sacramento) carried (i.e., introduced) a bill that was sponsored by the Ecology Council of Sacramento and intended to change the way that municipal utility district directors were elected. Previously at SMUD, all five of its directors were elected "at-large," and no incumbent had ever lost an election. The initiative passed and amended the Municipal Utilities Act, which provided for elections by ward. The initiative divided the SMUD service area into five wards, each of which would elect its own director. As a result, the SMUD incumbents did not win the next election. Instead, two newly elected SMUD board members, Rick Castro and Gary Hursh, for the first time represented concerns about the safety of Rancho Seco. SMUD board member John Kehoe recalled, "Then came the contentious period of the Castro-Hursh era in which they were continually questioning, particularly issues relating to Rancho Seco and nuclear power. Management took the position of 'we'll provide the Board with the least flow of information that could be deleterious to our decision-making.'" Kehoe noted his own discomfort performing as a board member with insufficient operational information.[25]

The Light Bulb Incident

In the larger context of a simmering antinuclear movement, Rancho Seco began to suffer significant technical problems that provided the public with reason to be concerned about the plant's safety. One of the earliest serious accidents reflected the apparent ease with which a simple misstep could lead to a potentially disastrous nuclear accident. On March 20, 1978, at about 4:30 a.m., a technician in the plant's control room was changing a small light bulb in a push-button switch located on the control panel console. In the process of this otherwise simple procedure, the bulb reportedly fell into the console and caused a short circuit that shut off power to the non-nuclear section of the control room instruments. The backup power did not engage, which led to an automatic shutdown of the reactor. In the process, according to a SMUD communications official, the automatic shutdown inadvertently caused a dangerously rapid cooldown of the reactor's cooling system.[26] Although the crisis was short-lived and the plant was able to restart four days later, the episode reminded the public that even a simple accident, such as this one involving the instrument panel, could result in a potentially disastrous event.

As one antinuclear activist recalled, "We could have had a major, major meltdown here. . . . We were very, very close. It's the worst overcooling accident of any nuclear plant that I've ever read about . . . in the United States."[27] This message was not the one that SMUD wanted to be broadcast to the public, but nevertheless it was. Rancho Seco's senior nuclear engineer, Dan Whitney, admitted that "the 'light-bulb incident' fit so nice[ly] into the popular jargon: how you trip up a whole nuclear power plant by a three cent light bulb. It was ridiculous to an extreme. But it really happened. And we dealt with it in a way that didn't cause a bad accident but it caused a lot of bad press, a lot of loss in confidence."[28] Despite the bad publicity, the plant soon returned to service.

Three Mile Island and Rancho Seco

The so-called "light bulb incident" occurred one year before what became known as the worst nuclear accident in US history. Early on the morning of March 28, 1979, unit II of the Three Mile Island (TMI) nuclear power plant suffered a partial core meltdown. Due to a series of events caused in part by inadequate operator training, as well as inaccurate instrument readings, about half of the core melted in the early stages of the accident. While this event did not result in a breach of the containment walls, there was a significant release of radiation from an auxiliary building. In response, Pennsylvania governor Dick Thornburgh, on the advice of the Nuclear Regulatory Commission (NRC), recommended that pregnant women and preschool-aged children within five miles of the plant evacuate; it is estimated that about 140,000 persons did leave the area at that time. Ironically, a Hollywood movie called *The China Syndrome,* which depicted a nuclear reactor meltdown, had been released only two weeks earlier, and it also contributed to the crisis atmosphere surrounding the event. One industry-wide result of the TMI accident was creation during December 1979 of the Institute of Nuclear Power Operations (INPO), a nuclear industry group that gathered information and established operating and safety standards for nuclear power plants.[29]

The Three Mile Island accident resonated quickly and intensely in Sacramento. Rancho Seco had already been plagued by numerous problems, outages, and a generally low level of power output relative to the plant's maximum electric power generation capacity. Even more ominous, particularly for the plant's detractors, was that the Three Mile Island plant used the same kind of Babcock & Wilcox nuclear reactor that Rancho Seco operated. The NRC was also concerned about possible safety issues with these B&W reactors, so it ordered that all plants using B&W reactors in the United States shut down until the cause of the TMI accident could be determined and addressed.[30]

Several days after the TMI accident became public, a group of thirteen activists in Sacramento went to the Rancho Seco plant to protest. They congregated just outside the plant's gate, adjacent to the road leading into it. In addition to Rancho Seco staff and local deputies, members of the media were also on hand. The protesters then decided to climb over the fence to emphasize their concerns about the plant's safety. As they climbed over the fence they were arrested for trespassing and then released. Subsequently, a trial was held in which a variety of issues were brought up relating to Rancho Seco's safety. One particular concern addressed at the trial was the detection of radioactivity in milk from dairy cows that were grazing in pastures adjacent to the plant. A Rancho Seco nuclear engineer suggested that the contamination was from a Chinese nuclear bomb test that had occurred three years earlier. Professor Ibser, who served as an expert witness, countered that that was extremely unlikely because the half-life of iodine 131 is only about eight days.[31] While the "Sacramento 13," as they had been dubbed, were eventually acquitted, the trial served to publicize the apparent safety problems at Rancho Seco.

The SMUD board meetings also began attracting more attention from local citizens. One of them was Martha Ann Blackman, a self-described poet. She recalled that "since I knew nothing about it [Rancho Seco]," except from fishing in the reservoir adjacent to the plant, "I decided . . . I had better learn."[32] Blackman, a thirty-five-year-old mother at the time, recalled, "So basically, I was going to SMUD meetings in my jeans. I was of the belief that I should be comfortable no matter what. So, I was just showing up looking like a twenty-nine year old hippie."[33] She quickly learned that Rancho Seco was not simply a local issue: "There were groups from the [San Francisco] Bay Area who were coming in. There were groups from here. Because it was such a large issue, we were getting a lot of peripheral people, not just people from . . . in town."[34]

Blackman observed the various individuals and representatives of groups who spoke against Rancho Seco at the board meetings. "And then there was this quiet little group called Citizens for Safe Energy . . . made up of a local group of people," she recalled. "They never shouted," she continued, "they never screamed, they never put people down when they were up on the podium talking to the board [SMUD]. They seemed to do things in an educational manner[,] . . . and that really impressed me. That's when I decided that that was the group that I would want to link up with. And so I did."[35] Blackman would not only join Citizens for Safe Energy, she would be one of its most effective advocates, in large part due to her calm, good-natured persistence and tenacity. However, anti–Ranch Seco sentiment seemed to dissipate somewhat over the next several years.

By the mid-1980s, Rancho Seco again began attracting more negative attention as serious accidents became public. According to SMUD board member Ed Smeloff, "Then things started catching up with SMUD. They did what I would call the minimum amount of maintenance that they could get by with on Rancho Seco and a minimum of compliance with the Nuclear Regulatory Commission."[36] The deaths of two workers at the plant in 1984 in an accident involving a ruptured high-pressure steam line emphasized again the dangers of working at Rancho Seco. And when SMUD announced in August 1985 that customers could expect rate increases of about 14 percent or more per year for the next three to four years, public dissatisfaction with the utility intensified.[37]

Overcooling Incident

The anti–Rancho Seco movement picked up steam in January 1986. In the early morning hours on December 26, 1985, Rancho Seco experienced its most serious accident. At 4:14 a.m., as the plant was operating at 76 percent power, the plant's integrated control system (ICS) suddenly lost power. In response, the automated system immediately repositioned valves and pumps to a halfway position, but this move caused the temperature in the reactor to increase from 582 degrees to 607 degrees within sixteen seconds. The rapid temperature rise then triggered the reactor's control rods to be inserted into the core in order to stop the nuclear reaction.[38] Next, a variety of alarms signaling fire, earthquake, and high temperatures in the spent fuel pool all began to sound, though they were unrelated to the initial technical issue. The most serious problem was noticed in the control room, where operators realized that cold water had begun flowing into the reactor's core, resulting in an extremely rapid cooldown. Within six minutes of the ICS failure, the temperature in the reactor had fallen 85 degrees. If the cooldown continued at that rate, the reactor walls could possibly become brittle and crack, releasing radioactivity into the containment building. In the resulting panic and confusion, technicians scrambled to manually adjust valves in order to stabilize the plant. In the meantime, a control room operator discovered that two recessed breaker switches on a control panel had tripped, causing the initial power outage and subsequent technical issues. The operator reset the switches and power was restored but not before water temperature had dropped a total of 180 degrees, 80 more in a one-hour period than NRC regulations allowed; the operator then collapsed with a minor heart attack. By 8:41 that morning, Rancho Seco's "unusual event" was over.

Rancho Seco suffered significant damage from the overcooling accident, in large part due to the actions of staff who sought to stabilize the plant after the loss of power. But no one in the control room had thought to check the breaker switches before initiating other action, possibly because they were located in a recessed panel and not easily visible.[39] The NRC immediately sent a team of five investigators to Sacramento to investigate the event. The NRC investigative report concluded, in part, that, "following the incident, it was found that licensees do not have a regular maintenance program that applies to every manual valve. The NRC does not have a requirement for maintenance and testing of convenience valves such as the locked-open manual valve involved in the Rancho Seco incident."[40] SMUD board member John Kehoe observed later that, "in the assignment of people during this Christmas period, training on this new system wasn't at as high a level as it could have been. The people on duty the day after Christmas were those seniority-wise who had the least time in grade. The shift didn't have the most experienced people on board."[41]

This accident, much more so than the "light bulb incident," attracted the investigative attention of the *Sacramento Bee*. Science writer Deborah Blum was assigned to the Rancho Seco story. "And frankly," she said, "once we got into looking at it very seriously after that accident, it was clear . . . that it was a really badly managed plant. But it was just kind of, you know, just cooking along, rates were low, it wasn't a squeaky wheel, and no one was paying any attention to it beyond your normal, what you think of as sort of your nuclear power hate groups. . . . So it was like that accident really woke people up."[42]

News of the overcooling incident dramatically ratcheted up the anti–Rancho Seco movement. The *Sacramento Bee* investigated the accident and reported that an otherwise minor problem had led to a near catastrophe. Deborah Blum's article, "One Switch Knocked Out Rancho Seco," noted that "failure of a tiny electrical switching box . . . plunged the plant's control system into chaos, setting off a dangerously fast cooldown of the reactor; triggering false emergency alarms throughout the plant; damaging valves, pumps, and monitors; and venting a small amount of radioactive gas to the atmosphere."[43] Further review indicated that a simple short circuit caused by a crimped wire in the electrical switching box had caused the ICS unit to lose power, resulting in a chain of events that resulted in a significant accident.[44]

FIGURE 11.3. Anti–Rancho Seco protesters. Courtesy Center for Sacramento History, Sacramento Bee Collection.

More and more, the Rancho Seco Nuclear Generating Station appeared to many local residents to be a problem that could not be fixed. Blum noted that "a lot of the mistakes, I think, with Rancho Seco were real human mistakes of simple technology. . . . All of the complicated stuff worked. It was the simple stuff that didn't work."[45] This perspective, of course, reflected on the management of Rancho Seco so that even those persons who were not opposed to nuclear power from the technological or even environmental standpoint would find fault with SMUD for its management. "Essentially," Blum said, "we made a decision at a certain point that [quietly] SMUD was inept and incompetent in running a nuclear power plant. If you read our stories, I think that would come through, that was our point of view. SMUD hated us, right?"[46] Ultimately, Blum said, "the impression I got was part of this was the rinky little provincial attitude of this SMUD board that was only interested in rates, and part of it was that they kept their nuclear staff really small."[47]

SMUD knew it had both a public perception problem as well as serious technical issues to resolve. It had hoped to get Rancho Seco back online as soon as possible. In fact, for each day that Rancho Seco was offline, SMUD had to purchase approximately $262,000 worth of power from PG&E, not to mention paying the ongoing regular labor and maintenance costs. But SMUD would not go online for many months. Due to a variety of issues documented by the NRC in its investigation of Rancho Seco after the accident, the NRC ordered SMUD "to conduct a complete review of every major system at the plant."[48] As a result of this major review and other repair work required to restart the plant, Rancho Seco remained offline for the next twenty-seven months, ultimately costing SMUD a total of $400 million in upgrade and related costs.

The overcooling incident was bad enough, but the timing could not have been worse for Rancho Seco's supporters. Four months later, on April 26, 1986, the Chernobyl nuclear reactor, located north of Kiev in the Ukrainian Soviet Socialist Republic, suffered a major catastrophe. During a testing phase for that reactor, a power surge followed by a series of attempts to control the problem, along with additional power abnormalities, caused an explosion that consequently exposed radioactive material to the air resulting in a large amount of radioactive smoke escaping into the atmosphere. The consequences of the Chernobyl disaster were immense: radioactivity from Chernobyl covered the western parts of the Soviet Union as well as western Europe, amid predictions of up to sixty thousand cancer deaths, not to mention the thirty-one deaths that resulted directly from the disaster. The Chernobyl accident was a dramatic event that again fueled a renewed effort to shut down Rancho Seco. Martha Ann Blackman recalled that while Citizens for Safe Energy had held a press conference each year on the anniversary of Three Mile Island, the group was otherwise largely inactive until Chernobyl. "When Chernobyl happened, we pulled out all the stops. It was really frightening for us," she recalled, "because we felt that we were so close ourselves to having a major problem at Rancho Seco that we didn't want to have to deal with that here. We wanted to stop it before it got that far."[49]

Initiatives B and C

With a renewed sense of purpose in publicizing the problems at Rancho Seco, Martha Ann Blackman met by chance a woman named Melinda Brown while making copies of newspaper articles about Rancho Seco at a local photocopy store. In discussing their mutual interest in Rancho Seco, Brown invited Blackman to a meeting of people concerned about Rancho Seco in light of the Chernobyl disaster. Blackman attended the meeting at Brown's house, where she met local attorney Michael Remy and others. At this meeting, the attendees formed a new group called SAFE (Sacramentans for SAFE Energy), and Blackman was elected to its board.[50] While SAFE began developing a sophisticated grass-roots effort to shutter Rancho Seco, in May 1986 the *Sacramento Bee* launched an in-depth five-part investigative series on the nuclear plant. With the *Bee* taking an active role investigating the problems at Rancho Seco, SAFE could focus on building public support for a political initiative to close the plant.[51]

SAFE developed a strategy to close Rancho Seco that was based on both environmental concerns as well as financial ones. Although much of the passion behind the group's efforts was certainly centered on an environmental and antinuclear agenda, it was clear that the group's message needed to appeal to ratepayers who were perhaps not opposed to nuclear power itself but were very concerned about their own electricity rates. Publicity about SMUD's plans for future rate increases tacked on to current rate increases led to increasing discontent among SMUD's customers. Blackman described the basic strategy: "We did not really have the right to shut it down on safety reasons, but we could shut it down for economic reasons. . . . It became dual purpose, with economics being the focal point."[52] SAFE's focus on economics was clearly a strategy meant to reach a broader audience. Gary Sprung, a SMUD computer system specialist, understood that Rancho Seco's opponents were using the economic argument to reach a broader audience: "I think the economic issue was a cover for the people who were really spreading fear. So their message was fear. And then when they were taken to task about the actual items of fear, they revert back to, well it doesn't make economic sense, or, no-no, we're only involved in economics."[53]

Michael Remy, the group's chair and legal advisor, who had earlier argued on behalf of Friends of the Earth against the AEC's order allowing the restart of Rancho Seco after the Three Mile Island incident, was instrumental in devising the group's strategy. In particular, he understood that SAFE had to have a clear goal— close Rancho Seco—and be ready to achieve it. This goal could be accomplished through the political process, but it would take careful planning and a great deal of hard work. "Because in politics of this type," Remy said, "when you're going to the people, there is only one thing, that is winning. Losing is absolutely worthless. And so part of the strategy was really to get to a position that we could sell to fifty plus one. And fifty plus one, I mean, and it turned out to be that close. Enough to get one vote over, more than the other side."[54] In order to achieve its goal of shuttering Rancho Seco, SAFE actively and aggressively planned to take advantage of California's voter initiative system.

In California, voter initiatives can be placed on the ballot if a requisite number of registered voters sign petitions for the proposed initiative. In October 1986, SAFE developed "The Rancho Seco Voters' Rights Initiative," which would become known as Measure B. With more than 50,630 signatures (well above the required 25,000 signatures), SAFE brought the petitions to SMUD on April 27, 1987, and demanded that voters be given the opportunity to decide whether Rancho Seco should keep operating or not. SMUD wanted the vote set for the following year, but the Sacramento Superior Court later set a compromise election date during June 1988.[55]

The effort to bring Rancho Seco's condition to the public's attention was also addressed by the Sacramento League of Women Voters. Anna Antos recalled that "Rancho Seco, the way we arrived at that [the decision to do a study] was at our annual meeting in May [1986]. Just before the annual meeting, a couple days before the annual meeting, Chernobyl went off [its reactor No. 4 exploded April 26, 1986]. That's how that issue came up."[56] The membership decided to study Rancho Seco, and it appointed Madlyne MacDonald as the Rancho Seco study chair, with Judy Painter as the resource chair, and Wendy Reid was the energy consultant. They would lead the effort to research Rancho Seco and compose the Every Member's

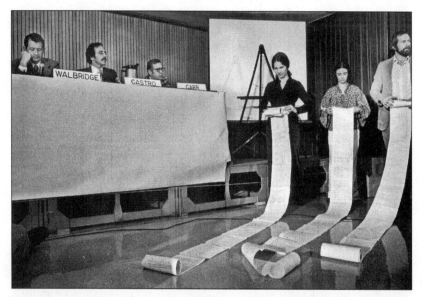

FIGURE 11.4. Presentation of petitions for a vote on the future of Rancho Seco to the Sacramento Municipal Utility District board. Courtesy Center for Sacramento History, Sacramento Bee Collection.

Toolkit, or EMT, which was an information packet used to inform the membership of the results of the issue under study.

MacDonald recalled, "We attended all of the SMUD meetings. And it was an amazing thing. It was standing room only at those SMUD meetings and those could get very vitriolic because they had people that were very much against nuclear power who were extremists, speaking out bluntly and emotionally."[57] The League of Women Voters in Sacramento ultimately endorsed a position to close Rancho Seco, but the measured and bipartisan nature of the league only underscored that this was not simply an anti- versus pro-nuke issue. MacDonald knew that local residents might take the position of the league more seriously than that of extremist groups: "I would say that, generally speaking, we were preferred over many other groups that were involved because we were measured, because we were non-emotional in our approach, and because we had a [favorable] reputation."[58]

While ongoing concerns about the plant's overall safety were addressed by the *Sacramento Bee* and could not be ignored in any case due to Rancho Seco's seemingly constant series of problems, as well as the ongoing issues related to Chernobyl, SAFE continued to push the economic argument. And it was becoming increasingly clear to many that Rancho Seco was actually becoming an economic liability that might take down all of SMUD. While SMUD's rates were still below those of PG&E, more rate increases were certainly on the way, and if SMUD's power became more expensive than that of PG&E, SMUD's reasons for being would be—understandably—questioned. Board president Cliff Wilcox considered whether SMUD should simply look for power on the open market and simultaneously investigate the possibility of selling Rancho Seco. PG&E also offered assistance, but it was not the offer the SMUD board wanted to hear. PG&E indicated it might be interested in buying SMUD outright and then shutting down Rancho Seco.[59] SMUD also received offers of power from Southern California Edison and the Bonneville Power Administration, and Portland General Electric offered to purchase SMUD's power generation facilities.[60]

In the meantime, SMUD hired a new general manager. After a difficult search process that at first focused on hiring S. David Freeman, formerly head of the Tennessee Valley Authority (TVA), the board hired Richard Byrne of the Massachusetts Municipal Wholesale Electric Company. Initially, the board had settled on Freeman but could not come to a compensation agreement with him, and this situation suited some members of the board who believed that Freeman was more likely to support closing Rancho Seco. Byrne, instead, was believed to be in favor of keeping Rancho Seco going. It was during this time, board member Smeloff recalled, that "I had made my mind up around January [1988] that the plant should be closed."[61] But this was a difficult position for a board member to take, he said, since "once I took the position to close the plant[,] . . . that isolated me."[62] One of Byrne's first moves as general manager was to contract for an independent study of Rancho Seco. The study, to be conducted by the Quality Energy for Sacramento's Tomorrow team (QUEST) issued a report on February 1, 1988, which did not support keeping Rancho Seco going. Byrne then shocked Rancho Seco's supporters by recommending that the plant be closed.[63]

Working at Rancho Seco during this time was not particularly pleasant for employees. The enthusiasm for nuclear energy had clearly dissipated, and SMUD was attempting to rectify the technical and managerial problems in order to keep the plant operating. The employees found themselves in a difficult position, working at their jobs while feeling the increasing anti–Rancho Seco pressure. Leon Grossheim, a tool repair subforeman, recalled, "It was just a lot of pressure, a lot of high pressure. And like I said, towards the end it was really bad because then you not only got it from all the different upper management doing their walkthroughs and the [Nuclear Regulatory Commission] coming through and checking on us, but also our own news media and things like that. And of course the news media got the general public fired up, and you just didn't tell people you worked at Rancho Seco."[64]

Rancho Seco's supporters believed that they needed to offer voters an alternative to simply voting to keep the plant operating or not. An employee group successfully urged the SMUD board to place an alternative initiative on the ballot (as a public agency, SMUD could sponsor an initiative without a signature petition drive). The new initiative, which became known as Measure C, would give voters the option of authorizing SMUD to operate Rancho Seco for an additional eighteen months, a "trial period," to be followed by a second vote to determine the plant's ultimate fate. Rancho Seco supporters hoped that voters would reject Measure B and approve Measure C, thereby giving Rancho Seco time to prove to the public that it could be operated safely and efficiently; otherwise, voters could shut the plant down in the subsequent vote.[65]

Carl Andognini, the engineer in charge of restarting Rancho Seco, was then actively seeking a buyer for the plant. He courted Duke Power, a large investor-owned utility headquartered in North Carolina that also had a strong interest in keeping Rancho Seco operating. Duke Power invested $100,000 in the campaign to save Rancho Seco, and it also had been negotiating with SMUD to manage Rancho Seco. As for the upcoming vote on Measures B and C, some observers believed that Duke Power perceived the vote as not simply an isolated issue about a problem-plagued plant but as a kind of general referendum on nuclear energy. Incensed by "interference" from Duke in the campaign, SMUD board member Smeloff traveled to a Duke Power stockholder meeting and told Duke to stay out of Sacramento's nuclear power issues. Duke Power had also been negotiating privately with SMUD to take over management of the plant, but the negotiations were not going well. Duke wanted $25 million per year plus performance bonus payments in return for providing one senior plant manager and unspecified additional staff and/or consultants. The management deal fell through.[66]

The effort to keep Rancho Seco operating was also intense.[67] The pro–Rancho Seco campaign had substantial financial and other support from groups such as the Sacramento Chamber of Commerce, as well as many local business leaders, farmers, and labor groups. Another ad hoc group, Citizens for Affordable Energy, supported the effort to keep Rancho Seco operating. But the local chapter of the League of Women Voters endorsed Measure B, and this endorsement also gave some "mainstream" legitimacy to SAFE, which appeared to many residents as simply an antinuclear organization.[68] SMUD directors John Kehoe and Ann Taylor also actively argued in favor of a "yes" vote on Measure C.

The movement to close Rancho Seco was perhaps more sophisticated and even more creative than many realized at the time. Fund-raising efforts, phone trees, and mailings were used effectively to garner support for the anti–Rancho Seco faction. Larger national and statewide organizations also played a role. Public Citizen, the national consumer rights advocacy group formed by Ralph Nader in 1971, actively supported SAFE's efforts. Martha Ann Blackman recalled that members of SAFE met with Ralph Nader at Sacramento State University during the campaign: "In fact, we had coffee with Ralph over here in the student union several times when he was in town. He was very gracious and helped us with the language of things we needed to do." Public Citizen was particularly important in assisting with research and information gathering.[69] Perhaps even more importantly, Campaign California, a political group founded by Tom Hayden, a cofounder of Students for a Democratic Society (SDS), also campaigned against Rancho Seco.

Michael Remy stated that the Rancho Seco voter initiative provided Campaign California with an opportunity to become more active and better known in Sacramento: "In this sense Campaign California was really looking . . . to build its constituency through door to door canvassing. And Rancho Seco was in Sacramento. . . . And Rancho Seco was actually a very good way for an organization like Campaign California to make some inroads in Sacramento."[70] Yet, the politics of the situation were "delicate." With Nader's Public Citizen and Hayden's Campaign California assisting their efforts, Sacramento's SAFE had to balance the support and assistance of these "outside groups" with the specter of a potential voter backlash. As Remy noted, "We knew where we could make inroads and we kind of also knew what voice it had to have, and what face. And it couldn't have their face, it couldn't."[71]

The election took place on June 7, 1988, and the results were very close. After more than 250,000 votes were counted, Measure B failed (49.4 to 50.4 percent), while Measure C passed, 51.6 to 48.4 percent; Rancho Seco would remain open for at least another year.[72] But more trouble was on the horizon. SMUD soon thereafter announced that it would have to implement two rate increases of 8 percent each over the next eighteen months. And the SMUD board fired Richard Byrne after what was described as a contentious board meeting; he was replaced by Dave Boggs, previously the head of the Sacramento Regional Transit Authority. Soon thereafter, engineer Carl Andognini resigned as well.[73]

The turnover of executive leadership at Rancho Seco served only to attract more attention from the *Sacramento Bee*. It printed articles about employee bonuses, large fees to consultants, and a costly plan to provide uniforms for Rancho Seco employees, ostensibly to project a more professional image to the public.[74] In addition, three of SMUD's board members were facing reelection in November. Two decided not to run again, and the third incumbent was defeated. The three new members included two who supported closing Rancho Seco and one who supported its continuation. However, one of the remaining two incumbents who initially supported the plant was beginning to support possible closure. And Rancho Seco's operational problems continued, with additional significant problems in December 1988 and January 1989. Further, both the NRC and the INPO now expressed concern over Rancho Seco's operations and operational procedures; a report issued by INPO criticized Rancho Seco for "lax operating procedures, engineering deficiencies, mechanical failures, and other problems."[75]

Making matters worse, there was a difficult relationship between Rancho Seco's executive staff, who were struggling to keep the plant operating, and the SMUD board, which was split on the issue. In this scenario, it could be an unpleasant task for a Rancho Seco executive to ask the board for more and more resources. Richard Oubre, who had served as manager of the nuclear operations department at Rancho Seco, recalled that "at the beginning of the '80s, the middle of the '80's, it was paranoia, I mean absolute paranoia, to go to the Board and ask for anything . . . and you just did not want to go through the chastising, the public chastising, that you received from those people."[76] He continued, adding that "the nuclear staff were right in between a Board that kept saying we were doing too much, and the NRC, who kept saying . . . and not just to us, they'd tell it to the industry . . . that we were doing the minimum."[77]

An important technical issue that was perhaps overshadowed by the larger safety concerns was the difference between Rancho Seco's nuclear and non-nuclear operating systems. Richard Oubre stated that "we were doing anything we could think of to prevent another outage due to turbine generators. Probably 75–80 percent of our outages were, in some way, the result of the turbine generator complex. Very, very disheartening . . . and disheartening to the local populace. They saw this plant not operating. Yet the nuclear steam supply system just hummed along. It was a good system."[78] Ultimately, it did not matter why the plant had problems; the fact remained that it clearly did. Inevitably, this situation raised concerns about safety as well as the impact of the outages on rates.

SMUD had set the date of June 6, 1989, for the public vote on Measure K, the next referendum on keeping Rancho Seco open, which had been authorized in Measure C. The forces strongly in favor of keeping Rancho Seco in operation were growing fewer, although they still had financial backing. Many Rancho Seco employees, labor groups and some businesses campaigned in support of Rancho Seco. And while Duke Power was now out of the picture, the engineering firm Bechtel, as well as Babcock & Wilcox, had offered to keep the plant running if Measure K passed.[79] SMUD board president Joe Buonaiuto also controversially suggested that if Measure K was defeated, he would try to find another company to run the plant. There was increasing concern within the nuclear power industry that the Measure K vote could be a watershed for the US nuclear power industry.

Leading up to the election, there was a power struggle of sorts between members of the more radical antinuclear movement and the political strategists working with SAFE. SAFE's attorney, Michael Remy, recalled,

Well, what happened is that five days or so before the '89 election, I mean we constantly were polling because that is one of the things we did do. . . . We were polling and we were very close. We were looking to see where was it that we could win over the people. And it was definitely not in the area of [anti-] nuclear. . . . We lost control. And they [antinuclear groups] had called for a big march on Sacramento. And we pretty much figured we were going to lose. Because they were going to go, you know, "The Crazies." And I could just see it on television. And God intervened and it rained. And it fell apart. It rained really hard. And it fell apart. And I always thought that sometimes the strangest things determine outcomes really.[80]

When the votes were counted, Measure K had failed, with 53.4 percent of voters casting ballots to close down the plant. Rancho Seco then became the first nuclear power plant to be voted out of operation; Scott Denman of the Safe Energy Communication Council called this a "shot heard around the world."[81] Remy later

FIGURE 11.5. Rancho Seco Recreational Area, 2010. Photograph by Terri A. Castaneda.

gave considerable credit to Campaign California for the successful effort to close Rancho Seco. "In many, many ways but for Tom Hayden," Remy said, "and Bob Mulholland who was the campaign manager, we wouldn't have held the line that we did. . . . I for one will tell that, but for Campaign California it would never have happened. We would have had all of the right ideas, but we couldn't have done it without Campaign."[82] From the perspective of SMUD employee Leon Grossheim, "We didn't stand a chance. There was just too much public opinion against us."[83] Another perspective, from Wendy Reid, the Sacramento League of Women Voters' energy advisor, was more concise: "It certainly was a long evolving process. . . . It was the poor performance of the Ranch during that period of time [preceding] the vote."[84]

The SMUD board did briefly investigate the possibility of selling Rancho Seco, and Quadrex Corporation expressed interest in running it. But Quadrex's offer was complex and mired in strident opposition from SAFE, which claimed that Rancho Seco had to be shuttered by the terms of the Measure K vote. SMUD finally rejected Quadrex's offer, and it was clear then that Rancho Seco would never operate again.[85] With a final decision made on Rancho Seco, there were serious concerns about SMUD's long-term viability. It was time to reinvigorate the utility and move forward. The SMUD board, doing now what it had not been able to do earlier, hired S. David Freeman as general manager.[86] Freeman, who stayed at SMUD for the next three and a half years, helped to turn SMUD around, in terms of both public perception and overall operations. As Illa Collin, a Sacramento County supervisor, stated, "For all the pros and cons about David Freeman . . . he certainly pulled that board together. And he made them come up with a way to make this utility successful and hold the rates down. Once the rates stabilized and people could see that the board was stabilizing and they had a director in there—he was a glad-hand, he was all over town—the business community came to have a lot of confidence, I think, in him."[87]

Half-Life

The closure of Rancho Seco was the result of a long-term and concerted effort by citizens who had a variety of strongly felt objections to nuclear power, both in terms of safety and cost. It is also clear that without Rancho Seco's history of operating problems, outages, and accidents, some of which coincided with two of the world's most serious nuclear accidents—Three Mile Island and Chernobyl—there would not likely have been a successful grass-roots effort to close the plant. As Martha Ann Blackman later recalled, "The way we closed Seco was by using its own mistakes. If it had no problems, we could not have closed it. . . . We just utilized everything that we could get our hands on that told about the things that had gone wrong there."[88] This is certainly true, yet there are other voices—voices that did not represent the "winning side"—that provide additional perspectives on the impact Rancho Seco had on the community.

Terry Dunden, an operations training supervisor at Rancho Seco, noted the basic safety concerns that seemed to drive the antinuclear activists. "Our introduction [to nuclear energy] was two bombs during World War II," he said. "So they think this thing can blow up like that. But it can't. It physically can't. We physically couldn't make it if we wanted to."[89] Responding at least in part to the same sentiment, George Pavia stated, "I think that the closure of Rancho Seco was based on false perceptions. It was kind of a feeding frenzy."[90] This observation may have in some respects underlined the effort to close Rancho Seco, but the issues were complex. Rancho Seco engineer Robert Nash moved this perspective further: "I thought it was emotional issues [leading to the vote that closed the plant]. People were convinced that the plant was dangerous and they were also convinced that the plant was not economically viable, but the economics was more or less a self-fulfilling prophecy."[91] Yet, one underlying and ongoing serious issue was concern about the nuclear waste generated by the plant and what would be done with it. Anna Antos remarked that when nuclear plants were built, the utility's management would say, "We don't know what to do with the radioactive garbage. But by the time that we have the garbage we'll find what to do. . . . And we believed it. We fell for that."[92]

Rancho Seco, as part of a municipal utility in the state's capital, was particularly vulnerable to politics, and SMUD, as a public agency, was restricted in the ways in which it could respond. Sacramento County supervisor Collin noted, "I think the biggest weakness was with that elected board—with the priority being keep the rates as low [as] possible, at all costs—what happened with that size utility, with the big pressure to keep the rates so low, was that they built, what one nuclear power expert called the Ferrari of nuclear power plants" and then did not allocate funds to properly maintain it.[93] Echoing this sentiment was Rancho Seco electrical engineer Keith Hartley, who pointed out that "the push from the board was: get the plant back on line, do what you have to do to keep it going. And along with that was kind of an attitude of: don't put a lot of money into it, or put as little money into it as you can get away with . . . do as much as you can for as little cost as you can get away with."[94] Hartley also observed that the public should have focused more attention on the board itself, because of its policies: "I think I was more surprised to see public sentiment come out as anti-nuclear when, to me, most of that should have been driven at the board. The board is an elected body. To me, if you didn't like the board of directors, what should have been done is that during the next election they should have been voted out of office."[95]

A municipal utility is subject to both economic as well as political concerns. Perhaps municipal utilities, as public entities, are intrinsically more responsive to the public, but they do not have to worry about stockholders. As engineer Oubre stated, "The private entity, like PG&E, has to worry about, 'Do we take the monies out of the ratepayers or do we take the monies out of the stockholders?' . . . In the case of an elected Board, where they physically go to be voted on, as with the SMUD Board, they are very, very sensitive to public comments."[96] Perhaps that sensitivity also engenders a longer-term social responsibility. Board member Smeloff, while supporting the closure of Rancho Seco, was also forward looking, to a time when deregulation of the industry was being explored and alternative energy sources were increasingly understood to be the future: " . . . since that time we chartered a new direction. Since the closure of the plant we made a major commitment to energy efficiency and renewable technologies."[97]

Ultimately, closing Rancho Seco did not permanently damage SMUD. In fact, it allowed the utility to focus on a different kind of energy future for its customers. At a speech delivered by SMUD general manager Richard Ferreira in New York City four years after Rancho Seco closed, he stated, "It was, however, the local citizenry that voted to close the Ranch, deciding the nuclear option was too risky for a small utility with limited technical, management and financial capabilities. The fact that an electorate voted down a nuclear plant and made the right economic decision should not be lost."[98] Indeed, ratepayers had voted through the political process on their electric power supply, and they chose a different path than SMUD had offered. The utility responded appropriately and began to move in a different direction itself, one that was more responsive to its customers as well as the changing dynamics of the energy industry and environmental concerns.

PART IV

Reclaiming the Past

CHAPTER 12

Dreams, Realizations, and Nightmares
THE AMERICAN RIVER PARKWAY'S
TUMULTUOUS LIFE, 1915–2011

Alfred E. Holland, Jr.

S acramentans proudly hail the American River Parkway as their region's crown
jewel. The nearly thirty-mile-long swath of riparian habitat straddling its
namesake river realizes a thinking man's good idea dating from 1915. A second
person reiterated and expanded that idea in 1927 and again at midcentury. After
four decades trying to break out of bureaucratic circles, a state bureaucrat and
streamside resident built a dream on the parkway idea and mobilized a cadre of
fellow insiders to apply public pressure at the city and county levels when rapid
suburban development encroached on the wild and ravaged lands bordering the
river. Between 1961 and 1978, the American River Parkway idea and the parkway
itself grew vigorously. Since then, not withstanding its merits and popularity, the
parkway has suffered from financial starvation—consequences of local, regional,
state, and national political machinations.

In contrast to other notable urban parks such as New York's Central Park and
San Francisco's Golden Gate Park, Sacramento's American River Parkway is for
the most part a natural environment rather than a rendition of a landscape architect's vision of "Nature." Far larger than other urban parks at more than forty-six
hundred acres, the American River Parkway is a unique public asset offering a
broad range of habitats and hosting profuse communities of flora and fauna. The
American River coheres the parkway, so this discussion of that good idea begins
with the river itself.

The River

The American River Parkway abuts the American River along its reach from the
river's mouth at Discovery Park upstream to Nimbus Dam, where it joins an additional seven miles of the Folsom Lake Recreation Area up to Beal's Point. Along its

FIGURE 12.1. American River Parkway. Map by Alfred E. Holland, Jr., 2011. Base layer from USDA-FSA-APFO Digital Ortho Mosaic Sacramento County, US Department of Agriculture National Agriculture Imagery Program, 2010.

twenty-three-mile course downstream of Nimbus Dam, the American River calms from a robust and rushing Sierra stream to the slow-moving but nonetheless second-largest tributary of California's largest stream, the Sacramento River.[1]

As is the case with all streams draining the western slope of the Sierra Nevada batholith, the American River has through the centuries gradually migrated northward from the higher southern end of that granitic block. The high bluffs that loom along the north bank of the American between Folsom and Carmichael, in contrast with the lower and relatively flat terrain of Rancho Cordova on the south bank, illustrate both this gradual northward migration and the consequence of the river's erosive power.[2]

Like Job's Lord, rivers give and rivers take away.[3] Whether moving quickly or slowly, rivers carve at impediments to their flow, corroding and eroding material and sweeping it away in the current, but the slower they flow the less they can carry.[4] Rivers are notorious litterbugs. Unless they maintain the speed at which they eroded their suspended sediment, they leave everything they carry strewn along behind as they rush headlong to their reunion with their mother, the ocean. The boulders, cobbles, gravels, sand, and silt dropped by the American River as it slowed debouching on to the Great Central Valley's floodplains mutely mark the torrent's transformation.[5] In a major 1917 study of the consequences of hydraulic mining, Grove Karl Gilbert estimated hydraulic mining in the American River watershed excavated 170.33 million cubic yards of material, all of which became potential detritus.[6] Most of that material along the American River's course in the

Sacramento region was deposited in a four-flood sequence—one routine, two major, and one superflood—in December 1861 and January 1862. In that greatest of Great Valley floods, debris loosened by hydraulic mining in the Sierra foothills was swept downstream by runoff from both torrential rainfall and precipitous snowmelt from a series of major storms, both arctic and tropical, buffeting the central Sierra.[7]

The American River's flow has varied between wide extremes during the period its flows have been recorded at Fair Oaks (1905 to the present). On several days during the summer drought of 1924, recorded flows dropped to less than 5 cubic feet per second. Its peak recorded flow of 132,000 cubic feet per second was recorded on November 21, 1950. The character of the American River changed abruptly in 1955, when construction of Folsom and Nimbus Dams was completed and their reservoirs began to fill. Since the dams began to buffer the river's flow, the peak stream flow is 131,000 cubic feet per second, recorded on February 19, 1986. But mean maximum flows have dropped by nearly one-third, from 39,300 cubic feet per second for the period from 1905 to 1954 to 26,400 cubic feet per second for the period from 1955 to 2010. Average minimum flows, on the other hand, have risen by a factor of 6.25 under the dams' river regulation regime, from 142 cubic feet per second from 1905 to 1954 to 887 cubic feet per second from 1955 to 2010. Mean daily stream flow has barely changed, declining just over 3 percent since the dams were built. Although Folsom's reservoir has provided flood protection during formidable storms, the dams have not limited high-water episodes. They have, however, reduced average high-water flows and significantly raised low flows. Whether the flood control improvements will suffice to protect Sacramento from the next superflood remains an open question. The US Geological Service estimates the American flowed at 318,000 cubic feet per second, more than twice the capacity of today's levees, on January 10, 1862. When another storm sequence of that magnitude batters the watersheds of the Sacramento River and the American River, Sacramento will flood. The river always wins.[8]

The American River systematically sorts its sediment load from coarsest to finest along its course. The boulders beneath Folsom's Rainbow Bridge, at the head of Lake Natoma, are the size of the automobiles zipping above them. Left behind by the river slowing precipitously as it exited the last canyon along its course and lost the powerful current of that confined channel upstream, those boulders have since hosted activities as varied as clambering opportunities for children of all ages and subject matter for landscape painters. Downstream the alluvial deposits become progressively smaller in diameter. The gravel bar on the right bank five and one-third miles downstream at Sailor Bar, however, is made up mostly of stones too large for skipping. At the point thirteen miles downstream from those Rainbow Bridge boulders, at the end of Rod Beaudry Drive in Rancho Cordova, skipping stones of appropriate size and sufficient plenty to exhaust a ten-year-old litter the beaches and bars at the former Goethe Park, now River Bend Park.[9] Beyond the levee behind Rio Americano and Jesuit High Schools, fifteen and three-quarters miles from Rainbow Bridge, the American River has become a mature, valley-bottom stream with abandoned meanders and horseshoe lakes on both banks. The expansive and alluring sandbar at Paradise Beach, twenty-one river miles downstream, attracts sunbathers and oglers throughout the warm months of the year. Protected from the seasonal high flows, the soil beneath the sod at Glen Hall Park immediately behind the levee at Paradise Beach, and throughout the East Sacramento and Campus Commons neighborhoods, is deep sandy loam, the fine silt and sand deposited in the backwaters during the centuries before the dams and levees constraining the American and Sacramento Rivers' floods were built.

Flora and Fauna

The biological communities calling the American River corridor home are richly diverse. The largest organisms along the parkway are the trees. Whether clustered hard by the streambed or scattered across the savannah-like uplands, trees first catch a parkway visitor's eye. Vegetation density strongly correlates to proximity to the river and its high water table.

Well-adapted to recurrent drowning and resilient to the damages inflicted by strong current, thickets of willows crowd from the water's edge across the ground inundated by winter high-water flows. The dominant riparian trees, those preferring to have their roots in the water but their trunks out, colonize the grounds elevated immediately above the willow thickets. Cottonwoods, sycamores, ashes, alders, and valley oaks predominate in the riparian groves' canopy. Blackberries and grapes comprise the most visible members of the riparian understory vegetation, their long vines and canes creating impenetrable brambles and tangles. In several shady but moist locations, grapes—masters of vertical encroachment— have climbed the trees, shaded out their host's leaves, and eventually pulled the thus-weakened trees down by the mass of vines. Sweet-loving avian and browsing species swarm to the grapes beginning in late August and through September, when the grapes ripen. Blackberries do not climb as well as grapes. They spread instead, forming five-foot-high mounds of tangled canes, festooned with succulent berries beginning in early July. The elderberry attracts a different sort of attention. It hosts throughout its entire life cycle the valley elderberry longhorn beetle, federally listed as threatened. The elderberries ripen, to the delight of most songbirds, in addition to rodents and opossums, from July through October. Deer browse on its leaves and twigs, particularly favoring its leaves after the first frost. The dense understory of the riparian groves provides bountiful food resources and protective cover to a broad variety of wildlife.

The higher and drier ground along the river, including the bluffs at Carmichael and upstream, hosts a forest, including the valley oaks familiar from the drier margins of the riparian community, but dominated by blue and interior live oaks, California walnut, California foothill pine, locusts, and California buckeye. The shrubs of the upland groves include ceanothus, covered with blue flowers in the spring, toyon, sporting red berries in the late fall, redbud, coffeeberry, some shrubby lupines, scotch broom, and the dastardly bane of woodland frolics, poison oak.

Two groups inventory the birds and other wildlife in the American River Parkway each winter during December. Zone 3 of the Sacramento Audubon Society's Christmas Count includes the dense riparian forest hard by the channel and the grasslands behind those groves on the right bank of the American from its mouth upstream to opposite Paradise Beach. Although the report does not break out birds by zone, the 2010–11 count spotted 160 individual species, one of the highest totals in nearly sixty years of counting.

The American River Natural History Association conducts a Parkway Wildlife Count covering the reach between Hazel Avenue and Discovery Park in early December each year. Several of the avian species counted in each of the count's twenty-six years are regulars along the river. Waterfowl include several duck species, the delightful diving pied-billed grebe, the double-crested cormorant, and nine species of gulls. Among the shorebirds, the elegant great blue heron and its smaller cousin the green heron, the great egret, and eight varieties of sandpipers scour the shallows and flats for tasty amphibians, crustaceans, and fish while the bank-living belted kingfisher hunts from branches above the stream. The grasslands host California's state bird, the California quail, the ring-necked pheasant (an imported game bird), the mourning dove, western meadowlarks, the yellow-billed magpie, and increasingly, in recent years, raucous wild turkeys. Soaring above, roosting in the trees, stooping to catch fish, and chasing their prey through the canopy are several species of raptors, including the ubiquitous turkey vulture, red-tailed hawks, an occasional Swainson's hawk that opted not to migrate to Mexico or South America for a year-round summer, ospreys, American kestrels and their larger cousins, the peregrine falcon and the hovering white-tailed kite. Occasionally both the bald and the golden eagle pass through and tarry to gorge on spent salmon. Swooping at low altitude, the northern harrier crisscrosses the marshes and grasslands. More often heard than seen during daylight hours, six species of owls hunt while the hawks sleep. The marshlands of the inlets and horseshoe lakes host cloudlike flocks of Brewer's, red-winged, and tri-colored blackbirds, and an avian weed, the European starling. Nine species of woodpeckers, sapsuckers, nuthatches, and flickers work the nut and acorn crops of the parkway forests, then switch to extracting grubs from the trunks and branches of the several tree and shrub species when the mast crop has passed. Their principal competition for the nuts is the western scrub jay, which, along with its corvid cousins, the yellow-billed magpie, American crow, and occasional raven, is making a slow comeback from the ravages of the West Nile virus. The bountiful insect resources of the parkway keep the flycatchers, mockingbirds, thrushes, bluebirds, and other insectivorous birds well fed.

Historically, mammals of the region included herds of tule elk, antelope, and deer, which in turn fed grizzly and black bears, wolves, and mountain lions. Of the ungulates, only a few deer remain in the parkway, seen most often in the vicinity of the Cal Expo event center and in Ancil Hoffman Park. The bears and wolves had been extirpated by the beginning of the twentieth century, but at least three times in the 1990s and 2000s an occasional mountain lion wandered into or through the parkway, causing great excitement among the parkway's neighbors. Repeated sightings and signs of lions have occurred far more often than reported in the local newspaper, confirming how wild the natural habitats of the parkway have remained in the heart of the Sacramento metropolis.[10] Several species of wild canids also reside in the parkway, including foxes and coyotes, and there are also the more elusive badgers and bobcats. Muskrats, beaver, river otters, and a rare sea lion make their living in and along the river. Mink, opossums, ground, gray, and red squirrels, and weasels forage in the thickets and brush of the parkway. Pocket gophers and moles burrow through the soil as alligator and fence lizards scurry about in search of insects.[11]

Several feral organisms use the parkway. Chief among them are humans who most visibly use the parkway as a residence. Homeless and otherwise marginalized men and women establish substantial yet ultimately ephemeral camps in the thickets along the lower reaches of the parkway, especially between the Sixteenth Street Bridge and Discovery Park, close by the metal and beverage container recycling yard, food kitchens, and indigent persons' services offices. These twenty-first-century camps are reminiscent of the Hoovervilles strewn along the banks of the American and Sacramento Rivers during the Great Depression.[12] Unlike the more permanent camps of the depression, modern camps last only until the police, goaded by single-room occupancy hotel and other flophouse proprietors into enforcing the city's prohibition against camping within the city limits, make one of their periodic sweeps, rousting campers and sometimes confiscating possessions. In addition, some solitary campers secret their individual camps away into thickets, holding down full-time, minimum-wage jobs paying less than enough to rent a roof over their head. Abandoned camps, whether abandoned voluntarily or by force, leave unsightly and unhealthful accumulations of refuse and other waste that must be cleaned up, further aggravating better-heeled parkway users.[13]

Feral household pets and backyard poultry find refuge in the parkway just like their human counterparts. Both dogs and cats slink about and lurk in the protective cover of parkway vegetation, subsisting on small rodents and bits of garbage strewn about by better-fed human users. Feral domesticated waterfowl work their way to or are abandoned in the waterway. The bizarre-looking ducks and geese paddling about Lake Natoma display the remarkable genetic diversity of their parent stock, mixed by opportunistic breeding. Fair Oaks chickens, descendants of resident artist and eccentric Hugh Gorman's street-ranging flock, now trapped by residents, have been "relocated" to the south end of the pedestrian bridge at the end of Bridge Street, augmenting a remarkable swarm of roosters and hens beaking and scratching in the leaf litter in and adjoining South Sunrise Park. Although rarely seen, on occasion a flock of feral, parrotlike cockatoos, escaped from their cages, makes its high-speed and noisy way through the parkway's groves.

The Parkway

The earliest use of the name American River Parkway appeared in a 1915 plan for Sacramento and its environs presented by pioneer urban planner John Nolen. In his proposal he envisioned maintaining the lands bordering the Sacramento River above and below the city and the American River all the way upstream to Folsom as a series of parklands. His "Preliminary Plan" illustrates two major objectives: an urban planner's "concern over the location and effects of unregulated private development on the urban landscape" and progressive social ideology.[14] Nolen's proposal was consistent with the reform philosophies of the Progressive era. Comfortable with the moral environmentalism ideology of his time, Nolen was convinced that providing beautiful places would improve society by providing a handy place to escape and that the natural environment would help alleviate the social tensions accompanying the urbanization and industrialization of the late nineteenth and early twentieth centuries. Nolen was among the first professional urban planners in the United States, was an influential thinker during the maturation of urban planning from the ideals of the City Beautiful movement to those of the City Practical, as well as a pioneer in adapting urban design to the rapidly evolving transportation modes, particularly the automobile. Robert Freestone has summarized Nolen's arguments for incorporating automobiles and roadways into professionally designed cities, observing, "New parkways were not just attractive pleasure drives but mechanisms for transforming unsightly corridors into impressive civic showpieces."[15] The Sacramento region's riverine corridors were not at all unsightly, but recurring floods rendered them marginal. Because the American and Sacramento Rivers rose with winter rains, the lands in their floodplains could not be fully developed. A high-volume thoroughfare in the boulevard parkway mode would be supremely impractical along the Sacramento's and the American's banks. Nolen instead proposed impressive civic showpiece scenic drives along both banks of six parks straddling the region's rivers: an American River Parkway extending from the mouth of the American beyond the edge of his plan at Brighton, Riverbank Park at the west end of Y Street on the left bank of the Sacramento, Sutterville Park at the intersection of Riverside and Sutterville Roads on the left bank of the Sacramento, Westside Park on the right bank of the Sacramento opposite Riverbank and Sutterville Parks, and Washington Park on the right bank of the Sacramento upstream of its confluence with the American.[16] A roadway cohered Nolen's proposed parkways through their entire length—a delightful place for a Sunday drive through the country without leaving town. Sacramento's city fathers neither implemented John Nolen's city plan nor pursued his proposed parkway. His parkway idea, however, endured as a dream.

A decade and a half later, the automobile had not only proliferated in California, it had also become even more important to recreational and scenic pursuits. California's State Park Commission in 1928 engaged Frederick Law Olmsted Jr., son of Central Park's designer and mentor to John Nolen in his studies at Harvard, to conduct a survey of the lands of the state, highlighting opportunities for creating state parks. Olmsted's *Report of State Park Survey of California,* although it emphasized more conventional "scenic and recreational assets" in mountainous, timbered, and coastal locales, focused briefly and innovatively on the riparian borders of the Sacramento River and its tributaries. Olmsted waxed rhapsodic on their merits: "For a distance of more than eighty miles, from Antioch past Sacramento to above Marysville, the river channels are enclosed by levees constructed by the state for flood protection. Along many of these levees there are roads, built and maintained by the state and its agents, the counties. From the levees, by automobile and otherwise, there are commanded delightful views of the river and its margins and of miles and miles of beautiful orchards and farming lands outside of and below the levees." He urged the State Park Commission to take advantage of the "situation which now offers admirable opportunities for scenic enjoyment by road and by water[,] and many pleasant natural recreation spots along the river could not only be maintained but greatly enhanced in scenic value" through State Park Commission collaboration with federal authorities (charged with maintaining navigation on the streams), other state authorities (managing debris control and flood protection), and local governments (armed with zoning authority) to achieve together what no single entity might alone.[17] In large part because of the severe restrictions in state expenditures consequent of the Great Depression and the distractions of World War II, California took no major action on Olmsted's suggestions.

Upon the end of hostilities, in 1946 California passed a substantial bond to finance the acquisition of additional lands for state parks. The California State Park Commission again sought guidance from Olmsted on establishing additional parks and recreation areas. Through the course of four years of study and analysis, Olmsted produced a *General Report on Potential State Park and Recreational Areas* (1950).[18] Olmsted's *General Report* summarized his findings at a statewide level. Prior to publishing the report, he and the State Park Commission published several preliminary reports, including one on the Sacramento River and its tributaries. The two-part report on the Sacramento River detailed specific proposals for park and parkway development along the river from the delta upstream to Yuba City and Marysville, and up its two major tributaries, the Feather and American Rivers. Olmsted was particularly taken with the scenic vistas offered by the roads atop levees built to protect valley bottoms from flooding. In his first, very general, supplementary report of December 1946, he noted how, during the nearly two decades between his earlier report and his present surveys, both freighting and passenger transport had shifted from steamboat to truck, rail, and automobile and that the levee-top roads were relieved of traffic as it was directed "away from the winding, crooked roads on to direct, modern, high-speed State Highways on the flat delta plain." He argued that the lands between the levees were "in general of little usefulness or value except for scenic enjoyment" because of their recurring flooding but that they should be easily acquired at bargain prices because they were "practically economic wasteland strips, unused and unusable" except as access to the river. In his conclusion, Olmsted far more strongly extolled the merits of levee roads as both access routes to riparian parkways and as sensible boundaries to those parklands: "Obviously this progressive diversion from the winding levee roads of through traffic bent on making high speed will tend to make these roads safer and more attractive than ever as *pleasure drives* for people from all the surrounding populous region," to the extent those drivers sought scenery and access to river recreation.[19]

In April 1947, Olmsted prepared an appendix to his December 1946 "Report on Sacramento River Parkways." In the later report, he described eight "divisions." Three of those divisions addressed the lands along the American River from the Folsom Bridge downstream to the river's mouth. He noted that the lands had already been put to use as parks, albeit informally: "Now this stretch of the American River is of great potential value for, and is considerably used by, the population of Sacramento and lower Placer Counties for a variety of recreational activities. Fishing is very popular; and all accessible areas along the south side of the river are heavily used for swimming, picnicking, etc.,—by trespass or on sufferance, and without any improvements or sanitary facilities or policing." He recognized the transition from foothill to valley bottom biotic communities and extolled the scenic interest, particularly of the right bank, where "the palisades . . . give the whole area a climactic sort of charm that makes it entirely worthy of consideration for State Park purposes."[20] Except for the lands along the shores of Lake Natoma, impounded behind Nimbus Dam, the California State Park Commission never acquired streamside lands for state parks along the American River but offered matching funds to assist local bodies in doing so.

John Nolen's good idea, reiterated twice by Frederick Law Olmsted, took root as a passionate dream. Movers and shakers in Sacramento rose to the matching funds lure offered by the State Park Commission. Chamber of commerce members and representatives of both the county and city governments joined together in a mainstream, quasi-official River Beautification Commission assembled in 1947.[21] The River Beautification Commission's efforts produced early results. In 1950, Sacramento mayor Herbert Eugene "Bert" Geisreiter successfully cajoled the city into purchasing Paradise Beach, a great expanse of sand roughly halfway between the H Street and Sixteenth Street Bridges across the American River on the left bank behind the levee protecting the River Park subdivision. Parklands had been acquired, but the city of Sacramento had gone into the parkway acquisition business on its own.

Elmer Aldrich, a conservation educator working for the California State Park Commission, learned of Olmsted's proposals and began to promote the parkway idea in his own neighborhood along the left bank of the American River just downstream of the H Street Bridge over the American.[22] His River Park neighbors and other river and riverbank users took up the dream and began to pressure city and county government agencies and elected officials to consider the proposals. Their citizen group sought to buttress the successes of the River Beautification Commission and especially to broaden the range of government entities organized to acquire riparian lands for a parkway. Those activists formed the River Recreation and Parks Association in 1951 to influence city and county authorities to endorse formation of a regional park district in order to raise funds through a property tax levy and to manage lands acquired thereby. Encouraged by a State Park Commission allocation of $200,000 to purchase property along the Sacramento, Feather, and American Rivers, the members of the River Recreation and Parks Association promoted a voter initiative to form a park district and to encourage private contributions to augment the funds raised through taxation. Elmer Aldrich penned an article in the Sacramento Audubon Society's journal, *The Observer,* announcing formation of the association and describing its objectives. He extolled Sacramento's opportunity: "We have in the Sacramento region a perfect stage for a conservation project of note. Sacramento at the Apex of two great river courses is perhaps the only city of its size in the country that has not developed them into parks or at least made them available for public use." Then he urged timely action: "This crusade will not be a new idea—it has been thought of many times. Waiting, however, makes it increasingly difficult to accomplish the purpose. In the last few years residential subdividing of the cream of the river frontage is a real threat towards ever securing an integrated park system for public enjoyment."[23]

The River Recreation and Parks Association enlisted support from three constituencies: conservation organizations, parks supporters in the progressive tradition, and neighbors who used the lands along and waters in the American River for refuge and recreation. Recruiting members of the two principal conservation organizations in the region, the recently organized Mother Lode chapter of the Sierra Club and the Audubon Society, came easily and quickly. Audubon members sought to preserve habitat for both wild and tame users—for their friends the birds and for their fellow bird watchers. The Sierra Clubbers, having drunk deeply of John Muir's praises of the outdoors as "no holier temple . . . consecrated by the heart of man," enthusiastically embraced preserving the wild lands in the heart of the rapidly expanding urban core.[24] The Sacramento Woman's Council, led by President Thelma McCullough, who simultaneously served on the board of directors of the River Recreation and Parks Association, lent its support and influence to the parkway proposal, consistent with its principles of preserving and beautifying parks.[25]

For the first few years of its existence, the River Recreation and Parks Association made little tangible progress in expanding the parkway of its dreams. Its members' motivation was spurred in 1955 when the Bureau of Reclamation and Army Corps of Engineers finished construction of Folsom and Nimbus Dams and the levees downstream. Characteristic of mid-twentieth-century water projects, that major construction effort was a multipurpose project designed to provide flood protection to downstream residents, to provide water storage and delivery for agricultural, industrial, and domestic water users, and to generate electricity and revenues from power sales. Reducing the threat of flooding posed a new threat, at least in the eyes of the River Recreation and Parks Association. Now that the river's rampages had been tamed, lands abutting the river could be reclaimed from the wilds and developed. Property owners along the American River who had held on to lands rendered nearly worthless by recurring flooding now stood to make great financial gains by selling to subdividers. The threat Aldrich had identified in 1951 had become far more acute as a consequence of the successful actions of those two federal agencies. Aldrich and his allies began to pursue Olmsted's most challenging recommendation—to promote regional cooperation, especially between the City and County of Sacramento.

Sacramento City and Sacramento County had since the earliest days approached the American and Sacramento Rivers very differently. City leaders had understood since the boom days of the 1850s their responsibility was to promote commerce and minimize the tax burden on those commercial operators. To protect the commercial core from flooding, the city had thrown up a series of woefully inadequate but inexpensive levees. Each time, the American punched through and filled the levee-enclosed basin with standing water. Finally, Sacramento merchants taxed themselves to finance raising the streets above routine high water beginning in the 1870s.

County officials, on the other hand, represented miners of a far broader expanse of landscape. Whether mining the rich bottomland soil's fertility in agriculture or mining the stream's prodigious gravel resources, the county's constituents sought protection from the American's floods on their river-bottom holdings upstream of the city.[26] Consistent with that historical division, when citizens began to call for aggressive acquisition of riparian lands for a parkway, city officials took the position that they had made the first move in acquiring Paradise Beach, the one site in the city ideally suited to parkway development. Buoyed by their success with the Paradise Beach purchase, the cadre of activists focused their attention on the county. They coherently argued that, because the city was so compact relative to the sprawl of the county, administration of the American River bottomlands ought logically fall to the county.

The Sacramento County Science Steering Committee had since the mid-1950s advocated setting aside lands throughout the county for natural history educational purposes. Organized by J. Martin Weber, the committee included Effie Yeaw, an elementary school teacher from Carmichael who had been taking her students to riparian groves for nature study. After retiring from full-time teaching, Yeaw served frequently as a long-term substitute. No matter the subject matter, she routinely incorporated the study of biological communities into her lessons. No matter which of the "three Rs" they studied at the moment, her elementary-school charges read about, wrote about, or calculated about creatures, their lives, and their homes. Weber later recalled, "Effie pushed us to start thinking of a natural area along the American River, and to consider an American River Parkway."[27]

In 1960, Sacramento County drafted a county-wide master plan. That plan, in large measure through the efforts of the River Recreation and Parks Association membership and of William Pond, who had been hired as the first chief of the county's Department of Parks and Recreation in March 1959, included an American River Parkway between Nimbus Dam and the river's mouth. The plan centered on Sacramento County's first major purchase, in December 1959, of parkway lands, the grazing and woodlot lands of San Juan Meadows on the right bank of the American beneath the bluffs in Carmichael, long held by the Deterding family. The woodland abutting San Juan Meadows had been long called Deterding Woods by Effie Yeaw, who had taken her students there on natural history field trips.[28] The county named the new park to honor the former manager of heavyweight boxer Max Baer and current member of the Sacramento County Board of Supervisors, Ancil Hoffman, adopted Yeaw's name for the woodland, and named the facility built there in 1976 as headquarters for nature study the Effie Yeaw Nature Center.

The history of the American River Parkway turned a key corner in mid-February 1961. A real estate developer announced the optioning of a substantial tract along the left bank in Rancho Cordova for the Rossmoor North subdivision, a development encroaching within 125 feet of the riverbank. The parkway advocates in the loosely organized and decidedly downstream River Recreation and Parks Association realized how much larger the campaign had become and sought to broaden their base of supporters in preparation for petitioning the Sacramento County Board of Supervisors to overturn the option agreement. Led by James C. (Jim) Mullaney, a director of the Cordova Recreation and Park District, and Effie Yeaw, the retired elementary school teacher and tireless, evangelical conservationist, they cast their net widely, recruiting both individual members and cosponsorships with other organizations in the region in the newly incorporated Save the American River Association. Cooperating with not only their familiar allies in the local Sierra Club and Audubon Society chapters and like-minded supporters from fishing, equestrian, and bicycling groups but also members of church groups, garden clubs, neighborhood associations, Boy and Girl Scout troops, chambers of commerce, and even realtor organizations, the Save the American River Association, in its own words, sought to "focus and coordinate the efforts of organizations and individuals in support of the Parkway."[29] Although the group failed to restrain or stop the Rossmoor North subdivision, they succeeded in creating and mobilizing a vocal constituency throughout the city and county and focused attention on applying for state and federal funds for park expansion and enhancement. In 1983, friends erected a bronze plaque on a granite boulder in Jim Mullaney's honor at the pinch point between Parkway and Rossmoor North. Ironically, that spot is, for users of walkers and wheelchairs, the most accessible place along the Parkway to visit the riparian thickets and groves and enjoy river vistas from their shade.

Sacramento County combined county funds and "open space" funds from the Kennedy-era Federal Housing and Home Finance Agency of the Urban Renewal Administration to go on a riparian lands buying spree. In November 1961, the Sacramento County Board of Supervisors approved purchase of both Discovery Park on the right bank of the American at its mouth and a parcel known briefly as American River Parkway South on the left bank across from the gravel pits at the east end of Arden Way. Two months later, on January 24, 1962, Sacramento formally adopted the American River Parkway Plan. J. Harold Severaid, professor of life sciences at Sacramento State College and one of the directors of the Save the American River Association, celebrated the plan as "the official mechanism for binding together in a continuous 23 mile-long parkway chain the many individual links which had already been or were yet to be forged."[30]

He had reason to celebrate. In the ten years since Elmer Aldrich's initial proposal had been politely deflected from the board of supervisors to oblivion in the county planning office, the county had come full circle and officially embraced an American River Parkway. The Save the American River Association has continued to serve as the front organization leading the parkway advocates and has seen its cause grow enormously in popularity. The association's successful campaign gradually enlisted not only the members of the board of supervisors but also owners of streamside lands. The supervisors made expanding the parkway one of the county's policies. Landowners enlisted in the policy and began to spurn lucrative offers from developers in favor of selling their lands to the county to augment the parkway.[31]

Economic Consequences

Dedicating streamside properties to a parkway had a profound effect on the sand and gravel business in the Sacramento region. No longer might private citizens drive to the nearest gravel bar and haul away as much cobble as they desired. Gravel mining had been driven upstream by Sacramento's expansion and suburban development throughout the twentieth century. Assembling the parkway drove gravel mining out of the riverbed. Pacific Coast Aggregates operated a massive gravel pit at Sixteenth and A Streets at the beginning of the twentieth century on lands now bearing diverse industrial and warehouse businesses. East Portal Park, in the heart of East Sacramento, sits atop a reclaimed gravel pit. As residential subdivisions encroached during the post–World War II building boom, existing sand and gravel mines along the river faced escalating pressure from their residential neighbors to cease their operations. The Pacific Coast Aggregates plant that was mining the left bank and Sacramento Bar on the right bank downstream from the Sunrise Boulevard Bridge faced a steady string of complaints about noise and dust from residents of the wooded streets on the bluffs of Fair Oaks. The Arden Sand

and Gravel plant on the eponymous bar at the foot of Arden Way weathered even greater pressures from even closer neighbors. The Teichert plant, crushing spoil piles left by Natoma Company dredges churning through Mississippi Bar to extract gold at the beginning of the twentieth century, was luckier in being farther away from residential subdivisions but nonetheless incurred the wrath of impatient citizen motorists delayed behind trucks bearing several tons of gravel grinding in the lowest of low gears up the steep grades on Winding Way into Fair Oaks or Main Avenue into Orangevale. All of those former gravel pits are today portions of the parkway, some reclaimed and improved and others remaining nearly as ravaged as when actively mined. All of the aggregate plants on the north bank of the American River between Arden Way and the town of Folsom finished their mining operations, closed down, and sold their lands to Sacramento County at below-market prices, in part a consequence of rising public enthusiasm for the parkway dream. Those lands make up nearly half of parkway acreage in the upper reach between Sacramento Bar and Mississippi Bar.

The other half belonged to a great extent to the remarkably resilient Natoma Company. The company had evolved from an 1852 ditch company delivering American River water for mining uses to the gravel-rich and water-poor regions southeast of Folsom, into granite quarrying in the foothills, then water delivery and hydroelectric generation. To fully use its water, the Natoma Water and Mining Company diversified into agriculture, especially high-value crops, including grapes, stone fruit, pears, and olives. In 1888, recognizing what had become the major arm of the enterprise, the company changed its name to Natoma Vineyard Company. When phylloxera infestation devastated its vines, the company redefined toiling in the vineyards as dredging the former vineyards, mining for gold at an industrial scale. The western edge of the Natoma Company dredging operations abutted the American River. As its mining operations wound down, Natoma Company sold off its lands, now covered with giant mounds of gravel.

The federal government built Mather Air Base and General Tire built the Aerojet General rocket engine plant on former Natoma Company ground. Largely through the influence of the company land officer, Dante Lembi, Natoma Company sold nearly half the acreage in the entire parkway to Sacramento County at bargain prices, sometimes as low as $250 per acre.[32]

Once construction of the dams at Folsom and Nimbus stopped the replenishment of American River gravels and the adoption of the American River Parkway Plan excluded mining from the American's course, gravel mining and aggregate processing operations relocated from the banks and channel of the American River to former farmlands strung along the Jackson Highway from Folsom Boulevard to the east and along South Watt Avenue and Bradshaw Road to the south. The alluvial deposits left beneath those farms by an earlier American River today supply construction products to the region. The gravel pit and aggregate plant sites left

FIGURE 12.2. Dredge tailings bisected by the bikeway. Photograph by Alfred E. Holland, Jr., 2011.

along the river by the aggregate makers have become the heart of the American River Parkway.

Most of those properties were purchased with $12.5 million in funds from Measure A in 1972. The electorate's support for Measure A was vigorous, with better than 70 percent voting to levy a new tax to repay bonds, the proceeds from which funded acquisition and development of lands for parks in the county. The Save the American River Association, especially Jim Jones, a rocket scientist with a fly fishing habit, served as initial promoter of the ballot measure.[33] The association's campaign burgeoned quickly into a coalition cutting across all manner of divides—political, social, economic, and regional. Jim Jones's boss, Jack L. Heckel, the head of the Aerojet plant at Rancho Cordova, joined by Dan Hall, editor of the *Sacramento Union,* emerged as principal spokesmen for the Measure A campaign. Jean Runyon, doyen of Sacramento public relations professionals, managed press and media affairs. Raymond T. Butler, insurance agent and behind-the-scenes political operator par excellence, handled the politicking.[34] In addition to lands along the American River, Sacramento County purchased the properties that became Elk Grove Park and Gibson Ranch County Park with Measure A funds.

The rapid conversion of extraction-ravaged riverbank into parkway focused attention on the river itself. All manner of institutions used the river's channel for diverse purposes. As with so many streams, the American River served as a drain for both surface runoff and sewage. Various sewage plants dumped superficially treated effluent into the American to the point its waters were unsafe for swim-

FIGURE 12.3.
Fisherman in
pool below
Nimbus Dam.
Photograph
by Alfred E.
Holland, Jr.,
2011.

ming. Mothers fearful of waterborne pathogens causing influenza, mononucleo-
sis, and hepatitis had since the 1960s admonished their children, "Don't go near
that river."[35] Fishing enthusiasts, especially those pursuing anadromous salmon
and steelhead, sought to stop the pollution of the waters so crucial for spawning
and so convenient for fishing. Not withstanding the contamination, the City of
Sacramento withdrew domestic water from the American downstream from those
sewage plants.

Flush with their recent success in raising funds for parkland acquisition, Save
the American River Association activists Jim Jones and Al Dreyfus initiated a second Measure A campaign in 1974 to create a regional sanitation district. Upon its
passage, the bond financed the massive sewage treatment plant on the Sacramento
River near Elk Grove, hundreds of miles of pipes collecting wastewater from most
of the cities and the unincorporated portions of Sacramento County, and the gradual decommissioning of the plants dumping insufficiently treated effluent into the
American.

The US Bureau of Reclamation uses the American River as a conveyance to
deliver water from behind Folsom Dam to urban, industrial, and agricultural us-

ers downstream, but reluctantly. The bureau's "Comprehensive Report," delivered to Congress in 1949, proposed diverting better than half the flow of the American River to primarily agricultural uses in the Sacramento–San Joaquin Delta, the lower San Joaquin Valley, and the upper San Joaquin Valley. The report proposed two major diversion canals—a Folsom Ione Mendota Canal, draining the reservoir impounded behind an expanded Folsom Dam, and a Folsom Newman Canal, draining the reservoir behind Nimbus Dam—to connect to a proposed San Luis West Side Canal serving the western side of the upper San Joaquin Valley. The net effect of the Bureau of Reclamation's proposal of 1949 was to reduce the wasted flows of nearly 11 million acre-feet per annum of water into the Pacific Ocean to a paltry 3 million acre-feet per year through the Golden Gate.[36] In the course of the political wrangling leading to authorization of construction of Folsom and Nimbus Dams, the Bureau of Reclamation conceded in California Water Rights Board Decision 893 of 1957 to deliver a minimum of 500 cubic feet per second during spawning season (September 15–December 31) and 250 cubic feet per second during nonspawning months to the lower American River.[37]

As fishing uses of the lower American River below Nimbus Dam increased due to establishment of the American River Parkway, widespread recognition of how woefully inadequate those minimum flows were for sustaining sport fishing species—salmon, steelhead, shad, and striped bass—spread across a broad group of citizens and organizations. Fisherfolk noticed a precipitous decline in salmon and steelhead spawners following the construction of Nimbus Dam, which blocked access to the five miles of gravels inundated by Lake Natoma, where an estimated 73 percent of successful spawning took place.[38] The California Department of Fish and Game and the US Fish and Wildlife Service both began in the 1960s to urge greater flows in the lower American River, especially during salmon and steelhead spawning in the fall. In 1963, well prior to congressional authorization of the Auburn–Folsom South Unit of the Central Valley Project in 1965, the Bureau of Reclamation began filing for appropriative water rights on the north fork of the American River and looking for buyers for that water. Those filings galvanized opposition in the Sacramento region. Most people committed to the American River Parkway, whether for fishing, boating, bicycling, or nature study, promptly recognized that the canal was designed to divert 3,500 of the pre Auburn–Folsom South project mean flow of 3,717 cubic feet per second immediately and unceasingly. The 217 cubic feet per second difference between the canal's design capacity and the mean stream flow could meet neither the 500 cubic feet per second spawning season flows nor the 250 cubic feet per second "off-season" flows. Overallocation of the American River by the Bureau of Reclamation would routinely dry the stream through the American River Parkway to levels equal to the lowest 10 percent of recorded flows throughout the 1904–55 period of record at Fair Oaks.[39] That grim calculus motivated both the federal Fish and Wildlife Service and the California Department of Fish and Game to reconsider their concurrence in the Decision

893 minimum flows and to petition California's Water Resources Control Board to raise the seasonal minimums. The California Department of Fish and Game formally protested the US Bureau of Reclamation's filings for water rights on the North Fork of the American in 1964. By 1967, the Water Resources Control Board had begun hearings on the dispute. This time, the Department of Fish and Game came prepared for the negotiations with Eric Gerstung's thorough analysis of the anadromous and sport fisheries of the American River and the ancillary biological communities along the river, all facing devastation by the draconian diversion and drying.[40] As such boards are wont to do, the Water Resources Control Board, after five days of hearings in January 1967, struck a bit of a compromise. Although in its ruling of December 17, 1970, it approved the permitted appropriations to the Bureau of Reclamation, the board reserved in its Decision 1356 a prerogative "jurisdiction over these permits for the purpose of conforming the season of diversion to later findings of the Board on prior applications involving water in the Sacramento River Basin and Delta."[41]

Construction on the Folsom South Canal, with a capacity of 3,500 cubic feet per second, began in 1968, before the board had issued its order granting the Bureau of Reclamation rights to water with which to fill its proposed Auburn Dam and to divert to users south of the American River. The Reclamation Bureau negotiated two contracts to deliver American River water through the Folsom South Canal: 75,000 acre-feet per year to the Sacramento Municipal Utility District's Rancho Seco nuclear power plant for cooling and 150,000 acre-feet per year to the East Bay Municipal Utility District for domestic and industrial uses. The water for Rancho Seco delivered through the Folsom South Canal allowed a reuse of water to which the Sacramento Municipal Utility District was already entitled for hydroelectric generation at facilities upstream of the Folsom South Canal's headgate at Nimbus Dam. The East Bay Municipal Utility District's flow had nowhere to go because the district had not begun to design or construct facilities to deliver water from the Folsom South Canal on the east side of the Great Valley to its customers on the east side of San Francisco Bay.

Decision 1356's reservations stimulated actions across the breadth of parties interested in the lower American River and American River waters. Their activities were both stimulated and reinforced by the National Environmental Policy Act of 1969, which became law on January 1, 1970, nearly a year prior to the issuance of Decision 1356. The Save the American River Association and the Environmental Defense Fund joined in a lawsuit against East Bay Municipal Utility District's contract for waters from the as yet unbuilt Auburn Dam. The California Department of Fish and Game augmented Eric Gerstung's 1967 report with input from private and public experts to conclude that, "although fish, wildlife, and recreational enhancement and water quality control are among the stated purposes of the Auburn–Folsom South Canal Project, present studies indicate the negotiated minimum flows of 250 cfs and 500 cfs provided for by the Folsom Project will not be adequate for maintenance of pre-project fish, wildlife, and related recreational resources including desirable water quality levels for these resources."[42] Gerstung's inclusion of recreational uses in his report marks a significant change in the dispute and is evidence of the increasing influence of parkway users in these negotiations. The Bureau of Reclamation responded to this shift in the terms of dispute in a far less confrontational manner than previously. The bureau conceded recreation and fishery uses required minimum flows in the 1,000 to 1,500 cubic feet per second range in a 1971 report on its collaborative study with many federal, state, and local agencies.[43] Under the letter of the law, the Bureau of Reclamation was not required by the National Environmental Policy Act to participate in evaluation of environmental consequences of its already negotiated contracts for Folsom South Canal deliveries. Nonetheless, it complied with the spirit of the law in this historic concession of instream flows to recreational uses.

The California State Water Resources Control Board conducted nine days of hearings in June, July, and August 1971, hearing testimony from the "Bureau [of Reclamation], and by prospective users of project water. Evidence regarding needs for recreational, fish, and wildlife purposes was presented by various public agencies, private organizations, and concerned individuals."[44] The East Bay Municipal Utility District, the Bureau of Reclamation, and the several San Joaquin irrigators with which the bureau had been negotiating fared poorly in the board's Decision 1400 compared to the fish, the fisherfolk, and those who floated and paddled the lower American River. In its decision, the board reserved its "jurisdiction . . . for the purpose of formulating terms and conditions relative to flows to be maintained from Nimbus Dam downstream to the mouth of the American River for recreational purposes and for the protection and enhancement of fish and wildlife." The board further ordered flows be maintained at a minimum of 1,250 cubic feet per second between October 15 and July 14 and at a minimum of 800 cubic feet per second between July 15 and October 14 for "maintenance of fish and wildlife," that flows of at least 1,500 cubic feet per second prevail between May 15 and October 14 "for recreational purposes," that diversion of American River waters to the East Bay Municipal Utility District take place downstream of the American's mouth at Hood rather than from the Folsom South Canal, and that all these stipulations faced an exception when drought conditions required proportionally reduced deliveries to all users of American River flows.[45]

Decision 1400 appropriated a water right for recreation uses for the first time in the contentious history of water regulation in the United States. This decision guaranteed that the river at the heart of the parkway would continue to flow except in the direst of drought circumstances. In its discussion of the validity of recreational flows, the board specifically cited the testimony of Sacramento paddling aficionado Ben Glading. Although he testified before the board in an unofficial capacity, he was coincidentally a biologist for the Department of Fish and Game who had documented "double clutching," or the successful rearing of two sets of

FIGURE 12.4. Sacramento Bar water fight. Photograph by Alfred E. Holland, Jr., 2011.

eggs in a single season, by breeding pairs of California valley quail.[46] His authoritative knowledge of recreational boating uses of the American River arose in the main from his key role as a leader of the river touring section of the Mother Lode chapter of the Sierra Club, which had been helping valley and Bay Area Sierra Clubbers paddle the American between the bridges at Sunrise Boulevard in Fair Oaks and Watt Avenue since the mid-1950s.

Boaters are among the most visible of parkway users, especially on summer weekends, when thousands of people beat the heat by drifting downstream. They employ all manner of craft, from simple innertubes to inflatable rafts, from ocean touring boats to sleek racing kayaks, from simple dinghies to elegant driftboats for guided fly-fishing. The lower American River is, however, segregated. Motorized boats are welcome on the American, but the entire river between Nimbus Dam and its mouth is a no-wake zone. Further, for the protection of spawning salmon and steelhead, no motorized craft are allowed upstream of mile point 15 at Hagan Community Park between November 1 and March 15.

Human-powered craft, on the other hand, at times swarm on the river. Several raft rental businesses cluster around the Sunrise Bridge in Fair Oaks and Rancho Cordova. In addition to renting out rafts and paddles, they also meet the floaters downstream with a shuttle bus to retrieve their boats and return customers to their cars parked at the Sunrise Bridge. When the temperature approaches or reaches triple digits on a summer weekend, the boat livery businesses enjoy a lucrative rush. Their customers enjoy floating downstream for a few hours, basking in the sunshine, and splashing in the cool waters. Typical summer floating conditions since the completion of the dams feature steady current and sufficient depth except those rare instances when releases are severely reduced for maintenance of the fish screens that force salmon and steelhead into the fish hatchery at Nimbus Dam. For three days during August 2011, flows plummeted during daylight hours to lows of 1,240 cubic feet per second, then rose during darkness back into the 2,500–3,500 cubic feet per second levels so daily average flows met the recreation flow requirements of Decision 1400. Such low flows require far more attention to the current in the channel. Flows below roughly 900 cubic feet per second require dragging one's craft across shoals separating pools with lethargic or less current. Although summer is peak season for boaters on the American River, a few people use it to float their craft year round.

When winter storms fill the American River's tributary streams, the dam managers at Folsom and Nimbus spill water to maintain flood protection capacity, driving flows from the "normal" levels of three thousand to four thousand cubic feet per second to ten times that. Such flows are dangerous to the beer-swilling, scantily clad, and distracted revelers of summer but excite appropriately equipped and experienced recreational boaters.[47] When the water level and current speed both increase noticeably, familiar riffles disappear, washed out by the high, swift flows, and exciting rapids appear in different locations. Being washed into the now-flooded riparian thickets poses greater risks to boaters during high flows than the current in the center of the river.

Most all of the lands in the lower reaches of the American River Parkway are within the levees lining the river to protect buildings constructed in the floodplain.[48] Consequently, when high releases from Folsom and Nimbus course downstream, they inundate and, in highest flows, inflict greater damage to those improvements in the park sites. During the greatest floods since the dams and levees were constructed, those of 1956, 1963, 1964, 1986, and 1997, streamside improvements have sustained expensive damage, ranging from debris that requires removal to the washing away of bike paths. Such damage is an anticipated consequence of the dam operators consciously releasing water from the reservoirs, carefully balancing releases against the capacity of the downstream plumbing system. On July 17, 1995, however, Folsom Dam released an uncontrolled flow when one of its eight floodgates broke during a routine operation. The million-acre-foot capacity reservoir was nearly full at the time and spilled nearly four hundred thousand acre-feet in a bit over a week, resulting in flows through the parkway of more than thirty thousand cubic feet per second. Such volumes are routine during winter storms but extraordinary during the summer. The risks to river users were far higher during the middle of July than in the winter periods because so many more use the river and its banks during warm weather. Inclement weather during storms keeps all but the most dedicated fisherfolk, swimmers, and boaters, not to neglect runners, bicyclists, and walkers, under cover in the winter and early spring.

High water flooded the parking lots at the Howe Avenue and Watt Avenue access points, some of the picnic facilities at Discovery Park, and a few sections of the Jedediah Smith Memorial Bicycle Trail in the vicinity of Hazel Avenue. To protect the public, Sacramento County officials closed all public access to the river for a week, at a painful loss of entrance gate revenues.[49]

Such concern for gate collections is symptomatic of the remarkable decline in political support for the parkway since the heady days of the early 1970s, when the electorate willingly taxed itself for acquisition, development, and protection of parkway resources. Passage of the infamous Proposition 13 in 1978 marks the turning point. Promoted by Howard Jarvis, the incorrigibly unscrupulous flack for southern California apartment owners and condominium associations, along with retired realtor and antitax ideologue Paul Gann, the initiative stripped local government entities of control over property tax assessment by holding real property assessments constant until the property sold and control over rate setting by both imposing a 1 percent of 1975 assessed valuation property tax ceiling and mandating any change in any tax or new tax subject to a two-thirds majority approval in an election of affected voters. The immediate consequences statewide were profound. First, real property owners, especially owners of commercial, rental housing, and industrial property, enjoyed a major reduction in property tax assessments. Second, the budgetary surplus enjoyed by California's state government quickly disappeared as the California legislature stepped in to finance local governments no longer able to raise revenues through property taxation. Third, county, city, and local government entities faced both draconian reductions in revenues and the fixity of those revenues to boot. Fourth, politicians of nearly every stripe clambered over each other trying to leap aboard the antitax bandwagon.

The City of Sacramento and Sacramento County shifted modes of operation in reaction to the new realities. Desperate for new sources of revenue to replace those that the Jarvis-Gann initiative had denied them, both the city and the county adjusted a number of significant policies. Several fees charged for county or city permits and services skyrocketed as the number of city and county workers providing the services for those fees declined. City and county policy makers sought to expand as rapidly as possible the volume of retail sales within their jurisdictions in order to increase collections of sales taxes. As a consequence, shopping center developers, whether of strip malls or major centers, became the new darlings of elected officials, extracting concessions on those newly increased fees in return for increased sales taxes collected.[50]

Budget discussions rapidly shifted from exercises in bureaucratic wrangling to pitched battles between departments over the limited funds to finance civic services. The results confirmed a basic law of human behavior: whether dealing with a mugger in a dark alley, a chief of police at a city council meeting, a county sheriff at a board of supervisors meeting, or the beribboned and braided Joint Chiefs of Staff at a congressional appropriation hearing, the guys with the guns get what they want. Elected officials earn the lion's share of their salaries performing the difficult task of doling out whatever remains to the less fear-mongering government services, ranging from education through health care for the destitute to recreation. The American River Parkway found itself lumped in with other less-influential rivals for limited funds.

Because so many of the parkway's dedicated users were politically sophisticated, financially comfortable, and idealistic, they stepped in to privately support services the city and county opted to abandon. As plummeting Sacramento County appropriations for the parkway operations led to slashing the ranger rolls and delayed cleaning and other maintenance of restrooms and picnic grounds, volunteer organizations stepped up to shoulder some of the burden. The American River Natural History Association took over the financing and operating of the Effie Yeaw Nature Center. The American River Parkway Foundation, organized by several of the men and women who had organized the successful bond measures in the years before Jarvis-Gann, supports the financially starving parkway in several ways. The foundation organizes the annual Great American River Clean Up, marshaling legions of volunteers, who gather tons of trash each fall. Routine trash pick-up responsibilities throughout the year have been assumed by "Volunteer Mile Stewards," who do the dirty work, and "Financial Stewards," who support the expenses of cleaning up a mile of the parkway and enjoy seeing their names and generosity touted on a signpost along the bikepath. The program has been so successful, no miles were available for sponsorship in 2012.

The facilities that private citizens now maintain in place of the increasingly impecunious city and county are used by a remarkable variety and number of people. Some are exercisers, working themselves to maintain fitness by running, skating, paddling, rowing, biking, or strolling along the river. Many are trim, toned, and tanned as a consequence of their compulsions. Bicyclists and runners fall into four basic groups. The fastest trail users are attired in bright Lycra clothing, sit atop lightweight bicycles, and make quite a whooshing sound as their loud spokes slice through the air as they fly by. The fastest runners show not an extra ounce of body fat, have remarkable shoes, but do not share the need to wear brightly colored, form-fitting garments. The second echelon of cyclists ride mountain bicycles with nubby and noisier tires, sport a less disciplined uniform, and generally smile more often and freely than the intent cyclists and runners. Their equivalent group of runners might better be termed joggers for the way they plod along. A subset of family units riding together is far more diverse in both equipment and attitude. Their bicycles range from fancy road bikes to classic "cruisers" beneath young parents, often with trailers or trailing bicycles attached to the parent's cycle for the youngsters. Their characteristic sounds range from squeals of glee to howls from grousing, disaffected adolescents. The slowest group of hikers and bikers are the cruisers and moseyers—those aged, infirm, obese, or simply disinclined to hurry. Only recently have the bikepaths of the American River Parkway been opened to

FIGURE 12.5. Cycling family. Photograph by Alfred E. Holland, Jr., 2011.

in-line skaters. A recent survey of users conducted along the length of the parkway found but a half dozen. Of that group, one couple displayed sound technique. The rest appeared to be getting more exercise than necessary per mile.

Not all activities pursued in the parkway are so widely considered healthful. The habitat offers concealment for people engaged in illicit activities, most notably drug use, sexual indiscretion, and poaching. Each of these activities is policed by its own authorities, both formal and informal. Drug and alcohol regulation are the purview of federal, state, and local police agencies. Offended moralists and aggrieved spouses are typically the front line of enforcement against errant mates. Game wardens and park rangers generally enforce laws against illegal taking of fish and game. All three groups have been the center of public attention in the parkway.

The popularity of floating down the river on a hot day, combined with the river's ability to keep canned beverages cold, has led to copious quantities of beer being quaffed by rafters. Several near riots, especially on three-day holiday weekends—Memorial Day at the beginning of the summer season, July Fourth in the middle, and Labor Day at season's end—have led Sacramento County to ban all alcohol from the parkway on those weekends. The campaign to restrict boozing in boats solidified over the Fourth of July weekend in 2005 when a mudpit frolic got entirely out of hand, resulting in some serious injuries.[51] As Labor Day approached a year later, the board of supervisors finally passed a holiday weekend alcohol ban for the banks of the American River through the parkway. Unable to regulate alcohol on the water because of details in state law, the board sought to intercept boys with beer on the banks.[52] Earlier, the supervisors had banned alcohol at several locations along the river—Paradise Beach, Rossmoor Bar, Gilligan's Island, and the Goethe Park boat ramp—because of repeated problems with public drunkenness.

Early in the life of the parkway, both the city and the county constructed facilities for more urban forms of recreation. Two golf courses were constructed in the first years of parkway development. At Ancil Hoffman Park in Carmichael, the county constructed an eighteen-hole golf course. Immediately downstream of the H Street Bridge the city constructed Campus Commons, a nine-hole course tucked between the river and the levee on the right bank opposite River Park. Although several regional parks adjacent to the parkway provide fields for baseball and soccer, no such facilities have been built within the parkway because of strident opposition by many parkway constituencies who favor retaining the natural character of the area. James Mullaney voiced the Save the American River Association's strident opposition to further such improvements in a letter to the Sacramento County Planning Commission wherein he "recommended that the plan contain a policy statement excluding organized competitive sports facilities, museums, and amusements center concession areas" from the parkway.[53] Lack of dedicated facilities has not suppressed pick-up games on the expanses of turf adjacent to picnic areas at many of the parkway sites.

The aversion to organized sports has not extended upstream from the American River Parkway into the Folsom Lake Recreation Area facilities on Lake Natoma. The Associated Students of California State University, Sacramento, operates an aquatic center there and provides equipment and instruction in its use to people of all ages. Activities range from paddling canoes and kayaks, rowing simple dinghies or racing shells, and sailing small craft on the lake waters, to instruction in waterskiing and wakeboarding on the larger reservoir upstream behind Folsom Dam. The women's crew team from CSUS practices there, along with the men's crew club. In addition, the aquatic center hosts a junior crew program so successful it has provided the start for competitors who became Olympic-level athletes. Its appeal is not limited to teenagers, however. National teams competing in world championship and Olympic contests train at these facilities when they can arrange it. The lower end of Lake Natoma is recognized throughout the world as one of the premier venues for crew regattas. The NCAA National Championship Regatta is held each spring at venues all over the United States, but every other year it comes back to the course Bob Woodford designed at Lake Natoma.

In the nearly one hundred years since Sacramentans first began considering an American River parkway, the region's population has surged from roughly seventy-five thousand to nearly one and a half million. During that time, nearly half of the American River's floodplain has been incorporated into the parkway. The American River throughout the parkway has been designated a California Wild and Scenic River for its extraordinary recreational values, a decision validated by the millions of visitors drawn to the parkway annually. As Sacramento County has reduced funding for the American River Parkway by nearly half over the first decade of the century, the parkway's backers have decided to return to the electorate rather than elected officials to try to raise funds through an additional one tenth of 1 percent sales tax and creation of an independent regional park district to manage the parks in Sacramento County. Not surprisingly, the Sacramento County Board of Supervisors is reluctant to endorse raising taxes and even less inclined to surrender its authority over the parkway.[54] Even in the face of vanished civic willingness to support the American River Parkway, an analysis by Joseph Karkowski Jr. concludes the following: "In summary, the evidence is compelling that homeowners living close to the Parkway are deriving a great deal of value from ensuring the Parkway is well maintained and crime kept to a minimum. The self-interest of those property owners and fundamental fairness commend those homeowners to provide the funds needed to keep this jewel of the Sacramento region shining."[55]

Whether the threat of seizing the crown jewels will galvanize elected officials to regain their lost love for the American River Parkway remains to be seen. The sights and sounds of the parkway and its diverse residents likewise remain to be seen. Go out and visit them.

CHAPTER 13   Thunder over the Valley

ENVIRONMENTAL POLITICS AND

AND INDIAN GAMING IN CALIFORNIA

Tanis C. Thorne

The remoteness of many reservations and rancherias is
becoming a thing of the past. . . . Many lie in the path of
approaching development and will be able to participate with
and, at times, compete with cities and counties in attracting
desirable economic activities.

—California Planning Roundtable, "Tribal Gaming and
Community Planning in California"

The Thunder Valley Casino owned by the United Auburn Indian Community
(UAIC) opened its doors on June 9, 2003, to an enthusiastic crowd that backed
up traffic more than seven miles. Located thirty miles east of Sacramento in the
Interstate 80 corridor, the casino is positioned to intercept much of the gambling
traffic going from the San Francisco Bay Area to Reno. Thunder Valley is a convenient distance from I-80 along Highway 65 and neighbors the city of Lincoln,
the fastest growing city in California in the first decade of the twenty-first century.
Since about 1990, the rural landscape in this area has undergone a radical transformation: the old Highway 65 is now a four-lane freeway, flanked by box stores,
shopping malls, and suburbs. In a major transportation corridor as well as on
the cusp of massive suburban expansion, the casino's success was to be expected,
but it proved to be phenomenal. Four short years after its opening, Thunder Valley was proclaimed "one of three most profitable casinos on earth." The largest
revenue-producing Indian gaming activity in the nation by 2010, the casino was
making $500 million a year, more than doubling the take of the most prosperous
Indian gaming tribes of southern California. Three and a half million people visit
Thunder Valley Casino each year, and ten thousand play its twenty-seven hundred
slot machines, stay in its luxury hotel, dine in its restaurants, and attend events in
its entertainment venue.[1]

As the adage goes, California is like the rest of the nation only more. The
California Indian experience in the gaming era is no exception. California has the
largest number of federally recognized tribes of any state of the union and the
second-largest number of tribes in the nation engaged in gaming: fifty-seven Cal-

FIGURE 13.1. Thunder Valley Casino (exterior). Photograph by Tanis C. Thorne.

ifornia Indian nations operate casinos and sixty-seven have compacts.[2] Arguably, California Indians experienced more genocide and injustice historically than Indians of other states. Landless and lacking basic rights as citizens, they experienced a demographic collapse in the second half of the nineteenth century, only to make an equally sudden and dramatic comeback from 1980 to 2010. "The success of tribal gaming caught many by surprise," a task force on gaming and community planning explains.[3] Living in one of the more densely populated and affluent states in the union, California tribes have the biggest market and command a staggering one-third of the national market share, garnering $8 billion in gaming profits in 2008.[4] In 2007, they hosted one million patrons a day. Many California Indian gaming nations, mired in poverty a generation ago, now have enormous prosperity. Growing up on the Auburn Rancheria, Jessica Tavares, chair of the UAIC, recalled living with her parents and six siblings in a shack where they "read by kerosene lamps and drank from ditch water until 1966."[5] Among the wealthiest Indian people of California are the San Manuel Band of Mission Indians and Santa Ynez Chumash, whose relatively small memberships mean very large per capita checks of between $30,000 and $53,000 per month.[6]

California's Indian gaming tribes skillfully converted wealth into political power. As legal scholar David Wilkins observes, "Indian gaming has wrought a revolutionary shift in the involvement of some tribes in state and federal politics on an unprecedented scale."[7] Morongo and Agua Caliente, southern California gaming nations, number among the top ten political contributors in the nation. Richard Milanovich, who died in 2012, was the longtime chair of the Agua Caliente and was once described as the "most powerful man in one of the most powerful Indian nations in North America."[8] Prosperous gaming nations are generous donors, giving millions each year to higher education, cancer research, victims of disasters, and a plethora of organizations in their local communities. San Manuel, Yocha Dehe (formerly Rumsey), Viejas, and the UAIC, among others, have well-deserved reputations for their generosity.

UAIC Exceptionalism

The UAIC experience with gaming is noteworthy because the group's 2004 compact represents a policy shift toward intergovernmental cooperation. The rapid expansion of the number and size of Indian casinos in California raised many questions about land use. A backlash to Indian gaming developed in the first years of the twenty-first century as conflicts with state, county, and municipal governments multiplied. According to some analysts, the tribal-state compacts of 2004 signify a major corrective or "rebalancing" after a tumultuous roller coaster of change in the environmental and economic landscapes of California. While many Indian sovereignty advocates vigorously disagree, Cheryl Schmit, director of Stand Up for California, a gaming watchdog organization, views the UAIC's compact as a model for decision making over land use that concerns multiple jurisdictions. The UAIC, argues Schmit, accommodated the needs of the local community, sharing increased costs for public services and infrastructure development.[9]

This chapter examines in some detail the UAIC's heavily contested journey through the process of acquiring trust land and establishing its lucrative Thunder Valley Casino. A pastiche of examples of other California gaming tribes' experiences across the state are also referenced to provide a succinct overview of the legal foundations, conflicts, and compromises over sovereign powers, cross-currents, and turning points like landmark California propositions, compact negotiations, and court challenges. This backdrop provides a context for understanding the UAIC's place in the arc of change from the early 1980s to 2011 regarding land use policy.

A necessary clarification at the outset is that Indian gaming profits are very unevenly distributed across California's native communities, as they are across the nation. Thirteen percent of the Indian casinos nationwide enjoy two-thirds of the gaming revenue. Only a tiny minority enjoys per capita payments in the thousands of dollars per month. A study of California Indian gaming completed in January 1997 reported that 47.3 percent of Indian people lived in poverty compared to 11.5 percent of non-Indians nationally. Poverty and high rates of unemployment remain the rule for the Indian majority in California and elsewhere in the nation. An estimated 9 percent of the Indians enrolled in California's federally recognized tribes are experiencing tangible economic change via gaming according to a report issued by the California Legislative Analyst's Office.[10]

A second important clarification: in addition to the fiscal disparities, there are wide variations in the environmental and historical experience of each of California's 110 federally recognized tribes. Hence, as most knowledgeable analysts emphasize, one must approach the subject of Indian gaming on a case-by-case basis.[11] Reflecting California's varied environment, prior to European contact, native California was culturally and linguistically diverse; there was a mosaic of hundreds if not thousands of politically autonomous territorial units, each occupying its own ecological niche and speaking different dialects.[12] Adding to the complexity, the eighteen federal treaties that set aside reservations in 1851–52 in California were not ratified by the US Senate. Historically, survivors of formerly autonomous political units merged as populations shrank due to disease, starvation, and warfare because there were no treaty-reserved lands. Land holdings were whittled down, until the small remnant of persons remaining were cornered and desperate; they were metaphorically and literally "pushed into the rocks." Belatedly, in the latter half of the nineteenth and early part of the twentieth century, the federal government reserved land by congressional action and executive order for some—but not all—of the hybrid communities of survivors.[13] California's reservations and rancherias are erratically scattered across the state, having come under federal trust protection at different times and under varying circumstances.[14] Up until the suburban expansion after 1950, most were remote, marginal lands in rural parts of the state.

Each Indian community's experience with non-Indian neighbors is unique and depends on a constellation of factors such as the economic potential of resources, terrain, demographics, and timing of federal trust protection. For example, the Wanakik lineages (dialect speakers of the larger linguistic unit of Cahuilla people), whose aboriginal territory was the San Gorgonio Pass in today's Riverside County, faced catastrophic smallpox epidemics just prior to an infusion of settlers who increased rapidly once the Southern Pacific Railroad bisected the territory. When the US government intervened in the 1880s and withdrew several sections of land for what would become the Morongo reservation, there remained on the Wana-kik's original land base in the Potrero canyon only one village, with one hundred desperate intermarried Cahuillas and Serrano. In the foothills of the Sierra Nevada in Nevada County, gold miners displaced the Nisenan-speaking people. The shrinking remnant of several formerly independent Nisenan villages clustered at the Wokodot Rancheria outside Nevada City after headman Charles Cully filed for a homestead in the 1880s. This privately owned acreage came under federal trust protection in 1917, a trust terminated in the 1960s subsequent to the California Rancheria Act of 1958; the eclectic band of Miwok and Nisenan tracing ancestry to the Nevada City Rancheria now seeks restoration of its status as a tribe and the re-acquisition of trust land.[15]

Location, Location, Location

These two sketchy examples of California tribal recognition highlight in very broad strokes some important regional differences that are critical to understanding the contours of California Indian gaming's development. Sovereignty emerges from the land and can find its tangible expression only in its regional setting, as the scholar Jessica Cattelino has observed.[16] Regional economics, history, demographic patterns, and infrastructural development—access to water, sewage, and transportation systems—are all components in evaluating gaming's fiscal success and its local impacts. About a third of California's federally recognized tribes and a third of those engaged in gaming today are located in two southern California counties—Riverside and San Diego—on desert or mountainous land with little water and minimal agricultural potential. These are the state's gaming powerhouses, with 45 percent of the licensed slot machines. San Diego County reservations alone enjoyed $1.7 billion (40 percent) of gaming profits of $7.7 billion statewide in 2007.[17]

Collectively described as "Mission Indians" because approximately three dozen reservations constitute a federal administrative unit called the Mission Indian Agency, the southern California Indians are highly politicized and have been for decades. Their past has been one of ongoing and vigorous defense of their resources and rights through political action. They were among the first to experiment with high-stakes gaming in the 1980s, testing the legal limits of what they could do, and they continue to test these limits. Morongo, Agua Caliente, and Cabazon border Interstate 10, which connects the affluent coastal urban and suburban population centers of southern California to Las Vegas. Other southern California gaming giants, like Pechanga, Viejas, Barona, and Sycuan, are being gradually engulfed by southern California's burgeoning suburban expansion into the Inland Empire. "Location, location, location" is the rule not only for prospective homeowners; it is also the hard and fast guide for California Indian tribes. Because of their markets, these Mission Agency tribes enjoy enrichment and empowerment. Access to markets alone does not explain the trajectory of gaming era politics. Because of their history of numerous battles to defend vital resources and

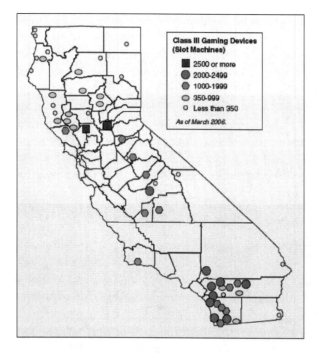

FIGURE 13.2. Map showing distribution of gaming devices (slot machines), across California, March 2006. From California Legislative Analyst's Office, "Questions and Answers: California Tribal Casinos," by Elizabeth G. Hill, legislative analyst, Feb. 2007, p. 7, http://www.lao.ca.gov/2007/tribal_casinos/tribal_casinos_020207.pdf.

land bases, often in adversarial relationships with local and federal authorities, these southern California nations are aggressive and sophisticated players in state politics. They take their sovereign status very seriously, and most are very wary of any compromise over principles.[18] "The most important understanding for California citizens is that California tribes are governments first and foremost," said Anthony Pico, who was Viejas chairperson in 2011. "There is nothing that is as important to California tribes. We are sovereign."[19]

Northern California Tribal Status Contested

By contrast, many tribes of the northern part of the state, like the United Auburn Indian Community, have a far more ambiguous, precarious, and controversial legal status. Though there are important exceptions, like Yocha Dehe (formerly the Rumsey Rancheria) and the Jackson Rancheria, northern tribes enjoy less desirable locations, and, generally speaking, they entered gaming much later than southern California's tribes. Critically, the small rancheria communities of the north bore the brunt of the termination movement; the Auburn and Nevada City Rancherias were among the forty-one rancherias that lost federal protection for their lands and their legal status as Indians in the 1960s and 1970s. In 1983, members of seventeen northern California bands that were terminated were restored to federal status by the *Tilly Hardwick v. United States* decision. Spurred by the success of Indian gaming, most of the other terminated tribes subsequently succeeded in getting their terminations reversed, most going through the courts, with three achieving their goals through congressional action. Many of the "restored" tribes (that is, those whose termination was reversed) lack trust land. Significantly, they need federal approval for converting private land to trust status (or they have trust land in areas too remote from population centers or transportation routes for a casino to provide economic uplift for their populations). The UAIC gained its forty-nine-acre site for its casino only after years of lobbying and litigation; others, like the Guidiville and Scotts Valley Pomo, were not as fortunate, though they spent years trying to surmount the legal obstacles to gaining trust land. Local political opposition is most effective in blocking trust land conversion when the location is an urban area and when the trust land requested is in another tribal group's aboriginal territory. Gaming watchdog activists oppose trust land conversions, off-reservation gaming (aka "reservation shopping"), and the acknowledgment of new tribes; some even contest the claim that restored "rancheria" communities have true reservation status. Litigation continues.[20] Advocates for stronger local voice in siting and the imposition of increased environmental regulatory control were most effective among these more vulnerable northern California restored tribes.

Background

The quasi-sovereign nature of federally recognized tribes is critical to understanding the rise of Indian gaming. Self-government over tribally held lands and tribal memberships is a contractual right established by treaties, subsequently affirmed by the Supreme Court in *Worcester v. Georgia* (1832) and reaffirmed by the Indian Reorganization Act (1934). Despite increased federal spending on Indians since the mid-1960s, in an effort to promote the prevailing policy of economic uplift via self-determination, the sovereign powers of tribal peoples on reservation lands have remained largely nominal until quite recently, and economic underdevelopment persists on Indian lands.

The dramatic comeback for the California Indians began in the late 1970s, but it was a shaky beginning fraught with risks. Inspired by the Seminole success in Florida, a few tribes in California, hoping for a path out of rural poverty, sought investors. Establishing card rooms or bingo parlors was a legally dubious move, and so were the investors. Several tribes experienced multiple failures with their initial gaming enterprises. The Jackson Rancheria's leader, Margaret Dalton, read about the Seminole in 1984 and found investors to open a bingo hall in 1985, but the hall failed three times before honest investors were found in 1991. All fledgling Indian gaming operations faced threats of closure by the state and counties. In 1980, the Cabazon tribe of Riverside County opened its first card room, and it was quickly shut down by police. The Barona group of San Diego County successfully mounted a legal action against the county undersheriff's police powers on Indian trust land in 1982.[21] In 1983, Morongo established the first high-stakes bingo parlor, quickly followed by Cabazon and San Manuel. In response to this burgeoning industry, California passed its pilot legislation to regulate Indian gaming in the state in 1984.

Indian gaming won a resounding victory with the Supreme Court's 1987 *California v. Cabazon* decision, which was quickly followed by national legislation, the Indian Gaming Regulatory Act (IGRA) of 1988. Congress endorsed economic opportunities for native Americans via gaming to "promote economic development, self-sufficiency, and strong tribal government." IGRA laid out the rules for high-stakes Indian gaming. Tribes were to be treated as sovereign governments within the states in which they reside and to enjoy limited immunity to state law. However, to give the state some regulatory control—which many tribal nations viewed as a compromise of their sovereignty—the tribal nation that wished to engage in high-stakes gaming (including operating slot machines—the casino cash cows) had to negotiate a compact with the state in which it resided. IGRA specified that each state-tribal compact be negotiated by the governor and ratified by the state legislature; the secretary of interior also had to approve it. Further, the National Indian Gaming Commission had to approve the gaming ordinance adopted by the tribe. Though Class II and III gaming was prohibited on lands put in trust after 1988, IGRA provided for exceptions and thus offered an avenue for unrecognized (aka "emerging") California tribes and landless, recognized restored tribes to enter the ranks of gaming nations.[22]

The State of California resisted compliance with IGRA's requirement that it negotiate gaming compacts in good faith. No compact was negotiated until 1997. In the interim, California gaming tribes pressed forward, eager to replicate the Pequot nation's success in Connecticut. The Pequots found foreign investors to build the palatial Foxwoods casino between Boston and New York and were grossing $1.2 billion a year for its six hundred members in the 1990s. Several southern California "Mission Indian" tribes opened casinos after IGRA became law in 1988. When the Chumash put in their first slot machines in 1994, yielding approximately $200 per machine per day, they began to make spectacular profits. The Agua Caliente had 210 slot machines in operation in 1995.[23] Yet, slot machines were technically illegal because there were no tribal-state compacts in place. Video games were confiscated by San Diego County law enforcement at the direction of the state attorney general, but a federal judge returned them. By 1998, forty-one California tribes were operating 13,000 illegal slot machines, up from 4,780 four years before.[24] More than half of these illegal machines were operating in San Diego County tribal casinos; used by fifteen thousand gamblers a day, they were bringing in revenues of $5.5 million a year by the late 1990s.[25] However, under the uncertain legal conditions, investors were hesitant to provide gaming tribes with the millions needed to construct casinos on the scale of the destination resorts of Las Vegas and Foxwoods.[26]

According to Cheryl Schmit, the "turning point" was when Sen. John McCain ushered the 1994 "List Act" through Congress in an effort to break the deadlock in California. This legislation named the "federally recognized" tribes of California and eliminated much of the ambiguity over the questionable sovereign status of many of the small "rancheria" groups in the northern part of the state and hence confirmed their identity so they could engage in high-stakes gaming. Eliminating much of the difficulty of getting backing from investors, the legislation made possible the "push" that began to expand gaming in California in 1994.[27] Investors approached small Indian communities, encouraging them to consider gaming as an economic option and offering their financial backing. Meanwhile, Gov. Pete Wilson's steadfast refusal to negotiate compacts for high-stakes gaming was unsuccessfully challenged in the courts in *Rumsey Indian Rancheria of Wintun v. Wilson* (1994). California passed additional legislation to regulate Indian gaming with the 1997 California Gaming Control Act.[28] Finally, in 1998, coming to terms with de facto gaming, the state legislature ratified the model compact the governor negotiated with the Pala tribe of southern California in 1998.

Though ten tribes reluctantly conceded, the California Indian Gaming Nations Association (CIGNA) characterized the response to the Pala compact as "explosive" because the agreement reduced tribal nations' powers to that of "quasi-municipalities." Politically mobilizing in 1998, gaming tribes organized to resist "political subjection." In 1998, they put Proposition 5, the Tribal Government Gaming and Economic Sufficiency Act, on the California state ballot. One of the "most expensive initiative campaigns in US history," Prop 5 authorized Indian casinos to operate slot machines and blackjack. The $70 million spent by tribes (primarily those in southern California) to promote its passage and the $28 million spent by the proposition's opponents resulted in a vote of 63 percent in favor of Prop 5.[29] The initial opposition to the institutionalization of gaming for moral or regulatory concerns—the potential for organized crime and other social problems—was overcome by the public's desire to compensate California Indians for historic injustices and to provide a path for economic self-sufficiency. Prop 5 was then struck down as unconstitutional by the California Supreme Court. Proposition 1A in 2000 again put the matter before California voters, and California voters favored it by a 2-to-1 margin. These two California ballot initiatives signaled an "inherent change in the landscape of the Indian gaming industry." According to CIGNA's historian, the passage of Prop 1A was "epic," as it overturned "California's 150 years of anti-Indian policy."[30] "Because of our affluence," said Viejas chairperson Pico, "we were able to access Sacramento . . . as never before. . . . Our emergence as a major political contributor allowed us to gain access and develop personal relationships with decision-makers. . . . For the first time in history, . . . tribes were framing the debate on Tribal issues—lawmakers weren't talking about us, they were talking with us."[31]

Pressured by Prop 1A's clear public mandate and by the federal government's call for compliance with IGRA, the newly elected California governor, Gray Davis, reentered compact negotiations in 1999. Subsequently, the California legislature approved sixty tribal compacts for 1999–2000, the terms of which were another political victory for the sovereign gaming nations. Tribes were required to contribute to two funds: the Indian Gaming Special Distribution Fund (IGSDF) and the Gaming Revenue Sharing Trust Fund (GRSTF). The former would compensate communities near the casinos for increased costs for fire protection, roads, and law enforcement; the second redistributed some of the gaming wealth of prospering tribes to poorer, nongaming California Indians. Compacting Indian tribes were permitted to install up to two thousand slot machines.[32] Although gaming tribes were advised to negotiate with local communities about off-reservation impacts such as higher costs to counties for road maintenance and policing, such mitigations were not compulsory, for there were no enforcement mechanisms. California gaming tribes rejoiced, as they had successfully vindicated their sovereign powers free of paternalistic regulatory control by local authorities. They had preserved their prerogatives by influencing the democratic process in legitimate ways: through campaign contributions, lobbying, petitions, supporting ballot initiatives, and advertising.[33] "We learned the value of Public Relations," said Pico, "as another arrow in our quiver to educate state and local political institutions and the public about who we are, and ensuring that we have a place and a voice in the future of California and San Diego County."[34]

Turning the Tables and the Backlash

By the turn of the century, California gaming tribes had decisively turned the tables, reversing historic power relationships. Few anticipated the phenomenal transformation in the state political economy from 1998 to 2004. The number of slot machines tripled, from 14,407 in 1996 to 58,100; gross revenues rose proportionately, with a 75 percent increase from 1999 to 2003.[35] In the early years of the twenty-first century, California represented a "vast potential market for continued expansion of gaming."[36] Wealthy investors prodded nongaming tribes to join the bonanza and eagerly put up vast sums for established gaming tribes to upgrade their bingo and card room operations to "destination resorts" on the scale of Las Vegas casinos, with golf courses, shopping outlets, and classy entertainment venues. In 2000, the Chumash were grossing $70 million a year, keeping 69 percent of profits for enrolled members. When they opened a new $157 million gaming complex in 2003 with 2,000 slots and a 106-room hotel, their revenues rose 40 percent within one year. By 2004, California Indians were being described as the "richest people on earth," though in truth this applied to a tiny minority. From 2002 to 2004, the southern California Agua Caliente, Pechanga, Cabazon, San Manuel, and Morongo tribes completed multimillion-dollar Vegas-style hotel and casino complexes. The Morongo Indians' twenty-seven-story, $250 million resort hotel and casino rose like a phalanx, dominating the landscape of the San Gorgonio Pass. With such expansion came many construction and service jobs. For example, the UAIC employs eighteen hundred people in its casino, three large restaurants, entertainment venue, and hotel. Morongo is the largest private-sector employer in Riverside County, Jackson Rancheria is the biggest employer in Amador County, and the Cachil Dehe Wintun are the largest employer in Colusa County.[37]

Indian casinos created jobs, but signs of public discontent began to appear, at first inchoate and easily dismissed as reactionary, then building into an audible, more broadly based public backlash. Criticisms ranged from resentment over traffic congestion, envy for new Indian wealth, and displaced non-Indian elites' nostalgia for the past; these complaints were joined by taxpayer concerns about increased costs of sewage, road, and water systems, as well as fire protection and law enforcement. A 2002 study by the California State Association of Counties revealed that thirty-two of fifty-eight California counties had Indian gaming facilities. The eight counties that kept records of fiscal impacts of Indian gaming calculated a $200 million fiscal impact; five of these counties received mitigation payments of $21.4 million.[38] Taxation and the conversion of fee land to trust status troubled county officials. Gaming tribes now had the capital to buy private land and businesses, and many applied to have these new properties converted to trust status. If the Department of the Interior approved these applications, counties would lose property tax revenues, thus putting the increased tax burden on non-Indian property owners. Native-owned businesses like gas stations or smoke shops have exemption from state sales taxes, giving these Indian businesses an advantage over local non-Indian businesses. Indian-owned hotels did not pay the transient tax, whereas non-Indian owned hotels were required to do so. The perception was growing among some gaming critics that Indians were getting an "unfair advantage" over non-Indian businesses.[39]

The friction between Indian and local non-Indian populations was exacerbated by a vigorous exercise of sovereign immunity in some locales. The Santa Ynez Chumash claimed exemption from compliance with county building codes when constructing a multistoried parking structure on their trust land. Wealthy Chumash who divorced non-Indian spouses claimed their tribal sovereignty rendered them immune from ex-spouses' demands for child support. Moreover, the Chumash were running afoul of their wealthy neighbors, many movie stars among them, who wanted the wine-growing country to remain rural. In partnership with the actor Fess Parker, the Chumash attempted to buy private land, convert it to trust status, and then subdivide and build homes in direct violation of county no-growth policies.[40]

For critics, the heart of the matter was that local jurisdictions were left out of the political process of casino siting and regulation. The federal government endorsed Indian gaming as benign national policy for economic uplift and delegated power to the state governments for hammering out the contractual agreements with sovereign tribal nations. County and municipal governments had no role in deciding if, when, and where a casino would be placed or in the negotiations over compensation for fiscal impacts on local services, nor did the local governments have any enforcement mechanisms to compel sovereign tribal governments to come to account.[41]

A Clash and a Compromise

Market-driven expansion of gaming collided with vigorous grass-roots activism in Placer County in the late 1990s, and the clash had ramifications for state gaming policy. In the UAIC compact, memorandums of understanding (MOUs) with local governments become mandatory. Watchdog activists championed the result of this hard-fought local contest as a model for not only California but also the nation. The UAIC's uphill struggle to establish a gaming operation is not unlike what other "restored" tribes experience. Today's UAIC had its origins as a rancheria with a heterogeneous membership of people of Nisenan, Miwok, Pomo, and Wailaki. The Auburn Indians were terminated following the Rancheria Act in 1958 and lost most of their forty acres of trust land outside the city of Auburn to privatization. In 1991, the band reorganized its tribal government, adopted a constitution as the UAIC, and petitioned to have federal recognition restored. The Bureau of Indian Affairs contested the UAIC's status as a tribe. With the political support of the Placer County supervisors, the City of Auburn, and Rep. George Miller, the tribe succeeded in getting Congress to pass the Auburn Indian Restoration Act in 1994. Section 4 provided for accepting newly acquired real property into trust elsewhere in Placer County in order to promote the UAIC's economic prospects. Economic prosperity for the tribe would defray the annual $500,000 expenditure for 150 Indian persons entitled to receive tribal services from the federal government.[42]

In the burgeoning expansion of Indian gaming at the turn of the twenty-first century, the Sacramento region was one of the most promising untapped markets. Having congressional authorization for choosing a location to site a casino was a significant advantage, but the UAIC still had to overcome organized resistance within Placer County. Shopping for a more auspicious site along Interstate 80 within Placer County in the late 1990s, UAIC chair Jessica Tavares recalled in a 2007 interview the "ugly" battle against casinos. The local community hated them initially because of the UAIC's exemption from local laws, she said. Fortunately for the UAIC, Tavares hired Sacramento lawyer Howard Dickstein, "Godfather of California Indian Law," at the recommendation of Jackson Rancheria and Yocha Dehe tribal chairpersons. (In late 2011, some members of the UAIC criticized Dickstein's $26 million in legal fees as excessive.)[43]

When the UAIC considered a piece of property in Penryn, off I-80, in March 1996, local resident Cheryl Schmit began her metamorphosis from a self-identified soccer mom into one of the state's most prominent and articulate spokespersons for citizens concerned about Indian gaming. Schmit and three hundred other community members met en masse with the UAIC's lawyers, and they were shocked to hear that there was "nothing you can do about this." The sixty-acre parcel the UAIC proposed to buy was clearly inappropriate for a gaming site. Not only was it not zoned for a large business, it lacked sewage hookups and was adjacent to a Zen center, churches, and children's play areas. The Placer Citizens for Community Rights (a precursor of the statewide watchdog organization, Stand Up for California) formed soon thereafter. Becoming educated about Indian gaming and making contacts with elected officials, the Placer citizens organized a conference and funded a trip to Washington, DC. Cheryl Schmit emerged as a leader because she had the free time to do the legwork for the organization—writing letters and making telephone calls—and because she had curiosity, drive, and personal connections. The Lungrens (Dan Lungren was then California attorney general) were neighbors and members of the same church. Schmit gained access to UAIC planning meetings and entered the fray of state referendum campaigns; she and her allies succeeded in including language that new casinos be located no closer than two miles from churches, homes, or schools. Schmit's overriding concern as a gaming watchdog was the nuts-and-bolts issue of land use raised by Indian gaming. She was determined to remedy the problem of locally elected officials who had lost their ability to protect citizens. Teaming up and taking the "bull by the horns," as she called it in a 2011 interview, Placer citizens demanded that the Auburn tribe work *with* them.[44]

What diffused the ugly confrontation between the UAIC and the Placer Citizens for Community Rights, according to both Tavares and Schmit, was the UAIC's accommodating stance and Dickstein's pragmatic attitude that no casino would be successful without the support of the community. After being shown an environmental impact statement on the proposed Penryn property and hearing the community's objections, the tribe and its advisors agreed to search for a more suitable location. Robert Weygandt, Placer County supervisor, located a more suitable forty-nine-acre site off Highway 65 in an area zoned for industrial use and buffered by open land. The UAIC agreed to some other major concessions regarding environmental protections and mitigation of off-reservation financial impacts, so that Placer County citizens would not have to subsidize an economic venture for which they received an unequal return. By 1998, prior to Governor Pete Wilson's compact negotiations, the UAIC had agreed to compliance with the California Environmental Quality Act. It is noteworthy that the tribe's memorandum of understanding with Placer was signed in December 1997, *before* the historic Proposition 5 and 1A battles and *before* the Wilson administration approved the 1999 compacts. The environmental protections and enforcement mechanisms for mitigating impacts were included in the language of UAIC's original 1999 compact, but it was later stripped of these progressive elements, said Schmit, for political reasons; ultimately, these features were restored when the UAIC compact was renegotiated in 2004.[45]

The collaborative effort with community organizations and county officials framed the Thunder Valley Casino's development within the county's police powers and growth plan. Compromise was a political necessity, for the UAIC needed the strong endorsement of Placer County to gain the Department of the Interior's

FIGURE 13.3. Thunder Valley Casino (interior). Photograph by Tanis C. Thorne.

endorsement of the trust conversion of the Thunder Valley site. Without trust land, there could be no casino. The UAIC signed a memorandum of understanding with Placer County (amended in 2003) in return for the county's support for trust land conversion. Following Department of the Interior approval and a federal appeals court decision in September 2002, the acreage for the Thunder Valley Casino was finally taken into trust. The UAIC "had integrity," Schmit said; if all California Indian nations were as reasonable as the UAIC, she would not have had objections to Indian gaming, she stated.[46]

Political expediency was a priority for the casino investors and the tribe. According to one source, meeting the construction deadlines was a priority, and success in doing so permitted investors to quickly recoup their capital investments for infrastructure development. (The Red Hawk Casino of the Shingle Springs Rancheria along Highway 50 was not so fortunate; that casino opened just as the economic downturn of 2008 hit the nation, and it totters on insolvency.) The UAIC is remarkably transparent and accommodating compared to other Indian gaming groups. Its management is pragmatic, rather than politically charged. The decision was made to avoid financial overextension by reducing the number of floors planned for the hotel, for example. The initial concerns of the Roseville and Rocklin communities about the presence of a casino have been allayed. There have not been protests in the non-Indian community about negative impacts on business. Generally there has been a trajectory of improving local attitudes toward the casino. Jobs have been created, and no apparent increase in crime or traffic congestion or gambling addiction has materialized.[47]

New Deals in California's Fiscal Crisis

When an energy shortage debacle caused a $35 million shortfall in the California state budget in 2003, the state economy faltered. Gov. Gray Davis looked to the prospering Indian gaming industry for needed revenues, as his successor, Arnold Schwarzenegger, would also do. Davis contemplated the possibility of allowing more slot machines (beyond the two thousand maximum per tribe allowed by the 1999 compacts) in return for the state's greater share of the gaming profits. Subsequently, Schwarzenegger launched a campaign to recall Davis in 2003, followed by his own successful bid for the California governorship in 2004. Schwarzenegger charged Davis and other Democratic candidates for reelection in 2004 with accepting tribal gaming contributions and being in the hands of "special interests." His banner campaign issue was calling for California Indians to "pay their fair share" as California's economy continued to stagger from deficits. Schwarzenegger's claim that California's political system had fallen into the hands of "special interests" was bolstered by the phenomenal sums—$120 million from 1998 to 2003—California gaming tribes were pouring into proposition battles, lobbying, and campaign contributions. His charge that California gaming tribes were not paying their fair share resonated because of the well-known fact that the Pequot, in their 1992 compact with Connecticut, had contracted to pay 25 percent of gaming profits to the state. By 2003, when California gaming was enjoying profits of $6 billion, Connecticut was collecting $400 million in revenue from tribal gaming whereas California was collecting only $131.6 million, a disparity Schwarzenegger was determined to correct. In his September 2004 preelection campaigning, Schwarzenegger expressed his determination to capture 25 percent for the state's general fund to lessen the state's budgetary shortfall of $300 million.[48]

In 2004, the Schwarzenegger gubernatorial campaign was a redefining moment in California's roller coaster ride over Indian gaming, uniting the various groups wishing to check Indian gaming, putting gaming tribes on the defensive, and polarizing politics. Significantly, the paternalistic rationale for California Indians' entitlement for gaming as self-help or compensation from past injustice was transformed; continued public support for Indian gaming now became a remedy for the state budgetary crisis. The representation of California Indians changed from victims to "special interests": "rich" or "greedy" people whose inordinate wealth was corrupting the democratic process, according to adversaries. California Indians realized that they were very vulnerable to changed public perceptions. If they were perceived as a homogeneous group of "rich" people who could afford to pay their own way, vital Indian welfare services, shared by the federal and state governments, might be cut for marginal or indigent tribes.[49]

In 2004, prosperous California gaming tribes, fortified by expensive legal talent, prepared for battle. They were resolved to defend themselves from "shakedowns" by the state government: sovereign entities cannot be taxed and IGRA explicitly prohibited it, they argued. Across the nation, many Indians viewed IGRA's requirement that tribes make compacts with states as an invasion of tribal sovereignty. Tim Giago, editor of *Indian Country Today*, went further; he viewed the Pequot compact that paid 25 percent of profits to Connecticut as extortion money. IGRA's requirement "opened a can of worms that crawled across America," wrote Giago.[50] In its amended 2003 MOU with Placer County and its 2004 amended compact with the state, the UAIC agreed to several concessions that other tribes interpreted as surrendering sovereignty.

Governor Schwarzenegger could not legally require the existing gaming tribes to pay a greater share, as their compacts would not expire until 2020. On the 2004 ballot, hardball politics were put into play. A coalition of non-Indian gaming interests put Proposition 68 on the ballot, which threatened the loss of the Indian monopoly on Class III gaming if the Indians did not agree to comply with more stringent regulations and to make more contributions to the state's coffers. The powerhouse southern California gaming tribes created a huge war chest of money to defend their sovereign rights, expending enormous sums to put Proposition 70 on the ballot. Proposition 70 would have given the gaming tribes virtual carte blanche to expand gaming operations as far as they wished. Neither proposition passed.

Spectacular Indian casino profits on the one hand and state budget crises on the other were feeding the multiplying worms. California, like many other states facing budgetary shortfalls, became heavily invested in Indian gaming. Schmit of Stand Up for California decried the imbalance created by Proposition 1A and the "unanticipated consequences of IGRA." What California voters had not anticipated—and did not know was a legal possibility when they approved Propositions 1A and 5, Schmit argued—was that market demands were driving relentlessly toward unchecked expansion of Indian gaming. The special circumstances in California, with its market demand and numerous "restored" tribes like the UAIC and an even greater number of "emerging" tribes—that is, those applying to be federally recognized—meant potential growth of gaming into dozens of new locales. As of 2007, twenty-three federally recognized tribes in California were seeking trust land under the exceptions provision of IGRA (the "Section 20 concurrence" rule).[51]

Ironically, the governor's goal of collecting money for the general fund and imposing stronger regulations fueled casino expansion. State politics went on a wild ride in 2004. The governor was determined to keep his campaign pledge and was also willing to gamble. His strategy against very sophisticated opponents from 2004 to 2007 could be compared to a game of roulette in which he put big piles of chips on certain Indian casinos, hoping for a big payout for the state.

Schwarzenegger hoped to leverage powerhouse gaming tribes with a tradeoff: more slots for more money to the state. Viejas, having "built up political muscle and experience interacting with California on a government-to-government basis," was one of the first California tribes to enter compact amendment negations. "The challenge was daunting and the stakes were high," said Anthony Pico.[52] Subsequent to amending its 1999 compact in 2004, the Viejas Band of Capitan Grande Indians had the legal right to install an unlimited number of slot machines (with a sliding scale of payments to the state's general fund) and to add another gaming facility. The Viejas compact extension went to 2030, instead of 2020, allowed for "a longer-term business plan to meet enterprise and government needs," and provided for "enhanced exclusivity in Viejas'[s] geographic market."[53]

Morongo, like Viejas, was one of the several tribes that had reached the two-thousand slot ceiling. It was completing its huge new casino/hotel and wanted to expand. When the governor made additional demands, which would lessen Morongo authority vis-à-vis local non-Indian governments, talks broke down. Facing defiant resistance from most tribes with existing compacts, the governor adopted the more promising approach of negotiating for a much higher percentage of profits from those California tribes that did not yet have compacts. By June 2004, things looked promising for the governor: ten new compacts promised to put a projected $350 million to $500 million into the state coffers. The California legislature approved compacts that promised $1 billion in immediate revenues for transportation bonds and 15 percent annually from slot-machine revenues. Ratifying only six new compacts in his administration, the governor ultimately could not fulfill his campaign promise because he encountered organized resistance from several of the well-financed, politically astute gaming tribes, legal obstacles to retroactive payments, and consolidated popular opposition to new urban and even rural casinos.[54]

Environmental Reforms of 2004

The 2004 compacts were qualitatively different than the 1999–2000 compacts. There were stronger environmental protections and increased input from local communities about casino siting, construction, and cost-sharing of off-reservation impacts. The post-2004 compacts incorporate many reforms pioneered by the UAIC in the late 1990s; tribes no longer contribute to IGSDF but must negotiate directly with local communities for mitigation. A little-known but excellent summary titled "Tribal Gaming and Community Planning in California: A Primer for Policymakers, the Public and the Press," published by the California Planning Roundtable in October 2007, argues persuasively that 2004 marked a significant shift toward gaming tribes' sensitivity and accommodation to the needs and demands of the city and county communities. These 2004 compacts require "intergovernmental agreements for off-site mitigation and public service costs." Previously, such agreements with local governments to share costs were prescriptive and voluntary. After 2004, the signing of memorandums of understanding with county and city governments became the norm prior to compact ratification or trust land acquisitions. Before the rise of Indian gaming, the report noted, "most jurisdictions had little interface with tribal land use," as Indian lands were in rural areas, far off the beaten path; economic activity there had minimal impact on non-Indians. However, suburban growth moved the non-Indian population toward Indian lands. "Increasingly, decisions related to tribal gaming have consequences for non-tribal lands," the roundtable concluded. Infrastructure extension—roads, sewage systems, and water service—is a necessary step to a casino's construction. "Off-site impacts" are a major concern both before and after casino construction.[55] Policy shifted to require each tribe entering a compact after 2003–4 to file a tribal environmental impact report (TEIR); before a project for casino development begins, tribes are required to enter agreements regarding mitigation of off-site environmental impacts. Expansion of existing gaming facilities also requires a TEIR. Establishing and operating casinos have important implications for land use and environmental planning for "growing numbers of California communities."[56] Viejas, to compensate San Diego County for its expansion to twenty-five hundred slot machines, agreed to pay $1.2 million for road improvement for off-reservation impacts in December 2005; this was the first intergovernmental agreement signed in San Diego County under the new compacts.[57] "We have made some compromises," said Pico, the Viejas chair. "We do our best to incorporate the public's concerns. . . . We value the input of our neighboring communities and local governments, and take their thoughts and concerns into consideration."[58] The Department of the Interior also developed new rules in the early twenty-first century requiring both environmental reviews and support from community leaders for Indian casino construction and expansion.[59]

While many California gaming tribes make very generous voluntary donations to their communities on a regular basis to maintain goodwill, the 2004 compacts included compulsory payments and ongoing and enforceable provisions for renegotiations. The concessions included agreements to pay the county the equivalent of property tax income lost when fee land is converted to trust status, compliance with county codes, and compliance with the environmental standards set by the state in the California Environmental Quality Act (CEQA). What Placer County gained from the compacts was quite significant: (1) payment of an amount equivalent to lost property taxes as well as the county right to a share of sales taxes and transient occupancy taxes collected by the tribe; (2) tribal compliance with the county general plan, ordinances, and building standards; (3) a review process using CEQA-like procedures; (4) mitigation for traffic, reimbursement for law enforcement and fire protection costs, and contributions to the county open-space program. The Sheriff's Department was slated to get $1.2 million a year from the UAIC, a sum that could be renegotiated as the tribe agreed to surrender its sovereign immunity to legal action. An anticipated $121 million under the MOU was expected to go to the county over twenty years.[60]

During the planning stage of the construction of the Thunder Valley Casino, the UAIC approached the City of Lincoln to negotiate a hookup to the city's wastewater treatment plant, a move that exemplifies the intergovernmental activity central to the effort. When some protests arose and this MOU was legally challenged and then tossed out, the tribe built its own treatment plant. Subsequently, another MOU was negotiated with Lincoln, which created the option of a future hookup to Lincoln as a backup; this agreement included a tradeoff in which the tribe would contribute financially to Lincoln's public library. City planner Rodney Campbell thought the UAIC's decision to build its own wastewater treatment plant was worse for the environment, as the city had higher standards for treatment before discharging the effluent into the Auburn Ravine; also, he added, the tribe was burdened with the unnecessary responsibility of building and maintaining its own wastewater treatment when it really would rather have avoided that undertaking. The UAIC has been making its "voluntary" contributions to the City of Lincoln, though it has not had to access the city's wastewater treatment system to date.[61]

These MOUs and their accommodations with city and county governments particularly apply to newcomers to the compact negotiation table and especially to restored tribes seeking trust land in prime locations such as urban areas. The Graton Rancheria, applying for trust land in Rohnert Park in Sonoma County, and the Guidiville Pomo and Scotts Valley Pomo (each seeking urban casino trust land in Richmond in Contra Costa County), for example, have gone through rigorous and costly environmental reviews over the last few years; they have signed MOUs with counties and cities, but their efforts to gain trust land approval from the federal government have failed.[62] The Enterprise Rancheria is a Maidu group of Butte County that wants to acquire additional trust land in a more promising location in Yuba County. In 2002, Enterprise signed a MOU with Yuba County. Marysville was offered $3.5 million over fifteen years to accept the trust land conversion, but, in November 2005, local voters said no to a Marysville casino. Graton Rancheria opens its casino in November 2013, but Guidiville and Scotts Valley were unsuccessful in their bids for trust land.

In a number of instances, California cities have been eager to embrace proposals that involve the creation of trust land in urban areas (so called "off-reservation gaming") because municipal governments are desperate for revenues. Barstow's willingness to host the combined Big Lagoon and Los Coyotes communities' casino was praised by one environmental historian as enlightened public policy. The argument is made by other leading analysts of Indian gaming that, as long as tribal sovereignty is respected, there is a win-win situation for all when compromises, or "mutual give and take between equals," are made via intergovernmental agreements.[63] Barstow needed the economic uplift the gaming enterprise would bring: jobs and guaranteed payments to the city. Los Coyotes needed a better casino site than its existing reservation; Big Lagoon's home reservation was too environmentally sensitive for a large development. However, the proposed compact for the Big

Lagoon–Los Coyotes casino created considerable controversy, and the Department of the Interior voted thumbs down on the project.[64]

Urban Casinos and Schwarzenegger's Waterloo at San Pablo

The governor's major triumph was an August 2004 compact for 25 percent of profits from the Lytton Band of Pomo. In San Francisco's East Bay region, a messy political fight disillusioned Californians about tribal reservation shopping. The homeland of the Lytton Band of Pomo is in Sonoma County, but, in 2000, Rep. George Miller, whose congressional district included San Pablo, introduced language into the fine print of an appropriations bill (the "stealth amendment," according to its critics) that granted a new 9.5-acre reservation off I-80 in the densely populated city of San Pablo. The governor's 2004 compact with the Lytton Band gave the tribe a monopoly over a thirty-five-mile radius for high-stakes gambling; in return for giving the state 25 percent of the take, the tribe could install up to five thousand slot machines in a planned, multistory six-hundred-thousand-square-foot facility that would cost $4.5 million. The Lytton Band's casino would be the biggest in the American West as well as the state's first urban casino. It would create sixty-six hundred new jobs in a town with a $2 million budget shortfall in 2004 and would give the state a projected $125 million of $500 million taken in annually at the casino. There were immediate protests, especially due to concerns about traffic congestion, and the tribe quickly agreed to scale down the casino to twenty-five hundred slots.[65] General opposition to urban casinos doomed the project, however, and the California legislature failed to ratify the Lytton compact. Cheryl Schmit nonetheless saw the failed Lytton compact as a good model of how locally empowered citizens could make the system work. The proposed compact had conformed to the environmental standards and intergovernmental compromises of the other 2004 compacts. Parties standing to gain, like unions seeking construction jobs, were involved, and there were county and city mitigations; for example, CalTrans would get money for road infrastructure improvement for the freeway, and the state would get a hefty amount of money that would help with budget balancing.[66]

Epitomizing the potential for expansion of Indian gaming into new areas, the San Pablo case had some important political by-products. In May 2005, Governor Schwarzenegger formally announced a new policy against urban casinos. The governor said that those seeking trust land for casinos must have approval from local jurisdictions. He also said that state agencies should review proposals for urban casinos.[67] In 2006, John McCain, head of the Senate Indian Affairs Committee, came out in opposition to "reservation shopping," stating it was not Congress's intent that gaming grow so fast. US senator Dianne Feinstein became committed to preventing any future Indian casinos in the San Francisco Bay Area. Feinstein opposed the plan to approve the billion-dollar casino/hotel complex the Guidiville Band of Pomo proposed for a former naval depot (Point Molate) near the Richmond–San Rafael Bridge, despite the fact that the tribe's investor reached an agreement with environmental groups to pay $48 million to buy and protect prime shoreline adjacent to the proposed casino.[68]

The general movement to empower local communities by requiring environmental impact studies and mitigations is opposed by several powerful California Indian gaming nations. The UAIC has been severely criticized for being traitors, and this situation has created a breach within the Indian gaming community.[69] Denying that the UAIC's compact is the "model" or template for future agreements, CIGNA in 2006 was developing its own guidelines. Agua Caliente's agreement with the City of Rancho Mirage is one of the sole exceptions to southern California gaming tribes' (those with 1999 compacts) stalwart and united refusal to make such intergovernmental compacts, as the tribes claim this is a violation of their sovereignty rights.[70]

The strongest southern California gaming tribes met with the governor to amend their 1999 compacts in 2006 because they wished to expand the number of slot machines they were operating and because investors were hesitant to provide capital on improvements with only fourteen years remaining on the existing compacts. Five of the richest gaming tribes in southern California—the San Manuel, Morongo, Sycuan, Agua Caliente, and Pechanga—engaged in negotiations for one of the "biggest gaming expansion[s] in recent national history," adding seventeen thousand to twenty-two thousand new slot machines and giving the state an anticipated $506 million in revenue. Morongo would be allowed to add up to fifty-five hundred slot machines to its existing two thousand, for example. An awkward coalition that mobilized to defeat the amended compacts was composed of the UAIC, Pala, and horse-racing groups, as well as labor unions and Stand Up for California. Doug Elmets, spokesperson for the UAIC, argued that the five compacts would give tribes with big casinos the power to "blow small and medium tribes out of the water." When the state assembly demanded concessions for increased regulation, San Manuel dropped out, but the other four agreed to compromise regarding environmental protections, building code compliance, and intergovernmental agreements. Compact ratification for the "Big Four" was a hard-fought battle nonetheless. Even after the California legislature and the Department of the Interior gave their approval, opponents demanded that the matter be put before California voters in a referendum. Agua Caliente tried unsuccessfully to get the referendum vote quashed in the courts three times. A tribal lawyer from Agua Caliente said the referendum was gratuitous and unfair because it amounted to changing the rules in the middle of the game. To Cheryl Schmidt, the 2007 compacts were a betrayal of the hard-won reforms of 2004 because they left cities and counties out of the process of determining what constitutes adequate mitigation for casino environmental impacts. For most California voters, the 2007 compacts promised tax relief. For Schmit and for the southern California gaming powerhouses, what was vitally at stake was the principle of sovereignty and how compacts were to be negotiated. Southern California tribes expended from $118 million to $124 million to gain

52.6 percent voter approval. The feared consequence of the 2007 compacts for many—the delivery of even more political power to the richest and most powerful tribes—was muffled by the financial recession that began in 2008.[71] The Sycuan tribal council voted down the compact the tribe had spent $6 million to secure.

Big Money and Charged Politics

Contradictions characterize California gaming's recent history. Indian gaming is obviously big business. Investors continue to provide the backing for dozens of California tribes to develop casinos in good locations where there are untapped markets. These efforts continue despite the fact that citizens—in various northern California counties in particular—have effectively mobilized to contest sitings of casinos and trust land conversions in various locales; various local, state, and federal authorities continue to press for stronger regulatory control of an industry that grew in a regulatory vacuum. There are confusing cross-currents as Indian gaming's further expansion promises needed local revenues, tax relief, and jobs in California's ailing economy, while Indian gaming also has some negative economic impacts on certain sectors of the population. California's federally recognized and unrecognized tribes continue to be dealt with on a case-to-case basis under the law, which inhibits the formation of standardized guidelines.

There are discernible trends, however; one indicates that community leaders have an increased voice in dealing with environmental impacts. Upon his election as California governor in 2010, Jerry Brown planned to open negotiations to amend the remaining 1999 compacts to bring the rest of the compact tribes in compliance with the new environmental standards and regulatory controls. As of 2012, he had negotiated two, one with the Habematolel Pomo of Lake County and one with the Pinoleville Pomo of Mendocino County. Regulatory controls are in place, and 15 percent of the Pinoleville casino net goes to local communities in exchange for operating nine hundred slots.[72] Another observable trend is that it is more and more difficult for a tribe to open a casino on recently acquired trust land.[73] It comes as little surprise to anyone in today's economy that those that have, get more, and those who don't, have less and less of a chance at the big jackpot. Those with ample reservation land in good locations are reasonably secure. Those without trust land face a dauntingly difficult uphill battle. Those with prosperous gaming operations already can apply to have trust land conversions of private property they have acquired with casino profits. However, gaming watchdog groups are chipping away at the Department of the Interior's broad discretionary power to make such trust conversions for either landed or landless Indian nations. In 2008, the Department of the Interior announced a more restrictive policy regarding fee-to-trust conversions after a district court judge found the fee-to-trust process to be flawed. The 2009 Supreme Court decision in *Carcieri v. Salazar* represents a more restrictive policy on trust conversions: only tribes under federal jurisdiction prior to 1934 are eligible. Section 20 of IGRA provides one of the few avenues remaining for a tribe without trust land before IGRA (1988) to gain it.[74] Sen. Dianne Feinstein introduced Senate bill S. 771, the Tribal Gaming Eligibility Act, to amend section 20 of IGRA and prohibit "off-reservation gaming" by requiring "substantial modern" as well as ancestral connection to newly acquired land. Schmit and Feinstein apparently shared the view that the intent of IGRA has been distorted, shifting from an original focus on tribal economic development and self-sufficiency to become a vehicle for constantly expanding casino operations. *Indian Country Today* denounced the Feinstein bill as a travesty that would make it nearly impossible for restored or newly recognized tribes to open casinos. Only five tribes nationally operate off-reservation casinos under the two-part determination of section 20 of IGRA, so some argue that the urgency to close this loophole is overblown.[75]

California voters seem to be content with any and all contributions by casino tribes to the state budget. Gaming tribes continue to give generously to sweeten relations with their communities. The established gaming tribes are less constrained by mandatory requirements to compensate counties, but they too have absorbed a lesson. Retiring an advertisement about the cruelties suffered by Santos Manuel, the reservation's first captain and stalwart defender, San Manuel currently airs a "Healthy Communities" video commercial on television stations. San Manuel's million-dollar donations for cancer research at Loma Linda University are showcased; an image of historic Indians helping white pioneers cross the difficult mountain passes is also featured. Both images underline the good neighbor theme. The commercial ends with the message, "Indian Tribes and California Together: One Community."[76] Cooperation is the watchword in California gaming for the foreseeable future.

CHAPTER 14   # The Invention of Old Sacramento
A PAST FOR THE FUTURE

Lee M. A. Simpson and Lisa C. Prince

Here is a unique opportunity to completely transform the heart
of a city . . . to clear away the debris of yesteryear and build
for tomorrow.
—Sacramento Redevelopment Agency, 1962

The City of Sacramento recognizes the importance of its
historic and cultural resources, which creates [*sic*] a distinct
sense of place for residents and visitors. . . . Preservation
and adaptive re-use of historic structures also promotes
sustainability.
—Sacramento 2030 General Plan

Old Sacramento, a twenty-eight-acre National Historic Site nestled between
Interstate 5 and the banks of the Sacramento River, reflects the evolution of
urban environmental politics and the historic preservation movement. Home to a
thriving business district in the mid- to late nineteenth century, the district slid
into a traditional skid row that, by the middle of the twentieth century, seemed an
ideal candidate for slum clearance and urban renewal. That the district survived is
testament to the tenacity and vision of a variety of individuals who, far before their
time, recognized that history and historic structures could be a valuable tool in the
economic revitalization of a city. The bulldozers stopped at Second Street, and a
new understanding of historic preservation, which would only become mainstream
forty years later, was born.

Preserving the Inner City

Sacramento's foray into historic preservation in Old Sacramento in the 1950s and
1960s puts it in the vanguard of the national historic preservation movement. Prior
to passage of the National Historic Preservation Act of 1966, the federal government limited its involvement in preservation to a few specific sites that had an
emphasis on archaeology or national glory. Even as individual cities in the late
nineteenth century became aware of the threat to colonial-era structures from rapid

development, no effort was made to protect entire districts. Lacking any cohesive vision or legal mechanisms for protection, the nation had only private initiatives to protect the Old Statehouse in Boston, the Betsy Ross house in Philadelphia, and the Fraunces Tavern, site of Washington's Farewell Address, in New York.[1]

The restoration of Williamsburg, Virginia, in the 1920s represents the first effort at district-wide preservation in the United States. Yet, this brilliant undertaking financed by John D. Rockefeller Jr., with its emphasis on establishing a place that would attract tourist dollars, did little to further understanding of the value of historic preservation as a tool for urban growth and development or to recognize historic structures as an important reflection of human interaction with the environment. Rockefeller had little interest in preservation beyond its ability to educate Americans to be good citizens. He argued that the importance of Williamsburg lay in "the lesson it teaches of the patriotism, high purpose, and unselfish devotion of our forefathers to the common good."[2]

As the twentieth century progressed, American cities pursued a growth model that emphasized development of new areas and the abandonment of older industrial sectors. By the middle of the century, these aging cores entered a period of crisis met with the innovative concept of urban renewal. The slash-and-burn philosophy of renewal, however, posited that cities could be revitalized only by demolition of old and obsolete buildings, especially when they appeared to impede construction of modern transportation infrastructure or profitable commercial ventures.

As thousands of structures and historic areas were razed through urban renewal, urban Americans came slowly to embrace historic preservation as a way to hold on to a sense of place and identity and as a tool to revitalize cities' aging cores. Unlike European cities, where structures are permitted to sit uninhabited for years before they are adaptively reused, Americans viewed older structures as derelict and worthy only of demolition. The federal government encouraged such thinking well into the 1970s with financial support of wholesale razing of neighborhoods and only limited backing of structural rehabilitation through tax credits.[3]

Passage of the National Historic Preservation Act in 1966 represented a direct challenge to the excesses of urban renewal and marked the federal government's recognition that the nation's architectural heritage was worthy of protection. Through listing on the National Register of Historic Places, inner cities now had a new tool and a new ally in their efforts to halt wholesale destruction. The register innovatively recognized both individual structures and entire districts; yet, its emphasis on freezing districts in a specific period of historical significance had unintended consequences. In many cities, including Sacramento, limited periods of significance have led to what some critics have called "phony" history or ahistorical representations of the past that fail to recognize and interpret districts as sites of change and diversity.[4] It is the challenge of the twenty-first century preservation movement to move beyond such limited understandings of historical resources and to redefine historic districts as vibrant and evolving components of the city.

Abandoning the River

The portion of the West End area that would eventually be designated as Old Sacramento was the birthplace of the city and the heart of commerce into the early twentieth century. From the city's founding in 1849, boats carrying global migrants, miners, and merchants plied the Sacramento River, arriving at Sutter's Embarcadero at the foot of J Street. The booming riverfront quickly became the commercial and social hub of the infant city, offering vital supplies and sanctuary to the multitudes of new residents and miners headed for the nearby gold fields.

The embarcadero remained the commercial nexus throughout the city's early decades. When the state legislature moved into the new capitol building along Tenth Street on December 6, 1869, the city center began its gradual shift eastward, away from the river. Four years later, the Central Pacific Railroad relocated its depot from Front and K Streets to the filled-in Sutter's Slough, thus moving this important transportation hub away from the riverfront. Construction of the Cathedral of the Blessed Sacrament at Eleventh and K, completed in 1886, a new city hall at Ninth and I, and a new city post office at Eighth and I Streets in the early twentieth century gave further evidence that the embarcadero no longer served as the city's center.[5]

While the West End's decline escalated dramatically during the Great Depression of the 1930s, its slide had begun long before. A 1915 map of Sacramento's West End lists hotels as "cheap lodgings," "Hindoo Lodgings," and "Jap Lodgings," indicating that once-fashionable hotels had become rooming houses to accommodate the second and third wave of immigrants arriving in Sacramento. Former theaters and fancy opera houses had become disreputable "moving picture galleries." Major businesses like Breuner's and Weinstock-Lubin moved to midtown locations, while the grand gold rush era hotels—the Orleans, Fremont, and Shasta House—became transient hotels.[6] As the city center and its former affluent residents moved eastward and to new suburbs outside the city, the West End's physical condition slowly deteriorated, undermining its economic base. By midcentury, Sacramento's West End was reported as being one of the worst slums west of the Mississippi.[7]

Envisioning the City of Tomorrow

Joining a growing national movement, the State of California put forth the California Redevelopment Act in 1945, which gave cities and counties the authority to establish redevelopment agencies to address the problems associated with blighted conditions like those found in Sacramento's West End.[8] The act specified that a city or county planning department could conduct surveys of blighted areas and make a preliminary plan for redevelopment. Blight was defined as the condition in urban areas that constituted physical and economic liabilities and which required redevelopment "in the interest of the health, safety, and general welfare of the people."[9]

In 1947, when the members of the Sacramento City Council looked at the West End area between the capitol and the Sacramento River, they saw deteriorating

FIGURE 14.1. Originally established in 1851, the Golden Eagle Hotel at 627 K Street was, by 1856, considered one of the largest and most impressive in the rapidly growing city of Sacramento. Along with visitors and residents, the Golden Eagle accommodated a restaurant, saloon, barbers, blacksmiths, bootmakers, and various manufacturers. A casualty of redevelopment, the Golden Eagle succumbed to demolition, which was a common sight in the early years of urban renewal projects, which sought to modernize deteriorating city cores. Courtesy of the Center for Sacramento History, Harry Sweet Collection.

streets lined with dilapidated housing and low-rent commercial buildings. Over the past twenty years they had witnessed the assessed valuation of the West End decrease by 50 percent. While tax revenue slid every year, demands on city services escalated. The area contained 8 percent of the total city area and 7.5 percent of the population, but it had 26 percent of the fires, 36 percent of the juvenile delinquency, 42 percent of adult crimes, and 76 percent of the tuberculosis cases.[10] Something had to be done to address the disparity. Redevelopment seemed the obvious solution, but it required strong public support since public monies would be used to relocate residents and businesses.

Sacramento Bee writer Hale Champion helped generate support through a series of articles in 1949 that described the West End as the "disease-ridden . . . rotting core" of a city desperate for change. He wrote, "Disease crawls out of the rooming houses and flophouses and chicken shacks of Sacramento's blighted areas. Crime and vice and their junior partner, juvenile delinquency, loot cars and roll drunks and pull knives in the asphalt jungle of Sacramento's west end. [The West End] is a row of shacks to call one's own—complete with dirt, rats, blistered, splintering boards and that stale, unwashed odor which is standard equipment in this area."[11] Perhaps exaggerated, Champion's observations nevertheless called attention to the fact that the city's once prosperous gold rush headquarters had deteriorated into a skid row.

The city's response was "not only to curtail the blight, but to wipe it out entirely."[12] In 1948, the city council appropriated $3,200 for a redevelopment survey. When this was completed and the need for action more clearly defined, the council asked the federal government's Housing and Home Finance Agency (later Housing and Urban Development, or HUD) to reserve $364,000 in federal funds under Title I for redevelopment activities.[13] In order to receive state and federal funds, the California Community Redevelopment Act of 1945 and the federal Housing Act of 1949 mandated that cities or counties create a local public agency to plan and manage redevelopment projects in their communities. The city created the Sacramento Redevelopment Agency on September 25, 1950, with a mandate to prepare the preliminary financial analysis, studies, and plans for redevelopment areas.[14] That same year, upon recommendation of the city's planning commission, the council adopted an ordinance designating the West End as blighted and requiring redevelopment. Redevelopment Area No. 1 included those city blocks from the Sacramento River east to Tenth Street and from I Street on the north to R Street on the south.[15] Although it was yet to be written into the city's plan, Sacramento's first urban redevelopment area included what would later become the nationally designated historic district called Old Sacramento.

Federal Policies of Slum Clearance and Urban Renewal

Like other cities in post–World War II America, Sacramento initiated its policies and projects according to guidelines set by the federal government. "Slum clearance" was the common terminology used to describe urban redevelopment policies implemented after passage of the Housing Acts of 1934, 1937, 1949, and 1954 and the Highway Act of 1956, all of which worked in tandem and informed the era for cities engaged in urban renewal.[16]

Ironically, the Housing Act of 1934, which sought to address problems of poverty and homelessness, contributed to the conditions that later led to areas being declared slums under the 1937 and 1949 acts. Essentially, the Federal Housing Administration (FHA) adopted criteria that denied mortgage insurance to many older buildings in low-income and high-minority urban neighborhoods.[17] The inability to purchase or restore such buildings led to the properties' further decline in condition and value. Later designated as blighted under the 1937 and 1949 housing acts, such buildings could be cheaply acquired by cities through eminent domain, and municipalities could then demolish them and sell or lease the cleared land for urban renewal projects or freeways built with funds provided by the Highway Act of 1956.[18]

Sacramento's West End, like many older districts in American cities, was one such redevelopment area designated for demolition and clearance. The area's racial and ethnic makeup reflected the national norm of low-income, high-minority urban neighborhoods that had evolved as the "white flight" of an expanding middle class departed the declining central city for suburbia. A 1951 Sacramento Redevelopment Agency survey of business in Sacramento's West End identified 50.3 percent Caucasian and 49.7 percent non-Caucasian ownership— "Negro, Chinese, Japanese, Mexican, East Indian," and other.[19] The report concluded, "Ownerships of business are distributed almost evenly as between Caucasians and the non-Caucasian-Mexican group. In general, income patterns seem to follow the type of business rather than the race of owner; however, Negro, Mexican, and East Indian business owners seem to be concentrated more in the lower revenue producing businesses."[20] Such an area would not be eligible for FHA mortgages and would soon become a prime target for urban renewal.[21]

In many cities, including Sacramento, this paradigm better served the redevelopers and city planners of central business districts than the residents living in the redevelopment areas. Sacramento's Redevelopment Area No. 1 included the worst slum in the city's West End, but it also included established areas whose residents did not consider their neighborhoods "blighted."

The Housing Act of 1954 increased the flexibility of the 1949 act, which had triggered the blight designation and slum clearance policies that reshaped American cities. The act provided federal funds for two-thirds of the costs for planning, acquisition, demolition, and site improvement, while local entities paid the remaining one-third. The 1954 act specified that the earlier act's funding for redevelopment be expanded to include commercial and industrial development. This change constituted a shift in emphasis from replacement residential housing (urban redevelopment) to commercial development (urban renewal), which meant that low-income areas being redeveloped could be demolished and replaced with commercial structures or high-end apartments.[22] State and local governments combined with local business interests to divide the one-third share of redevelopment costs to rebuild their city cores and central business districts. Viewing this move

FIGURE 14.2. Playing on the dilapidated front porch of a home in the West End redevelopment zone in the early 1960s, these boys represent the predominantly low-income mix of ethnic groups that populated the area. Neighborhoods such as this one were marked for demolition to make way for renewal projects, forcing residents to relocate their families and businesses. Courtesy of the Center for Sacramento History, Ted Leonard Collection.

as a profitable and painless means of dealing with distressed neighborhoods, the Sacramento Redevelopment Agency accelerated its urban renewal applications for federal funds after passage of the Housing Act of 1954.

Working with the redevelopment agency and state planners to conceive a new direction for the capital area, in 1959 Sacramento's planning commission and the city council adopted a new general plan. The plan was a broad statement of community objectives, including standards, policies, and principles to address growth problems. The first of a series of precise plans was for the "Old City" of Sacramento—the area bounded by the Southern Pacific Railroad levee on the north, Broadway Boulevard on the south, Alhambra Boulevard on the east, and the Sacramento River on the west—essentially, the original city grid.[23]

Between 1960 and 1962, the city and state completed a series of studies to analyze the area's function and map its growth. The city hired the consulting firm of Leo A. Daly and Associates to prepare a comprehensive central city plan for Sacramento, which served as a guide upon which all subsequent plans were based. At the same time, the state legislature commissioned a state capitol building plan, which both the city and state adopted in 1961. The city adopted a new general plan in 1963, which updated the 1959 plan. This new plan included the freeway routes (for Interstate 80 and Highway 50) adopted in 1962, which the state's highway division, in conjunction with the city planning commission and the redevelopment agency, had spent several years planning. It also included an area to be developed that was marked "Historical Center."[24]

The Relentless Advance of the Bulldozer

In the meantime, the Sacramento Redevelopment Agency's projects were well under way. As noted, the city designated its first effort, Redevelopment Area No. 1, in 1950. The first project was a fifteen-block portion of the area called the Capitol Mall Project No. 2-A, approved in 1955. The first large-scale demolitions began in January 1957, and by March 15, 1961, all 310 parcels in the project area had been cleared. The number of people displaced totaled 1,867, which included 408 families, 308 single householders, 417 single persons, and 350 businesses, all of which the agency assisted in relocating.[25]

The first new development to break ground was the $7 million federal building on Capitol Mall between Seventh and Eighth Streets. Sacramento was the first city in the nation to use an innovative financing measure called tax increment financing, or TIF, for urban renewal projects. Using TIF, the tax yield for the new federal building was estimated to bring in 70 percent of the tax revenue formerly collected from the entire fifteen-block Capitol Mall Project area.[26] Next came the award-winning Capitol Towers and Garden Apartments taking up the four blocks bounded by N, Seventh, P, and Fifth Streets in 1960, also part of Capitol Mall Project No. 2-A. In that same year, the agency began Capitol Mall Extension Project No. 3, a ten-and-one-quarter-block area that bordered the Capitol Mall Project No. 2-A on three sides, encompassed 222 parcels, and was "planned to be exclusively commercial in re-use character." By 1962, more than a third of the parcels had been demolished and cleared. This renewal project resulted in the displacement (and partial relocation) of 1,000 single men, 117 families, 400 businesses, and 12 institutions.[27]

City leaders could not have been happier over the obliteration of blight and increased revenues from redevelopment. Describing its future vision for the city, the triumphant redevelopment agency claimed, "Sacramento's commitment to transform the western portion of its Central Business District from a shabby run-down area into an environment of urban grandeur is rapidly being honored."[28] Listed as a future project in a 1962 Sacramento Redevelopment Agency report was Project No. 4 (later named Capitol Mall Riverfront Project No. 4), comprising the fifty-one blocks remaining in Redevelopment Area No. 1. Tentatively planned for this project area was a "four block 'Old Sacramento' historic area, a new Chinese community, a three-block cultural area, a multiple residential area, a heavy commercial corridor, and a State Office Building complex."[29] The redevelopment agency approved Capitol Mall Riverfront Project No. 4 on June 20, 1966, and soon commenced with the detailed planning, final acquisitions, and site preparation for the historic district.

FIGURE 14.3. "Redevelopment Dedicated to a Finer Future Sacramento," reads a sign posted on the 1852 D. O. Mills & Company bank building at 226 J Street in Old Sacramento in the early 1960s. Arriving in Sacramento from New York in 1849, Darius Ogden Mills established the first banking institution in the state, dealing in gold dust, nuggets, and New York exchange. The "finer, future Sacramento" would include the preservation of this pioneering banking firm's early building. Courtesy of the Center for Sacramento History, City of Sacramento Collection.

The redevelopment plan emphasized "preservation, restoration and reconstruction of properties" of the period from 1849 to 1870.[30]

The final approval and adoption of this agency plan for Old Sacramento did not happen quickly or without serious controversy, public debate, further local, state, and national studies, and what ultimately played out as a contest between opposing visions for the city's future. The battle lines were drawn between historic preservation advocates, increasingly alarmed at the wholesale demolition practices of urban renewal, and those favoring the perceived promise of a high-tech modern city. The fight reached its peak during the freeway controversy of 1960–61.

The Freeway Is the Future

Sacramento, by the late 1950s, had come a long way from the days when the Sacramento River provided the main artery for travel and commerce. The city experienced tremendous growth and urbanization during and especially after World War II. No fewer than four military bases, along with expanding industrialization, altered the region's environment and increased its population. Suburban tracts multiplied, and travel by automobile, whether for work or leisure, became the norm. New highway systems crisscrossing the nation quickly replaced the aging travel routes of roads and rivers.

The Federal Highway Act of 1956 committed the government to invest billions of dollars in a national network of interstate highways. The federal government provided 90 percent of the cost, while states paid the remaining 10 percent. Designed for civilian needs, the highways were meant to provide congestion relief, spur economic development, and connect principal metropolitan areas. Additionally, better roads would make it easier to move military convoys in case of attack and to evacuate large cities more efficiently.[31] The new highway system also addressed changing traffic patterns associated with postwar population growth and suburban life as millions nationwide fled decaying inner cities. The idea was to provide speedy transport through or around urban centers. Unfortunately, state highway commissions, with the authority and responsibility to plan freeways and highways with the most direct and cost-efficient routes available, often routed them directly through established urban neighborhoods or historic sites, isolating or destroying many in the process. This was the case with the routing of Interstate 5 through Sacramento's West End.

In 1962, Sacramento's city council, planning commission, and redevelopment agency, working with the state's division of highways and highway commission, adopted plans to route Interstate 5 through the city's western edge, by then recognized as its most historic area. Before adopting this route, the city engaged two consulting firms to study traffic routes through the city. The first effort, the Deleuw-Cather study in 1958, recommended the freeway be routed through the West End on the east side of the Sacramento River, approximately at the site of the final adopted route. Next, the city's 1961 central city plan, by Leo Daly and Associates, also recommended the freeway be placed east of the river, approximately between Second and Third Streets. The Daly plan, however, considered not only traffic arteries but also all sorts of land uses for the downtown redevelopment area, including a historical section in the West End.[32]

The city's reigning political powers of the time supported the West End freeway route. These supporters included members of Sacramento's city council, redevelopment agency, chamber of commerce, downtown merchants association, and the realty board, as well as the county road commissioner and the *Sacramento Union,* among others.[33] The redevelopment agency's interest in the adopted freeway route cannot be overstated. The agency had lured retail enterprises, such as Macy's, to the redevelopment area with the promise of easy freeway access.[34] In addition, the agency's ability to use federal highway funds to clear blighted areas in the freeway's path also helped it finance such a large area of redevelopment.[35] Although the central city plan and the redevelopment agency's tentative renewal plans recognized the possibility of creating a historic district, doing so was certainly not the chief priority.

Preservationists who wanted the freeway routed on the Yolo (west) side of the river were outraged and soon mounted a strong campaign against allowing a freeway to tear through the remaining historic heart of the city.[36] Significant opposition came from the Sacramento Historic Landmarks Commission, the State Division of Beaches and Parks, the National Park Service, US representative John Moss, and the *Sacramento Bee,* whose publisher at the time, Eleanor McClatchy, "waged an all-out campaign in the paper's editorial pages and led the preservationists' fight."[37] Ultimately, the West End freeway proponents won the battle, but not without a long and drawn-out fight. A compromise of sorts was made when the division of highways agreed to bulge the freeway route to the east to preserve what became the Old Sacramento Historic District.

Old Sacramento

The initial basis for the creation of Old Sacramento grew out of several significant reports on the area. In 1957, the state authorized the Division of Beaches and Parks to "provide for the study of the development of a zone of preservation in the historic West End of Sacramento."[38] The effort produced a three-part report, *Old Sacramento: A Report on Its Significance to the City, State, and Nation, with Recommendations for the Preservation and Use of Its Principal Historical Structures and Sites,* and recommended the establishment of a state historical monument. The report expressed the importance of protecting historical sites to develop and sustain public memory: "The very things that Americans adore abroad they destroy systematically at home. Old buildings are broken up in the United States as fast as used packing boxes, to make way for new ones . . . without them we are perpetual juveniles, starting over and over, a people without a memory."[39]

In May 1960, the Sacramento Historic Landmarks Commission, at the request of the city council, submitted its own report, *Telling the Sacramento Story by the Preservation and Enhancement of Historic Landmarks: A Report of the Ways and Means of Restoring and Preserving Historic Landmarks and Heritage of "Old Sacramento."* The report included recommendations to establish a state park, a city-county museum, to impose architectural controls through a zoning ordinance in the proposed preservation plan, and to establish an Old Sacramento authority to operate the project. Also included was the understanding that the proposed Old Sacramento area met the National Trust for Historic Preservation's criteria for suitability, particularly that the structures had outstanding historical and cultural significance in the nation, state, or region in which they existed and that they retained their integrity of original materials and location.[40]

In 1961, the National Park Service, the agency responsible under law for preserving historic sites and materials of national significance, prepared its own study, which temporarily stalled the freeway project. The study investigated the impact of I-5 on plans for Old Sacramento. In its statement of findings, the report noted that a freeway route on the west side of the Sacramento River in Yolo County would not affect Old Sacramento but that any of the proposed routes on the east side of the river would require demolition or removal of old buildings of considerable historic interest and value to the community, the state, and the nation. The report continued, "Old Sacramento contains 31 old structures importantly associated with broad aspects of Western history and with notable men and events. . . . These buildings offer an opportunity to re-create and preserve a significant segment of the pioneer western scene for the inspiration, education, and enjoyment of future generations."[41] The National Park Service urged preservation and restoration of Old Sacramento as far as possible, emphasizing that large-scale demolition of so many historic structures should be a "matter of deep concern and determined efforts should be made to avoid such destruction." The findings recommended that if a choice had to be made, the removal of historic buildings was preferable over demolition.[42]

The publication of the three reports established the importance of the local, state, and national significance of Old Sacramento, an area that some believed to be the West's most historic city. The old Sutter Embarcadero and surrounding buildings marked an important part of American history—the opening of the West to the nation and the world. The gold rush, Pony Express, first telegraph and transcontinental railroad lines, and the headquarters of banking and agricultural firms, among others, were all represented in Old Sacramento.

The efforts of preservation advocates persuaded the city's urban renewal planners to commission a master study plan for the Old Sacramento Historic District in 1963. The Candeub, Fleissig & Associates consulting firm was hired to prepare a plan for the development of the Old Sacramento Historic Area and Riverfront Park with the objective of achieving "practical re-creation of a living, self-sustaining community reflecting the atmosphere, character, architecture, enterprise and color of the early gold mining period for the inspiration, use and enjoyment of the people and to stimulate their appreciation of historical values as they pertain to our national heritage."[43]

The Candeub, Fleissig master plan helped coordinate the renewal efforts for Sacramento's West End. The Division of Highways modified the adopted freeway route in order to save more buildings, although the roadway would still cut through the city and isolate the district from downtown. The master plan included the following assumptions:

- The district should be commercial and self-sustaining.

- It should be achieved through a maximum of private investment.

- In so far as possible, it should be an authentic re-creation of Old Sacramento, recognizing the significant stages of Sacramento's growth and development.

- Development of the area should be practically and economically feasible.

- The plan should maximize the educational, cultural and historical values of the area, presenting an accurate portrayal of life and activities in Old Sacramento.[44]

Preservation efforts received another boost on January 12, 1965, when the secretary of interior declared Old Sacramento a "Historic District" and therefore eligible for nomination as a registered National Historic Landmark, provided that its rehabilitation satisfied the guidelines and standards of the pending Historic Preservation Act of 1966. Soon after, the State of California designated a portion of the district as a state historic park.

Preservation for Use

While many people and agencies worked toward creating Old Sacramento, one individual stands out for his untiring efforts to make it happen: Vernon Aubrey Neasham. Aubrey Neasham was a trailblazer in the historic preservation movement, leaving his mark on an impressive legacy of prominent sites across the western United States. Born in 1908, Neasham began his long career in history in 1936 when he was appointed supervisor of a Works Progress Administration research project on California's historical landmarks shortly after obtaining his PhD in history from the University of California, Berkeley. He later worked as regional historian for the National Park Service in New Mexico, Hawaii, and Alaska. Appointed state historian for the California Department of Natural Resources Division of Beaches and Parks in 1953, he led projects to preserve historic areas in Monterey, Coloma, Columbia, the Pueblo de Los Angeles, Hearst Castle, Donner Memorial State Park, Fort Ross, Sonoma Mission, Sutter's Fort, and Old Sacramento.[45]

Neasham's work with the state's Division of Beaches and Parks included research on Old Sacramento's historic buildings and sites, which was used in the initial 1957 state study on the area. He left the division in 1960 to form Western

Heritage, Inc., a historical consulting firm, after which he became heavily involved in the efforts to protect, preserve, and restore Old Sacramento. Neasham took a leading role in navigating the complex relationships and controversial issues that shaped the project from its beginning. He understood the politics involved in working with so many disparate governmental agencies, civic groups, and economic concerns. Although initially an opponent of the West End freeway route, he worked with the parties involved for a solution to save the district and had a leading role in persuading the planners to move the freeway eastward to save both sides of Second Street.

Neasham's Western Heritage, Inc., was the historical consulting firm used for the Candeub, Fleissig master plan. His idea of using historic preservation as a tool for urban renewal was a new idea that could be applied to an entire district. His theory of "preservation for use" informed the master plan and likely sold the idea to city planners, who liked the promise of commercial redevelopment in an area that had so recently been a drain on city services and its tax base. "Preservation for use" implied that the area would be an integral and self-sustaining part of the city's business district. The restored and reconstructed buildings would operate as shops, restaurants, hotels, bars, theaters, offices, and residences. The buildings and sites would tell the monumental stories that occurred there. As Neasham himself explained it, "'Preservation for Use' shall be its guideline. No dead museum piece will this be, but a living, pulsating element of modern life, to be enjoyed by the living. To integrate the old with the new shall be its challenge. Preserved, with an economic as well as a cultural reason for being, it will have nationwide importance. As a model and guide in historical restoration, interpretation, and use, its influence will be exerted throughout the land, thus enabling us to better understand what made America great."[46]

A charter member of the National Trust for Historic Preservation, Neasham understood, advocated, and implemented the early ideas of preserving the historic environment. His idea was to "freeze" Old Sacramento in the era of the Old West of early glory and triumph; the stories of remarkable firsts and great men were historically significant not only for the city but for the state and nation as well. The rehabilitated or reconstructed buildings in the historic district would represent the early developmental stages of Sacramento within the 1849–70s period, although they had never actually existed this way in fact. Some critics later claimed the decision to select only certain historical aspects of the period was an attempt to mythologize it for commercial purposes. It is important to remember that Neasham was not only informed by the era's historic preservation standards but also bound by its political and economic conditions. But it might also be argued that savvy redevelopers collaborating with city officials and preservationists "co-opted the preservation movement for their own interests while capitalizing on the public's nostalgia for yesteryear."[47] Nevertheless, creating Old Sacramento was an enormous undertaking that overcame many obstacles to become the city's largest draw for visitors to the region. The project also corrected the area's unsustainable decline as the city's former skid row.

When finally approved in 1966, and funded in 1967, Old Sacramento still required several more years before it resembled a cohesive historic district. Surrounded and isolated by the "bombed-out" look of massive demolition and freeway construction until the early 1970s, the Old Sacramento project took time. The Sacramento Redevelopment Agency, working with planning, historical, and architectural consultants, was creating one of the first "historical developments" in the United States and using a combination of federal urban renewal funds, local TIF financing, and special tax incentives for private investors. By 1976, in time for the nation's bicentennial, a number of the buildings had been restored or reconstructed, the waterfront had been cleared, and while streets, sidewalks, and waterfront docks had yet to be built, businesses were operating and visitors were coming.

The Historic Buildings and Sites of Old Sacramento

While Aubrey Neasham and the early proponents of Old Sacramento saw the district's structures as emblematic of a period of great men and heroic firsts, recent research has provided evidence of a more nuanced and inclusive story that includes tangible evidence of Sacramentans' intense interactions with their environment. More than a story of miners and entrepreneurs, the buildings of Old Sacramento tell a story of inundations—of people, commerce, and culture converging at the confluence of the Sacramento and American Rivers. Yet, despite their best-laid plans, nature struck back in the form of fires and floods. It is in the built environment where visitors can best witness the often-epic struggle between inundations of people and inundations of nature that shaped Sacramento's development.

Several of the district's buildings stand testament to that story. The Lady Adams building, located at 119 K Street, is one of the oldest buildings in the district and a survivor of the 1852 fire that destroyed most of the city. Rising in 1849, the building was constructed by shipwrights who used reclaimed timber from the *Lady Adams* ship and locally made brick. Roofed with a mixture of rough planking, tin, brick, and sand, and with steel shutters, the building proved to be impenetrable. The structure survived intact until 1970, when a city work crew trenching in the adjoining alley undermined its foundation, causing a wall to topple and the roof to cave in. Given its significance as one of the oldest surviving buildings, it became one of the first buildings restored in the district.

Like the Lady Adams building, the B. F. Hastings building, located at the corner of Second and J Streets, stands testament to the importance of building with brick in a commercial district. Built to replace a structure destroyed by the 1852 fire, the B. F. Hastings building housed Wells Fargo, the telegraph, the Pony Express, an office for Theodore Judah (whose ideas created the transcontinental railroad), the Sacramento Valley Railroad, and the California State Supreme Court.

FIGURE 14.4. Located on K Street, the Lady Adams building is one of the oldest surviving structures in Sacramento, one of only four to survive the 1852 fire that destroyed much of the city. In this photograph, the sloping alley provides evidence of the street-raising project that elevated the city following the floods of the 1860s. Photograph by William Simpson.

In 1976, the building became part of the state park portion of Old Sacramento, and it is listed on the National Register of Historic Places.

The Lady Adams and B. F. Hastings buildings provide evidence of the city's battle against inundations of water. Devastating floods in 1852, 1858, and 1862 led to construction of a massive levee system and a decade-long engineering project to raise the city streets. While some property owners chose to raise the buildings to meet the new street levels, others, like the owners of the Lady Adams, chose to turn first floors into basements. It is in the basement of the Lady Adams building where visitors can see the original beams used to construct the building in 1849. Evidence of the street raising can also be seen in the semiburied window openings of buildings like the Mechanics Exchange building on I Street and in the sloped alleys between Front and Second Streets. These traces of history would be gone had the bulldozers continued their relentless assault on the city, just as the floodwaters had ravaged it a century before.

Bridging Interstate 5

By the turn of the twenty-first century, the city was more than forty years into its experiment in historic preservation in Old Sacramento. By several measures, the experiment could be deemed a success. First and foremost, a blighted district that had been home to the city's skid row had been converted into a vibrant commercial district and the city's premier tourist attraction, host to the Sacramento Jazz Jubilee (Memorial Day weekend) and Gold Rush Days (Labor Day weekend). Travel writers across the nation and around the globe have written favorable reviews of the district, encouraging their readers to make a trip to Sacramento part of their travel plans for northern California. *The Travel Trade Gazette of the UK and Ireland* described the district in 2002 as "a nugget often overlooked," while Australia's *Sunday Mail* found it in 2007 to be "much more than a tourist trap." *Washington Post* travel writer Cindy Loose suggested in 2004 that the district had clearly achieved Aubrey Neasham's vision of "preservation for use." She wrote that "it could easily have become one of those dead, re-created-village places where people in period [costumes] run around, not fooling you for a minute. Instead, the city allowed merchants to open real restaurants and shops in some of the 53 historic buildings, making it feel historic but alive."[48]

Yet, the district's disconnection from downtown, created by the construction of I-5 and touted by proponents as a positive outcome of construction that would protect the integrity of the district, had become one of its biggest hindrances. While the freeway essentially isolated the district from the city's modern core, the hoped-for nineteenth-century atmosphere failed to materialize, as the freeway became both a visual and auditory hindrance to history and a hulking barrier to visitors, despite the pedestrian tunnel underneath I-5 on K Street. Although recommending a visit to Old Sacramento, a travel writer for the *New Zealand Herald* captured the problem in this 2008 review: "Across from the Hastings Building is a statue erected to the memory of the Pony Express riders. It is of a heroic young man on a rearing horse, his mouth agape, determination in his piercing eyes. Behind him is the cutting edge of a freeway and, on this clear morning, I try to take an emblematic photograph of this monument to a brief, defining period in Sacramento's life 150 years ago. But the freeway is there in every snap of the shutter, the new imposing itself on the old."[49]

In the late 1990s, the city started what has become a concerted yet unfortunately abortive effort to end Old Sacramento's isolation. The variety of proposed fixes provides evidence of changing sensibilities regarding the environment and appropriate use of urban space. The once revered interstate highway, celebrated as a catalyst for urban and economic revitalization, has come to be seen as a contributor to blight or, at the very least, an obstacle to implementing the city's vision of becoming "the most livable city in America."[50] In 1998, the city began to take a serious look at various alternatives for undoing the damage of a previous generation. With removal of the interstate an unfeasible alternative, a new generation of city leaders and planners suggested reconceptualizing the freeway as "usable public space." Looking to Seattle's successful decking of I-5, Sacramento planners gave serious thought to bridging the freeway as a means to "make downtown whole." While waiting for completion of lengthy environmental and engineering studies on bridging, the city moved forward with an enhanced pedestrian underpass as a first step in reconnecting the old city with the new.[51]

FIGURE 14.5. Dedicated in 1976 as part of the national bicentennial celebration, the Pony Express statue in Old Sacramento memorializes one of western history's legendary entities. Situated across the street from the B. F. Hastings building at the corner of J and Second Streets, the statue is often overshadowed by the traffic flying by on Interstate 5. Photograph by William Simpson.

The $1.5 million enhancement of the K Street pedestrian tunnel in 2000 provided a better connection for pedestrians wanting to access Old Sacramento, but it failed to address the visual and noise pollution caused by the interstate and did not significantly alter the district's isolation from the rest of the city. City leaders continued to explore the decking option and in 2000 commissioned the first of a series of feasibility studies. Conducted by the city's Department of Transportation, the project overview illustrates the city's altered understanding of its relationship to both its history and to its natural environment. In explaining the need for the project, officials noted that the opening of I-5 forty years previously had effectively cut off downtown Sacramento from its riverfront, "isolating the community from its historic origin and the Sacramento River." Noting that construction of the interstate between Capitol Mall and the Crocker Art Museum at O Street put the freeway below grade and lower than city streets, the department proposed decking I-5 at this location.[52]

In the initial development phases, residents and officials put forth an ambitious plan to create new usable space over the freeway that would accommodate "shops, parks, housing and other uses." That plan carried a price tag in excess of $250 million, however, so the city decided to pare back its plans and focus on a nondecking alternative that would still meet the project's main goal of connecting downtown to the waterfront and Old Sacramento.[53] In September 2009, the Department of

Transportation presented this new alternative to the city council for approval before beginning work on an environmental impact report.

The bridging proposal reflects Sacramento's vision of a future that demonstrates a radically different vision of growth from that of the past. The 2030 General Plan, adopted in March 2009, emphasizes the need for the city to follow "smart growth principles" that encourage green building technology, infill projects, and protection of both built and natural resources. The plan notes the importance of historic and cultural resources to the creation of "a distinct sense of place for residents and visitors . . . that differentiates Sacramento from all other cities." In addition, the plan recognizes that "preservation of historic and cultural resources is important because cities with distinctly identifiable places and history are generally more livable for residents and more attractive to new businesses that sustain the economy. Preservation and adaptive re-use of historic structures also promote sustainability by reducing the need for new construction materials."[54] No longer does the city envision the type of wholesale destruction of neighborhoods seen as vital to growth in the 1950s and 1960s. How successful the plan will be in implementing that vision, especially given the economic impact of the deep recession that began in 2008 and brought an abrupt end to discussions of bridging or decking I-5, remains to be seen.

The Issue of Integrity

In 2004, the Old Sacramento Historic District found itself on a watch list maintained by the National Historic Landmarks Program. The program report noted that the district suffered "from both the deterioration of contributing buildings and the cumulative [effect] of incompatible treatments, such as signage and the district-wide installation of parking meters. The result is the erosion of the overall integrity."[55]

Old Sacramento's status as a threatened historic resource reflects one of the potential outcomes of the policy of "preservation for use." How does a historic district protect its historic integrity while remaining usable in the modern world? Sacramento turned to parking meters, for example, in response to the modern problem of lack of funding. In 1999, facing budget cuts, the city chose to divert $415,000 in general funds from Old Sacramento to other parts of the city. Proponents of the installation of parking meters hoped they would provide a secure and reliable funding source and anticipated a revenue stream of about $400,000 annually.[56] Even at the time of installation, however, city officials were aware that the meters threatened the district's integrity. They conducted an eight-month study of the issue and looked at alternatives to meters, including installation of sticker-dispensing boxes that would be less obtrusive. Their consultant, along with the city and state preservation officers, all concluded that parking meters would create a serious threat to historic integrity.[57]

Threatened removal from the National Register of Historic Places galvanized the city and Old Sacramento property owners to reexamine the balance between preservation and use in the district. The city took a more active role in enforcing sign ordinances and maintenance agreements with property owners so that, by 2010, other than the parking meters, most of the criticisms of the National Historic Landmarks Program had been addressed. In addition, the city instigated reorganization of the various nonprofit entities that managed Old Sacramento to increase cooperation and help develop a cohesive vision for the district. The resulting Historic Old Sacramento Foundation, formed in 2008, has succeeded admirably in building a coalition between state parks, the Old Sacramento Business Association, and the city that is finally bridging the gap between preservation and use through an intensive and concerted interpretive program.

At the center of the new vision for Old Sacramento is a desire to reconnect to the environmental history of Sacramento. No longer is it sufficient to preserve or rebuild historic structures to either celebrate a mythic gold rush past or sell T-shirts and candy to tourists. Gone are the Mark Twain audio boxes and the majority of knick-knack shops. In their place are new business ventures, including high-end loft housing and well-developed living history tours emphasizing a variety of gold rush experiences that extend beyond the stereotypical male forty-niner. Each summer the foundation sponsors a series of weekend street performances that bring visitors into some of the most historic structures in the district, including the Eagle Theater and the Central Pacific Railroad Passenger Station. Most impressively, the foundation sponsored the creation of underground tours that explore Sacramento's most significant environmental history episode: the raising of the streets in response to flooding. As tour author Heather Downey notes, "The underground's eerie, musty spaces are portals to the past that tell a variety of stories about Sacramento's unique history. These architectural relics are more than symbols of Sacramentans' early struggle with nature. They spark people's imaginations, and help them to become more familiar with the city's landscape. They are significant resources for the Sacramento region, reminding us of this city's singular origins. They are material proof of the physical, financial and political effort Sacramentans exerted to save their city in the wake of frequent natural disasters."[58] In essence, the tours remind visitors of the city's intimate and precarious relationship to the river that gave it life and continues to shape its destiny.

The river provides the central focal point for the revised Old Sacramento State Historic Park general plan. Developed in 2010–11, the plan outlines a new vision for the state-owned portion of the district that seeks to uncover the traces of early Sacramento history that can still be found both above and below ground. Building on the underground tours, the state plans to develop an excavation exhibit where visitors can view the remnants of the gold rush era buried underground. Above ground, the state plans to reconstruct certain commercial buildings from the 1860s and 1870s to explore the commercial history of the district.[59]

In addition, the state plans extensive development of the waterfront to help refocus the district on the site where Sacramento began. First, the plan envisions creating an exhibit space from which to view a sunken nineteenth-century ship currently hidden from view. Second, the plan proposes facilitating visitor access to the river via water taxi tours or some other form of historic boat tour. The river, however, remains hidden from view by the Central Pacific freight and passenger depots. Like the river, the railroad is another defining feature of Sacramento history, and the new general plan calls for emphasizing the railroad as the second focal point of the district. The plan calls for reconstruction of historic train tracks for use by excursion trains and restoration of the freight and passenger depots to their 1870s appearance.[60]

While the revised general plan received favorable reviews from the city council and in public comment, the ability of the state to implement the plan over the next twenty years is far from certain. In 2010, voters rejected a ballot measure proposing to increase vehicle registration fees by eighteen dollars to finance a state park system trust fund. Faced with millions of dollars in deferred maintenance and an additional slashing of the department's general fund in the 2011–12 fiscal year, there is little money for implementing an ambitious general plan like that for Old Sacramento.

Why Save Old Sacramento?

What inspired preservation advocates to save this district of outdated and dilapidated buildings while modernizing efforts were progressing all around them? Why was it important to do so, and who would benefit? Walter Frame, vice president of the Conference of California Historical Societies and an advocate for Old Sacramento, echoing concerns across the country, explained, "We are deeply concerned with the destruction of California's landmarks throughout the State. The mushrooming population of our State, the careless redevelopment of the older parts of our cities and the witless urge to bulldoze history into dust has destroyed much that is of great value and threatens what we have left."[61]

Yet, the threat to historic sites came not only from the razing of buildings. It came also in the form of stagnant historic districts cut off in time from the rest of their history. In a 1977 article entitled, "Everyone Applauds Preservation—But Something's Missing," history curator Thomas Frye criticized preservation that "is impersonal and anonymous, which endeavors to conjure up what 'used to be'— preservation that treads on the pretext of history." Historic districts, old towns, and pioneer parks are areas where "the politics of preservation, economic forces and stereotyped views of history are likely to combine to create the outcome." The outcome, Frye suggested, is the nineteenth-century lithograph—the bird's-eye view—in other words, inauthentic, a construct. Recognizing that such adaptive use is a good way to preserve old structures and get neighborhoods back on the tax rolls, somehow it all made Frye uneasy. It was not just the bisecting freeway soaring nearby. "No," Frye argued, something is missing. My history is missing. It wasn't like this. I am a stranger here. . . . Old Town's 20th century history has been eradicated as systematically as possible. The successive layers of the buildings have been peeled back and thrown away, leaving no evidence of their varied use as rooming houses, bars, wholesalers, pawnshops, and labor headquarters. These middle years are not represented in the restoration, not even a few examples . . . are being kept for future interpretation by the urban historian. Some of my history was destroyed when they peeled off those layers and threw them away.[62]

Perhaps Frye missed the whole point of creating an Old Sacramento Historic District, which aimed to celebrate the city's dynamic early years. Nevertheless, Frye asked painful but necessary questions about how we consider, select, and interpret the history of our built environment. Who is it for? What does it serve? Can it help us make sense of a past to which we may not feel a connection?

The preservation of Old Sacramento provides stunning evidence of the changing environmental sensibilities of urban America. It reveals competing visions of urban identity in relation to preserving a glorious past or looking forward to a promising future. The collision between urban renewal and historic preservation interests in Sacramento exposes the ways disparate civic groups, business interests, and local, state, and federal officials negotiated and competed for public support, limited funds, and control to recreate a contested urban identity.

In hindsight, there are aspects about the creation of Old Sacramento to criticize, most notably its isolation from the rest of the city and its celebratory focus on the gold rush era, yet the district remains a valuable historic resource with much to contribute to the past, present, and future vision of Sacramento. Is this a district worthy of preservation? Are there solutions to the district's many problems? The answer is an unequivocal yes. It will take the concerted vision and effort of the next generation of Sacramento preservationists, along with city and state planners who, it is hoped, will be as innovative as their predecessors.

Sacramento, Before and After the Gold Rush

Ty O. Smith

To drive or walk in Sacramento's downtown core is to witness the clash of time. New high-rise buildings blend with old brick façades, and multiple generations of advertising messages peek from behind peeling paint and maintain a faded vigilance over the bustling metropolis. On a building near the corner of Twelfth and J Streets hangs an example of one of Sacramento's many public art projects. Pasted to the side of the Masonic Temple is a huge version of Charles Christian Nahl's famous gold rush era painting, *Sunday Morning at the Mines*. This painting illustrates the extremes of camp life, with one side depicting a raucous horse race and drunken miners and the other, miners engaged in Bible study and domestic tasks. It is a comment on the uneven nature of piety, virtue, and excess among the men living in the mining camps of the Sierra. But urban artists also added images of miners emerging from the painting and climbing down a ladder; as they descend the ladder, they evolve into modern Sacramentans, one complete with sports coat and briefcase in tow. The message is clear: our presence here today is the product of our literal and figurative descent from our gold rush past. In short, it is Sacramento's genesis story. Sacramento, like Minerva, the Roman goddess who graces the Great Seal of the State of California, was born of only a father.

The ladder that extends from the region's past to the present, however, extends back farther than the gold rush, and the human dramas, as the chapters in this volume demonstrate, were no less tumultuous. While one can center the activities related to the gold rush on Sacramento, one cannot fully understand Sacramento through such a narrow lens. Sacramento, once a land occupied for millennia exclusively by native peoples and then loosely governed by Spain and later Mexico, saw the influx of gold-seeking adventurers and the merchants who sold them supplies. With the founding of the city and the continuation of an entrepreneurial spirit, the "Big Four" established the Central Pacific Railroad and the western leg of the transcontinental railroad. Agriculture boomed, as did the need for water, irrigation systems, and flood control. By the twentieth century, the entrepreneurial boom-town had been transformed into a government town: the state's capital and home to three major military bases. The city grew but was eclipsed in stature and status by California's coastal cities. By the early twenty-first century, Sacramento once again confronted dramatic change as its military bases were shuttered and its own name became used to simply describe the place where state government dysfunction occurred. Taken as a whole, the various eras of Sacramento's development, before and after the gold rush, are nothing short of epic. And each of them has formed the tributaries that flow into the river of Sacramentans' daily lives.

Sacramento's history as an urban area is often dated to the gold rush. Local habitation, of course, did not begin in the Sacramento region with the "days of '49," when, as historian J. S. Holliday characterized it, "the world rushed in."[1] If not rushing, the fact is, the "world" was already at least trickling into California. For those departing from the East, the gold rush only served to accelerate a process of western migration that had been going on for more than a decade. Before a single ounce of gold ever hit the assessor's scale, Anglo families risked it all to come to places like California, many swearing off allegiance to their former country and receiving land and citizenship in Mexico. The covered wagons that rolled west through prairie and over mountains to destinations like Sutter's outpost, in what would later become Sacramento, were not traveling to the edge of nowhere, just the edge of somewhere else. Hudson's Bay Company trappers and Russian explor-ers exploited resources in the Central Valley for years before that. Such activities had already begun to drastically reshape the environment, in intended and unin-tended ways.

Although not writing specifically about the Sacramento region, William Pres-ton in his study "Serpent in the Garden," describes the process of environmental and demographic change brought by a host of "companions of conquest," from germs to plant seeds to ideologies, all of which would transform the California environment, before, during, and after the mission period.[2] Indeed, if there was a "serpent in the garden" in the Sacramento context, it slithered in well before the gold rush. While on paper Mexico claimed half of the continent in 1824, Mex-ico occupied very little of this land. The Mexican republic in California actually hugged a thin strip of land along the coast. Mexican officials, from the confines of their offices in coastal Monterey or Yerba Buena (now San Francisco), imagined the Sacramento interior as the wilds. They, like Spain before them, had tried and failed to settle the interior.[3] Valley tribes repelled military expeditions and otherwise resisted missionization. This resistance did not mean, however, that the Indian nations of the Central Valley were not affected by coastal settlement. As detailed by George Harwood Phillips in *Indians and Intruders in Central California, 1769–1849*, interactions between interior Indians and the Spanish and Mexicans ranged from violent confrontations to the even more deadly spread of diseases. On the one hand, interior Indians grew in military power by siphoning off mission resources, such as cattle and especially horses. But contact with Spanish and later Mexican pueblos and with Anglo and Russian trappers working for Hudson's Bay Company spread diseases, and outreach during the mission period served to undermine native societal structures.[4]

The Sacramento region during the 1830s was an incredibly complex area, one where these disruptions put distinct Indian groups in competition with one another for increasingly scarce resources, and commercial activities such as trapping accelerated such scarcity. As Albert Hurtado reminds us, however, this was no wilderness region. It would be a mistake to imagine the region's native American inhabitants as simply living lazily off the fat of the land, leaving their sustenance completely to fate. This is the impression left by early anthropological studies, but as M. Kat Anderson's *Tending the Wild* demonstrates, California Indians throughout the state did much to augment nature's bounty through land management practices.[5] Indians had been living in the Sacramento region from time immemorial, and while, by the 1840s, it was a world increasingly in peril, it still was a world of native logic and control.

It was into this complex world that Johann Sutter (John Sutter) floated in 1839. He was not after gold, he was not motivated by any notion of helping Anglos succeed in any sort of "manifest destiny." Sutter's goal, as Hurtado elucidates, was to establish an agricultural settlement, but this is not the memory of Sacramento's founding. As government agencies and nonprofit organizations attempt to market the city's history, they focus on the gold rush and its resulting urban development, in the process erasing from the public memory the environmental history of the city and the continuity between past and present. Largely missing from this memory is the region's Spanish and Mexican past, the California Indians who lived and continue to live there, environmental change, and the agricultural production that fueled it all and that would itself become the "gold" after the gold rush.

Sutter's dream of an agricultural empire was short lived. By 1850, just eleven years after its founding and in the same year that the city of Sacramento incorporated, Sutter's Fort lay in ruin. First went the roofs of the perimeter buildings. Early Sacramentans scavenged beams and roof shakes, and they literally wove the fragments of the fort into the fabric of the emerging city. Meanwhile, the exposed adobe melted back into the Sacramento earth, leaving only the fort's central building. The fort's community, once vibrant, multicultural, and polyglot, spilled out into Sacramento and into the mining towns of the Sierra foothills. A desperate Sutter had sold his fort in 1849 for seven thousand dollars, and, saddled with a mountain of debt, he left Sacramento. He would eventually pay those debts with sections of his remaining land, all of which he received as a result of becoming a naturalized citizen of Mexico.

Sutter was lucky to escape with that much. Many Mexican era grantees lost their land after the Mexican republic ceded most of what is now the western half of the United States after the US-Mexico War. Some grantees, like Sutter, retained title to most of their land, but not before proving legitimate title through the California Land Commission. But even with the legal victory, Sutter could not turn away the stream of creditors. In Sutter's mind, he was a victim of an uncontrollable mass of rough and rowdy settlers, who, hell bent on attaining easy riches, held no respect for property rights. Had it not been for his own failed businesses and personal excesses, however, these losses might not have stung so badly.

Near the end of his life, Sutter and his wife established a comfortable home in Lititz, Pennsylvania. It was a mansion by most people's standards, but it was likely a small consolation for Sutter. Sutter's own pride undoubtedly judged his new home by the impossible standards and nostalgia for his former life, where he ruled as monarch in his own imagined empire, where, as he often recalled, he "had the power of life and death over both Indians and white people."[6] In Pennsylvania and on the streets of Washington, DC, citizens met him with deference. Sutter's personal fortune and legacy, however, at least in his own mind, seemed to rest with winning recompense from the US government, which he lobbied for compensation, year in and year out, until his death. In the meantime, the California legislature doled out his day-to-day expenses in the form of a relief bill. To Sutter, it was rightful compensation for the lands lost to squatters and progress, but it was charity in both intent and deed. Just two days after Congress adjourned in the summer of 1880, as had been the case in years past, without considering that year's Sutter relief bill, Sutter died of a heart attack in a Washington, DC, hotel.

In the 1880s, sons and daughters of "pioneers," safely removed from the tumult of the gold rush, turned reflective. Wanting to preserve the memory of the romance of the founding of the state, they staged expositions, marked pioneer sites, and otherwise created monuments to pioneers from which they claimed descent (literal or imagined). It was in this context of pioneer hero worship that the Native Sons of the Golden West purchased the remnants of Sutter's Fort and the small plot of property on which it stood. They gifted it to the state and participated in its reconstruction, which they had completed by 1905. Workers accomplished the physical reconstruction with brick, mortar, and roof tiles. Just as they reconstructed "his" fort, so too did pioneer boosters remake Sutter. They refashioned him not as who he was but who they wanted him to be. They propped up his image, and, like puppeteers, they made him perform, but not without first cloaking him in clothing that was not his own and making him speak in a clarity of English his own lips had never uttered. In the re-presentation, they made him into an archetype of western, Anglo expansion. They turned Sutter—the Swiss immigrant, the naturalized citizen of Mexico, the failed trader, the debtor to Russia, the subjugator of California Indians—into an Anglo pioneer. And they turned his settlement, which historically was populated primarily by California Indians, Hawaiians, and non-Anglo Europeans, into a haven for Anglo American settlement, the cradle of the gold rush, and the birthplace of California. Like any good work of fiction, this vision had elements of truth, but the historical figures who once called the place home would not recognize either the restored fort or the resurrected Sutter. Both, however, satisfied the needs of early twentieth-century Sacramentans, but the re-packaging also set into motion a vision of the past that would extend well beyond that generation into the present.

As with many expressions of public memory, the reconstruction of Sutter's Fort was a product of the advocacy work of a few but with the indirect and tacit approval of many. Supporters of the reconstruction cast a wide net to garner public support. The reconstruction was about not just rebuilding a physical structure but also fashioning the site into a repository and shaper of public memory related to Sacramento's gold rush "heritage." The *Sacramento Union* published articles encouraging citizens to bring "relics of the pioneer era" to the fort. Soon, in the spirit of community participation, the fort became the locus of one version of the city and state's past. People brought remnants of the era, passed down from family members, to add to the material representation of the glorious gold rush. Lanterns, gold pans, pantaloons, tintypes, and various other materials and personal effects multiplied. The fort did not shy away from this role, and, in short order, it morphed into the "state's attic." As the moniker implied, items, some of questionable provenance, burst the seams of the fort. A half century after the restoration, family mementos continued to trickle in, the most notable instance of which was when descendants of the infamous Reed-Donner party donated a number of objects to the fort in the 1940s. Over the years, the collection, which has held both treasure and oddity, witnessed and was subjected to the professionalization of the curator's science, and while curators culled some of the original collection, the remaining objects are still referred to as the "Stronghold of Pioneer Memories"—so much so that the fort's Mexican era context, California Indian reality, and environmental legacy are all but lost in the cacophony.

There is now a weekly tradition in this vein: on Tuesdays and Thursdays, a small wagon train starts its journey in Old Sacramento and winds its way down the busy streets of modern Sacramento. Students, often dressed in some version of pioneer garb, smile and wave. After a forty-five-minute journey, the groups approach the front gates of Sutter's Fort State Historic Park, where park staff and docents greet them with shouts of welcome. Emulating pioneers who have crossed the Sierra, these students spend the next twenty-four hours "living history." They make soap, do laundry, twine rope, view a cannon drill, and, as night falls, they sit by the campfire and sing songs; it is a program that they will never forget, which is, at once, the good and bad news, the gift and the curse. The curriculum and information upon which the park bases this program emphasizes the Anglo migrant experience, while ignoring the fact that the site was primarily populated by California Indians, Hawaiians, and other European settlers. The curriculum also focuses on activity *in* the fort, with little exploration of the impact of the fort on the surrounding land. Perhaps future park planners will more fully account for these histories in their public programming. California State Parks and its partners have embarked on the preliminary steps in building a state-of-the-art California Indian Heritage Center. Located along the banks of the confluence of the Sacramento and American Rivers, in West Sacramento, the center will provide a venue to explore the experiences of California Indian people, past, present, and future. Pioneer memories at existing venues, however, continue to have a strong hold.

Perhaps Sutter had it right all along. His vision was based on commerce and agriculture, not gold. As miners harvested the last bits of gold from the hills and mountains, the earth provided abundance and wealth of a different sort. For the generation after the argonauts, "gold" grew and, in most of the valley, continues to grow, on trees and vines, and, for much of its life, Sacramento has served as a hub of both agricultural production and distribution.

The signs of the significance of Sacramento's agricultural heritage are fading. Visitors to communities such as Orangevale and Citrus Heights may be hard pressed to find the fruit orchards for which the towns were named, but the place names bear witness to this history. And agriculture is not abandoned. Today, numerous farmers' markets in and around Sacramento remind residents of the region's agricultural heritage. That heritage is also recalled as a museum exhibition at the Heidrick Ag History Center, located fifteen miles north in Yolo County.

Agriculture contrasts with Sacramento's urban reality. While Sacramentans and city boosters once extolled the virtues of the region's rural and urban nexus in the nearby communities of Elk Grove, Fair Oaks, and Rio Linda, Sacramento today is a sprawling metroplex with a past built upon many phases of urban development. As recently as the mid-1970s, it would have been hard to envision the many acres of houses extending northward almost to the Sacramento International Airport, but there they stand, obscuring the physical traces of the hop yards, fields, and orchards that once surrounded the city. This land is almost all the product of massive reclamation work; where people had once put their hopes and dreams to arm and shovel, there now stand suburban developments and commercial and state office complexes.

Such development has caused an improbable city built at the confluence of two major rivers to rise like a mirage from the vast valley expanse. Indeed, the city of Sacramento stands smack dab in the middle of the Great Central Valley, one of the world's richest agricultural regions. Billboards remind travelers that they are in the "bread basket of the nation." Writer Gerald Haslam has labeled the Central Valley "the other California," divergent in landscape, politics, and culture.[7] But where does Sacramento fit into this other California? Is it an island unto itself or part of the "other" California? While farmers on the southern end of the Central Valley decry the "congress created dustbowl," sprinklers water the grounds of the capitol in the midday sun and residents lament the recent addition of water meters at their homes. Gone are the days of the flat-rate water bills for Sacramento's residents. In southern California, people have learned to rejoice in the rain, but, in Sacramento, abundance in the form of water and agricultural products has been seemingly a part of daily life. This is changing now as the city moves farther away from its rural roots and takes its place as a major California metropolitan area.

While Sacramento's agricultural past may seem less important today than history tells us it should be, it is clear that history is a remarkably important part of Sacramento's identity. In fact, Sacramento promotes its present and future through other aspects of its history, especially the gold rush and the building of the transcontinental railroad. One year's batch of promotional material for Gold Rush Days, held yearly in Old Sacramento, encourages visitors to "hitch up the team to your buckboard and come on down! Bring the young'uns and the in-laws, the neighbors and the new folk just off the stage from Back East. Heck, bring your sweetheart along for a thrill. . . . During Labor Day Weekend in Old Sacramento you'll find yourself transported back to the days of Gold and Glory, when California was a brand-new state with brand-new ideas. Join in the truly old-time fun in the world of Yesterday!"[8] Gold and Glory? Old-time fun? Mock Old West shoot-outs and salty but lovable old-timey miners obscure the historic and ongoing environmental degradation wrought by the gold rush. Certainly, this is a celebration with a selective memory. It is not interested in recalling bounties on Indian scalps or the fact that, even to this day, mercury, used to extract gold 150 years ago, flows through the Sacramento River, just one example of what some historians have labeled as the "toxic legacies" of the gold rush.[9]

The fact that Old Sacramento is now a tourist draw reflects a remarkable episode in its own right. In the 1940s, most residents saw downtown Sacramento's west side as a "slum." To city leaders' eyes, the area now known as Old Sacramento was one of the worst representations of urban blight. That Sacramento was built at the confluence of two major rivers almost led to its demise, and much of early Sacramento's history is about the steps that citizens took to make their city safe from seasonal floods. But as new modes of transportation emerged, the city literally developed away from the river and grew in various phases of urban and suburban growth to the east. As Lee Simpson and Lisa Prince detail, reformers and early preservationists created a plan to "restore" this area. Their idea was to preserve this aspect of the city's past to benefit the future, but, in so doing, they were asking Sacramentans to crane their necks back to an area they had collectively abandoned. What outsiders called a slum, however, was a community, a disadvantaged community to be sure, but a community nonetheless and a place where people experienced a full range of emotions as they attempted to make a life of their own.

Part of the process of rebuilding Old Sacramento was displacing its residents. It is here that we return full circle to the question highlighted by Steven Avella in the introduction to this volume: "How does one accurately and honestly capture the historical memory of a community?" Or, as Lee Simpson and Lisa Prince question in their chapter on Old Sacramento, "In hindsight, there are aspects about the creation of Old Sacramento to criticize, most notably its isolation from the rest of the city and its celebratory focus on the gold rush era, yet the district remains a valuable historic resource with much to contribute to the past, present, and future vision of Sacramento. Is this a district worthy of preservation? Are there solutions to the district's many problems?" "The answer," they conclude, "is an unequivocal yes." A similar case may be made for Sutter's Fort. This generation has the opportunity to re-inscribe onto the site that which was vital to the site's history but not important to past planners: the California Indian story and the environmental story. As Hurtado reminds us, "in 1847, about 280 white men, women, and children were associated in one way or another with New Helvetia. At the same time, the New Helvetia area was home to about 2,800 Indian men, women, and children." But it is more than just a story of numbers. Sutter's Fort was built on the backs of California Indian and Hawaiian labor, and the land of Sacramento was made usable by their labor and the labor of later immigrants from China, Japan, South America, and Europe. In this sense, the great wealth generated by the California gold rush and the opening of transportation, such as the transcontinental railroad, came at an enormous human cost.

"The past didn't go anywhere," the musician Utah Phillips once proclaimed. In Sacramento, this assertion seems like more than a folk singer's lament. Indeed, despite the travails of history, every fall, during Native American Day at the state capitol, Miwok and Maidu dancers unite past and present through dance, the heels of their bare feet stomping the ground so hard that one wonders if 160 years of state history might not collapse back on itself. Meanwhile, the Theodore Judahs, Stanfords, and Crockers of our own time imagine how they might revolutionize the world and line their own pockets with one or another business startup. Contrary to Western romance, the West was not settled at the end of a gun barrel; the story of Sacramento reveals that it was also "won" through more mundane but just as powerful modes. The progress of the conquest of humanity and nature can just as easily be measured by the movement of the surveyor's chain and its strength tested by property case law. City founders chose for their motto the Latin phrase "Urbs Indomita," or "the indomitable city," but this was perhaps as much a hope for the future as a reflection of their present. It is true that in Sacramento nature pushed people and that people pushed back, but under the surface there remains an anxiety, and, still, at least some Sacramentans must wonder if there is not some more shoving to be done in this now timeless pushing match. But no matter what the future holds for Sacramento's residents, responses to ongoing challenges, whether posed by the environment, human interactions, or the legacies of history, can be aided by a broader understanding of the region's environmental history before and after the gold rush.

NOTES

Introduction: The Indomitable City and Its Environmental Context

1. Sarah T. Phillips, "Environmental History," in *American History Now,* ed. Eric Foner and Lisa McGirr (Philadelphia: Temple University Press, 2011), 286.

2. Louis S. Warren, ed., *American Environmental History* (Malden, MA: Blackwell, 2003), 1.

3. William Cronon, *Nature's Metropolis: Chicago and the Great West* (New York: Norton, 1992).

4. Joseph A. McGowan, *History of the Sacramento Valley,* 3 vols. (New York and West Palm Beach, FL: Lewis Historical Publishing, 1961).

5. Carl Abbott, *How Cities Won the West: Four Centuries of Urban Change in Western North America* (Albuquerque: University of New Mexico Press, 2008), 1–10.

6. Ibid., 164.

7. Mark A. Eifler, *Gold Rush Capitalists: Greed and Growth in Sacramento* (Albuquerque: University of New Mexico Press, 2002), 15.

8. Hal K. Rothman, "Selling the Meaning of Place: Entrepreneurship, Tourism, and Community Transformation in the Twentieth Century American West," *Pacific Historical Review* 65, no. 4 (1996): 525–57. See also David Glassberg, *Sense of History: The Place of the Past in American History* (Amherst: University of Massachusetts Press, 2001).

Chapter 1. John A. Sutter and the Indian Business

This chapter is a revised version of a chapter by the same name that appeared in Kenneth N. Owens, ed., *John Sutter and a Wider West* (Lincoln: University of Nebraska Press, 1994), 76–92.

1. Albert L. Hurtado, *John Sutter: A Life on the North American Frontier* (Norman: University of Oklahoma Press, 2006), 3–66 and passim.

2. The fur trade literature is huge. For interpretive treatments of the impact of the trade on Indians, see David J. Wishart, *The Fur Trade and the American West, 1807–1840* (Lincoln: University of Nebraska Press, 1979); Calvin Martin, *Keepers of the Game: Indian-Animal Relationships and the Fur Trade* (Berkeley: University of California Press, 1978); William Cronon, *Changes in the Land: Indians, Colonists, and the Ecology of New England* (New York: Hill and Wang, 1983); James P. Ronda, *Lewis and Clark among the Indians* (Lincoln: University of Nebraska Press, 1984); and Richard White, *The Roots of Dependency: Subsistence, Environment, and Social Change among the Choctaws, Pawnees, and Navajos* (Lincoln: University of Nebraska Press, 1983). On the Canadian trade, see Arthur J. Ray, *Indians in the Fur Trade: Their Role as Hunters, Trappers, and Middlemen in the Lands Southwest of Hudson Bay, 1660–1870* (Toronto:

University of Toronto Press, 1974); Arthur J. Ray and Donald Freeman, *"Give Us Good Measure": An Economic Analysis of Relations between the Indians and the Hudson's Bay Company before 1763* (Toronto: University of Toronto Press, 1978); and W. J. Eccles, "The Fur Trade and Eighteenth-Century Imperialism," *William and Mary Quarterly* 40, no. 3 (1983): 341–62.

3. White, *Roots of Dependency,* 95–96; Robert A. Trennert Jr., *Indian Traders on the Middle Border: The House of Ewing, 1827–54* (Lincoln: University of Nebraska Press, 1981) 114–16 and passim.

4. James A. Bennyhoff, *Ethnogeography of the Plains Miwok,* Center for Archaeological Research at Davis, no. 5 (Davis: University of California, 1977).

5. James P. Ronda, *Astoria and Empire* (Lincoln: University of Nebraska Press, 1990).

6. Robert Archibald, "Acculturation and Assimilation in Colonial New Mexico," *New Mexico Historical Quarterly* 53, no. 3 (1978): 205–17; Christon I. Archer, "The Deportation of the Barbarian Indians from the Internal Provinces of New Spain," *Americas* 29, no. 3 (1973): 376–85. On the Columbian origins of Spanish labor practices, see Carl Ortwin Sauer, *The Early Spanish Main* (Berkeley: University of California Press, 1969), 66–67; and Charles Gibson, *Spain in America* (New York: Harper and Row, 1966), 48–67.

7. Sherburne F. Cook, *The Indian versus the Spanish Mission* (Berkeley: University of California Press, 1943); Sherburne F. Cook, *The Physical and Demographic Reaction of Nonmission Indians in Colonial and Provincial California* (Berkeley: University of California Press, 1943); Robert Archibald, "The Economy of the Alta California Mission, 1803–1821," *Southern California Quarterly* 58 (1976): 227–40; Albert L. Hurtado, "California Indians and the Workaday West: Labor Assimilation, and Survival," *California History* 69, no. 1 (1990): 2–11.

8. John Augustus Sutter, "Personal Reminiscences of General John Augustus Sutter," MS., Bancroft Library, University of California, Berkeley.

9. Ibid.

10. William J. Breault, *John A. Sutter in Hawaii and California, 1838–1839* (Rancho Cordova, CA: Landmark Enterprises, 1998), 41–42.

11. Richard Dillon, *Fool's Gold: The Decline and Fall of Captain John Sutter of California* (New York: Coward-McCann, 1967; repr., Santa Cruz, CA: Western Tanager, 1981), 75; Erwin G. Gudde, *Sutter's Own Story: The Life of General John Augustus Sutter and the History of New Helvetia in the Sacramento Valley* (New York: G. P. Putnam's Sons, 1936), 25.

12. See, for example, James Peter Zollinger, *Sutter: The Man and His Empire* (New York: Oxford University Press, 1939), 44–45; and Marguerite Eyer Wilbur's fictionalized biography, *John Sutter: Rascal and Adventurer* (New York: Liveright Publishing, 1949), 42–46.

13. Sherburne F. Cook, *The Population of the California Indians, 1769–1970* (Berkeley: University of California Press, 1976), 42. Cook gives the figures as 76,100 and 83,800, respectively, but this estimate was for the period prior to the introduction of the European diseases that devastated the population. The numbers that I give in the text are extrapolated from Cook's calculations.

14. Robert F. Heizer and Albert B. Elsasser, *The Natural World of the California Indians* (Berkeley: University of California Press, 1980), 37–45.

15. Lowell John Bean, "Social Organization in Native California," in *Native Californians: A Theoretical Retrospective,* ed. Lowell John Bean and Thomas C. Blackburn (Socorro, NM: Ballena Press, 1976), 99–124; Joseph L. Chartkoff and Kerry Kona Chartkoff, *The Archeology of California* (Stanford: Stanford University Press, 1984), 205–42; Robert F. Heizer, ed., *Handbook of North American Indians,* vol. 8., *California* (Washington, DC: Smithsonian Institution, 1978), 370–97.

16. Richard White, "John Sutter and the Natural World," in *John Sutter and a Wider West,* ed. Kenneth Owens (Lincoln: University of Nebraska Press, 1994), 95–96 and passim.

17. Albert L. Hurtado, *Indian Survival on the California Frontier* (New Haven: Yale University Press, 1988), 24, 32–35; Edith Buckland Webb, *Indian Life at the Old Missions* (Los Angeles: W. F. Lewis Publications, 1952; repr., Lincoln: University of Nebraska Press, 1982).

18. Hurtado, *Indian Survival,* 32–54.

19. William Heath Davis, *Seventy-Five Years in California: Recollections and Remarks by One Who Visited These Shores in 1831, and again in 1833, and Except When Absent on Business Was a Resident from 1838 until the End of a Long Life in 1909,* ed. Harold A. Small, 3rd ed. (San Francisco: J. Howell Books, 1967), 16.

20. Sutter, "Personal Reminiscences."

21. Bennyhoff, *Ethnogeography of the Plains Miwok.*

22. Hurtado, *John Sutter,* 72–73.

23. Sherburne F. Cook, *The Epidemic of 1830–1833 in California and Oregon,* University of California Publications in American Archaeology and Ethnology 43, no. 3 (1955): 303–25.

24. Sutter, "Personal Reminiscences"; Heinrich Lienhard, *A Pioneer at Sutter's Fort, 1846–1850: The Adventures of Heinrich Lienhard,* trans. and ed. Marguerite Eyer Wilbur (Los Angeles: Calafia Society, 1941), 68.

25. Sutter, "Personal Reminiscences"; Webfoot [William D. Phelps], *Fore and Aft; Or, Leaves from the Life of an Old Sailor* (Boston: Nichols and Hall, 1871), 258; Sutter to William A. Leidesdorff, Aug. 8, 1844, MS. 22, Leidesdorff Collection, Henry E. Huntington Library, San Marino, CA (hereafter, LC); Sutter to Antonio Suñol, May 14 and June 13, 1842, Sutter Collection, California Room, State Library, Sacramento (hereafter, SuC).

26. Sutter, "Personal Reminiscences."

27. Dillon, *Fool's Gold,* 206–8, 221–22, emphasizes Sutter's self-interest in encouraging immigrants to settle near him.

28. See, for examples, Sutter to Pierson B. Reading, May 11, 1845, Reading Collection, California Room, State Library, Sacramento (hereafter, RC); John A. Sutter et al., *New Helvetia Diary: A Record of Events Kept by John A. Sutter and His Clerks at New Helvetia, California, from September 9, 1845, to May 25, 1848* (San Francisco: Grabhorn Press, 1939), 50–96; and Sutter to William A. Leidesdorff, Apr. 17, 1846, MS. 122, and May 11, 1846, MS. 129, LC.

29. Sutter, "Personal Reminiscences."

30. Ibid.; Johann August Sutter, *The Diary of Johann August Sutter* (San Francisco: Grabhorn Press, 1932), 8.

31. Sutter, "Personal Reminiscences."

32. Ibid.; John S. Missroon to Edward Kern, Aug. 8, 1846, MS. 27, and Aug. 16, 1846, MS. 28, Fort Sutter Papers, Henry E. Huntington Library, San Marino, CA (hereafter, FSP); John B. Montgomery to Edward Kern, Aug. 26, 1846, MS. 63, FSP; Edwin Bryant, *What I Saw in California: Being the Journal of a Tour by the Emigrant Route and South Pass of the Rocky Mountains, across the Continent of North America, the Great Desert Basin, and through California in the Years 1846, 1847* (New York: D. Appleton and Company, 1848; repr., Berkeley: University of California Press, 1985), 359–60; "Muster Roll of Company H," Feb. 18, 1847, Selected Records of the General Accounting Office Relating to the Frémont Expeditions and the California Battalion, 1842–90, Records of the United States General Accounting Office, Record Group 217, National Archives Microfilm Publication T135; Donald Jackson and Mary Lee Spence, eds., *The Expeditions of John Charles Frémont,* 3 vols. (Urbana: University of Illinois Press, 1970–73), 2:235, 302.

33. Sutter to Pierson B. Reading, May 8, 1845, RC.

34. Lienhard, *Pioneer at Sutter's Fort,* 3.

35. Sutter to Pierson B. Reading, Feb. 15, 1845, RC; Sutter et al., *New Helvetia Diary,* 2.

36. Sutter et al., *New Helvetia Diary,* 2.

37. The account about stock pens was attributed to Lizzie Enos, a prominent Maidu woman, by Bernice Pate of Auburn, California, in an interview with the author, July 1, 1976. For other stories by and about Lizzie Enos, see Richard Simpson, *Ooti: A Maidu Legacy* (Millbrae, CA: Celestial Arts, 1977). On housing within the fort, see Lienhard, *Pioneer at Sutter's Fort,* 68. On using force to control Indian workers, see Sutter to Antonio Suñol, May 19, 1845, SuC; Sutter to Pierson B. Reading, May 11, 1845, RC.

38. John Bidwell, *Echoes of the Past about California,* and John Steele, *In Camp and Cabin,* 2 vols. in 1, ed. Milo Milton Quaife (Chicago: R. R. Donnelly and Sons, 1928), 82–83.

39. Account of W. A. Leidesdorff, Aug. 1, 1844, to Jan. 27, 1846, MS. 32, Marsh Collection, California Room, State Library, Sacramento (hereafter, MC).

40. John Marsh to Antonio Suñol, Mar. 16, 1845, MC.

41. John Chamberlain, "Memoirs of California since 1840," MS., Bancroft Library, University of California, Berkeley.

42. Sutter to Antonio Suñol, May 19, 1845, SuC.

43. Sutter to William A. Leidesdorff, May 11, 1846, MS. 129, LC.

44. See the discussion in Fernand Braudel, *Civilization and Capitalism, 15th–18th Century,* vol. 1, *The Structures of Everyday Life,* trans. Siân Reynolds (New York: Harper & Row, 1981), 93–102 and passim. At the same time, we should recognize that Sutter's reliance on Indian enslavement provided him with a margin of available cheap labor at a time when labor was scarce. Indian slavery may well have made for John Sutter the critical difference between profit and loss during New Helvetia's most prosperous years; see Hurtado, *Indian Survival,* 59–60. On forced labor as an alternative to free labor in regions of frontier commercial and agricultural expansion, see Howard R. Lamar, "From Bondage to Contract: Ethnic Labor in the American West, 1600–1890," in *The Countryside in the Age of Capitalist Transformation: Essays in the Social History of Rural America,* ed. Steven Hahn and Jonathan Prud (Chapel Hill: University of North Carolina Press, 1985); Peter Kolchin, *Unfree Labor: American Slavery and Russian Serfdom* (Cambridge, MA: Harvard University Press, 1987); and Thomas Barfield, *The Perilous Frontier: Nomadic Empires and China* (Cambridge: Basil Blackwell, 1989).

45. Census data are in [George McKinstry], Nov. 1846, MSS. 12–13, McKinstry Papers, Bancroft Library, University of California, Berkeley (hereafter, MKP); and Sutter, "Estimate of Indian Population," Dec. 20, 1847, MSS. 14–15, MKP. The best-known slave-raiding episode is described in Sutter to José de Jesus Vallejo, Oct. 15, 1840, SuC.

46. Sutter et al., *New Helvetia Diary,* 58–101; Robert F. Heizer, "Walla Walla Indian Expeditions to the Sacramento Valley," *California Historical Society Quarterly* 21, no. 1 (1942): 1–7.

47. Sutter, *Diary,* 45–46.

48. Sutter to Thomas Henley, Feb. 9, 1856, Letters Received by the Office of Indian Affairs, California Superintendency, 1849–80, Records of the Bureau of Indian Affairs, Record Group 75, National Archives Microfilm Publication M234, reel 35 (hereafter, M234).

49. Ibid.

50. Thomas Henley to George Manypenny, Dec. 4, 1856, M234, reel 35.

51. Dillon, *Fool's Gold,* 341–50.

52. Hurtado, *Indian Survival,* 55–71, 100–17.

53. Stephen W. Kearny to Sutter, Apr. 7, 1847, Letters Sent by the Governors and

Secretary of State of California, 1847–48, Records of the Adjutant General's Office, Record Group 94, National Archives Microfilm Publication M182; D. C. Goddard to A. S. Loughery, Mar. 22, 1849, M234, reel 32; and Sutter to the secretary of the interior, May 23, 1850, M234, reel 32.

54. Hurtado, *Indian Survival,* 125–48, 150–53.

55. [McKinstry], [Population Enumeration of the Sacramento Valley], Nov. 1846, MSS. 12–13, MKP; Sutter, "Estimate of Indian Population," Dec. 20, 1847, MSS. 14–15, MKP.

Chapter 2. River City: Sacramento's Gold Rush Birth and Transfiguration

1. Charles Wilkes, *Narrative of the United States Exploring Expedition during the Years 1838, 1839, 1840, 1841, 1842,* 5 vols. (Philadelphia: Lee and Blanchard, 1845), 5:154–55.

2. Richard White, "John Sutter and the Natural World," in *John Sutter and a Wider West,* ed. Kenneth N. Owens (Lincoln: University of Nebraska Press, 1994), 93–119; Raymond F. Dasmann, "Environmental Changes before and after the Gold Rush," in *A Golden State: Mining and Economic Development in Gold Rush California,* ed. James J. Rawls and Richard J. Orsi (Berkeley: University of California Press for the California Historical Society, 1998), 105–22.

3. See Albert L. Hurtado, *John Sutter: A Life on the North American Frontier* (Norman: University of Oklahoma Press, 2006), for the most authoritative appraisal of Sutter's California career. On his labor system, see also Hurtado's essay, "John A. Sutter and the Indian Business," in *John Sutter and a Wider West,* ed. Owens, 51–75.

4. The first of Brannan's 1847 visits came in the spring as he was traveling eastward to meet Brigham Young on the overland trail leading from Missouri. He then expected to guide President Young and the Latter-day Saints pioneer migration party to northern California. To his extreme dismay, Young insisted on stopping and planting his Zion church colony in the Salt Lake basin. Brannan then returned to California, a very disappointed promoter, and again passed by Sutter's Fort with hardly a pause in his trip back to San Francisco. Will Bagley, ed., *Scoundrel's Tale: The Samuel Brannan Papers* (Spokane, WA: Arthur H. Clark Company, 1999), 197–203, 223–24; Kenneth N. Owens, *Gold Rush Saints: California Mormons and the Great Rush for Riches* (Spokane, WA: Arthur H. Clark Company, 2004), 50–52.

5. Rodman W. Paul, *California Gold: The Beginning of Mining in the Far West* (Cambridge, MA: Harvard University Press, 1947), 39–42, has an excellent summary of Mother Lode geography and geology. More detailed treatments will be found in Rodman W. Paul, *Mining Frontiers of the Far West* (New York: Holt, Rinehart and Winston, 1963); and Mary Hill, *Gold: The California Story* (Berkeley: University of California Press, 1999), 94–113, 149–78. David Beesley, *Crow's Range: An Environmental History of the Sierra Nevada* (Reno: University of Nevada Press, 2004), 44–47, also presents a concise summary of the Sierra's geological history, emphasizing the power of the Sierra waterways. The term *placer* (plaah-sur) is of Hispanic origin and refers to unalloyed gold found free in nature, eroded from its original hard rock encasement.

6. Quoted in Erwin G. Gudde, ed., *Bigler's Chronicle of the West: The Conquest of California, Discovery of Gold, and Mormon Settlement as Reflected in Henry William Bigler's Diaries* (Berkeley: University of California Press, 1962), 102.

7. The elementary technology of placer gold mining is described and fully illustrated in Hill, *Gold,* 86–93.

8. The geological events forming these gold-bearing deep gravels and the record of their exploitation are admirably synthesized in Hill, *Gold,* 105–13.

9. Technological advances in gold rush mining are nicely summarized in Duane A. Smith, "Mother Lode for the West: California Mining Men and Methods," in *Golden State*, ed. Rawls and Orsi, 149–73.

10. The political battle against hydraulic mining is well summarized in Hill, *Gold*, 114–32. The classic work on this subject is Robert L. Kelley, *Gold vs. Grain: The Hydraulic Mining Controversy in California's Central Valley; A Chapter in the Decline of the Concept of Laissez Faire* (Glendale, CA: Arthur H. Clark Company, 1959). The Sawyer Decision language is quoted in Hill, *Gold*, 129.

11. The leading work on this topic is Alfred L. Hurtado, *Indian Survival on the California Frontier* (New Haven: Yale University Press, 1988). For the history of racist stereotyping, see James J. Rawls, *Indians of California: The Changing Image* (Norman: University of Oklahoma Press, 1984).

12. Regarding the absence of any federal law governing mining at the start of the gold rush, consult Robert W. Swenson, "Legal Aspects of Mineral Resources Exploitation," in *History of Public Land Law Development*, ed. Paul W. Gates (Washington, DC: US Government Printing Office, 1968), 699–716; and Carl J. Mayer and George A. Riley, *Public Domain, Private Dominion: A History of Public Mineral Policy in America* (San Francisco: Sierra Club Books, 1985), 34–50. An excellent summary appears in Donald J. Pisani, "'I am resolved not to interfere, but permit all to work freely': The Gold Rush and American Resource Law," in *Golden State*, ed. Rawls and Orsi, 123–48. The situation in the upper Mississippi tri-state lead region is summarized in Kenneth N. Owens, *Galena, Grant, and the Fortunes of War: A History of Galena, Illinois during the Civil War Era* (DeKalb: Northern Illinois University with the Galena Historical Society, 1963), 4–7. A fuller account appears in Duane K. Everhart, "The Leasing of Mineral Lands in Illinois and Wisconsin," *Journal of the Illinois State Historical Society* 60, no. 2 (1967): 117–36. Since the upper Mississippi lead mines were in steep decline by 1848, news of the California gold discoveries set off an exodus of miners who brought their skills and organizational experience to northern California's placer diggings. On Hispanic precedents for California's self-constituted mining regulation, see also Ray August, "Gringos vs. Mineros: The Hispanic Origins of Western American Mining Laws," *Western Legal History* 9 (summer–fall 1996): 147–75.

13. The best account of these circumstances remains William Henry Ellison, *A Self-Governing Dominion: California, 1849–1860* (Berkeley: University of California Press, 1950). In 1850, the first session of the state legislature took action to improvise rules regarding land rights that might serve in the absence of federal land law. The Possessory Act of 1850, amended in 1852, declared that duly constituted local law officers should protect any persons using public lands for grazing or farming purposes against interference with their peaceable possession. Exception was made, however, in the case of mineral-bearing lands. Miners, the state law established, had a usufruct right superior to the rights of farmers and stock raisers. It was not an act of trespass to enter on public lands already occupied and in use for agricultural purposes if the interloper intended to work deposits of gold or other precious metals. In addition, the state legislature in 1851 legitimized the locally constituted codes of the placer mining districts, requiring that in cases involving mining claims, state courts must recognize and shape their decisions according to the established customs, usages, and rules of the mining camps. This privileged position for mining and miners received reinforcement when Congress, at long last, approved a very flawed measure that became the Mining Act of 1866. See Swenson, "Legal Aspects," 701–11.

14. Donald J. Pisani, *To Reclaim a Divided West: Water, Law, and Public Policy* (Albuquerque:

University of New Mexico Press, 1992). As this code developed, the dry-country principle of prior appropriation—the first to lay claim to a given stream of flowing water became forever the first in legal right to that water—became paramount over the wet-country principle of riparian rights, based on land ownership.

15. Mildred Brooke Hoover et al., *Historic Spots in California*, 4th ed., rev. Douglas E. Kyle (Stanford: Stanford University Press, 1990), 290.

16. This topic is thoroughly reappraised in Martin Ridge's essay, "Disorder, Crime, and Punishment in the California Gold Rush," in *Riches for All: The California Gold Rush and the World*, ed. Kenneth N. Owens (Lincoln: University of Nebraska Press, 2002), 176–201.

17. The evidence regarding California gold discoveries before 1848 is well surveyed in Hill, *Gold*, 4–20.

18. For details of these events, see Owens, *Gold Rush Saints*, 91–138.

19. "Autobiography of Major Stephen Cooper," quoted in Bagley, *Scoundrel's Tale*, 266.

20. Edward Kemble quoted in Bagley, *Scoundrel's Tale*, 265.

21. [John M. Letts,] *A pictorial view of California; including a description of the Panama and Nicaragua routes, with information and advice interesting to all, particularly those who intend to visit the golden region. By a returned Californian* (New York: H. Bill, 1853), 132.

22. Bonita Louise Boles, "The Advent of Malaria in California and Oregon in the 1830s," *Golden Notes* 36, no. 4 (winter 1990); Joseph A. McGowan, "Miasma in Sacramento, 1860–1950," *Golden Notes* 24, no. 3 (fall 1978); Sherburne F. Cook, *The Epidemic of 1830–1833 in California and Oregon* (Berkeley: University of California Press, 1955).

23. On the disease dangers of city life, see William H. McNeill, *Plagues and Peoples* (Garden City, NY: Anchor Press/Doubleday, 1976); Arno Karlen, *Man and Microbes: Disease and Plagues in History and Modern Times* (New York: G. P. Putnam's Sons, 1995), 47–63 and passim; Sir MacFarlane Burnet and David O. White, *Natural History of Infectious Disease*, 4th ed. (Cambridge: Cambridge University Press, 1972), 13–14 and passim.

24. These developments are best described in Hurtado, *John Sutter*, 236–46. Sutter senior had already launched a rival townsite promotion on a bluff along the river a few miles to the southwest, where the high bank afforded better protection against flooding. Always name proud, he called it Sutterville. Under hectic circumstances in mid-1849, Brannan and his associates duped the senior and junior Sutters into signing over five hundred Sacramento lots to them in order to counter a supposed similar competitive offer from the Sutterville merchant promoters. This deal in effect ended Sutterville's prospects for besting Sacramento's shrewd merchant cabal. Allan Ottley, "Biography of John A. Sutter, Jr.," in John A. Sutter, Jr., *The Sutter Family and the Origins of Gold-Rush Sacramento*, ed. Allan R. Ottley (Sacramento: Sacramento Book Collectors Club, 1943; repr., with an introduction by Albert L. Hurtado, Norman: University of Oklahoma Press, 2002), 22–26, 98–99; Hurtado, *John Sutter*, 246–47.

25. The plan is described and pictured in John William Reps, *Cities of the American West: A History of Frontier Urban Planning* (Princeton: Princeton University Press, 1979), 209–11.

26. The grants are recorded in the Sacramento City Tax Assessment Rolls, Book A, Sacramento Archives and Museum Collection Center. An appreciative volume, prepared by the students of McClatchy Senior High School in 1948, describes the status of the park blocks at that date: *Park Grants of John A. Sutter, Junior* (Sacramento: Nugget Press, 1948).

27. Dorothea J. Theodoratus and Kathleen McBride, *History of the Sacramento City Block 6th and 7th, K and L Streets, 1848–1920* (Sacramento: Redevelopment Agency of the City of Sacramento, 1978); Luzena Stanley Wilson, *'49er: Memories Recalled Years Later for Her Daughter Correnah Wilson Wright* (Oakland, CA: Eucalyptus Press, 1937), 17–18.

28. Jerry MacMullen, *Paddle Wheel Days in California* (Palo Alto: Stanford University Press, 1944), 12. MacMullen states that the *Lady Washington*, a flat-bottomed stern-wheeler assembled at Sutter's Embarcadero, earlier that year "chugged bravely up the Sacramento and American Rivers to Coloma, started back, struck a snag, and went to the bottom." Ibid., 11. Anyone conversant with local geography recognizes the impossibility of such a trip. Today, above the landing site for Sutter's Fort, normally only kayaks, small fishing boats, and recreational rafts can run the river.

29. A. C. W. Bethel, "The Golden Skein: California's Gold-Rush Transportation Network," in *Golden State,* ed. Rawls and Orsi, 250–75, provides an excellent survey of this topic. For river travel, see also the introduction in Roger R. Olmsted, *Square-Toed Packets: Scow Schooners of San Francisco Bay* (Cupertino: California History Center, 1988); and MacMullen, *Paddle Wheel Days in California,* 19–22.

30. Joseph A. McGowan, *History of the Sacramento Valley,* 3 vols. (New York: Lewis Historical Publishing, 1961), 1:89.

31. Bethel, "Golden Skein," 261.

32. John Letts reminiscence, quoted in Reps, *Cities of the American West,* 209.

33. For a full, carefully detailed description of road development in the gold region, see Kenneth Davies and Loren Hansen, *Mormon Gold: Mormons in the California Gold Rush,* 2nd ed., rev. (North Salt Lake City: Granite Mountain Publishing, 2010).

34. Will Bagley, *So Rugged and Mountainous: Blazing the Trails to Oregon and California, 1812–1848* (Norman: University of Oklahoma Press, 2010), 368–70, 371–74.

35. Details of the Mormon veterans' trail-making effort are found in Owens, *Gold Rush Saints,* 157–200. The broader significance of this route is discussed in Kenneth N. Owens, "The Mormon-Carson Emigrant Trail in Western History," *Montana: The Magazine of Western History* 42, no. 1 (winter 1992): 14–27.

36. An excellent summary of population movement into northern California during the gold rush era appears in the prize-winning study by Walter Nugent, *Into the West: The Story of Its People* (New York: Knopf, 1999), 54–65.

37. John Morse, *The First History of Sacramento City, Written in 1853, with a Historical Note on the Life of Dr. Morse by Caroline Wenzel* (Sacramento: Sacramento Book Collector's Club, 1945), 37.

38. Wilson, '*49er,* 17.

39. Ibid., 18.

40. Ibid., 24–25.

41. Accounts of Sacramento's early experiences with fires can be found in Edward H. Howes, "The World's Gateway to the Gold, 1848–1860s," in *Sacramento: Gold Rush Legacy, Metropolitan Destiny,* ed. John F. Burns (Carlsbad, CA: Heritage Media, 1999), 36–37; Thor Severson, *Sacramento: An Illustrated History* (San Francisco: California Historical Society, 1973), 106–7; and Charles E. Nagel, "A Fight for Survival: Floods, Riots and Disease in Sacramento, 1850" (MA thesis, California State University, Sacramento, 1965).

42. Mary Crocker to Mrs. Lydia Seymour, Mar. 25, 1853, manuscript box 5, State Library Collection, California Room, California State Library, courtesy of the California History Room, California State Library.

43. Eugene M. Itogawa, "The Natural Ice Industry in California" (MA thesis, California State University, Sacramento, 1974).

44. Morse, *First History,* 50; Charles E. Nagel, "Sacramento Cholera Epidemic of 1850," *Golden Notes* 4, no. 1 (Oct. 1967); Mitchel Roth, "Cholera, Community, and Public Health in

Gold Rush Sacramento and San Francisco," *Pacific Historical Review* 66, no. 4 (1997): 527–51. A colorful description appears in George W. Groh, *Gold Fever: Being a True Account, Both Horrifying and Hilarious, of the Art of Healing (so-called) During the California Gold Rush* (New York: William Morrow, 1966), 215–23. For the circumstances that brought cholera to the western United States in 1849 and 1850, see Charles S. Rosenberg, *The Cholera Years: The United States in 1832, 1849, and 1866* (Chicago: University of Chicago Press, 1962).

45. Darius Ogden Mills, "Biography of Darius Ogden Mills," Bancroft Library, University of California, Berkeley; Burelle Press Clipping Service, "In Memoriam Darius Ogden Mills," Special Collections, California Room, California State Library; Willard Thompson, "D. O. Mills," *Golden Notes* 30, no. 4 (winter 1984).

46. Kenneth N. Owens, *Sutter's East Adobe: A Cultural Resources Report for Sutter Hospitals,* culture resources management report, on file with Peak and Associates, Inc., El Dorado Hills, CA.

47. Wilson, *'49er,* 14.

48. Ibid., 15–16.

49. Crocker to Seymour, Mar. 25, 1853.

50. The adventurous course of the younger Sutter's life in Mexico is described in Ottley, "Biography of John A. Sutter, Jr.," a lengthy introduction to Sutter junior's *Sutter Family and the Origins of Gold Rush Sacramento.*

51. Charles V. Hume, "The Sacramento Theater, 1849–1885" (PhD diss., Stanford University, 1955); Hume, "The Eagle Theater, 1849," *Golden Notes* 19, no. 3 (August 1973); Hume, "First of the Gold Rush Theaters," *California Historical Society Quarterly* 46, no. 4 (1967): 337–44.

52. Literature on the Sacramento squatters' rebellion includes Dennis M. Dart, "Sacramento's Squatter Riot of August 14, 1850," *Pacific Historian* 24, no. 2 (1980): 156–67; Mickey Knapp, "The Squatters' Riot: A Dramatic Episode in Sacramento's History," *Golden Notes* 38, no. 3–4 (fall–winter 1992); Mark A. Eifler, *Gold Rush Capitalists: Greed and Growth in Sacramento* (Berkeley: University of California Press, 2002); Donald J. Pisani, "Squatter Law in California, 1850–1858," *Western Historical Quarterly* 25, no. 3 (1994): 277–310; Nicolai Laquaglia, "Hardin Bigelow, the First Mayor of Sacramento" (MA thesis, California State University, Sacramento, 1968); and Tamara H. Venit, "A Squatters' Republic: Land Rights, Reform, and Anti-Monopoly in California and the Nation, 1850–1920" (PhD dissertation, Stanford University, 2008).

53. Charles Christian Nahl to his Family, various dates, Nahl Family Letters, 1842–1867, Bancroft Library, University of California, Berkeley.

54. Carol Radovich and Kira Russo Bauer, "The Prostitute as Business Woman: Sacramento, 1850–1880," graduate seminar paper, Jan. 1992, on file, Special Collections Library, California State University, Sacramento.

55. K. D. Kurutz, "Sacramento's Pioneer Patrons of Art: The Edwin Bryant Crocker Family," ed. John F. Wilhelm, *Golden Notes* 31, no. 2 (summer 1985). Steven M. Avella has in preparation a full-scale history of the McClatchy family.

56. See the biographical sketch of Dr. Morse by Caroline Wenzel in Morse, *First History of Sacramento City.*

57. Jeremy Mouat, "After California: Later Gold Rushes of the Pacific Basin," in *Riches for All,* ed. Owens, 264–95; Charlene Porsild, "The Last Great Gold Rush," in *Riches for All,* ed. Owens, 317–27; Smith, "Mother Lode for the West," *Golden State,* ed. Rawls and Orsi, 149–73.

58. The Sacramento Museum and History Division, with funding from the California

Council for the Humanities, sponsored a series of Sacramento ethnic community studies during the 1980s, coordinated by Prof. Joseph Pitti of California State University, Sacramento. The narratives for these studies are on file at the Sacramento Archives and Museum Collection Center. Particularly relevant are the following works in this collection: the Chinese, by Sylvia Sun Minnick; the Portuguese, by Joseph d'Allesandro; the Irish, by Elizabeth McKee; the African Americans, by Clarence Caesar; the Italians, by Bruce Pierini; the Germans, by Thomas D. Norris; and the Jews, by Alice Kingsnorth. Other pertinent works include Rudolph Lapp, *Blacks in Gold Rush California* (New Haven: Yale University Press, 1977); Clarence Caesar, "The Historical Demographics of Sacramento's Black Community, 1848–1900," *California History* 75, no. 3 (1996): 198–213; Susan Bragg, "Knowledge Is Power: Sacramento Blacks and the Public Schools, 1854–1860," *California History* 75, no. 3 (1996): 214–21; Marlene S. Gaines, "The Early Sacramento Jewish Community," *Western States Jewish Historical Quarterly* 3, no. 2 (1971): 65–85; Gottard Deutsch, "David Lubin: A Remarkable Jew," *Western States Jewish Historical Quarterly* 14, no. 4 (1982): 316–201; Willard Thompson, "David Lubin: Sacramento's Pioneer Merchant-Philosopher," *Golden Notes* 32, no. 1 (spring 1986); Bernard M. Kaplan, "An Historical Outline of the Jews of Sacramento in the Nineteenth Century," *Western States Jewish Historical Quarterly* 23, no. 3 (1991): 256–67; and John Francis Dulury, "Irish Nationalism in Sacramento, 1850–1890," *Golden Notes* 36, no. 2 (summer 1990). On the religious history of pioneer Sacramento, see especially Steven M. Avella, "Phelan's Cemetery: Religion in the Urbanizing West, 1850–1869, in Los Angeles, San Francisco, and Sacramento," in *Rooted in Barbarous Soil: People, Culture, and Community in Gold Rush California,* ed. Kevin Starr and Richard J. Orsi, special edition of *California History* 74, no. 2 (summer 2000): 250–315; and also Avella's excellent study, *Sacramento and the Catholic Church: Shaping a Capital City* (Reno: University of Nevada Press, 2008).

59. Cindy Baker, "Sacramento's Sophisticated Ladies: Prostitution in 1860," *Golden Notes* 41, no. 2 (summer 1995).

60. In addition to the Sacramento Museum and History Division–sponsored narrative on the Chinese by Sylvia Sun Minnick, cited above, substantial information will be found in Thomas W. Chinn, Him Mark Lai, and Phil Choy, eds., *A History of the Chinese in California: A Syllabus* (San Francisco: Chinese Historical Society, 1969). The history of Chinese agricultural workers in the Sacramento–San Joaquin Delta is brilliantly explored in Sucheng Chan, *Bittersweet Soil: The Chinese in California Agriculture, 1860–1910* (Berkeley: University of California Press, 1986). General accounts include Sucheng Chan, *Asian Californians* (San Francisco: MTL/Boyd Fraser, 1991); Gunther Barth, *Bitter Strength: A History of the Chinese in the United States, 1850–1870* (Cambridge, MA: Harvard University Press, 1964); and Roger Daniels, *Asian America: Chinese and Japanese in the United States since 1850* (Seattle: University of Washington Press, 1990).

61. Mary Evangelist Morgan, *Mercy, Generation to Generation: History of the First Century of the Sisters of Mercy, Diocese of Sacramento, California* (San Francisco: Fearon Publishers, 1957). On the history of Sacramento women, see, among other items, Allan R. Ottley, "Angels without Wings: The Scarcity of Women in Pioneer Sacramento," *Golden Notes* 37–38, no. 4 (winter 1991); Terry R. Willis, "Sacramento Women in 1872" (MA thesis, California State University, Sacramento, 1979); Wendy Welles Franklin, "The Capital and Women's Rights, 1850–1911," *Golden Notes* 34, no. 4 (winter 1988); Irma West, *Walking Tour of Medical Pioneer Gravesites* [Sacramento Pioneer Cemetery] (Sacramento: Sacramento–El Dorado Medical Society Historical Committee, n.d.); Elaine Connolly and Dian Self, *Capital Women: An Interpretive History of Women in Sacramento, 1850–1920* (Sacramento: Capital Women's History Project,

1995). The role of women in education is described in Jane L. Jensen, "The Development of Sacramento Public Schools, 1854 to 1900" (MA thesis, California State University, Sacramento, 1954); and Bragg, "Knowledge Is Power."

62. E. J. Hobsbawm, *The Age of Capital, 1848–1875* (London: Weidenfeld and Nicolson, 1975).

63. While most published research on anti-Chinese and anti-Japanese agitation in northern California has centered on San Francisco, Sacramento was also a focal point for propaganda efforts directed toward the restriction of immigration from eastern Asia. James McClatchy, an Irish immigrant who became publisher and editor of the *Sacramento Bee*, was prominent in the anti-Chinese cause. His son, Valentine McClatchy, who succeeded his father as the newspaper's publisher, became a leading propagandist for the anti-Japanese movement during the early decades of the twentieth century.

64. Barbara Lagomarsino, "Early Attempts to Save Sacramento by Raising Its Business District" (MA thesis, California State University, Sacramento, 1969); Justin Turner, "The Sacramento Floods in the 1850s," *Pacific Historian* 8, no. 3 (1964): 129–33; Marvin Brienes, "Sacramento Defies the Rivers, 1850–1878," *California History* 58, no. 1 (1979): 2–19.

65. These projects are described most fully in Severson, *Sacramento*, 114–15; and Hubert Howe Bancroft, *California*, 7 vols. (San Francisco: A. L. Bancroft and Company, 1884–90), 6:456–63.

66. Joseph A. McGowan, "California's Capitol, 1849–1854," *Golden Notes* 14, no. 3 (Apr. 1968); Severson, *Sacramento*, 185–91.

67. This controversy is best followed in the pages of the *Sacramento Bee*, whose editor, C. K. McClatchy, was a vehement opponent of the measure. Charles M. Goethe, the son of Sacramento's first German Lutheran minister, became a leading advocate and activist on behalf of the measure. Goethe's role is inadequately documented in the C. M. Goethe Papers housed in the University Archives at California State University, Sacramento.

68. Joseph A. McGowan, "Miasma in Sacramento, 1860–1950," *Golden Notes* 24, no. 3 (fall 1978); Joseph A. McGowan, "Clear, Clean Water, 1850–1923," *Golden Notes* 24, no. 4 (winter 1978); Cedrik R. Zemitis, "Garbage in Sacramento: The Transition from Private Enterprise to Municipal Control, 1892–1922" (MA thesis, California State University, Sacramento, 1998).

69. For the early development of this style, see Kenneth N. Owens, *Alkali Flat Historical Overview*, cultural resources management report for the Sacramento City Redevelopment Agency, 1979, on file in Special Collections and University Archives, California State University Library, Sacramento.

70. Richard C. Wade, *The Urban Frontier: The Rise of Western Cities, 1790–1830* (Cambridge, MA: Harvard University Press, 1950).

71. Engels to Marx, Aug. 24, 1853, quoted in Hobsbawm, *Age of Capital*, 62.

Chapter 3. "We Must Give the World Confidence in the Stability and Permanence of the Place": Planning Sacramento's Townsite, 1853–1870

1. William Dane Phelps, *Alta California, 1840–1842: The Journal and Observations of William Dane Phelps, Master of the Ship "Alert"* (Glendale, CA: Arthur H. Clark Company, 1983), 202–6.

2. Quoted in "Meeting of J Street Property Owners," *Sacramento Daily Union*, Mar. 17, 1862.

3. Quoted in "Street Grade Meeting," *Sacramento Daily Union*, Mar. 19, 1862.

4. Robert Fishman, "The American Planning Tradition: An Introduction and Interpreta-

tion," in *The American Planning Tradition: Culture and Policy,* ed. Robert Fishman (Washington, DC: Woodrow Wilson Center Press, 2000), 2.

5. Kenneth Thompson, "Riparian Forests of the Sacramento Valley, California," *Annals of the Association of American Geographers* 51 (Sept. 1961): 299.

6. Albert L. Hurtado, *John Sutter: A Life on the North American Frontier* (Norman: University of Oklahoma Press, 2006), 237.

7. John A. Sutter Jr., *The Sutter Family and the Origins of Gold-Rush Sacramento* (Norman: University of Oklahoma Press, 2002), 89.

8. Mark A. Eifler, *Gold Rush Capitalists: Greed and Growth in Sacramento* (Albuquerque: University of New Mexico Press, 2002), 38–55.

9. Sutter Jr., *Sutter Family and Origins of Gold-Rush Sacramento,* 90.

10. Marguerite Eyer Wilber, trans. and ed., *A Pioneer at Sutter's Fort, 1846–1850: The Adventures of Heinrich Lienhard* (Los Angeles: Califia Society, 1941), 162.

11. Sutter Jr., *Sutter Family and the Origins of Gold-Rush Sacramento,* 92.

12. Wilber, *Pioneer at Sutter's Fort,* 186.

13. William Tecumseh Sherman, *Memoirs of General W. T. Sherman* (New York: Penguin, 2000), 58–59.

14. Ibid., 105.

15. John W. Reps, *The Making of Urban America: A History of City Planning in the United States* (Princeton: Princeton University Press, 1965), 308.

16. Mead B. Kibbey, "A History of Sacramento to 1851," in *Facsimile Reproduction of the California State Library Copy of J. Horace Culver's Sacramento City Directory for the Year, 1851,* ed. Mead B. Kibbey (Sacramento: California State Library Foundation, 2000), 63. For a description of Brannan's Addition, see *The Pacific Reporter, Volume 52* (Saint Paul, MN: West Publishing, 1898), 52.

17. Quoted in Allan R. Ottley, "Biography of John A. Sutter, Jr." in Sutter Jr., *Sutter Family and the Origins of Gold-Rush Sacramento,* 20.

18. Peter H. Burnett, *Reflections and Opinions of an Old Pioneer* (New York: D. Appleton and Company, 1880), 293.

19. Bayard Taylor, *Eldorado, or, Adventures in the Path of Empire,* 18th ed. (New York: G. P. Putnam, 1859), 219, 225.

20. J. Horace Culver, "Historical Sketch" in *Facsimile Reproduction of the California State Library Copy of J. Horace Culver's Sacramento City Directory,* ed. Kibbey, 270.

21. Sarah Royce, *A Frontier Lady: Recollections of the Gold Rush and Early California* (New Haven: Yale University Press, 1932), 91.

22. Ibid., 94.

23. "Tremendous South-east Storm—Overflow of the City—Great Loss of Property," *Placer Times,* Jan. 19, 1850.

24. Andrew C. Isenberg, *Mining California: An Ecological History* (New York: Hill and Wang, 2005), 68–69.

25. Marvin Brienes, "Sacramento Defies the Rivers, 1850–1878," *California History* 58, no. 1 (1979): 5–10.

26. "The Levee and the Streets," *Sacramento Daily Union,* Jan. 7, 1853.

27. "The City," *Sacramento Daily Union,* Jan. 19, 1853.

28. Eifler, *Gold Rush Capitalists,* 177.

29. "Report and Estimates in the Matter of Raising the Streets in the City of Sacramento," *Sacramento Daily Union,* Mar. 23, 1853.

30. "Amendments to City Charter," *Sacramento Daily Union,* Apr. 26, 1853.

31. "Grading the Streets," *Sacramento Daily Union,* Apr. 29, 1853.

32. *Reproduction of Thompson and West's "History of Sacramento County California" with Illustrations* (Berkeley, CA: Howell-North, 1960), 204; "The City," *Sacramento Daily Union,* June 8, 1853; "The City," *Sacramento Daily Union,* July 12, 1853.

33. Reprinted in *Golden Notes* 1, no. 1 (1954): 2.

34. "Taxation Statistics from 1850 to 1857—Sacramento City and County," *Sacramento Daily Union,* Oct. 10, 1857; "Valuation of Property," *Sacramento Daily Union,* Jan. 1, 1859; "Valuation of Property," *Sacramento Daily Union,* Jan. 2, 1860.

35. John W. Reps, *Cities of the American West: A History of Frontier Urban Planning* (Princeton: Princeton University Press, 1979), 215.

36. *Journal of the Fifth Session of the Legislature of the State of California, Begun on the Second Day of January, 1854, and Ended on the Fifteenth Day of May, 1854, at the Cities of Benicia and Sacramento* (Sacramento: B. B. Redding, State Printer, 1854), 77.

37. "History of the Seat of State Government," *Governmental Roster* (Sacramento: State Office, J. D. Young, Supt. State Printing, 1889), 207–8.

38. Ibid., 210.

39. Ibid., 210–11.

40. Clark quoted in "California Legislature," *Sacramento Daily Union,* Mar. 23, 1860.

41. McDougal quoted in "California Legislature," *Sacramento Daily Union,* Mar. 23, 1860.

42. "History of the Seat of State Government," 211; "Board of Supervisors," *Sacramento Daily Union,* Apr. 5, 1860.

43. Stanford quoted in "History of the Seat of State Government," 213.

44. "History of the Seat of State Government," 215–16.

45. *Williams' Illustrated Trans-Continental Guide of Travel from the Atlantic to the Pacific Ocean* (New York: Henry T. Williams, 1877), 246.

46. For a history of the state fair, see "History of the State Agricultural Society of California," *Transactions of the California State Agricultural Society: The Year 1879* (Sacramento: State Printing Office, 1880), 176–211.

47. Quoted in "History of the State Agricultural Society of California," 179.

48. For a description of the Agricultural Pavilion, see *Transactions of the California State Agricultural Society during the Year 1859,* 364–69.

49. "History of the State Agricultural Society of California," 184–87.

50. "Our Sacramento Correspondence," *Daily Alta California* (San Francisco), Jan. 24, 1860.

51. "History of the State Agricultural Society of California," 190–93.

52. "Annual Session of the State Agricultural Society," *Sacramento Daily Union,* Jan. 20, 1860.

53. For American River statistics, see "Water-Data Report 2009, 11446500 American River at Fair Oaks, CA," accessed Aug. 19, 2011, http://wdr.water.usgs.gov/wy2009/pdfs/11446500.2009.pdf; *The National Almanac and Annual Record for the Year 1863* (Philadelphia: George W. Childs, 1863), 519.

54. George Tisdale Bromley, *The Long Ago and the Later On: Or Recollections of Eighty Years* (San Francisco: A. M. Robertson, 1904), 57.

55. "Terrible Inundation," *Daily Alta California* (San Francisco), Jan. 12, 1862.

56. Eugene Itogawa, "New Channels for the American River," in *Sketches of Old Sacramento: A Tribute to Joseph A. McGowan* (Sacramento: Sacramento County Historical Society, 1976), 215–16.

57. *The Statutes of California, Passed at the Thirteenth Session of the Legislature, 1862* (Sacramento: State Printer, 1862), 151–52.

58. *The State Register and Year Book of Facts: For the Year 1859* (San Francisco: Henry G. Langley and Samuel Morison, 1859), 84. Jackson left Sacramento around 1865 to perform surveying duties for the State Land Office in the Tulare basin; Jackson eventually settled in this area and helped found the town of Bakersfield.

59. "Straightening the American," *Sacramento Daily Union,* Sept. 11, 1862.

60. Itogawa, "New Channels for the American River," 221–27; "The Work Done," *Sacramento Daily Union,* Dec. 11, 1862.

61. Itogawa, "New Channels for the American River," 221–27.

62. Barbara Lagomarsino, "Early Attempts to Save the Site of Sacramento by Raising Its Business District" (Master's thesis, Sacramento State College, 1969), 46.

63. Ibid., 90–126.

64. "Mark Twain's Interior Notes," *San Francisco Bulletin,* Nov. 30, 1866.

65. "State Correspondence," *Daily Alta California* (San Francisco), Sept. 12, 1866.

66. Sherman, *Memoirs,* 69.

Chapter 4. Railroads and the Urban Environment: Sacramento's Story

1. *Sacramento Union,* Jan. 9, 17, 1863, reprinted Feb. 27, 1926; *San Francisco Chronicle,* Feb. 28, 1926; Raymond Momboise, "The Day the Central Pacific Began," *Golden Notes* (Sacramento County Historical Society) 9 (Jan. 1963): 3–19; Norman E. Tutorow, *The Governor: The Life and Legacy of Leland Stanford, a California Colossus,* 2 vols. (Spokane, WA: Arthur H. Clark Company, 2004), 1:219–20; Salvador A. Ramirez, *Inside Man: The Life and Times of Mark Hopkins of New York, Michigan, and California,* 2 vols. (Carlsbad, CA: Tentacled Press, 2007), 1:237–40.

2. The CPRR, through acquisitions and mergers, controlled many lines, one of which, in 1868, was the Southern Pacific Railroad, which dwarfed its parent by the early 1880s. When a new holding company was formed in 1884 to integrate dozens of companies, it took the name Southern Pacific Company, and the name "Central Pacific" faded into disuse. In this chapter, "Central Pacific" will refer to the railroad before 1884 and "Southern Pacific" after 1884.

3. James John Campilio, "A History of the Sacramento Valley Railroad up to 1856" (MA thesis, University of Southern California, 1934); Robert O. Briggs, "The Sacramento Valley Railroad" (MA thesis, Sacramento State College, 1954); Dorothy Kupcha Leland, *A Short History of Sacramento* (San Francisco: Lexikos, 1989), 24ff.; Tutorow, *Governor,* 1:229, 256–59; Thor Severson, *Sacramento, an Illustrated History: 1839–1874* (San Francisco: California Historical Society, 1973), 170–72; Ramirez, *Inside Man,* 1:145ff., 272ff. On the SVRR's bankruptcy and sale to the CPRR, see *Sacramento Union,* Aug. 17, 1865.

4. Tutorow, *Governor,* 1:316–318; Severson, *Sacramento,* 179–82; Ramirez, *Inside Man,* 1:447–48, 466–70, 2:752, 771ff.

5. David F. Myrick, *Western Pacific: The Last Transcontinental Railroad,* Colorado Rail Annual no. 27 (Golden: Colorado Railroad Museum, [2006]); Alfred E. Perlman, *Western Pacific Railroad: The Feather River Route* (New York: Newcomen Society in North America, 1975).

6. *Sacramento Union,* Oct. 8, 1905. See also Thomas H. Irion, "An Historical Geography of the Sacramento Northern Railway" (MA thesis, California State University, Hayward, 1997); George W. Hilton and John F. Due, *The Electric Interurban Railways in America* (Stanford: Stanford University Press, 1960); Paul C. Trimble, *Sacramento Northern Railway* (Charleston,

SC: Arcadia Publishing, 2005); William Burg, *Sacramento's Streetcars* (Charleston, SC: Arcadia Publishing, 2006).

7. Earlier works include Bradford Luckingham, *The Urban Southwest: A Profile History of Albuquerque, El Paso, Phoenix, and Tucson* (El Paso: Texas Western Press, 1982), 17ff.; Lawrence H. Larsen, *The Urban South: A History* (Lexington: University Press of Kentucky, 1990); Andrew C. O'Dell and Peter S. Richards, *Railroads and Geography* (London: Hutchinson University Library, 1971), esp. 191ff. Recent studies include Carl Abbott, *How Cities Won the West: Four Centuries of Urban Change in Western North America* (Albuquerque: University of New Mexico Press, 2008); Michael F. Logan, *Desert Cities: The Environmental History of Phoenix and Tucson* (Pittsburgh: University of Pittsburgh Press, 2006); Andrew C. Isenberg, ed., *The Nature of Cities* (Rochester, NY: University of Rochester Press, 2006); Char Miller, ed., *Cities and Nature in the American West* (Reno: University of Nevada Press, 2010); and Paul Stanton Kibel, ed., *Rivertown: Rethinking Urban Rivers* (Cambridge, MA: MIT Press, 2007), esp. chapters by Kibel, "Bankside Urban: An Introduction," 1–21, and by Robert Gottlieb and Andrea Misako Azuma, "Bankside Los Angeles," 23–46, which overlook railroads' influence on urban riversides.

8. Joel A. Tarr and Gabriel Dupuy, eds., *Technology and the Rise of the Networked City in Europe and America* (Philadelphia: Temple University Press, 1988), xiv–xv.

9. See sources listed in notes 7 and 8 above. Also Joel A. Tarr, *Transportation Innovation and Social Change in Pittsburgh, 1850–1934* (Chicago: Public Works Historical Society, 1978), 1–24, on the centrality of streetcars.

10. William Cronon, *Nature's Metropolis: Chicago and the Great West* (New York: Norton, 1991); John R. Stilgoe, *Metropolitan Corridor: Railroads and the American Scene* (New Haven: Yale University Press, 1983); Carlos A. Schwantes and James P. Ronda, *The West the Railroads Made* (Seattle: University of Washington Press with the Washington State Historical Society, the John W. Barriger III National Railroad Library at the St. Louis Mercantile Library, et al., 2008).

11. Blake Gumprecht, *The Los Angeles River: Its Life, Death, and Possible Rebirth* (Baltimore: Johns Hopkins University Press, 1999), esp. 111ff., 151ff.; Gumprecht, "Who Killed the Los Angeles River?," in *Land of Sunshine: An Environmental History of Los Angeles,* ed. William Deverell and Greg Hise (Pittsburgh: University of Pittsburgh Press, 2005), 125–26; Christopher G. Boone, "Zoning and Environmental Inequity in the Industrial East Side," in *Land of Sunshine,* ed. Deverell and Hise, 173–75; Ari Kelman, *A River and Its City: The Nature of Landscape in New Orleans* (Berkeley: University of California Press, 2003), 117–26, 142ff., 150ff.; Matthew Klingle, *Emerald City: An Environmental History of Seattle* (New Haven: Yale University Press, 2007), 49–110; David M. Young, *The Iron Horse and the Windy City: How Railroads Shaped Chicago* (DeKalb: Northern Illinois University Press, 2005), esp. vii–viii and chap. 14; Jared Orsi, *Hazardous Metropolis: Flooding and Urban Ecology in Los Angeles* (Berkeley: University of California Press, 2004), 11, 15–28, 31–40, 156–59. For flooding effects of the Sacramento Valley Railroad in Sacramento city, see Andrew C. Isenberg, "Banking on Sacramento: Urban Development, Flood Control, and Political Legitimization, 1848–1862," in *Nature of Cities,* ed. Isenberg, 115. See also earlier studies, including Joseph Konvitz, *Cities and the Sea: Port City Planning in Early Modern Europe* (Baltimore: Johns Hopkins University Press, 1978), 180–86; and Tarr, *Transportation Innovation,* 1–24.

12. For a more extensive environmental history of railroads, see Richard J. Orsi, "The Iron Horse in the Garden: The Ambiguous Environmental Legacy of the Southern Pacific

Railroad" (paper presented at the American Society for Environmental History conference, Portland, OR, Mar. 2010).

13. Sutter Lake has variously been called Sutter Slough and China Lake or China Slough.

14. Marvin Brienes, "Sacramento Defies the Rivers, 1850–1876," *California Historical Quarterly* 58 (spring 1979): 3ff.; Eugene Itogawa, "New Channels for the American River," in *Sketches of Old Sacramento: A Tribute to Joseph A. McGowan,* ed. Jesse M. Smith (Sacramento: Sacramento County Historical Society, 1976), 211ff.; Heather Lavezzo Downey, "The Force of Nature and the Power of Man: Historic Walking Tours of Old Sacramento's Underground and Hollow Sidewalks" (MA thesis, California State University, Sacramento, 2010), 20ff.; Isenberg, "Banking on Sacramento," 103–21; Albert L. Hurtado, *John Sutter: A Life on the North American Frontier* (Norman: University of Oklahoma Press, 2006), 110–11, 269; Ramirez, *Inside Man,* 1:195–96. On hydraulic mining, see Robert L. Kelley, *Gold vs. Grain: The Hydraulic Mining Controversy in California's Sacramento Valley; A Chapter in the Decline of the Concept of Laissez Faire* (Glendale, CA: Arthur H. Clark Company, 1959), passim. On the American River–Sutter Lake flood corridor, see *Sacramento Union,* July 2–12, 1860. For the Southern Pacific Railroad's long battle against hydraulic mining, see Richard J. Orsi, *Sunset Limited: The Southern Pacific Railroad and the Development of the American West, 1850–1930* (Berkeley: University of California Press, 2005), 54–55, 206–20.

15. *Sacramento Union,* June 4, 1857.

16. See flood control plans in Ramirez, *Inside Man,* 1:196; and Brienes, "Sacramento Defies the Rivers."

17. Meetings of Feb. 7, 10, 1855, Sacramento Common Council Records, Sept. 1855–Aug. 1856, Public Documents, Center for Sacramento History; *Sacramento Union,* Feb. 12, 1855.

18. Meetings of Jan. 1, 24, 30, 31, 1855, Feb. 7, 10, 19, 1855, Sacramento Common Council Records; *Sacramento Union,* Jan. 23–26, 31, 1855, Feb. 8–9, 12–13, 20, 1855.

19. Downey, "Force of Nature," 20–44; Brienes, "Sacramento Defies the Rivers," 11ff.; Joseph A. McGowan and Terry R. Willis, with pictorial research by Lucinda Woodward, *Sacramento: Heart of the Golden State* (Woodland Hills, CA: Windsor Publications, 1983), 39, 58.

20. Itogawa, "New Channels for the American River," 211–27.

21. Ramirez, *Inside Man,* 1:270ff.; *Sacramento Union,* Dec. 12–19, 1861.

22. Ramirez, *Inside Man,* 1:270.

23. For the city's conflict with the SVRR over the 1861–62 flood, see meetings of Dec. 16, 17, 19, 21, 1861, Jan. 6, 8, 1862, Feb. 5, 1862, Mar. 4, 1862, 519–80, Minute Records, Sacramento County Board of Supervisors, vol. F, Public Documents, Center for Sacramento History; Downey, "Force of Nature," 22.

24. *Sacramento Union,* Dec. 20, 1862, Mar. 28, 1863; Ramirez, *Inside Man,* 1:274; McGowan and Willis, *Sacramento,* 58. The city lost its lawsuit against the railroad in 1864.

25. *Sacramento Union,* Mar. 17, 1862; *Sacramento Bee,* June 23, 1862; Ramirez, *Inside Man,* 1:204–7 and note 88, 242, 2:739ff.

26. Accounts of the meeting from Ramirez, *Inside Man,* 1:219–21; *Sacramento Union,* Oct. 9, 10, 1862.

27. Meetings of Oct. 8, 9, 20, 21, 22, 1862, Nov. 4, 6, 17, 18, 1862, Minute Records, Sacramento County Board of Supervisors, vol. G; *Sacramento Union,* Oct. 10, 18, 22, 1862, Nov. 13, 20, 22, 24, 25, 26, 27, 29, 1862, Dec. 20, 22, 1862. The ordinance and related documents were published in *General Railroad Laws of California, the Pacific Railroad Act of Congress, and the By-Laws of the Central Pacific Railroad Co. of California Together with City Ordinance of Sacramento and Act of Donation of Swamp Land* (Sacramento: H.S. Crocker & Co., 1862), esp. 73–75.

28. Robert T. Devlin, *Statutes of the State of California Relating to the City of Sacramento, with the Ordinances Now in Force* (Sacramento: Valley Press, 1881); Tutorow, *Governor,* 1:226.

29. Meetings of Nov. 4, 6, 17, 18, 1862, Dec. 1, 15, 1862, Minute Records, Sacramento County Board of Supervisors, vol. G.

30. For the concept of "second nature," see Cronon, *Nature's Metropolis.*

31. *Sacramento Union,* Sept. 11, 18, 1862, Nov. 12, 1862, Mar. 23, 1863; Itogawa, "New Channels for the American River," 211–27; V. Aubrey Neasham, "Old Sacramento: Its Historical Significance" (typescript, May 27, 1964), Henry E. Huntington Library, San Marino, CA,

32. Barbara Lagomarsino, "Sacramento on the Rise," in *Sketches of Old Sacramento,* ed. Smith, 193–210; Downey, "Force of Nature," 26ff., 229; Stephen Helmich, *Sacramento's 1854 City Hall and Waterworks* (Sacramento: Sacramento County Historical Society, 1986); Ramirez, *Inside Man,* 1:205ff., 242ff.

33. *Sacramento Union,* Mar. 1, 1863, Feb. 23, 27, 28, 1863, Jan. 17, 21, 1864, Mar. 1, 1865; Helmich, *Sacramento's 1854 City Hall and Waterworks,* 23; Ramirez, *Inside Man,* 1:396–97; Neasham, "Old Sacramento," 14ff; "Uncovering History: Finding a Piece of the Original Transcontinental Railroad," *On Track: Official Newsletter of the California State Railroad Museum,* (spring 2009): 1, 3; Kyle Wyatt, "Central Pacific Trestle—CSRM [California State Railroad Museum]" (typescript, 2009), California State Railroad Museum Library, Sacramento. Focusing on the period up to 1862, Isenberg, "Banking on Sacramento," 115–17, does not examine the CPRR's role in combating Sacramento's flooding problem.

34. *Sacramento Union,* Oct. 25, 1865.

35. *Sacramento Bee,* Jan. 30, 1865, Sept. 5, 1875, Sept. 5, 1976; Kyle Wyatt, curator railroad technology, California State Railroad Museum, interview by the author, Sacramento, Sept. 9, 2010.

36. *Sacramento Record-Union,* Aug. 25, 1877, Oct. 20, 1877, June 17, 1879, Oct. 13, 1880, Dec. 2, 1880, Aug. 25, 1887, Dec. 2, 1887, Sept. 17, 1904, Oct. 4, 1904, June 25–26, 1906; *Sacramento Bee,* Oct. 12, 1955; unidentified newspaper clipping, ca. Feb. 1926, scrapbook, n.p., Alexander J. Gardiner Collection, California State Railroad Museum, Sacramento; D. L. Joslyn, "The Southern Pacific Shops, 1863–1950," *Golden Notes* 19 (Nov. 1973): 1–23; Ramirez, *Inside Man,* 1:220–28, 247, 396–97, 2:741, 778; Robert A. Pecotich, *Southern Pacific's Sacramento Shops: Incubator of Innovation* (Berkeley and Wilton, CA: Signature Press, 2010), 18, 22–25, 148–49; Alfred Yee, "What Happened to China Slough?," *Golden Notes* 40 (summer 1994): 1–33; Carolyn Dougherty et al., "A SP Shops History," *American Engineering Record,* author's collection.

37. Ramirez, *Inside Man,* 2:737–41, 778; Leland, *Short History of Sacramento,* 45ff.; Neasham, "Old Sacramento," 12ff.; Pecotich, *Southern Pacific's Sacramento Shops,* 11ff.; *Sacramento's Alkali Flat: Special Collections of the Sacramento Room* (Charleston, SC: Arcadia Publishing, 2010), 55, 60–62. For the early history of the rail shops' development, see *Sacramento Union,* Nov. 6, 1863, Dec. 10, 1866, July 17, 1867, Aug. 9, 1867, Sept. 27, 1867, Dec. 18, 1867, Apr. 14, 1868, Oct. 31, 1868; and *Sacramento Record-Union,* Nov. 28, 1887, May 21, 1892, Oct. 4, 1896.

38. On similar conditions in other cities, see Tarr and Dupuy, *Technology and the Rise of the Networked City,* 5, 8, 12–13; Cronon, *Nature's Metropolis,* 273–74; Mark Aldrich, *Death Rode the Rails: American Railroad Accidents and Safety, 1828–1965* (Baltimore: Johns Hopkins University Press, 2006), esp. 16–18, 94, 120ff., 217ff., 263ff., 334ff.; Stilgoe, *Metropolitan Corridor;* Orsi, "Iron Horse in the Garden," 6ff.

39. See, for example, Leland, *Short History of Sacramento,* 34ff.

40. Helmich, *Sacramento's 1854 City Hall and Waterworks,* 21ff.; *Sacramento Bee,* Feb. 23, 1956.

41. Alfred W. Crosby, *Epidemic and Peace: 1918* (Westport, CT: Greenwood Press, 1976), 56–68, 91–120; Gerald F. Pyle, *The Diffusion of Influenza: Patterns and Paradigms* (Totowa, NJ: Rowman and Littlefield, 1986), 30–33; Linda Ann Johnson, "The Invisible Enemy: Epidemic Influenza in Sacramento, 1918–1919" (MA thesis, California State University, Sacramento, 1994), 11.

42. On crime around railroad yards, including in Sacramento, see Orsi, "Iron Horse in the Garden."

43. *Sacramento Union,* Jan. 23, 1855.

44. Ramirez, *Inside Man,* 2:773. On accidents and violence bred by Sacramento trains, see *Sacramento Union,* Nov. 14, 1855; *Sacramento Bee,* Jan. 1, 1865, May 12, 13, 1869, July 30, 31, 1869; *San Francisco Alta California,* Nov. 15, 1855, Dec. 15, 1867, June 6, 1872; *Sacramento Tribune,* Nov. 14, 1855; *San Francisco Call,* June 16, 1889, Sept. 1, 1891, July 19, 1892. On general safety problems caused by urban railroads, see Aldrich, *Death Rode the Rails,* esp. 25, 124, 213.

45. Undated clipping, *Sacramento Union,* ca. May 1926, scrapbook, Gardiner Collection.

46. Ramirez, *Inside Man,* 1:150ff, 270; *Sacramento Union,* Jan. 14, 1858, Oct. 10, 1862, Oct. 5, 1864, Feb. 16, 1870; *Sacramento Bee,* Feb. 22, 1947.

47. On pollution at Sacramento Shops, see the editorial "The Plague Spot of Sacramento" in *Sacramento Record-Union,* Oct. 2, 1877, as well as Oct. 20, 1877, June 17, 1879 (about Board of Health's scathing report on the lake). See also album photographs numbered 72/212/07, -08, -35, and -144, Center for Sacramento History; Joslyn, "Southern Pacific Shops," esp. 3ff.; McGowan and Willis, *Sacramento,* 104; *Sacramento's Alkali Flat,* 104, 113; Pecotich, *Southern Pacific's Sacramento Shops,* esp. 46. On underground pollution plumes and current cleanup status, see information, esp. 4.6.8 "Historic District Boundaries," and 4.8.1 "Extent of Soil and Groundwater Contamination and Status of Cleanup," accessed Dec. 5, 2010, at http://www.cityofsacramento.org/dsd/projects/railyards/feir/.

48. Pecotich, *Southern Pacific's Sacramento Shops,* 46.

49. Yee, "What Happened to China Slough?"; Joslyn, "Southern Pacific Shops," 14–15.

50. Pecotich, *Southern Pacific's Sacramento Shops,* 76–78; Joslyn, "Southern Pacific Shops," 14–15.

51. *Sacramento Record-Union,* July 21, 1879, Nov. 7, 1898, Apr. 10, 11, 16, 1905; Pecotich, *Southern Pacific's Sacramento Shops,* 77–78, 146ff.; Joslyn, "Southern Pacific Shops," 14–15.

52. Sacramento's site, subject to millennia of native occupation and harvesting, as well as decades of intrusive modification by Spaniards, Mexicans, and especially immigrant developers such as grantee John Sutter and subsequent gold rush settlers, had ceased to be "natural" long before railroads intervened.

53. *San Francisco Alta California,* Dec. 15, 1867; McGowan and Willis, *Sacramento,* 57. On the railroad's role in street paving and the environmental benefits deriving from it, see Anthony Sutcliffe, "Street Transit in the Second Half of the Nineteenth Century," in *Technology and the Rise of the Networked City,* ed. Tarr and Dupuy, 26–27.

54. On CPRR and early infrastructure modernization, see Ramirez, *Inside Man,* 2:737–41.

55. *Sacramento County and Its Resources: Souvenir of the Bee* (Sacramento: Bee, 1894), 114–17.

56. Pecotich, *Southern Pacific's Sacramento Shops,* 32, 44–45; Rowena Wise Day, "Carnival of Lights," in *Sketches of Old Sacramento,* ed. Smith, 28–29.

57. On Southern Pacific as a pioneering water utility serving many communities, see Orsi, *Sunset Limited,* chap. 7.

58. *Sacramento Record-Union,* Sept. 8–10, 1879; Day, "Carnival of Lights," 28–29. On

the *Sacramento Record-Union*'s and Mills's efforts for more efficient use of natural resources, including water, see Orsi, *Sunset Limited.*

59. Pecotich, *Southern Pacific's Sacramento Shops,* 44–45; *Sacramento Bee,* Aug. 16, 1927.

60. *Sacramento Record-Union,* Sept. 9, 10, 1895; *Sacramento Bee,* July 13, 1895, Sept. 10, 11, 1895; *San Francisco Chronicle,* May 3, 11–15, 1903; Native Sons of the Golden West, *The New Sacramento,* pamphlet, Sept. 1895; Day, "Carnival of Lights," 28–29. On inventions that came from the shops, see *Sacramento Union,* Oct. 23, 1938.

61. McGowan and Willis, *Sacramento,* 61ff. On electrification in other cities, see Harold Platt, "City Light," in *Technology and the Rise of the Networked City,* ed. Tarr and Dupuy, 260.

62. "Articles of Incorporation of the Sacramento Electric Power and Light Company" (typescript, Dec. 28, 1892), no. 610; "Amended Articles of Incorporation of the Sacramento Power and Light Company" (typescript, Mar. 21, 1896), no. 704; and "Articles of Incorporation of the Sacramento County Water Company" (typescript, Nov. 11, 1892), no. 609, all in Sacramento County Corporation Files, Center for Sacramento History; *Sacramento County and Its Resources . . .* (Sacramento: Bee, 1894), 92–94; Day, "Carnival of Lights," 46ff.; Burg, *Sacramento's Streetcars,* 7–39; Pecotich, *Southern Pacific's Sacramento Shops,* 43–44; Gallatin biography in Elizabeth Mims and Kevin Mitchell Mims, *Sacramento: A Pictorial History of California's Capital* (Virginia Beach, VA: Donning Company, 1981), 72–73.

63. *Sacramento Bee,* June 27, 1956.

64. Pecotich, *Southern Pacific's Sacramento Shops,* 29; *Sacramento Record-Union,* Apr. 27, 1878.

65. See, for example, "Shop Pattern Book, 1894–1899," Sacramento Shops Records, Southern Pacific Railroad Collection, California State Railroad Museum Library; *Sacramento Bee,* Aug. 16, 1927; news clipping, ca. 1927, scrapbook, Gardiner Collection; Pecotich, *Southern Pacific's Sacramento Shops,* esp. 81ff, 94ff, 146ff.

66. Pecotich, *Southern Pacific's Sacramento Shops,* 34–36, 57, 191ff., 273ff.; *Southern Pacific Bulletin* 6 (Feb. 15, 1918): 4; various photographs of recycling, recycling machinery, and assembly lines, Southern Pacific Shops and Stores Albums, California State Railroad Museum Library and California State Library, Sacramento.

67. Cronon, *Nature's Metropolis,* 79ff, 230ff; Orsi, *Sunset Limited,* 116ff and chap. 12; Richard J. Orsi, "Truckee: Ultimate Railroad Town" (paper presented at Sierra College, Truckee, CA, Feb. 11, 2011), 13–14; Richard J. Orsi, "The Southern Pacific Railroad and Monterey Bay History" (paper presented at Naval Postgraduate School, Del Monte Hotel, Monterey, CA, Feb. 5, 2007), 6–9; Bruce A. MacGregor, *South Pacific Coast: An Illustrated History of the Narrow Gauge South Pacific Coast Railroad* (Berkeley: Howell-North Books, 1968), chap. 4.

68. *Sacramento Union,* Apr. 23, 1869, Sept. 21, 1872; Central Pacific Railroad, *Annual Report* (Sacramento, 1873), 8; "Health Precautions on Railroads," *Sunset Magazine* 14 (Jan. 1905): 307; *Sacramento's Alkali Flat,* 29, 45ff.; J. Roy Jones, MD, *Memories, Men, and Medicine: A History of Medicine in Sacramento, California* (Sacramento: Sacramento Society for Medical Improvement, 1950), 140ff., 156, 406–30, 449, 453; J. Roy Jones, MD, *The Old Central Pacific Hospital* (Sacramento: Western Association of Railway Surgeons, 1960); Aldrich, *Death Rode the Rails,* 157, 168–69; Charles E. Rosenberg, *The Care of Strangers: The Rise of the American Hospital* (New York: Basic Books, 1987), 113–14.

69. For a brief review and discussion of future plans, see "Old Sacramento State Historic Park—General Plan," accessed Dec. 14, 2010, http://www.parks.ca.gov/?page id=26346.

70. See brief reviews and recent status report in "Key Railyard Deadline Passes," *Sacramento Bee,* Aug. 24, 2010, B1; "Curtis Park Project Moves Forward," *Sacramento Bee,* Apr. 2, 2010, B1.

71. On other cities and more suburban and rural districts, where rail corridors are giving way to public redevelopments, hiking trails, and nature preserves, see Young, *Iron Horse and the Windy City*, 169ff., esp. chap. 14; Kibel, *Rivertown*, esp. 1–21, 92–96; Orsi, *Hazardous Metropolis*, 156–59; Gumprecht, *Los Angeles River*, 226–28; Konvitz, *Cities and the Sea*, 181; Klingle, *Emerald City*, 78ff; John R. Stilgoe, *Train Time: Railroads and the Imminent Reshaping of the United States Landscape* (Charlottesville: University of Virginia Press, 2007), 26ff.; Orsi, "Truckee," 22–23; "Ballpark a Home Run for Neighborhood," *San Francisco Chronicle*, Nov. 2, 2010, E1; "New Tenant Boosts Mission Bay," *San Francisco Chronicle*, Nov. 21, 2010, D1; "6 Abandoned Railroads, Subways, and Train Stations," *WebUrbanist*, accessed Oct. 29, 2010, http://weburbanist.com/2008/09/30/6-abandoned-railroads-subways-and-train-stations.

72. For further elaboration, see Orsi, *Sunset Limited;* and Orsi, "Iron Horse in the Garden."

Chapter 5. The Perils of Agriculture in Sacramento's Untamed Hinterland

1. E. Dyer, Deputy Surveyor, "Field Notes of the Subdivision Lines in Township 8 North, Range 3 East of the Mt. Diablo Base and Meridian in the State of California," 1862, Surveyor Records, Bureau of Land Management, California State Office, Sacramento (quotes); Joann Leach Larkey, *Davisville '68: The History and Heritage of the City of Davis, Yolo County, California* (Davis, CA: Davis Historical and Landmarks Commission, 1969), 31.

2. *California Statutes* (1855), 189; Yolo County, "Swamp and Overflowed Lands Record Book," Yolo County Archives, Woodland, CA (hereafter, YCA); C. P. Sprague and H. W. Atwell, *The Western Shore Gazetteer and Commercial Directory, for the State of California, . . . Yolo County* (San Francisco: Press of Bancroft, 1870), 48–51; Richard H. Peterson, "The Failure to Reclaim: California State Swamp Land Policy and the Sacramento Valley, 1850–1866," *Southern California Quarterly* 56 (spring 1974): 45–60.

3. The literature on the development of agriculture in the Sacramento Valley is fairly extensive; for a good starting point, see the "Essay on Sources" in both David Vaught, *After the Gold Rush: Tarnished Dreams in the Sacramento Valley* (Baltimore: Johns Hopkins University Press, 2007), 295–300; and Vaught, *Cultivating California: Growers, Specialty Crops, and Labor, 1875–1920* (Baltimore: Johns Hopkins University Press, 1999), 259–70. On California's reputation as the "granary of the world," see Morton Rothstein, "West Coast Farmers and the Tyranny of Distance: Agriculture on the Fringes of the World Market," *Agricultural History* 49 (Jan. 1975): 272–80. See also William Cronon: *Nature's Metropolis: Chicago and the Great West* (New York: Norton, 1992).

4. On the persistence of settlers in the region, see Vaught, *After the Gold Rush*, chap. 7, esp. note 1, 263–64. The Sacramento County Historical Society published a previous version of this essay, "A Swamplander's Vengeance: R. S. Carey and the Failure to Reclaim Putah Sink, 1855–1895," in *Sacramento History Journal* 6 (2006): 161–76, in a special issue, "Water: Our History and Our Future."

5. This is the central theme of Vaught, *After the Gold Rush;* see esp. chap. 1.

6. *California Statutes* (1855), 189; Sprague and Atwell, *Western Shore Gazetteer*, 48–51; Joseph A. McGowan, *History of the Sacramento Valley*, 3 vols. (New York: Lewis Historical Publishing, 1961), 1:283–84; Vaught, *After the Gold Rush*, 45–56.

7. *US Statutes at Large*, 10:519; Samuel A. Smith to J. W. Mandeville, Dec. 13, 1859, Correspondence, Board of Swampland Commissioners, Predecessor Agencies, Reclamation Board Records, California State Archives, Sacramento (quote); Peterson, "Failure to Reclaim," 46–48; McGowan, *History of the Sacramento Valley*, 1:283–84.

8. *Sacramento Daily Union*, Dec. 9, 1862; Yolo County, "Swampland Surveys," Book A, 14,

20, 28 (quote), 40, 41, County Surveyor's Office, Woodland, CA; Sprague and Atwell, *Western Shore Gazetteer*, 48–51.

9. *Sacramento Daily Record-Union*, Dec. 10, 1892; Elna Bakker, *An Island Called California: An Ecological Introduction to Its Natural Communities* (Berkeley: University of California Press, 1971), 123–57; Robert Kelley, *Battling the Inland Sea: American Political Culture, Public Policy, and the Sacramento Valley, 1850–1986* (Berkeley: University of California Press, 1989), 3–6; Kenneth Thompson, "Riparian Forests of the Sacramento Valley, California," *Annals of the Association of American Geographers* 51 (Sept. 1961): 294–314; Sue Coggins, *Puta-To to North Fork of Putah Creek* (n.p., 1970), Department of Special Collections, University of California Library, Davis.

10. *Sacramento Daily Union*, Dec. 9, 1862, Jan. 10, 1863; *Knights Landing News*, Jan. 25, 1862 (quote); Frank T. Gilbert, *The Illustrated Atlas and History of Yolo County* (San Francisco: De Pue and Company, 1879), 40, 54; Francis P. Farquhar, ed., *Up and Down California in 1860–1864: The Journal of William H. Brewer* (Berkeley: University of California Press, 1974), 241–44.

11. Yolo County, "Swamp and Overflowed Lands Record Book," YCA; Yolo County, "Assessment Rolls," 1865, YCA; *Sacramento Daily Record-Union*, June 19, 1895; J. M. Guinn, "Exceptional Years: A History of California Floods and Drought," *Publications of the Historical Society of Southern California* 1 (1890): 36–37; Gilbert, *Illustrated Atlas and History of Yolo County*, 40–41; Hazel Adele Pulling, "California's Fence Laws and the Range-Cattle Industry," *Historian* 8 (spring 1946): 144.

12. *California Statutes* (1861), 355–61; Peterson, "Failure to Reclaim," 48–56.

13. *California Statutes* (1861), 355–61 (quotes); *Sacramento Daily Union*, May 16, 1861, Jan. 1, 1862; Kelley, *Battling the Inland Sea*, 48–50; Peterson, "Failure to Reclaim," 50–51.

14. Yolo County, "Swampland District No. 18 Boundary Petition Description," YCA; *Sacramento Daily Union*, Mar. 15, 1859 (quote); *First Annual Report of Swamp Land Commissioners for 1861* (Sacramento: State Printer, 1862), 23–24; *Annual Report of the Swamp Land Commissioners for the Year 1862* (Sacramento: State Printer, 1863), 3–6; *Report of the Board of Swamp Land Commissioners for the Years 1864 and 1865* (Sacramento: State Printer, 1866), 10–11; *Sacramento Daily Union*, Jan. 1, 1862, Mar. 12, 1862; Jan. 1, 1864, Nov. 24, 1864, Jan. 2, 1865, Jan. 1, 1866, Dec. 25, 1866; Gilbert, *Illustrated Atlas and History of Yolo County*, 57; Peterson, "Failure to Reclaim," 53.

15. Yolo County, "Board of Supervisors, Swampland District No. 18, Supervisors' Record, 1866–1873," 81–159 (quote, 157), YCA; Gilbert, *Illustrated Atlas and History of Yolo County*, 54–55; *Woodland News*, Mar. 9, 1867; *Sacramento Daily Union*, Jan. 20, 1868, Apr. 10, 1869.

16. Kelley, *Battling the Inland Sea*, 52–53; Yolo County, "Board of Supervisors, Swampland District No. 18, Supervisors' Record, 1866–1873," 159–61, YCA; *California Statutes* (1865–66), 799–801; *California Statutes* (1867–68), 514–21.

17. *Sacramento Daily Record-Union*, June 19, 1895; Yolo County, "Board of Supervisors, Swampland District No. 18, Supervisors' Record, 1866–1873," 3–80; Yolo County, "Assessment Rolls," 1866, YCA; Kelley, *Battling the Inland Sea*, 57.

18. Yolo County, "Board of Supervisors, Swampland District No. 18, Supervisors' Record, 1866–1873," 79–80, 119–26; Kelley, *Battling the Inland Sea*, 57–59.

19. *California Statutes* (1867–68), 514–21; Kelley, *Battling the Inland Sea*, 60–61.

20. *Yolo County Democrat*, May 30, 1868; Yolo County, "Swamp and Overflowed Lands Record Book," YCA; US Census, Agricultural Schedules for Putah Township, Yolo County, California, 1860 (microfilm), California Room, California State Library, Sacramento.

21. Rodman W. Paul, "The Beginnings of Agriculture in California: Innovation vs. Continuity," *California Historical Quarterly* 52 (spring 1973): 16–37; Morton Rothstein, "Frank

Norris and Popular Perceptions of the Market," *Agricultural History* 56 (Jan. 1982): 53; Vaught, *After the Gold Rush,* chap. 8.

22. Yolo County, "Board of Supervisors, Swampland District No. 18, Supervisors' Record, 1866–1873," 161–232; Yolo County, "Board of Supervisors, Swampland District No. 18, Accounts," 228, 230, YCA; Henry Cowell v. R. S. Carey (1895), Yolo County, Superior Court Case Files, no. 1531, YCA; S. H. Cowell v. Lydia T. Armstrong (1930), California State Supreme Court, no. 4341 (SAC), "Transcript on Appeal," 73–75, 312, California State Archives; *Sacramento Daily Union,* Jan. 20, June 2, 1868; *Weekly Solano Republican,* Feb. 16, 1871.

23. *Yolo County Democrat,* Dec. 23, 1871 (quotes); *Dixon Tribune,* Nov. 5, 1887; *Sacramento Daily Record-Union,* Dec. 20, 1871; Cowell v. Armstrong, "Transcript on Appeal," 73.

24. Gilbert, *Illustrated Atlas and History of Yolo County,* 50; Yolo County, "Board of Supervisors, Swampland District No. 18, Supervisors' Record," 39, 50, 60, 81, 166, YCA; Cowell v. Armstrong, "Transcript on Appeal," 66–75, 85; George W. Pierce, Daily Journals, 1867–90, entry for Dec. 19, 1871, Pierce Family Papers, Department of Special Collections, University of California, Davis (hereafter, Pierce journal); "Why Putah Creek Changed Its Course," undated clipping (1968) from the *Dixon Tribune* on file at the Dixon Public Library, Dixon, CA; *Woodland News,* Mar. 9, 1867; *Yolo Weekly Democrat,* Dec. 23, 1871; *Yolo Weekly Mail,* Jan. 4, 1872; *Dixon Tribune,* Sept. 18, 1886, Nov. 5, 1887.

25. Cowell v. Armstrong, "Transcript on Appeal," 68, 80; Pierce journal, Dec. 19, 1871 (quote); "Why Putah Creek Changed Its Course"; *Yolo Weekly Democrat,* Dec. 23, 1871; *Dixon Tribune,* Sept. 18, 1886, Nov. 5, 1887.

26. Yolo County, "Board of Supervisors, Swampland District No. 18, Accounts," 230, YCA; Yolo County, "Board of Supervisors Minutes," Book D, Feb. 7, 1872, YCA; Yolo County, "Reclamation District Formation," Book A, 23, YCA.

27. *California Statutes* (1872), 941; *Sacramento Daily Union,* Mar. 28, 1872; *Weekly Solano Republican,* May 2, 1872; *Yolo County Democrat,* Aug. 21, 1869, May 11, 1872; State of California, *Journal of the Assembly* (Sacramento: State Printer, 1872), 833, 846, 875.

28. *California Statutes* (1872), 941–45 (quotes); *Yolo County Democrat,* May 11, 1872; *Sacramento Daily Record-Union,* Mar. 23, 1872.

29. Yolo County, "Board of Supervisors Minutes," Book D, Apr. 22, 1872, May 7, 1872, YCA; *Yolo County Democrat,* May 11, 1872 (quotes).

30. Solano County, "Board of Supervisors Minutes," Book 4, Apr. 25, 30, 1872, County Administrator's Office, Fairfield, CA; *Yolo County Democrat,* May 11, 1872 (quote); *Dixon Tribune,* Sept. 18, 1886, Nov. 5, 1887; *California Statutes* (1874), 84.

31. "Why Putah Creek Changed Its Course"; Cowell v. Armstrong, "Transcript on Appeal," 312–13; *Dixon Tribune,* Sept. 18, 1886, Nov. 5, 1887.

32. "Why Putah Creek Changed Its Course"; Cowell v. Armstrong, "Transcript on Appeal," 69–75; *Dixon Tribune,* Jan. 19, 1878; *Yolo Weekly Mail,* May 16, 1878; *Historical Atlas Map of Solano County, California* (San Francisco: Thompson and West, 1878), 27.

33. *Sacramento Bee,* Dec. 31, 1873; *Marysville Daily Appeal,* Jan. 3, 1874; Cowell v. Armstrong, "Transcript on Appeal," 69–87 (quote 85), 312–13; *Yolo Weekly Mail,* Jan. 21, 1875, Feb. 21, 1878, May 16, 1878; *Dixon Tribune,* Nov. 11, 1876, Jan. 19, 1878 (quotes), Feb. 2, 23, 1878, Mar. 8, 15, 1879, Jan. 17, 1880, Apr. 24, 1880; *Sacramento Daily Record-Union,* Dec. 31, 1873, Jan. 17, 1874, Nov. 18, 1875, Jan. 17, 1878, Feb. 19, 1878, Oct. 12, 1878, Dec. 1, 11, 1879, Jan. 19, 1880, Apr. 21, 1880, Jan. 27, 1890, Dec. 10, 1892; Gilbert, *Illustrated Atlas and History of Yolo County,* 55–56.

34. *Dixon Tribune,* Mar. 15, 1879; *Sacramento Daily Record-Union,* Dec. 10, 1892; "Why

Putah Creek Changed Its Course"; Cowell v. Armstrong, "Transcript on Appeal," 69–76; *Historical Atlas Map of Solano County, California*, 27; Edward Nelson Eager, *Official Map of the County of Solano* (San Francisco: Britton & Rey, 1890); California Commissioner of Public Works, *Yolo Basin* (San Francisco: Britton & Rey, 1895); P. N. Ashley, *Official Map of the County of Yolo* (San Francisco: Britton & Rey, 1900).

35. Cowell v. Armstrong, "Transcript on Appeal," 73–75, 298 (quote), 312; *Dixon Tribune,* Apr. 21, 1888, Nov. 3, 1888, Feb. 8, 1892, Dec. 30, 1892, Jan. 11, 1895, Feb. 1, 8 (quote), 1895, July 5, 1895 (quote), Oct. 11, 1895; *Sacramento Daily Record-Union,* Jan. 25, 1890.

36. Cowell v. Carey (1895); Yolo County, "Mortgages," Book 28, 327, YCA; Yolo County, "Deeds," Book 54, 383, YCA; Cowell v. Armstrong, "Transcript on Appeal," 142, 312; *Sacramento Daily Record-Union,* June 19, 1895; *Dixon Tribune,* Nov. 2, 1889, June 28, 1895.

37. Kelley, *Battling the Inland Sea,* 297–316; Paul Rhode, "Learning, Capital Accumulation, and the Transformation of California Agriculture," *Journal of Economic History* 55 (Dec. 1995): 773–800 (quote, 773); Vaught, *After the Gold Rush,* 197–219; Vaught, *Cultivating California,* 110–14.

38. Kelley, *Battling the Inland Sea,* 297–316; Coggins, *Puta-To to North Fork of Putah Creek,* 4.

Chapter 6. Rivers of Gold, Valley of Conquest: The Business of Levees and Dams in the Capital City

1. Kenneth Thompson, "Historic Flooding in Sacramento Valley," *Pacific Historical Review* 29, no. 4 (1960): 349–60; Hubert Howe Bancroft, *History of California,* 7 vols. (San Francisco: History Company, Publishers, 1888), 6:453; James Henley, "Flooding in the Sacramento Valley: A Seething and Boiling Force That Threatens the Monuments of Our Enterprise," *Sacramento History Journal* 6, no. 1 (2006): 7–40. Also see Mark Eifler, *Gold Rush Capitalists: Greed and Growth in Sacramento* (Albuquerque: University of New Mexico Press, 2002), 83–101. Eifler notes the double floods of miners and water.

2. Joseph McGowan and Terry Willis, *Sacramento: Heart of the Golden State* (Woodland Hills, CA: Windsor Publications, 1983), 36; Entry for Dec. 21, 1852, Benicia, CA, folder 13 (1852), box 1, Alfred Sully Papers, Beinecke Rare Book and Manuscript Library, Yale University, New Haven, CT. Special thanks to Marcel Garcia for bringing the Sully Papers to my attention.

3. For examples of California and the arid West, see Donald Worster, *Rivers of Empire: Water, Aridity, and the Growth of the American West* (New York: Pantheon, 1985); Donald Pisani, *From the Family Farm to Agribusiness: The Irrigation Crusade in California and the West, 1850–1931* (Berkeley: University of California Press, 1984); Marc Reisner, *Cadillac Desert: The American West and Its Disappearing Water* (New York: Penguin, 1986); William Smythe, *The Conquest of Arid America* (New York: Harper & Brothers, 1899). The works of Robert Kelley offer an important exception to this trend. See Kelley, *Gold vs. Grain: The Hydraulic Mining Controversy in California's Sacramento Valley* (Glendale, CA: Arthur H. Clark Company, 1959); and Kelley, *Battling the Inland Sea: American Political Culture, Public Policy, and the Sacramento Valley, 1850–1986* (Berkeley: University of California Press, 1989). A great debt is owed to Kelley for his work on flood control in the Sacramento Valley.

4. Kenneth Thompson, "Riparian Forests of the Sacramento Valley, California," *Annals of the Association of American Geographers* 51, no. 3 (Sept. 1961): 294–315; Thompson, "Historic Flooding," 350–52; David Vaught, *After the Gold Rush: Tarnished Dreams in the Sacramento Valley* (Baltimore: Johns Hopkins University Press, 2007), 28–29; Kelley, *Battling the Inland Sea,* xv.

5. Thompson, "Riparian Forests," 297–99; Erwin G. Guddee, *Sutter's Own Story: The Life of General John Augustus Sutter and the History of New Helvetia in the Sacramento Valley* (New York:

G. P. Putnam's Sons, 1936), 220; Bancroft, *History of California*, 6:447. According to Bancroft, to escape creditors Sutter transferred his assets to his son, who upon his father's travels began to develop the current river site of Sacramento. Charles Wilkes, *Narrative of the United States Exploring Expedition 1838–1842*, 5:189, Beinecke Rare Book and Manuscript Library, Yale University. Mark Eifler's work demonstrates how mining interests trumped geography and rational planning in regard to Sacramento's waterfront location. See Eifler, *Gold Rush Capitalists*.

6. Bancroft, *History of California*, 6:458; Thompson, "Historic Flooding," 359; J. W. Wooldridge, *History of the Sacramento Valley, California* (Chicago: Pioneer Historical Publishing, 1931), 1:64, Beinecke Rare Book and Manuscript Library, Yale University.

7. Norris Hundley Jr., *The Great Thirst: Californians and Water, 1770s–1990s* (Berkeley: University of California Press, 1992), 79–80; Bancroft, *History of California*, 7:16–17; McGowan and Willis, *Sacramento*, 39; "Flooding in the Sacramento Valley," 9; Karen Marie O'Neill, "State Building and the Campaign for U.S. Flood Control, 1824–1936" (PhD diss., University of California, Los Angeles, 1998), 223; newspaper quotation in Vaught, *After the Gold Rush*, 73. For an analysis of Republicans and Democrats regarding state projects over the nineteenth and twentieth centuries, see Kelley, *Battling the Inland Sea*, 317–38.

8. Bancroft, *History of California*, 6:458; McGowan and Willis, *Sacramento*, 39–40; Joseph A. McGowan, *History of the Sacramento Valley*, 3 vols. (New York: Lewis Historical Publishing, 1961), 1:187–88.

9. Hundley, *Great Thirst*, 79–82; Kelley, *Battling the Inland Sea*, xvii, 160–70; "The Rivers," *Woodland Daily Democrat*, Dec. 12, 1890.

10. Andrew C. Isenberg, *Mining California: An Ecological History* (New York: Hill and Wang, 2005), 40–44; McGowan and Willis, *Sacramento*, 39; McGowan, *History of the Sacramento Valley*, 1:286–91, 2:172. Also see Kelley, *Gold vs. Grain;* and Thompson, "Historic Flooding." Thompson challenges Kelley's earlier work, emphasizing that hydraulic mining *exacerbated* rather than *caused* the flooding of the Sacramento Valley. Hydraulic mining was finally banned in 1876, a ban that the California Supreme Court upheld in 1878 and again in 1883.

11. Kelley, *Battling the Inland Sea*, 288–89. Also see Spencer C. Olin Jr., *California's Prodigal Sons: Hiram Johnson and the Progressives, 1911–1917* (Berkeley: University of California Press, 1968); Samuel P. Hays, *Conservation and the Gospel of Efficiency: The Progressive Conservation Movement, 1890–1920* (1959; repr., Pittsburgh: University of Pittsburgh Press, 1999).

12. Natoma Water and Mining Company Articles of Incorporation, June 25, 1851, Natomas file, Public Utility Commission, F3725:7100, Earl Warren Papers, California State Archives, Sacramento (hereafter, EWP). The company's name changed numerous times over the century: Natomas Water & Mining (1851), Natoma Vineyard Company (1889), Natoma Development Company (1906), Natomas Consolidated of California (1908–9), Natomas Company of California (1914), Natomas Company (1928). Antonia Castaneda, Robert Docken, Edith Pitti, and Chandler Ide, "The Natomas Company, 1851–1984" (unpublished manuscript, 1984), 5, Center for Sacramento History, Sacramento.

13. Castaneda et al., "Natomas Company," 28, 36–40, 49–51 (quote, 51), 92.

14. Natomas Background, Application 6975, Jan. 3, 1923, Public Utility Commission, Part II, Group 2, F3725:7098, EWP; Castaneda et al., "Natomas Company," 6, 96, 124, 145.

15. Natomas Background, Application 6975, Jan. 25, 1922, Public Utility Commission, F3725:7099, EWP; Castaneda et al., "Natomas Company," 5, 100–105, 112–14. For the conflict between miners and farmers in the valley, see Kelley, *Gold vs. Grain*.

16. *Walker's Manual of California Securities and Directory of Directors, 1911,* 104, Beinecke Rare Book and Manuscript Library, Yale University. For corporate links of directors, see Louis Sloss, Frank Griffin, Joseph Grant, E. J. de Sabla Jr., W. P. Hammon, Albert Hanford, and E. R. Lillenthal in *Walker's Manual.*

17. Natomas Real Estate Guide and Holdings, Public Utilities Commission F3725:7100; Natomas Background, Application 6975, Jan. 3, 1923, Public Utility Commission, Part II, Group 2, F3725:7098, both in EWP; Castaneda et al., "Natomas Company," 241–45; *Natomas News* 2 (Aug. 1912): 12 (quote).

18. *Natomas News* 1 (May–June 1911): 15; Castaneda et al., "Natomas Company," 247–49, 252.

19. Thompson, "Riparian Forests"; Titus Fey Cronise, *The Natural Wealth of California* (San Francisco: H. H. Bancroft & Company, 1868), 309, Beinecke Rare Book and Manuscript Library, Yale University; historian quoted in Vaught, *After the Gold Rush,* 28; Isenberg, *Mining California,* 6–9; Castaneda et al., "Natomas Company," 248, 250; Kenneth Thompson, "The Fever Tree in California: Eucalypts and Malaria Prophylaxis," *Annals of the Association of American Geographers* 60, no. 2 (June 1970): 230–44.

20. *Natomas News* 2 (May 1912): 9–13, 2 (Oct. 1912): 13–14; Castaneda et al., "Natomas Company," 249–54; Kelley, *Battling the Inland Sea,* xvi (quote).

21. *Natomas News* 2 (Aug. 1912): 17–18.

22. O'Neill, "State Building," 349–51.

23. Ibid., 377–80, 393–95; Kelley, *Battling the Inland Sea,* 307–8.

24. "Both Sides of Central Valley Water Project," *Los Angeles Times,* Dec. 15, 1933, 13; California Chamber of Commerce, "California's Central Valley Project" (San Francisco, 1943); "Heavy Rains in North Flood Capitol Offices," *Los Angeles Times,* Apr. 8 1935, 1; "Flood Peril Passes Sacramento Area," *Boston Globe,* Apr. 10, 1935, 10; "30 California Towns Flooded," *Washington Post,* Dec. 12, 1937, 1; "Floods Take Heavy Toll in California," *Hartford Courant,* Dec. 13, 1937, 16; "Floods Up—Pacific Coast Storm Ceases on Its 19th Day," *New York Times,* Feb. 15, 1938, 3; "California Floods Extend Ravages," *New York Times,* Feb. 13, 1938, 24; "Flood Refugees Begin Trek Back to Homes," *Los Angeles Times,* Mar. 3, 1940, 5.

25. US Bureau of Reclamation, *Central Valley Project Information Packet* (Washington DC, 1941); Kelley, *Battling the Inland Sea,* 308. For more on Shasta Dam and the Winnemem Wintu, see Mary Ngo, "Loss of Sacred Spaces: The Winnemem Wintu Struggle against a Cultural Genocide by California Water Demands" (MA thesis, California State University, Long Beach, 2010).

26. "The Central Valley Project—Troubled Water," news clipping dated Nov. 28, 1945, EWP; Earl Warren, speech delivered Nov. 1, 1945, Water Control Board F3640:4325, EWP; Henley, "Flooding in the Sacramento Valley," 8; Jordan Fisher Smith, *Nature Noir: A Park Ranger's Patrol in the Sierra* (New York: Mariner Books, 2006), 28–29. Also see Royal Miller, Chair, State Water Resource Board, to Earl Warren, Sept. 13, 1946, Water Pollution F3640: 4325, EWP; Miller testimony, House Appropriations Committee, June 1947; State Water Resource Board Resolution, Mar. 7, 1947, Water Pollution F3640:4326, all in EWP. California's fight with Washington on flood control money spanned from 1945 to 1948.

27. Reclamation Board, *Flood Control and Reclamation in California* (Sacramento, 1916), 17–18 (quote); Stephen B. Adams, *Mr. Kaiser Goes to Washington: The Rise of a Government Entrepreneur* (Chapel Hill: University of North Carolina Press, 1997), 36–50, 180–81; Jordan A. Schwarz, *The New Dealers: Power Politics in the Age of Roosevelt* (New York: Knopf, 1993), 297–312; Gerald D. Nash, *World War II and the West: Reshaping the Economy* (Lincoln:

University of Nebraska Press, 1990), 46–65; *Walker's Manual*, 1965, 425–27; Hundley, *Great Thirst*, 268–69.

28. Kelley, *Battling the Inland Sea*, 309. For an example of Natomas's promotional literature, see *Natomas News*, volumes 1–3 (1911–13), available online at Google Books.

29. California Department of Water Resources, "Fact Sheet: Sacramento River Flood Control Project," Dec. 2010, www.water.ca.gov/newsroom/docs/WeirsReliefStructures. pdf; Vaught, *After the Gold Rush*, 230; Kelley, *Battling the Inland Sea*, 313–15; Ken Calhoon, "Flood Insurance for Natomas," *Real Estate News*, Jan. 5, 2007, http://kencalhoon.blogspot. com/2007/01/flood-insurance-for-natomas.html. For more on suburban Natomas, see "Natomas to Vote on Property Tax for Levee Repairs," *Sacramento Bee*, Mar. 3, 2011, 1B.

Chapter 7. Forging Transcontinental Alliances:
The Sacramento River Valley in National Drainage and Flood Control Politics, 1900–1917

1. *Appendix to the Congressional Record*, 65th Cong., 1st sess., n.d., 735–36.

2. Studies of flood control and drainage in the Sacramento Valley generally overlook both the USGS's strategy of institutional aggrandizement and the transcontinental vote-trading alliance between the Sacramento and Mississippi River valleys. The classic study on the subject remains Robert L. Kelley, *Battling the Inland Sea: Floods, Public Policy, and the Sacramento Valley* (Berkeley: University of California Press, 1989). Also important are Kelley, "Taming the Sacramento: Hamiltonianism in Action," *Pacific Historical Review* 34 (Feb. 1965): 21–49; Philip Garone, *The Rise and Fall of the Wetlands of California's Great Central Valley* (Berkeley: University of California Press, 2011); and Karen O'Neill, *Rivers by Design: State Power and the Origins of U.S. Flood Control* (Durham: Duke University Press, 2006).

3. The classic work on the Progressive era conservation movement is Samuel P. Hays, *Conservation and the Gospel of Efficiency: The Progressive Conservation Movement, 1890–1920* (Cambridge, MA: Harvard University Press, 1959). Also see Donald J. Pisani, "The Many Faces of Conservation: Natural Resources and the American State, 1900–1940," in *Taking Stock: American Government in the Twentieth Century*, ed. Morton Keller and R. Shep Melnick (New York: Cambridge University Press, 1999), 123–55; Martin Reuss, *The Corps of Engineers and Water Resources in the Progressive Era (1890–1920)* (Kansas City, MO: Public Works Historical Society, 2009); Elmo Richardson, *The Politics of Conservation: Crusades and Controversies, 1897–1913* (Berkeley: University of California Press, 1962); and Donald C. Swain, *Federal Conservation Policy, 1921–1933* (Berkeley: University of California Press, 1963).

4. Donald J. Pisani, *Water and American Government: The Reclamation Bureau, National Water Policy, and the West, 1902–1935* (Berkeley: University of California Press, 2002), 1–2.

5. Donald J. Pisani, "Water Planning in the Progressive Era: The Inland Waterways Commission Reconsidered," *Journal of Policy History* 18 (fall 2006): 396; House Committee on Irrigation of Arid Lands, "Hearings before the Committee on Irrigation of Arid Lands," 58th Cong., 3rd sess., Mar. 2, 1905, H. Doc. 381, 44.

6. Anthony E. Carlson, "The Other Kind of Reclamation: Wetlands Drainage and National Water Policy, 1902–1912," *Agricultural History* 84 (fall 2010): 451–78. For American attitudes toward wetlands, see Jeffrey K. Stine, *America's Forested Wetlands: From Wasteland to Valued Resource* (Durham: Forest History Society, 2008); Ann Vileisis, *Discovering the Unknown Landscape: A History of America's Wetlands* (Washington, DC: Island Press, 1997).

7. For Congress's nineteenth-century river improvement program, see Paul F. Paskoff, *Troubled Waters: Steamboat Disasters, River Improvements, and American Public Policy, 1821–1860* (Baton Rouge: Louisiana State University Press, 2007). For federalism and water resource

development, see Carlson, "Other Kind of Reclamation"; Kelley, *Battling the Inland Sea,* 28–29; Pisani, *Water and American Government,* 253; and Martin Reuss, "The Development of American Water Resources: Planners, Politicians, and Constitutional Interpretation," in *Managing Water Resources Past and Present,* ed. Julie Trottier and Paul Slack (New York: Oxford University Press, 2004), 51–71.

8. Kelley, *Battling the Inland Sea,* 4–7; Kenneth Thompson, "Historic Flooding in the Sacramento Valley," *Pacific Historical Review* 29 (Nov. 1960): 349–60; House Committee on Irrigation of Arid Lands, "Hearings before the Committee on Irrigation of Arid Lands," 58th Cong., 3rd sess., Mar. 2, 1905, H. Doc. 381, 122.

9. "Irrigation Investigations in California," 56th Cong., 2nd sess., Jan. 24, 1901, S. Doc. 108, 26–28; Donald J. Pisani, *From the Family Farm to Agribusiness: The Irrigation Crusade in California and the West, 1850–1931* (Berkeley: University of California Press, 1984), 5–11, 286–88, 324–25.

10. James R. Kluger, *Turning on Water with a Shovel: The Career of Elwood Mead* (Albuquerque: University of New Mexico Press, 1992), 28–38; Donald J. Pisani, *To Reclaim a Divided West: Water, Law, and Public Policy, 1848–1902* (Albuquerque: University of New Mexico Press, 1992), 304–10.

11. Donald J. Pisani, "A Conservation Myth: The Troubled Childhood of the Multiple-Use Idea," *Agricultural History* 76 (spring 2002): 154–71. On the Reclamation Service's early support of multiple-use planning in the Sacramento Valley, see Frederick H. Newell to George Pardee, Dec. 30, 1904, Jan. 23 and Feb. 8, 1905, Newell folder, George Pardee Collection, Bancroft Library, University of California, Berkeley; J. B. Lippincott, "General Outlook for Reclamation Work in California," *Forestry and Irrigation* 11 (Aug. 1905): 353; "Reclamation Scheme," *Woodland (CA) Daily Democrat,* Jan. 21, 1905.

12. Abraham Hoffman, *Vision or Villainy: Origins of the Owens Valley–Los Angeles Water Controversy* (College Station: Texas A&M University Press, 1981), 19–24; Kenneth Q. Volk, "Joseph Barlow Lippincott," *Transactions of the American Society of Civil Engineers* 108 (1943): 1543–50. For the expansion of the USGS's gauging program on the Sacramento River, see J. B. Lippincott, *Irrigation of the Sacramento Valley: An Address at the Reception of the Congressional Irrigation Committee at Red Bluff, Cal., June 15, 1905* (San Francisco: n.p. 1905), 5–9.

13. S. G. Bennett, "Synopsis of Progress Report on Hydrographic Investigation in Sacramento Basin," to Governor Pardee, Jan. 14, 1905, folder 991, "Sacramento Valley Project—California—Miscellaneous," box 831, General Administrative and Project Records, 1902–19, entry 3, Records of the Bureau of Reclamation, RG 115, National Archives and Records Administration (hereafter, NARA), Denver, CO; Lippincott, "General Outlook," 353. For Bennett's final unpublished report, which was completed in July 1906, see Bennett, "Report on Hydrographic Investigations in the Sacramento Basin, California," July 18, 1906, untitled folder, box 2, Hydrologic Data and Reports, Water Resources Division: Unpublished Manuscripts, 1904–6, entry 501, Records of the Geological Survey, RG 57, NARA, College Park, MD.

14. *A Bill Authorizing and Empowering the Secretary of Interior to Include Swamp and Over-flowed Lands in Reclamation Projects,* H.R. 18001, 58th Cong., 3rd sess., Jan. 19, 1905; House Committee on Irrigation of Arid Lands, "Hearings before the Committee on Irrigation of Arid Lands," 58th Cong., 3rd sess., Mar. 2, 1905, H. Doc. 381, 124; "The Charming Simplicity of the Swamp-Land Ring," *Oakland Tribune,* Sept. 18, 1905; *San Francisco Chronicle* quoted in "Current Comment," *Woodland (CA) Daily Democrat,* Aug. 29, 1905. Also see "Bell Speaks on Irrigation," *Ukiah (CA) Dispatch-Democrat,* Mar. 31, 1905.

15. "Considers Plan," *Woodland (CA) Daily Democrat,* Jan. 13, 1905; Kelley, *Battling the Inland Sea,* 265–70. For Dabney's report, see House Committee on Rivers and Harbors, "Sacramento, San Joaquin, and Feather Rivers, California," 59th Cong., 1st sess., Dec. 19, 1905, H. Doc. 262.

16. "Secretary Taft as Presidential Timber," *Oakland Tribune,* Sept. 30, 1905; "Taft on the River," *Woodland (CA) Daily Democrat,* Sept. 29, 1905.

17. "For Benefit of Navigation," *Oakland Tribune,* Nov. 11, 1905; *Biographical Directory of the United States Congress, 1774–Present,* accessed July 22, 2011, http://bioguide.congress.gov/scripts/biodisplay.pl?index=F000207.

18. Resolution quoted in "New President Defines Policy," *San Francisco Call,* Dec. 3, 1905; O'Neill, *Rivers by Design,* 114.

19. Justice B. Detwiler, ed., *Who's Who in California: A Biographical Directory, 1928–29* (San Francisco: Who's Who Publishing, 1929), 282; Kelley, *Battling the Inland Sea,* 190, 238–41.

20. C. E. Grunsky to Charles D. Walcott, Jan. 16, 1906, folder 989, "Sacramento Valley Project—California—General Reports," box 831, entry 3, RG 115, NARA, Denver, CO.

21. "Reclamation Fund Exhausted," *Irrigation Age* 22 (Apr. 1906): 180–81.

22. Carlson, "Other Kind of Reclamation," 454–59.

23. Ibid., 458–60.

24. "Pardee Talks of Irrigation," *Los Angeles Herald,* Aug. 8, 1906; *A Bill Providing for Examinations and Surveys for the Location of Reclamation and Irrigation Works in the Sacramento and San Joaquin Valleys, in the State of California,* S. 5944, 59th Cong. 1st sess., Apr. 27, 1906; *A Bill Providing for the Reclamation of Lands in the Sacramento and San Joaquin Valleys in the State of California,* S. 5376, 59th Cong., 1st sess., Mar. 27, 1906.

25. Charles D. Walcott to Ethan A. Hitchcock, Apr. 6, 1906; "Memorandum by C. E. Grunsky," Apr. 1906, both in folder 287–4, "Senate Bills, 59th Congress, 1st Session," box 153, entry 3, RG 115, NARA, Denver, CO.

26. Anthony E. Carlson, "'Drain the Swamps for Health and Home': Wetlands Drainage, Land Conservation, and National Water Policy, 1850–1917" (PhD diss., University of Oklahoma, 2010), 244–48; *A Bill for the Establishment of a Drainage Fund and the Construction of Works for the Reclamation of Swamp and Overflowed Lands,* S. 6626, 59th Cong., 2nd sess., Dec. 5, 1906.

27. "Touches California Closely," *San Francisco Call,* Oct. 13, 1907; "Reclamation of the Sacramento Valley," *San Francisco Call,* Dec. 2, 1907; Ira E. Bennett, "Western Affairs at Washington," *Pacific Monthly* 18 (Nov. 1907): 610–20; Fortier quoted in "Would Reclaim Vast Areas for Public Use," *Oakland Tribune,* July 2, 1906.

28. Carlson, "'Drain the Swamps for Health and Home,'" 265–67; "Gossip of Washington," *Charlotte (NC) Observer,* Dec. 24, 1907.

29. Frederick H. Newell to James R. Garfield, Jan. 21, 1908, file 2–9, box 734, Central Classified Files, 1907–36, entry 749, Records of the Office of the Secretary of the Interior, RG 48, NARA, College Park, MD; "Memorandum of meeting held in the office of the Secretary of the Interior at 10 a.m., January 25, 1908"; Morris Bien, "Memorandum on conference held in the office of the Secretary of the Interior, 10 a.m., Saturday, February 1, 1908"; and Bien, "Memorandum," Feb. 1, 1908, all in folder 110-G, "General Correspondence re. Federal Legislation for Drainage of Swamp and Overflow Lands," box 97, entry 3, RG 115, NARA, Denver, CO; *A Bill Appropriating the Receipts from the Sale and Disposal of Public Lands in Certain States to the Construction of Works for the Drainage or Reclamation of Swamp and Overflowed Lands,* S. 4855, 60th Cong., 1st sess., Feb. 3, 1908; Asbury Latimer to Napoleon Broward, Jan.

30, 1908, folder "January 1908," box 6, Napoleon Bonaparte Broward Papers, University of Florida Special Collections, Gainesville, FL.

30. *Congressional Record,* 60th Cong., 1st sess., Apr. 15, 1908, 4769–74; Apr. 17, 1908, 4859–66; Apr. 20, 1908, 4970–71.

31. Ibid.

32. Pisani, *Water and American Government,* 8, 58, 104–15. For Taft's opposition to federal drainage and flood control in the Mississippi River valley, see "'I Would Run for President,'" *Los Angeles Herald,* Oct. 11, 1910.

33. For Maxwell's promotion of federal irrigation and political and social beliefs, see Pisani, "George Maxwell, the Railroads, and American Land Policy, 1899–1904," *Pacific Historical Review* 63 (May 1994): 177–202; Pisani, *From the Family Farm to Agribusiness,* 273–75, 290–301; and Laura L. Lovett, *Conceiving the Future: Pronatalism, Reproduction, and the Family in the United States, 1890–1938* (Chapel Hill: University of North Carolina Press, 2007), chap. 3.

34. Roland M. Smith, "The Politics of Pittsburgh Flood Control, 1908–1936," *Pennsylvania History* 42 (Jan. 1975): 5–13; Donald J. Pisani, "Water Planning in the Progressive Era: The Inland Waterways Commission Reconsidered," *Journal of Policy History* 18 (fall 2006): 389–418; "For Strong Government Levees, Supplemented by Reservoirs," *New Orleans Daily Picayune,* May 15, 1912.

35. "For Strong Government Levees, Supplemented by Reservoirs," *New Orleans Daily Picayune,* May 15, 1912; "Reclamation Club Put on Solid Base," *New Orleans Daily Picayune,* July 12, 1912; Fowler quoted in "Fowler Is Opposed to Absorption of Congress," *Albuquerque Journal,* Nov. 28, 1911; Maxwell quoted in "A Message to Louisiana on Drainage of Lands," *Bayou Sara (LA) True Democrat,* Jan. 27, 1912; Hays, *Conservation and the Gospel of Efficiency,* 223–30.

36. John M. Barry, *Rising Tide: The Great Mississippi Flood of 1927 and How It Changed America* (New York: Simon & Schuster, 1997), 158; Pisani, *Water and American Government,* 253; Reuss, *Corps of Engineers and Water Resources in the Progressive Era,* 38; Woodrow Wilson to Edmund T. Perkins, Mar. 27, 1913, folder 110-G, "General Correspondence re. Federal Legislation for Drainage of Swamp and Overflow Lands," box 97, entry 3, RG 115, NARA, Denver, CO.

37. John Sharp Williams to Walter L. Fisher, July 24, 1912, folder "General Land Office Swamp Lands Legislation," box 83, Legislation Files, 1905–36, entry 753, RG 48, NARA, College Park, MD; *A Bill to Establish a Drainage Fund and to Provide for the Reclamation of Swamp and Overflowed Lands in Certain States,* S. 7194, 62nd Cong., 2nd sess., June 24, 1912; *A Bill to Establish a Drainage Fund and to Provide for the Reclamation of Swamp and Overflowed Lands in Certain States,* S. 1139, 63rd Cong., 1st sess., Apr. 17, 1913; *A Bill to Establish a Drainage Fund and to Provide for the Reclamation of Swamp and Overflowed Lands in Certain States,* S. 459, 64th Cong., 1st sess., Dec. 7, 1915; *A Bill to Establish a Drainage Fund and to Provide for the Reclamation of Swamp and Overflowed Lands in Certain States,* S. 753, 65th Cong., 1st sess., Apr. 6, 1917.

38. "What Newlands Proposes for California," *San Francisco Call,* May 4, 1912; "California Is Interested," *San Francisco Call,* Apr. 12, 1913; Kelley, *Battling the Inland Sea,* 278–86; *Congressional Record,* 63rd Cong., 1st sess., July 5, 1913, 2337. For Jackson's report, see House Committee on Rivers and Harbors, "Flood Control—Sacramento and San Joaquin River Systems, California," 62nd Cong., 1st sess., June 29, 1911, H. Doc. 81.

39. "Flood Protection, Drainage and Reclamation of Overflowed and Swamp Lands in the United States," n.d., 4–8, 12–20, folder 110-G, "General Correspondence re. Federal Legislation for Drainage of Swamp and Overflow Lands," box 97, entry 3, RG 115, NARA, Denver, CO.

40. Quoted in *Proceedings of the Conference on Irrigation Held at Denver, Colorado, April 9, 10, and 11, 1914, Pursuant to Invitations Issued by Secretary Lane to Western Governors and other Interested Parties,* 122–33, file 2–187, box 835, entry 749, RG 48, NARA, College Park, MD.

41. McClatchy quoted in *Official Proceedings of the Sixth Annual Meeting of the National Drainage Congress at Cairo, Illinois* (Cairo, IL: National Drainage Congress, 1916), 69–70; House Committee on Rivers and Harbors, "Flood Control—Sacramento and San Joaquin River Systems, California," 62nd Cong., 1st sess., June 29, 1911, H. Doc. 81, 7; Kelley, "Taming the Sacramento," 42–47.

42. Quoted in *Official Proceedings of the Sixth Annual Meeting of the National Drainage Congress,* 42–46.

43. Pisani, *Water and American Government,* 253–57; Kelley, *Battling the Inland Sea,* 291–93.

Chapter 8. Both "Country Town" and "Bustling Metropolis":
How Boosterism, Suburbs, and Narrative Helped Shape Sacramento's Identity and Environmental Sensibilities

1. William Holden, *Sacramento: Excursions into Its History and Natural World* (Fair Oaks, CA: Two Rivers Publishing, 1988), 9.

2. Sacramento Chamber of Commerce, *Sacramento Facts* (Sacramento: Chamber of Commerce, 1952, 1953, and 1954). The pamphlet shows the tagline on the front cover.

3. For sources elucidating the power of narrative to affect behavior and shape beliefs, see Jerome Bruner, *The Culture of Education* (Cambridge, MA: Harvard University Press, 1996), 130; David Carr, "Narrative and the Real World: An Argument for Continuity," *History and Theory* 25, no. 2 (May 1986): 117; Fredrick Jameson, *The Political Unconscious: Narrative as a Socially Symbolic Act* (Ithaca, NY: Cornell University Press, 1981); Alasdair MacIntyre, *After Virtue: A Study in Moral Theory* (Notre Dame, IN: University of Notre Dame Press, 1984), 216; L. O. Mink, "Narrative Form as a Cognitive Instrument," in *The Writing of History: Literary Form and Historical Understanding,* ed. R. H. Canary and H. Kozicki (Madison: University of Wisconsin Press, 1978), 129–49; James V. Wertsch, *Voices of Collective Remembering* (New York: Cambridge University Press, 2002), 57; and Hayden White, "The Value of Narrativity in the Representation of Reality," in *On Narrative,* ed. W. J. T. Mitchell (Chicago: University of Chicago Press, 1984), 1–23.

4. Thomas Jefferson quoted in Charles N. Glaab and A. Theodore Brown, *A History of Urban America* (New York: Macmillan, 1967), 55.

5. For more on the rural ideal, see, first and foremost, Thomas Jefferson's 1781–82 *Notes on the State of Virginia: With Related Documents,* ed. and with an introduction by David Waldstreicher (New York: Palgrave, 2002). See also David F. Allmendinger Jr., *Ruffin: Family and Reform in the Old South* (New York: Oxford University Press, 1990); John Archer, "Country and City in the American Romantic Suburb," *Journal of the Society of Architectural Historians* 42, no. 2 (May 1983): 139–56; Joyce E. Chaplin, *An Anxious Revolt: Agricultural Innovation and Modernity in the Lower South, 1730–1815* (Chapel Hill: University of North Carolina Press, 1993); David B. Danbom, *Born in the Country: A History of Rural America,* 2nd ed. (Baltimore: Johns Hopkins University Press, 2006), 65–69; Robert Fishman, *Bourgeois Utopias: The Rise and Fall of Suburbia* (New York: Basic Books, 1987), 53–54, 127; R. Douglas Hurt, *American Agriculture: A Brief History,* rev. ed. (West Lafayette, IN: Purdue University Press, 2002), 72–77; Leo Marx, *The Machine in the Garden: Technology and the Pastoral Ideal in America* (New York: Oxford University Press, 1964); Peter D. McClelland, *Sowing Modernity: America's First Agricultural Revolution* (Ithaca, NY: Cornell University Press, 1997); Morrill D. Peterson,

The Jefferson Image in the American Mind (New York: Oxford University Press, 1960); Henry Nash Smith, *Virgin Land: The American West as Symbol and Myth* (Cambridge, MA: Harvard University Press, 1950); Sam Bass Warner Jr., *Streetcar Suburbs: The Process of Growth in Boston, 1870–1900* (New York: Athenaeum, 1976), 11–12, 14, 45, 90; and Raymond Williams, *The Country and the City* (New York: Oxford University Press, 1973).

6. For more on suburbs and their relationship to democracy, republicanism, citizenship, and civic participation, see John Archer, *Architecture and Suburbia: From English Villa to American Dream House, 1690–2000* (Minneapolis: University of Minnesota Press, 2005), 173–202; Archer, "Country and City," 147; Clifford Edward Clark Jr., *The American Family Home, 1800–1960* (Chapel Hill: University of North Carolina Press, 1986), 24; Kenneth T. Jackson, *Crabgrass Frontier: The Suburbanization of America* (New York: Oxford University Press, 1985), 65–66; Margaret Marsh, *Suburban Lives* (New Brunswick, NJ: Rutgers University Press, 1990), 5; and Warner, *Streetcar Suburbs,* 158.

7. Robert Kirkman, "Reasons to Dwell on (If Not Necessarily in) the Suburbs," *Environmental Ethics* 26 (spring 2004): 77–95; Adam Ward Rome, *The Bulldozer in the Countryside: Suburban Sprawl and the Rise of American Environmentalism* (New York: Cambridge University Press, 2001); Mary Corbin Sies, "The City Transformed: Nature, Technology, and the Suburban Ideal, 1877–1917," *Journal of Urban History* 14, no. 1 (Nov. 1987): 81–111. For more on how suburbia represented the desire to relocate to rural-like environments away from the city, see Archer, *Architecture and Suburbia;* Fishman, *Bourgeois Utopias,* 53–54; Dolores Hayden, *Building Suburbia: Green Fields and Urban Growth, 1820–2000* (New York: Vintage Books, 2003), 3; Jackson, *Crabgrass Frontier,* 128; and Warner, *Streetcar Suburbs,* 11–12.

8. Archer, "Country and City"; Fishman, *Bourgeois Utopias;* Hayden, *Building Suburbia;* Jackson, *Crabgrass Frontier;* Warner, *Streetcar Suburbs.* The list of outstanding works concerning suburbs is large; however, the following are useful when considering the late nineteenth century: Archer, *Architecture and Suburbia;* Robert M. Fogelson, *Bourgeois Nightmares: Suburbia, 1870–1930* (New Haven: Yale University Press, 2005); Hayden, *Building Suburbia;* Jackson, *Crabgrass Frontier;* Robert Lewis, ed., *Manufacturing Suburbs: Building Work and Home on the Metropolitan Fringe* (Philadelphia: Temple University Press, 2004); Marsh, *Suburban Lives;* Becky M. Nicolaides and Andrew Wiese, eds., *The Suburb Reader* (New York: Routledge, 2006); Mary Corbin Sies, "Paradise Retained: An Analysis of Persistence in Planned, Exclusive Suburbs, 1880–1980," *Planning Perspectives* 12, no. 2 (1997): 165–91; John R. Stilgoe, *Borderland: Origins of the American Suburb, 1820–1939* (New Haven: Yale University Press, 1989); Jon C. Teaford, *City and Suburb: The Political Fragmentation of Metropolitan America, 1850–1970* (Baltimore: Johns Hopkins University Press, 1979); and Warner, *Streetcar Suburbs.*

9. Henri Lefebvre, *The Production of Space* (1974; repr., Oxford: Blackwell, 1991), 336–38; John R. Logan and Harvey Molotch, *Urban Fortunes: The Political Economy of Place* (Berkeley: University of California Press, 1987), 280–81.

10. Raymond F. Dasmann, *California's Changing Environment* (San Francisco: Boyd & Fraser, 1981), 20.

11. Quoted in Holden, *Sacramento,* 213.

12. Rachel Carson, *Silent Spring,* 40th anniversary edition, with essays by Edward O. Wilson and Linda Lear (New York: Houghton Mifflin, 2002), 297.

13. Danbom, *Born in the Country,* 65–66.

14. H. L. Mencken, "The Sahara of the Bozart," in *Prejudices: A Selection* (Baltimore: Johns Hopkins University Press, 2006), 74; H. L. Mencken, "In Memoriam: W.J.B.," in *H. L. Mencken: Prejudices, Fourth, Fifth, and Sixth Series* (New York: Library of America, 2010), 216.

15. Thomas Jefferson, letter to Benjamin Rush (1800), quoted in Jackson, *Crabgrass Frontier,* 68.

16. The "growth machine" referred to here is a rough application of Harvey Molotch's "growth machine" thesis in which municipalities, under the control of land-based elite, particularly newspaper editors and other professionals, represent "growth machines" that produce wealth through real estate development. Suburbs, and entire metropolitan landscapes, are thus social spaces that are essentially material products shaped by a society's social relations, which encompass class interests, experts, the grassroots, and other contending forces. See Harvey Molotch, "The City as a Growth Machine: Toward a Political Economy of Place," *American Journal of Sociology* 82, no. 2 (Sept. 1976): 309–22. See also David Harvey, *Social Justice and the City* (Baltimore: Johns Hopkins University Press, 1973); Andrew E. G. Jonas and David Wilson, eds., *The Urban Growth Machine: Critical Perspectives Two Decades Later* (Albany: State University of New York Press, 1999); Lefebvre, *Production of Space;* and Logan and Molotch, *Urban Fortunes.*

17. David Harvey, *The Condition of Postmodernity* (Oxford: Blackwell, 1989), 295. According to Harvey, "The active production of places with special qualities becomes an important stake in spatial competition between localities, regions, and nations." Ibid. See also William Cronon, "A Place for Stories: Nature, History, and Narrative," *Journal of American History* 78, no. 4 (Mar. 1992): 1347–76; William Cronon, *Nature's Metropolis: Chicago and the Great West* (New York: Norton, 1991), 5–19; Mike Davis, *City of Quartz: Excavating the Future in Los Angeles* (London: Verso, 1990), esp. chap. 1, "Sunshine or Noir," 17–97; Jackson, *Crabgrass Frontier,* 296; Lefebvre, *Production of Space,* 89, 335; Logan and Molotch, *Urban Fortunes,* 236; Gyan Prakash, introduction to *The Spaces of the Modern City: Imaginaries, Politics, and Everyday Life,* ed. Gyan Prakash and Kevin M. Kruse (Princeton: Princeton University Press, 2008), 7; and Stephen Victor Ward, *Selling Places: The Marketing and Promotion of Towns and Cities, 1850–2000* (New York: Routledge, 1998).

18. For more on the power of local history to affect identity and community, see David Glassberg, *Sense of History: The Place of the Past in American Life* (Amherst: University of Massachusetts Press, 2001), 126; Carol Kammen, ed., *The Pursuit of Local History: Readings on Theory and Practice* (Walnut Creek, CA: AltaMira, 1996); Michael Kammen, *Selvages and Biases: The Fabric of History in American Culture* (Ithaca, NY: Cornell University Press, 1989), 156; Friedrich W. Nietzsche, *On the Use and Abuse of History for Life* (Sioux Falls, SD: NuVision Publications, 2007), 23–24; Lydia R. Otero, *La Calle: Spatial Conflicts and Urban Renewal in a Southwest City* (Tucson: University of Arizona Press, 2010); and Michel-Rolph Trouillot, *Silencing the Past: Power and the Production of History* (Boston: Beacon Press, 1995).

19. The list of booster materials I consulted is extremely long. In the interest of conserving space (which is hard to believe when you look below), I have provided reference here to only a small sampling of such materials. To see more, visit the Sacramento Room at the Central Library of the Sacramento Public Library system, the California Room at the California State Library, and the Center for Sacramento History, all in Sacramento, as they have vast collections of chamber of commerce and local history materials. *History of Sacramento County, California[,] with Illustrations Descriptive of Its Scenery, Residences, Public Buildings, Fine Blocks, and Manufactories* (Oakland: Thompson & West, 1880); *Souvenir of Sacramento, California* (San Francisco: C. P. Heininger, 1887); *Sacramento: The Commercial Metropolis of Northern and Central California* (Sacramento: A. J. Johnston & Company, 1888); Winfield J. Davis, *An Illustrated History of Sacramento County, California: Containing a History of Sacramento County from the Earliest Period of its Occupancy to the Present Time* (Chicago: Lewis Publishing, 1890); James

McClatchy & Company, *Sacramento County and Its Resources: A Souvenir of the Bee* (Sacramento: James McClatchy & Company, 1894); Sacramento Board of Supervisors and Sacramento Chamber of Commerce, *Resources of Sacramento County, California* (Sacramento: Sacramento Board of Supervisors and Chamber of Commerce, [1899]); William H. Bryan, *Souvenir of the Capital of California: Sacramento City and Country as Seen through the Camera,* issued by the Sacramento Union (San Francisco: Stanley-Taylor, 1901); H. A. French, *California's Sacramento: Story of the Strawberry* (Sacramento: Chamber of Commerce, 1902); H. A. French, *California's Sacramento: The Story of the Grape* (Sacramento: Chamber of Commerce, 1903); Sacramento Chamber of Commerce, *Resources of Sacramento County, California* (Sacramento: Press of the H. S. Crocker Company, [1903]); Sacramento Chamber of Commerce, *Fruit Growing Is California's Greatest Industry: Sacramento County Is the Very Heart of its Greatest Production; Possesses a Climate Unsurpassed for its Equilibrity* (Sacramento: Chamber of Commerce, [1904]); Sacramento Chamber of Commerce, *Sacramento and Its Tributary County* (Sacramento: Chamber of Commerce, [1904]); Winfield J. Davis, *Sacramento County, California: Its Resources and Advantages* (Sacramento: Board of Supervisors, 1905); John C. Ing, *Sacramento City and County, California* (Sacramento: Sacramento Chamber of Commerce, 1905); William E. Terwilliger, *Sacramento Souvenir Guide,* approved by the Chamber of Commerce and the Sacramento Retail Merchants Association (Sacramento: [Chamber of Commerce], 1911); *Greater Sacramento: Her Achievements, Resources and Possibilities* (Sacramento: Kelman & Company, 1912); William L. Willis, *History of Sacramento County, California* (Los Angeles: Historic Record Company, 1913); *Sacramento Valley and Foothill Counties of California,* comp. and ed. Emmett Phillips and John H. Miller, under the direction of the Sacramento Valley Exposition (Sacramento: Sacramento Valley Exposition, 1915); Bureau Service, Sacramento Chamber of Commerce, *Sacramento: The Gateway to California* (Sacramento: The Bureau, 1922); G. Walter Reed, ed., *History of Sacramento County, California* (Los Angeles: Historic Record Company, 1923); Sacramento Chamber of Commerce, *Industrial Survey of Sacramento* (Sacramento: Chamber of Commerce, 1925); Women's Bureau, Better Home Week Committee, Sacramento Chamber of Commerce, *Home Builders Blue Book* (Sacramento: The Bureau, 1925); Sacramento Chamber of Commerce, *Sacramento, California: The World's Garden Valley* (Sacramento: Anderson Printing, [1926]); Industrial Department, Sacramento Chamber of Commerce, *Sacramento: California's Inland Industrial Center* (Sacramento: The Department, 1926); Sacramento Chamber of Commerce, *Capital Business* (Sacramento: Chamber of Commerce, printed monthly Mar. 1927–Dec. 1927, and Sept. 1933); Jesse Walton Wooldridge, *History of the Sacramento Valley, California,* 3 vols. (Chicago: Pioneer Historical Publishing, 1931); Industrial Department, Sacramento Chamber of Commerce, *Industrial Facts: Source of Raw Materials, Extent of Market, Vital Concentration Center, Hub of Transportation* (Sacramento: The Department, 1932); Harry C. Peterson, *The Romance of California* (Sacramento: Sacramento Chamber of Commerce, [1938]); Sacramento Chamber of Commerce, *Sacramento Business Barometer* (Sacramento: Chamber of Commerce, 1938, 1939, 1940, 1944); Sacramento Bee, *Sacramento Guide Book* (Sacramento: Sacramento Bee, 1939); *Visiting the Mother Lode of California,* text courtesy of the Sacramento Chamber of Commerce (Los Angeles: Touring Bureau, Automobile Club of Southern California, 1940); Sacramento Chamber of Commerce, *The Good Earth That Is Sacramento's* (Sacramento: Sacramento Bee, [1941]); Sacramento Chamber of Commerce, *Greater Sacramento Survey* (Sacramento: Chamber of Commerce, 1944); Sacramento Chamber of Commerce, *The California Farm Home: Sacramento Region* (Sacramento: Chamber of Commerce, [1944]); Sacramento Chamber of Commerce, *Hub of Western Industry: Sacramento, California* (Sacramento: Chamber of Commerce, 1944); Myrtle Lord Shaw, *A Sacramento Sage: Fifty Years of Achievement—Chamber of Commerce Leadership* (Sacramento: Sacramento Chamber of Commerce, 1946); Sacramento Chamber of Commerce, "Sacramento Facts," 1952–1963; Sophie Price, *The Sacramento Story* (New York: Vintage Press, 1955); Joseph A. McGowan, *History of the Sacramento Valley*, 3 vols. (New York: Lewis Historical Publishing, 1961); Research Department, Sacramento City-County Chamber of Commerce, *Pertinent Information about Metropolitan Sacramento* (Sacramento: The Department, 1962); Sacramento City-County Chamber of Commerce, *Sacramento, California: "Camellia Capital of the World"* (Sacramento: Chamber of Commerce, [1965]); Joseph A. McGowan, *The Sacramento Valley: A Students' Guide to Localized History* (New York: Teachers College Press, [1967]); Thor Severson, *Sacramento: An Illustrated History, 1839 to 1874; From Sutter's Fort to Capital City* (San Francisco: California Historical Society, [1973]); Marion M. Young, *Sacramento: A Tour Guide and Coloring Book* (Auberry, CA: Homestead Press, 1974); Sacramento Metropolitan Chamber of Commerce, *Sacramento Area Analysis* (Sacramento: Chamber of Commerce, 1979); Diane P. Muro, *A Complete Guide to Sacramento and Surrounding Areas* (Sacramento: Camellia Press, 1981); Joseph A. McGowan and Terry R. Willis, *Sacramento: Heart of the Golden State* (Woodland Hills, CA: Windsor Publications, 1983); Dorothy Kupcha Leland, *A Short History of Sacramento* (San Francisco: Lexikos, 1989); John F. Burns, ed., *Sacramento: Gold Rush Legacy, Metropolitan Destiny* (Carlsbad, CA: Heritage Media, 1999); Steven M. Avella, *Sacramento: Indomitable City* (Charleston, SC: Arcadia Publishing, 2003); Steven M. Avella, *The Good Life: Sacramento's Consumer Culture* (Charleston, SC: Arcadia Publishing, 2008); and Paula Bowden, ed., *The Golden Hub: Sacramento, including Folsom, Fair Oaks, Galt, Elk Grove, Walnut Grove and Surrounding Communities,* written by California pioneers and nineteenth-century historians (Pilot Hill, CA: 19th Century Books, 2008).

20. Muro, *Complete Guide to Sacramento,* 4.

21. *Visiting the Mother Lode of California.*

22. Chamber of Commerce, *Sacramento and Its Tributary County,* 14.

23. *Sacramento: The Commercial Metropolis,* 35.

24. The entire Mediterranean region, in fact, and not just Italy, became the standard for what boosters and others considered the perfect climate. Kevin Starr's treatment of the Mediterranean metaphor in *Americans and the California Dream* is the best on the subject. See Starr, *Americans and the California Dream, 1850–1915* (New York: Oxford University Press, 1973), 365–414.

25. Chamber of Commerce, *Good Earth That Is Sacramento's;* Chamber of Commerce, *Sacramento and Its Tributary County,* 5; Chamber of Commerce, *Sacramento, California: The World's Garden Valley.*

26. Chamber of Commerce, *Sacramento and Its Tributary County,* 5; *Sacramento: The Commercial Metropolis,* 11; Chamber of Commerce, *Fruit Growing Is California's Greatest Industry.* See also *Sacramento: The Commercial Metropolis,* 26.

27. *Sacramento: The Commercial Metropolis,* 47.

28. McClatchy & Company, *Sacramento County and Its Resources,* 34.

29. *Sacramento: The Commercial Metropolis;* Chamber of Commerce, *Hub of Western Industry;* Chamber of Commerce, *Industrial Facts;* Chamber of Commerce, *Sacramento Business Barometer;* Bryan, *Souvenir of the Capital,* 14.

30. On suburbia being a blend of city and country, see Archer, "Country and City," 139–56; Fishman, *Bourgeois Utopias,* 53–54, 128; and Jackson, *Crabgrass Frontier,* 12, 24, 31–32, 128. On California's agricultural areas mixing urban and rural qualities, see Matt Garcia, *A World of Its Own: Race, Labor, and Citrus in the Making of Greater Los Angeles, 1900–1970* (Chapel Hill: University of North Carolina Press, 2001), 25–28; Carey McWilliams, *Southern Califor-*

nia: An Island on the Land (New York: Duell, Sloan & Pearce, 1946), 12–13, 194, 207; Donald J. Pisani, *From the Family Farm to Agribusiness: The Irrigation Crusade in California and the West, 1850–1931* (Berkeley: University of California Press, 1984), 73, 120–21; Starr, *Americans and the California Dream,* 202, 416; Kevin Starr, *Inventing the Dream: California through the Progressive Era* (New York: Oxford University Press, 1985), 45–47, 134, 139; Kevin Starr, *Material Dreams: Southern California through the 1920s* (New York: Oxford University Press, 1990), 15–16; and David Vaught, *Cultivating California: Growers, Specialty Crops, and Labor, 1875–1920* (Baltimore: Johns Hopkins University Press, 1999), 9–10, 30–31, 53.

31. Bryan, *Souvenir of the Capital,* 15, 11–12, respectively.

32. Chamber of Commerce, *Sacramento and Its Tributary County,* 2; Bryan, *Souvenir of the Capital,* 7, 13, 3; *Sacramento: The Commercial Metropolis,* 47; McClatchy & Company, *Sacramento County and Its Resources,* 34.

33. Paul J. P. Sandul, "The Agriburb: Recalling the Suburban Side of Ontario, California's Agricultural Colonization," *Agricultural History* 84, no. 2 (spring 2010): 195–223. The suburban process and form are highlighted in two other works (though, in them, I do not employ the term *agriburb*): Paul J. P. Sandul and Tory D. Swim, *Orangevale* (Charleston, SC: Arcadia Publishing, 2006); and Lee M. A. Simpson and Paul J. P. Sandul, *Fair Oaks* (Charleston, SC: Arcadia Publishing, 2006). Finally, I delimit what an "agriburb" is in detail in Paul J. P. Sandul, "Harvesting Suburbs: Recalling the Suburban Side of California's Agricultural Colonization" (PhD diss., University of California, Santa Barbara and California State University, Sacramento, 2009); and Sandul, *Harvesting Suburbs, Cultivating Memory: Legacies of Rural and Urban Land Boosterism in California* (Morgantown: West Virginia University Press, forthcoming in 2014).

34. Sandul, "Agriburb," 195–223.

35. McWilliams, *Southern California,* 12; Starr, *Inventing the Dream,* 134.

36. "Orangevale," *Sacramento Union,* May 8, 1888, 3. For more promotional literature on Orangevale, see "Orangevale: A Sacramento Fruit Colony Enterprise," *Sacramento Daily Union,* May 8, 1888, 3; "Wake Up Sleepy Folsom," *Sacramento Union,* May 28, 1889, 2; "Orange Vale's Water System," *Sacramento Union,* July 27, 1889, 5; Orange Vale Colonization Company, *Map of Sacramento County Showing Location of Orange Vale: Property of The Orange Vale Colonization Company, Sacramento County, Cal., comprising 3,200 acres cultivated land* ([Sacramento: The Company, 1892]), available at the California History Room, California State Library, Sacramento; "Orange Vale: An Excursion to the Sacramento Colony near Folsom," *Sacramento Union,* June 16, 1890, 1; "Orange Vale: Making Rapid Progress," *Folsom Telegraph,* Feb. 18, 1893, 2; Orange Vale Colonization Company, *A Souvenir of Orange Vale* (Sacramento: Orange Vale Colonization Company, 1894), on file at the California History Room, California State Library, Sacramento; Orange Vale Water Company Papers (Orangevale, CA: The Company, [1896]), on file at the Sacramento Room, Central Library, Sacramento. For more on the history of Orangevale, see Sheila LaDuke, *The History of Orangevale* ([Orangevale, CA]: Vintage Typographics, 1980), available at the Orangevale Public Library, Orangevale, CA; Catherine Hack, *A History of the Orangevale Community* (N.p., 1990), on file at the California History Room, California State Library, Sacramento; Carol Anne West, *Northern California's First Successful Colony: The Orange Vale Legacy* ([Orangevale, CA]: Carol Anne West, 2001), available at the California History Room, California State Library, Sacramento; Sandul and Swim, *Orangevale.*

37. "Arcade Park: Ideal Suburban Home Sites," *Sunset* (May 1911), clipping, Ephemera: Real Estate Developments, Sacramento Room, Central Library, Sacramento; *Arcade Park: The*

Pasadena of Northern California (Sacramento: News Publishing Company, 1912), in California History Room, California State Library, Sacramento. For more on the history of Arcade Park, see James R. Cowan, *A History of the Arcade School District with Information on the Growth and Development of the North Area of Sacramento County, California, 1885–1960* (Sacramento: California Retired Teachers Association, Division V, History Committee, 1990).

38. For more on Daniel Carmichael and the history of Carmichael, see Kay Muther, *Carmichael* (Charleston, SC: Arcadia Publishing, 2004); and James R. Cowan, *A History of the Carmichael School and Community, 1880–1960* (Sacramento: The Author, [1995]), on file at the Sacramento Room, Central Library, Sacramento.

39. "Big Real Estate Deal," *Folsom Telegraph,* Oct. 1, 1909; unidentified newspaper article or pamphlet, ca. 1909, SM&HC # 268–63, Land Colonization 9, 80/18/518, Center for Sacramento History, Sacramento.

40. "Ten Acres and Independence," advertisement, *Sacramento Valley Monthly* 5, nos. 5–6 (Oct.–Nov. 1915): 13; *Carmichael Colony: In the Heart of California* (Sacramento [1911]), [6]; *Carmichael Colony,* [3–4].

41. "Your Ten Acres in Citrus Heights," advertisement clipping, ca. 1913, SM&HC # (not catalogued), Land Colonization 7, 80/18/520, Center for Sacramento History, Sacramento. For more Citrus Heights promotional material, see "Picking Oranges at Fair Oaks adjoining Citrus Heights," advertisement clipping, ca. 1911, SM&HC # 286–107, Land Colonization 8, 80/18/520, Center for Sacramento History, Sacramento; Cate and Marshall Phinney, Map of Citrus Heights Addition No. 16, "Located on the beautiful boulevard leading to the country club," drawn for the Trainor-Desmond Real Estate Co. (Sacramento: Trainor-Desmond Real Estate, 1912), available at the California History Room, California State Library, Sacramento. For more on the history of Citrus Heights, see Lillian A. Cross, *Sylvan Recollections: A History of the Sylvan District, Sacramento County, California* (Sacramento: Office of the County Superintendent of Schools, 1943); Roeley Giusti, *A Century of History* ([Citrus Heights]: Citrus Heights Historical Society, 1994); and James Van Maren, *Citrus Heights* (Charleston, SC: Arcadia Publishing, 2011).

42. *Carmichael Colony,* [9–13].

43. "Ten Acres and Independence," 13.

44. Unidentified newspaper article or pamphlet, ca. 1909.

45. *Carmichael Colony,* [5–6].

46. "Secure a Home in Park View in the Heart of the Rancho Del Paso," advertisement clipping, *Sacramento Valley Monthly,* ca. 1911, 80/18/514, Center for Sacramento History, Sacramento. Also see J. C. Boyd, *Ranch Del Paso: Ideal Tracts for Oranges, Lemons, Grape Fruit, Olives, Almonds, Grapes, Alfalfa, Hops, Deciduous Fruits* (Sacramento: Sacramento Valley Colonization Company, 1910); Sacramento Valley Colonization Company, *Rancho Del Paso (Ranch of the Pass)* (Sacramento: Sacramento Valley Colonization Company, [1910]); Official plat of East Del Paso Heights (N.p., 1912); Reynolds & Whitman, Plat of Del Paso Park View tract no. 2: Located in sec's. 27 & 30 of the Rancho Del Paso, Sacramento County, California (Sacramento: Sacramento Valley Colonization Company, [1913]); Sacramento Suburban Fruit Lands Company, Plat of New Prague: Located in section 6, Rancho Del Paso, Sacramento County, California (San Francisco: Sacramento Suburban Fruit Lands Company, [1913]); and Sacramento Suburban Fruit Lands Company, *Romance and History of Rancho del Paso, Sacramento, California* (Sacramento: Sacramento Suburban Fruit Lands Company, [1914]). For history on the area, see Barbara Austin, *A Story of Rancho Del Paso: Straight from the Horse's*

Mouth (Sacramento: Sacramento State College Alumni Association, 1962); and K. W. Lee, *Del Paso Heights: The City Apart* (Sacramento: Sacramento Union, [1973]).

47. Sacramento Suburban Fruit Lands Company, Plat of Rio Linda subdivision no. 5: located in sections 23 and nos. 1–2 22, Rancho Del Paso, Sacramento County, California, owned and for sale on easy terms by Sacramento Suburban Fruit Lands Co. (Sacramento: Sacramento Suburban Fruit Lands Company, [192–?]); Sacramento Suburban Fruit Lands Company, *The Most Progressive Suburb of the City of Sacramento Is Rio Linda* (Sacramento: Sacramento Suburban Fruit Lands Company, [1926]); Sacramento Suburban Fruit Lands Company, *Rio Linda[,] California: The Home of Four Hundred Families from Minnesota and Other Northern States* (Sacramento: Sacramento Suburban Fruit Lands Company, [192–?]); and Sacramento Suburban Fruit Lands Company, *Why Rio Linda?* (Sacramento: Sacramento Suburban Fruit Lands Company, [192–?]). For more on the history of Rio Linda and surrounding areas, see Margaret Posehn, *Rio Linda and Elverta Early History, 1850–1929* (North Highlands, CA: published by author, [2008]); and Joyce Buckland, *Rio Linda and Elverta* (Charleston, SC: Arcadia Publishing, 2006).

48. *Carmichael Colony,* [9].

49. Ibid., [10].

50. *Carmichael Colony,* [23]; unidentified newspaper article or pamphlet, ca. 1909.

51. Olmsted, Vaux, and Company, *Preliminary Report upon the Proposed Suburban Village at Riverside, near Chicago* (New York: Sutton, Browne and Company, 1868), 7.

52. Ibid., 7.

53. Unidentified newspaper article or pamphlet, ca. 1909.

54. Brooke Realty Company, *North Sacramento* (Sacramento: Brooke Realty, [1910s]), 12, Michael Benning Collection, 1983/232, box 1 of 2, 28:5D, Center for Sacramento History, Sacramento. More early promotional ads can be found in the Sacramento Room, Central Library, Sacramento; and in V. Ehrenreich-Risner, *North Sacramento* (Charleston, SC: Arcadia Publishing, 2010). For more on the history of the area, see Ehrenreich-Risner, *North Sacramento;* and Austin, *Story of Rancho Del Paso.*

55. Fair Oaks Development Company, *Fair Oaks, Sacramento County: In the Heart of the Fruit-Growing Section of California* (Sacramento: Fair Oaks Development Company, 1900), 3–4. For more promotional literature about Fair Oaks, see Howard & Wilson Publishing, *The Heart of California* (Chicago: Howard & Wilson Publishing, 1897); Howard & Wilson Publishing, *Sunset Colonies: Fair Oaks and Olive Park, In the Heart of California; Farm, Field and Fireside and Western Rural, Colony Department* (Chicago: Farm, Field and Fireside and Western Rural, Colony Dept., 1896); Howard & Wilson Publishing, *Fair Oaks, In the Heart of California* ([Chicago: Howard & Wilson Publishing], 1897). For more on the history of Fair Oaks, see Fair Oaks Historical Society, *Fair Oaks: The Early Years* (Fair Oaks, CA: Fair Oaks Historical Society, Centennial History Book Committee, 1995); and Simpson and Sandul, *Fair Oaks.*

56. *Carmichael Colony,* [2–3].

57. "70,000 Acres to Be Reclaimed," advertisement, ca. 1911, SM&HC #269–87, Floods and Reclamation 9, 80/18/531, Center for Sacramento History, Sacramento. For more promotional material, see *Natomas News* 1, nos.1–3 (1911).

58. "Natomas," advertisement, ca. 1911, City of Sacramento Collection, 1980/018/0536, Center for Sacramento History, Sacramento. For more on the history of the reclamation project and Natomas Company, see Carson Hendricks and Lisa C. Prince, "From Swampland to Farmland: Reclamation and Irrigation in the Natomas Basin," *Sacramento History Journal* 6, nos. 1–4 (2006): 177–86; and Antonia Castaneda, Robert Docken, Edith Pitti, and Chandler

Ide, "Natomas Company, 1851–1984," prepared under the direction of the Sacramento History Center (now Center for Sacramento History) for the Natomas Company (unpublished manuscript, 1984), 237–66, on file at the Center for Sacramento History, Sacramento.

59. Castaneda et al., "Natomas Company," 237–66.

60. Joseph A. McGowan et al., *Report on the Historical Development of the City of Sacramento Blocks Bounded by H and I, 5th and 6th* (Sacramento, 1978), 1, on file at the Center for Sacramento History, Sacramento; John C. Jenkins, "Sutter Lake or China Slough," *Golden Notes* (Dec. 1966): 1–3; Brienes, West, and Schuly, "Overview of Cultural Resources in the Central Business District, Sacramento, California" (1981), 61, identified by authors' last names only and on file at the Center for Sacramento History, Sacramento; Mary Praetzellis and Adrian Praetzellis, *Archeological Study of the IJ-56 Block, Sacramento, California: An Early Chinese Community* (Sonoma, CA: Anthropological Studies Center, Sonoma State University, 1982), 17, on file at the Center for Sacramento History, Sacramento; Willis, *History of Sacramento County*, 198.

61. "Grand Auction Sale! Oak Park Addition," advertisement, *Sacramento Union*, Sept. 1887, reprinted in Lee M. A. Simpson, ed., *Sacramento's Oak Park* (Charleston, SC: Arcadia Publishing, 2004), 10.

62. "Grand Auction Sale! Of the Highland Park Tract," advertisement, *Sacramento Union*, Oct. 1887, reprinted in Dan Murphy, *Sacramento's Curtis Park* (Charleston, SC: Arcadia Publishing, 2005), 23.

63. Avella, *Good Life*, 99.

64. Wooldridge, *History of the Sacramento Valley*, 2:149–50.

65. Amanda Paige Meeker, "Wright & Kimbrough Tract 24: Review of National Register Eligibility" (MA thesis, California State University, Sacramento, 2000), 51; "Pioneer Sacramento Realty Firm Golden Anniversary in 1943," *California Real Estate Magazine*, May 1943, clipping found in SAC PAM—Businesses—Wright & Kimbrough, Sacramento Room, Central Library, Sacramento; "William P. Wright, Realtor, Dies at 67; Funeral Today," *Sacramento Bee*, Aug. 24, 1978, B23; "Charles Wright, Sacramento Real Estate Man, Dies," unidentified newspaper article, 1939, clipping found in SAC PAM—Businesses—Wright & Kimbrough, Sacramento Room, Central Library, Sacramento; and "A. Russel Gallaway, Jr., 89, a Developer in the Capitol [*sic*]," *Sacramento Bee*, May 3, 2001, B5.

66. "Pioneer Sacramento Realty Firm Golden Anniversary in 1943"; "William P. Wright, Realtor, Dies at 67; Funeral Today"; "Charles Wright, Sacramento Real Estate Man, Dies."

67. "Choice East Sacramento Lots at the Lowest Prices in Ten Years," unidentified advertisement, ca. 1920s, SAC PAM—Neighborhoods—Fabulous Forties, Sacramento Room, Central Library, Sacramento.

68. "Choice East Sacramento Lots at the Lowest Prices in Ten Years"; "Wright & Kimbrough Tract 33," unidentified advertisement, ca. 1920s; "Wright & Kimbrough Tract 24 Addition (East Sacramento)," unidentified advertisement, ca. 1920s, all in SAC PAM—Neighborhoods—Fabulous Forties, Sacramento Room, Central Library, Sacramento.

69. "The Old Golf Links"; and "East Sacramento (Wright & Kimbrough Tract 24 Annex)," unidentified advertisements, ca. 1920s, both in SAC PAM—Neighborhoods—Fabulous Forties, Sacramento Room, Central Library, Sacramento.

70. Paula S. Fass, *The Damned and the Beautiful: American Youth in the 1920s* (New York: Oxford University Press, 1977); Nathan Miller, *New World Coming: The 1920s and the Making of Modern America* (New York: Scribner, 2003).

71. "These Homesite Values Cannot Be Duplicated," unidentified advertisement, ca. 1930s;

"Wright & Kimbrough College Tract," unidentified advertisement, ca. 1930s, both in SAC PAM—Neighborhoods—Land Park, Sacramento Room, Central Library, Sacramento.

72. Wright & Kimbrough, "Arden Park Vista, Unit 8," promotional brochure, 1945, SAC PAM—Neighborhoods—Fabulous Forties, Sacramento Room, Central Library, Sacramento; Wright & Kimbrough, "Wright & Kimbrough; Arden Park Vista," promotional brochure, 1945, 2002/116/004, MC 13:01, Center for Sacramento History, Sacramento; Wright & Kimbrough, "Wright & Kimbrough Arden Park Vista, Unit 4," promotional brochure, 1945, SAC PAM—Neighborhoods—Fabulous Forties, Sacramento Room, Central Library, Sacramento.

73. Avella, *Good Life,* 102–18.

74. "Sierra Oaks: Sacramento's Ideal Residential Development," brochure, ca. 1950s, SAC PAM—Neighborhoods—Sierra Oaks, Sacramento Room, Central Library, Sacramento; "Greenhaven 70," *Sacramento Bee,* Mar. 11, 1962, G1–G5; Morris Newman, "FOCUS: A Transit-Oriented Approach to Suburbia," *New York Times,* Nov. 10, 1991, http://www.nytimes.com/1991/11/10/realestate/focus-a-transit-oriented-approach-to-suburbia.html?scp=6&sq=Laguna%20West%20california&st=cse; Luxury Real Estate CA, company website, advertisements, and real estate listings, accessed online at http://www.luxuryrealestateca.com.

75. John Bodnar, *Remaking America: Public Memory, Commemoration, and Patriotism in the Twentieth Century* (Princeton: Princeton University Press, 1992), 115–37. For more on "public memory," see Martha K. Norkunas, *The Politics of Public Memory: Tourism, History, and Ethnicity in Monterey, California* (Albany: State University of New York Press, 1993); Dolores Hayden, *The Power of Place: Urban Landscapes as Public History* (Cambridge, MA: MIT Press, 1996); and Glassberg, *Sense of History.*

76. An example of this can be seen in Fair Oaks. See *A History of Fair Oaks* (Fair Oaks, CA: Fair Oaks Historical Society, 2005), accessible at http://www.fairoakshistory.org; *Fair Oaks Guide,* contributing writers Judy Kemper, Hugh Gorman, Maggie Upton (Fair Oaks, CA: P. D. Willey, 1984), available at California History Room, Sacramento; *Fair Oaks Guide* ([Fair Oaks, CA]: Fair Oaks Chamber of Commerce, 1988), available at California History Room, Sacramento; Fair Oaks Historical Society, *Fair Oaks: The Early Years;* Fair Oaks Woman's Thursday Club, *Fair Oaks: The Way It Was, 1895–1976* ([Fair Oaks, CA: Woman's Thursday Club of Fair Oaks, 1976]), available at the Sacramento Room, Sacramento; Peter J. Hayes, ed., *The Lower American River: Prehistory to Parkway* (Carmichael, CA: American River Natural History Association, 2005); Selden Menefee, Patricia Fitzgerald, and Geraldine Fitzgerald, eds., *Fair Oaks and San Juan Area Memories* (Fair Oaks, CA: San Juan Record Press, 1960); and Sacramento County Planning Department, "The Fair Oaks Community Plan," adopted by the Sacramento County Board of Supervisors, Resolution no. 75–12, Jan. 8, 1975. The following material sites of public memory are also relevant: (1) Fair Oaks Historical Society and History Center; a museum is operated out of the Old Fair Oaks Library Building, erected in 1912; (2) Fair Oaks Plaza mural by Hugh Gorman, a local resident and artist's public art of the history of Fair Oaks; (3) Fair Oaks Bluff, overlooking the American River, a favorite site of locals for more than one hundred years and also a favorite of promoters in advertising images. The organization Citizens to Save the Bluffs has worked to purchase the property to conserve the area; see http://www.savethebluffs.org; (4) Old Fair Oaks Downtown Area, or Fair Oaks Village, is the old central business district of Fair Oaks and has served as the main business thoroughfare in the community for more than one hundred years. In addition to the Fair Oaks Plaza, Slocum House, and the Old Library Building (which are mentioned elsewhere), the area is also the site of several older buildings, built in the early to mid-twentieth century, such as

the Bank Building (ca. 1910), Community Center (site of the first schoolhouse), and Tudor-style business offices (though they were built in the 1980s); (5) the Old Fair Oaks Bridge, Bridge Street, spans the American River and is on the National Register of Historic Places; (6) "Old Fair Oaks Bridge," memorial plaque spearheaded by Jason Marty and located on the north side of the Fair Oaks Bridge on Bridge Street; (7) Slocum House & Restaurant, 7992 California Avenue, a California Historical Landmark, is the former home of Charles Slocum, a prominent businessman and civic leader in the late nineteenth and early twentieth century. In addition, the Fair Oaks Fiesta, renamed the Fair Oaks Spring Fest, has been held every May since the 1950s. It features such entertainments as frog jumps, the "Sun Run," a car show, parade, food and craft vendors, special entertainment, and children's games. Another event, the Fair Oaks Chicken Festival, began in 2006; locals and neighbors come out to dance, dine, and drink yet again in the center of town. The festival pays tribute to Fair Oaks's legendary roosters and chickens that frolic freely throughout the downtown district.

77. Fitzgerald and Fitzgerald, *Fair Oaks and San Juan Area Memories*. For Fair Oaks population figures, see California, Department of Finance, "Population Totals by Township and Place for California Counties: 1860 to 1950," compiled by Dr. Campbell Gibson, 2005, www.dof.ca.gov.; US Bureau of the Census, 1990 Census of Population and Housing, Summary Tape File 1, Fair Oaks, California CDP; US Census Bureau, Census 2000 Summary File 4, Fair Oaks, California CDP; and US Census Bureau, 2005–2007 American Community Survey, Fair Oaks, California CDP, all at www.census.gov.

78. "The History of Fair Oaks," http://www.fairoakshistory.org/history/fohist.htm.

79. "Fair Oaks History and Walking Tour," http://www.fairoakshistory.org/walktour/fowt.htm.

80. William Deverell, *Whitewashed Adobe: The Rise of Los Angeles and the Remaking of Its Mexican Past* (Berkeley: University of California Press, 2004), 4–5.

81. Paul J. Crutzen, "Geology of Mankind," *Nature* 415 (Jan. 3, 2002): 23. For more on the Anthropocene, see Paul J. Crutzen and Eugene F. Stoermer, "The 'Anthropocene,'" *IGBP Newsletter* 41 (May 2000): 17–18; Paul J. Crutzen, "The 'Anthropocene,'" *Journal de Physique IV France* 12 (2002): 447; and William F. Ruddiman, "The Anthropogenic Greenhouse Era Began Thousands of Years Ago," *Climatic Change* 61, no. 3 (Dec. 2003): 261–93.

82. See also "Welcome to the Anthropocene," *Economist*, May 28, 2011, 11.

83. Bruner, *Culture of Education*, 130; Carr, "Narrative and the Real World," 117; Mink, "Narrative Form as a Cognitive Instrument," 129–49; Wertsch, *Voices of Collective Remembering*, 57; White, "Value of Narrativity in the Representation of Reality," 1–23.

Chapter 9. Unseen Investment: New Deal Sacramento

1. *Fresno Bee*, May 19, 1940.

2. Works Progress Administration director Harry Hopkins insisted that all WPA projects would be identified by a red, white, and blue sign, explaining that "frequently people observe activities under private contract or municipal or county enterprises and make critical comment about the WPA. We want our projects marked so that if anybody wants to see them they can be sure of what they are looking at." "Hopkins Sets Signs to Mark All WPA Projects," *Sacramento Bee*, Mar. 10, 1936.

3. "Ickes Says Federal Government Is Good for California," *Architect and Engineer*, Dec. 1939.

4. Steve Avella, *Sacramento: Indomitable City* (Charleston, SC: Arcadia Publishing, 2003), 97; Paul Sandul, "Harvesting Suburbs: Recalling the Suburban Side of California's Agricul-

tural Colonization" (PhD diss., University of California, Santa Barbara, and California State University, Sacramento, 2009).

5. Joseph A. McGowan, *History of the Sacramento Valley*, 3 vols. (New York: Lewis Historical Publishing, 1961), 2:257.

6. Avella, *Sacramento: Indomitable City*, 98.

7. Ibid., 98–99.

8. Joan Hoff Wilson, *Herbert Hoover, Forgotten Progressive* (Boston: Little, Brown, 1975), 143–57; Avella, *Sacramento: Indomitable City*, 99.

9. Avella, *Sacramento: Indomitable City*, 100.

10. Franklin D. Roosevelt, "Address Accepting the Presidential Nomination at the Democratic National Convention in Chicago," July 2, 1932, online at Gerhard Peters and John T. Woolley, *The American Presidency Project*, http://www.presidency.ucsb.edu/ws/?pid=75174.

11. C. W. Short and R. Stanley-Brown, *Public Buildings: A Survey of Architecture of Projects Constructed by Federal and Other Governmental Bodies between the Years 1933 and 1939 with the Assistance of the Public Works Administration* (Washington, DC: Government Printing Office, 1939).

12. Henry G. Alsberg, *America Fights the Depression: A Photographic Record of the Civil Works Administration* (New York: Coward-McCann, 1934).

13. *Sacramento Bee*, Jan. 27, 1934.

14. Deterding Scrapbook, Center for Sacramento History, Sacramento. Deterding also procured extensive WPA and PWA aid for infrastructure, parks, and Grant Union High School in Rancho Del Paso and Hagginwood. He was a large local landholder; others may determine if he profited from public investment in that area.

15. *Sacramento Bee*, Apr. 18, 1934.

16. William R. Lawson, *Achievements, Federal Works Agency: Work Projects Administration, Northern California* (San Francisco, 1940).

17. Supervisors from eleven important California counties met in San Diego to oppose the WPA, issuing a statement that "the program will be a financial impossibility, would lead to unionizing of all relief workers and finally to overthrow of the government. They protested it would yield only about 20% in real value and lastly that it would be an insult to the mentality of every man and woman in the state." "Supervisors Attack New U.S. Program for Relief," *San Diego Sun*, July 6, 1935.

18. "New Deal Save[s] City, County $3,115,479 to Help Projects," *Sacramento Bee*, Oct. 31, 1936.

19. "WPA Project Is Started in City," *Sacramento Bee*, Sept. 23, 1935. Two weeks before, Hopkins reported that the WPA had employed 837,563 workers nationally. *Sacramento Bee*, Sept. 6, 1935.

20. "Men Beyond 50 Erect Thirty WPA Buildings," *Sacramento Bee*, June 26, 1936.

21. "Sacramento County's WPA Accomplishments Are Listed," *Sacramento Bee*, Oct. 17, 1940.

22. A cap of twenty-five thousand dollars was imposed on WPA projects, but Hopkins would often aggregate them to exceed that amount.

23. "New Fire Alarm System Is Assured for Sacramento," *Sacramento Bee*, Sept. 11, 1936. The article mentions that the system would be operated from a central station, apparently the concrete structure in the center of Winn Park.

24. Information provided by Robert Leighninger from research he has conducted at the National Archives and Records Administration in College Park, MD.

25. The tanks were featured as elements of Sacramento's municipal water system in a compilation of outstanding public works built by the PWA. Short and Stanley-Brown, *Public Buildings*, 491.

26. The Bridge Act of 1906 revised the River and Harbor Act of 1899 and clarified War Department authority over the construction of bridges. US Congress, *The Statutes at Large of the United States from March 1897 to March 1899 and Recent Treaties, Conventions, Executive Proclamations and Current Resolutions of the Two Houses of Congress*, vol. 30 (Washington, DC: Government Printing Office, 1899), 1151; US Congress, *The Statutes at Large of the United States from December 1905 to March 1907 and Concurrent Resolutions of the Two Houses of Congress and Recent Treaties, Conventions, Executive Proclamations*, vol. 34 (Washington, DC: Government Printing Office, 1907), 84–86.

27. US Department of Agriculture, Bureau of Public Roads, "Memorandum to District Engineers," Aug. 8, 1933, Sacramento, Record Group 30, National Archives San Bruno Division.

28. US Department of Agriculture, Bureau of Public Roads, "Grade Crossing Elimination and Protection," Nov. 21, 1933, Sacramento, Record Group 30, National Archives San Bruno Division.

29. "An Act to Add a New Section to the Political Code, to Be Numbered 363dd, Authorizing the Director of Public Works to Enter into Agreements for the Construction, Maintenance, and Use of State Highway Bridges Jointly by the Public and Private Owners," *California State Political Code 363dd*, Assembly (1933).

30. US Department of the Interior, Historic American Engineering Record, "Sacramento River Bridge (Tower Bridge) (M Street Bridge)," HAER No. CA-73 (undated) by James F. Fisher and John W. Snyder.

31. W. P. Dwyer, Sacramento, to Frank H. Reynolds, Sacramento, Sept. 19, 1933, Bridge Construction Project Files, III-YOL, Sac (M Street [Tower] Bridge) F3778:3415–34200, California State Archives.

32. Purcell (by F. W. Panhorst, Acting Bridge Engineer, Caltrans) to Cortelyou, Jan. 4, 1934, Bridge Construction Project Files, III-YOL, Sac (M Street [Tower] Bridge) F3778:3415–34200, California State Archives.

33. Harrington & Cortelyou to Purcell, Jan. 30, 1934, Bridge Construction Project Files, III-YOL, Sac (M Street [Tower] Bridge) F3778:3415–34200, California State Archives.

34. "Highway Bids and Awards for July," *California Highways and Public Works* 12, no. 8 (Aug. 1934): 30.

35. US Department of the Interior, Historic American Engineering Record, "Sacramento River Bridge (Tower Bridge) (M Street Bridge)."

36. W. A. Douglas, "Progress on M Street Bridge at Sacramento Promises Opening in Fall," *California Highways and Public Works* 13, no. 5 (May 1935): 18.

37. Ibid., 4.

38. Ibid., 2.

39. Ibid.

40. Everett L. Walsh, "Tower Bridge Wins National Award," *California Highways and Public Works* 14, no. 7 (July 1936): 8.

41. Avella, *Sacramento: Indomitable City*, 103; Sacramento Air Depot, National Register nomination, 1988, http://pdfhost.focus.nps.gov/docs/NRHP/Text/91001969.pdf. The structure was listed in 1991.

42. Kyle Byard and Tom Naiman, *McClellan Air Force Base* (Charleston, SC: Arcadia Publishing, 2007), 9.

43. Ibid.; Avella, *Sacramento: Indomitable City,* 104; Sacramento Air Depot nomination.

44. Sacramento Air Depot nomination.

45. Byard and Naiman, *McClellan Air Force Base,* 9; Sacramento Air Depot nomination.

46. Sacramento Air Depot nomination.

47. Ibid.

48. Short and Stanley-Brown, *Public Buildings,* 1.

49. "500 Will Work on Tree Project," *Sacramento Bee,* Jan. 15, 1936.

50. When the Sacramento Army Depot was dedicated on April 29, 1939, an article in the *Bee* said that it alone had pumped $7 million into the local economy.

51. See also "Johnson Is Prepared to Push Capitol Park Plans," *Sacramento Bee,* Apr. 16, 1935.

Chapter 10. The Legacy of War: Sacramento's Military Bases

1. Defense Base Closure and Realignment Commission, "2005 Final Report to the President," http://www.brac.gov/Finalreport.html.

2. Ibid.

3. The BRAC process has been widely documented. Basic information on BRAC considerations can be found at the Defense Base Closure and Realignment Commission website, http://www.brac.gov/. For basic information related to CERCLA, see http://www.epa.gov/superfund/policy/cercla.htm.

4. For information related to former military facilities with Superfund status, see the Environmental Protection Agency's website, http://www.epa.gov/region9/superfund/, and search by facility name.

5. Maj. Frank W. Tate, "Army Aviation as a Branch, Eighteen Years after the Decision: A Monograph," School of Advanced Military Studies, United States Army Command and General Staff College, Fort Leavenworth, KS, Second Term AY 00–01, 3.

6. Maurer Mauer, *Aviation in the U.S. Army, 1919–1939* (Washington, DC: Office of Air Force History, US Air Force, 1987), xix–xxii.

7. Robert Mueller, *Air Force Bases,* vol. 1, *Active Air Force Bases within the United States of America on 17 September 1982* (Washington, DC: Office of Air Force History, US Air Force, 1982), 375, 378.

8. Mauer, *Aviation in the U.S. Army, 1919–1939,* 131–34; Mueller, *Air Force Bases,* 1:378.

9. Mauer, *Aviation in the U.S. Army, 1919–1939,* 90, 136–38; Mueller, *Air Force Bases,* 1:378.

10. Mauer, *Aviation in the U.S. Army,* 1919–1939, 70–74, 191, 196–97.

11. Ibid., 196–202.

12. Mueller, *Air Force Bases,* 1:378.

13. William A. Goss, "Origins of the Army Air Forces," in *Men and Planes,* vol. 6 of *The Army Air Forces in World War II,* ed. Wesley Frank Craven and James Lea Cate (1955; repr., Washington, DC: Office of Air Force History, 1983), 8–19.

14. Mueller, *Air Force Bases,* 1:378; Goss, "Origins of the Army Air Forces," 19–27; JRP Historical Consulting Services, "California Historic Military Buildings and Structures Inventory," vol. 2, "History and Historic Resources of the Military in California, 1769 to 1989," (prepared for US Army Corps of Engineers, 2000), 5–14.

15. Mueller, *Air Force Bases,* 1:378; "B-25," *The Simon and Schuster Encyclopedia of World War II,* ed. Thomas Parrish (New York: Simon and Schuster, 1978), 42–43.

16. Mueller, *Air Force Bases,* 1:378.

17. Frank H. Heck, "Traffic Homeward Bound," in *Services around the World,* vol. 7 of *The Army Air Forces in World War II,* ed. Wesley Frank Craven and James Lea Cate (1955; repr., Washington, DC: Office of Air Force History, 1983), 197–198, 226; "B-29," *Simon and Schuster Encyclopedia,* 41.

18. "The Mather AFB 'Incident,'" *Manhattan Project Heritage Preservation Association Homepage,* accessed May 10, 2010, http://www.mphpa.org/classic/CG/CG_09A.htm.

19. Heck, "Traffic Homeward Bound," 226.

20. National Security Act of 1947, 61 Stat. 495, Public Law 80–253, July 26, 1947; Mueller, *Air Force Bases,* 1:375, 378.

21. Lt. Gen. C. A. Spaatz, CG AAT, to CG SAC, Subj: Interim Mission, Mar. 12, 1946, in Hq Continental Air Forces, Organization and Missions, Hq Continental Air Forces, Dec. 15, 1937–Mar. 21, 1946, Doc. 59, AFHRA 415.01, quoted in Walton S. Moody, *Building a Strategic Air Force* (Bolling AFB, Washington, DC: Air Force History and Museums Program, 1995), 66.

22. JRP Historical Consulting Services, "Historic Context: Themes, Property Types, and Registration Requirements," vol. 3, "California Historic Military Buildings and Structures Inventory" (prepared for US Army Corps of Engineers, 2000), 8–29; Mueller, *Air Force Bases,* 1:378.

23. Charles A. Revenstein, *Air Force Combat Wings: Lineage and Honors Histories, 1947–1977* (Washington, DC: Office of Air Force History, US Air Force, 1984), 170–71; California State Military Museum, "Known Units at Mather Field," accessed Mar. 12, 2010, http://www. militarymuseum.org/MatherAFB.html.

24. Defense Base Closure and Realignment Commission, "2005 Final Report to the President"; GlobalSecurity.org, "Mather Army Aviation Support Facility (AASF)," http:// www.globalsecurity.org/military/facility/mather.htm.

25. "Mather Air Force Base," Pacific Southwest Superfund Site Overviews, US Environmental Protection Agency, http://yosemite.epa.gov/r9/sfund/r9sfdocw.nsf/bysite/ mather%20air%20force%20base?opendocument.

26. California State Military Department, California State Military Museum, "Historic California Posts: McClellan Air Force Base," accessed June 27, 2011, http://www.militarymuseum.org/McClellanAFB.html.

27. "James Ben Ali Haggin," from *History of Kentucky* (Louisville, KY: J. S. Clarke Publishing, 1928), last updated Jan. 20, 2006, http://haggin.org/JBAH_Biography.html.

28. California State Military Department, California State Military Museum, " Historic California Posts: McClellan Air Force Base."

29. Maurice A. Miller, ed., *McClellan Air Force Base, 1936–1982: A Pictorial History* (Sacramento: Office of History, Sacramento Air Logistics Center, McClellan Air Force Base, 1982), 41; Michael P. Malone and Richard W. Etulain, *The American West: A Twentieth-Century History* (Lincoln: University of Nebraska Press, 1989), 107.

30. Miller, *McClellan Air Force Base,* 42; Livingstone Porter, comp., "History of Sacramento Air Service Command" [ca. 1943], 333–34. Copy originally on file at the Office of History, McClellan Air Force Base.

31. Miller, *McClellan Air Force Base,* 43–45; Porter, "History of Sacramento Air Service Command," 348; real property records, Real Property Department, McClellan Air Force Base.

32. Miller, *McClellan Air Force Base,* 47; Porter, "History of Sacramento Air Service Command," 368–69.

33. Porter, "History of Sacramento Air Service Command," 148–49, 169, 348–50, 368–73; Quartermaster Form Q117 and Real Property Cards, stored with the Real Property Department, McClellan Air Force Base, ca. 1995.

34. Miller, *McClellan Air Force Base,* 50–52.

35. Ibid., 53–55, 57–59, 61.

36. Letters can be found at the BRAC Commission website, accessed June 30, 2012, http://www.brac.gov/DocSearch1995.aspx.

37. McClellan Air Force Base data, US Environmental Protection Agency, Superfund Site Information, available at www.epa.gov. See also "McClellan Air Force Base (Groundwater Contamination)," Pacific Southwest Superfund Site Overviews, US Environmental Protection Agency, http://yosemite.epa.gov/r9/sfund/r9sfdocw.nsf/ViewByEPAID/ca4570024337?OpenDocument.

38. JRP Historical Consulting Services, "HABS Documentation for Building 252, McClellan Business Park," 2012.

39. Ron Starbuck, "Sacramento Army Depot History," California State Military Department, California State Military Museum, accessed July 1, 2012, http://www.militarymuseum.org/SacramentoArmyDepot.html.

40. JRP Historical Consulting Services, "California Historic Military Buildings and Structures Inventory," Vol. II, 7–2–7–4, 7–23–7–25.

41. Thomas D. Norris, "The Sacramento Signal Depot during World War II" (unpublished paper, 1980), 3–7.

42. Ibid., 8–12.

43. Starbuck, "Sacramento Army Depot History."

44. Ibid.

45. "Sacramento Army Depot," Pacific Southwest Superfund Site Overviews, US Environmental Protection Agency, accessed June 27, 2011, http://yosemite.epa.gov/r9/sfund/r9sfdocw.nsf/ViewByEPAID/ca0210020780?OpenDocument.

46. Starbuck, "Sacramento Army Depot History."

47. "Walerga Assembly Center," Historical Marker Database, accessed June 28, 2011, http://www.hmdb.org/marker.asp?marker=16850.

48. US Environmental Protection Agency, "Site Summary Sheet for DERP-FUDS Site No. J09CA706300, Camp Kohler," accessed June 28, 2011, http://www.corpsfuds.com/php/siteindex.php?site=J09CA7063&state=California999.

Chapter 11. Recalling Rancho Seco: Voicing a Nuclear Past

This chapter is based in large part on oral history interviews that represent a variety of viewpoints and experiences of the Rancho Seco episode. The interviews were conducted during the spring of 1995 by students enrolled in my graduate oral history seminar at California State University, Sacramento, regarding the shutdown of Rancho Seco Nuclear Generating Station No. 1. I express appreciation to all of the interviewers and narrators for their participation. Thanks also to Terri Castaneda, Patrick Ettinger, and James Shaw for reading and commenting on drafts of this chapter.

1. David Kaplan, interview by Andrew Varga, Apr. 12, 1995, transcript, 9, Department of Special Collections and University Archives, Library, California State University, Sacramento (hereafter, Special Collections, CSUS).

2. Richard A. Ferreira, speech at the annual meeting of the EEI [Edison Electric Institute] Finance Committee, New York City, May 14, 1993, 3.

3. SMUD's service area as of 2011 included a nine-hundred-square-mile service territory encompassing Sacramento County along with small adjoining portions of Placer County and Yolo County.

4. Ruth Sutherland Ward, "... For the People": The Story of the Sacramento Municipal Utility District (Sacramento: Sacramento Municipal Utility District, 1973), 9.

5. Ibid., 13–14.

6. Charles M. Coleman, PG&E of California: The Centennial Story of Pacific Gas and Electric Company, 1852–1952 (New York: McGraw Hill, 1952), 321–22; Ward, "... For the People," 45–46.

7. Ward, "... For the People," 74.

8. George Pavia, interview by Jeff Crawford, May 21, 1995, transcript, 10, Special Collections, CSUS.

9. Ward, "... For the People," 76–80.

10. Ibid., 80.

11. Ed Smeloff and Peter Asmus, Reinventing Electric Utilities: Competition, Citizen Action, and Clean Power (Washington, DC: Island Press, 1997), 28.

12. Pat Macdonald, interview by Rosie Ramirez, May 15, 1995, transcript, 20, Special Collections, CSUS.

13. Ibid., 3–4.

14. Ibid., 6. This shift from antiwar to antinuclear can also be seen with the national organization Mothers for Peace. See Thomas Raymond Wellock, Critical Masses: Opposition to Nuclear Power in California, 1958–1978 (Madison: University of Wisconsin Press, 1998), 154.

15. Homer W. Ibser, interview by Kelly Ann Bitz, Apr. 27, 1995, transcript, 9, 51, Special Collections, CSUS.

16. Homer Ibser, Physics 186 course syllabus, Writing & Correspondence, 1978, Homer W. Ibser Papers, Department of Special Collections and University Archives, Library, California State University, Sacramento (hereafter, Ibser Papers).

17. Macdonald interview, 5.

18. Myra Schimke to John B. Farmakides, Apr. 16, 1973, Ibser Papers.

19. Macdonald interview, 9.

20. Ibid., 12.

21. Kaplan interview, 12.

22. Macdonald interview, 12–15.

23. Thomas Raymond Wellock, Critical Masses: Opposition to Nuclear Power in California, 1958–1978 (Madison: University of Wisconsin Press, 1998), 147–72.

24. "SMUD Official Expects Public Projects to Lift Power Needs," Sacramento Bee, Oct. 25, 1974, B1.

25. John T. Kehoe, interview by James L. Shaw, May 15, 1995, transcript, 6, Special Collections, CSUS.

26. James K. Staley, "Short Circuit Gets Blame for Rancho Seco Shutdown," Sacramento Bee, Mar. 21, 1978.

27. Martha Ann Blackman, interview by Patricia J. Johnson, Apr. 17, 1995, transcript, 17, Special Collections, CSUS.

28. Daniel D. Whitney, interview by Robert Hull, Apr. 12, 1995, transcript, 30, Special Collections, CSUS.

29. The INPO was established in response to the recommendation of the Kemeny Commission, which Pres. Jimmy Carter established to investigate the Three Mile Island nuclear power plant accident.

30. Smeloff and Asmus, *Reinventing Electric Utilities*, 29.

31. Ibid., 29.

32. Blackman interview, 2, 4.

33. Ibid., 10–11.

34. Ibid., 9.

35. Ibid., 11.

36. Edward Smeloff Jr., interview by Tracey Panek, Apr. 8, 1995, transcript, 28, Special Collections, CSUS.

37. Mark Glover, "No Quick End Seen to Hefty SMUD Hikes," *Sacramento Bee*, Aug. 25, 1985, B2. See also "SMUD Rates: Up 14% and Rising" (editorial), *Sacramento Bee*, Jan. 24, 1985.

38. Smeloff and Asmus, *Reinventing Electric Utilities*, 25.

39. Ibid., 25–27.

40. US Nuclear Regulatory Commission Resolution of Generic Safety Issues, Issue 127: Maintenance and Testing of Manual Valves in Safety-Related Systems (NUREG-0933, Main Report with Supplements 1–33).

41. Kehoe interview, 17.

42. Deborah Blum, interview by R. Meta Bunse, Apr. 26, 1995, transcript, 7, Special Collections, CSUS.

43. Deborah Blum, "One Switch Knocked Out Rancho Seco," *Sacramento Bee*, Jan. 19, 1986, 1.

44. Smeloff and Asmus, *Reinventing Electric Utilities*, 27.

45. Blum interview, 16.

46. Ibid., 21.

47. Ibid., 27–28.

48. Smeloff and Asmus, *Reinventing Electric Utilities*, 27.

49. Blackman interview, 21–22.

50. Ibid., 22–23.

51. Smeloff and Asmus, *Reinventing Electric Utilities*, 31.

52. Blackman interview, 26.

53. Gary Sprung, interview by Morgan P. Yates, May 26, 1995, transcript, 28, Special Collections, CSUS.

54. Michael Remy, interview by Natalie Thompson, May 22, 1995, transcript, 12, Special Collections, CSUS.

55. Smeloff and Asmus, *Reinventing Electric Utilities*, 33.

56. Anna Antos, interview by Theresa Saputo, May 12, 1995, transcript, 15, Special Collections, CSUS.

57. Madlyne A. MacDonald, interview by Robert E. Hull, Apr. 17, 1995, transcript, 25, Special Collections, CSUS.

58. Ibid., 26.

59. Richard A. Clarke to President [Cliff Wilcox], SMUD, Sept. 3, 1987, Special Collections, CSUS.

60. Smeloff and Asmus, *Reinventing Electric Utilities*, 33–35.

61. Smeloff interview, 46.

62. Ibid., 64.

63. Smeloff and Asmus, *Reinventing Electric Utilities,* 37.

64. Leon Grossheim, interview by Jenan Shabbas, Apr. 14, 1995, transcript, 9, Special Collections, CSUS.

65. Smeloff and Asmus, *Reinventing Electric Utilities,* 39.

66. Ibid., 39–41.

67. "Seco Backers, Foes Raising War Chests," *Sacramento Bee,* Apr. 10, 1988, B1.

68. Macdonald interview, 33.

69. Blackman interview, 37.

70. Remy interview, 28–29.

71. Ibid., 33.

72. Smeloff and Asmus, *Reinventing Electric Utilities,* 41.

73. Ibid., 41–42.

74. Ibid., 42–43.

75. Ibid., 43; Ferreira speech at the annual meeting of the EEI Finance Committee, 12.

76. Richard P. Oubre, interview by James Shaw, Aug. 14, 1995, transcript, 28, Special Collections, CSUS.

77. Ibid., 29.

78. Ibid., 17.

79. Smeloff and Asmus, *Reinventing Electric Utilities,* 44.

80. Remy interview, 21–22.

81. Smeloff and Asmus, *Reinventing Electric Utilities,* 45–46.

82. Remy interview, 28.

83. Grossheim interview, 18.

84. Wendy Reid, interview by Robert Hull, Apr. 4, 1995, transcript, 22, Special Collections, CSUS.

85. Smeloff and Asmus, *Reinventing Electric Utilities,* 46.

86. Ibid., 47–48.

87. Illa Collin, interview by Loorie Toohey, Mar. 30, 1995, transcript, 24, Special Collections, CSUS.

88. Blackman interview, 39–40.

89. Terry Dunden, interview by Carl Schmid III, May 5, 1995, transcript, 12, Special Collections, CSUS.

90. Pavia interview, 6.

91. Robert Nash, interview by Robert Miller, Apr. 19, 1995, transcript, 33, Special Collections, CSUS.

92. Antos interview, 32.

93. Collin interview, 10.

94. Keith Hartley, interview by Amanda Meeker, Apr. 26, 1995, transcript, 23, Special Collections, CSUS.

95. Ibid., 27.

96. Oubre interview, 73.

97. Smeloff interview, 78.

98. Ferreira speech at the annual meeting of the EEI Finance Committee, 16.

1. US Bureau of Reclamation, "Natural Run-off of Central Valley Streams (1904–1943 Average), Table 1," in *Central Valley Basin: A Comprehensive Departmental Report on the Development of the Water and Related Resources of the Central Valley Basin, and Comments from the State of California and Federal Agencies, 81st Cong., 1st sess. S. Doc. 113* (Washington, DC: Government Printing Office, 1949), 100.

2. For example, the river's elevation immediately downstream of the Hazel Avenue Bridge is 80 feet above mean sea level and the high point in the Curragh Downs subdivision atop the north bank bluff is 170 feet higher. See the topographical map, USGS Folsom Quadrangle, 7.5 Minute Series (Topographical), N3837.5—W121107.5/7.5 (1967; photorevised 1980).

3. See Job 1:21.

4. John Wesley Powell, "The Laws of Hydraulic Degradation," *Science* 12, no. 302 (Nov. 16, 1888): 229.

5. Erwin Gudde attributes first use of "Great Valley" to describe the valley formed by the Sacramento and San Joaquin Rivers to Lansford Hastings in his *Emigrants' Guide to Oregon and California* (1845). See Erwin Gudde, *California Place Names: The Origin and Etymology of Current Geographical Names*, 4th ed., rev. and enl. William Bright (Berkeley: University of California Press, 1998), *s.v.* "Great."

6. Grove Karl Gilbert, *Hydraulic-Mining Débris in the Sierra Nevada*, Professional Paper 105 (Washington, DC: US Geological Survey, 1917), 35.

7. On the floods, see Leon Hunsaker, "Dr. Snell's Precipitation Measurements of December 1861–January 1862 Floods Are Valid" (paper presented at the California Extreme Precipitation Symposium, University of California, Davis, June 23, 2010). On the debris and its source, see Jeffrey F. Mount, *California Rivers and Streams: The Conflict between Fluvial Process and Land Use* (Berkeley: University of California Press, 1995), 205–6.

8. To understand a flow specified in cubic feet per second (ft³/sec), visualize a torrent of regulation-sized basketballs. Each basketball nestled between all the others occupies mighty close to one cubic foot. A flow of five cubic feet per second is the equivalent of five basketballs passing by a given point each second. US Geological Service, "USGS 11446500 American River at Fair Oaks CA: Daily Mean Discharge in ft³/sec," accessed July 18, 2011, http://waterdata.usgs.gov/nwis/dv?cb_00060=on&format=html&begin_date=1904–10–01&end_date=2011–07–18&site_no=11446500&referred_module=sw.

9. Charles M. Goethe (1875–1966), a successful banker and subdivider in addition to generous philanthropist in Sacramento, has, because of his close ties to the eugenics movement, endured a rash of political rectitude–fueled scouring of his name from various sites. It is now gone from his former T Street home (now renamed the Julia Morgan House for its architect), from the streamside facilities in the parkway, and even from the arboretum on the campus of California State University, Sacramento. See Tony Platt, "Curious Historical Bedfellows: Sac State and Its Racist Benefactor—After Receiving Honors Aplenty from University, C. M. Goethe Left Most of His Big Estate to It," *Sacramento Bee*, Feb. 29, 2004, E3; Bill Lindelof, "Old Goethe Signs Replaced at Renamed River Bend Park," *Sacramento Bee*, Aug. 5, 2008.

10. "Picnickers' Surprise Guest at CSUS: A Lion," *Sacramento Bee*, Jan. 2, 1991, B3; "State to Kick Mountain Lion Out of School and Back into Nature," *Sacramento Bee*, Jan. 4, 1991, B4; "The Lion at the Gates," *Sacramento Bee*, May 16, 1992, B6; Kathy Lachenauer, "Captured Mountain Lion May Go Back to Foothills," *Sacramento Bee*, Aug. 23, 1993, B2; Nicole

Williams, "Wildlife—Mountain Lion Sighting Sparks Excitement in West Sacramento," *Sacramento Bee*, July 19, 2009, B1.

11. Riparian community descriptions based upon author's lifetime of visiting and exploring the banks and waters of the American River, bolstered by the Audubon Society Christmas Count, Dec. 26, 2010, http://cbc.audubon.org/cbccurrent/current_table.html; the American River Natural History Association Parkway Wildlife Count, Dec. 4, 2010, http://www.arnha.org/images/ARHNA_Wildlife_Count_2010.pdf; and Eric R. Gerstung's admirable *A Report to the California State Water Resources Control Board on the Fish and Wildlife Resources of the American River to Be Affected by the Auburn Dam and Reservoir and the Folsom South Canal and Measures Proposed to Maintain These Resources* (Sacramento: California Department of Fish and Game, 1971).

12. See, for example, the State Emergency Relief Administration photographs of Sacramento's Hoovervilles, available at http://www.calisphere.universityofcalifornia.edu/browse/azBrowse/Great+Depression,+hooverville.

13. Dale Maharidge and Nancy Weaver, "Capital Cops Roust Homeless: Early-Morning Sweep Infuriates Advocates," *Sacramento Bee*, Apr. 27, 1989, A1; Ilana DeBare and Dale Maharidge, "Council Was Kept in Dark[,] Not Told about Sweeps," *Sacramento Bee*, Apr. 29, 1989, B1; Elizabeth Hume, "Homeless Camper Arrested Again," *Sacramento Bee*, Oct. 31, 2002, B2; Ramon Coronado, "Camper Claims Bias by Sheriff—The Homeless Man Will Ask a Judge to Order That He Be Allowed in a Work Program," *Sacramento Bee*, Dec. 24, 2003, B1; Matt Kawahara, "Homeless—Campers Are Told They Must Find New Home—American River Parkway Residents Worry They Won't Be Able to Locate Shelter," *Sacramento Bee*, Feb. 10, 2011, B1; Carlos Alcala, "Parkway Volunteers Help Clean Up Messes Left by Homeless Campers," *Sacramento Bee*, Mar. 6, 2011, B2. See also Phoebe S. Kropp Young, "Sleeping Outside: The Political Natures of Urban Camping," in *Cities and Nature in the American West*, ed. Char Miller (Reno and Las Vegas: University of Nevada Press, 2010), 171–91.

14. Steven T. Moga, "Marginal Lands and Suburban Nature: Open Space Planning and the Case of the 1893 Boston Metropolitan Parks Plan," *Journal of Planning History* 8, no. 4 (Nov. 2009): 309. See also Frederick Law Olmsted Jr., "Introductory Address on City Planning," in *The Urban Community: Housing and Planning in the Progressive Era*, ed. Roy Lubove (Englewood Cliffs, NJ: Prentice-Hall, 1967), 81–94.

15. Robert Freestone, "Reconciling Beauty and Utility in Early City Planning: The Contribution of John Nolen," *Journal of Urban History* 37, no. 2 (Mar. 2011): 259.

16. John Nolen, "Sacramento California Preliminary Plan: Showing Conditions, Improvements and New Planning of Old City and Annexed Territory" (blueprint, scale 5.25 inches = 1 mile), City of Sacramento Collection, 1978/31/722, Center for Sacramento History, Sacramento. Nolen's "Preliminary Plan" also proposed a dozen new bridges, eight crossing the American and four crossing the Sacramento. The most monumental of his proposals entailed an Eleventh Street Parkway offering an unobstructed view of the state capitol from his proposed Capitol View Bridge.

17. California State Park Commission and Frederick Law Olmsted, "Part II—Review of the Scenic and Recreational Resources of California and of Various Means of Conserving and Utilizing Them, of Which Means State Parks Comprise Only One," in *Report of State Park Survey of California* (Sacramento: California State Printing Office, 1929), 25. Frederick Law Olmsted Jr. (1870–1957) dropped the "Jr." from his name after his father's death in 1903, sowing potential confusion for the unwary, especially inasmuch as both Frederick and Frederick Jr. (Rick) made major contributions as landscape architects and urban planners.

18. California State Park Commission and Frederick Law Olmsted, *General Report on Potential State Park and Recreational Areas* (Sacramento: State Park Commission, 1950).

19. Frederick Law Olmsted, "Report on Advisability of Establishing Parkways along Sacramento River and Its Tributaries Consistent with Chapter 1422, Statutes of 1945, Part I, to December," pp. 2–3, box 1, folder 42, Frederick L. Olmsted Reports 93/138 c, Manuscripts Division, Bancroft Library, University of California, Berkeley (hereafter, Olmsted Reports).

20. Frederick Law Olmsted, "Report on Sacramento River Parkways, Part II, to April [1947]," p. 20, box 1, folder 32, Olmsted Reports 93/138 c.

21. William C. Dillinger, *A History of the Lower American River,* rev. and updated ed. (Carmichael, CA: American River Natural History Association, 1991), 149.

22. Planning Division, California State Parks, "Dedication to Elmer C. Aldrich, 1914–2010," in *Planning Milestones for the Park Units and Major Properties Associated with the California State Parks System, July 1, 2010* (Sacramento: Planning Division, California State Parks, 2010), iii.

23. Elmer Aldrich, "A Long Needed Park System for Sacramento," *The Observer* 2, no. 2 (Mar.–Apr. 1952): 2–3.

24. John Muir, *The Yosemite* (New York: Century, 1912), 121.

25. Sacramento Woman's Council, *A Silhouette of Service* (Sacramento: Printed by News Publishing Company for Sacramento Woman's Council, 1955).

26. See Andrew C. Isenberg, *Mining California: An Ecological History* (New York: Hill and Wang, 2005), 53–74, on city policies and priorities; and Dillinger, *History of the Lower American River,* 113–28, on agricultural development along the lower American floodplain.

27. Quoted in Frederic R. Gunsky, "A Sketch of the Life of Effie Yeaw: The Children, the River, the Trees," *Golden Notes* 36 (May 1990): 11.

28. Among the myriad anecdotes about Effie Yeaw, one of the most telling relates how she, while focused on teaching her charges about the wild communities sharing her revered Deterding Woods, accosted a stranger there and insisted he identify himself and explain why he was trespassing. The stranger was ranch manager Arch MacDonald, son-in-law of landowner Mary Deterding and the author's neighbor at the time.

29. Quoted from the masthead of the Save the American River Association's newsletter, *Riverwatch,* summer 1988.

30. J. Harold Severaid, "A Step by Step Progress Report on the American River Parkway Plan," introductory remarks prepared for delivery as master of ceremonies at the dedication of the Boat Launching Facilities at Discovery Park, May 16, box 12, MSS 1991/02, Joye Harold Severaid Papers, Department of Special Collections and University Archives, Library, California State University, Sacramento.

31. William C. Dillinger, Lucinda Woodward, Jesse M. Smith, Ed Littrell, Felix Smith, and the American River Natural History Association, *The Lower American River: Prehistory to Parkway,* ed. Peter J. Hayes (Carmichael, CA: American River Natural History Association, 2005), 114.

32. Jim Jones, interview by the author, Aug. 22, 2011.

33. Frank Cirill, interview by the author, Aug. 22, 2011.

34. Jones interview.

35. Lyric by Bob McDill and Allen Reynolds from "Catfish John," first performed by Johnny Russell on an RCA single of the same name from 1972; since covered by, among others, the Jerry Garcia Band, Old and In the Way, and Alison Krauss with the Nitty Gritty Dirt Band.

36. US Bureau of Reclamation, "Stream Flow Diagram: Future Conditions of Development, Plate 11," in *Central Valley Basin: A Comprehensive Report on the Development of the Water and Related Resources of the Central Valley Basin for Irrigation, Power Production and Other Beneficial Uses in California, and Comments by the State of California and Federal Agencies,* 81st Cong., 1st sess., S. Doc. 113 (Washington, DC: Government Printing Office, 1949), facing 116.

37. California Water Rights Board, Decision 893, accessed July 18, 2011, http://www.waterboards.ca.gov/waterrights/board_decisions/adopted_orders/decisions/d0850_d0899/wrd893.pdf.

38. Sacramento County Planning Department, Sacramento Planning Department, and California Department of Fish and Game, *Lower American River Waterway Management Plan* (Sacramento: California Department of Fish and Game, 1977), 1-3.

39. Water years 1904–55 total 18,627 days. On 1,859 of those days, the Fair Oaks gauge recorded flows of 217 cubic feet per second or less. See US Geological Service, "USGS 11446500 American River at Fair Oaks Ca: Daily Mean Discharge in Ft³/Sec."

40. Eric R. Gerstung, *A Report to the State Water Resources Control Board on the Fish and Wildlife Resources of the American River to Be Affected by the Auburn Dam and Reservoir and the Folsom South Canal and Measures Proposed to Maintain These Resources* (Sacramento: California Department of Fish and Game, 1967).

41. California State Water Resources Control Board, Decision 1356, Order, p. 13, http://www.waterboards.ca.gov/waterrights/board_decisions/adopted_orders/decisions/d1350_d1399/wrd1356.pdf. Order 13, sustaining Decision 1356, may be found at http://www.waterboards.ca.gov/waterrights/board_decisions/adopted_orders/orders/1970/wro70_wrd1356.pdf.

42. Eric R. Gerstung and California Department of Fish and Game, *A Report to the California State Water Resources Control Board on the Fish and Wildlife Resources of the American River to Be Affected by the Auburn Dam and Reservoir and the Folsom South Canal and Measures Proposed to Maintain These Resources* (Sacramento: California Department of Fish and Game, 1971), i.

43. US Bureau of Reclamation, *Lower American River Flows: A Discussion of Alternatives* (Sacramento: US Department of the Interior, Bureau of Reclamation, 1973), 12–13.

44. California State Water Resources Control Board, Decision 1400, 2, http://www.waterboards.ca.gov/waterrights/board_decisions/adopted_orders/decisions/d1400_d1449/wrd1400.pdf.

45. California Water Resources Control Board, Decision 1400, Order, 22–24, http://www.waterboards.ca.gov/waterrights/board_decisions/adopted_orders/orders/1972/wro72_wrd1400.pdf.

46. T. I. Storer, F. P. Cronemiller, E. E. Horn, and B. Glading, "Studies on Valley Quail," in *The San Joaquin Experimental Range,* University of California College of Agriculture, Agricultural Experiment Station Bulletin no. 663 (Berkeley: University of California Press, 1942).

47. Sam Stanton, "Water Releases: Swollen Rivers Entice Paddlers; Kayakers Revel in High Flows; Warning Issued," *Sacramento Bee,* Mar. 3, 2011.

48. US Army Corps of Engineers Sacramento District, US Bureau of Reclamation Mid-Pacific Regional Office, and California Department of Water Resources Central District, "Levees in Study Area, Plate 2," in *Special Study on the Lower American River, California* (Sacramento: Army Corps of Engineers, 1987).

49. Dorsey Griffith, "Broken Dam Thwarts Lake, River Activities—Boaters, Swimmers, Bicyclists Clear Area," *Sacramento Bee,* July 18, 1995, B1; Kimberly A. Moy, "Folsom Dam Gate Fails—Flow Poses No Flood Threat, Officials Reassure Residents," *Sacramento Bee,* July 18,

1995, A1; Nancy Vogel, "Folsom Dam Gate Fails—Lake Level Must Drop 40% before Repairs Can Start," *Sacramento Bee,* July 18, 1995, A1.

50. Peter Schrag, "The Spirit of 13," in *Paradise Lost: California's Experience, America's Future* (Berkeley: University of California Press, 1999), 129–87.

51. Christina Jewett and Phillip Reese, "Melee on River Sparks Talk of Alcohol Ban," *Sacramento Bee,* July 6, 2005, A1.

52. Ed Fletcher, "Holiday Drinking on River Banned," *Sacramento Bee,* Aug. 9, 2006, B2.

53. James C. Mullaney to Sacramento County Planning Commission, Dec. 6, 1967, box 6, MSS 2007/23, Save the American River Association Records, 1965–2002, Special Collections and University Archives, Library, California State University, Sacramento.

54. Charlie Willard, "Give Voters a Say on Rescuing Regional Parks," *Sacramento Bee,* May 21, 2011, A13.

55. Joseph Karkowski Jr., "A Hedonic Pricing Model of the Effect of the American River Parkway on Home Prices in Sacramento County, California, USA" (MA thesis, California State University, Sacramento, 2009), 102.

Chapter 13. Thunder over the Valley: Environmental Politics and Indian Gaming in California

1. Gus Thomson, of the *Auburn (CA) Journal,* interviewed on "Insight: News Network," Capital Public Radio (Sacramento Valley–Tahoe/Reno), Nov. 15, 2011; United Auburn Indian Community (UAIC), accessed May 6, 2011, http://www.auburnrancheria.com. Lincoln, with a 258 percent increase from 2000 to 2006 and two thousand new housing units per month at the peak of the boom, was named by Bloomberg Businessweek in October 2010 as the fastest growing city in California. "Lincoln, California," accessed May 1, 2011, http://en.wikipedia.org/wiki/Lincoln,_California.

2. A total of sixty-five thousand gaming devices are operated by California tribes. "Feb, 15, 2011: Indian Gaming Special Distribution Fund," accessed June 27, 2013, http://www.standupforca.org/reports.

3. California Planning Roundtable, "Tribal Gaming and Community Planning in California: A Primer for Policymakers, the Public and the Press," Oct. 2007, 24, http://cproundtable.org/cprwww/docs/TGnCP.bw.pdf.

4. Ironically, those states with the largest Indian populations enjoy far less gaming wealth than California and Connecticut, which have relatively small Indian populations. California, Florida, and Connecticut, with 3 percent of the Indian population, haul in 44 percent of the national revenue. In 2008, California and Oklahoma together generated 38 percent of the total national Indian gaming revenues; Oklahoma had eighty-two casinos, bringing in $1.2 billion in 2004. Jan Golab, "Indian Casinos Have No Obligation to Share Profits with the Government," in *Indian Gaming,* ed. Stuart Kallen (Detroit: Thomson Gale, 2006), 44; Stephen Magagnini, "The New Chiefs," *Sacramento Bee,* Sept. 2, 2007, http://technews.tmcnet.com/business-video/news/2007/09/02/2904959.htm.

5. Magagnini, "New Chiefs," A1, A20.

6. The Santa Ynez Chumash counted 153 members who received $1 million each from 2000 to 2004. Glenn F. Bunting, "Chumash: Sudden Wealth," *Los Angeles Times,* Dec. 3, 2004, A1, A34–35, reprinted in Kallen, *Indian Gaming,* 28.

7. Quoted in Steven Andrew Light and Kathryn R. L. Rand, *Indian Gaming and Tribal Sovereignty: The Casino Compromise* (Lawrence: University Press of Kansas, 2005), 65; Duane Champagne and Carole Goldberg, "Ramona Redeemed: The Rise of Tribal Political Power in California," *Wicazo Sa Review* 17, no. 1 (2002): 43–63.

8. Magagnini, "New Chiefs."

9. California Planning Roundtable, "Tribal Gaming and Community Planning," 24; Cheryl Schmit, interview by the author, Penryn, CA, June 24, 2011.

10. Donald Barlett and James Steel, "Wheel of Misfortune," *Time*, Dec. 16, 2002, 47; Roger Dunstan and California Research Bureau, *Gambling in California* (Sacramento: California State Law Library, 1997); California Legislative Analyst's Office, "Questions and Answers: California Tribal Casinos," by Elizabeth G. Hill, legislative analyst, Feb. 2007, http://www.lao.ca.gov/2007/tribal_casinos/tribal_casinos_020207.pdf; "The Great California Casino Caper," *Los Angeles Times*, Mar. 11, 2007.

11. Cheryl Schmit, as well as Steven Light and Kathryn R. L. Rand of the Institute for the Study of Tribal Gaming, Law, and Policy, University of North Dakota, share this view.

12. There were 150 rancherias in Chumash territory alone. John Johnson, e-mail to the author, July 17, 2011. Within the linguistic grouping labeled as "Pomo" on maps reconstructing pre-contact native culture, Pomo territory had 80 autonomous "tribelets" or "miniature tribes," as anthropologist Alfred Kroeber has called them, with 125 to 1,500 persons each. "The Nature of Land-Holding Groups in Aboriginal California," *University of California Archaeological Survey Reports* 56, no. 1 (1954).

13. Fifty-four of California's fifty-nine rancherias came under federal trust protection as "federal fee lands" from 1906 to 1934; some were deeded to individuals (possibly Indian homesteads with trust protection) or a specific band; forty-one or forty-two of these were terminated after 1958; federal status was subsequently restored to all but four.

14. The word *rancheria*, as used by ethnographers, referenced the independent territorial unit owned by different lineages and clans, and it later referred to post-contact reconsolidated Indian communities. However, it is used here in a more narrow sense to refer to the landless northern California groups who received federal protection in the northern part of the state after 1900.

15. T. Thorne and Heather Daly, "William Pablo: Man of Malki" (unpublished ms., 2010); Tanis C. Thorne, *The Campoodie of Nevada City: The Story of a Rancheria* (Sanssouci Publications, 2000); Dan Baumgart, "Will the One True Indigenous Tribe of Nevada County Please Stand Up?," *Indian Country Today*, Aug. 1, 2011, http://indiancountrytodaymedianetwork.com/2011/08/will-the-one-true-indigenous-tribe-of-nevada-county-please-stand-up/.

16. See, for example, Jessica Cattelino, *High Stakes: Florida Seminole Gaming and Sovereignty* (Durham: Duke University Press, 2008).

17. California Legislative Analyst's Office, "Questions and Answers"; *San Diego Union-Tribune*, June 28, 2007. For an excellent synoptic map, "The Location of Indian Casinos Operating Class III Gaming Devices in California," see "Feb. 15, 2011: Indian Gaming Special Distribution Fund," fig. 2, at www.standupca.org/reports.

18. See, for example, Florence Shipek, *Pushed into the Rocks: Southern California Indian Land Tenure, 1769–1986* (Lincoln: University of Nebraska Press, 1987); Richard Carrico, *Strangers in a Stolen Land: Indians of San Diego County from Prehistory to the New Deal* (San Diego, CA: Sunbelt Publications, 2008); Tanis C. Thorne, "The Death of Agent Stanley and the Cahuilla Uprising of 1907–1912," *Journal of California and Great Basin Anthropology* 24, no. 2 (2004): 233–58; Tanis C. Thorne, "On the Fault Line: Political Violence at Campo Fiesta, 1927, and National Reform in Indian Policy," *Journal of California and Great Basin Anthropology* 21, no. 2 (1999): 182–212; and Tanis C. Thorne, *El Capitan: Adaptation and Agency on a Southern California Indian Reservation, 1850 to 1937* (Banning, CA: Malki-Ballena Press, 2012).

19. Anthony Pico, interview by author, Viejas Reservation, Sept. 21, 2011.

20. California Planning Roundtable, "Tribal Gaming and Community Planning," 5. A full exposition of the various contests is impossible here, but the ongoing *Amador County v. Salazar* is a key case, challenging as it does the federal government's approval of a casino for the Buena Vista Me-Wuk (near Ione) when the local population opposes it. Restored to federal status in 1985, the Buena Vista Rancheria was still trying to open a casino after a ten-year legal battle. See "Ione Band of Miwok Indians Seek Casino near Plymouth," *500 Nations*, Feb. 20, 2009, http://500nations.com/news/California/20090220.asp. *Carcieri v. Salazar* (2009) is another key case, because the decision stated that land cannot be taken into trust for a tribe if it did not have federal trust acknowledgment by 1934. Citizens groups in Contra Costa, Napa, Sonoma, and Santa Barbara Counties are contesting casino development, the legitimacy of recognized groups as Indians, and expansion of existing tribes' trust land.

21. The Santa Ynez Chumash casino folded twice before 1999; Barona's casino closed three times from 1988 to 1991. *Barona Group of Capitan Grande Band of Mission Indians v. Duffy* (694 F.2d 1185); Jackson Rancheria, accessed June 10, 2011, www.jacksoncasino.com/tribal/history.asp.

22. The "Section 20 concurrence" rule of IGRA states that, if the state governor concurred with the secretary of the interior that it is in the best interests of the tribe and not detrimental to the local community, a casino was permissible. Trust lands need to be either contiguous or within the tribe's last recognized reservation. California Planning Roundtable, "Tribal Gaming and Community Planning," 5–6.

23. Bunting, "Chumash," 33.

24. Dunstan and California Research Bureau, *Gambling in California*, V-9.

25. Per capita distributions of gaming profits at Barona reached forty-five hundred dollars per month by the late 1990s. Joseph G. Jorgensen, "Gaming and Recent American Indian Economic Development," *American Indian Culture and Research Journal* 22, no. 3 (1998): 157–72.

26. Jorgensen, "Gaming and Recent American Indian Economic Development." IGRA wisely limited the time period for non-Indian investors to have a controlling share of profits. Outside firms can invest and even manage casinos but cannot have more than 30 percent of profits for the first five years. California Indians gradually began absorbing the lion's share of profits for their memberships. One estimate was that 65 to 85 percent of the revenues went to management companies in the 1990s. Dunstan and California Research Bureau, *Gambling in California*, IV-1.

27. Schmit interview. Indians nationally were facing in the late 1990s what one scholar says was the "most direct assault on their sovereignty" since the termination era. W. Dale Mason, *Indian Gaming: Tribal Sovereignty and American Politics* (Norman: University of Oklahoma Press, 2000), 254. This new assault was a two-tiered ranking system in which only higher ranking tribes would have full recognition of sovereign rights. The Federally Recognized Indian Tribe List Act of 1994 did away with that distinction in California, and legal challenges in the courts have not been successful to date. Allogan Slagle, "Unfinished Justice: Completing the Restoration and Acknowledgment of California Indian Tribes," *American Indian Quarterly* 13, no. 4 (fall 1989): 325–36.

28. Dunstan and California Research Bureau, *Gambling in California;* California Planning Roundtable, "Tribal Gaming and Community Planning." In *Rumsey Indian Rancheria of Wintun v. Wilson*, the right to operate slots was rejected by the federal court.

29. Michael Lombardi, "History of California Gaming: The Long Road Travelled,"

accessed Aug. 5, 2011, at www.cniga.com; California Tribal-State Gambling Compacts, 1998–2006, California Research Bureau (Feb. 2007), 19, California State Association of Counties, accessed Aug. 4, 2011, www.csac.counties.org/default.asp?id=297.

30. Lombardi, "History of California Gaming"; R. Ranat, "Tribal-State Compacts: Legitimate or Illegal Taxation on Indian Gaming in California, *Whittier Law Review* 26 (spring 2005): 955. Light and Rand, *Indian Gaming,* also agree on these propositions as historical markers.

31. Pico interview.

32. The potential ceiling in total number of slot machines was debated; 58,100 were in operation by 2004; not all those with compacts had operational casinos. In 1999, fifty-seven tribes signed compacts (eight of these were subsequently renegotiated); from 2000 to 2003, three more compacts were ratified, with La Posta, Santa Ysabel, and Torres-Martinez. California Planning Roundtable, "Tribal Gaming and Community Planning," 5. The Revenue Sharing Trust Fund delivers $1.1 million a year in quarterly payments to each California nongaming tribe, with the state picking up the large shortfall (the lion's share). The compacts of 1999 provided for payment based on a sliding scale according to the number of slot machines operative: for 350 to 750 machines, $900 per machine per year; 750 to 1250 slots, $1,950 per machine; 1,250 to 2,000 (maximum), $350 per year per machine. Light and Rand, *Indian Gaming,* 70. Most money collected by the state for the Special Distribution Fund comes from Riverside County tribes, which require that the money in the fund (42 percent from 2003 to 2006) be returned to that county; hence, the other counties receive negligible amounts in terms of offsets. *San Diego Union-Tribune,* Apr. 2, 2006. The Coyote Valley Band of Pomo Indians operated a casino without having a state compact until 2004. "Pact May Allow First Major Urban Casino," *Los Angeles Times,* Aug. 17, 2004, A17.

33. Cheryl Schmit suspects that the governor and other elected official who received campaign contributions watered down the environmental protections and enforcement mechanisms and that this represents the corrupting influence of "checkbook" politics. Schmit interview; Fred Dickey, "Who's Watching the Casinos?," *Los Angeles Times Magazine,* Feb. 16, 2003. Light and Rand, *Indian Gaming,* argue that tribal conversion of financial power to political power is legitimate.

34. Pico interview.

35. California Tribal-State Gambling Compacts, 1998–2006, accessed Aug. 4, 2011, www. csac.counties.org/default.asp?id=297, 8, 15.

36. Steven Light, Kathryn R. L. Rand, and Alan Meister, "Spreading the Wealth: Indian Gaming and Revenue Sharing Agreements," *North Dakota Law Review* 80, no. 4 (2004): 699.

37. Bunting, "Chumash"; Hugo Martin, "Tribe Unveils Its Casino Royale," *Los Angeles Times,* Dec. 10, 2004, B1, 7; Jackson Rancheria website, http://www.jacksoncasino.com/; Stephen Magagnini, "In Colusa, a Tribe Uses Gambling to Reclaim Its Culture," June 8, 2013, http://www.standupca.org/tribes/.

38. Critics called this "cost shifting": county/local taxpayers bear the costs, but the tribe benefits. California State Association of Counties, "CSAC Fact Sheet on Indian Gaming in California" (2003), accessed Aug. 2, 2011, http://www.csac.counties.org/legislation/ indian_gaming/fact_sheet2.pdf.

39. Golab, "Indian Casinos Have No Obligation to Share Profits," 44, 48; *San Francisco Chronicle,* Oct. 24, 2004, E1, E6.

40. Bunting, "Chumash," 37; Eve Darian-Smith, *New Capitalists: Law, Politics, and Identity Surrounding Casino Gaming on Native American Land* (Belmont, CA: Thomson Wadsworth,

2004). The Agua Caliente refused to reveal their campaign contributions until forced to by a court ruling. Michael Garden, "Disclosure Laws Apply to Tribes, Court Rules," *San Diego Union-Tribune,* Dec. 22, 2006.

41. Cheryl Schmit, "Indian Gaming and Community Rights: The California Story," Feb. 2002, excerpt available on the Stand Up for California website, http://www.standupca.org.

42. Twenty acres were put in trust in 1917 and 20 in 1953; all but 2.8 acres were privatized in 1967. The City of Auburn made a failed attempt to annex the lands of the former rancheria in 1989. For legal history, see the UAIC website, http://www.auburnrancheria.com/about/the-history.

43. Magagnini, "New Chiefs," A20.

44. Ibid.; Schmit interview.

45. Schmit interview; Fred Dickey, "Going, Going, Gone: How Gray Davis Gave Up California's Last Chance to Settle Environmental Issues at Indian Casinos," *Los Angeles Times Magazine,* Feb. 29, 2004.

46. UAIC tribal website, www.auburnrancheria.com/about/; Schmit interview; Placer County Board of Supervisors to Department of the Interior, May 16, 2000, www.csac.counties.org/images/public/Advocacy/hlt/ig_mous.pdf.

47. Rodney Campbell, director of development services, City of Lincoln, interview by the author, Lincoln, CA, June 14, 2011.

48. The State of California was second in the nation in its income from gaming. Light and Rand, *Indian Gaming,* 87; Eric Bailey, "Weighing Casino Cash vs. Problems," *Los Angeles Times,* July 7, 2004, B1, B7.

49. Light and Rand, *Indian Gaming,* 16, 64–66. There were 65,000 persons enrolled in the 109 federally recognized tribes in 2011, according to the Inter-Tribal Council of California website, http://www.itccinc.org/index.asp. The state and the federal governments each pay half of the annual $90 million budget for Indian welfare programs administered by Indians.

50. Tim Giago, "Tribes Have Traded Sovereignty Rights for Casino Profits," *Indian Country Today,* Apr. 2003, reprinted in Kallen, *Indian Gaming,* 34.

51. As of early 2007, 67 of 302 or 22 percent of those on the waiting list for federal recognition since the process (federal acknowledgment process or FAP) was established in 1978 were California groups; as of 2013, the number of California groups applying was up to 79, with 10 rejected and 69 currently in process. As of 2007, 23 different tribes were seeking the "after-acquired" trust lands with local community support. California Tribal-State Gaming Compacts, 1998–2006, accessed Aug. 4, 2011, www.csac.counties.org/default.asp?id=297, 25–35.

52. Pico interview.

53. Ibid. The UAIC, Pala, Pauma, and Rumsey also have rights to "unlimited" gaming devices.

54. California Planning Roundtable, "Tribal Gaming and Community Planning," 21. The 2004 compacts required five tribes to finance a $1 billion transportation bond; payments to the state from gaming tribes reached $400 million in 2010. The Rincon tribe wanted to add another nine hundred slot machines to the sixteen hundred it already had, permissible under its early compact; in return, the state demanded $38 million for its general fund. The Rincon tribe successfully appealed to the Ninth US Circuit Court, with the court ruling that the governor could not demand money without offering something in return. Fees paid under the terms of tribal compact were only to be used to mitigate impacts, protect public safety, and to establish a framework of regulations with the tribes. Onell R. Soto, "Court Rules for

Tribes on Profit Sharing," *San Diego Union-Tribune,* Apr. 21, 2010. The Rincon case, in which the state attempted to "tax" slots in play after 2004 to support the general fund, was appealed to the Supreme Court, but the High Court chose not to review the case in June 2011. "Court Deals Victory to Local Tribe," *San Diego Union-Tribune,* June 28, 2011; Schmit interview. *Amador County v. Plymouth* challenged the Department of the Interior's ability to approve Buena Vista Me-Wuk's Flying Cloud Casino. The county's legal challenge failed, but the US Court of Appeals, District of Columbia Circuit, recently revived the lawsuit *Amador County v. Salazar.*

55. California Planning Roundtable, "Tribal Gaming and Community Planning in California," 1, 16, 21.

56. "Feb. 15, 2011: Indian Gaming Special Distribution Fund" report. In 2004, there were two new compacts, with the Coyote Valley and Fort Mojave tribes, and seven amended compacts, with the Pala, Pauma, Rumsey (Yocha Dehe), UAIC, and Viejas (all in June 2004) and the Buena Vista Me-Wuk and Ewiiaapaayp (both in August 2004). California Planning Roundtable, "Tribal Gaming and Community Planning in California," 1, 13, 15, 20.

57. Chet Barfield, "Viejas to Pay for Casino Addition's Traffic Impacts," *San Diego Union-Tribune,* Dec. 8, 2005. An environmental review was required before casino expansion. The Viejas plan to build an $800 million casino-hotel, the most expensive in the state, and to buy water from northern California was tabled because of the recession. *San Diego Union-Tribune,* Aug. 24, 2007. Viejas has been making $210 million or more a year and contributed $19.1 million to politicians between 1999 and 2007.

58. Pico interview.

59. California Legislative Analyst's Office, "Questions and Answers," 15. Exec. Order No. 13,352, Aug. 26, 2004, promoted collaboration among local, state, and federal governments.

60. California Planning Roundtable, "Tribal Gaming and Community Planning in California," 15; Magagnini, "New Chiefs."

61. The MOU dealing with the wastewater treatment and "contributions" to the public library is on file at the City of Lincoln clerk's office. Contingencies like the negotiations over wastewater treatment delayed the opening of the Thunder Valley Casino. Campbell interview.

62. A $1.5 billion casino overlooking San Francisco Bay was proposed by the Guidiville Band of Pomo (whose home territory is near Ukiah), which agreed to pay the city of Richmond $20 million annually for twenty years and hire half of the casino workforce locally and thus revitalize a crime-ridden city. Frances Dinkelspiel, "Plan for Casino in Richmond Raises Fears of a Bad Precedent," *New York Times,* Feb. 11, 2010, accessed at http://www.standupca.org/tribes/Guidiville%20Rancheria/plan-for-casino-in-richmond-raises-fears-of-a-bad-precedent?searchterm=Guid.

63. Light and Rand, *Indian Gaming,* 162. See also Matthew Murphy, "Betting the Rancheria: Environmental Protection as a Bargaining Chip under the IGRA," *Boston College Environmental Affairs Law Review* 36, no. 17 (2009): 171–205.

64. In its willingness to consider a casino, the municipality of Barstow offered an $850,000 deal. A third group, the Chemehuevi, opposed the deal because they claimed the region as their ancestral territory and wanted to build a casino in Barstow themselves. Ashley Powers, "Barstow Voters to Place Their Bets," *Los Angeles Times,* June 1, 2006, B4. Big Lagoon dropped out of the application, and Los Coyotes has continued to pursue its quest for a Barstow casino.

65. Dan Morain, "Pact May Allow First Major Urban Casino," *Los Angeles Times,* Aug. 17, 2004, A1, A7; Peter Nicholas, "Gov. Signs Pacts with 5 Tribes," *Los Angeles Times,* Aug. 20, 2004, B1, B7; Dan Morain, "Tribe Scales Back Casino Plan," *Los Angeles Times,* Aug. 23, 2004, B1, B7. Investors in the planned casino at San Pablo included longtime casino developer Jerome Turk, the Rumsey Band of Wintun, the Pala Band of Mission Indians, and Sacramento NBA team owner George Maloof.

66. Schmit interview. It worked out better for Lytton that politics gutted the deal, as Class II gaming met the Lytton Band's goals.

67. "Governor Schwarzenegger Issues Proclamation on Tribal Gaming Policy: Proclamation by the Governor of the State of California," May 18, 2005, accessed at http://www .standupca.org/off-reservation-gaming/Off%20Reservation%20Proclamation-2005.pdf; California Planning Roundtable, "Tribal Gaming and Community Planning in California," 7.

68. John Simerman, "Tribe, Developer, Environmental Groups Announce Major Shoreline Deal," *San Jose Mercury News,* Oct. 20, 2010. The newly elected Richmond city council withdrew its support after voters rejected the tribe's bid for the site in November 2010. On May 11, 2011, the Bureau of Indian Affairs privately told the Guidiville Band and Scotts Valley Band of Pomo that the Obama administration would approve their casino projects, but neither application was approved. Unlike the Guidiville proposal, the Scotts Valley casino project in Richmond is on unincorporated land not subject to city vote. Scotts Valley efforts to build an urban casino have lasted nearly a decade; it is one of four landless tribes restored in 1992 court action.

69. There are two big tribal business groups: the Tribal Alliance of Sovereign Indian Nations (TASIN) and the California Tribal Business Alliance (CTBA); the UAIC opposed the southern California compacts made in 2007.

70. Schmit interview.

71. "The Great California Casino Caper," *Los Angeles Times,* Mar. 11, 2007 (quotes). A suspicious aspect of the compact ratification process was that the agreements were "lost" when they were sent to the Department of the Interior (DOI); because they were not officially rejected during a predetermined time period, they received federal approval automatically. After this mistake, the DOI announced new guidelines on January 14, 2008. Schmit interview. Schmit claims the southern California tribes "built out" their gaming operations before 2007 so that they would not be subject to mitigations after their compacts were amended. Magagnini, "New Chiefs"; Michael Hiltzik, "State Holds Valuable Cards in Its Fight for a Bigger Share of Casino Money," *Los Angeles Times,* Jan. 19, 2004, C6, C8. See also *San Diego Union-Tribune* articles on ratification: Dec. 17, 2006; Apr. 2, 20, 2007, June 27, 2007, and Sept. 7, 2007 (on the San Manuel refusal to accept the state assembly's terms), and Dec. 1, 2007. Agua Caliente is now entitled to up to five thousand gaming devices and Morongo, Pechanga, and San Manuel, up to seventy-five hundred.

72. "Governor Signs Compact with Pinoleville Pomo," *Lake County (CA) News,* Aug. 9, 2011; Pinoleville compact, http://gov.ca.gov/docs/Pinoleville_Compact.pdf. Governor Brown also negotiated compacts with the Ramona tribe and Mono of Madera County in 2013.

73. California Legislative Analyst's Office, "Questions and Answers," 15.

74. Applications for section 20 exceptions increased threefold from July 2005 to November 2006. The Stand Up for California website, http://www.standupca.org, has a list of California fee-to-trust applications in process as of August 3, 2010.

75. "Feinstein's New Bill: It's a Travesty," Apr. 13, 2011, http://indiancountrytodaymedianetwork.com/tag/the-tribal-gaming-eligibility-act/. The California state senate approved the first "off-reservation" gaming in Madera County on June 27, 2013. Marc Benjamin, "Madera Casino a Step Closer with State Senate Support," *Fresno Bee,* June 27, 2013.

76. "San Manuel Band of Serrano Indians Gets the Message Out with Television Advertising," *Indian Country Today,* May 13, 2011. Videos and other commercials produced by San Manuel can be downloaded at http://sanmanuel-nsn.gov.

Chapter 14. The Invention of Old Sacramento: A Past for the Future

1. Andrew Hurley, *Beyond Preservation: Using Public History to Revitalize Inner Cities* (Philadelphia: Temple University Press, 2010), 3.

2. Quoted in ibid., 4.

3. Norman Tyler, *Historic Preservation: An Introduction to Its History, Principles, and Practice* (New York: Norton, 2000).

4. Hurley, *Beyond Preservation,* 9–23; David Hamer, *History in Urban Places: The Historic Districts of the United States* (Columbus: Ohio State University Press, 1998).

5. Richard Trainor, *Flood, Fire, and Blight: A History of Redevelopment in Sacramento* (Sacramento: Sacramento Housing and Redevelopment Agency, 1992), 14.

6. Ibid., 19.

7. *Sacramento Bee,* Nov. 29, 30, 1949, Dec. 1, 2, 3, 4, 5, 1949.

8. California Redevelopment Association, accessed June 27, 2007, http://www.redevelopmentdissolution.lacounty.gov/. The California Redevelopment Act was later renamed the Community Redevelopment Law.

9. California Health and Safety Code, section 33030, accessed Aug. 1, 2011, http://codes.lp.findlaw.com/cacode/HSC/1/d24/1/1/3/s33030.

10. Redevelopment Agency of the City of Sacramento, *Sacramento Redevelopment: The Sacramento of Tomorrow* (Sacramento: Sacramento Redevelopment Agency, ca. 1962), 1.

11. *Sacramento Bee,* Nov. 29, 1949, cited in Brian Roberts, "Redevelopment at the Crossroads: How Sacramento City Chose between Priorities in the 1950s," *Golden Notes* 35, no. 2 (summer 1989): 3.

12. Redevelopment Agency, *Sacramento Redevelopment,* 2.

13. The federal Housing Act of 1949 states, "Title 1. Slum Clearance and Community Development and Redevelopment. This title authorizes the Housing and Home Finance Administrator to make loans and grants to localities to assist locally initiated, locally planned, and locally managed slum clearance and urban redevelopment undertakings. A local public agency would, after public hearing, acquire (through purchase or condemnation) a slum or blighted or deteriorating area selected in accordance with a general city plan for the development of the locality as a whole." Housing Act of 1949, Pub. L. No. 171, 63 Stat. 413, summary accessed Aug. 1, 2011, http://ftp.resource.org/gao.gov/81-171/00002FD7.pdf.

14. City of Sacramento, *Sacramento Urban Redevelopment: Existing Conditions in Blighted Area* (Sacramento: Sacramento Planning Commission, 1950).

15. Redevelopment Agency, *Sacramento Redevelopment,* 2. The federal government's Reorganization Plan No. 3 established the Housing and Home Finance Agency to assist cities and counties with housing and slum clearance projects. Redevelopment Project No. 1 was later enlarged to sixty-two blocks in 1951 and to sixty-five and a quarter blocks in 1958.

16. Paul Stanton Kibel, *Rivertown: Rethinking Urban Rivers* (Cambridge, MA: MIT Press, 2007), 2.

17. Jon C. Teaford, *The Rough Road to Renaissance: Urban Revitalization in America, 1940–1985* (Baltimore: Johns Hopkins University Press, 1990), 17, cited in Kibel, *Rivertown,* 2.

18. Kibel, *Rivertown,* 2.

19. Redevelopment Agency of the City of Sacramento, *Survey of Business in Sacramento's West End,* report by Harold F. Wise (Sacramento: Sacramento Redevelopment Agency, 1951), 6.

20. Ibid., 10.

21. Kenneth T. Jackson, *Crabgrass Frontier: The Suburbanization of the United States* (New York: Oxford University Press, 1985), 208–13; Richard Moe and Carter Wilkie, *Changing Paces: Rebuilding Community in the Age of Sprawl* (New York: Holt, 1997), 50, cited in Kibel, *Rivertown,* 2.

22. What-When-How In Depth Tutorials and Information, "Housing Act of 1954," accessed July 26, 2011, http://what-when-how.com/the-american-economy/housing-act-of-1954/.

23. City of Sacramento, "A Community Plan for the 'Old City,'" Sacramento Planning Commission, 1963, Center for Sacramento History.

24. Ibid.; City of Sacramento, "A Community Plan for the 'Old City,'" Sacramento Planning Commission, 1966. The "Community Plan for the 'Old City'" was again revised and updated in 1964 and 1966.

25. Redevelopment Agency, *Sacramento Redevelopment,* 3–8.

26. Ibid., 11. This innovative type of funding used for the redevelopment agency's projects was a first in the nation for urban renewal projects. "A California constitutional amendment authorizing Tax Increment Financing (TIF) was approved in 1950, and in 1951 the California legislature enacted implementing legislation." TIF, called the "Sacramento Plan," was later adopted by redevelopment agencies in other cities, including Portland, Oregon. "The concept of TIF is simple. Tax revenue generated by the incremental increase in value ('increment') in the renewal area can be used to pay for improvements in the area being renewed. Once an urban renewal boundary is defined, the county assessor 'freezes' the assessed value of real property within the urban renewal district. When property values go up as a result of investment in the area or appreciation, the taxes on the increase in assessed value above the frozen base are used to pay for the improvements in the urban renewal area. . . . In the long term, the increment goes back at full value onto the tax rolls, from which all taxing districts benefit." *Urban Renewal in Oregon: History, Case Studies, Policy Issues, and Latest Developments,* researched and written by Nina Johnson and Jeffrey Tashman for Tashman Johnson LLC, Consultants in Policy, Planning & Project Management, accessed Aug. 1, 2011, http://www.pdc.us/pdf/about/oregon_urban_renewal_history.pdf.

27. Redevelopment Agency, *Sacramento Redevelopment,* 15.

28. Redevelopment Agency of the City of Sacramento, *Urban Renewal Sacramento: A Testament to the Past and a Promise of the Future,* progress report (Sacramento: Sacramento Redevelopment Agency, ca. 1965).

29. Redevelopment Agency, *Sacramento Redevelopment,* 16.

30. Redevelopment Agency of the City of Sacramento, "Redevelopment Plan: Capitol Mall Riverfront Project–Project No. 4 (Calif. R-67)," 1966, 9.

31. "Roads to Somewhere: The Highways That Have Changed America's Social and Economic Face," *The Economist,* June 22, 2006.

32. Frank D. Durkee, testimony before the California Assembly Committee on Natural Resources, Planning, and Public Works, "Transcript of Proceedings: Highway and Freeway

Planning Procedures and Criteria: (Historical Values)," Sacramento, Sept. 29, 1964, 36–37. Frank D. Durkee was a member of the Sacramento Redevelopment Agency and its Old Sacramento Historical Committee, as well as a former employee and representative of the California Division of Highways and the California Highway Commission from 1923 until 1958.

33. Trainor, *Flood, Fire, and Blight*, 41.

34. *Sacramento Bee*, and *Sacramento Union*, Jan. 31, 1961, cited in Trainor, *Flood, Fire, and Blight*, 47.

35. Durkee testimony, 41. The federal highway funds paid 90 percent of costs.

36. The *New York Times* reported on October 15, 1961, that the National Park Service of the Department of the Interior recommended the freeway be taken across the Sacramento River and back again to preserve Old Sacramento. "The cost of the bridges by some estimates would be about $12 million, which is not much more than the $10 million that the United States expects to contribute toward saving ancient monuments in Egypt and the Sudan." Ibid.

37. Trainor, *Flood, Fire, and Blight*, 41.

38. Division of Beaches and Parks, Department of Natural Resources, State of California, *Old Sacramento: A Report on Its Significance to the City, State, and Nation, with Recommendations for the Preservation and Use of Its Principal Historical Structures and Sites, Part I* (Sacramento: Division of Beaches and Parks, 1958), 3. This study included reports issued as Part II, also in 1958, and Part III, in 1960.

39. *Architectural Forum* editorial, quoted in *Reader's Digest*, Dec. 1957; Division of Beaches and Parks, *Old Sacramento, Part I*, 2.

40. Sacramento Historic Landmarks Commission, *Telling the Sacramento Story by the Preservation and Enhancement of Historic Landmarks: A Report of the Ways and Means of Restoring and Preserving Historic Landmarks and Heritage of "Old Sacramento"* (Sacramento: Sacramento Historic Landmarks Commission, May 1960).

41. US Department of the Interior, National Park Service, *Old Sacramento: A Statement of Findings* (Oct. 2, 1961), Center for Sacramento History.

42. Ibid.; John C. Cannon, "Historic Old Sacramento and U.S. Interstate Route 5," *Traffic Quarterly* (July 1965): 407.

43. Candeub, Fleissig & Associates Planning Consultants, "Old Sacramento Historic Area and Riverfront Park: Technical Report Prepared for the Redevelopment Agency of the City of Sacramento," San Francisco, CA, ca. 1964, 2.

44. Ibid., 51.

45. Finding Aid Biography, Aubrey Neasham Collection, Center for Sacramento History.

46. V. Aubrey Neasham, *Old Sacramento: A Reference Point in Time* (Sacramento: published by the Sacramento Historic Landmarks Commission in cooperation with the Redevelopment Agency of the City of Sacramento, 1965), 19.

47. "Death by Nostalgia," *New York Times*, June 10, 2011.

48. *Travel Trade Gazette of the UK and Ireland*, Mar. 18, 2002; Liz Johnston, "This Is Arnie's Kingdom," *Sunday Mail* (Adelaide, Australia), Feb. 4, 2007; Cindy Loose, "Sacramento: The Two Day Tour," *Washington Post*, Oct. 10, 2004.

49. "California: The Ghosts of Old Sacramento," *New Zealand Herald*, Mar. 16, 2008.

50. Sacramento 2030 General Plan, adopted Mar. 3, 2009, available online at http://www.sacgp.org/.

51. *Sacramento Bee*, June 14, 1998.

52. City of Sacramento, Department of Transportation, Engineering Services, "I-5 Riverfront Connection: Project Overview," accessed July 18, 2011, http://www.cityofsacramento.org/transportation/engineering/bridging_I-5/.

53. Ibid.

54. City of Sacramento 2030 General Plan, Historic and Cultural Resources (2009), 2, available online at http://www.sacgp.org/.

55. "Old Sacramento Historic District," National Historic Landmarks Program, accessed July 18, 2011, http://tps.cr.nps.gov/nhl/detail.cfm?ResourceId=124&ResourceType=District.

56. *Sacramento Bee,* June 3, 1999.

57. *Sacramento Bee,* June 27, 2000.

58. "Old Sacramento Underground: Get the Low Down," Official Souvenir Guide, Historic Old Sacramento Foundation, 2010.

59. Old Sacramento State Historic Park General Plan Draft Preferred Alternative, Apr. 20, 2011, http://www.parks.ca.gov/?page_id=26346.

60. Ibid.

61. Walter Frame, testimony before the California Assembly Committee on Natural Resources, Planning, and Public Works, "Transcript of Proceedings: Highway and Freeway Planning Procedures and Criteria: (Historical Values)," Sacramento, Sept. 29, 1964, 62.

62. Thomas Frye, "Everyone Applauds Preservation—But Something's Missing," *Museum of California* (Oakland), July 1977, 10–11.

Epilogue

1. J. S. Holliday, *The World Rushed In: The California Gold Rush Experience* (New York: Simon and Schuster, 1981).

2. William Preston, "Serpent in the Garden: Environmental Change in Colonial California," *California History* 76, no. 2–3 (summer–fall, 1997): 260–98. Steven Hackel presents a similar argument related to what he terms the "dual revolutions," "ecological change and demographic collapse," in *Children of Coyote, Missionaries of Saint Francis: Indian Spanish Relations in Colonial California, 1769–1850* (Chapel Hill: University of North Carolina Press, 2005).

3. For information on Mexican attitudes toward Indians in the California interior, see David J. Weber, *The Mexican Frontier, 1821–1846* (Albuquerque: University of New Mexico Press, 1982), and Robert F. Heizer and Alan F. Almquist, *The Other Californians: Prejudice and Discrimination under Spain, Mexico, and the United States to 1920* (Berkeley: University of California Press, 1971).

4. George Harwood Phillips, *Indians and Intruders in Central California, 1769–1849* (Norman: University of Oklahoma Press, 1993). Although Phillips's work deals primarily with Indian groups in the southern San Joaquin Valley, some of the general patterns he describes relate to the Sacramento Valley mission hinterlands, especially in the chapter on foreign infiltration. Ibid., 117–34.

5. M. Kat Anderson, *Tending the Wild: Native American Knowledge and the Management of California's Natural Resources* (Berkeley: University of California Press, 2005).

6. Quoted in Albert L. Hurtado, *John Sutter: A Life on the American Frontier* (Norman: University of Oklahoma Press, 2006), 112.

7. See Gerald Haslam, *The Other California: The Great Central Valley in Life and Letters* (Reno: University of Nevada Press, 1990); and Gerald Haslam, *Haslam's Valley* (Berkeley, CA: Heyday Books/Great Valley Books, 2005).

8. Such text has been presented in printed and online promotional materials. See, e.g., http://www.sacramento365.com/event/detail/441779347/Gold_Rush_Days.

9. Pratap Chatterjeem, *Gold, Greed and Genocide: Unmasking the Myth of the '49ers* (Berkeley, CA: Project Underground, 1998).

CONTRIBUTORS

Steven M. Avella is a professor of history at Marquette University in Milwaukee, Wisconsin. He is the author of two books on Sacramento: *Sacramento: Indomitable City* (Arcadia, 2003) and *Sacramento and the Catholic Church* (University of Nevada Press, 2008). He has completed a biography of Sacramento Bee editor and publisher C. K. McClatchy.

Gray Brechin, a historical geographer, is a visiting scholar in the Department of Geography at the University of California, Berkeley. He is the author of *Imperial San Francisco: Urban Power, Earthly Ruin* and a collaborator with photographer Robert Dawson on *Farewell, Promised Land: Waking from the California Dream.* He is founder and project scholar of California's Living New Deal Project. His chief interests are the state of California, the environmental impact of cities upon their hinterlands, and the invisible landscape of New Deal public works.

Anthony E. Carlson holds a PhD in environmental history from the University of Oklahoma. He is the author of several articles and chapters on national and transnational water policy. He currently serves as a Department of Defense historian at Fort Leavenworth, Kansas.

Christopher J. Castaneda is professor of history at California State University, Sacramento. He has served as director of the Oral History of the Houston Economy project and coordinator of the Sacramento State Oral History Program. He has written extensively on the history of the energy industry and energy regulatory policy and is the author of *Gas Pipelines and the Emergence of America's Regulatory State* (1996, 2002), *Invisible Fuel: Manufactured and Natural Gas in America, 1800–2000* (1999), and "Natural Disasters in the Making: Fossil Fuels, Humanity, and the Environment," in the *OAH Magazine of History* (2011).

Nathan Hallam is a PhD candidate in Public History at Arizona State University. His research focuses on urban history and local history in the U.S. West. He has worked in the field of historic preservation in Northern California and Central Arizona and currently serves as the coordinator of the North Central Information Center in Sacramento.

Rand Herbert has been a researcher, writer, and project manager for more than thirty-five years. As a consulting historian, he has worked on projects for federal, state, and local agencies and private businesses, and he has provided expert witness services and testimony in trials or administrative proceedings. He earned his MAT in history from the University of California, Davis, and his BA in history from the University of California, Berkeley.

Throughout his three score and seven years, three things have commandeered the lion's share of **Alfred E. Holland, Jr.'s** professional attention: flowing rivers, trees, and teaching. He floats every river he can, whether placid or tumultuous. He remains grateful for the trees' contribution to the twenty-year privilege of making fine hardwood furniture. But teaching about humankind and its past is the best job anyone ever had.

Todd Holmes received his PhD in history from Yale University in 2013 and is a postdoctoral fellow with the Bill Lane Center for the American West at Stanford University. A native of Sacramento and alumnus of California State University, Sacramento, he is the author of numerous articles on California agricultural, business, and political history. He is finishing a book manuscript on the corporate West and the rise of Reaganism in American politics.

Albert L. Hurtado, now retired, held the Travis Chair in Modern American History at the University of Oklahoma, where he taught courses on the American West and native American history. His books and articles on these subjects have won awards, including the Billington Prize for *Indian Survival on the California Frontier* (1988), the Neuerburg Award for *Intimate Frontiers: Sex, Gender and Culture in Old California* (1999), and the Caughey Prize for *John Sutter: A Life on the North American Frontier* (2006). Professor Hurtado's most recent book is *Herbert Eugene Bolton: Historian of the American Borderlands.* Hurtado lives in Folsom, California.

Richard J. Orsi, professor emeritus of history, California State University, East Bay, specializes in western America and California, with emphasis on social, economic, and environmental development. He is the author of *Sunset Limited: The Southern Pacific Railroad and the Development of the American West* (University of California Press, 2005) and coauthor of four editions of *The Elusive Eden: A New History of California* (McGraw-Hill, 1987–2012). He also is a former editor of *California History,* the quarterly journal of the California Historical Society.

Kenneth N. Owens, a native of the Pacific Northwest, is professor emeritus of western history at California State University, Sacramento. He was the founder of the Capital Campus Public History Program, and he has published extensively on northern California during the gold rush era.

Lisa C. Prince has worked as an independent historical consultant, oral historian, archivist, and curator. She is currently a lecturer in the Department of History at California State University, Sacramento. She is the author of "Community Life: Adaptive and Culturally Diverse," in *Old Sacramento and Downtown;* "The Colonials," in *Sacramento's Elmhurst, Tahoe Park and Colonial Heights;* and "James Purcell, Mitsuye Endo, and Constitutional Challenge, 1942–1944." She has curated several exhibits on California and Sacramento history.

Paul J. P. Sandul is an assistant professor of history at Stephen F. Austin State University. The author of previous publications on suburbs, culture, and memory, he has a new book, tentatively titled *Harvesting Suburbs, Cultivating Memory: Legacies of Rural and Urban Land Boosterism in California,* scheduled for publication by West Virginia University Press in 2014. He is also a coeditor and contributor for a new anthology, tentatively titled *Making Suburbia,* scheduled for publication by the University of Minnesota Press, also in 2014.

Lee M. A. Simpson is a professor in the Department of History and director of the General Education Honors Program at California State University, Sacramento. She served as review editor for the *Public Historian* from 2006 to 2012. She is the author of *Selling the City: Women and the California City Growth Game, 1880–1920.* Her current research explores the role of various justices on the Ninth Judicial Circuit Court of Appeals in historic preservation and urban development.

Ty O. Smith is a PhD candidate in the University of California, Santa Barbara, and California State University, Sacramento, joint PhD program in public history. He has worked as the museum services manager of the California State Capitol Museum and currently holds the position of chief of museum interpretation at Hearst San Simeon State Historical Monument. He also serves on the board of directors of the California Mission Studies Association.

Tanis C. Thorne teaches Native American studies courses at the University of California, Irvine. Her publications include *The Many Hands of My Relations* (1996), *The World's Richest Indian* (2003), and *El Capitan: Adaptation and Agency on a Southern California Indian Reservation, 1850–1935* (2012).

David Vaught is department head and professor of history at Texas A&M University. He is the author of four books: *Cultivating California: Growers, Specialty Crops, and Labor, 1875–1920* (1999), *After the Gold Rush: Tarnished Dreams in the Sacramento Valley* (2007), *The Farmers' Game: Baseball in Rural America* (2013)—all published by Johns Hopkins University Press—and *Teaching the Big Class: Advice from a History Colleague* (Bedford/St. Martin's, 2011).

INDEX

Note: Page numbers in italics refer to figures.

Abbott, Carl, 3
acorns, Indians' use of, *19*, 21
agriburbs. *See* suburbs, agricultural
agriculture, 137, 186; development of, 116, 139, 156; effects of Sutter's introduction of, 33; efforts to farm in Putah Sink, 103–4, 115; flood control and, 6; Indians and, 14, 17–19; Indians as Sutter's workforce in, 24, 26; mining and, 36–37, 125, 144–45; Natomas and, 125; railroads' influence on, 47, 96–97; rural roads built by New Deal workers for, 189; Sacramento boosters boasting about, 164, 168–69, 170–71; in Sacramento's development, 30, 59, 314, 318–19; small-scale recommended for suburban homeowners, 164–71; in Sutter's dream of empire, 315, 318; transients seeking work in, 187–88; water policies and, 39, 143, 256–57; wheat, 103, 110, 139
Agua Caliente Indians, 269, 274, 276, 287, 376n40
air defense, cities' promotion of, 195
Aldrich, Elmer, 249, 251
Alkali Flats, 172–73
Alsip, Edwin K., 173
American basin: high grade lifting Sacramento out of, 74; landscape of, 65; Natomas land in, 126, 128–30; Sacramento in, 62, 72, 119
American River, 32; as California Wild and Scenic River, 265; dams taming, 124, 132, 242–43; discovery of gold in, 40; diversion of water from, 219, 256–59; flora and fauna along, 244–47; flow of, 243, 257–61; flow required for fish spawning, 257, 259–61; hydroelectric

plants on, 95, 218, 258; levees on, 56, 66, 72, 81, 120; pollution of, 255–56; recreation on, *256, 260*, 260–61, 264–65; rerouting of, 5, 56, 62, 68, 72–74, *73*, 80–81, 84–85, 121; sediment and debris from, 243–44, 253–55; topography along, 242, 243–44
American River Natural History Association, 245, 263
American River Parkway, *255*; effects on sand and gravel business, 253–55; facilities damaged by flooding, 261–62; land for, 251–53, 255; original proposals for, 247–49; promoters of, 249–51; reduced funding for, 262–63, 265–66; route of, 241–42, *242*; Sacramentans' pride in, 241, 266; varied uses of, 263–64, *264*, 265
Amtrak, using Southern Pacific depot, *99*
Anderson, M. Kat, 315
Andognini, Carl, 232-33
Anthropocene era, 180–81
Arcade Park, 166–67
architecture: to avoid floods, *58*, 58–59; in Fair Oaks' local histories, 179; of McClellan Field buildings, 196; of suburban homes, 175–78
Arden Park Vista, 176–77
Army Corps of Engineers, 132, 143; focus on levees, 131, 140; US Geological Service competing with, 136, 139
Arrowsmith, A. T., *124*
Astor, John Jacob, 14
Atomic Energy Commission, 219–20
Auburn Dam, opposition to, 258
Auburn-Folsom South Unit, of Central Valley Project, 257–59
Auburn Indians, in UAIC, 278

Audubon Society, 245, 250, 252
automobiles, 194; urban planners incorporating, 247, 299–300

B. F. Hastings building, in Old Sacramento, 304–5
Babcock & Wilcox nuclear reactor, 219, 224, 234
Bacon, Augustus O., 150–51
Barden, Mary, 177
Barstow, welcoming Indian gaming, 285, 378n64
Base Realignment and Closure Commission (BRAC), 202, 207, 211, 213–14
Bear River, Natomas dredging, 128
Bechtel Corporation, and Rancho Seco, 219, 234
Beecher, Catherine E., 169
Bell, Theodore A., 141, 145
Benicia, as rival for state capital, 69
Bennett, Ira E., 148–49
Bennett, S. G., 141
Bercut-Richards Cannery, Sacramento Army Depot using, 212–13, 213
Bidwell, John, 26, 29, 53
Bigelow, Hardin, 53, 117–18
Big Lagoon and Los Coyotes communities, 285
Bigler, John, 69
Blackman, Martha Ann, 224–25, 228–29, 232, 236
Blum, Deborah, 226–27
Board of Swampland Commissioners, 120–21
Boggs, Dave, 233
boosters, Sacramento's, 159, 163; as growth machine, 162, 352n16; in suburbanization, 160, 167, 173
BRAC. See Base Realignment and Closure Commission
Brannan, Samuel, 33, 40, 53, 325n4; gold rush and, 40, 44; Sutter and, 63–64, 327n24
Brannan's Addition, to original grid, 64
bridges, 91, 370n16, 382n36. See also Tower Bridges
Bromley, George, 72
brothels, 53, 55, 57
Broward, Napoleon Bonaparte, 149–50
Brown, Jerry, 288
Brown, Melinda, 228
Buonaiuto, Joe, 234
Bureau of Reclamation, 132; proposals to divert American River water, 219, 256–59
Burnett, Peter, 43, 65, 68
business, 277; boosterism by, 57, 165; in

development of Sacramento, 62, 313–14, 318; effects of floods on, 49–50, 66; gold rushers abandoning mining for, 67; influence on routing of Interstate 5, 299–300; merchants as civic leaders, 56; Natomas in, 124, 126; in "preservation for use" model, 303–4; profiting from gold rush, 40, 42, 46–48, 63; railroads and, 90, 93; riverfront and, 40, 292; sand and gravel, 253–55; uses of former military facilities by, 207, 211; in West End/Old Sacramento, 290, 295, 309
Butler, Raymond T., 255
Byrne, Richard, 231, 233

Cabazon Indians, 273–74, 276
Cachil Dehe Wintun Indians, 277
California, 167; fiscal crisis in, 262–63, 281–83; Indian gaming in, 267–68, 272, 273–76, 282; Indians in, 14–15, 268, 270, 275, 282, 377n51; initiative process in, 216, 221, 229; lack of regulation of mining and water, 38–39; market for expanded gaming in, 276; under Mexico, 13, 314; military base closures in, 202; New Deal projects in, 185; population growth in, 48; wheat industry in, 103, 110, 139. See also government, state
California Community Redevelopment Act (1945), 292
California Environmental Quality Act (CEQA), 279, 284
California Indian Gaming Nations Association (CIGNA), 275, 287
California Indian Heritage Center, 318
California Mining Association (CMA), 144–45, 147
California Pacific Railroad, 78
California Rancheria Act of 1958, 271
California Reclamation Board, 123
California Redevelopment Act (1945), 292
California State Military Museum, 214
California State Railroad Museum, 98, 100
California State Water Resources Control Board, 257–58
California Steam Navigation Company, 45, 85, 88
California Supreme Court, on hydraulic mining, 36–37
Calthrope, Peter, 178
Campaign California, 232–35

Campbell, Rodney, 285

Camp Kohler, 200, 210, 214

canals: to divert American River water, 257; drainage, 129–30; in flood control efforts, 108–9, 111–12, 114; for irrigation, 125

Candeub, Fleissig master plan, for redevelopment of West End, 302–3

Cannon, Thomas L., 148

capital, state, 163; Sacramento's advantages as site for, 68–69; Sacramento winning, 57, 68, 120

capitol, state, *126*, 292; city giving land for, 44, 69–70

capitol building plan, 296

Capitol Mall Project, for redevelopment, 297

Capitol Mall Riverfront Project, for redevelopment, 297–99

Capitol Park, 70, 199

Carey, Joseph M., 155

Carey, Ransom S., 106; buying more swamplands, 109–10; efforts to reclaim Putah Sink, 104, 109–15; financial collapse of, 115–16

Carlucci, Frank, 202

Carly, J. C., 175

Carmichael, 166–67, 170

Carmichael, Daniel W., 167

Carson, Kit, 16

casinos, Indian: becoming "destination resorts," 276, 378n57; in California, 267–69; cities welcoming, 285, 378n64; expansion of, 268; jobs in, 276–77; local communities and, 277–78, 280–81, 287, 375n20; locations of, 277–79, 283, 285, 372n4; negotiations in establishing, 269, 286; opposition to, 273, 278, 286, 288, 375n20; profits from, 268–70, 280; slot machines in, 274, 376n32; urban, 286–87. *See also* Indian gaming

Castro, Rick, 222–23

casualties, from floods, 72, 106, 117, 120, 131

Catlin, Amos P., 69, 124

Cattelino, Jessica, 271

Central Pacific Railroad. *See* Southern Pacific Railroad

Central Valley, 119, 189, 314, 318. *See also* Sacramento Valley

Central Valley Project (1930s), 131–32, 257

Cesar Chavez Plaza, 44

Chamberlain, John, 26

Champion, Hale, 294

Chinese: discrimination against, 172, 331n63; neighborhoods of, 55

Chinese Exclusion Act (1882), 55, 172

cholera, 51, 53

Chumash Indians (Santa Ynez Band of Chumash Indians), 269, 274, 276–77

cities, 3; amenities of, 165–66, 171; effects of highways routed through, 299; growth models of, 291; railroads' environmental influences on, 77–80, 89–90, 92–94; relation to hinterlands, 59; rural ideal *vs.*, 159, 177; Sacramento claiming rural virtues compared to other, 162, 180; welcoming Indian gaming, 285, 378n64

Citizens for Affordable Energy, supporting Rancho Seco, 232

Citizens for Safe Energy, 221, 225, 228

Citizens to Stop Rancho Seco, 220–21. *See also* Citizens for Safe Energy

Citrus Heights, 166–68

city council, Sacramento's: early projects of, 56–57; on Old Sacramento, 300–301. *See also* government, city

city planning: altering original grid plan, 62, 69–70; changing visions of Sacramento's future, 308; failings of original grid plan, 43, 69; freeways incorporated into, 296–97; layout and naming of streets, 64; original grid plan for Sacramento, 43, *65*, 296; original proposals for American River Parkway in, 247; Sutter's gift of blocks, 65; for West End redevelopment, 296

Civil Works Administration (CWA), 188

Clark, Champ, 153, 156

Clark, Robert, 69–70

Clarke, James, 150

Clay, Alexander, 150

climate: railroad mitigating effects of, 96–97; Sacramento's boosters boasting about, 6, 163–64, 168, 170; unattractiveness of, 50–51; weather and, 31–32

cold war, Sacramento's military facilities in, 200, 206–7, 211, 213, 215

Collin, Illa, 236, 237

Colonial Heights, 173

community institutions/civic improvement: lack of women and, 52, 55; slow development of, 50

Comprehensive Environmental Response, Compensation, and Liability Act (CERCLA). *See* Superfund sites

Congress, US. *See* government, federal

Coolidge, Calvin, 204

Cortelyou and Harrington, 192–93

county courthouse, 68, *75*

Cowell, Henry, 115–16

Craig, J. L., 153

Crocker, Charles, 53–54, 83

Crocker, E. B., 58, 71

Crocker, Edwin, 83

Crocker, Mary, 52–54

Crocker Art Museum, 58

Cronon, William, 2, 96

Crutzen, Paul J., 180

Cully, Charles, 271

cultural diversity: of immigrants, 47, 54–55; of New Helvetia, 315, 317, 320

Culver, J. Horace, 66

Curry, Charles, 156

Curtis Park, 173

D. O. Mills & Company bank building, *298*

Dabney, T. G., 143

Dalton, Margaret, 273

dams, 253; on American River, 124, 218; for flood control, 131, 261. *See also* specific dams

Dasmann, Raymond F., 161

Davis, Arthur P., 140

Davis, Gray, 275–76, 281

Davis, William Heath, 21–22

Dean, James S., 187, 189

DeCuir, Charles D., 175

Denman, Scott, 234

Department of Agriculture (USDA), 136, 191; Office of Irrigation Investigations (OII) of, 139–40; US Geological Service competing with, 139

Department of Defense (DOD), 202

Department of the Interior, 190; on conversion of trust lands, 279–80, 288–89; on Indian gaming, 284, 379n71. *See also* US Geological Service (USGS)

Deterding, Charles W., 188–89, 361n14

Deterding Woods, 252

Deverell, William, 180

Dickstein, Howard, 278–79

Diggs, Marshall, 167

Discovery Park, 241

diseases: among Indians, 22, 27–28, 37, 270–71, 315; causes of, 41–42, 51, 138; cholera, 51, 53; effects of, 51–53; malaria, 22, 27–28, 41, 51; scurvy, 51–52; spread by rail, 89–90; in West End, 293–94

Downey, Heather, 309

Downey, John, 70

Downing, Andrew Jackson, 169

drainage: in competition for reclamation funding, 146, 148–51, 156; interference with flood-waters', 79, 120; relation to flood control, 152–53

Dreyfus, Al, 256

droughts, 71–72, 85, 107, 243

Dudley, Arthur S., 195–96

Duke Power, and Rancho Seco, 232

Dunden, Terry, 236

Dupuy, Gabriel, 79

Durkee, Frank D., 382n32

Dwyer, W. P., 192

Eagle Theater, 53

East Bay Municipal Utility District, 258

East Sacramento, 173, 175

economy, 308; California's fiscal crisis, 262–63, 281–83; contribution of military facilities to, 215, 363n50; effects of gold rush on California's, 28; of fur trade, 14; Great Depression and, 186–88; importance of Indians' labor in, 14–15; influx of New Deal money into Sacramento's, 188–89; railroads' influence on, 78–79, 88–89; rural *vs.* urban, 4; strategy for closing Rancho Seco based on, 228–29

education: historic preservation and, 303, 309, 317; natural history and, 251–52. *See also* schools

Effie Yeaw Nature Center, 251, 263

Eifler, Mark A., 4, 67

Electric Carnival, *126*

electricity: cost of production, 219; hydroelectric generation of, 95, 125, 218, 251, 258; Natomas's involvement in, 125–26, 133; SMUD wanting

to generate *vs.* distribute, 218. *See also* Rancho
Seco Nuclear Generating Station (RSNGS)
elites, 56; in suburbanization, 167, 175; transience
of, 48–49, 53–54
Elk Grove, 178
Elmets, Doug, 287
Elmhurst, 173
Elverta, 173
Engels, Friedrich, 59
Enterprise Rancheria, 285
Environmental Defense Fund, 258–59
environmental protection, and casinos, 273, 279,
283–88
Environmental Protection Agency (EPA), 208, 211
esplanade, railroads' improvements on, 86–87

Fair Oaks, 166–67, 169, 179, 359n76
Fair Oaks chickens, 246–47
Farmakides, John B., 220
Feather River, 32, 36, 61
Federal Highway Act of 1956, 299
Federal Housing Administration (FHA), 295
Feinstein, Dianne, 286, 289
Ferreira, Richard, 237–38
festivals, in Old Sacramento, 305–6, 319
fires: in development of Sacramento, 50, 53, 304;
Indians' use of, 20; protection from, 56, 191;
Southern Pacific Shops as hazard, 92; US
Army Air Service detecting forest, 203–4
fish: effects of American River flow and, 257–61;
effects of gold mining on, 37; pollution of
American River and, 256
Fisher, Walter L., 153
fishing: in American River, *256*, 257; by Indians,
18, 21
Fishman, Robert, 62
Flint, Frank P., 144, 147–51
flood control, 6; assumed adequate during
droughts, 71–72; city projects for, 56, 62, 120;
cost of, 132; dams in, 131, 261; demand for,
117, 156; effects of, 128, 243, 251; failed efforts
at, 110–11, 114–15, 146; federal responsibility
for, 130–31, 138, 153, 155–57; first levee for, 66;
funding for, 109, 112–14, 148–51; growing interest in large-scale, 123, 128, 151–52; hydraulic
mining and, 123, 155; inadequacy of, 66–67,
72, 123; irrigation *vs.*, 131, 148–51; levees in,

66–67, 81, 140; in multiple-use plans, 152–54,
251; by Natomas Company, *127*, 127–30,
170–71; obstacles to, 80; politics in, 120–21;
public and private collaboration in, 118, 123,
126, 130; for Putah Sink, 107–15, *111*; railroads'
role in, 5, 82, 84–85, 93; Sacramento achieving
some success in, 120–21; in Sacramento Valley,
121; state Board of Swampland Commissioners
planning, 107–8
Flood Control Act (federal, 1917), 130, 156–57
Flood Control Act (federal, 1928), 130, 136
Flood Control Act (federal, 1936), 131
Flood Control Act (state, 1911), 123
floods: 1849-1850, *49*, 49–50, 117, 120; 1850,
66; 1861-1862, 72, 82–83, 84, 106, 120, *121*;
1867-1868, 108; 1904, 143; 1928, 130; 1935, 131;
boat travel during, 44–45; costs of, 62, 133;
county *vs.* city approaches to, 251; damage
from, 32–33, 82–83, 106, 108, 120, *121*, 261–62;
effects of, 105, 106, 243; efforts to avoid damage from, *58*, 58–59, 61; hydraulic mining and,
36, 81, *122*, 122–23, 155, 344n10; inevitability
of, 32, 133–34; lesser threat from Sacramento
River, 80; levels of, 66, 81; limiting uses of
river corridors, 247, 249; in Mississippi and
Ohio river valleys, 130, 136, 152–53, 157;
railroads and, 77, 79, 82–83; respite from, 105;
in stories told by Old Sacramento, 304–5
Folsom: first earthen dam in, 118, 125; hydroelectric power plants near, 95, 125; proposals
for parkland along river to, 247; railroad
connection to, 78; Sacramento Valley Railroad
to, 46–47
Folsom Dam, 132–33; as best flood control, 118;
broken floodgate on, 261–62; effect on
American River flow, 243; in multipurpose
water projects, 250–51
Folsom Lake, 219
Folsom Lake Recreation Area, 241, 265
Folsom South Canal, 257–58
forests: along American River, 244–45; destruction
of, 36, 171; fires in, 203–4; in flood control,
140–41; Sutter's *vs.* Indians' use of, 21
Fortier, S., 149
Fort Ross, 17, 24–25, 33
Fowler, Benjamin, 152
Foxwoods Casino, 274

Frame, Walter, 310
Freeman, Frank S., 112–13
Freeman, S. David, 231, 236
Friant Dam, as New Deal project, 185
Frye, Thomas, 310–11
fur trade, 20; Indians and, 14, 315; Sutter and, 16–17, 33

Gallatin, Albert, 95
Gallaway, Alfred, Jr., 175
Gaming Revenue Sharing Trust Fund (GRSTF), 276
Gann, Paul, 262
Garfield, James R., 149–50
gas works, for lighting, 57
Geisreiter, Herbert Eugene "Bert," 249
gender imbalance: cities needing to attract women, 42; effects of male dominance in cities, 50, 52; shortage of women, 42, 55, 57
General Land Office (GLO), 147
George Pollack Company, Tower Bridge built by, 194
Gerstung, Eric, 258
Giago, Tim, 282
Gilbert, Grove Karl, 242
Gillett, James Norris, 149
Glading, Ben, 259–60
Glaha, Ben, 132
Goethe, Charles M., 8, 331n67, 369n9
gold, 34; discovery of, 38–40. See also mining
Golden Eagle Hotel, 293
gold rush: effects of, 28, 38, 271; effects on population, 42, 47–49; fueling Sacramento's development, 39, 48, 59; heritage of, 78, 199, 317, 319; immigrants in, 45–46, 118, 172; influence on siting of Sacramento, 80, 292; miners turning to farming after, 104–7; Sacramento frozen in era of, 163, 303, 310–11, 313–15, 319–20
Gold Rush Capitalists: Greed and Growth in Sacramento (Eifler), 4
Gorman, Hugh, 246
government, California state: capitol building and, 69, 296; collaborations with USGS, 140–41; compacts for Indian gaming by, 274–76, 287–88; fleeing floods in Sacramento, 120–21; flood control and, 72, 112–13, 120, 138;

funding for state parks, 248; implementation of federal swampland acts, 107, 145; Indian gaming and, 268, 274, 275, 377n54; legislation on nuclear industry, 221; military, 38–39; Natomas Company and, 124–25; negotiations with railroad about Tower Bridge, 192; resource management and, 38–39, 123, 326n13; in Sacramento's development, 90, 309–10, 314; sharing redevelopment costs, 295; swampland sales by, 105, 107, 109–10; title to Sutter Lake and, 81, 84
government, county: American River Parkway and, 249, 251; Indian gaming and, 268, 277–80, 283–85; management of swampland turned over to, 108–9; redevelopment and, 207, 292, 294; response to Proposition 13, 262–63; unable to meet relief needs in Depression, 187. See also Sacramento County
government, federal: budget reductions by, 203–4; Central Valley Project of, 131–32; encouraging urban renewal, 291; expanding powers of, 136–38; flood control and, 130–31, 141–43, 155–57, 156; funding for highway construction, 299; in fur trade, 14; on historic preservation, 290–91; on Indian gaming, 274, 277–78; Indians and, 270–73, 278; on navigability of waterways, 138; reclamation and, 135–36, 146–51; regulation of mining, 38, 326n13; in resource management, 123; states' rights vs., 137, 151, 153; swampland acts of, 105, 145; water projects and, 130, 132, 151. See also New Deal
government, municipal: Indian gaming and, 268, 276–77, 279–80, 283–85; redevelopment and, 292, 294–95
government, Sacramento city, 57; American River Parkway and, 251; buildings for as PWA projects, 191; flood control efforts by, 56, 66–68, 80, 120; giving land for statehouse, 69; inadequacy of flood control measures by flood, 67, 72; leadership of, 56; matching funds for park land purchases, 249; Old Sacramento and, 292–94, 308; quality of life improvements by, 56–57, 68; railroads and, 82–84, 92; regaining control of riverfront, 90, 98; response to Proposition 13, 262–63; unable to meet relief needs in Depression, 187
grade, raising Sacramento's. See also street grading

Grant Union High School, as New Deal project, 186, 198

Graton Rancheria, 285

"Great Calamity," 1862 flood as, 72

Great Depression, 185; effects on Sacramento, 186–87, 246, 292. *See also* New Deal

Green, Will S., 109

Green Act (1868), 109, 112, 121

Greenhaven, 177–78

Gregory, Dick, 220

Gronna, Asle, 146

Grossheim, Leon, 231, 235

groundwater, pollution of, 90, 208, 214

growth machine, boosters as, 162, 352n16

Grunsky, C. E., 144–48

Haggin, James Ben Ali, 208

Hall, Dan, 255

Hansbrough, Henry C., 146

Hartley, Keith, 237

Haslam, Gerald, 318

Hawaii, Sutter in, 16–17

Hayden, Tom, 232–33, 235

health care: for Southern Pacific employees, 97–98. *See also* hospitals

Heckel, Jack L., 255

Heidrick Ag History Center, 318

Henley, Thomas, 28

Hensley, Samuel, 53

Highland Park, 173–74

highways: debate about routing through West End, 382n36; effects of freeway location on Old Sacramento, 299–301, 303, 306–7; freeways incorporated into city planning, 296–97; New Deal improvements of, 191; proposals to bridge Interstate 5, 306–8

Hilgard, Eugene W., 144–45

historic preservation: danger of stagnation in, 310–11; education through, in Old Sacramento, 309; growing awareness of, 291; of homes, not districts, 290–91; importance of, in Old Sacramento, 310–11; under National Park Service, 301; Neasham as pioneer in movement, 302; in redevelopment plans, 299; as tool for urban renewal, 303; in visions of Sacramento's future, 308

histories, local, 159, 163, 316; danger of stagnation in, 310–11; of Fair Oaks, 359n76; frozen periods of, 291, 303; Indians neglected in, 320; of suburbs, 178–80; transforming reality, 316–17

Hock Farm, Sutter retiring to, 28–29

Hoffman, Ancil, 252

Holliday, J. S., 314

Hoover, Herbert, 187–88

Hoovervilles, 187, 246

Hopkins, Harry, 188, 189, 360n2

Hopkins, Mark, 68, 83

horses, trade in stolen, 16, 20–21

hospitals, 68, 207; Southern Pacific's, 89–90, 97–98

Housing Act of 1934, 294–95

Housing Act of 1949, 199, 294, 380n13

Housing Act of 1954, 295–96

Housing and Urban Development (HUD), 294

Howard & Wilson, 167

Hudson's Bay Company, 41

Hughes, Rosanna, 53

Humphreys, Benjamin, 156

hunting and gathering, Indians', 17–20

Huntington, Collis P., 83, 95

Huntington, Thomas, 97–98

Hurricane Katrina, increasing fear of floods, 1, 9

Hursh, Gary, 222–23

Hurtado, Albert, 315

hydraulic mining, *35*, 124; agriculture and, 144–45; court cases limiting, 36–37, 344n10; effects of, 36–37, 44, 141, 155, 242–43, 344n10; efforts to revive, 144; floods and, 81, *122*, 122–23, 155; railroads *vs.*, 5

Ibser, Homer, 220, 224

Ickes, Harold, 185, 188

immigrants, 41, 314; crowding into hotels in West End, 292; in development of Sacramento, 56, 163; discrimination against, 172–73, 331n63; gold rush causing influx of, 42, 54, 118; incentives to relocate to reclaimed land, 137; swamplanders as, 104–5

Indian gaming: backlash to, 268, 276–78; benefits to local communities, 288; in California, 267–69, 273–76; compacts for, 268–69, 274–76, 278–79, 281, 283–88, 379n71; distribution of profits from, 270, 276, 284,

289; environmental protection in compacts for, 283–85; expansion of, 282, 286, 287; federal government endorsing, 277; governors negotiating compacts for, 275–76, 279, 286, 287; illegal slot machines in, 274; investors in, 273–76, 280, 288, 375n26; location and viability of, 271; locations of, 271, *272*, 277; negotiations with local communities for, 269, 276, 283–85; off-reservation, 273, 285, 289; opposition to, 275, 282; political battle over, 282; profits from, 268–69, 271, 274, 276, 378n57; public support for, 275, 281; Sacramento market for, 278; sharing revenues from, 281–83, 288, 376n32, 377n54; slot machine limits in, 276, 283; sovereignty and compacts, 269, 271, 274, 275–78, 282–83, 285, 287; threats to monopoly of, 282. *See also* casinos, Indian

Indian Gaming Regulatory Act (IGRA) of 1988, 274, 282, 289, 375n26

Indian Gaming Special Distribution Fund (IGSDF), 276

Indians: agriculture and, 14, 17–19; California Indian Heritage Center and, 318; competition among, 315; diseases among, 22, 27–28, 37, 270–71, 315; effects of wage labor on culture of, 23–24, 27; enslavement of, 16, 26–27, 324n44; environment and, 20, 61, 161, 315; foods of, *18–19*; homes of, *23*; labor of, 14–17, 19–20, 28; lands of, 37–38, 131; legal status of, 271, 272–73, 275; in local histories, 318, 320; mingling of tribes, 270–71, 278; mining and, 28, 37–38; missionaries' influence on, 20; population of, 22, 27–28, 270, 372n4; recognition of tribes of, 275, 282; relations with Mexico and Spain, 314–15; relations with non-Indian neighbors, 270; resentments against, 277, 281; in Sacramento's development, 313–14; sovereignty of, 268, 271–78, 282–83, 287, 375n27; Sutter and, 16, 21–26; Sutter and labor of, 13, 15–21, 26–27, 61; Sutter paying for labor of, 22–23, 27–28; Sutter's army of, 24–25; Sutter's control of, 16, 25–26, 30; trade in stolen horses, 20–21; treatment in California, 268, 270; village of, *18*; wealth and poverty of, 268, 270, 276, 377n49. *See also specific tribes*

industrialization: after WWII, 299; railroads' influence on, 79, 89; rural ideal *vs.,* 159; of Southern Pacific Shops, 90

industry, 6, 162; decline in Great Depression, 186–87; water for, 256–57

Inland Waterways Commission, 152, 154–55

Institute of Nuclear Power Operations (INPO), 224, 233

insurance, for floodplain residents, 133

Interstate 5, routed through West End, 299–301

interurban railroads, 78–79

irrigation, 141; in competition for reclamation funding, 146–47, 148–51; in diversification of agriculture, 125, 139; reclamation and, 118, 137, 141, 146; relation to drainage and flood control, 131, 137, 152–54, 156; USDA and USGS sparring over authority for, 139–40

Isenberg, Andrew, 66

Jackson, Andrew R., 72, 334n58

Jackson, Thomas H., 153

Jackson Rancheria, 272–73, 277

Jackson Report, 153

Japanese Americans, interned at Camp Kohler, 200, 214

Japantown, 172

Jarvis, Howard, 262

jobs: from casinos, 276–77, 281, 286; at military facilities, 195, 209–10, 212, 215; with railroads, 88, 90, 95, 97, 186–87; in state government, 88; through New Deal programs, 188, 189, 190

Johnson, Hiram, 123, 125, 130, 195, 199

Johnson, Lyndon, 202

Johnson, R. P., 82

Johnson Cutoff Wagon Road, 46

Jones, Jim, 255, 256

Judah, Theodore, 46–47, 83

Kaiser Industries, 132–33

Kaplan, David, 216–17, 221

Karkowski, Joseph, Jr., 266

Kehoe, John, 223, 226

Kelley, Robert, 3

Kennedy, John F., 201–2

Kimbrough, Howard, 175

labor: for gold mining, 34–35; of indentured
servants, 16–17; Indians', 14–15, 19–20, 23–24,
320, 324n44; Sutter and Indians', 13, 15–23,
26–28, 61
Lady Adams building, in Old Sacramento, 304,
305
Laguna West, 178
Lake Natoma, 246, 249, 265
Land, William, 8–9
land grants, Mexican, 38, 105, 125, 195, 208, 315–16
Land Park, 173, 176, *176*
land prices, 68, 156, 251
land speculation: after floods, 107, 109; gold
rush causing, 42; in suburbanization, 167; on
Sutter's Embarcadero, 40
Lane, Franklin, 154–55
Latimer, Asbury, 146, 149–50
law and order: on American River and parkway,
264–65; crime in West End, 293–94; during
early gold rush years, 48
lead mining, 38–39
League of Women Voters: study of Rancho Seco
by, 229–30; support for Measure B, 232
Lembi, Dante, 253
Leo A. Daly and Associates, central city plan by,
296, 299–300
Leonard, Ben, 167
levees: on American River, breaking, 72, 120;
Army Corps of Engineers focus on, 140;
Carey rebuilding repeatedly, 115; Central
Pacific Railroad and, 83–84; city funding
construction of, 120; competition in placing,
145; cost of, 67; effects of American River new
course on, 74; failure of Natomas's, 131; federal
government taking responsibility for, 130–31;
first on American River, 56; fortified by PWA,
197; Hoovervilles below, 187; inadequacy of,
5, 67, 80, 118, 120, 152; misplaced, increasing
flood damage, 81; in multipurpose water projects, 250–51; Natomas building, 171; Natomas
constructing, *127*; pitting land owners against
one another, 122; proposed scenic drives
along, 247–49; on Putah Creek, 111–12; PWA
improvements in, 191; railroads built on, 82;
railroads improving, 85; raised after 1861-1862
floods, 121; on Sacramento River, 108;

Natomas building, 129; not breaking, 120; to
shield city from flooding of Sutter Lake, 81
Liedesdorff, William, 26–27
Lienhard, Heinrich, 23, 63–64
lighting, first gas works for, 57
Lincoln, 267, 285, 372n1
Lippincott, J. B., 140–41
livestock: flooding and, 106, 109; Sutter's influence
increasing, 30, 33
Loose, Cindy, 306
Louisiana Reclamation Club (LRC), 152
Lubin, David, 167
Lungren, Dan, 279

MacDonald, Madlyne, 229–30
Macdonald, Pat, 220–21
Maidu, 285
malaria, 41, 51; among Indians, 22, 27–28
Marshall, George C., 205
Marshall, James, 38–40
Marx, Karl, 59
Marysville, 70–71, 141, 285
Mather Air Force Base, 177, *205,* 253; history of,
200, 202–8; New Deal improvements at,
194–96, 199
Maxwell, George H., 151–52, 154–55
McCain, John, 274–75, 286
McClatchy, C. K., 5–6, 331n67
McClatchy, Charles, 6, 8
McClatchy, Eleanor, 300
McClatchy, James, 53, 331n63
McClatchy, Valentine S., 6, 155–56, 167, 331n63
McClatchy High School, as New Deal project,
186, 198
McClatchy papers, support for Roosevelt in, 188
McClellan Air Force Base, 177, 199; advantages
of Sacramento location for, 195–96; history
of, 208–11; on National Register of Historic
Places, 196
McClellan Airport, 214
McClellan Business Park, 211
McClellan Park, as New Deal project, 186
McConnell, W. H., 185
McCullough, Thelma, 250
McDougal, James, 70
McGowan, Joseph, 3

McNamara, Robert S., 201–2

McWilliams, Carey, 166

Mead, Elwood, 139–40

Measure A, to buy land for American River Parkway, 255; to create regional sanitation district, 256

Measure B ("Rancho Seco Voters' Rights Initiative"), 229; Measure C *vs.*, 231–33

Measure C, as SMUD's alternative initiative, 231–33

Measure K, on keeping Rancho Seco open, 234

media: on American River Parkway, 255; on Rancho Seco, 224, 231; on routing of Interstate 5, 300. *See also* Sacramento Bee

mercury, used in gold mining, 37

Mexico: California under, 13, 314; relations with Indians, 314–15. *See also* land grants, Mexican; US-Mexico War

middle class: rural ideal of, 159; Sacramento's lifestyle as, 56–57, 60, 169

Midtown, 173

Milanovich, Richard, 269

military: advantages of Sacramento location for facilities, 195–96, 200, 202, 208, 212; closure and realignment of bases, 201–2; effects of bases, 299, 363n50; highway construction allowing movement by, 299; map of facilities, *201*; New Deal money for facilities, 194–96, 199; pollution on installations of, 201–2; redevelopment of facilities of, 206–7, 215; in Sacramento's development, 314; Sacramento's facilities in WWII, 200, 214–15; suburbs ground around installations of, 177, 199, 201, 203. *See also specific facilities*

Miller, George, 278, 286

Miller, Maurice, 209

Mills, Darius Ogden, *298*

Milton J. Brock & Sons, 177

miners' courts, 39

mining, 78; agriculture and, 103, 125; gold, 28, 34–39; gold rushers abandoning for business, 67; lack of governmental regulation of, 38–39; lead, 38–39; Natomas and, 125–26; regulation of, 326n13; riverbed, 124; sand and gravel business, 252–53. *See also* hydraulic mining

Mining Act of 1866, 326n13

mining towns, freight shipped to, 45

Mission Indians, 271–72, 274

missions, Franciscan, 314; Indians and, 15, 20, 315; secularization of, 15, 17

Mississippi River: coalition with Sacramento Valley, 136, 151, 155–57; demands for federal flood control help, 156; flooding of, 130, 152, 157; lead mining along, 38–39; multiple-use plan for watershed of, 152

Missouri, 15–16, 38

Miwok Indians: horse stealing by, 20–21; Sutter and, 22, 25; in UAIC, 278

modernization, railroads encouraging, 96–97, 100

Moraga, Gabriel, 158

Mormon Battalion, trail established by, 46

Mormon-Carson Pass Wagon Road, 46

Mormons, 39–40, 44, 325n4

Morongo Indians, 269, 276, 283; gaming by, 273–74, 277, 287; reservation of, 271

Morse, John, 47–48, 53

Moss, John, 300

M Street Bridge, Tower Bridge replacing, 192, 194

Mullaney, James C. "Jim," 252, 265

multiple-use conservation, 144, 152; USGS and, 140, 146; water projects as, 250–51

Munson, Marsden, 145

Museum of Railroad Technology, 100

museums: California Indian Heritage Center, 318; Heidrick Ag History Center, 318; Museum of Railroad Technology, 318; Sutter's Fort as repository of artifacts, 317

Nader, Ralph, 232–33

Nahl, Charles Christian, 53, 313

narratives, developed by Sacramento's boosters, 159; able to be changed, 181; claiming rural and urban advantages, 164–66; environment in, 160, 180–81; influence of, 180; minorities excluded from, 172–73; suburban developers using, 166–71, 173–77, 180; in suburbs' local histories, 178–80

Nash, Robert, 236–37

National Air Defense Frontier Association, 195

National Drainage Association (NDA), 148–49

National Drainage Congress (NDC), 152–55

National Historic Landmark, Old Sacramento as, 302, 308–9

National Historic Preservation Act of 1966, 202, 290–91, 302

National Historic Site, Old Sacramento as, 290
National Industrial Recovery Act (NIRA), 191
National Irrigation Association (NIA), 151
National Irrigation Congress, 147
National Park Service, Old Sacramento, 300–301
National Register of Historic Places: McClellan
   Field on, 196, 211; uses of, 291
National Trust for Historic Preservation, Old
   Sacramento, 301
Native Sons of the Golden West, 316
Natomas Company, 133; declining influence of,
   132–33; in development of suburbs, 126–27,
   170–71; in flood control and reclamation, *127,*
   127–31; land of, 126–27, *129*; land sales by, 125,
   130, 253; original Folsom dam by, 118, 132–33;
   range of businesses of, 124; relations with state
   government, 124–25
natural history education, 251–52
natural resources: conservation of, 135–36; expanding federal powers over, 136–37; extraction of,
   33, 35–36; Mission Indians' defense of, 271–72;
   planning for, 152; Sacramento narratives
   boasting about, 163, 165; Sutter's plan to
   exploit, 13, 17–21, 33
nature: American River Parkway retaining feeling
   of, 265; human exploitation of, 159–60,
   160–61, 180–81; Indians' relationship with,
   161
Nature's Metropolis: Chicago and the Great West
   (Cronon), 2, 96
Neasham, Vernon Aubrey, 302–4
New Deal, 199; lack of signs on projects of,
   185–86, 189, 198; legacy of, 196–98; money
   for military facilities from, 194–96, 199;
   preparations for war under, 191; Roosevelt's
   vision of, 188; Sacramento projects of, 186;
   Tower Bridge as project of, 191–94
Newell, Frederick H., 137, 139–40, 149, 156
New Helvetia, 22, 27; cultural diversity of, 29,
   320; as Sutter's dream of agricultural empire,
   13, 33, 315, 318
Newlands, Francis, 152
Newlands Reclamation Act (1902), 123
Nimbus Dam, 242–43, 250–51, 257
Nisenan Indians, 22, 271; Sutter and, 21–22; in
   UAIC, 278
Nolen, John, 247, 370n16

North Highlands, 199, 211, 214
North Sacramento, 166–67, 169
North Sacramento Land Company, 167
nuclear power, 217; accidents in, 228; initiatives
   seen as general referenda on, 232, 234;
   opposition to, 220–21; public dissatisfaction
   with, 216, 231; safety concerns about, 223–24,
   236–37; SMUD's choice of, 216–19. *See also*
   Rancho Seco Nuclear Generating Station
   (RSNGS)
Nuclear Regulatory Commission (NRC): on
   Babcock & Wilcox nuclear reactors, 224; on
   Rancho Seco, 226–27, 231, 233–34; Rancho
   Seco's minimal compliance with, 225; on
   Three Mile Island accident, 224

Oakland, as rival for state capital, 69
Oak Park, 173, *174*
Office of Irrigation Investigations (OII), of USDA,
   139–40
Ohio River, flooding of, 152–53, 157
Old Sacramento: attractions in, 304–6, 309, 319;
   effects of freeway location on, 299–301, 303,
   306–7; gold rush heritage of, 317, 319–20;
   historic significance of, 301, 310–11; integrity
   of, 308–9; as National Historic Site, 290, 302,
   308–9; politics in development of, 299, 303;
   Pony Express statue in, 306, *307;* "preservation
   for use" model in, 303, 306; redevelopment
   of, 296, *298;* Southern Pacific and, 89, 98;
   tourism in, 304–6; various stories told by,
   304, 309
Old Sacramento Historic Area and Riverfront
   Park, 301–2
Old Sacramento State Historic Park, 98, *99,* 309
Olmsted, Frederick Law, 169, 248–49, 370n17
Orangevale, 166–67
Ord, Edward, 64
Oubre, Richard, 233–34, 237
overland trails, 33, 41, 45–46

Pacific Gas & Electric (PG&E), 95, 133; considering buying Rancho Seco, 231; SMUD and, 217,
   219, 227, 230
Painter, Judy, 229–30
Pala tribe (Pala Band of Mission of Indians), 275,
   287

Paradise Beach, 249, 251

Pardee, George C., 141, 143, 147

parks, 8–9, 250; American River Parkway compared to other, 241; American River Parkway proposal linking, 247, 249; around statehouse, 70; funding for state, 248; New Deal projects in, 185, 190, 198; Old Sacramento as state historic park, 302; regional park district for, 250; Sacramento County and, 255; Sutter's gift land becoming, 44, 65. *See also specific parks*

Pavia, George, 219, 236

Pechanga Indians (Pechanga Band of Luiseño Indians), 276, 287

People for Proof, 221

Pequot Indians, 274

Perkins, Edmund T., 153, 156

Phelps, William Dane, 61

Phillips, George Harwood, 314–15

Pico, Anthony, 272, 275, 283, 284

Pierce, George W., Jr., 116

Pisani, Donald J., 140

place, sense of, 159; historic preservation and, 291; packaging of, 162, 172; in visions of Sacramento's future, 308

Placer Citizens for Community Rights, 279

police, 95, 277

politics, 130, 188; California's initiative process in, 216, 221, 229; in closing Rancho Seco, 229, 234–35, 238; in development of Old Sacramento, 299, 303; in drainage, reclamation, and flood control projects, 120–21, 136, 146–51; Indians in, 269, 272, 275, 287–88, 376n40; interagency, 136; sectional, 153; SMUD's limited responses to, 237

pollution: of American River, 255–56; in cities along rivers, 41–42; on military installations, 201–2, 207–8, 211, 213–14; from railroads, 79, 89–92; sources of, 123, 307; of Sutter Lake, 92

Pomo, 374n13; Guidiville Band, 273, 285–87, 378n62, 379n68; Habematolel, 288; Lytton Band, 286; Pinoleville, 288; Scotts Valley Band, 273, 285, 379n68; in UAIC, 278

Pond, William, 252

population, cities' needing to replace, 41–42

population, Sacramento's, 161, 194, 265; arrival of multigenerational families, 54–55; California's and, 126; effects of gold rush on, 42, 47–49;

growth of, 162, 187–88, 299; Indian, 22, 27–28, 270, 372n4; postwar growth, 171, 177; railroads' influence on growth of, 79, 93; slow growth of, 49–51; transiency of, 48–49

port cities, railroads' influence on, 79

post office building, 188, 292

Powell, Robert C., 177–78

power: Southern Pacific emphasizing efficiency, 93–94. *See also* electricity

"preservation for use" model, 303, 306, 308–9

Preston, William, 314

prisoners of war, at Sacramento Army Depot, 212, 213

Progressive era, 136, 138, 247

property owners, 62, 68, 251; in Old Sacramento, 308–9; promoting American River Parkway, 250, 266; small-scale farming recommended for, 164–71; street grading and, 67, 74–75

Proposition 13, effects on American River Parkway, 262–63

Proposition 68, threatening Indian monopoly on gaming, 282

Proposition 70, to protect Indian gaming, 282

Propositions 5 and 1A (Tribal Government Gaming and Economic Sufficiency Act), 275, 279

Public Citizen group, in opposition to Rancho Seco, 232–33

publicity campaigns, effects of, 159

Public Works Administration (PWA): legacy of, 196–98; projects of, 188, 190

Purcell, C. H., 192–93

Putah Creek: flooding of, 106, 108, 110–11, 114–16; levees on, 111–12; rerouting of, 112, 114–15

Putah Sink: efforts to farm in, 103–4; failed flood control efforts for, 110–11, 114–15; flood control efforts for, 107–10, *111*, 112–14, 116; flooding of, 108, 114–15; map of, *104*; sale of swamplands of, 109–10

quality of life, 89; city improvements for, 56–57; in suburban narrative, 169–71, 176–78

railroads: blocking development of riverfront, 79, 310; declining importance of, 98; in development of suburbs, 126–27; diseases spread by, 89–90; effects of, 5–6, 47, 89; environmental effects of, 77–80, 89, 100; in flood control efforts, 5, 82, 84–85; jobs with, 88, 90, 95, 97, 186–87; military and, 195, 212; public complaints about, 90; reuse of land of, 10, 99–100; in Sacramento's development, 314; Sacramento Valley Railroad as first, 46–47; sharing Tower Bridge with highways, 191–92; transcontinental, 77, 83, 85; vs. hydraulic mining, 5. See also Southern Pacific Railroad

Railyard, planned as infill community, 99–100

rancherias, 278, 374nn13–14; Indians relocated to, 37–38; loss of federal protection of, 272–73; reservation status vs., 273. See also reservations, Indian

rancheros, Indians on, 15

Rancho Cordova, 199, 207, 252

Rancho Del Paso, 167, 169, 188–89, 208

Rancho Del Paso Land Company, 166–67

Rancho Seco Nuclear Generating Station (RSNGS), 217, 258; accidents at, 223, 225–26; concerns about waste generated by, 237; control room of, 222; as economic liability, 227–28, 230, 234; effects of closing on SMUD, 237–38; maintenance problems at, 225–26; management of, 223, 231–34, 237; Measure C giving 18-month extension, 231–33; moderates vs. extremists in opposition to, 225, 230; operating problems at, 217, 224, 230, 233–34, 236; opposition to, 220–22, 225, 232–34; protests at, 224, 227; safety concerns about, 223, 234; SMUD board's changing opinions about, 233; SMUD considering selling, 231–32, 236; SMUD trying to fix problems at, 231, 234; strategies in campaign to close, 228–29, 236–37; studies of, 229–31; support for, 231–32, 234; vote to close, 216, 234–35

Rancho Seco Recreation Area, 219, 235

Raphero, Sutter's execution of, 25–26

Reading, Pierson B., 25, 29, 53

reclaimed land, 6, 9; incentives to relocate immigrants and slum dwellers to, 137; as misnomer, 170; suburbs on, 170–71, 318

reclamation, 120, 136; competition for funding for, 141, 148–51, 156; federal authority for, 138, 141–43, 151; private efforts in, 156; stigmatization of swamps and, 137–38; of swampland, 144

Reclamation Act (1902), 137, 151

Reclamation and Swampland Act of 1861, 120–21

Reclamation Service. See under US Geological Service (USGS)

Reconstruction Finance Corporation, 188

recreation: on and along American River, 249, 252, 255–57, 256, 260, 260–61, 264–65; first water rights for, 259; at Folsom Lake Recreation Area, 265; during gold rush, 42–43, 57; at Mather Park, 207; at Rancho Seco Recreation Area, 219, 235

recycling, by Southern Pacific, 96

redevelopment funding: business and government sharing, 295; federal, 294; for Old Sacramento, 304, 310; tax increment financing, 297, 381n26

Reid, Wendy, 229–30, 235

relief, during Great Depression, 187, 199

religion, diversity of, 55

Remy, Michael, 229, 232–35

Reps, John, 64, 68

reservations, Indian: in California, 28–29, 270; location and viability of gaming, 271, 286; self-government on, 273

reservoirs, 243, 261; uses of water from, 140–41, 144, 219, 257

resource management, as government responsibility, 123

Reynolds, F. H., 192

Richards, W. A., 147

Rincon, 377n54

Rio Linda, 169, 173, 211

River Beautification Commission, 249–50

riverfront, 250; businesses servicing gold rush on, 40, 42–43; Central Pacific Railroad facilities and, 84; city regaining control of, 90, 98; railroads' improvements on, 86–87; redevelopment of, 99, 199, 309–10; relation to downtown, 292, 307; Southern Pacific's dominance of, 88–90, 91; Southern Pacific's expansion on, 88. See also Old Sacramento; Sutter's Embarcadero

River Improvement and Drainage Association of California (RIDA), 143–44

River Recreation and Parks Association, 250, 252

rivers, 3, 90, 370n16; cities located along, 41–42, 119; county vs. city approaches to, 251; debris in, 123, 144, 242–43; draining Sierra Nevada, 34, 242; flow measurement of, 139–41, 369n8;

improvements to, 130, 140, 144; mining and, 34–36, 123–24, 144; Natomas Company and, 124, *127,* 128; navigability of, 32, 138, 328n28; park land purchases along, 250–51; steam-powered boats on, 44–45. See also *specific rivers*

Rizer, H. C., 147–48

roads: built by New Deal projects, 197–98; casino traffic on, 277, 284; proposed scenic drives along river corridors, 247–49

Robertson, O. A., 167

Robinson, Joseph Taylor, 149

Robinson, Lester, 82–83

Rockefeller, John D., Jr., 291

Rodda, Albert, 222

Rodgers, William, 69

Roosevelt, Franklin, 205; New Deal programs under, 185, 188–89

Roseville, 178

Rossmoor North subdivision, 252

Royce, Sarah, 66

Rufino, Sutter's execution of, 25–26

Runyon, Jean, 255

rural ideal: Sacramento's boosters using, 159, 160–62, 166–71, 180; suburban developers using, 175–77

Russian-American Company, and Sutter, 17, 33, 63, 65

Sacramentans for SAFE Energy (SAFE): legitimacy of, 232, 234; opposition to sale of Rancho Seco, 236; strategy for closing Rancho Seco, 228–29, 233

Sacramento (Sutter's schooner), 44

Sacramento Air Depot. *See* McClellan Air Force Base

Sacramento Army Depot, 200, 212–14, *213,* 363n50; New Deal money for, 194–96, 199

Sacramento Bee, 331n67; anti-Asian campaigns in, 331n63; on Rancho Seco, 226, 228, 230, 233; on redevelopment of West End, 294, 300; tree-planting campaign of, 57–58

Sacramento City College: auditorium of, *197,* 198; as New Deal project, 186

Sacramento County, 194; American River Parkway and, 251–52, 255, 265–66; effects of Propo-

sition 13 on, 262–63; voting to shut Rancho Seco, 216. See also government, county

Sacramento County Airport System, 206–7

Sacramento County Science Steering Committee, 251

Sacramento Electric Power and Light Company, 95, 125–26

Sacramento Flood Control Project, 116, 133, 153

Sacramento Flood Control System, 130

Sacramento Historic Landmarks Commission, 300–301

Sacramento Municipal Airport, 199

Sacramento Municipal Utility District (SMUD): board considering selling Rancho Seco, 231, 236; board of, 233, 237; board's changing opinions about Rancho Seco, 231, 233; choice of nuclear generating station, 216–19; contracting for water for Rancho Seco, 219, 258; cost of Rancho Seco being offline, 227–28; effects of closing Rancho Seco on, 236–38; election of board, 221, 222–23; Freeman hired as general manager of, 236; hydroelectric generation by, 258; improved public perceptions of, 236; management of Rancho Seco by, 225, 227, 231; Rancho Seco Nuclear plant shut down, 216; petitions on shutting Rancho Seco to board of, 229, *230;* PG&E and, 217, 219, 230; public attendance at board meetings of, 220–21, 224–25, 230; public dissatisfaction with, 216, 225; Rancho Seco management and, 223, 231–34, 237; rate increases by, 225, 233; rates of, 228–30, 234, 237; responses to initiatives to close Rancho Seco, 229, 231–32

Sacramento Northern Railway, 78, 192

Sacramento Park Association, 71

Sacramento Redevelopment Agency, 294, 296; development of Old Sacramento, 299, 304; on routing of Interstate 5, 299–300

Sacramento River, 32; American River as largest tributary of, 242; bridges over, 78, 191–92; drainage basin of, *142;* dredging of, 80, 85, 129; early importance of, 40, 292; effects of American River's new course on, 74, 84–85; flooding by, 80, 119, 131; Putah Sink, 106; flows of, 139, 140–41, 155; geography of Sacramento Valley and, 119; levees on, 108, 120, 129; McClellan's freight docks on, 208, 210–11; military transports on, 195, 208; navigability of, 136, 141; proposals for parkland along, 247; routing of Interstate 5 and, 299–301; sewage treatment plant on, 256; Shasta Dam on, 131; traffic on, 156; uses for water of, 56, 57, 141

Sacramento Shops, of Central Pacific Railroad. *See* Southern Pacific Shops

Sacramento Suburban Fruit Lands Company, 169

Sacramento townsite: advantages and disadvantages of, 62, 68–69, 119; in American River flood basin, 62; choice of, 4, 63–64; disadvantages of, 41–42, 80, 318–19; gold rush's influence on, 40, 80; slow population growth due to, 49–51; surveying and sale of lots in, 43; Sutterville as alternative, 327n24

Sacramento Union, 300

Sacramento Valley, 41; agriculture in, 103–4, 143; flood control in, 121, 123, 130, 133; geography of, 119, 139; as inland sea, 119–20, 131, 133–34, 139, 143; isolation of, 32–33; Mississippi River valley's coalition with, 151, 155–57; reclamation efforts in, 147, 149, 156; Sutter's influence on, 29–30; as testing ground for USGS multiple-use conservation, 140, 147; Trans-Mississippi Commercial Congress asking for federal aid to, 135–36; US Geological Service wanting institutional dominance in, 136, 138–39; water policies in, 143–46

Sacramento Valley Colonization Company, 167

Sacramento Valley Railroad (SVRR), 46–47, 78, 82–83, 93

Sacramento Women's Council, 250

safety: of nuclear power, 223–24, 228, 236; railroads and, 90–91, 96–97; of Rancho Seco, 223–24, 228–30, 234, 237; traffic, 192

sand and gravel business, American River Parkway's effects on, 253–55

San Diego County, Indian gaming in, 271, 273–74, 284

San Francisco, 40, 198, 202; hosting state fair, 70–71; proposed casinos around, 286–87, 378n62; railroad connection to, 78; as rival for state capital, 69; Sacramento River as access

to, 44–45, 191, 208; Sacramento's isolation from, 32

San Gorgonio Pass, 270–71, 276

San Joaquin River, Friant Dam on, 185

San Joaquin River valley, 147, 149

San Jose, 69, 70–71

San Juan Meadows, 252

San Manuel Band of Mission Indians, 269, 274, 276, 287, 289

San Pablo, 286, 379n65

Savage, Thomas, 29

Save the American River Association, 252, 255, 258–59, 265

Schmit, Cheryl, 269, 274–75; in opposition to casino expansion, 278, 282, 286; on UAIC working with local community, 279–80

schools, 44, 68; built as New Deal projects, 189, 190–91, 198; Sacramento's first, 55; in suburban narrative, 176–77

Schwarzenegger, Arnold, 281–83, 286

scurvy, 51–52

sewage/waste disposal, 41; for casinos, 277, 284, 285; efforts to upgrade, 191, 256; first system for, 56–57; water pollution from, 92, 255–56

Shasta Dam, 131

Sheldon, Jared, 39

Sherman, William Tecumseh, 43, 64, 76

Sierra Club, 250, 252, 260

Sierra Nevada, 31; gold mining in, 35; overland trails crossing, 45–46; rivers draining, 34, 242; snowpack on, 32, 119

Sinclair, John, 61

slavery: effects on California's status, 38; of Indians, 26–27, 324n44

slickens, from hydraulic mining, 36, 144–45

slum clearance, 290, 294. *See also* urban renewal

Small, John Humphrey, 146

"smart growth principles," in visions of Sacramento's future, 308

Smith, Jedediah, 20

Solano County, and flood control for Putah Sink, 112–14

Southern Pacific Railroad, 47, 334n2; building across Sutter Lake, 86; depots of, 99, 292, 310; dominance of riverfront by, 86–87, 91, 310; employee health care of, 89–90, 97–98;

encouraging modernization, 94–95, 96–97; environmental influences of, 92–94, 100; facilities (*See* Southern Pacific Shops); filling Sutter Lake, 85, 87–88, 91–92; in flood control, 5, 87; formation of, 83; groundbreaking for, 77; name change from Central Pacific, 78, 88; renewal of land of, 98–100; streetcars converging at depots of, 88–89, 95; utilities and, 94–96; workforce of, 88

Southern Pacific Shops, *81, 84, 91*; closing down, 98, *99*; construction of, 85, *86–87*, 88; danger of, 90–92; emphasizing energy efficiency, 93–94; expansion of, 88, 90; recycling at, 96

Spanish Empire, Indians and, 14–15, 314–15

Sprung, Gary, 229

Spry, William, 155

squatters' rebellion, 53

Stand Up for California, 268, 279, 282, 287

Stanford, Leland: Central Pacific Railroad and, 47, 77, 83–85; as governor, 57, 77

Stanford Mansion, 58

Starr, Kevin, 166

State Division of Beaches and Parks, 300, 302

State Fair, California, 70–71, 189, 209, 212

State Park Commission, California, 248–50

State Reclamation Board of California, 155

states' rights, *vs.* federal role in reclamation and flood control, 137, 151, 153, 157

Steenerson, Halvor, 146

Stevens, A. J., 95–96

streetcars/trolleys: converging at Southern Pacific's depots, 88–89, 95; horse-drawn and electric, 78–79; paving streets for, 93; spread of electricity and, 95; in suburbanization, 173, 175

street grading: after 1861-1862 floods, 121; by CWA and WPA workers, 189; first attempt at, 68, 72; high grade of, 68, 74–76; hopes for, 5, 81; property owners raising buildings after, 67–68; raised to railroad's new grade, 85; in stories told by Old Sacramento, 305

streets: naming of, 64; paving of, 93; planking of, 56, 62, 67; PWA improvements in, 191; railroads and, 84, 89–90, 93; raising level of, 56, 62; in suburban narrative, 176–78

Streng, James and William, 177

Strizek, Jere, 177

suburban ideal, 169, 172

suburbanization, 159, 267; after WWII, 177, 299; decline of West End and, 292; impacting Indian rancherias and reservations, 270–71, 284; Natomas in, 126–27; New Deal programs facilitating, 199; pattern of, 166, 172–73; role of transportation in, 78–79, 173, 175

suburbs: agricultural, 165–71, 186; amenities promised by, 169–70, 173–77; developed around military installations, 199, 201, 203, 215; first as ethnic neighborhoods, 172–73; on floodplain, 133; green-belts in, 9; for growing population, 126; local histories of, 178–80; rural ideal and, 160; sprawl of, 177, 318

Suffern, Edward, 67–68

Superfund sites: former military bases as, 202–3, 207–8, 213–14; Southern Pacific Shops as, 90

Sutter, John, 44, 46; control of Indians, 25–26; dependence on Indians' labor, 17–24, 324n44; discovery of gold and, 40; exploitation of natural resources by, 17–21, 33; exposure to Indian business, 15–17; financial failures of, 28–29, 33, 43, 63, 65, 315–16; in Hawaii, 16–17; on inappropriateness of Sacramento's site, 80, 119; as Indian agent in US-Mexico War, 29; Indian army of, 24–25; influence on Sacramento Valley, 29–30; leaving Sacramento, 53; plans of, 13, 33, 315; relations with Indians, *18,* 21–26, 28–29; reputation of, 17, 28; Sacramento narratives focused on, 163; transformed image of, 315–16

Sutter, John A., Jr., 53; embarcadero's accessibility over Sutterville, 63–64; giving lots to city, 44, 65; sale of lots by, 43, 63

Sutter Lake: desire to fill, 56, 80–81; flooding of, 66, 72, 80; levees on, 66, 81; pollution of, 90, 92; Southern Pacific and, 83–84, *86*; Southern Pacific filling in, 85, 87–88, 91–92

Sutter's Embarcadero: gold rush causing development of, 40, 42, 45; as Sacramento River landing, 44, 63–64, 292; silting of, 72–73. *See also* riverfront

Sutter's Fort, 33, 61, 315–17

Sutter's Fort State Historic Park, 317, 320

Sutter's Slough (China Slough), 172

Sutterville, 63–64, 74, 327n24

Swampland Act. *See also* Reclamation and
Swampland Act of 1861

Swamp Land Act (1850), 105

swampland districts, 107–8, 112–13

swamps/wetlands, 144; federal government in
drainage of, 137–38, 189; railroads filling in,
79; state implementation of federal acts on,
145; stigmatization of, 137–38, 153. *See also* Tule

Sycuan Indians, 287–88

Taft, William Howard, 143–44, 151

Tarr, Joel, 79

Tavares, Jessica, 269, 278–79

taxes: counties losing due to Indian trust lands,
277, 284; declining revenues from, 186–87,
262, 293; effects of casinos on, 277; federal
credits for urban renewal, 291; increasing
revenues, 93, 297; Indians' immunity to, 277,
282; levied for flood control, 62, 107–9; for
park funding, 250, 266; to pay for raising
Sacramento's grade, 5; to purchase land for
state buildings, 70–71; suburbs avoiding
Sacramento's, 173, *174*

tax increment financing, as Sacramento innovation, 297, 381n26

technology, railroads encouraging, 93, 96–97

Tending the Wild (Anderson), 315

Thornburgh, Dick, 224

Three Mile Island, nuclear accident at, 223–24,
228

Thunder Valley Casino, 267, *280, 288*; jobs
in, 276–77; UAIC negotiating with local
community about, 279–80, 285

Tirrell, Charles Q., 137

tourism, in Old Sacramento, 304–6, 319

Tower Bridge: aesthetic design of, 192–94; as
New Deal project, 186, 191–94, 198–99; as
Sacramento icon, 192–94, *193*, 198–99

townsite. *See* Sacramento townsite

trade, 22–23, 40

trees, 66; along American River, 244–45; efforts
to restore, 8, 57–58; eucalyptus, 92, 128; flood
control destroying riparian forests, 128; in
original Sacramento landscape, 65–66; in
suburban narrative, 176–78

"Tribal Gaming and Community Planning"
(California Planning Roundtable), 283–84

Truckee River-Donner Pass route, 46

trust lands, Indians', 271, 273–74, 278, 375n20,
377n41; acquisition process for, 279–80,
377n51; conversion of fee lands into, 277,
284; increasing limitations on, 288–89; tribes
seeking, 282, 285

Tule (Yolo Basin), 106, 139; efforts to drain, 108,
149; plan to deprive of water, 140

Twain, Mark, 74

unemployment: among Indians, 270; in Great
Depression, 186–87

Union Pacific Railroad, land of, 98, 100

United Auburn Indian Community (UAIC):
compact of, 268, 278; legal status of, 272–73;
sovereignty issues, 282, 287; Thunder Valley
Casino of, 267, 276–77, 278; working with
local community, 279–80, 285

Upper American River Project, 218

urban renewal: historic preservation as tool for,
303; housing acts and highway act promoting,
294; National Historic Preservation Act
challenging, 291; Old Sacramento and, 290,
301; urban redevelopment *vs.*, 295

US Geological Service (USGS): gauging stations
of, 139–41; institutional aggrandizement
and water imperialism of, 136, 138–39, 141,
143, 147, 157; Reclamation Service of, 137,
141, 145–46, 148, 151; Sacramento Valley as
showplace for, 138–39, 146–47

US-Mexico War, 25, 29, 38

utilities, 133; municipal *vs.* private, 237; Southern
Pacific purchasing *vs.* producing, 95–96;
Southern Pacific's stimulation of, 93–96. *See
also* Rancho Seco Nuclear Generating Station
(RSNGS); Sacramento Municipal Utility
District (SMUD)

Van Pelt, John, 44

Van Winkle, Isaac, 62

Vaught, David, 133

Viejas Band of Capitan Grande Indians, 268, 283,
284, 378n57

Wailaki Indians, 278

Walcott, Charles D., 140, 145, 147–48

Warner, William, 43, 64

water, in development of Sacramento, 318–19

water policies, 143; coalition of Sacramento Valley and Mississippi River regions for, 155–57; effects of uncoordinated water projects, 143, 145–46; and funding for projects, 146–47, 151; multiple-use approach to, 140, 144, 251

water rights, 326n14; Bureau of Reclamation and, 257–59; lack of governmental regulation of, 38–39; for recreation, 259

Waters, Reginald, 195

water supplies: competition for, 6; drawn from American River, 256; Natomas supplying, 124; for Rancho Seco nuclear plant, 219

water works/water systems, 56, 68; casinos and, 277, 284; New Deal projects in, 189–90, 191, 197; Southern Pacific stimulating improvements in, 95–96

wealth: from Indians' gaming, 269, 275–76; taken out of Sacramento, 48, 51–54

Weber, Charles, 29

Weber, J. Martin, 251

Weinstock, Harris, 167

West, development of cities of, 3

West End: cost of services to, 293; decline of, 89, 187, 290, 292, 294, 304; desire to redevelop, 292–94; ethnicities of, 295; housing in, 295, 296; plans for redevelopment of, 302, 319; routing of Interstate 5 through, 299–301, 382n36; Southern Pacific and, 89, 98. *See also* Old Sacramento

Western Heritage, Inc., 302–3

Western Pacific Railroad, 78, 100

West Sacramento, 173, 191, 199

wetlands. *See* swamps/wetlands

Weygandt, Robert, 279

White, Richard, 33

Whitney, Dan, 223

Wilcox, Cliff, 230–31

Wilcox, J. Mark, 195

wildlife, 61; along American River, 244–47; decimation of, 37, 160–61; flood control destroying habitat of, 128; Sutter's exploitation of, 21, 33

Wilkes, Charles, 32–33, 119–20

Wilkins, David, 269

Williams, Frank E., 175

Williams, John Sharp, 153

Williamsburg, Virginia, 291

Williamson, R. S., 120

Wilson, Charles L., 46–47

Wilson, Luzena Stanley, 48–50, 52

Wilson, Pete, 275, 279

Wilson, Woodrow, 153–54

Winnemem Wintu 131

Works Progress Administration (WPA): opposition to, 361n17; projects of, 189–90, 196, 199; PWA and, 190–91; signs on, 360n2

World War II: Camp Kohler in, 214; expansion of automobile traffic after, 299–300; Mather Air Force Base in, 205–6; McClellan Air Force Base in, 208–11; New Deal preparations for, 191, 194–96; Sacramento Army Depot in, 212–13; Sacramento's growth after, 171–72, 177; Sacramento's military facilities in, 200, 214–15; US Army Air Service in, 203

Wright, Charles E., 175

Wright, William P., 175

Wright & Kimbrough, 175–77, 176

Yeaw, Effie, 251–52, 371n28

Yerba Buena. *See* San Francisco

Yocha Dehe Indians (Yocha Dehe Wintun Nation, formerly Rumsey Band of Wintun Indians), 268, 272, 278, 378n56

Yokut Indians, 20–21

Yolo County, 6, 85, 112–14, 194. *See also* Putah Sink

Youngs, Thomas, 68, 72, 74

Yuba River, hydraulic mining and, 36